JUDICIAL PROCESS

By

Prof. G.P. TRIPATHI, Ph.D.

Senior Professor KIIT Law School

KIIT & KISS University, Bhubaneshwar (Odisha)

and

G.G. Padmakar Tripathi

Advocate, Supreme Court of India

Second Edition

Reprint 2025

CENTRAL LAW PUBLICATIONS

ISBN : 978-93-86456-32-8

FIRST EDITION	:	2013
REPRINT	:	2015
SECOND EDITION	:	2018
REPRINT	:	2021
REPRINT	:	2023
REPRINT	:	2025

Published by :
Central Law Publications
107, Darbhanga Castle, Prayagraj
Phone : (0532) 2461178, 2461123
e-mail : clp.editorial@gmail.com
Web-site : www.clplawbooks.com

Price : Rs. 450.00
(Rupees Four Hundred Fifty Only)

Published by : **Central Law Publications,** 107, Darbhanga Castle, Prayagraj
Laser Typesetting : **N & T Computers,** Prayagraj
Printed at : **Caxton Press,** Prayagraj

Dedicated to

My Wife (Smt.) Girish Tripathi

LL.M. (MATS), M.A. (Sagar)

(31-7-1954 to 28-3-2012

Preface to the Second Edition

Obliged to the readers for patronising the book on judicial process, obliged also to the publishers for publishing this in book form.

Now the current edition of this book, thoroughly revised and enlarged.

A judicial process is basically whole complex phenomenon of court working and what wrong has come in it is the issue in this edition, cost, corruption and delay are the three maladies that are crying for remedy. All the three are cancer to the justice delivery system of this sentinel of democracy. How to get it cured and to ensure it does not return is of concern to all of us. A reader who has to read the book has every reason to know, of course, in few words, prior to he pays for the book. The reasons why should he pay for it? Work of payment and information, he would get that he cannot get otherwise elsewhere? True Author has to tell him the truth.

In fact, this book came in existence initially as text book for students of judicial process that was introduced s subject in course structure of law schools. As a teacher associated with this subject, a challenge confronted me to make a text book available to may students since more than 5 decades (since September 23, 1967).

The request of my students and colleagues could not have gone unheard and unattended . Judicial process was taught to budding lawyers of those times as part of what we taught in jurisprudence. Law was two years course. Later on, it was converted into three years course. (Training as advocate trainee was merged in University curriculum). After 5 years law (that too after 10+2) transformation came in legal education. Judicial process started being taught as independent paper in 5 years integrated (Hon.) degree programmes.

Hence acute shortage of a text book was felt and that necessitated writing of this book on judicial process. The first edition has been sold out; re prints are finished; now revised brand new edition before brand new young readers' doing law from reputed universities and their faculties.

Some clarifications were asked for by few. This edition takes care of many of these. Obliged to my learned friends for assisting me to do better.

First chapter on Nature of Judicial Process has been explained more and enlarged. Some theories of judicial process have been added. Some comments on "slowness" of judicial process are mounted afresh. Few lines of accountability of judicial system have been added. Court of future is conceived *de novo*.

Chapter 2 is on Adjudication of Constitutional issues and judicial process is modified. Issues arising out of judicial review have been re-examined a judicial activism and judicial restraint have been re-visited.

Chapter 3 deals with judicial process and court structure. The whole chapter is re-written. Hierarchy of courts in several countries of world have become part of this work. See what courts are there in countries through out the world? What and how do these operate?

Chapter 4 deliberates on creativity of judicial process and precedent legal arguments (7) when there are precedent on issue concerned? Arguments (3) When there are no precedent? How the judicial process responds to first (7) or next (3)? Courts effort to clean election and the political process are added to this Chapter in current edition.

Chapter 5 deals with judicial method under statutory and codified systems. Principles of interpretation are basic issue for discussion here. But Hon. (now retd. judge) Markanday Katju J. heralded a new era by reading Mimansa rules, with English rules of interpretation putting together. Many of English rules of interpretation have similarity in content of Mimansa rules in existence prior to birth of England and U.S.A. Some of these (Mimansa rules) have been applied by Courts in present day India and these have made our judicial system richer. In this Chapter, some observations are included for the information of students of judicial process who can boast of richness we had and lost in judicial process and judicial system. They would feel proud to go through these.

Chapter 6 deals with response of judicial process to cases of first impression. Cardozo's contribution here is acknowledged. Cardozo suggested that when constitution, statutes, precedents ditch you; go to philosophy (analogy), Go to history (Traditions) or to Sociology. These or all these or any of these would help you (the judge) to sail through in first impression cases.

Chapter 7 deals with custom and the judicial process. In fact, if new chapter carved out of Chapter 6 of first edition of this book, the cases of first impression have been given in now redrafted Chapter 6. Custom in law is the established pattern of behaviour that can be objectively verified within a particular social setting. When does a custom become law? Does it require judicial stamping. The whole of Modern Hindu Law, and Muslim law are developed through judicial decisions of the Privy Council. So is the contribution of our Supreme Court in re-writing of Muslim Law. Specially on Section 125, Cr. P.C. and right of a Muslim woman. Tripple talak and bigamy are being examined by Supreme Court in light of the constitutional provisions and human rights.

Chapter 8 is recast Chapter on legal reasoning, philosophy and judicial process. The ethical aspect of legal reasoning. The philosophy or analogy that is permissible for court's seeing cases of first impression. This is a judicial method acceptable to Cardozo even.

Chapter 9 deals with Cardozo's third way out open to a judge facing a case of first impression, that is sociology. If History does not help, philosophy fails; Go to third that is sociology of parties and sociology of law and find the way out to decide the cases that have come to you as a judge mainly that of a trial court.

Chapter 10 deals with comparison as an aid to judicial method. This method is quite often made use of by lawyers and judges to build wall as Romans did. Certainty comes. Precedents are born, elaborated, extended and explained, a comparison is effective tool in armoury of judicial process. The partial incorporation of due process, or Basic feature doctrine, world common law common core of legal principles are few examples developed by judiciary through comparative method.

Chapter 11 deals with the application of theories of justice, theories of punishment; legal injustices, civil disobedience, theories of justice and impact of vision on them, utilitarianism, libertarianism, comparative capitalism; theories of justice as fairness, original position and its significance in 'Rawl's Theories', Dependency and Development Theories and modernization theories.

Chapter 12 deals with judicial process and the Administrative structure. Dicey in Rule of Law (Ist principle) refused to recognize Administrative law being in line with Rule of Law. Both exist now. Relationship in between the two has to be discussed in post-Dicey period. The present century is century of Tribunals and Forums. The traditional judicial process is almost eaten up by these developments. Almost the whole world now accepts these and existence of Administrative process running side by side the judicial process. Delegated legislations are products of Administrative structures.

Chapter 13 Procedure is handmaid of justice. There was a time when rights ensured out of writs of action issued by Chancery Courts. Birth and growth of Public Interest Litigations (Social Interest Litigations as Baxicalls) are latest entrants almost doing away with *'locus standi'* doctrine in areas where such litigations are resorted to PIL is confined only to Article 32 and 226 matters in Supreme Court and High Courts. Still Section 482, Cr.P.C. and 151 (CPC) play significant role in judicial process.

Chapter 14 deals with Judicial Process and legislation (Legislative Process). Bentham and Marx views on law and the legislation are discussed. In addition legislative procedure (Article 107-111), Money bill (Article 109), Appropriation Bill (Art. 114), vote on account votes on credit and exceptional grants and legislative procedures are also discussed in this Chapter.

Chapter 15 deals with Rule of Law and judicial process. Concept and development of Rules of law have been newly written. Concept as developed by Raz is part of this Chapter. Need of police force and rule of Law. Rule of Law and Good governance are innovations in this Chapter.

Chapter 16 deals with Constitutionalism and the Judicial Process. Constitutionalism has been explained *de novo* constitutionalism, the fix view and living tree views of the Constitution have been explained. Textualism and the Constitutionalism; originalism; Hypothetical Intent theory, Moral Theory of Dworkin (interpretive theory); Critical theory (Hercules); Political philosophy, Gerhard Casper's as descriptive and prescriptive connotation, features of Constitutionalism, Limited form of government entrenched form of these rules, separation of powers; U.S.A., U.K. Accountability and the Constitutionalism.

Chapter 17 deals with independence of judiciary and judicial process; Basic Components of an independent judiciary; Basic Principles of Independence of Judiciary. Latent dangers of independence of judiciary, and some basic notes on Independence of a judges and the judiciary.

Chapter 18 talks about Democracy and role of the judicial process in its composition, running and what does each expect from the other and what people want.

Bhubaneshwar
KIIT University

Prof. G.P. Tripathi (Dr)
Mr. G.G. Padmakar LL.M.

Preface to First Edition

The erstwhile jurisprudence that we studied in law classes during LL.B. and LL.M. was a general study of entire literature on law. It meant legal theory, (concept of law), elements of law (concepts of law) and sources of law. Much water has flown under the bridges in Ganges since those days when LL.B./LL.M. both used to be two years course. The Bar Council in its effort to improve the quality of legal profession devised three years law degree programme after graduation in any stream, *i.e.* arts, science, commerce. agriculture, medicine, engineering, dental or pharmacy had nothing to do with law as degree. So the graduates in these did not bother to study law after graduating in these areas. The management was a discipline added to commerce so BBA and MBA were not heard as separate disciplines for studies.

Traditionally the 10+2 students had arts, science, commerce, medicine and engineering as choice to chalk out their future. Law as choice was not available to 10+2 pass outs.

The Bar Council of India resolved to create 'Law' as another option to 10+2 pass outs. They opened a 5 years law degree integrated (honours) course as option to other professional courses like engineering and medicines. It clicked and young 10+2 students who had seen engineering and medicine graduate falling out of demand in job market turned towards this course. National Law School, Bangalore started on experimental basis. Law graduates created a good market for themselves better than what was available to engineers and medicine graduates. The medicine and engineering courses did not remain that popular in job market.

The cost on their studies escalcated beyond what even richest could bear out. Blackmarketers entered. The schooling in these areas went beyond average families in India. Banks started Educational loans students got help. Hon's courses have clicked.

Legal education turned out to be cheaper and better option in professional courses. the judges, advocates and law professors grabbed this 'opportunity created by Bar Council of India and patronised these schools imparting 5 years legal education. The position is that law course has become choice No. 1 of new generation. We have got 14 National Law Universities wherein trimester/ semester pattern of schooling is going on. Many of these universities are giving B.A., LL.B. Course, some are giving B.Sc., LL.B./B.Com.,LL.B. 5 yrs. law degree. State Universities, Central Universities and Private Universities have joined hands with these national law universities and are running 5 years law degree courses.

B.B.A.–LL.B./B.Tech.–LL.B are latest option now in legal education. MATS Law School is out to offer facilities for these courses.

All these are specialised career providing courses. As such, need specialists professors for handling it. The jurisprudence is now divided in legal method, legal theory and judicial process for giving specialisation in these as foundation course.

The courses are running but there is no text book which may be readily available to help students to know as to what would they need to study in judicial process. Hence this book.

The book contains 12 chapters, Chapter 1 deals with Nature of Judicial Process. Chapter 2 : Constitutional adjudication, Chapter 3 : Court Structure, Chapter 4 : Precedent, Chapter 5 : Statutory interpretation, Chapter 6 : Methods of Judicial Process, Chapter 7 : Method of History and Judicial Process, Chapter 8 : Comparative Method, Chapter 9 : Law and Justice, Chapter 10 : Administrative Structure, Chapter 11 : Private Law, Chapter 12 : Procedure and Chapter 13 : Legislation, Chapter 14 : Rule of Law and Judicial Process, Chapter 15 : Constitutionalism, Chapter 16 : Independence of Judiciary, Chapter 17 : Democracy, Chapter 18 : Constitution and Election.

Now thanks and acknowledgments. MATS Law School is one of the top few in the country. Let anybody examine from any angle. Being in recently established State of Chhattisgarh, (Raipur, Tahsil Arang village Gullu), it provides best academic climate for study and research to the faculties and students who hail from throughout the country from Assam to Kerala and from Bengal to Odisha, Rajasthan, Delhi, Tamilnadu, Andhra and beautiful seven sisters of the country what to say of M.P., U.P. and Maharashtra and locals. 70% students of our school are hostellers. We are English medium co-education Institution running BB.A, LL.B, B.A., LL.B, LL.B. (three years) and LL.M. (trimester/semester/annual one year and distance mode), Ph.D. and LL.D.

The school gives 10 short-term placements to each student during his/her schooling here, each is of 6 weeks. We have collaboration with many National Law Universities in India like NLIU Bangalore, NLU Maharashtra, Bombay, CNLU Patna and Patna Law College Patna University and abroad. Our journal MATS University journal is published twice a year. This gives wonderful weather for academics and research.

So I thank first to management. Chief Patron of the University, Shri Gajraj Pagariya and the Administration, Director General Shri Priyesh Pagaria Vice Chancellor Prof. (Dr.) Byju John and Mr. Gokul Panda Registrar for giving such a trouble free academic climate wherein the writing of this book has been possible.

My sons, daughters and daughter-in-laws, Mr. Kamlakar-Vandana, Satish-Sunita, Santosh-Savita, Karunakar-Vandana, Ratnakar-Garima and Shivalkar Priyanka and Padmakar Swati and grand-son Prakhar, Daksha, Krishna, Parth and grand daughters, Peehu and Shivi and Betu deserve my blessings on this pious occasion. The credit for this work goes to my wife

(Smt.) Girish Tripathi M.A. LL.M. for leaving me tension-free and carefree for completing this assignment.

My old friend Mr. Ram Nath Arora (Nathi Bhai) and his son in law Mr. Rajiv Arora Proprietors of Central Law Publications Allahabad deserve special thanks for nice get up and flawless printing.

The book is presented to my students of MATS, HNLU, NLIU Bangalore, CNLU, Patna Law College Patna University, ICFAI, Meerut, Subharti, Agra, Lucknow, Kanpur, Gorakhpur and Allahabad Universities. In some of which I got opportunity to teach. Let them take benefit of it as they or their elder generations (Many of whom are Supreme Court and High Court Judges) have done by my earlier publications since 1969.

Gullu, Arang
MATS University Campus
28-3-2012

Prof. G.P. Tripathi (Dr)
Mr. G.G. Padmakar LL.M.

CONTENTS

Chapter 1

Meaning and the Nature of the Judicial Process

Chapter 5

Judicial method under statutory and codified system Application of legal reasoning

Chapter 6

Response of the Judicial Process to the cases of first impression

Chapter 7

Custom and judicial process

Chapter 8

Ethical Reasoning Philosophy and the judicial process

Chapter 10

Comparison as an Aid to the Judicial Method

Chapter 11

Application of Theories of Justice and Judicial Process

Chapter 15

Judicial Process and the Legislation (Legislative Process)

Chapter 16

Rule of Law and Judicial Process

Chapter 17

Independent Judiciary and Judicial Process

Chapter 18

Democracy : Expectation from Judiciary

Chapter 1

Meaning and the Nature of the Judicial Process

'Process' is a way for doing something which lends validity to action processed. Registering a plaint reply (W.S.) witness, argument, judgment and order are processes which result in decree. No decree will be there till these process are followed. So is the legislative process for passing an Act, Administration process for issuing Administrative order, *fatwa* given otherwise than Mufti is not *fatwa* that binds; so is the judicial process.

The most important understanding of the judicial process requires us to think about more than formal law and procedure. The first question which often comes in one's mind is what do you exactly mean by critical analysis of judicial process? Is it merely a statement of criticism or something beyond the imagination of one's thinking? However, if we closely analyse, then all the doubts become crystal clear because 70 years after independence, the entire judicial system is said to be on the verge of collapse. While the superior courts have earned praise from citizens for intervening in citizen's concerns raised through public interest petitions, only those with resources or cunning can hope to get ordinary justice. Over three crore cases are presently pending in various courts. In most cases, citizens have little hope of getting justice in their lifetime. Cost corruption and abuse of court processes are rampant.

So, what exactly judicial process is?

Everything done by judge in the process of delivery of justice is called judicial process. It basically confines itself to the study of "is" to "ought" of the law.

One should be very clear from the outset that judicial process from trial court to the Appellate/Revision goes on and a case is decided on facts searched, tested and established by evidence and in the light of law relevant and applicable therein. It is not decided on the basis of any theory of law. We apply theories to these decisions if consistent on any view or theory.

The judicial process is a set of interrelated procedures and roles for deciding disputes by an authoritative person or persons whose decisions are regularly obeyed. The disputes are to be decided according to previously agreed upon set of procedures and in conformity with prescribed rules. As an incident, or consequence, of their dispute-deciding function, those who decide make authoritative statements of how the rules are to be applied, and these statements have a prospective generalized impact on the behavior of many besides the immediate parties to the dispute. Hence the judicial process is both a means of resolving disputes between identifiable and specified persons and a process for making public policies.

Development of the concept of judicial process

For centuries hundreds of writers in thousands of articles and books have tried to determine what is the essence of the judicial or adjudicatory process, what distinguishes it from the legislative and administrative processes. During the last several centuries this exercise in political taxonomy has taken on special urgency and normative concerns. For under the doctrine of separation of powers it became improper for legislatures to engage in the judicial process—issuance of bills of attainder, for example, or for judges to assume functions that are thought to be within the scope of the legislative process.

The classic doctrine of separation of powers divided the world of political activity into the three familiar divisions based both on what was thought to be the behaviour of political actors and on what were thought to be the requirements for the maintenance of liberty. The judiciary was assigned the function of applying the laws that the constitution makers and the legislatures had created and that the administrators enforced.

Today political analysts have abandoned these categories in favor of a continuum. At one pole is the legislative process for making law (formulating norms) and at the other the administrative and judicial processes for administration or applying the law (individualizing the norm). (These categories are analytic, and the activities are not necessarily performed by agencies with corresponding labels). As to the distinction between the administrative and judicial, some writers such as Hans Kelsen and Otto Kirchheimer insist that these processes cannot be distinguished functionally and that it is more or less a historical accident whether some disputes are assigned to what are known as courts whereas others are assigned to what are known as administrative agencies. Others, such as Roscoe Pound, insist that the difference grows out of the fact that administrators are not obliged to make their decisions by following prescribed procedures or in accord with legal doctrines. Administration is seen by these writers as power and discretion, whereas adjudication is rational and controlled.

The orthodox theory

According to what is variously called the "mechanical", "slot-machine", "photographic", "formalistic", "conceptual", or "orthodox" theory of the judicial process, judges, like doctors or scientists, are trained technicians who apply their specialized knowledge to discover answers to legal disputes. Judging is to be sharply distinguished from politics. Political forces determine what the rules are; the judge merely applies the given rules to the facts. If the judges come across a novel situation for which there is no agreed upon rule, by a process of analogy and logic they discover what rule should be applied; to this extent, and to this extent only, they may be said to create rules. Some commentators have even gone further : to them the judicial process is a self contained world with its own dynamics and is totally divorced from the political system. And even those who recognize that legal rules and judicial decisions are related to the political community insist that the judges and the law they apply are neutral among competing interests within the community. The judge is a spokesman for the more enduring values of the society, not merely the wishes of those who are for the moment governing it. As the noted English barrister Sir Carleton Kemp Allen phrased it :

> Our law has had its political vicissitudes, and at certain periods of its history it has been threatened with degradation into an instrument of government; it might, indeed, have suffered that dismal fate but for the resistance of men like Sir Edward Coke. But today there is nothing more repellent to Anglo-Saxon legal instinct than the corruption of law by political "ideology".

Major assertions—The realists criticism

The formalistic conception of the judicial process has always been questioned. But beginning towards the end of the last century, and with great zeal in this century, there has been a mounting criticism of it. The attack has come from many sources and from many different writers. The skeptics represent a wide variety of different kinds of analyses, many of which contradict one another, and it is difficult to present the skeptics' views as a consistent whole. They are often grouped together under the label of "legal realists", although at times this appellation is reserved for a smaller number of American writers of the 1920s and 1930s. Using the term "realists" in its broadest sense to include all who are skeptical of the traditional analysis, we might mention three of the major assertions :

(1) Legal rules do not determine judicial decisions.—"The theory that rules decide cases seems for a century to have fooled, not only library-ridden recluses, but judges". "The half explanatory, half apologetic reference to the judge's subservience to the law is at best a playful protective device; at worst it testifies to his unwillingness to understand his own role in the social process."

The point here and about it there remains, much confusion is not that there are no legal rules or that there is always uncertainty as to what the law requires. The skepticism relates to the extent to which rules determine judicial decisions. There are rules, for example, conferring jurisdiction on courts and making their decisions authoritative. Clearly understood laws govern the great bulk of human transactions; most men know what they must do if they wish the contracts they make to be valid and enforceabl by courts. Most legal conflicts do not give rise to litigation, since the law provides relatively precise answers to most questions without the necessity of bringing the matter before a judge. Furthermore, often the judge is not asked which rule should be applied but what happened, that is, to determine who did what to whom. And in other instances, especially at the trial level, the judge's function is to legitimize a transaction by applying a rule about which there is no dispute. No judge is likely to make a decision in such a case contrary to the widely accepted rule; if he did so his decision would not long survive, and he would be unmasked as an incompetent. In this sense he has no discretion, and the rule does provide a guideline.

However, when a judge must resolve a conflict and there is a dispute as to which rule should be applied, the traditional explanation of the judicial process is misleading. According to this explanation judges look to past precedents or to constitutions, statutes, or codes and find the proper rule to resolve the dispute. But there are conflicting precedents and an infinite variety of factual situations to which the uncertain precedents can apply. Nor do constitutions, statutes, and codes provide certain guidelines. "Much of the jurisprudence of this century has consisted of the progressive realization (and sometimes the exaggeration) of the important fact that the distinction between the uncertainties of communication by authoritative example (precedent), and the certainties of communication by authoritative general language (legislation) is far less firm than this naive contrast suggests."

(2) The formal theory of interpretation and the fiction of legislative intent are methods of "paying lip service to the prevailing myth of statutory interpretation and to the equally mythical notion that judicial legislation is both unconstitutional and improper. Attempts to hide that fact of the creative function of statutory interpretation behind a cloak of verbiage are fatuous at best. And the judicial creative activity applies, to some degree at least, to all statutes."

Judges do and must make law. But this is not to say that when judges make law they are acting improperly, for such lawmaking is inherent in their function. A judge may be neutral between the parties to a lawsuit and dedicated to the principles of his craft, but he must choose; and the difference between one judge's choice and another's does not stem from any difference in their technical knowledge of the law, but from their differing response to the conflicting values which the case presents.

To recognize that judges make law is not to conclude that they are "free" to make any law they wish; and while one strand of the realist ferment emphasizes the choice-making, creative role of the judge, another searches for the variables that condition and restrict that choice.

(3) The decisions are not personal choices of the judges, accidental, arbitrary, or divorced from the rest of the political system. Although some American realists of the 1930s seemed to suggest that judicial rulings were determined by the personality traits of the jurists which some wag labeled the "breakfast-food theory" of jurisprudence—most writers have concluded that to add personality to precedent does not substantially advance our understanding of the judicial process.

Statutory directions, traditional procedures, the demands of the judicial role, and the organizational and political connections between the judicial process and the political system set limits to and give a direction to judicial decision making.

Underlying much of the work of the realists is the view that since judges must inevitably choose between competing values, awareness of the fact that they are making such choice, some knowledge on which to base these choices, and concern for the social consequences of the choice are desirable.

One looks around, after war and foreign danger have sweated some of this silliness out of us, and sees vastly different scene. The danger lies now in altogether different quarters. The danger now is that men will lose confidence in their judges, thinking that they operate without regard to generalizable standards.

Neo-orthodox theory

A group of scholars for whom there is as yet no label but who may be called the "neo-orthodox" have redirected attention not to how the judicial process is like the legislative but to how it differs. The whole purpose of the judicial process, they argue, is to permit knowledge and argument to lead to a reasoned decision. To reduce the analysis of the judicial process to the same terms that are used to describe the legislative process is to strip the judicial of that distinguishes it from the other ways to order human affairs. Although it is not to be assumed that judges are superhuman logicians or even that their decisions always are the deductive application of legal rules, nonetheless their decisions are products of a different set of conditions than are those of political actors who are directly accountable to political majorities and who are assigned different tasks and different roles.

Some skeptics of the orthodox ideology concede that the judges sometimes do make value choices and that the law does not necessarily determine their behavior. Nonetheless, they argue, the policy-making activity of the judges is an exception to the general course of judicial business and stems primarily from giving judges the power of judicial review.

Whether a synthesis between the realist and formalist concepts of the judicial process will result and whether such a synthesis will provide a better tool for understanding the dynamics of the judicial process is yet to be determined. As it stands, in the world of scholarship the formalist view has been modified, and the statement of the realist position is no longer so shrill. Among sophisticates the orthodox explanations of judicial behavior are no longer in good standing. On the other hand, there is no longer much shock value in pointing out that the judges are men and like all men are subject to limited perspectives. Few scholars now deny that the judicial process operates within and is conditioned by the political system and that judges make policy, but because of their adjudicatory function they make policy in special ways. Outside the world of scholarship, the orthodox position still holds. The prevailing expectations still require judges to state their decisions as controlled by statutes or precedents, and the official explanation of public men and practicing lawyers remains that the law is independent of the judges and controls their behavior.

Organization of the judicial process

The organization of the judicial process is determined by its purpose : to adjudicate particular kinds of disputes. (There must be a conflict between parties presenting the judges with a "yes" or "nay" choice.) By definition, among the factors that distinguish adjudication from the other techniques of dispute deciding—bargaining, electioneering, voting, fighting—is that each side in the conflict is entitled to be heard by an outside to the dispute who is to make his decision solely on the evidence presented to him and in accord with a standard of right and wrong.

In democratic societies adjudication is based on an entirely different set of expectations than those that underlie the legislative or executive functions. What the majority wishes is what the legislators should decide. But adjudication called for decisions in accord with standards of right, to be made by persons who are free to apply these standards without concern for the popularity of their decisions. Adjudication rests on the conviction that some kinds of differences are best resolved by an appeal to a specially qualified elite.

Based on these expectations and in accord with its defined function, the judicial process is deliberately organized to "disconnect" it from the rest of the community. The judicial system ordinarily does not have direct lines of accountability to the political authorities. (In some American states where judges are elected for short terms obviously this is not so.) This independence of the judicial system from the community is based on the need for dispute deciders who are not subject to outside instructions or coercion. Both realist and orthodox analyses support this independence in order that those who come before the judges may have a hearing by a tribunal free to make a decision on the basis of the evidence and arguments presented to it. The orthodox ideology has the additional advantage of squaring this judicial independence with the principles of democratic politics, for portraying the judges as technicians who do not participate in the resolution of policy conflicts makes it unnecessary to hold them politically accountable.

Selection procedures and tenure arrangements vary from nation to nation, but their design is to reduce considerations of partisan politics and to maximize attention to professional qualifications. Although, lay participation still survives in the form of jury and lay judges, the definition of the "best qualified" now carries the expectations that the judges will be men trained in law. As early as the seventeenth century the celebrated Lord Code told King James that since he lacked knowledge of the "artificial reasons and judgment of the law" even the king was not entitled to decide cases but must act through his law-trained officers. Nowadays the legal profession has much to say as to who among them shall be selected as a judge, even if the actual selection process vests the final choice in political authorities. (The Supreme Court of the United States is to a considerable extent an exception in that the president exercises something like a personal prerogative in choosing justices for this Court.) Once selected, judges are expected to perform in accordance with professional standards, and they are measured by these standards : judges are members of distinctive professional group who look to that group for their prestige.

Courtroom access and judicial scope

Since judges are expected to approach each case with an open mind, in all nations they lack authority to initiate proceedings for if permitted to do so, it is felt, they would be compelled to pre-judge the case. "It is the fact that such application of person claiming rights must be made to him, which distinguishes a judge from an administrative officer. Of greater significance, however, than the fact that the judges may not start lawsuits is the fact that an ordinary individual through a regular lawsuit may raise fundamental questions of public policy. Whereas only those with some political strength may command legislative attention, a single individual may compel a judge to make a ruling. The litigant may be concerned only with his own problems : to secure ownership of a piece of property, to dissolve a marriage contract, or to stay out of prison; but the decision he secures will create or confirm a rule that governs the behavior of many persons other than himself.

In the Anglo-American nations there are no distinctions between courts created to adjudicate disputes and those established to hear conflicts involving questions of "high politics". The higher appellate courts, however, operate under rules specifying that they are not to hear cases merely to do justice between litigants but only where the public interest is paramount. Nonetheless, they are organized like and function as ordinary law courts. Civil law nations do attempt to distinguish more sharply between courts created to adjudicate law-suits and those established to deal with questions of more general public significance. In the German Federal Republic and in Italy, for example, special courts deal with constitutional questions. Their jurisdiction does not depend on the ordinary litigant but may be invoked by public authorities. In France a separate court system deals with disputes between citizens and administrative officials.

There are limits to courtroom access. Generally speaking, only those who are able to persuade the judges that they are personally and directly involved in a dispute may seek a judicial resolution of it, and there are some kinds of disputes judges will not attempt to decide. The technical rules and rationalizations to distinguish between "justiciable" and "non-justiciable" issues vary from nation to nation and time to time. The widest range of subjects are dealt with by courts in nations such as the United States, Australia, and Canada, where the constitution is a legal as well as a political document, that is, a document subject to construction by judges. In the United States judges have the broad jurisdiction characteristic of the common law countries, plus the authority to treat the constitution as a legal instrument. The Supreme Court of the United States has been squarely in the middle of almost every major political conflict that has arisen within the American republic. But even in the United States the judicial process has played a minor role in some areas : conflicts over control of the machinery of government; price policies for the distribution of goods and services; and the whole area of American relations with foreign nations.

Civil law nations attempt to restrict the impact of decisions to the immediate cases, and except in a few nations—and here only since World

War II—constitutional documents are not considered to be subject to judicial construction. The French judiciary, for example, has never been the pivot for any major political interest. It is impossible to cite a single judicial ruling that has had a substantial impact on the political life of that nation, which is all the more remarkable in view of the highly divisive nature of French politics.

Litigation as a device for making policy depends upon the ability to formulate a lawsuit that presents judges with a year or nay choice. However, for some issues a day in court is easier to secure than a day before the legislature. The "chips" for winning the judicial "game" are different from those for winning the legislative "game", since judges are related to the political community in a different fashion than are legislators. Groups who lack electoral strength may, therefore, find it more profitable to resort to litigation than to legislation. However, without some political strength in the community, major alterations of public policy through litigation are as unlikely as through legislation. For the chance of securing favorable judicial rulings is not unrelated to the political configurations of the community. Unpopular minorities whose activities have been restricted by legislation seldom have more success before the courts than they have had before the legislature. Yet in many nations because of such factors as federalism, bicameralism, election district geography, rules of debate in the legislature, and so on, even relatively widely supported values may not secure legislative expression. The judicial process thus provides a forum for raising issues in a different context from the one provided by legislative or executive decision makers.

The formal requirements of judicial process

By definition adjudication is distinguished from other techniques of dispute deciding in that it calls for the open presentation of evidence and reasoned argument before impartial judges who are to make their decisions in accord with the evidence and arguments presented to them and in accord with established standards. Courts exist to settle lawsuits, and this function imposes certain requirements on judicial procedures. Whether these requirements accurately describe how judges behave is for the moment irrelevant, for they have a significance divorced from consideration of whether they are descriptively accurate.

Judicial decisions are expected to be based only on the information formally fed into the system. In contrast legislators and administrators (except when they are expected to perform as judges) may secure information whenever and however they please, may contact rival claimants in private, and are under no obligation to give each claimant an opportunity to respond to the other side. Judges, however, are forbidden to discuss a case or to gather evidence outside the formal proceedings. Although in the misleadingly named "inquisitorial system" of civil-law countries, judges have somewhat more leeway in making independent investigations, they too operate under narrowly prescribed procedures designed to exclude from consideration any fact or arguments except those which the participants have presented in formal proceedings. (The doctrine of "judicial notice" provides an exception. Judges are permitted to make rulings in the light of knowledge that is so widely known and acceptable that it may be taken into account without being formally presented to them.)

Judges must explain decisions.—Other decision makers are often called on to justify their actions and to put their decisions into the rhetoric of the public well-being. But only judges are compelled to provide detailed, formally stated, and—at the appellate level—frequently written justifications of why they decided as they did. The fact that a judge knows that he will have to justify his ruling and expose his arguments to the critical attention of a professional audience of his peers has an impact on the decisions he makes which is easy to see, difficult to measure, and little studied. The formally written opinion, of course, tidies up a much more complex decision-making process. Many students have been concerned with the various forms of reasoning judges use and have wondered whether they make decisions first and then seek rules to justify them, or whether they move from general rules to the particular dispute.

Judicial rulings as political forces

A judicial opinion justifying a decision, especially of an appellate court, itself becomes a factor in the political process. For the opinion is both an explanation of a particular decision and instruction to law officers, including subordinate judges, as to how they should dispose of similar disputes. And these opinions, like statutes, are themselves subject to a variety of constructions.

Both the traditional and realist analysis of the judicial process tend to emphasize the finality of a judicial ruling. Chief Justice Charles Evans Hughes' famous quip that the constitution is what the judges say it is frequently cited to demonstrate that although the Congress may pass a law, it is the Supreme Court which determines whether it will be applied. To the same point is the often quoted remark by Gray, one of the intellectual fathers of the realist movement : "Statutes are sources of law, not part of the law itself". In the same tradition Kirchheimer writes, "The validity of a norm does not follow from its existence, but from the fate it suffers in the administrative and judicial process."

Judicial process consists likewise of how a suit or complaint is filed, processes issued, evidence and witnesses on facts in issue, arguments and the judgment, decree or punishment takes shape, and executed. The journey starts when plaint is instituted and registered (in civil cases) or FIR is lodged or complaint is filed (criminal case) passing through enquiry and trial, the criminal case results into punishment or acquittal. In civil case, statement of plaintiff and his witnesses, that of defendant and his witnesses, examination in chief, cross examination, judgment, order and then decree, its execution and satisfaction. The appeal, revision or judicial review are all different steps in judicial process. The court and the judges are the mechanism of this process and Code of Civil Procedure, Criminal Procedure Code and Law of Evidence and Rules of Courts are laws that lead and regulate the exercise of this process.

The judicial process is judgment or decree or sentence producing mechanism. It has its special features, weakness and strengths. It needs reforms and the shortcoming can be improved. Alternative Dispute Resolutions like Arbitration, Conciliation, Mediation, Lok Adalats, Panchayats and Gramin Nyalaya are coming up to add or to improve upon the current judicial process. Judicial Accountability Bill 2011 is before Parliament that is in legislative process.

Judicial Process includes what the presiding officer of the court of law does or how he works or behaves on the way to delivery of justice. What he does and what he ought to do is the basic question that we address in discussion on judicial process. That is the study of journey from 'is' to 'ought' of law. It is an analysis of whole complex of phenomenon of court working. What is court structure? What is its present status? satisfactory, good, bad or excellent. Does it need any reform? Whether reforms made hitherto are or are not productive? What else is needed?

What happens is that courts sit and work everyday. Through out the world, process is identical. Suits or complaints are filed in registry or court. Proper draft of plaint is prepared. It is duly stamped and filed. Processes are issued through summons to the opposite parties. Sometimes through process server and sometimes through registered post. The date is mentioned for appearance of the opposite party either in person or through counsel duly authorised and briefed. That is how the process begins.

Civil Procedure Code, Court Fee Act, Suit Valuation Act and Court Rules are all made use of hitherto. Evidence Act and Limitation Act are very helpful in judicial process. Process continues in appeal, second appeal, revision, reference, review and writs for judicial review. It extends to executions proceedings in civil matters and conviction, sentencing and sending convict to jail in criminal process. Judicial process ends after convict is handed over to jail authorities for serving jail term or till execution in death penalty cases. Death warrant is issued by the court that initially gave death punishment.

Non-judicial functionaries in judicial process

Judicial process does not depend on the hierarchy of Presiding Officers alone. It is process of Courts from subordinate to Supreme Court. Loophole anywhere tarnishes the image of the whole judicial system :

Criminal system.—Main functionaries are :

Constable Munshi who records the FIR;

Beat constables who bring the culprit;

Investigation officer (I.O) who records the statement of victims under Section 161 and 164, Cr.P.C. and submits report either under Section 169 (final report) or under Section 173 (challani report, chargesheet or police report).

Medical officer who conducts post-mortem;

Compounder of police hospital who manages injury report and post-mortem report.

Sweeper (hela) who for all practical purposes conducts *'cheerfad'* (post-mortem). He decides on the spot whether wound is; incised, piercing, or inflated (deflated). This decision is acted upon through out the judicial system and how does it function is well known to those connected with judicial process?

Civil system.—Civil system means what is known as "Diwani". Hierarchy of Civil Courts is regulated by Provincial Civil Courts Act of each State. Some of the Courts are called Institution Courts; like Civil Judge Junior Division; Civil Judge Senior Division. The former has jurisdiction upto fixed amount; jurisdiction of the latter is unlimited (in civil matters). The Courts of District and Session Judge is First Appellate Court (under Section 96, C.P.C.). High Court is Court of Second Appeal on substantive questions of law. Special appeals go to Supreme Court under Article 136.

Non-judicial officer.—Institution clerk maintains register of suits filed. The matter after registry goes to Court through *peshi* clerk to Presiding Officer. Copy section issues copy of orders passed. In final disposal matters, decrees are issued and proceedings of execution ensue.

In Revenue Matters, Highest revenue Court is Board of Revenue. Next down to it are Court of Commissioner, Collector, C.R.O. S.D.O, Tehsildars and Naib-Tahsildars. The Qanungo and Lekhpals are revenue officials.

Other courts are consolidation courts, Family Courts, Labour Courts and Tribunals like CAT or SATS.

Any sickness or slackness anywhere would go to damage the reputation of judicial process.

Judicial process as instrument of social ordering

No society would survive when there is chaos and disorder around. The survival of society is ensured by 'Dharma' (the right path) its members follow. May be family, village, community, religion, caste, race, creed, region, State, country or international community. The order keeps it organised and chaos makes any of these or all disorganized. Job of law is to establish peace, and order. There is every court as 'dharma'. King has his own dharma (Rajdharma), so father (Pitra dharma), Putra dharma, Pati-Patni dharma etc. Every unit moves on this path. Sun, moon, earth, stars have their own dharma. So has nature; summer, rain, winter come in order (dharma). It cannot be broken.

So is in society. dharma-religion—moral—love—culture/law all operate to keep order in the society. All must go together. All must cooperate to assist order in society and also all unite. Law is very effective if all these pull on in same direction as society wants. If any or all pull in different directions, there is disorder, discontentment and feeling generated is of something being wrong. Law alone can not pull or push the society ahead. It needs cooperation of all these factors.

Law is a weapon pulled out of weaponry of state. It is as such very powerful. Therefore, expectations from law are great. Responsibilities are great. Be it legislature, executive or judiciary, all the three are three wings of Government. Constitutional governance requires all three to operate in three areas; law making. law implementation and law interpretation. Legislature is constituted by election in democracy, Executive is by selection or election somewhere direct, elsewhere indirect. It is judiciary which is constituted on merit like administrators. People have great faith in judiciary. It is the sentinel of people's interests. It is the last resort to which people look for remedies. It is guardian of people, rights, their liberties, their life, their property. All are safe if judicial system is on track.

In many European countries, judiciary is a department of Government. It works like other departments. People do not have more expectation from court than what they have from the Government in power. Judiciary does not enjoy any special status or protection of law in these countries. Rule of law ensures that the law is respected. Things move according to law. It is law that has responsibility to keep law and order in society. It aims social welfare, people's comfort and survival of society. It may create paternal government, or maternal government or government of law, by law and for law for the welfare of society through law, legal institutions and rule of law. For ensurng survival of all these, the delivery of justice according to law is a must.

Functions of law and the legal system

The law serves many purposes and functions in society. Four principal purposes and functions are establishing standards, maintaining order, resolving disputes, and protecting liberties and rights. The law is a guidepost for minimally acceptable behavior in society.

What law does? What is the function of social order that the law establishes in the society? When we talk about function of legal system in society, concept or theories of law are not relevant. These theories explain why behind? The organisation of law, the system of law and the Government is relevant. The function of legal order is basically maintenance of peace in the society. The individuals living together and the institutions that the men set for regulating their living are kept in order so as to ensure that these institutions survive and the individuals flourish to see these organisations surviving. This is the basic job of the legal system, and this is done by norms set by the individuals while living in the society. Social order is not much different from legal order.

Kelsen described the legal system as pyramid of norms over norms. These legal norm pyramids are different from morality or religion which also restrain arbitrary and undesirable conducts of the individuals constituting social order with one difference. The difference lies in how deviance is handled. In socio-legal order, the deviance is tackled by another person who is part of the same socio legal order and is designated by the socio-legal order itself to handle the deviance. The person so designated can inflict the punishment on the deviant. The punishment is also prescribed by the same socio-legal order. How it is inflicted is also given in the same socio-legal order. The whole process is in—house arrangement; so does it operate within as such.

Moral or religious restraints are equally or sometimes with more telling effect but role of super human authority is relevant. Moreso, their effect is only on believers.

Law and order

Law is when order is; there can be no law, when there is disorder. When disorder prevails, law flies out and keeps watching that goes on when disorder continues. Law pounces upon when disorder is replaced by order and takes account of what has been done during disorder. There is nothing like law of disorder. Laws of war are there but law does not regulate war. It is one that takes care of when war ends.

Law and Dharma in

Change is the law of nature. An infant becomes child, child to adolescent—youth—adult and old. In case of Dharma, it never changes because it is the foundation. Any change in dharma destroys the unit whose dharma is disturbed by the change, or non-observance. Dharma does not change, it adjusts the changes all around while keeping the basics unchanged. It is like Constitution which can be changed except as regards its basic features which can not be amended. Dharma is life, basis and breath of every unit, may be individual, family, community, caste, society or country. India cannot be Russia, China, or America. Their foundations are different. Religion is not 'dharma'. It may, at the most, be one of the indices of dharma along with culture, morality, love and law.

Dharma does not change. It can not change. It sustains the unit. Religions are so many. Religions change and people change religion. Religion relegates one to self. That is 'God' or any thing else if there is something other than God. Morality is Individual's morality to public morality through social morality; differs from time to time, place to place, culture to culture, man to man. What is moral to one is contrary to morality of the other. What is approved by moral in year 2012 may be disapproved by moral sense of 2020. Living together without proper marriage and sharing bed and board was immoral. It is now tolerated as new morality of 'live in relationship'. Same sex marriage'; could it be thought of few years back; say in 1980? It is advocated today. Intercaste marriage; think of it in Haryana, West U.P. you will see how family prestige, and family ego react? Love of family, parents, grand parents, brothers and sisters is now confined to fascination amongst young immature youths for opposite sexes. These are forgotten *quo* sex infatuations. The guardians of law (Police) have to show sometime violent reactions which may come nearer to savagery.

Law always tries to keep society within dotted lines but changes itself when it appears to it that new lines are required by the same society. It changes itself to keep abreast with changes. Indian Penal Code 1860 (with amendments) is still main criminal code in 2012. It is still working. New crimes like cyber crimes and others are being taken care of by society going for new enactments. Sometimes law changes as per need of society, whereas some other time society adjusts howsoever painfully with enacted law. Reservation laws, dowry laws, domestic violence laws. S.C., S.T. atrocities prevention laws all have come, society has adjusted.

Judicial process and social change; whether law leads social change or vice-versa?

In Civil legal system, legislature makes law, executes law and interprets law, so do the executive, administrative and judicial departments of the Government. All three wings act unitedly to give effect to the policy of the Government. In common law systems, the three do three jobs differently. One makes law, the second executes law and the third interprets law. All the three are three specialists doing the job. Each checks and cross checks the other. The relationship is that of check and balance. The judiciary reviews whether laws are made keeping in view the Constitution and rule of law, whether the law made is not violative of rule of law. It can declare any law crossing permissible limits as ultravires or unconstitutional. The Constitution is not a rigid statute. It is living law and it is by judicial process that it is kept abreast as living law.

The Acts made in 1860, 1872, 1881 are still alive and are still accepted, for this, credit goes only to judicial process which has remained alert and updated to solve problems of the people and those statutes that are in disuse or non-use have become obsolete. The legal system survives, it is all due to healthy judicial response to changes in society.

Shaken faith of people in legislators does not affect the system directly. That is the position when loss of faith concerns the executive or the administrators. These leave enough leverages to save public confidence in law, system of law and the Government. But shaken faith of people (the parties, their families, the accused) in court leaves wound that are not easily filled up. It is faith of common man in judicial process and the courts that keeps the society alive, lively and liveable. Judicial process has responsibility to preserve it and prove that it has done. The uproar of judicial accountability indicates that there is an erosion in it. The sooner it is repaired, the better it is for us and the system and also for the society.

Judicial process; as it is now

Our judicial system is admirable though it may be, (it) is at once slow and costly. It is a finished product of great beauty, but entails an immense sacrifice of time, money and talent.

This 'beautiful' system is frequently a luxury, it tends to give a high quality of justice only when for one reason or another, parties can surmount the substantial barriers, which it erects to most people and to many types of claims."

Why drive common people to public interest action? Where Directive Principles have found statutory expression in Do's and Don't's, the court will not sit idly by and all municipal government to become a statutory mockery. The law will relentlessly be enforced and the plea of poor finance will be poor alibi when people in misery cry for justice. The dynamics of the judicial process has a new 'enforcement' dimension not merely through some of the provisions of the Criminal Procedure Code (as here), but also through activated tort consciousness. The officers in-charge and even the elected representatives will have to face the penalty of the law, if what the Constitution and follow-up Legislation direct them to do or defied or denied wrongfully."

In a landmark judgment delivered between *Gujarat Steel Tubes Ltd.* v. *Gujarat Steel Tubes Mazdoor Sabha and others* reported in 1980 SCC (II) 593, while commenting upon the rationale of oral arguments by the lawyers community, justice Iyer made the following observations :

> "Orality ad libitum may be the genius of Victorian Era advocacy but in our 'needy' Republic with crowded dockets, forensic brevity is a necessity. The Bench and the Bar must fabricate a new shorthand form of court methodology, which will do justice to the pockets of the poor, who seek right and justice and to the limited judicial hours humanly available to the court if the delivery system of justice is not to suffer obsolescence."

The judiciary is one of the pillars on which the edifice of the constitution is built. It is the guiding pillar of democracy, what is happening inside it is a fascinating study. Its logbook shows that often the judgments of the Apex Court degenerated into a dismal failure. There are many self inflicted wounds. This is the story of 70 years of the Supreme Court. Speaking of the Supreme Court of United States of America, Jackson J., of the court said, "we are final, not because we are infallible, we are infallible because we are final." the judgments of the Supreme Court are final but not infallible. They require constructive criticism, especially to take them out of the morass of alien concept and ideas foreign to the land and culture. The Supreme Court is virtually the proverbial ivory tower, with the judges sitting on the top. Disturbed by some of its judgments, Pt. Nehru once said in a diatribe, "judges of the Supreme Court sit on ivory towers, far removed from ordinary men and know nothing about them." The Supreme Court is sometimes said to be beyond the reach of a common person.

Now, a question arises;

What is justice? Is an age long question since the beginning of civilization? It is an elusive term. What appears justice to one person and from one viewpoint may be injustice to another or in another prospective. We cannot have such elusive concept as a yardstick. There must always be some objective test to form a foundation of just society. Jurisprudence formulates that test as "justice according to rules". Therefore, W. Freidmann said, "justice is an irrational concept". He concludes that justice as a generally valid concept is the goal to which every order aspires as a "purposeful enterprise".

The question arises as to what actually went wrong to judicial process in India? Because the Supreme Court, instead of searching and basing its judgments on first principles or fundamentals of jurisprudence has sometimes taken a shortcut by resorting to the supposed fiat of Article 142.

This Article was employed as a tool to pass final decisions, apart from and without recourse to the law of the land. The concept of expanding universe is not confined to astronomy alone. There is fast expanding judicial firmament. The expansion of judicial world sometimes reads on fields occupied and reserved for others. It is very necessary that Supreme Court acts with self restraint. Let us remember the adage, "power corrupts and absolute power corrupts absolutely".

There are certain questions which are needed to be answered in the working of judicial process, like :

1. What is the need of Court fees?
2. Why advocates are needed?
3. Why we are bound to pay advocate fees when they are called as officers of court?
4. Why we have chosen adversarial process of justice?
5. What is wrong with this system?
6. Is there any justification of having Limitation Act which is pro British legislation?

Critical analysis of the present system of Judicial Process

An introductory analysis of Indian judicial process

A vision of equal, expeditious and inexpensive justice for India's millions, a passion for effective delivery of social justice for the victimized masses and a mission of constitutional fulfilment through a dynamic rule of law geared to democratic values, operated by a fearless judicial personnel with a positive people oriented jurisprudence broad based an access to a sensitive, streamlined, functional jurisprudence—that is the command of the Preamble to the Constitution and the categorical imperative of Article 39-A. Our socialist Republic now hungers for human justice through human law and staggers towards nowhere since courts have lost their credibility and are writing their own obituary through retiring chief justices. Today judicial justice has come to a grinding halt, the judicature has caricatured itself and the Bench and the Bar, alas, have become a law into themselves, Indian humanity having alienated itself from the feudal forensic system and the cult of the robbed process. If all the judges and lawyers of India pull down the shutters of their law shops nationwide, injustice may not anymore escalate, if at all litigative waste of human and material resources may be obviated.

Now, a situation arises that the entire Indian justice system is now under severe threat. With the police force that has been condemned by everyone as being incompetent and corrupt, with the prosecution system that is inept and selective and a judiciary that is corrupt where is the room for justice in the Indian context?

Indian Judicial system has collapsed totally.--Be it the justice delivery system existent in criminal side or civil side, there is no hope for justice for common man. Entire fabric has been exploited and doomed. The condition of Indian judicial system worsened so much that Attorney General of India, Mr. Soli Sorabjee remarked, "Criminal Justice system in India is on the verge of collapse owing to inordinate delay in getting judicial verdict and many a potential litigant seem to take recourse to a parallel mafia dominated system of 'justice' that has sprung up in metros like Mumbai, Delhi *etc.*".

"Hamlet's lament about the laws delays still haunts us in India and the horrendous arrears of cases in courts is a disgraceful blot on our legal system, especially the criminal justice delivery system, "Striking an alarm bell, Sorabjee said : "criminal justice system is on the verge of collapse. Because Justice is not dispensed speedily, people have come to believe that there is no such thing as justice in courts".

"This perception has caused many a potential litigant who has been wronged to settle out of court on terms which are unfair to him or to secure justice by taking the law into his own hands or by recourse to a parallel mafia dominated system of 'justice' that has sprung up in metropolitan centres like Mumbai".

"The gravity of this development cannot be underestimated. Justice delayed will not only be justice denied, it will be the rule of law destroyed". The Attorney General said the time has come to ask, "Have the ideals of justice, liberty, equality and fraternity proclaimed in the preamble in grandiloquent language been realised in the working of the Constitution during the last 53 years? Have we redeemed our tryst with destiny? Have fundamental rights been merely in the realm of empty rhetoric or have become living realities for the people of India."

Apart from that there are number of questions which require answer in the working of judicial process, like :

1. What is the need of Court fees?
2. Why advocates are needed?
3. Why we are bound to pay advocate fees when they are officers of court?
4. Why we have chosen adversarial process of justice?
5. What is wrong with this system?
6. What is the use of *locus standi*?
7. Are these provisions violative of Article 14 of the Constitution? If yes, then why there is nobody to take reformative steps?

Mutual appreciation of society of judges and advocates constitute extra constitutional power and this lead to imbalance of power spectrum in society. What we need is, whatever the SC said, don't take it as gospel of God. We should be able to discover the truth; we should be able to analyze that whether the particular question is in conformity with Fundamental Rights. We should have the ability to identify what is wrong, where? Now, the analysis of governmental functioning is "the executive is failing, the legislature is failing and the judiciary has failed."

Article 13(2) clearly provided "the state shall not make any law which takes away or abridges the rights conferred by this part and any law made in contravention of this clause shall, to the extent of the contravention, be void."

Now, question arises, who is the custodian of this right? The answer is President of India under Article 60 and Governor under Article 159. President is not bound to sign the Bill which is unconstitutional, as an obligation is imposed under Article 60 that he shall preserve, protect and defend the constitution and the law. There has to be unity of command to direct state and we have President and Governor for that purpose. Article 14 compels every functionary including the judges to decide according to the provisions of the Constitution.

According to professor Burgess, the idea of complete constitution is like this :

1. Amending power of the Constitution is given under Article 368 of the Constitution.
2. Liberty : consists in three modules :
   - (i) Declaration of liberty.
   - (ii) Guarantee of liberty.
   - (iii) Suspension of liberty under Articles 358 and 359.

Organs of Governmental power.—Legislature, executive and judiciary. Professor Bluntschli, added one more, Presidential form of government has power to choose policy, what he required is only support from legislature.

If one analyzes the recent opinion of CJI that judges are not bound to disclose their assets. What the CJI is trying to do? He is just claiming unequal protection of law which is not guaranteed under Article 14 of the Constitution as he is attempting to take more protection of law; therefore, the equality clause is violated by the judges.

Education and economic development are the only two methods of correctness mentioned under Article 46 of the Constitution. But in the recent decision of SC regarding reservation policy for weaker section of the society is totally a blunder created by it. Nobody has grievance that the weaker section of society should prosper, but it does not mean robbing upper strata of society of their opportunities and development. Forward section of society cannot be pulled down to promote weaker section of the society. The basic funda is "unless there is capacity building from primary level, reservation does not help."

The answer of all the grievances are given under Article 14 of the Constitution but the judiciary has lost the beauty of this particular Article through classification. By and large Courts failed to deliver complete justice. Article 14 talks of restitutive justice and restitutive justice has the touchstone of time count. Moreover, procedural complexities should not hamper the way to justice. As laid down by SC that if you move the High Court under Article 226 then you can come to SC only under Article 136. What is this nonsense? Is it the denial to the people that by way of procedural complexities they cannot enforce their rights against the wrong doer? It is highly unconstitutional. Nobody can forfeit your right to move to SC under Article 32 if you exhaust your first remedy under Article 226, because it is violative to the protection given under Article 14. What is wrong here is the manner of working, though system is good enough to lead to equality.

The following are some of the shortcomings of the present day Judicial system :

Procedural hurdles in Access to Justice

Procedural laws are not merely a body of rules meant for facilitating the dispensation of justice on substantive questions. It also represents the value choices of the makers of law. What are their priorities—facilitating access to justice or creating hurdles to access to justice? The answer is better understood by everybody. From institution of a suit to the execution of a decree, it is the onus of private individuals, not the government. The lacuna is due to the adversarial process of justice system. Under the said model, there is no duty of the court to ascertain the truth. Adopting an adversarial system leads to number of hurdles in access to justice, especially procedural hurdles in access to justice.

It does not reflect the fundamental policy choices made in the Constitution of India. Instead it reflects the values chosen by the colonial masters, the British, who were least interested in the plight of Indians and thus placed several hurdles in access to justice by prescribing several technicalities. Though the Supreme Court has said that "procedure is hand-maiden to the substantive rights of the parties", the practical working of this hand-maiden leads to the perception that the handmaiden has had her revenge by overpowering the queen, *i.e.*, the substantive laws. Procedural laws prescribe the procedure for enforcement of substantive laws however procedural laws have been used, time and again, to defeat substantive rights.

We can say and many would agree that judicial process has not stood the test of the time. We appoint judges, give them recognition and reputation because they are amongst good brains of the society. The system wherein they work makes them decree minting machines.' We have been amending law of procedure to give a meaning to judicial process but it is still not beyond doubt whether it has worked to give us a better judicial process?

The cost, corruption and delay are out to derail the judicial process. The courts are there for deciding cases coming before them by litigating parties. The parties keep on and die without getting that dispute decided. How long the play would continue, only God knows. One thing remains; their names are called out through years to come and their heirs fight out. Sometimes the property, for which dispute was itself, is finished and in criminal cases, the accused dies pending trial or appeal. That is the situation wherein justice delivery process is at present. This reality is known to everybody. The planners as such devised Alternate Dispute. Resolutions forums but rush there too is devastating. The decisions of any or many are not final or acceptable. Lok Adalats are working but how? only the lawyers know it. Cases decided in regular sittings are listed in Lok Adalat just to complete the quota to show that system of Lok Adalat is working.

Do we need replacement of present judicial process? The court, advocate, witness, appeal and further appeal or revision process. Most of the jurisdiction erstwhile in civil courts has shifted to A.D.R. or to the tribunals or forums. Now what remains in 'Hauda khoonta' and injunctions matter before civil courts. For criminal courts, bail is the only thing that matters for an accused. The whole lower subordinate court structure is ripe for re-incarnation. The cost, corruption and delay would go with the courts.

A vision of equal, expeditious and inexpensive justice for India's millions, a passion for effective delivery of social justice for the victimized masses and a mission of constitutional fulfilment through a dynamic rule of law geared to democratic values, operated by a fearless judicial personnel with a positive people oriented jurisprudence broad based, an access to a sensitive, streamlined, functional jurisprudence—that is the command of the Preamble to the Constitution and the categorical imperative of Article 39-A is what is required to do magic that the society expects and needs from the courts and the judicial process. Our socialist Republic, now hankers for human justice through human law and staggers towards nowhere since courts are alleged to have lost their credibility and are writing their own obituary through retiring chief justices.

Today judicial justice has come to a grinding halt, the judicature has caricatured itself and the Bench and the Bar, alas, have become a law into themselves. Indian humanity having alienated itself from the feudal forensic system and the cult of the robbed process. If all the judges and lawyers of India pull down the shutters of their law shops nationwide, injustice may not anymore escalate, if at all, litigative waste of human and material resources may be obviated.

Is this view correct? Now, a situation arises that the Indian justice system is now under severe threat. With the police force that has been condemned by everyone as being incompetent and corrupt, with the prosecution system that is inept and selective and a judiciary that is corrupt where is the room for justice in the Indian context? Can we agree to it? Has Indian Judicial system collapsed totally? Be it the justice delivery system existent in criminal side or civil side. Is there no hope of justice for common man. Has the fabric been exploited and doomed. Is criminal justice system in India on the verge of collapse owing to inordinate delay in getting judicial verdict and is it the reason why many a potential litigants seem to take recourse to a parallel mafia dominated system of 'justice' that has sprung up in metros like Mumbai, Delhi and naxal dominated areas of states of Chhattisgarh, Odisha and Andhra Pradesh.

Do the "Hamlet's laments about the laws delays still haunt us in India and the horrendous arrears of cases in courts is a disgraceful blot on our legal system, especially the criminal justice delivery system. Is "criminal justice system on the verge of collapse? Because Justice is not dispensed speedily, people have come to believe that there is no such thing as justice in courts.?

"This perception has caused many a potential litigants who have been wronged to settle out of court on terms which are unfair to him or to secure justice by taking the law into his own hands or by recourse to a parallel mafia dominated system of 'justice' "The gravity of this development cannot be underestimated. Justice delayed will not only be justice denied. But it will be the rule of law destroyed." How can we balance justice delayed is justice denied with justice hurried is justice buried.

Have the ideals of justice, liberty, equality and fraternity proclaimed in the preamble in grandiloquent language been realised in the working of the Constitution during the last 66 years? Have we redeemed our tryst with destiny? Have fundamental rights been merely in the realm of empty rhetoric or have become living realities for the people of India."

The Judicial process : spectrums;

Mutual appreciation of the judges and the advocates constitutes extra constitutional power and this leads to imbalance of power spectrum in society. What we need is, whatever the Supreme Court said, don't take it as gospel of God. We should be able to discover the truth; we should be able to analyze that whether the particular question is in conformity with Fundamental rights. We should have the ability to identify what is wrong and where it is? The analysis of government functioning of the moment can be said to be; "the executive is failing, the legislature is failing and the judiciary has failed." Article 13(2) clearly provides "the State shall not make any law which takes away or abridges the rights conferred by part III and any law made in contravention of this clause (Art. 13(2)) shall to the extent of the contravention, be void."

Who is the custodian of this right? Is it the President of India (under Article 60) or the Governor (under Article 159). President is not bound to sign the Bill which is unconstitutional, as an obligation is imposed under Article 60 that he shall preserve, protect and defend the Constitution and the law. There has to be unity of command to direct State and we have President and Governor for that purpose. Article 14 compels every functionary including the judges to decide according to the provisions of the Constitution. Point to remember is; that it is our constitution that is Supreme, it is we the people of India, that are sovereign; none of the functionaries created by the Constitution are supreme; Neither Parliament, nor President nor Supreme Court. They can be said to be supreme within the areas assigned but all are subordinate to Constitution of India as by law established.

The answer of all the grievances is given under Article 14 of the Constitution but the judiciary has lost the beauty of this particular Article through classification. By and large Courts failed to deliver complete justice. Article 14 talks of restitutive justice and restitutive justice has the touchstone of time count. Moreover, procedural complexities should not hamper the way to justice only. If you move to High Court under Article 226 then you can come to Supreme Court under Article 136. Is it the denial to the people that by way of procedural complexities, they cannot enforce their rights against the wrong doer? Nobody can forfeit your right to move to SC under Article 32 if you exhaust your first remedy under Article 226, because it is violative to the protection given under Article 14. What is wrong here is the manner of working though system is good enough to lead to equality? Can the judiciary consider these?

Procedural hurdles

Procedure is whether for Justice or creating hurdles in access to justice? The answer is better understood by everybody. From institution of a suit to the execution of a decree, it is the procedure, is to be taken care of by the private individuals, not the government. The lacuna is due to the adversarial process of justice system. Under the said model, there is no duty of the court to ascertain the truth. Adopting an adversarial system leads to number of hurdles in access to justice, especially procedural hurdles in access to justice. It does not reflect the fundamental policy choices made in the Constitution of India. Instead it reflects the values chosen by the colonial masters, the British, who were least interested in the plight of litigants and thus placed several hurdles in access to justice by prescribing several technicalities. Though the "procedure is hand-maiden to the substantive rights of the parties", the practical working of this hand-maiden leads to the perception that the hand-maiden has had her revenge by overpowering the queen, *i.e.*, the substantive laws. Procedural laws prescribe the procedure for enforcement of substantive laws; however, procedural laws have been used, time and again to defeat the substantive rights. The Procedural laws hamper judicial process, tie up the judicial process and sometimes even if the court wants one thing but is forced to go the other way where it is taken by destined process. Section 151 of Code of Civil Procedure helps but only where there is no clear cut way out elsewhere.

Cost of litigation, judicial process and the ethical court.

(Order IX, R 2, Order XVI, R 2 of CPC) The most disadvantageous feature of judicial process is its cost. The costly nature of litigation compels parties not to pursue even just claims and defences. The cost of litigation consists of court fees, process fees, advocate fees and the principle of the losing party paying the cost of litigation. This cost system is peculiar to British administration. It was British who imposed such fees for reducing filing of frivolous claims. The motive of this was to delay and the denial of access to the Courts and also to extract money from the people. In independent India, we followed the same legislation *i.e.* The Court Fees Act of 1870. Apart from that, parties are required to pay process fees like fee for filing of plaints, for issuing summons and for getting the copy of judgment and decree. The access to justice in India depends much on the financial capabilities of the parties that is unconstitutional and encourages inequality between the parties. Here, ethical count is defeated. Judicial process has to be litigant friendly. Court is not a source of income to the Government. It can not be self-financing institution. Cost has to be the responsibility of the State. Legal aid has come up to help poor and needy. It is commendable.

With the institution of the suit, a court fee has to be paid. As per Section 35 of the CPC, the award of the costs of and incidents of all suits shall be in the discretion of the Court and the Court has the full authority to determine the extent of costs. As per Order IX R. 2 of CPC, a suit can be dismissed if the summons has not been served upon the defendant in consequence of the failure of the plaintiff to pay he Court fee or postal charges.

Court fees

Court Fee is a colonial baggage being carried by the Indian courts till today. The policy of selling justice is against the constitutional scheme. The charging fee for rendering justice is all on negative side when seen in the light of power spectrum. Court fee has to be low on ethical spectrum as it is against the basic premises of the foundation of a welfare Sate. With the institution of the suit, a court fee has to be paid. As per Section 35 of CPC, the costs of and incidents of all suits shall be in the discretion of the Court and the Court has the full authority to determine the extent of costs. As per Order IX, R. 2 of CPC, a suit can be dismissed if the summons has not been served upon the defendant in consequence of the failure of the plaintiff to pay the Court fee or postal charges. Court fee is a colonial baggage being carried by the Indian Courts till today. The policy of selling justice is against the constitutional scheme. When seen in the light of the power spectrum as elucidated by Prof. Julius Stone in his book, the aspect of power relations in charging a fee for rendering justice is all on negative side. Court fee is low on ethical spectrum as it is against the basic premises of the foundation of a welfare state as envisaged in the Constitution. Since a multitude of citizens are involved in civil litigation process, the head count component is quite high and so is the interest affected component as civil cases cover a broad ambit of interests. The Court fee, being a hurdle in access to justice, has a large degree of influence in discouraging honest litigants who do not have sufficient financial resources to pay the fee from approaching the courts. Since the non-payment of court fee can result in dismissal of the suit, it is very high on coercion band.

The judicial dicta on entry fee hurdle in access to justice are quite interesting. In *Central Coal Fields Ltd.* v. *V. Jaiswal Coal Co.*, AIR 1980 SC 2125, observed that effective access to justice is one of the basic requirements of a system and high amount of court fee may amount to sale of justice. The Court observed that :

> "It is more deplorable that the culture of the magna carta notwithstanding, the Anglo-American forensic system and currently free India's court process—shall insist on payment of court fee on such a profiteering scale without corrective expenditure on the administration of civil justice that the levies often smack of sale of justice in the Indian Republic where equality before the law is a guaranteed constitutional fundamental right and the legal system has been directed by Article 39A "to ensure that opportunities for securing justice are not denied to any citizen by reason of

economic....disabilities."

It is submitted that sale of justice whether for a penny or for a pound is a sale. The basic premise for accessing the court for redressal of an injury is that the State is liable to protect the individual and having failed to do so, it should redress the injury. For this no fee can be charged. It is a settled principle of law that no one can profit from their own wrong. Thus, State ought not and cannot profit from its own lapse in performance of duty.

Later in *Secy. to Govt. of India* v. *P.R. Sriramulu*, 1996 (1) SCC 345, the Court pointed out that it could not be disputed that the administration of justice is a service which the State is under an obligation to render to its subjects. However, yet again, the Court failed to declare the Court Fee Act as unconstitutional.

Advocate fees

A question now arises, what is the need of advocate fees? William Shakespeare is correct when he said, "the first thing we do, let's kill all the lawyers."

The money power and influence power comes into play, thus the principle of equality as envisaged under Article 14 stands violated. The adversarial system does not impose a positive duty on judges to discover the truth; he merely plays a passive role. However, under Section 57(1) of the Indian Evidence Act, a judge is presumed to know every law, then he is the best person to discover the truth, then why at all, he needed the help of advocates?

Advocates are considered to be the officer of the Court under Advocates Act, they are regarded to assist the Court in the administration of justice. Then why parties are required to pay advocate fees? It is clear cut violative of Article 14, as the court is required to administer justice without the aid of advocate. Even if you want advocates then go for public advocates aided and supported by states. In the process of delivery of justice there is no parity of power. There is need for rethinking or revamping whole judicial system. Time count is very important to determine the scope of Article 14.

Head component count and interest affected Count

Levying court fee can be examined from either of these angles; in Civil or Criminal Cases. It is not justified from either. The history of court fee itself proves that it was levied for discouraging access to the court. It is a punitive measure. It can not be justified in judicial process of welfare state. Judicial process can not be revenue generating unit of Government. Judicial process is a long term investment of the society. Since a multitude of citizens are involved in civil litigation process, the head count component is quite high and so is the interest affected component as civil cases cover a broad ambit of interests. The Court fee, being a hurdle in access to justice, has a large degree of influence in discouraging honest litigants who do not have sufficient financial resources to pay the fee from approaching the courts. Since the non-payment of court fee can result in dismissal of the suit, it is very high on coercion band.

Entry fee hurdle and opinions of courts

The Judicial dicta on entry fee hurdle in access to justice are quite interesting. In *Central Coal Fields Ltd.* v. *Jaiswal Coal Co.*,[1] it was observed that effective access to justice is one of the basic requirements of a system and high amount of court fee may amount to sale of justice. It is more deplorable that the culture of the magna carta notwithstanding, the Anglo-American forensic system and currently free India's court process—shall insist on payment of court fee on such a profiteering scale without corrective expenditure on the administration of civil justice that the levies often smack of sale of justice in the Indian Republic where equality before the law is a guaranteed constitutional fundamental right and the legal system has been directed by Article 39A "to ensure that opportunities for securing justice are not denied to any citizen by reason of economic disabilities."

The sale of justice whether for a penny or for a pound is a sale. The basic premise for accessing the court for redressal of any injury is that the State is liable to protect the individual and having failed to do so, it should redress the injury. For this, no fee can be charged. It is a settled principle of law that no one can profit by their own wrong. Thus State ought not and cannot profit from its own lapse in performance of duty.

Later in *Secy. to Govt. of India* v. *P.R. Sriramulu*,[2] the Court pointed out that it could not be disputed that the administration of justice is a service which the State is under an obligation to render to its subjects. However, yet again, the Court failed to declare the Court Fee Act as unconstitutional.

Justice is only for rich. interaction of money power and influence power

Do we need lawyers? William Shakespeare said, "the first thing we do, let's kill all the lawyers.' Is he correct? 'No' is the answer, judicial system survives on shoulders of bar. A competent and independent Bar is the *sine quo non* of justice according to law. The money power and influence power comes into play, thus the principle of equality as envisaged under Article 14 stands violated. The adversarial system does not impose a positive duty on judges to discover the truth; he merely plays a passive role. Under Section 57(1) of the Indian Evidence Act, a judge is presumed to know every law, then he is the best person to discover the truth.

Advocate and his fee are separate issues. We need lawyers. The exorbitant fee causes serious concern. Advocates are the officer of the Court under Advocates Act. They assist the Court in the administration of justice. Even if you want advocates then go for public advocates aided and supported by States. In the process of delivery of justice, there is no parity of power. There is need for rethinking or revamping of the whole judicial system. Time count is very important to determine the scope of Article 14. The judicial process for being more meaningful and effective must think in terms of

1. A.I.R. 1980 S.C. 2125.
2. 1996(1) SCC 345.

Advocacy being integral part of process at the cost of State.

Complaint against high fee is a universal phenomenon. Advocacy is one of the noblest profession. It needs high investment in library and equipments. There is no certainty in life and income-risk factors are more as compared to other professions. Advocate's fee are not unreasonable. They fight the case on fee paid. Maintenance and champerty are prohibited. The Bar Council is the body of advocates. It has done something for security of its members. Much more is required. Advocates should also think of charging minimum, must consider the capacity of client. My experience is; that I never settled my fee but was never denied fee. This enhances work for the counsel.

The law of Limitation : Defeats time Spectrum

The Limitation Act of 1963 read with Order 7 Rule 6 of the C.P.C. provides for the specific period for a person to enforce his rights. This bars the remedy after certain period of time but the rights subsist. The Act was passed during British in the year 1793 and was amended and consolidated later. The same was adopted by Independent India, the effect of this is that it denies justice after a period of time, thus invalidating and defeating the time spectrum as a person is denied of his right after certain period of time, thereby denying interest spectrum as interests of such persons who cannot approach to Court. Thus, their interests get affected and influence of laws, on such aggrieved persons was unable to get remedy. Limitation Act basically does not defeat right but basically the remedy is denied. Article 14 guarantees moment to moment protection because the idea of justice under Article 14 is restitutive justice. Sanction for prosecution abridges my right to file suit. If any aggrieved person failed to file suit within limitation time, then wasn't it the duty of the court to take judicial notice of this as clearly provided under Article 57(1) of Indian Evidence Act? How long can we allow cause of action to rule from the grave. How long can one sleep over his right to sue? Limitation says hitherto no more. We have evidence based process. Judicial process based on witness. The Act balances right of one suing and the other sued.

Arrears of cases

There is huge backlog of cases which are pending in all courts and it may take approximately 20 years for a case to be disposed off. This snail pace speed of dispensation of cases throughout the years is affecting the ethical count, and also adversely affecting the time count spectrum and interest spectrum is affected when litigant suffers throughout the years. Code of Civil Procedure has been amended in 1999 and 2002 wherein process has been changed to tackle arrears. Satisfactory results are expected. Awareness of its frightening condition is coming up.

National Legal Services Authority

National Legal Services Authority of India (NALSA) was formed on 5th December, 1995 under the authority of the Legal Services Authorities Act, 1987. Its purpose is to provide free legal services to eligible candidates (defined in Sec. 12 of the Act), and to organize Lok Adalats for speedy resolution of cases. The Chief Justice of India is patron-in-chief of NALSA while second senior-most judge of Supreme Court of India is the Executive-Chairman. There is a provision for similar mechanism at state and district level also headed by Chief Justice of High Courts and Chief Judges of District courts respectively. The prime objective of NALSA is speedy disposal of cases and reducing the burden of judiciary.

The National Legal Services Authority (NALSA) has been constituted under the Legal Services Authorities Act, 1987 to provide free Legal Services to the weaker sections of the society and to organize Lok Adalats for amicable settlement of disputes.

Hon'ble Mr. Justice Tirath Singh Thakur, the Chief Justice of India is the Patron-in-Chief and Hon'ble Mr. Justice Anil R. Dave, Judge, Supreme Court of India is the Executive Chairman of the Authority. NALSA is housed at 12/11, Jam Nagar House, New Delhi-110011.

In every State, State Legal Services Authority has been constituted to give effect to the policies and directions of the NALSA and to give free legal services to the people and conduct Lok Adalats in the State. The State Legal Services Authority is headed by the Hon'ble Chief Justice of the respective High Court who is the Patron-in-Chief of the State Legal Service Authority.

In every District, District Legal Services Authority has been constituted to implement Legal Services Programmes in the District. The District Legal Services Authority is situated in the District Courts Complex in every District and chaired by the District Judge of the respective district.

Legal aid movement in India—Its development and present status

Article 39A of the Constitution of India provides that State shall secure that the operation of the legal system promotes justice on a basis of equal opportunity, and shall in particular, provide free legal aid, by suitable legislation or schemes or in any other way, to ensure that opportunities for securing justice are not denied to any citizen by reason of economic or other disability. Articles 14 and 22(1) also make it obligatory for the State to ensure equality before law and a legal system which promotes justice on a basis of equal opportunity to all. Legal aid strives to ensure that constitutional pledge is fulfilled in its letter and spirit and equal justice is made available to the poor, downtrodden and weaker sections of the society.

The earliest Legal Aid movement appears to be of the year 1851 when some enactment was introduced in France for providing legal assistance to the indigent. In Britain, the history of the organised efforts on the part of the State to provide legal services to the poor and needy dates back to 1944, when Lord Chancellor, Viscount Simon appointed Rushcliffe Committee to enquire about the facilities existing in England and Wales for giving legal advice to the poor and to make recommendations as appear to be desirable for ensuring that person in need of legal advice are provided the same by the State. Since 1952, the Government of India also started addressing to the question of legal aid for the poor in various conferences of Law Ministers and Law Commissions. In 1960, some guidelines were drawn by the Government for legal aid schemes. In different states legal aid schemes were floated through Legal Aid Boards, Societies and Law Departments. In 1980, a Committee at the national level was constituted to oversee and supervise legal aid programmes throughout the country under the Chairmanship of Hon. Mr. Justice P.N. Bhagwati then a Judge of the Supreme Court of India. This Committee came to be known as CILAS (Committee for Implementing Legal Aid Schemes) and started monitoring legal aid activities throughout the country. The introduction of Lok Adalats added a new chapter to the justice dispensation system of this country and succeeded in providing a supplementary forum to the litigants for conciliatory settlement of their disputes. In 1987 Legal Services Authorities Act was enacted to give a statutory base to legal aid programmes throughout the country on a uniform pattern. This Act was finally enforced on 9th of November, 1995 after certain amendments were introduced therein by the Amendment Act of 1994. Hon. Mr. Justice R.N. Mishra the then Chief Justice of India played a key role in the enforcement of the Act.

National Legal Services Authority was constituted on 5th December, 1995. His Lordship Hon. Dr. Justice A.S. Anand, Judge, Supreme Court of India took over as the Executive Chairman of National Legal Services Authority on 17th July, 1997. Soon after assuming the office, His Lordship initiated steps for making the National Legal Services Authority functional. The first Member Secretary of the authority joined in December, 1997 and by January, 1998 the other officers and staff were also appointed. By February, 1998 the office of National Legal Services Authority became properly functional for the first time.

In October, 1998, His Lordship Hon. Dr. Justice A.S. Anand assumed the Office of the Chief Justice of India and thus became the Patron-in-Chief of National Legal Services Authority. His Lordship Hon. Mr. Justice S.P. Bharucha, the senior-most judge of the Supreme Court of India assumed the office of the Executive Chairman, National Legal Services Authority.

Section 12 of the Legal Services Authorities Act, 1987 prescribes the criteria for giving legal services to the eligible persons. Section 12 of the Act reads as under :—

> 12. Every person who has to file or defend a case shall be entitled to legal services under this Act if that person is :—
>
> (a) a member of a Scheduled Caste or Scheduled Tribe;
>
> (b) a victim of trafficking in human beings or begar as referred to in Article 23 of the Constitution;
>
> (c) a woman or a child;
>
> (d) a mentally ill or otherwise disabled person;
>
> (e) a person under circumstances of undeserved want such as being a victim of a mass disaster, ethnic violence, caste atrocity, flood, drought, earthquake or industrial disaster; or
>
> (f) an industrial workman; or

(g) in custody, including custody in a protective home within the meaning of clause (g) of Section 2 of the Immoral Traffic (Prevention) Act, 1956 (104 of 1956); or in a juvenile home within the meaning of clause;

(j) of Section 2 of the Juvenile Justice Act, 1983 (53 of 1986) or in a psychiatric hospital or psychiatric nursing home within the meaning of clause (g) of Section 2 of the Mental Health Act, 1987 (14 of 1987); or

(h) in receipt of annual income less than rupees nine thousand or such other higher amount as may be prescribed by the State Government, if the case is before a court other than the Supreme Court, and less than rupees twelve thousand or such other higher amount as may be prescribed by the Central Government, if the case is before the Supreme Court."

(Rules have already been amended to enhance this income ceiling).

According to Section 2(1)(a) of the Act, legal aid can be provided to a person for a 'case' which includes a suit or any proceeding before a court. Section 2(1) (aaa) defines the 'court' as a civil, criminal or revenue court and includes any tribunal or any other authority constituted under any law for the time being in force, to exercise judicial or quasi-judicial functions. As per Section 2(1)(c) 'legal service' includes the rendering of any service in the conduct of any case or other legal proceeding before any court or other authority or tribunal and the giving of advice on any legal matter.

Legal Services Authorities after examining the eligibility criteria of an applicant and the existence of a *prima facie* case in his favour provide him counsel at State expense, pay the required Court Fee in the matter and bear all incidental expenses in connection with the case. The person to whom legal aid is provided is not called upon to spend anything on the litigation once it is supported by a Legal Service Authority.

A nationwide network has been envisaged under the Act for providing legal aid and assistance. National Legal Service Authority is the apex body constituted to lay down policies and principles for making legal services available under the provisions of the Act and to frame most effective and economical schemes for legal services. It also disburses funds and grants to State Legal Services Authorities and NGOs for implementing legal aid schemes and programmes.

In every State, a State Legal Service Authority is constituted to give effect to the policies and directions of the Central Authority (NALSA) and to give legal services to the people and conduct Lok Adalats in the State. State Legal Services Authority is headed by the Chief Justice of the State High Court who is its Patron-in-Chief. A serving or retired Judge of the High Court is nominated as its Executive Chairman.

District Legal Services Authority is constituted in every District to implement Legal Aid Programmes and Schemes in the District. The District Judge of the District is its ex-officio Chairman.

Taluk Legal Services Committees are also constituted for each of the Taluk or Mandal or for group of Taluk or Mandals to coordinate the activities of legal services in the Taluk and to organise Lok Adalats. Every Taluk Legal Services Committee is headed by a senior Civil Judge operating within the jurisdiction of the Committee who is its ex-officio Chairman.

After the constitution of the Central Authority and the establishment of NALSA office towards the beginning of 1998, following schemes and measures have been envisaged and implemented by the Central Authority :—

(a) Establishing Permanent and Continuous Lok Adalats in all the Districts in the country for disposal of pending matters as well as disputes at pre-litigative stage;

(b) Establishing separate Permanent and Continuous Lok Adalats for Government Departments, Statutory Authorities and Public Sector Undertakings for disposal of pending cases as well as disputes at pre-litigative stage;

(c) Accreditation of NGOs for Legal Literacy and Legal Awareness campaign;

(d) Appointment of "Legal Aid Counsel" in all the Courts of Magistrates in the country;

(e) Disposal of cases through Lok Adalats on old pattern;

(f) Publicity to Legal Aid Schemes and programmes to make people aware about legal aid facilities;

(g) Emphasis on competent and quality legal services to the aided persons;

(h) Legal aid facilities in jails;

(i) Setting up of Counselling and Conciliation Centers in all the Districts in the country;

(j) Sensitisation of Judicial Officers in regard to Legal Services Schemes and programmes;

(k) Publication of "Nyaya Deep", the official newsletter of NALSA;

(l) Enhancement of Income Ceiling to Rs. 1,25,000/- p.a. for legal aid before Supreme Court of India and to Rs. 1,00,000 p.a. for legal aid upto High Courts; and

(m) Steps for framing rules for refund of court fees and execution of Awards passed by Lok Adalats.

The First Annual Meet of the State Legal Services Authorities was held on 12th of September, 1998 at Vigyan Bhawan, New Delhi which was presided over by His Lordship Hon. Dr. Justice A.S. Anand, the then Executive Chairman, NALSA. His Lordship Hon. Mr. Justice S.B. Majmudar, Judge, Supreme Court of India and Chairman, Supreme Court Legal Services Committee, the Members of the Central Authority and the Executive Chairman and Member Secretaries of the State Legal Services Authorities attended this Meet. In this Meet, the progress of on-going schemes which had been initiated by NALSA was examined and decisions of far reaching implications were taken with a view to strengthen and streamline legal aid programmes in the country. The Second Annual Meet of the State Legal Services Authorities was held at Jubilee Hall, Hyderabad on 9th October, 1999. This Meet was inaugurated by His Lordship Hon. Dr. Justice A.S. Anand, the Chief Justice of India and Patron-in-Chief, NALSA. Hon. Mr. Justice S.P. Bharucha, Executive Chairman, NALSA delivered the Keynote address. Other dignitaries present at the inaugural function included Hon. Mr. Justice S.B. Majmudar, Judge, Supreme Court of India and Chairman, Supreme Court Legal Services Committee, Hon. Mr. Justice M.S. Liberhan, Chief Justice of Andhra Pradesh High Court and Members of Central Authority.

In pursuance of the call given by His Lordship Hon. Dr. Justice A.S. Anand, the Chief Justice of India in the First Annual Meet, 9th of November is being celebrated every year by all Legal Services Authorities as "Legal Services Day". NALSA issues Press Release in almost all the leading newspapers in the country in English, Hindi and regional languages to convey to the public salient provisions of the Legal Services Authorities Act, the important schemes introduced by NALSA for providing legal aid and the utility of Lok Adalats, so that people should know about the facilities being provided by Legal Services Authorities throughout the country. State Legal Services Authorities all over the country organise Lok Adalats, legal literary camps and undertake legal awareness campaign to make people aware of their legal rights.

Permanent and Continuous Lok Adalats are being established in all the Districts in the country. NALSA has been providing and shall continue to provide funds to State Legal Services Authorities for the implementation of the Legal Aid Schemes and Programmes but the infrastructure has to be provided by the State Governments. Separate Permanent and Continuous Lok Adalats in Government Departments are aimed at amicably settling pending cases as well as the matters at pre-litigative stage between Government Departments and general public so that the inflow of litigation to regular Courts is reduced. In so many Government bodies these Lok Adalats have become functional. In Delhi, Permanent Lok Adalats have been established in Delhi Vidyut Board, Delhi Development Authority, Municipal Corpn. or Delhi, MTNL and General Insurance Corpn. These Lok Adalats are becoming popular day-by-day and it is expected that very soon a large number of disputes between public and statutory authorities would start getting settled at pre-litigative stage itself saving the parties from unnecessary expense and litigational inconvenience. In other States also State Legal Services Authorities have initiated steps to persuade the State Governments and statutory bodies, *etc.* to set up separate Permanent Lok Adalats for amicable settlement of their legal disputes.

"Legal Aid Counsel" Scheme which was conceived and introduced by His Lordship Hon. Dr. Justice A.S. Anand when His Lordship was the Executive Chairman, NALSA has been well received all over country. Legal Aid Counsel have been provided in most of the courts of the Magistrates in the country to provide immediate legal assistance to those prisoners who are not in a position to engage their own counsel.

Hon. Mr. Justice S.P. Bharucha, Executive Chairman, NALSA in the course of working season of the Second Annual Meet of the State Legal Services Authorities held at Hyderabad, had emphasised that Counselling and Conciliation Centers should be established in all the Districts in the country to bring about negotiated settlement of disputes between the parties. All the State Legal Services Authorities are taking steps to establish these Centers which would prove immensely useful for settling legal disputes at pre-litigative stage and would also help legal services functionaries to find out as to whether a person approaching them for legal aid has or not a *prima facie* case in his favour which is a pre-requisite for grant of legal aid. Hon. Executive Chairman has repeatedly emphasised that legal aid must not be given as a matter of routine and frivolous cases should not be supported by legal aid authorities.

Hon. Mr. Justice S.P. Bharucha, Executive Chairman, NALSA while writing in 'Nyaya Deep' and in the course of his keynote address in the meeting of the Member Secretaries held in NALSA office on 19.2.2000 emphasised the need for improving the quality of legal aid that is being given by legal aid advocates. His Lordship observed that teeming millions of this country who live below poverty line in tribal, backward and far flung areas look to Legal Services Authorities for help and support in resolving their legal problems. When involved in litigation they very often feel that they are fighting an unequal battle in which the party that has better financial resources can secure more able legal assistance. His Lordship is of the view that these poor and weaker sections must not remain under the impression that they are getting comparatively inferior legal assistance. His Lordship has called upon legal services authorities to revise the payment schedule for legal aid panel advocates and also compress the panels so that panel advocates get more work and better remuneration from legal services authorities and thus get encouraged to render effective legal assistance to aided persons.

His Lordship Hon. Mr. Justice B.N. Kirpal, Judge, Supreme Court of India and Chairman, Supreme Court Legal Services Committee has a very long association with legal aid movement. Under the guidance and control of His Lordship, Supreme Court Legal Services Committee is providing legal aid to eligible persons in a very effective and meaningful way. Upto 31.12.99 Supreme Court Legal Services Committee has provided legal aid and assistance to 10,125 applicants.

'Nyaya Deep', the official news letter of NALSA is promoting a healthy working relationship between legal services functionaries throughout the country and is proving immensely useful for exchange of views and sharing of ideas. Statistical information in regard to legal aid schemes and programmes is also included in this newsletter which is printed on quarterly basis. The editorials written by Hon. Mr. Justice R.C. Lahoti reflect the soul of 'Nyaya Deep' and measure the depth of the material included therein. These provide a window to the reader who in one glance through it can appreciate the content and purpose of the articles.

Need culture of settling disputes amicably outside courts

Supreme Court judge and executive chairman of the National Legal Services Authority (NALSA) appealed for developing a culture in India for settlement of disputes through amicable resolution instead of lining up in courts.

Access to justice for all is a pledge that could be fulfilled more effectively if people are encouraged to resort to an alternate dispute resolution system.

"In our country, there has to be development of a settlement culture." It was a duty incumbent upon the chairmen of the legal services authorities, as "captains of his army", to realise NALSA's motto of "access of justice for all".

Appealing to judges and judicial officers associated with legal aid and services to display exemplary dedication and sincerity, Justice Misra emphasised that people's right to access justice is not only a constitutional and statutory right but also a "basic human right".

"Anyone involved in legal aid cannot conceive an idea of scepticism and cynicism, no one should entertain any doubt with regard to realisation of service, there has to be complete dedication and sincerity", said the judge.

The chairman of the legal services authority spoke about the importance of providing access to justice to the needy and marginalised sections of society amid obstacles arising from financial and geographical constraints, and time consuming litigation.

NALSA spearheaded significant public interest litigation in the top court, such as getting legal recognition for transgenders and measures for improving the condition of Vrindavan widows in 2012. "But I don't see anything moving in this direction now, NALSA should consider this aspect.

There could be a debate on whether the Legal Services Act should be amended to substitute serving judicial functionaries as heads of these bodies so that a "more satisfying and fulfilling end" could be achieved.

Statistics on disposal of cases in Lok Adalats and those given legal aid demonstrated a good picture but it must also be remembered that they could just be "a drop in the ocean" in a country having population of 130 crores, out of which 30 per cent live below the artificially drawn poverty line. A more "proactive role" by NALSA is required so that a "just social order" is achieved in a country where poverty, unemployment and oppression are still rampant.

Selection of judges in higher judiciary;

As far as selection of judges is concerned, according to the text of the Constitution, President has the power to appoint judges, he has discretion to choose and he can consult the Chief Justice of India as well as senior most judges of Supreme Court in matter of appointment. But *S.P. Gupta and others* v. *Union of India* held that consultation by CJI means his consent. If consultation means consent then the power spectrum shifted from the President to CJI, and it is this interpretation of the Constitution which is under challenge at the moment in current judicial process. Peer selection is under criticism.

Added to all these, immunity to judiciary is the power of contempt of Court, which can be used by the judiciary to stifle public criticism, or even an honest evaluation of the judiciary. This threat of contempt has prevented a frank discussion or a healthy debate on the functioning of judiciary. The judiciary recommended that the Chief Justice should be the final word in deciding whether any information about the Court should be given out or not. Most High Courts have not even appointed a public information officer under the RTI Act. The Delhi High Court has framed rules which prohibit the release of non judicial information about the court, such as purchases and appointments. All this has ensured that the judiciary becomes a law unto itself, totally non transparent, and accountable to none.

Independence of the judiciary

The principle of the independence of the Judiciary has its origins in the doctrine of Separation of Powers, which basically states that the three arms of government, that is the Executive, Legislature and the Judiciary, must be independent of each other and separate from one another. The doctrine was most famously expounded by Montesquieu, a French Jurist :

> "Political liberty is to be found only when there is no abuse of power. But constant experience shows us that every man invested with power is liable to abuse it, and to carry his authority as far as it will go...To prevent this abuse, it is necessary from the nature of things that one power should be a check on another... When the executive and legislative powers are united in the same person or body... there can be no liberty if the judicial power is not separated from the legislature and the executive... There would be an end of everything, if the same person or body, whether of the nobles or of the people, were to exercise all three powers."

It goes without saying that there is no country in the world where there is complete separation of power, as this would bring governments to a standstill. In many countries, there are various overlaps. It is generally accepted that what the doctrine advocates is a system of checks and balances aimed at the prevention of tyranny by conferment of too much power on any one person or body and the checking of one power by another.

The principles of the independence of the Judiciary is also closely tied to the doctrine of the rule of law. The primary meaning of this doctrine is that everything must be done according to law. A good example for the application of the primary meaning of the rule of law is the Latin maxim "*nullum crimen sine lege*," meaning, "There can be no crime outside the law." Applied to the powers of government, it means that every act involving the exercise of governmental power must be shown to be authorised by law. Secondly, it means that government should be conducted within a framework of recognised rules and principles, which restrict discretionary power. It also means that disputes regarding the legality of governmental action must be decided by judges who are wholly independent of the executive.

Furthermore, when such disputes are being adjudicated upon, the law should be even-handed between the government and the citizen; in other words, there must be equality before the law.

All in all, an independent Judiciary is the cornerstone of democratic government and the surest guarantor of human rights.

Key tenets of the Principle of the Independence of the Judiciary

(1) "Total separation of judicial power is not possible in the real world."—In many countries, including Uganda, the Executive appoints Judges, subject to the approval of the legislature. the legislature enacts laws that define the jurisdiction and structure of the courts. In spite of these overlaps, the Constitution of the Republic of Uganda reiterates that :

(2) "In the exercise of Judicial Power, the courts shall be independent and shall not be subject to the control of direction of any person or authority."—However, the principle goes beyond merely not being "subject to the control or direction of any person or authority." In Interventions and interference by the state and other powerful interests in society is bound to take more subtle forms. Accordingly, in order to ensure that judicial officers are not subject to the control or direction of any person or authority, various other factors must be taken into account.

Firstly, the requirements regarding the qualifications, training and selection or appointment of judges should ensure that persons selected for judicial office should be individuals of integrity and ability with appropriate training or qualifications in law. Any method of judicial selection should safeguard against judicial appointments for improper motives.

Secondly, the term of office of judges, their independence, security, adequate remuneration, conditions of service, pensions and the age of retirement shall be adequately secured by law.

Basic Principles on the Independence of the Judiciary

Adopted by the Seventh United Nations Congress on the Prevention of Crime and the Treatment of Offenders held at Milan from 26 August to 6 September 1985 and endorsed by General Assembly resolution 40/32 of 29 November 1985 and 40/146 of 13 December 1985.

Whereas in the Charter of the United Nations the peoples of the world affirm, *inter alia*, their determination to establish conditions under which justice can be maintained to achieve international co-operation in promoting and encouraging respect for human rights and fundamental freedoms without any discrimination,

Whereas the Universal Declaration of Human Rights enshrines in particular the principles of equality before the law, of the presumption of innocence and of the right to a fair and public hearing by a competent, independent and impartial tribunal established by law,

Whereas the International Covenants on Economic, Social and Cultural Rights and on Civil and Political Rights both guarantee the exercise of those rights, and in addition, the Covenant on Civil and Political Rights further guarantees the right to be tried without undue delay,

Whereas frequently there still exists a gap between the vision underlying those principles and the actual situation,

Whereas the organization and administration of justice in every country should be inspired by those principles, and efforts should be undertaken to translate them fully into reality,

Whereas rules concerning the exercise of judicial office should aim at enabling judges to act in accordance with those principles,

Whereas judges are charged with the ultimate decision over life, freedoms, rights, duties and property of citizens,

Whereas the Sixth united Nations Congress on the Prevention of Crime and the Treatment of Offenders, by its resolution 16, called upon the Committee on Crime Prevention and Control to include among its priorities the elaboration of guidelines relating to the independence of judges and the selection, professional training and status of judges and prosecutors,

Whereas it is, therefore, appropriate that consideration be first given to the role of judges in relation to the system of justice and to the importance of their selection, training and conduct,

The following basic principles, formulated to assist Member States in their task of securing and promoting the independence of the judiciary should be taken into account and respected by Governments within the framework of their national legislation and practice and be brought to the attention of judges, lawyers, members of the executive and the legislature and the public in general. The principles have been formulated principally with professional judges in mind, but they apply equally, as appropriate, to lay judges, where they exist.

Independence of the judiciary

1. The independence of the judiciary shall be guaranteed by the State and enshrined in the Constitution or the law of the country. It is the duty of all governmental and other institutions to respect and observe the independence of the judiciary.

2. The judiciary shall decide matters before them impartially, on the basis of facts and in accordance with the law, without any restrictions, improper influences, inducements, pressures, threats or interferences, direct or indirect, from any quarter or for any reason.

3. The judiciary shall have jurisdiction over all issues of a judicial nature and shall have exclusive authority to decide whether an issue submitted for its decision is within its competence as defined by law.

4. There shall not be any inappropriate or unwarranted interference with the judicial process, nor shall judicial decisions by the courts be subject to revision. This principle is without prejudice to judicial review or to mitigation or commutation by competent authorities of sentences imposed by the judiciary, in accordance with the law.

5. Everyone shall have the right to be tried by ordinary courts or tribunals using established legal procedures. Tribunals that do not use the duly established procedures of the legal process shall not be created to

displace the jurisdiction belonging to the ordinary courts or judicial tribunals.

6. The principle of the independence of the judiciary entitles and requires the judiciary to ensure that judicial proceedings are conducted fairly and that the rights of the parties are respected.

7. It is the duty of each Member State to provide adequate resources to enable the judiciary to properly perform its functions.

Freedom of expression and association

8. In accordance with the Universal Declaration of Human Rights, members of the judiciary are like other citizens entitled to freedom of expression, belief, association and assembly; provided, however, that in exercising such rights, judges shall always conduct themselves in such a manner as to preserve the dignity of their office and the impartiality and independence of the judiciary.

9. Judges shall be free to form and join associations of judges or other organizations to represent their interests, to promote their professional training and to protect their judicial independence.

Qualifications, selection and training

10. Persons selected for judicial office shall be individuals of integrity and ability with appropriate training or qualifications in law. Any method of judicial selection shall safeguard against judicial appointments for improper motives. In the selection of judges, there shall be no discrimination against a person on the grounds of race, colour, sex, religion, political or other opinion, national or social origin, property, birth or status, except that a requirement, that a candidate for judicial office must be a national of the country concerned, shall not be considered discriminatory.

Conditions of service and tenure

11. The term of office of judges, their independence, security, adequate remuneration, conditions of service, pensions and the age of retirement shall be adequately secured by law.

12. Judges whether appointed or elected, shall have guaranteed tenure until a mandatory retirement age or the expiry of their term of office, where such exists.

13. Promotion of judges, wherever such a system exists, should be based on objective factors, in particular ability, integrity and experience.

14. The assignment of cases to judges within the court to which they belong is an internal matter of judicial administration.

Professional secrecy and immunity

15. The judiciary shall be bound by professional secrecy with regard to their deliberations and to confidential information acquired in the course of their duties other than in public proceedings, and shall not be compelled to testify on such matters.

16. Without prejudice to any disciplinary procedure or to any right of appeal or to compensation from the State, in accordance with national law,

judges should enjoy personal immunity from civil suits for monetary damages for improper acts or omissions in the exercise of their judicial functions.

Discipline, suspension and removal

17. A charge or complaint made against a judge in his/her judicial and professional capacity shall be processed expeditiously and fairly under an appropriate procedure. The judge shall have the right to a fair hearing. The examination of the matter at its initial stage shall be kept confidential, unless otherwise requested by the judge.

18. Judges shall be subject to suspension or removal only for reasons of incapacity or behaviour that renders them unfit to discharge their duties.

19. All disciplinary, suspension or removal proceedings shall be determined in accordance with established standards of judicial conduct.

20. Decisions in disciplinary, suspension or removal proceedings should be subject to an independent review. This principle may not apply to the decisions of the highest court and those of the legislature in impeachment or similar proceedings.

Independence of Judiciary—Some Latent Dangers

The Constitution has tried to insulate the Judiciary from outside influence both from the Executive and the Legislature. Independence of the judiciary constitutes the foundation on which rests the edifice of Democratic Polity. The general concept of Judicial Independence is that a judge should be free from any pressure from the government or any one else (as to how to while deciding) any particular case; and for that reason, salary of a judge is not dependent on the Executive decision and his conditions of service are secured and not to be varied at the whim of the Executives.

Things have changed in the recent past, particularly in the last 20 years. There has been a great upsurge in crime and criminal litigation, and equally in the number of civil disputes. So to say, there is unmanageable docket explosion in every court. To meet this challenge there has to be a large increase in the number of judges, court, court staffs and other infrastructure. But no such increase has been made. Even in the existing courts, the working conditions in most of them are unsatisfactory. The courts do not have financial independence, since finance falls under the Executive control. The judges are not provided with the up-to-date statutes or law books. They are generally under the mercy of lawyers to provide copies of the decisions or enactments relied during the course of arguments. The judges are not given proper training either at the induction level or periodical refresher courses. Commenting on the similar conditions in the British Justice System which existed at one time, Lord Devlin opined :

"If our business methods were as antiquated as our legal system, we would have become a bankrupt nation long back."

Power spectrum and judicial process;

Power is "the ability to affect another by its exercise." Power has a close interrelation with the law. So in order to understand the role of power in creating, supporting, and changing or subverting law Julious stone enumerates six power bands to verify the proper exercise of power.

Power band and results: These results are :—

(1) Coercion Component Spectrum.—The coercion spectrum is concerned with the degree of coercion involved in the power relation. A valid exercise of power or any valid law must be devoid of coercion or if at all necessary to the minimum. It is beyond doubt that the non accessibility of justice because of high cost and other procedural hindrances can be termed as the "vulgar notion" of power by the power holder. Rich party can put down the opponents by endless delays and they can drive up expenses by costly discoveries. Poorer parties often cannot afford to pay for investigators, expert testimony, and lawyer's time and so on. Many possible witnesses are reluctant to come forward because of the possible harassment and humiliation in cross examination, time lost from work and so forth. All these acts as excessive coercion.

(2) Ethical component spectrum.—This count deals with ethical and moral aspects of law as it emphasizes that every law, decision, or policy must satisfy minimum standards of ethics and morality of the society, which differ from society to society. A uniform standard of ethics cannot be laid down for it differs from society to society. Justice in the present system is hugely influenced by the counsel representing the party. There is no parity of power. Many times justice is not delivered. Adversarial process hinders peaceful resolution of disputes. Lawyers tend to be partisan advocates to promote the interest of the clients, create discord and tensions. We have introduced professional ethics in Law Schools. How much lawyers and Judges put it in practice is an open question.

(3) Interest affected spectrum.—This count draws attention to the problems faced by the subject (in this case litigants) as a consequence of improper exercise of power, that is when their interests are affected by and subordinated to the interests of power wielders (State). In this case victim has to fight himself for justice and State does not provide for any considerable assistance. There are many procedural hindrances in his way and many times such victim is not able to access justice.

Lawyers are accepted as officers of court. They must not treat adversary of their client as their own adversary. The Counsel for opposite party is addressed as learned friend. Corporate lawyering is coming up new replacing litigation lawyering. The lawyers have to adjust with this new phenomenon.

(4) Influence spectrum.—This spectrum means the degree of influence exerted on the person subject to power. This band differs from the coercion band as influence is a positive but sanctions are a negative concept Influence has independent existence whereas coercion is a non-entity without fear and sanction. In adversarial system, this spectrum stands completely demolished. Rich can easily dodge the clutches of law; advocates can give him ample support. Such thing sets up as an example for other law abiding citizens who feel that they can also get away with law.

(5) The head count spectrum.—This spectrum is an inherent feature of all the four above mentioned spectrums barring the ethical component. This count signifies the number of persons affected by any decision or law. The underlying idea of this band is to protect the interests of maximum number of persons. Justice is the first virtue of social institutions. Basic aim of legal system is to provide justice to every man in the society. But today, in India, our legal system has undergone such a deep state of crisis that it is not able to provide justice to common man. Justice is not delivered to the majority of citizens because of various flaws embodied in the present system. Few among them are mentioned above. Justice delivery mechanism has badly failed to come up to the aspirations of half-clad and half-hungry masses of independent India.

(6) The time count spectrum.—This is by far the most important aspect of all the six power spectrums, because violation of the time count spectrum nullifies all other aspects. The time-count spectrum concerns itself with the stability of the other power spectrums through time. This band has two facets.

One, *they are self-promotive* in the sense that they grow stronger by their own continuance.

The second *facet of time count is delay i.e.*, delay acts as an impediment to access and realization of justice and that preventive, as well as protective remedies should be provided without delay. Both these facets are not fulfilled in the adversarial system. There is inordinate delay in the present system because of various reasons. Moreover it has not changed to a stronger position.

Some errors of judicial process; court decisions

There are numerous instances of cases where Apex Court wrongly interpreted the provision of Constitution like *Joshi* v. *Madhya Bharat* where it was held that place of birth is relevant or in *Balaji* v. *State of Mysore* case where caste was given prominence. Here, court indirectly held that caste and religion is important which is wholly unconstitutional. By upholding pro government attitude, courts are cheating the citizens who belong to socially advantageous sections of society but are economically backward enough not to get an opportunity of education. Reservation in the matter practised today cannot lead to the fulfilment of Article 45. We should make the quest to achieve all this on the bedrock of Article 14. Judges have to act strictly in accordance with law, on the matter of judicial process, the duty of the court is to ascertain the law and apply it and judge the fact in the light of that law.

The Constitution has conferred a very wide jurisdiction on Supreme Court of India. It shows that the Constitution makers placed great confidence in the sagacity and the wisdom of those who were to exercise such enormous power. When any court is vested and is invested with wide jurisdiction, it necessarily follows that the court must exercise that jurisdiction with utmost care and caution. When power is conferred on constitutional machinery, it is always to be understood by the functionary as a duty; others may view it as power. When the functionary is a judicial officer, he must be extra careful, lest he may appear to be carried away by emotion or bias. Self imposed discipline and judicial restraint should be his armament, otherwise there is the fear that he may not be viewed as impartial. It is difficult to draw the line but one can say, without fear of contradiction that the power must be exercised with restraint and should not appear to be an immature impulse. In a democratic set up, when the Constitution confers wide powers and jurisdiction on any institution, the constitutional functionaries exercising those powers are in effect called upon to perform certain duties and functions and, therefore, they must carry out those obligations with great care and caution. The constraint and restraint of judicial office demand a self imposed discipline in the exercise of the power and jurisdiction conferred by the Constitution and the law. There can, therefore, be no doubt that the jurisdiction must be exercised responsibly, and with restraint and circumspection.

In *Chiranjeet Lal Chowdhary* v. *Union of India*,[1] the Court held that the constitutionality of a statute is presumed. The Supreme Court abdicated its power in the hands of the executive and laid down the doctrine of the constitutionality of Statute" in which the petitioner has to prove the unconstitutionality of the statute and court assumes its constitutionality. This judgment defeats all the bands of the power spectrum, as it is unethical on the part of the Court to presuppose the constitutionality of the statute without looking into its essence so it clearly violates the power principle. This approach affects the interest, influence, head count and time bands of the power spectrum, because the interests of the majority of people are affected by his approach when an individual is entrapped in dilatory legal battle for justice.

In *Maneka Gandhi* v. *Union of India*,[2] the passport of the Petitioner was seized on the ground of interest of public by the Central Government under Section 10(3)(c) of the Passport Act 1967 without giving her opportunity of any hearing. Hence she filed a writ petition under Article 32 on following grounds—

1. Section 10(3)(c) is violative of Article 21 as it does not prescribe any procedure for the seizure of the passport.
2. Section 10(3)(c) is violative of Article 14 as power conferred to delegate is excessive.
3. Section 10(3)(c) is violative of Article 19(1)(a) and Article 19(1)(g).
4. She was denied the opportunity of hearing which amounted to the arbitrary exercise of the power violating Article 14.

In this case, Supreme Court observed (not given the judgment) after assessing the evidences that the seizure of the passport was *mala fide* in violation of Article 14, 19, 21. Procedure established by the law means a procedure which is just, fair and reasonable. Rule of *Audi Alteram Partem*

---

1. AIR 1951 SC 41.
2. 1978 AIR 597.

is a part of natural law protected under Article 21. Illegal seizure of passport violates Article 19(1)(a), 19(1)(g) having a direct bearing on right to food protected under Article 21. Realising that there was fatal defect and decision of the court would render the Central Government's order, as void, the Attorney General gave the assurance that—"The opportunity of hearing and representation shall be given to the petitioner within two weeks and representation will be dealt with expeditiously in accordance with the law. On getting this assurance the Supreme Court disposed of the case.

Did it discharge its duty as court? The observation is criticised that the duty of the Supreme Court was to render restitutive justice under Article 14 but it failed to render the complete justice hence , Article 142 remained unanswered.

The judgment of Supreme Court holds the authority of law under Article 141, and so it is expected from it to resolve all the issues once for all in the form of judgment and not observations. It is a justice delivery institution not a compromise making body. Supreme Court failed to take the notice of Section 166 of IPC and Section 57(1) of the Indian Evidence Act, 1872, and failed in punishing the wrongdoers.

In *ADM Jabalpur* v. *Shivkant Shukla*,[1] the President on the advice of the P.M. declared emergency in 1975 under Article 352 on the ground that the security of India was threatened by internal disturbance and also issued an order under Article 359 suspending the right to access to the courts for the enforcement of the fundamental rights. The questions which fell for the consideration in this case were the two—

> "Whether in view of the Presidential order under clause (1) of Article 359 of the Constitution any writ petition under Article 226 before a High Court for *habeas corpus* or any other writ or order or direction to challenge the legality of an order of detention on the ground that the order is not under or in compliance with the Act is maintainable or is vitiated by *mala fides* factual or legal or is based on extraneous considerations.
>
> Second, if such a petition is maintainable, what is the scope or extent of judicial scrutiny. Supreme Court by majority (except Justice H.R. Khanna) held that emergency is declared to overcome certain imminent contingencies, and permission to enforce one's fundamental right would frustrate the object of emergency, hence no person has *locus standi* to challenge the validity of his detention during the operation of Article 359(1), howsoever wrong his detention may be.

Did the judicial process not cause injustice. Rule of law is the antithesis of arbitrariness; the State has got no power to deprive a person from his life or liberty without the authority of law. The vesting of power of detention without trial in the executive, has the effect of making the same authority both the prosecutor as well as the judge and is bound to result in arbitrariness which is violative of Article 14 read with Article 19(1)(a) to (g), 20, 21 and 22.

---

1. AIR 1976 SC 1207.

A Presidential order under Article 359(1) can suspend during the period of emergency only the right to move any court for enforcement of the fundamental rights mentioned in the Order. It can't deny to avail the procedural safeguards in the Preventive Detention Act. The court failed to take notice of the law of tort and IPC and Section 57(1) of Indian Evidence Act regarding wrongful confinement of the petitioner and penalising the wrongdoing authorities. Nowhere in the Constitution is prescribed that suspension of enforcement of fundamental rights means denial of testing the legality of exercise of the power under the Constitution, hence Supreme Court and High Court both are competent to issue the writ of *habeas corpus* under Article 32 and Article 226 respectively.

In *Kasturilal* v. *State of U.P.*,[1] and *Vidyawati* cases, the appellant was apprehended by police and some silver and gold were seized and deposited by the police in police Malkhana, from where the gold was misappropriated by a constable who fled to the Pakistan. The court held depositing of gold by police in police Malkhana is a sovereign function and hence the government is not liable for the misappropriation of the gold. This was absolutely wrong judgment because the court found that there was gross negligent on the part of police authorities but it failed to punish the wrongdoing authorities under Section 166 of I.P.C. Neither keeping gold in Malkhana nor its misappropriation amount to the sovereign function, sovereign functions are those functions which can be performed by the State only in comparison to a private person. Even if keeping gold was a sovereign function of the State, the State (Judiciary) is duty bound to give restitutive justice under Article 14. The court also failed to take judicial notice of law of tort and Section 57(1) of Indian Evidence Act, 1872 the maxim, "where there is infringement of a legal right, there exists remedy". Thus in this case there was absolute denial of justice.

In *Dhananjay Chatterjee* alias *Dhana* v. *State of West Bengal and Ors.*,[2] the Petitioner filed an appeal against the death penalty awarded by Calcutta High Court for committing an offence under Section 376 and 302 of I.P.C. against a minor girl. The court held that the act of petitioner amounts to the rarest of rare case and hence accused is liable for death penalty. Death penalty can be given when we have fair and reasonable procedure. We have an evidence and witness based procedure. Truth remains Utopia. As such, death penalty needs to be considered whether it is desirable. However, it is a matter of policy to be decided by appropriate body or authority which 'law' definitely is not.

According to Article 21, No person shall be deprived from his personal life and liberty except through a procedure established by 'law' and that law must be just, fair and reasonable. Where a death penalty is given to a person, he cannot exercise the rights under Article 19(1)(a) to (g), because it amounts to the absolute restriction on those freedoms which is unconstitutional because law requires only reasonable restriction on those

---

1. AIR 1965 SC 1039.

2. 1994 SCR (1) 37.

freedoms on grounds prescribed under Article 19(2) to (5). Besides it, Section 302 of I.P.C. is a pre-constitutional law which may be argued as hit by the Article 13(2) of the Constitution. Doctrine of rarest of rare case cannot be said to have the quality of predictability according to law but life of a person is kept at the sweet will of the judge which is against the rule of law envisaged by the Constitution under Article 14. Petitioner could be said to have been given double punishment for the same offence in violation of the Article 20(2) first punishment he faced was 14 years living in jail under death row and second was the capital punishment itself. Examples of gross constitutional faults can also be seen in Ramjawaya Kapoor, A.K. Gopalan and Champakam Dorairajan cases.

Public Interest litigation—Product of judicial process.

In Public interest litigation the court is taking affirmative action by issuing directions in cases of governmental inaction or lethargy. Scheduled Caste residents of hilly area of Shimla district addressed a letter to the Chief Justice of Himachal Pradesh, High Court complaining that there was no proper road in their area. This not only affected their livelihood but also their development. They also pointed out that the sum allocated by the Government for the construction of the road was insufficient. The Court treated the letter as writ petition and held that every person is entitled to life as enjoined in Article 21 and in the fact of this case read in conjunction with Article 19(1)(d) in the background of Article 38(2), right to life embraces not only physical existence but the quality of life and for residents of hilly area, access to road is access to life itself. The court also directed the Superintending Engineer of P.W.D. to proceed with the construction of the road and to complete the work assigned to it before the end of that financial year. The court further directed the Engineer to make an application to the State Government demanding an additional sum of Rs. 50,000 for the purpose and to report the progress in construction with regard to the case. The State of Himachal Pradesh filed a petition for special leave to appeal before the Supreme Court challenging the High Court's power to regulate financial matters in the State under Article 226. The Supreme Court held that the High Court was within the limits of its jurisdiction in directing the P.W.D. authorities to complete the construction of a road in a poor and Harijan *basti* and also to the Government to make available an additional sum of Rs. 50,000 for the completion of the work. It is submitted that the High Court in this case has exceeded its domain and taken over the functions of the executive.

Judicial Legislation—Basu and Vishaka cases

In an unprecedented manner the Supreme Court, in *D.K. Basu* v. *State of W.B.*,[1] issued 11 requirements to be followed in all cases of arrest or detention till legal provisions are made in that behalf. The requirements were held to be flowing from Articles 21 and 22(1) of the Constitution. In its anxiety to protect the interests of the arrested person, the court has exhibited an instance of judicial hyper-activism rather judicial waywardness.

1. (1997) 1 SCC 216.

The case sounds death-knell to Montesquieu's theory of separation of powers amongst three organs of the State. The Supreme Court arrogated to itself the constituent or at least legislative power in laying down these requirements. The Supreme Court while interpreting a provision of the Constitution may fill in the interstices but the zeal to create such interstices and then fill it should be deprecated. The judiciary should restrain from trespassing in the field of another organ under the guise of interpretation of the Constitution or doing complete justice. Though these eleven requirements comprise human rights jurisprudence and it would be in the fitness of the things, if these were law, these sweeping eleven requirements laid down by the Supreme Court, it is submitted, cannot have the status of law as its source is not legislature but judiciary.

The Supreme Court did not hesitate to assume direct legislative function in the case of *Vishaka* v. *State of Rajasthan.*[1] In this case, the Supreme Court has virtually enacted a piece of legislation on the ground that there is a vacuum in the legislative field of sexual harassment of working women. There is a paragraph similar to the statement of objects and reasons. There is a definition clause and there are 12 points similar to 12 sections. The Supreme Court laid down some guidelines and norms which are directed to be treated as law. It is submitted that these guidelines cannot be treated as laying down a precedent under Article 141, but this should be treated as unauthorized *ad hoc* legislation by the judiciary. Interpreting certain provisions of the existing law and laying down certain principles in the form of the precedent is what is envisaged under Article 141 and not *ad hoc* legislation by the judiciary when there is vacuum in the field. *Vishaka* is an example of judicial trespass in legislative domain.

How to reform our judicial process

In today's era, it becomes crystal clear that our judicial process is on the verge of total collapse. The adversarial system which Indian legal system follows has failed to answer the test of Article 14 read with Article 256 as it is required that the party must do everything for paying court fees to execute the decree which actually is the task of the State. Constitution is the supreme law of the land governing conduct of government and semi-governmental institutions and their affairs.

Trans personalized—Power System.—In ancient India king is the fountain head of justice. Sage Yajnavalkaya declared that "the king, divested of anger and avarice, and associated with the learned should investigate judicial proceedings conformably to the sacred code of laws." In ancient India, legal procedure was governed by the principles of *rajadharma*. All the dharmas merged into the philosophy of *'rajadharma'* and it was paramount dharma. It is a classic example of trans-personalized power system.

The adversarial system lacks dynamism because it has no lofty ideal to inspire. It has not been entrusted with a positive duty to discover the truth as is in the inquisitorial system. When the investigation are perfunctory and ineffective. The judges seldom take any initiative to remedy the situation.

1. AIR 1997 SC 3011.

During the trial, the judges do not bother if relevant evidence is not produced and play passive role as they don't have any duty to search for the truth. As the prosecution has to prove the case beyond reasonable doubt, the system appears to be skewed in favour of the accused. It is therefore, necessary to strengthen the adversarial system by adopting suitable modification and taking some of the good and useful feature of the inquisitorial system.

An epiloguic thought repeating what has been said earlier may be needed to strength submission that the court will commit blunder if it does not guard its reputation more seriously. A post script in this prospective, may drive home the point, treating the bench and the bar as a complex agency of public justice. A learned Judge mild in his words, who retired last year from the Supreme Court, wrote with restraint to a former colleague of his still on the High Court, what makes poignant reading : "the judiciary is sinking. The destruction is from within; it is for judges like you to restore the fast disappearing credibility of the High Courts and the Apex Court."

Equal protection of the laws is the fundamental right of the citizen which has a forensic dimension and procedural projection. The obligation of every court from the summit to base is to afford the same facility for hearing of case to the rich and the poor, to the dubious billionaire, to the bonded labourer. Now, there exists a mutual appreciation of society between judges and advocates which led to the failure of justice delivery system. The judiciary is the fiduciary of people's justice and has accountability to the country for scrupulously equal judicial process.

The crisis is not resolved by some martyrs from the class of advocates courting displeasure by exposure of oblique events but by a people's movement which will compel the judges and advocates against the privatisation of judicial process. Your monopoly obligates accountability and if there is culpability, it cannot be gagged by contempt proceedings. In our system, both the robe and the gown must remember that the court is what it does. The new dimension of justice delivery and new vision of alternative justicing will have to be explored and executed if the first promise of the Constitution were to be actualised. Therefore, today, in adversarial system of justice, what we need to reform are :

Measures recommended for reforming justice delivery system

The Constitution only furnishes a framework in which different organs of the State, including the judiciary, have to function. Nevertheless, the law making power rests with the legislative wing of the State. When once a law has been validity made in exercise of legislative power that is binding on every citizen as well as the executive and the judiciary, the court cannot administer justice in accordance with their subjective perceptions. They are as much bound by law of the land as any other person. Although Article 12 does not expressly refer to judiciary being an organ of the State, it is certainly bound by Article 14 of the Constitution. Article 142 cannot be resorted by the Supreme Court to circumvent the law.

However, the Supreme Court, instead of searching and basing its judgments on first principles or fundamentals of jurisprudence has sometimes taken a shortcut by resorting to the supposed fiat of Article 142. This article was employed as a tool to pass final decisions, apart from and without recourse to the law of the land.

The concept of expanding universe is not confined to astronomy alone. There is fast expanding judicial firmament. The expansion of judicial world sometimes treads on fields occupied and reserved for others. It is very necessary that Supreme Court acts with self restraint. Let us remember the adage, "power corrupts and absolute power corrupts absolutely."

Arrears eradication scheme

Filling of all posts lying vacant is must.—Government of India, Ministry of Law and Justice has created fast track courts which has jurisdiction only in Session cases and also having practical problems which restrict it to this work in all States. To overcome this problem an Arrears Eradication Scheme for the purpose of tackling all cases has been worked out that are pending for more than 2 years.

Court fees to be rationalised

The purpose of delivering justice is the promise of law and hence the role of State is not limited merely to establish the judicial institutions but also to fulfil the expectations of the people which they attach to the State while conferring role and seat of power. To charge fees for justice is like selling the promise of law and flouting the constitutional duty of State to provide justice to the people at their door step. Merely laying down the foundations of judicial shops and washing their hands of from the process of justice delivery is not warranted on the part of the State. To seek revenue for the enforcement of rights and to collect it in rigorous ways may create a situation wherein the failure to pay may mean the justice being not accessible to because one cannot afford to pay it in terms of money. It is the misery and apathy wherein, the courts in India are continuing with. The proper course is restricting the court fee to the minimum because it seriously undermines the parity of power principles insofar as it places the richer one in advantageous position which offends the spirit of Constitutional goals.

Advocate's fee to be regulated

As it is clearly provided under the provisions of Advocates Act that advocates are the officers of the Court, then why the clients are bound to pay hefty fees to lawyers for contesting their cases. There should be provision for public advocates who are available to everyone and should be paid by State. One alternative is that let the fee be paid in registry and provision be made for allotment of work by turn as is the practice in appointment of Survey Commissioners in courts.

Selection of Judges : must be transparent;

The Supreme Court seems to have committed blunder when in one of the most controversial cases it held that consultation with CJI means his consent. Here, by this observation the power of President is reduced to zero and whole spectrum of power given under the Constitution is disturbed. The judges should be appointed by President only with the consultation of CJI and not by his consent.

Moreover, the provision of advocates becoming judges after certain required years of practise should be abolished. Judges and advocates are different profession and they should not be intermingled. There should not be any mutual appreciation of society. In civil law countries, this arrangement is working successfully. A research can be done to find out the feasibility.

Adversarial system : needs to be re-visited

The present adversarial system should be abolished and replaced with inquisitorial system of justice. The Universities may conduct researches to see whether this change is feasible in India. Abrupt change just for change and experiment is to be avoided. Judicial process is essentially deductive reasoning and it is to tell authoritatively what law is. The judge should take judicial notice of all the law. The judge is to investigate the case before him, by approximating 'is' to the 'ought', after the parties present their case.

By virtue of Article 14 read with 256, there should be an affirmative action by the policy implementing organ. It should protect the citizens with their affirmative action, just like the ancient Indian system. The present Indian legal system is continuing the colonial legacy where the ends justify the means, but since now, we are living under the umbrella of a controlling Constitution, the means should justify the ends.

The Limitation Act needs readjustment

The Limitation Act should be struck down as unconstitutional since it is violative of Article 14. Under Article 14 there is no distinction between State action and private action. If any person's fundamental rights are infringed, how can the State fix a time limit to curtail the right to move the court for justice. Why should it withstand the test of Article 14, or the fix counts of the power spectrum. Hence, Limitation Act, doctrine of delay and laches and procedural hassles are undoubtedly unconstitutional and needs to be revisited in light of free and unhampered access to courts.

Judges should be made accountable

The judges should not have immunity because the functions of a judge are twofold; the judicial function is only to state authoritatively what law is. All others are administrative functions. The fundamental law is the Constitution and it is the only supreme authority. If judges commit any negligence or there is designed and calculated dereliction of duty on their part, then such judges should be punished under Section 166 of the I.P.C. because they are the public officers and hence liable for punishment for negligence of duty.

Rajdharma principle—need of the day

According to Rajadharma principles, the king himself is liable to be punished for an offence by penalty which would be one thousand times more than what would be inflicted on an ordinary citizen. Perhaps, it is high time that this principle needs to be enforced by law in India especially as under the Constitution none is above the law and there is no immunity for crime. If judges of the Supreme Court in China and Japan can be prosecuted and punished for violations of law, why not in India which has a basic structure command to ensure equal subjection of all to the law. Lex is Rex in our country. This be made specific and be shown to be so by suitable legislation.

Judicial Process under the Indian Constitution

Judicial process is basically the path or the method of attaining "justice". Justice is the approximation of the 'is' to 'ought'. Judicial power is involved in the legal ordering of facts and is under the obligation to approximate 'is' with the 'ought'. This ordering is nothing but the performance of administrative duties. Supremacy of law implies that it is equally applied and nobody is above the law. Everyone is equal in the eyes of law so that a level playing field is created in order to strengthen parity of power.

Indian Constitution adopted this principle in Article 14 and the Preamble which provides equality of status and opportunity. Thus, Constitution ensures to establish parity of power which requires that every person must be on the same plane. The wording of Article 14 made it an 'umbrella' Article under which all other rights, both constitutional and statutory, find protection. This is so because all laws treat all with equality and the protection of laws is extended to all without any discrimination, then all other rights are automatically enforced. This duty to guarantee equality before the law and equal protection of the laws has been cast on the State.

Articles 256 and 258-A make it obligatory upon the executive of every State to ensure compliance with the law made by Parliament and any existing law which applies in the State. The Union executive is empowered to give such directions to a State as may appear necessary to ensure the compliance of the laws by the State executive. Thus, according to Article 256, it is the duty of the executive to ensure compliance with the laws and that too in a manner that satisfies the mandate of Article 14.

Articles 256 and 258-A are in fact, the reflection of the true tradition of the Rajadharma Principles which regarded it the responsibility of the executive to deliver justice through affirmative executive action to ensure strict compliance with the applicable law. Articles 256 are 258-A State the whole mechanism to ensure the implementation of every law by the ecutive power. It thus, envisages the delivery of justice through administrative mode. The administrative mechanism of providing justice as promised under Article 14 is provided in Article 256 and 258-A. It is well established that the judiciary is the outcome of the dissatisfaction of the working of the administrative machinery. The need for a dispassionate judgment of the executive action has given rise to judiciary. Essentially, the judiciary while resolving disputes is ensuring implementation of laws. Thus, its functions are basically administrative in nature. Law is always based on the policy when the judiciary implements or reverses the action of the executive, the judiciary acts as a policy controller. This view has been endorsed by Karl Lowenstein who held the view that adjudication is basically execution.

But the present Indian judicial system is by all accounts unusual. The proceedings of the Courts are extra ordinarily dilatory and comparatively expensive. A single issue is often fragmented into a multitude of court actions. Execution of the judgment is haphazard. Tutoring of the witness is part of the job of lawyer who is all out to win the case. Justice is not the first aim, to win the case at all cost is the mission of a counsel. It needs to be controlled but is very difficult. To win the case is practical for counsel and also far client. Do not expect advocate to be 'dharmaraj'. The job of counsel is to present his client's case quite dispassionately. That he does without getting personally involved.

In India, the judiciary is separate and independent organ of the State. The legislature and the executive are not allowed by the Constitution to interfere in the functioning of the judiciary. The functioning of the judiciary is independent but it doesn't mean that it is not accountable to anyone. In a democracy the power lies with the people. The judiciary must concern with this fact while functioning. The High Courts have the power of control over the subordinate courts under Article 235 of the Constitution of India. The Supreme Court has no such power over High Court. The CJ of High Courts/India have no power to control or make accountable other judge of the High Court. Judicial Accountability bill is before Parliament.

Reluctant approach of Supreme Court to accept petition under Article 32.

The rule made by Supreme Court under Article 145 laying down the procedure to be followed by the Supreme Court in performing its functions involves lot of technicalities. It is the duty of the Supreme Court to grant relief under Article 32 and it is mandatory as it is obvious from the word "the Supreme Court shall" in Article 32. But the Supreme Court is not very enthusiastic to perform its functions.

To conclude one can say that whatever may be the system the procedural laws must be minimum, simple and must be litigant friendly.

Delay should be avoided

The delay in our legal system is well known evil. There are over 30 million cases pending in various Courts. The average time span for dispute to be resolved through the court system is about 20 years. Litigation has become a convenient method for avoiding prompt retribution by many people on the wrong side of law. The Bible says that the path to hell is paved with good intention. The legal system is meant to punish the criminal and to protect the law abiding citizens. But Many a times, criminals exploit the legal process itself to escape punishment.

Supreme Court benches to sit elsewhere; needs consideration

Article 130 of the Constitution provides that the Supreme Court shall sit in Delhi or in such other place or places, as the CJI may with the approval of President, from time to time appoint. This provision of the Constitution has not been applied so far. If the Supreme Court has a seat on other places, that is seat in every State, then it will be relief to the aggrieved and justice will be assessible to them, which will result in reduction of cost of litigation and will cause less hardship to the litigant. It is quite different whether such benches of Supreme Court are desirable or are feasible and can the country afford it, keeping cost, ethics, security, facilities and merit in mind.

Presumption of constitutionality; does it need any review?

The presumption is always in the favour of constitutionality of statute. It is a gross misapplication of justice as it tends to presume the preponderance of power in favour of one party and tilts the balance unjustly. This totally upsets the balance of parity of power, which is ensured through the guarantee of "equal protection of laws' under Article 14 as well as Article 13(2) and (3) of the Constitution, respectively. The burden of justifying the constitutional validity of the law as well as the fact that the State action was in accordance with such law should be on the State, and not on the person who challenges its constitutional validity. Asking the injured party to prove the wrong or injury suffered, destroys the guarantee of equal protection of laws. Such a position on the part of court is extremely low on the ethical count of the power spectrum.

Judges should play active and not passive role while deciding cases

Article 14 of the Indian Constitution made it obligatory on the State to provide justice to all at the door step. Thus, the Indian Constitution necessarily envisages inquisitional mode. So, the judges should go few miles extra in deciding cases as the judges supervising the cases are independent and are bound by law to direct their inquiries either in favour or against the guilt of any suspect and play an active role while deciding cases.

Other areas of concern that need to be addressed are like shortage of judges and staffs, lack of infrastructure and funds, political interference, accessibility, and misuse of power etc.

Judicial activism and judicial process; new chapters opened

There is always a conflict between judicial activism and judicial restraint, the latter jurisprudence adheres by and large, to a legal positivist approach while the former is basically having realist approach.

The word judicial activism, judicial overreach, judicial credibility sounds to be quite synonymous to judicial review and judicial creativity, until the judiciary works with its full competency and honesty. The judges would not in any manner fail to police themselves. It was Hon'ble Speaker Mr. Somnath Chatterjee who had marked that the M.P.'s are working hard to destroy the democracy. But after detection of several cases of corruption of the judges, it's hard to say that the judiciary is working with its full credibility. A learned judge of today remarked that when he had joined the judiciary there were less than 20% of corrupt judges and when the time comes towards his retirement after serving the nation for more than three decades he with tears in his eyes stated that today we have more than 80% of corrupt judges in the system. It's shameful for the nation when we see a sitting Supreme Court Judge involved in the Ghaziabad P.F. Scandal, when we see a Chief Justice of a certain High Court as among one of the most corrupt judges in the system. It was the then Hon'ble President Mr. A.P.J. Abdul Kalam who had refused to elevate such a judge but sooner or later he was there.

The Indian Judiciary tends to be a den of corruption. The extortion of litigants has become a regular business of today's judicial servants. The whole money extorted from the litigants is being collected by the reader of the court. From this booty, the allegations are that the lunch is being served for the Judiciary presiding officers and; their monthly households are met. The remaining booty is being distributed among the staff of the judge. The litigants should be protected from this exploitation by the system. It should be the judges who should police themselves without any kind of discrimination on any basis.

The real question lies in, whether such a judicial system leads to a reign of tyranny or adds anything to moralty behind just activism. As far as the system is working towards nation building and in national interest, it cannot be called a tyranny but as judicial creativity. Judicial activism can be called as quite synonymous to judicial credibility or creativity. Where judiciary is known as the paterfamilias of the organs of the government and the nation, it should work for the welfare of the nation and its citizens, in order to protect the rights of the citizens. And such a system should not be absolute in nature; changes, reformations are must for a better today and tomorrow, with a balanced amount of check over each other.

Is Indian judiciary cause of great concern

Indian judiciary has become a decaying institution that has no internal mechanisms or will or strength to adapt to the changing times. The judiciary has become almost a law unto itself, answerable to none and under no pressures to reform or change with time. Indian judiciary started as an extension of the colonial regime. British set up a poor copy of the British judicial system as Indian judicial system. The judges (generally British in pre-independence India) were the symbol of imperial power and all the systems and procedures of the court were intended to humiliate the natives. Even after Indians were appointed as judges, any contact between judges and the common people was discouraged. The concept of jury was anathema since it would have involved the local people in decision making process.

The role of judiciary in policy control.—It comes into picture when the executive fails to deliver the justice. In order to make judicial process effective the court must observe following guidelines—

(1) Judiciary must keep in mind that its work is to say authoritatively what the law *i.e.* policy is controlling. Provisions of Article 142 and 226 of Constitution, Section 482 Cr.P.C. and 151 of C.P.C. though give inherent power to the Supreme Court and High Court to render complete justice, it means only to fill the gap within the parameter of the Constitution and statutes and it does not mean to supersede the Constitution or statute as it did in Ramjawaya Kapoor and S.C. Advocates on Records case. The decision that consultation means concurrence amounts to the amendment in the Constitution without following prescribed procedure and the statement that Indian Government system is based on Westminister form of Government and not on advanced presidential form of Government amounts to change the nature of Government from republic democracy to oligarchic democracy which is not permitted to the judiciary.

(2) When a petition is made to test the legality of the decision of any subordinate court/tribunal the court should only issue the writ of *certiorari* if grounds are satisfied, it must not issue other writs unless the statutory remedies are exhausted.

(3) Constitution of new benches—The Chief Justice of India in exercise of his power under Article 130 should constitute at least its four regular benches in and for the eastern, western, northern and southern regions to hear the appeals from the State High Courts. It will help the people to have easy access to the Supreme Court. It is also in consonance with the time, ethical and influence bands of the power spectrum.

(4) Judiciary must accept the norm of democracy that justice not only be done but it appears to be done. How Government could fight against corruption if judiciary itself is against the Right to Information Act regarding disclosure of assets of its judges on ground of being not a public servant but constitutional authority. It amounts to double standing as on one hand they claim salaries and other benefits on ground of being public servant and denying the liability to disclose the assets by saying not to be a public servant. However, true fact is that they are public servant within the meaning of Section 21 I.P.C. However, this issue ceases in view of fact that disclosure is now made to Chief Justice of India.

(5) Curative petitions—Supreme Court must also correct its illegal wrong judgments which are being followed in the country in the name of precedent.

(6) They must provide the justice when the aggrieved party knocks its door and not try to compromise the dispute as it did in Maneka Gandhi case, because Article 14 guarantees restitutive justice.

(7) Judges should play an active role in bringing the truth and not merely being a silent spectator of the dispute.

(8) Whether there should not be presumption of constitutionality of the Act because it tends to presume a preponderance of power in favour of one party and tilts the balance unjustly. This totally affects the principle of parity of power which is ensured through guaranty of equal protection of laws under Article 14 as well as Article 13(1) and 13(2) respectively, asking the injured party to prove the wrong or injury suffered destroys the guaranty of equal protection of laws. Such an opinion on part of court is extremely low on the ethical count of power spectrum.

(9) Section 166 of IPC, 1860 should be enforced 'which provides— "Whoever, being a public servant, knowingly disobeys any direction of the law as to the way in which he is to conduct himself as such public servant, intending to cause, or knowing it to be likely that he will, by such disobedience, cause injury to any person, shall be punished with simple imprisonment for a term which may extend to one year, or with fine, or with both.

(10) "Under Article 14 of the Constitution it is the duty of judiciary (Judiciary is a State as laid down in *A.R. Antulay* v. *R.S. Nayak)*,[1] to render justice but where it fails, it amounts to injury under Section 44 IPC. Judges being public servant within the meaning of Section 21 of IPC, injury caused by them amounts to offence under Section 166 and accordingly they should be punished.

(11) Since section 197 Cr.P.C. is hindrance and violative of equality provisions of Article 14 it should be modified by legislature.

(12) Alternative mode of adversarial system, that is inquisitorial system may be implemented, as it is also envisaged by Article 14 and is in consonance with the objective of the preamble to secure justice, social, economic and political.

Accountability, public faith and judicial process

Judicial Accountability : Why there is a need?

The word 'accountable' as defined in the Oxford Dictionary means 'responsible for your own decisions or actions and expected to explain them when you are asked. Accountability is the *sine qua non* of democracy.

Associated with the higher cause of truth and justice, judiciary and the judges have been accorded a distinct position. What the Constitutional provisions provide for is that "there should be an impartial and independent judicial body to adjudicate upon the matters and to act as the interpreter and guardian of the Constitution." It is also a well settled principle of modern day governance that an authority deriving its existence from same source cannot claim to be absolute and unaccountable. It must be accountable either to the source of its origin, to the institution and more importantly to the people. All wings of Government belong to the people. when the legislature and the executive both are accountable, the judiciary

1. A.I.R. 1988 S.C. 1531.

cannot remain unaccountable and absolute. No person, howsoever high is above the law similarly, no institution howsoever sanctified can claim to be unaccountable. Ultimately, every institution is accountable to the people in every democratic polity like ours. Several countries in their constitutions have already provided for ensuring accountability of judiciary. This to prevent concentration of power in the hands of a single organ of the state especially in countries where judicial activism interferes with and invades into the domain of other organs. But at the same time judicial independence is a pre-requisite for every judge whose oath of office requires him to act without fear or favour, affection or ill-will and to uphold the constitution and laws of the country. Thus, here arises a tension between judicial independence and judicial accountability.

Ethics of judges

Hon'ble Mr. Justice S.H. Kapadia, Chief Justice of India said : "When we talk of ethics, the judges normally comment upon ethics among politicians, students and professors and others. But I would say that for a judge too, ethics, not only constitutional morality but even ethical morality should be the base.

The basic code of ethics is the principle that no man can be a judge in his own cause; it means that a judge should not adjudicate those cases in which he has any kind of interest. A judge should follow the motto of "*Fiat justitia, ruat caelum*" that is "let justice be done though the heavens fall". A judge should guard against intimidation of powerful outside interests, which often threatened the impartial administration of justice and keep himself free from application of crude pressure, which may result in manipulation of the law for political purposes at the behest of the government in power or anybody else.

A judge is the judge of all people. He does not belong to any person or any section of society. A judge must follow the principle of equity in treating the parties to the dispute. The Supreme Court said in the celebrated case "No man's right should be affected without an opportunity to ventilate his views". The Supreme Court in *Ram Pratap Sharma* v. *Daya Nand*,[1] issued a note of caution to the effect that it is proper for a Judge not to accept any invitation and hospitality of any business or commercial organization or of any political party or of any club or organization run or sectarian, communal or parochial lines. Lord Widgery, Lord Chief Justice of England since 1971 to 1980, said that "the best judge is the man who should not court publicity and should work in such a way that they don't catch the eyes of the newsmen". Lord Hailsham said that the "best judges are those who do not find their names in the Daily Mail and still, who abhor it."

Constitutional provisions for making the judiciary accountable

Definition of "misbehavior" : According to Black's Law Dictionary : III-conduct; improper or unlawful behavior.

The fact that the powers of judge are very wide is in itself an indication

---

1. AIR 1977 SC 809.

that the powers may not be allowed to be absolute. Among the constitutional limitations on the judges, the most important one is the provision for 'removal' of judges of the High Courts/Supreme Court by address of the Houses of Parliament to the President on the ground of 'proved misbehavior or incapacity'. This is provided in Constitution of India, Article 124(2) and (4) in respect of judges of the Supreme Court and in view of Article 217, that procedure is attracted to the 'removal' of judges of the High Court also.

In pursuance of the provisions of Article 124(5) of the Constitution the Judges (Inquiry) Act, 1968 was enacted to regulate the procedure for investigation and proof of the "misbehavior" or incapacity of a Judge of the Supreme Court or of a High Court and for the presentation of an address by Parliament to the President and for matters connected therewith.

Judicial Standards and Accountability Bill, 2010

The Judicial Standards and Accountability Bill, 2010 replaces the Judges (Inquiry) Act, 1968. It seeks to create enforceable standards for the conduct of judges of High Courts and the Supreme Court, change the existing mechanism for investigation into allegations of "misbehaviour" or incapacity of judges of High Courts and the Supreme Court, change the process of removal of judges, enable minor disciplinary measures to be taken against judges, and require the declaration of assets of judges.

Questions raised against the Bill

- Whether the balance between independence and accountability is maintained by the proposed mechanism in the Bill?
- It is not clear whether the power of the Oversight Committee to impose minor measures is constitutionally valid?
- The Bill does not mention whether a judge has the right to appeal to the Supreme Court against an order of removal issued by the President after Parliament finds him guilty of "misbehaviour"?

The issues of Judicial Standards must be seen in the context of Article 124(4) of the Constitution which provides for the process of impeachment of a judge on the grounds of proved "misbehaviour" or "incapacity". Article 124(5) empowers Parliament only to make laws to regulate the procedure for presentation of address of impeachment, and for the investigation and proof for the "misbehaviour" or incapacity of a judge. Article 124(5) does not empower Parliament to create any other forum for recommending impeachment proceedings, or allow complaints to be made by any person or to make a judge liable for minor penalties. What can be done only by a hundred or more members of the Lok Sabha or fifty or more members of the Rajya Sabha (*i.e.*, initiation of impeachment proceedings) can now theoretically be done by only one person.

Loopholes in the Bill

- the Bill seeks to provide a straight definition of "misbehaviour" in clause 2(j), but by laying down a strict definition, the concept loses its elasticity and becomes both under inclusive and over-inclusive.
- The Bill also provides a list of standards of judicial conduct to

which all judges are expected to adhere. The very idea of statutorily providing for judicial standards, irrespective of their content, is violative of judicial independence.

- Under the Bill, "any" person may file a complaint in a prescri format. This is likely to lead to a multiplicity of complaints even though the Bill prescribes false and vexatious complaints under Clause 53, this is unlikely to prove much of a deterrent and since each of them will have to be checked by the Scrutiny Panel. It is also likely to result in a huge waste of time.
- The Attorney-General has the responsibility of regularly appearing on behalf of the government before the court. The possibility of his appearing before a judge against whom a complaint has been filed cannot be ruled out in such a circumstance, there is clearly a conflict of interest since the Attorney-General will be a member of the Oversight Committee to look into the complaints made against the former.
- The Scrutiny Panel is to consist of three members, two of whom will be judges sitting in the same court as the judge against whom the complaint is made. Since these judges would be colleagues sitting in the same court, it is likely that this will, either way, influence their conduct.
- The idea of "minor" punishments is unworkable and has the potential to seriously undermine judicial status.
- The Bill completely excludes the operation of the RTI. This establishes an atmosphere of total secrecy more regressive than the present system, and for which, there does not appear to be any rational reason to make a change.
- The Bill makes no mention of whether a judge who has been removed has a right to appeal to the Supreme Court. The Standing Committee has stated that there should not be any provision for appeal as the finality of a Presidential order should not be challenged.

Thus, it is totally impermissible for the legislature to strike upon the independence and fearlessness of the judiciary. A judge of a superior court cannot be treated as an employee of the government. The present Bill is incapable of salvage and must be rejected in totality. In a system where half the litigants must necessarily lose their cases, and where most of the complaints against judges are frivolous and made by disgruntled litigants, this bill, if implemented, would mark the beginning of the ends of the judiciary.

Judicial Accountability in other Nations of the World

South Africa

South Africa is currently in the process of adopting new laws on judicial ethics and discipline, financial disclosure, judicial codes of conduct and training for judges. Issues of judicial accountability have been on the legislative agenda since the late 1990s the subject of wide publicity during the current parliamentary term (January to May 2007). Parliament's Portfolio Committee on Justice and Constitutional Development will be deliberating the latest versions of two judiciary bills—the Judicial Services Commission Amendment Bill B-2007 (dealing with judicial discipline and ethics) and the South Africa Judicial Education Institute Bill B 4-2007 (dealing with judicial education).

Australia

The federal judiciary enjoys constitutional protection in terms of appointment and removal of judges by virtue of Section 72 of the Federal Court of Australia Act. Removal can only occur through proved misbehavior or incapacity. Removal must be effected by the Governor General on an address from both houses of parliament in the same sitting on either of the two grounds listed above. A more formal mechanism for considering complaints was established to address the Judicial Commission of New South Wales. The New South Wales statute requires the Commission to dismiss complaints in a number of specified circumstances : including where there is a right of appeal, where the complaint is frivolous or trivial, or where further consideration is unnecessary or unjustifiable.

Canada

In Canada the independence of the federally appointed judiciary is guaranteed by the Canadian Constitution (namely sections 96 to 100 of the Constitution Act, 1867) which provides for the appointment, security of tenure and financial security of superior court judges. This provision aims to ensure judicial independence by making it extremely difficult to remove judges from office for political or other reasons. The 1971 amendments to the Judges Act created the Canadian Judicial Council and gave it statutory authority to investigate complaints against federally appointed judges. Judicial Independence is also guaranteed by the Canadian Charter of Rights and Freedoms, Schedule B to the Constitution Act, 1982. Under Section 63(2) of the Judges Act, any member of the public (including a provincial attorney general or the federal Minister of Justice) may make a complaint about a federally appointed judge by writing to the Canadian Judicial Council.

United States

Article III of the US Constitution establishes the judiciary as an independent third branch of government. Article III gives the judiciary the power to hear and adjudicate all cases arising out of the Constitution and laws of the USA with impartiality. Article III also states that federal judges can only be removed through impeachment by the House of Representatives and conviction by the US Senate for "treason, bribery or other high crimes or misdemeanours." Short of removal, federal judges can be disciplined for violations of the Code of Conduct for United States Judges—a set of ethical principles and guidelines adopted by the Judicial Conference of the United States.

Most States have adopted the Model Code of Judicial Conduct compiled by the American Bar Association in 1990, which governs judges' conduct during judicial proceedings, as well as speech, business activities, civil, charitable, political and other associations. The detail of the actual complaints procedure at federal district level is set out in the Judicial Council Reform and Judicial Conduct and Disability Act.

To bring a complaint, individuals submit written statements to the clerk for the chief judge of the relevant court. A chief judge can also initiate a proceeding based on informal complaints received. Complaints about this behavior of state court judges can be filed as a grievance with the state's judicial conduct organization referred to above.

Corruption in India

"Corruption is like a hidden tiger in the bushes, waiting to pounce on the deer (rule of law), catch it by the neck and finally strangulate it to death. Unless the tiger is caged it will continue to wreak havoc."

Indian Judiciary system is the most powerful judiciary in the world after USA. Judiciary in India being a democratic country is vested with the highest power by the people and is considered as strongest pillar of the democracy. Judiciary in India has been given Supreme powers by the Legislature which has lead to the non-accountability of the judiciary to anyone. Judiciary in India enjoys judicial independence but this independence sometimes results in misuse of the powers and privileges by the Judges. Thus, the concept of Judicial Accountability is nowadays is in question. All over the world various conferences and discussions are going on as to whether judiciary can be held accountable for actions. The author of this paper would deal with the need for judicial accountability and meaning of ethics in context with the judges. The author would like to discuss the Judicial Standard and Accountability Bill, 2010 in detail and would like to suggest some measure along with conclusion which can be used to improve standard of judicial accountability in India. The author would also deal with the fact as to how corruption is hampering the judicial system in India. The author would throw some light on the status of judicial accountability in other nations of the world like USA. Australia *etc.*

Democracy means rule of law and it is the primary duty of the government to ensure that the rule of law is obeyed. Wherever rule of law is broken, corruption and injustice will flourish. Every unpunished crime will give birth to a thousand new crimes, creating conditions of anarchy. Corruption corrodes the values people cherish and projects the State as predatory and unjust. Corruption tends to undercut the legitimacy of the State and make a mockery of the rule of law. Corruption, which springs from the basic human tendency of greed, distorts the whole process of law.

The basic defect in the manner in which the candidates are elected to the legislature has its impact on the law making. Corruption distorts not only the composition of the legislatures but also the process of law making and implementation.

Due to corruption, the very constitutional institutions, which are supposed to protect and uphold liberty and rule of law, turn against them. Therefore, to the majority of Indians, the only way left is resorting to the local mafia, who are more than willing to dispense rough and ready justice for a price, leading to criminalisation of Indian society. Rule of law and access to justice are the very essence of a modern democracy and without them we cannot call ourselves a great democracy in any sense.

A report by Transparency International (TI) is called the "Global Corruption Report 2007". The report, based on a 2005 countrywide survey of "public perceptions and experiences of corruption in the lower judiciary", conducted by the Centre for Media Studies, finds that a very high 77 per cent of respondents believe that the Indian judiciary is corrupt. It says that "bribes seem to be solicited as the price of getting things done". The estimated amount paid in bribes in a 12 months period it found was around 580 million dollars. "Money was paid to the officials in the following proportions : 61 per cent to lawyers; 29 per cent to court officials; 5 per cent to middlemen.

So, just as predator kills the pray, corruption kills Rule of Law therefore wherever corruption exists rule of law has no place there.

Instances

Justice Sinha is the only Judge impeached. Our Fore-Fathers represented by Constituent Assembly of India, framers of Constitution of India then in 1949 impeached Mr. Justice Sinha finding him "guilty of improper exercise of judicial functions, the cumulative effect of which was to lower the dignity of his office and undermine the confidence of the public in the administration of justice".

Justice V. Ramaswamy, May 11, 1993 will be remembered as a black day for Parliament and for the judiciary in this country. The impeachment motion against Justice V. Ramaswamy of the Supreme Court was established. Thus, despite the motion for removal being passed unanimously by the members who voted, it failed. The result, therefore, is that despite a high-power inquiry committee of three eminent judges having come to the conclusion that Ramaswami was guilty of several acts of gross mis-behaviour which warranted his removal, the judge is still entitled to discharge judicial functions from the highest court of the lands. It is another matter that after the impeachment motion failed, Ramswami was persuaded to resign by the Congress (I) a belatedly behavior lest it would have to pay a heavy price for being seen to have supported a corrupt judge. The failure of the motion, especially after the tortuous course it went through, raises several grave issues for the future of the administration of justice in this country and indeed for probity in public life in general.

Sex for Acquittal

In November 2002, Sunita Malviya, a Jodhpur-based doctor, alleged that a deputy registrar of the Rajasthan High Court had sought sexual favours for himself and for Justice Arun Madan to "fix" a case in her favour. A committee set up by former CJI, G.B. Patnaik found *prima facie* evidence against Madan, who does not attend court anymore. Judge Resigned.

"If not now than when"?

The legal system in India and the judiciary has reached a stage now where the public openly criticise the judiciary and the News Channels debate even the judgments delivered by the Constitutional Courts. It is an open fact in author's opinion that the public opinion at the legal system in India and as to how the judiciary is not able to deliver results meeting the expectations of the public, has taken away the caution to be exercised while referring to the judiciary or the legal system. The respect can never forcibly be received and the respect should come voluntarily. The functioning of judiciary or the legal system has a direct impact on the society and the rights of the people. If a criminal could manage a magistrate or court dealing with his case, then, who will protect the society from evil forces? We cannot expect the government to be very clean and responsive given the complications in the Indian political system. As such, the Judiciary or the legal system has a big role to play in protecting the rights of the people, ensuring orderliness in the system and even making a judgment on the executive actions when those are not in conformity with the public interest. There are critics on the allegations of corruption and lack of transparency in the Judiciary. In my opinion, many people talk about the judiciary and the judicial reforms only because people have the hope that judiciary can protect their rights and ensure 'right to life' as guaranteed under Article 21 of Constitution of India and further expanded.

Suggestions for reform in judicial process

The problem with judicial reforms in India is that we lack clarity as to who is ultimately responsible to the citizens. But, with experience, the collegiums system has invited so much criticism and the executive do not bother to address the issue showing judicial independence and they will say that they can do nothing given the legal position in this regard. Likewise, the problem is where to start and whose responsibility it is to address the issue of delay in disposal of cases before various courts in this country. It is for sure that we can certainly curtail the delay in justice delivery and can ensure speedy justice to the citizens. For which what we need is commitment from Government and the concerned ministry. We have so many eminent judges with vast experience who also command great respect among the professionals and people. We need to utilize their services and get their guidance as to how to cure the system and make the speedy disposal of cases a reality. Judicial reforms will transform his country to a great extent and we can see lot of change in the things in the society if we are able to bring the judicial reforms. There will not be any illegality in the society or at least we can see substantial reduction in illegal activities in the society if there is an effective judicial system in place. This is the impact of effective judicial system in the country.

Alleged corruption in Judiciary and particularly lower judiciary is a matter of grave concern. We need to address the issue of corruption in Higher Judiciary first and we need to concentrate on the issue of judicial appointments. The judge's accountability is a serious issue as options are less to deal with the judge who is not accountable or who is corrupt. So, the responsibility of appointing efficient and clean judges is to be given to executive and they should not be allowed to take a defence that they are not concerned with the appointments and as such they can do nothing when it comes to corruption in judiciary. Our country is really facing a serious problem with the allegations of corruption in judiciary and the public are slowly losing their faith in judiciary or finding the ways to get relief by adopting unethical means. When we make the system very transparent, then, there is a chance of reducing the corruption to a great extent and as such the executive should concentrate as to how to make the entire judicial system in the country transparent.

All that is needed is :

1. Speedy justice not amounting to justice buried.
2. Simplistic procedures where even a common man with basic knowledge can directly approach the court.
3. Transparency in the system and reduction of corruption to a great extent.
4. Appointment of efficient and clean professionals as judges.
5. Ensuring the required standards in the legal professional or the person concerned.

It is odd indeed that the Delhi High Court seems to believe that sensational media coverage can sway the Supreme Court into prejudice against one of its own retired judges. Justice Manmohan Singh of the Delhi High Court has said in *Swatanter Kumar* v. *Indian Express and Others*, that the pervasive sensational media coverage of the sexual harassment allegations against the retired Supreme Court judge "may also result in creating an atmosphere in the form of public opinion wherein a person may not be able to put forward his defence properly and his likelihood of getting fair trial would be seriously impaired." This Delhi High Court judgment has drawn upon the controversial 2011 Supreme Court judgment in *Sahara India Real Estate Corp. Ltd.* v. *SEBI*,[1] (referred to as the Gag Order case in this piece), to prohibit the media from publishing headlines connecting retired Justice Swatanter Kumar with the intern's allegations and from publishing his photograph in connection with the allegations.

Reporting proceedings

Although the Gag Order judgment was criticised at the time that it was delivered, *Swatanter Kumar* v. *Indian Express* illustrates its detractors' argument more clearly than anyone could have imagined. Sukumar Muralidharan wrote of the Gag Order case that the postponement (of media coverage) orders that it set up as a remedy, could become an "instrument in the hands of wealthy and influential litigants, to subvert the course of open justice." Here we find that although a former Supreme Court judge is pitted against a very young former intern within a system over which he once

1. AIR 2012 SC 3448.

presided, Justice Manmohan Singh seems to think that it is the judge who is in danger of being victimised. The High Court's Swatanter Kumar judgment was enabled by both the Gag Order case as well as the 1966 Supreme Court judgment in *Naresh Shridhar Mirajkar* v. *State of Maharashtra*,[1] which in combination created a process for veiling court proceedings. Naresh Mirajkar stated that the inherent powers of courts extend to barring media reports and comments on ongoing trials in the interests of justice, and that such powers do not violate the right to freedom of speech; and the Gag Order case created an instrument—the "postponement order"—for litigants, such that they can have media reports of a pending case restricted. The manner in which this is used in the Swatanter Kumar judgments raises very worrying questions about how the judiciary views the boundaries of the right to freedom of expression, particularly in the context of reporting court proceedings.

Broad power to restrict reporting

The Gag Order case was problematic : it used arguments for legitimate restraints on media reporting in exceptional circumstances, to permit restrictions on media reporting of court proceedings under circumstances "where there is a real and substantial risk of prejudice to fairness of the trial or to proper administration of justice." The Supreme Court refused to narrow this or clarify what publications would fall within this category, saying that this would depend on the content and context of the offending publication, and that no "straitjacket formula" could be created to enumerate these categories. This discretionary power is broad and ambiguous. It imperils openness and transparency in the context in which the public needs it the most—when powerful public figures whose actions have public implications are under trial.

Court proceedings are usually open to the public. This openness serves as a check on the judiciary and ensures public faith in the judiciary. In countries as large as ours, media coverage of important cases ensures actual openness of court proceedings—we are able to follow the arguments made by petitioners who ask that homosexuality be decriminalised, the trial of suspected terrorists and alleged murders, and the manner in which our legal system handles sexual harassment complaints filed by young women.

When court proceedings are closed to the public (known as "in-camera" trials) or when media dissemination of information about them is restricted, the openness and transparency of court proceedings is compromised. Such compromise of transparency does take place in many countries, to protect the rights of the parties involved, or prevent the miscarriage of justice. For example, child-participants are protected by holding trials in-camera; names of parties to court proceedings are withheld to protect their privacy sometimes; and in countries where juries determine guilt, news coverage that may prejudice the jury is also restricted.

---

1. AIR 1967 SC 1.

Damage done

Although the Supreme Court stated in principle that the openness of court proceedings should only be restricted where strictly necessary, this appears to lend itself to very varied interpretation. For example, it is very difficult for some of us to understand whey it was strictly necessary to restrict media coverage of sexual harassment proceedings in the Swatanter Kumar case. Justice Manmohan Singh on the other hand seems to argue that the adverse public opinion will affect the retired judge's chance of getting a fair trial. However, his judgment also seems to indicate his concern that the sensational headlines will impact public confidence in the Supreme Court.

The Delhi High Court's concern about the effects of the newspaper coverage on the reputation of the judge did not need to translate into a prior restraint on media coverage. They may better have been addressed at a later stage by evaluating whether there was defamation once the facts were determined. His concern about the reputation of the judiciary may also have been better addressed by transparency. If powerful public figures, especially those with as much influence as a former Supreme Court judge are not subjected to transparent court proceedings, the opacity in the face of such a critical issue is likely to undermine public faith in the judiciary. Such opacity undermines the purpose of open courts.

Since the Delhi High Court ruling, there has been little coverage of the sexual harassment case. The suppression of media coverage leaves the young woman comparatively isolated, without all the support that media coverage can bring. Wide coverage of the other sexual harassment complaint involving Justice Ganguly helped the intern in that case find support. The circulation of information led to other former interns in a similar position as well as from a larger network of lawyers and activists reaching out to her. Media coverage is often critical to whether someone relatively powerless is able to assert her rights against a very powerful person, and it is the reason that we protect the freedom of expression in our democracy.

If the Supreme Court was confident that the high courts in India would use their broad discretionary power under the Gag Order case sparingly and only the interests of justice, the Swatanter Kumar case should offer it grounds to reconsider. Openness and freedom of expression are not meant to be diluted to protect the powerful—they exist precisely to ensure that even the powerful are held accountable by state systems that they might otherwise be able to sway.

❑❑

Chapter 2

Constitutional Adjudication and the 'Dimensions' of Judicial Activism

The dominant approach to constitutional law, and even more so to constitutional theory, is undoubtedly judicial review-centered. The debates on the role of courts in constitutional legal orders, on the related process of adjudication, and on the proper balance of power between the judiciary and the political process have filled libraries for centuries, with an overwhelming body of literature on almost every imaginable aspect of the so-called domain of 'judicial policy-making'. This is true for the United States as well as other legal orders, including continental European orders, despite deep-rooted cultural differences. The general attempt is to construct—directly or indirectly—organic theories of judicial review, trying to justify it or to reject it, and dictating its parameters.

At the level of principle, the eternal question of the legitimacy of the constitutional jurisdiction appears to be of fundamental importance in all modern democratic legal orders, establishing a structural link between the theory of the Constitution, on the one hand, and the theory of constitutional interpretation, on the other. This has historically drawn a sort of osmotic *continuum* of the characterizing factors and called for systemic criteria in the study of them. But it has also led to a kind of *'foundationalist'* structure of constitutional scholarship, in a sort of continuous effort to discover a general and unified principle that can provide the basis for judicial decisions : and it seems to me that most of the leading constitutional theories—regardless of their favour or disfavour for judicial role—share this vocation.

Numerous diverse approaches to this popular research topic have been proposed by scholars, ranging from different historical and methodological premises. In the last years and in the resulting works of systematization, these have been persuasively grouped under three typical *'families of theories of judging'*, namely the socio-political the legal-positivist, and the normative-prescriptive. Of course, all these varieties and their work of systematization have come at the expense (or at the risk) of some generalizations, sometimes even at the expense of some form of 'native legal realism' : an undeniable difficulty to be considered, but also a price to pay in comparative theoretical studies, facing the methodological necessity, at a certain point, the drawing *'abstract forms of reference'*, or rather, in our filed, defining a kind of *'prototype of courts'*. Regardless—for now—of the different scientific insights and different tools used in the research, one can say that the common denominator of most modern accounts on the work of the various *'least dangerous branches'* seems to be the search for a realistic approach, at least in intention. Scholars have emphasized that, nowadays, the *'repudiation of Montesquieu* and the *'expansion and legitimacy of constitutional justice'* are both to be regarded as historical truths, in parallel with the growth of the judicial role in modern societies. They have spoken of necessary developments in increasingly complex systems of checks and balances, which face, generally speaking, "*a proliferation of legislative regulation*" and a variation in the role itself of the legislative source. They have depicted powerful legislatures and bureaucracies needing a judiciary subject to a commensurate expansion in power, for a proportionate, coherently expanded system of checks and balances; and the related, arising *'distrust'* of the political branches of government would be reflected not only in the growth of judicial power, but also in the modification of the very nature of the judicial tasks.

The *'revolt against formalism'* and the transformation of the role of the state (and of the law itself) in post-modern welfare systems have represented two basic phenomena of the second postwar orders, probably two of the first really global legal phenomena. Undoubtedly, they have created a very different model of the judicial bodies' role, and this is particularly true for supreme and constitutional tribunals, increasingly central to the arbitration of political and social disputes in their political communities. In has been usual to argue that both in common law and civil law countries 'the veil has been lifted', calling for realist and pragmatist studies, discovering new dynamics of interpretation, and going far beyond the mechanic-logical-deductive processes declared by judges bound by the legal text. A supposedly sharp contrast between *interpretation* and *law-making* has been highlighted not only, as is well known, by continental thinkers, but already by Jeremy Bentham and, subsequently, by other common law scholars : it was thought to mirror the supposedly broader, sharper boundaries between the powers of the *trias politica*, although nowadays all these boundaries are increasingly blurring, subject to extensive rethinking. The constitutionalization of political life has promoted the judicialization of political disputes. Therefore, in its new broader context, judicial interpretation is widely regarded as *'unavoidably creative'*, even in the case *'of apparently simple or direct language, in which legislative intent may have been expressed'*

The inherent, mighty problem of the democratic legitimacy of judicial law-making is not negated, in this fluid context, by these modern streams of thought. In general terms, it is simply not considered to be a 'fatal' issue, involving *ex se* the democratic character of an order and of a country, and an issue to be studied as such, in a limited way. From our perspective, as explicitly suggested by Cappelletti, an analysis of judicial creativity only begins with this awareness. Taking for granted the unavoidably creative function of judicial interpretation, the inquiry must refer to the *degree* of such creativity, as well as to the questions of the *mode*, the *limits*, and the level of *acceptability* of law-making through the courts. "*In the real political world it is senseless to carry on examinations of any branch of government in simple terms of the voice of the majority or 'democratic' and 'undemocratic' labels. There are undoubtedly many instances in which the policy decisions...reflect and/or result from majority sentiment, but there are many instances in which they do not.*" In assessing mode, degrees, limits, alternative strengths and weaknesses, new basic questions arise, both as premises and consequences, but for the institutional capabilities of the judiciary and of the political process, vis-a-vis societal goals. As a result, we simultaneously move from and towards a new assessment of the traditional distinction "*between 'reason', the realm of adjudication, and 'will', the realm of policies*", in search of a feasible and acceptable balance. It is through this broadening process of interpretation that the boundaries between the legislative and the judicial branches (set more or less clearly by the constitution) are continuously reshaped.

Some of the most modern legal theories, defined as 'neo-realist' in a recent mapping exercise, start precisely and directly from this point. It is particularly interesting to consider here the positive of Neil Komesar and his 'comparative institutional' analysis, whose main features, with regard to the theories of judicial review, stem precisely from a sense of discontent with grand theoretical foundations and which call for a pragmatic appraisal of concrete institutional capabilities in decision-making. His more general lesson, already proved influential for other new theoretical appraisals of constitutional adjudication, comes directly from his comparison with traditional constitutional theories. The main suggestions is to abandon debates at a high level of abstraction, by raising questions about the nature of interpretation, making large claims about democracy, legitimacy, and constitutionalism, mainly by following a 'master principle' of constitutional authority, being moral philosophy, societal consensus or original intent. All these approaches, in his opinion, have important and useful ideas to offer, and can provide useful heuristic and analytical tools. However, they embody—in his lawyer-economist's jargon—the 'Nirvana fallacy' of juxtaposing the picture of an idealized judge (Hercules or a more conservative colleague) with the real-world judge, who actually operates "*as part of a decision-making committee staffed by multiple actors*". In short, from an institutional viewpoints, the important questions about judicial review (as well as about any other decision-making institution) are not in the form of first-best principles, but in the form of second-best enquiries about institutional performances and systemic effects : and "*a second-best assessment of institutional issues might, in some cases, be not only necessary but indeed sufficient to resolve conflicts over interpretative theories, simply because the assessment might lead people with different views on the theoretical issues to agree on the appropriate practices.*"

It is probably no coincidence, but—instead—is evidence of an evolution in the debate, that some scholars even see institutional analysis as a new common ground and the "*basis of a new synthesis of scholarly discourse about law*". Several major constitutional theories set the stage—knowingly or unknowingly—for comparative institutional analysis, often just starting, as mentioned, from an analysis of judicial review. The more we distance ourselves from the ideas of purely rational decision, ideal institutions, clearly defined boundaries, optimal solutions, the more we need a realistic understanding of institutional capabilities and inter-branch dynamics. It thinks that the guidance of Komesar in this realm of "*highly imperfect alternatives*" can provide particularly valuable insight.

Some reflection on Law and Politics

Assumption is that the phrase 'judicial activism', however typical of a particular context such as the American one and eve:. though occasionally regarded as a gross, not strictly dogmatic or even legal category, can be comparatively exported and used as helpful tool for reflection by the constitutional justice scholar. If properly substantiated, it may represent (and to some extent make concrete) the latent and often intractable tensions inherent in traditional constitutional theories of judicial review. It can also serve precisely as the external, common thread of these. Moreover, it may also represent the inherent tensions which a comparative institutional analysis undertaken from the perspective of a constitutional adjudicator entails, including many of the 'Institutionalists reflections, primarily Komesar, on judicial review.

The phrase 'judicial activism' has popular origins. Recent works concerning the term and its conceptualization have emphasized its first recorded use in a magazine article meant for a general audience, written by a non-lawyer, as a symbol of an intrinsic *'-ism difficulty'* in definition. The same scholars have, however, insisted on the utility of a conceptual and historical analysis of 'judicial activism', since it has already become a tool that is too widespread in making critical reviews of judges' behaviour to be ignored or avoided. This, the authors believe, should yield clearer perceptions of judicial behaviour and "*might reduce destructive schisms between expert and non-expert discussions of judicial role*".

Various exercises of categorization have been proposed : their usefulness, like all comparative 'ideal types', needs to be tested when applied to the study of a single peculiar order. As already mentioned, the risk of *a contextual* research in this field, where several context-specific factors cross each other 'politically', seems particularly strong. On the other hand, it also seems necessary to clear the field of those overly 'politicized' approach that have made the term laden with clearly pejorative connotation, automatically linked to a certain political vision : in other words, the problem needs to be assessed on a value-free level, in order to avoid 'judicial activism' from simply being used to mean 'a decision one does not like." This initial, basic difficulty in the transition from popular/political jargon to a legal conceptualization is also the reason why it seems better to make a judicious use of these works and their attempts to clarify this issue. Rather than making an abstract use of them for quantitative, statistical inquiries, it seems more appropriate to take advantage of the aforementioned works by considering them as attempts to outline composite models and composite categories : one can then collect around them a number of issues raised by the study of the function of the judiciary in constitutionalist climates, at least the most sensitive ones relating to the variety of ways in which courts can impact society. This seems, in fact, to be the same concern that has inspired, *ex ante*, the recent works of those scholars who, belonging to different environments and moving from different cultural backgrounds, have proposed *'multi-layered'/multi-dimensional'* models of activism. Facing a historical lack of clarity, it has seemed better to avoid the search for a clear-cut definition based on a single criterion, and to benefit from recognising the variety of meanings, the variety of expressions of 'activism'. Each of these meanings should be assessed separately, as a single question about the function of the judiciary and as a facet of the debate on the 'third branch of government' in its role as a "*participant in a network of interaction with other social, political and institutional players*". It also seems better to rely on exercise of broad categorization, free from excessive particularism, which can best fulfil his function in the light of these reflections, rather than using the dozens of strict parameters for evaluation identified in one of the most recent works on the matter.

Constitutional Functionaries

The Constitution has three tier Governance First Union of India (President-Parliament-Supreme Court) second; the States (Government-Legislature-High Courts) and 3rd, Local self Governments like Municipalities, the Panchayats and the Scheduled and Tribal Areas.

Judicial Process consists of Supreme Court, High Courts, Subordinate District Courts and Law Officers; (Attorney General, Solicitor-General and Comptroller and Auditor General of India), Advocate General, and Auditor. General for States.

Judicial Process and the Separation of Power

We do not have it in the strict sense it is in U.S.A. In fact, we have division of Governmental powers. It should not be confused with separation of power *struct sensu*.

Separation of power means

(1) Same person should not form part of more than one of the three organs of Government;

(2) No interference with other organ;

(3) Should not exercise power of the other organ.

In India, we do not have anything like separation of power amongst three organs (Executive-Legislature-Judiciary) of the Government. Separation of Power is essential requirement of strict Federal Constitution which is based on the principle of rivalry in Centre and the States. In Indian system, we do not provide for strict Federal Constitution. Our constitution has everything that is good in Federal Constitution and all best of unitary Constitution. It is based on Cooperative federalism'. As such we provide for division of power (Part XI) in our Constitution.

Executive (Chapter 1, Article 52-78) for purposes of Union means President, Vice-President and council of Ministers headed by the Prime Minister. For purposes of states (Chapter II, Part VI, Articles 153 to 167) it means, the Governor and Council of Minister headed by the Chief Minister.

Parliament, (Chapter II, Part V Articles 79-122) means both Houses of the Parliament, Lok Sabha (House of Peoples) and Rajya Sabha, (Council of States) and officers of the Parliament (Chairman and Deputy Chairman of Rajya Sabha, Speaker and Dy. Speaker of Lok Sabha) State, Vidhan Sabha (Legislature Assembly) and Vidhan Parishad (Legislative Council).

Judiciary

Judiciary means Supreme Court—High Court of States and 'District Courts'.

Separation of Power or its Indian modified version division of power survives on check and balance doctrine which is a constitutional doctrine that is operated by courts. Articles 245-246 of the Constitution of India, provide for two principles of law making. First territoriality; Parliament can make law for whole country and even beyond for countrymen expatriate non-resident Indians or non-nationals coming to India. No law made by Parliament shall be deemed to be invalid on the ground that it would have extra territorial operation. It is message for judiciary that has liberty to declare so under Article 13(2).

The legislature of a State may make laws for the whole or any part of State. These principles have far reaching implications and may be construed to delimit the area of work for all functionaries. The second thing that is here is in Article 246 which describes, subject-matter of laws on which law can be made by Parliament and by the State legislatures. Parliament can make law on any item given in list I (Union List). It is exclusive power of Parliament described in Seventh Schedule (97 items). Art. 246(2) says that State legislatures have exclusive power to legislate on any item contained in list II (State list) Seventh Schedule (66 items). Both Parliament and Legislatures of States have concurrent legislative power to make laws on items contained in concurrent list (List III, 47 items).

In these lists new items have been inserted. In List I, 2-A, is new insertion, Entry 92 has been redrafted and expanded in Entry 92-A, 92-B, and 92-C. Entry 79 has been re-written. Entry 33 has been deleted. Entry 63, 67, 78 have been expanded. In List II, no new entry has been added; Entries 11, 20, 29, 36 have been deleted. Entry 54 and 55 are re-drafted. List III (Concurrent List, 47 entries), 11-A, 17-A, 17-B, 20-A, 33-A are new additions, Entry 25, 33, 40, 42 are modified.

In context of liberalisation, privatisation and globalisation, separation means community of power exercised in cooperation in best interest of the people.

Judicial Process and the Judicial Review, The issues relevant in study of judicial review

(1) The Problem of Judicial Review—The practice of judicial review has become an important problem for democratic and liberal theory and for descriptive political science in the twentieth century. But of course it began as the assertion by a judicial body of a legal power under the written Constitution. The legality of that initial assertion has itself been controversial. Was the power of judicial review implicit in the Constitution, or was it the creation of the Marshall Court? Is *Marbury* v. *Madison*[1] an instance of careful legal judgment or early judicial activism? Is judicial review a legal doctrine or a political power, or both?

(2) The "Activism" debate—The public debate over judicial review primarily revolves around denunciations of judicial "activism". Unfortunately the term does not have any clear content, though it does have a fairly clear valence (nobody likes "activism", whatever it might be). Nonetheless, some basic notion of activism underlies the normative scholarly debate over judicial review as well. Is there anything worth salvaging here? Is judicial activism a bad thing?

(3) Democracy, reason and neutrality—The *Lochner* era (1905) of the late nineteenth and early twentieth centuries provoked a crisis for the Court and the power of judicial review. By the time of the New Deal, a substantial body of Progressive-minded legal thought questioned the value and process of judicial review. The Court's capitulation to the Roosevelt administration was seen by many to mark the beginning of a new era of judicial restraint. The Warren Court (1953-1959) forced a rethinking of the value of judicial review in the light of progressive judicial activism. The core concerns of modern constitutional theory were laid out in this era. How can democracy and judicial review be reconciled? How can judicial review be anything other than the exercise of raw political power? Can the courts be distinguished from legislatures in any meaningful way? In particular, are courts more principled and reasonable than legislatures, and is that sufficient to justify judicial review?

(4) Fundamental Values—The "legal process" school of the 1950s and early 1960s emphasized principle, but their conception of principle was relatively thin and legalistic. As scholars became more comfortable with the Warren Court, a more explicitly and substantively rich values approach to constitutional jurisprudence was developed. Judicial review might be justified by the important values that it advanced. If the children of the New Deal were centrally concerned with establishing the primacy of democracy over controversial rights claims, the children of the Warren Court (1953-1959) were centrally concerned with identifying rights as "trumps" over democratic outcomes. Can the enforcement of fundamental values provide an adequate justification for judicial review? Must the Court be limited to those values contained within the Constitution or traditionally recognized in the law? Can the fundamental values approach be rationalized with the Court as a judicial institution and with the inherited Constitution as written? What values should be enforced? How should they be generated? Can the Warren Court be justified without also justifying the *Lochner* Court? (198 US 45).

(5) Reinforcing Democracy—The common response to Bickel's "countermajoritarian difficulty" is to deny that countermajoritarianism raises any problems at all-to defend an activist Court and constitutional

1. 5 US 137 (1803).

rights as trumps. Another option is to seek to avoid the difficulty by charging the Court with reinforcing and facilitating democracy rather than checking it. Limiting the Court to actions that can reinforce democracy has also been advocated as a way for the Court to avoid the *Lochner* problem of making controversial value judgments. What does democracy require and how might the Court reinforce it? Can the Court claim democratic credentials? Is reinforcing democracy an adequate role for the Court? Is it a possible role for the Court? Would this mission resolve the Court's legitimacy problems?

(6) Originalism and Interpretation—Fundamental values and democratic justifications for judicial review offer substantive, functional defenses of the Court. A more traditional alternative that received renewed attention over the past two decades reemphasizes the legal role of the Court as an interpreter of the Constitution. Rather than going "beyond the Constitution" to enforce some particular value, the Court should instead focus on interpreting the Constitution as written and enforcing its various commitments. Constitutional theory joined the "interpretive turn" that was made by much of the humanities and social sciences, exploring the implications and possibilities of textual interpretation and the role that texts play within interpretive communities. A prominent-but not the only-interpretive theory is originalism, that the Court should enforce the Constitution as the Founders understood it. Why interpret? What is the authority of the text? What is "the Constitution"? What is required by constitutional interpretation? Is interpretation possible? Can interpretation be distinguished from originalism? What is the authority of the Founders? What does originalism require?

(7) Judicial Supremacy v. Popular Constitutionalism.—Two related debates have dominated constitutional theory over the past few decades, a debate over how "activist" or "restrained" the Court should be in exercising the power of judicial review and a debate over the proper foundations and purposes of the power of judicial review. In recent years, another strand of debate has emerged focusing on how "supreme" judicial interpretations of the Constitution should be and how authoritative other interpreters of the Constitution might be. The debate over judicial supremacy has both normative and empirical elements, introducing a more explicit institutional element to the debate over judicial review. Who should interpret the Constitution? Under what circumstances? Should the judiciary defer to other political actors? Does judicial review make sense in the absence of judicial supremacy? What is "popular constitutionalism", and is it consistent with the modern constitutionalism of legally constrained government? Do non-judicial actors take the Constitution seriously? How are constitutional values best defined and enforced?

(8) The Countermajoritarian Court?—The starting point for contemporary normative theorizing about judicial review is the assumption that the Court is a countermajoritarian institution. That counter-majoritarianism created both possibilities and difficulties. It created the possibility that the Court could protect minorities and individuals from majority power. It created the difficulty that judicial review was in conflict with democracy. The dramatic conflict between the *Lochner* Court and the New Deal exposed the central feature of American judicial review. The normative debate essentially begins with from that core empirical assumption. But through most of the nineteenth century, no one would have given credence to that assumption, and James Madison himself doubted the value of constitutional rights because he thought the popular will was the only significant political force in a republic. Is the countermajoritarian Court a myth? Can the Court be countermajoritarian? Will it want to be countermajoritarian? What would it mean to be countermajoritarian? What is the relationship of the Court to other political actors? Are the assumptions of normative theory consistent with our understandings of how politics works and how political power is accumulated and exercised?

(9) Constructing Judicial Review—Landes-Posner helped put the question of how independent judiciaries are created and sustained on the agenda for empirical social science. Placing the problem of judicial independence within a larger framework of interest group efforts to "buy" legislation, Landes-Posner suggested that private actors-and through them legislators-might value independent judges who could help provide some assurance of temporal stability for legislative bargains (which in turn made those bargains-legislation-more valuable). There are a number of puzzles about the Landes-Posner model (why, for example, would judges be interested in enforcing past legislative bargains, and why would current legislators want them to do so?), but it emphasized that a political explanation was needed for an independent judiciary and suggested that such an explanation might be found in the varying incentives and times horizons of courts, legislators and private actors. Subsequent models have tended to emphasize either internal or external factors supporting judicial independence. Internal models focus on the incentives of elite political actors that lead them to desire an independent judiciary (the Landes-Posner model is an example). External models focus on external constraints on political actors that prevent them from subverting an independent judiciary (*e.g.*, mass public opinion that supports the judiciary). Do political models of judicial independence capture what we mean by "judicial independence"? What do we mean by "judicial independence"? How do we observe it? Are internal and external models incompatible? What do judges do these models?

(10) Entrenchment and Judicialization—Judicial review may be understood as a mechanism by which powerful political actors entrench their interests against future displacement. The Constitution itself may be understood as an entrenchment device, identifying certain commitments as particularly important and handicapping future political actors who may want to violate those commitments. The entrenchment logic may help explain both the political supports for judicial review and the substantive content of the constitutional decisions that courts render. How does Court fit within the political system? How does it advance, resist or complicate the goals of the dominant political coalition? What makes a commitment stick? Under what conditions are efforts at entrenchment successful? Does this approach make judicial review more or less normatively attractive? We might distinguish between two somewhat separate dynamics-the entrenchment of currently preferred policy against easy displacement by future political actors, and the judicialization of political disputes by shifting issues from the legislative and electoral arena into the judicial arena for resolution.

(11) Dialogues and Constraints—Rather than a bolt from the blue, the exercise of judicial review and constitutional interpretation by the courts might be understood as part of a process that includes other actors and institutions. The Court has an ongoing relationship with the other branches of government, and it may be in dialogue with them in both a strategic sense and a deliberative sense. How does the Court and Congress relate to one another? The Court and the executive branch? What is the Court's role in the constitutional dialogue? What are the limits of judicial action? What are the spurs to judicial action? What responses to judicial decisions are available to elected officials? Are judicial and non-judicial actors speaking the same language? What is the value of judicial review to political actors? How is constitutional law shaped by its historic and political context? Can a strategic Court be consistent with our normative theories of judicial review and constitutionalism? Can a strategic Court be justified? Should the Court take into account strategic considerations in deciding constitutional cases?

(12) Litigation and Impact—Prior to the twentieth century, the Supreme Court's appellate jurisdiction was mandatory. The Court had to hear any case meeting certain criteria. In the twentieth century, the Court has been given discretionary jurisdiction, leaving it up to the justices to decide which cases to accept for decision. In either case, the justices only have control over the case for a short time. The Court cannot determine what cases are brought to it, and they must ultimately rely on others to implement their decisions. Although normative theories of judicial review often portray the Court as a lone and omnipotent crusader, the justices actually operate within their own extended institutional environment. How does this context affect judicial power? How might it affect? How the power of judicial review is exercised? Does the litigation environment affect our view of judicial independence? Does the litigation context matter to judicial decision-making? Does it affect outcomes? How should it be integrated into theories of judicial policy-making, such as the attitudinal model? How powerful is the Court? What can it accomplish? How should this context be integrated into our normative theories of judicial review? Should the Court worry about the impact of its rulings? What might the regime development perspective say about Rosenberg's analysis of desegregation?

Judicial Activism

'Judicial activism' means different things to different people. It seems that a 'multidimensional' approach, like the one I have tried to adopt throughout the paper, can represent the most effective attempt to conceptualize the related discussion, or at least to provide a taxonomy of the critical perceptions on judicial decision-making. The result is a brief journey through some well-recognised problems of constitutional theory, highlighting the latent and often intractable tensions inherent in them.

A pragmatic discussion in this perspective starts acknowledging the function of judicial interpretation as often creative, sometimes even unavoidably creative. Firstly, it is necessary to identify the spaces, the 'dimensions', in which such a role is placed; and then, as already pointed out, the inquiry must turn to the *degree* of creativity, and to the question of the *mode*, the *limits*, and the level of *acceptability* of law-making through the courts. The first stage is therefore heuristic, while the second is clearly empirical and casuistic.

Often, however, leading constitutional theories add to their reflections a clear normative option on the work of courts, and this obviously orientates any subsequent investigation. As I tried to explain, what is interesting in institutional analysis, and in Komesar's works in particular, is the focus on second-best enquiries about institutional performance and systemic effects, rather than about first-best principles. 'Judicial activism' is about tensions between decision-making bodies, each with its own characteristics and neither of which is working in an institutional vacuum. If it is true that, after the definition of a heuristic framework, "*the case for constitutional judicial review varies from one setting to another*", understanding "*what factors determine or should determine this variation*" is more related to a kind of "*not indifferent*" but "*agnostic*" position, than to a constitutional scholarship which is "*strong on positions and weak on analysis*".

The phrase 'judicial activism' carries more than one connotation. The common law tradition conceives of courtroom litigation as an adversarial process where the onus is on the pleaders to shape the overall course of the proceedings through their submissions. In this conception, the role of the judge is cast in a passive mould and the objective is to dispassionately evaluate the arguments made by both sides.

However, the actual experience of a courtroom clearly bears witness to the tendency on part of some judges to pose incisive questions before the practitioners. This may have the consequence of proceedings being judicially-directed to a certain degree. While this literal understanding of activism from the bench may have its supporters as well as detractors, the focus of my talk will be on another understanding of 'judicial activism'. In the Indian context, there has been a raging debate on the proper scope and limits of the judicial role—especially of that played by the higher judiciary which consists of the Supreme Court of India at the Centre and the High Courts in the various States that form the Union of India. The terms of that debate have been broadly framed with respect to the considerations of ensuring an effective 'separation of powers' between the executive, legislature and the judiciary as well as concerns about the efficacy and legitimacy of judicial interventions in the long-run. In the course of this talk, I will attempt to present some background information as well as the main themes of these debates.

The place of 'judicial review'—In post-independence India Article 13(2), the inclusion of explicit provisions for 'judicial review' were necessary in order to give effect to the individual and group rights guaranteed in the text of the Constitution. Dr. B.R. Ambedkar, who chaired the drafting committee of our Constituent Assembly, had described the provision related to the same as the 'heart of the Constitution'. Article 13(2) of the Constitution of India prescribes that the Union or the States shall not make any law that takes away or abridges any of the fundamental rights, and any law made in contravention of the aforementioned mandate shall, to the extent of the contravention, be void.

While judicial review over administrative action has evolved on the lines of common law doctrines such as 'proportionality', 'legitimate expectation', 'reasonableness' and principles of natural justice, the Supreme Court of India and the various High Courts were given the power to rule on the constitutionality of legislative as well as administrative actions. In most cases, the power of judicial review is exercised to protect and enforce the fundamental rights guaranteed in Part III of the Constitution. The higher courts are also approached to rule on questions of legislative competence, mostly in the context of Centre-State relations since Article 246 of the Constitution read with the 7th schedule contemplated a clear demarcation as well as a zone of intersection between the law-making powers of the Union Parliament and the various State Legislatures.

Hence the scope of judicial review before Indian courts has evolved in three dimensions—firstly, to ensure fairness in administrative action, secondly to protect the constitutionally guaranteed fundamental rights of citizens and thirdly to rule on questions of legislative competence between the centre and the states. The power of the Supreme Court of India to enforce these fundamental rights is derived from Article 32 of the Constitution. It gives citizens the right to directly approach the Supreme Court for seeking remedies against the violation of these fundamental rights.

The entitlement to constitutional remedies is itself a fundamental right and can be enforced in the form of writs evolved in common law—such as *habeas corpus* (to direct the release of a person detained unlawfully), *mandamus* (to direct a public authority to do its duty), *quo warranto* (to direct a person to vacate an office assumed wrongfully), prohibition (to prohibit a lower court from proceeding on a case) and *certiorari* (power of the higher court to remove a proceeding from a lower court and bring it before itself). Besides the Supreme Court, the High Courts located in the various States are also designated as constitutional courts and Article 226 permits citizens to file similar writs before the High Courts.

PIL—A product of judicial activism

With the advent of Public Interest Litigation (PIL) in recent decades, Article 32 has been creatively interpreted to shape innovative remedies such as a '*continuing mandamus*' for ensuring that executive agencies comply with judicial directions. In this category of litigation, judges have also imported private law remedies such as 'injunctions' and 'stay orders' into what are essentially public law-related matters. Successful challenges against statutory provisions result in reliefs such as the striking down of statues or even reading down of statues, the latter implying that courts reject a particular approach to the interpretation of a statutory provision rather than rejecting the provision in its entirety.

Beginning with the first few instances in the late-1970s, the category of Public Interest Litigation (PIL) has come to be associated with its own 'people-friendly' procedures. The foremost change came in the form of the dilution of the requirement of 'locus standi' for initiating proceedings. Since the intent was to improve access to justice for those who were otherwise too poor to move the courts or were unaware of their legal entitlements, the Court allowed actions to be brought on their behalf by social activists and lawyers. In numerous instances, the Court took *suo moto cognizances* of matters involving the abuse of prisoners, bonded labourers and inmates of mental institutions, through letters addressed to sitting judges. This practice of initiating proceedings on the basis of letters has now been streamlined and has come to be described as 'epistolary jurisdiction'. In Public Interest Litigation (PIL), the nature of proceedings itself does not exactly fit into the accepted common-law framework of adversarial litigation. The courtroom dynamics are substantially different from ordinary civil or criminal appeals. While an adversarial environment may prevent in cases where actions are brought to highlight administrative apathy or the government's condonation of abusive practices, in most public interest-related litigation, the judges take on a far more active role in the literal sense as well by posing questions to the parties as well as exploring solutions.

Considering the objections to the doctrine of 'judicial review' in many jurisdictions—questions have been asked about the proper understanding of 'judicial review' as well as its expansion. There are two principled objections offered against the very idea of 'judicial review' in a democratic order. The first idea is that the judiciary being an unelected body is not accountable to the people through any institutional mechanism. In most countries judges are appointed through methods involving selection or nomination, in which ordinary citizens do not have a say. It is argued that allowing the judiciary to rule on the validity of the enactments passed by a popularly elected legislature amounts to a violation of the idea of 'separation of powers'. Skepticism is also voiced against judges using their personal discretion to grant remedies in areas in which, they have no expertise. This critique locates the role of the judiciary as purely one of resolving disputes between parties and deferring to the prescriptions of the elected legislature while doing so. In the Common Law realm, this critique is based on the age-old notions of 'parliamentary sovereignty', with respect to the inherent value of a written constitution that also incorporates 'judicial review'. It would be appropriate to refer to an observation made by Justice Aharon Barak : "To maintain real democracy and to ensure a delicate balance between its elements a formal constitution is preferable. To operate effectively, a constitution "should enjoy normative supremacy, should not be as easily amendable as a normal statute and should give judges the power to review the constitutionality of legislation. Without a formal constitution, there is no legal limitation on legislative supremacy, and the supremacy of human rights can exist on the grace of the majority's self-restraint. A constitution, however, imposes legal limitations on the legislature and guarantees that human rights are protected not only by the self-restraint of the majority, but also by constitutional control over the majority. Hence, the need for a formal constitution."

Milestones of Public Interest Litigation in India

One of the earliest cases of public interest litigation was reported as *Hussainara Khatoon (I)* v. *State of Bihar.*[1] This case was concerned with a series of articles published in a prominent newspaper—the Indian Express which exposed the plight of undertrial prisoners in the state of Bihar. A writ petition was filed by an advocate drawing the Court's attention to the deplorable plight of these prisoners. Many of them had been in jail for longer periods than the maximum permissible sentences for the offences they had been charged with. The Supreme Court accepted the locus standi of the advocate to maintain the writ petition. Thereafter, a series of cases followed in which the Court gave directions through which the 'right to speedy trial' was deemed to be an integral and an essential part of the protection of life and personal liberty.

Soon thereafter, two noted professors of law filed writ petitions in the Supreme Court highlighting various abuses of the law, which, they asserted, were a violation of Article 21 of the Constitution. These included inhuman conditions prevailing in protective homes, long pendency of trials in court, trafficking of women, importation of children for homosexual purposes, and the non-payment of wages to bonded labourers among others. The Supreme Court accepted their locus standi to represent the suffering masses and passed guidelines and orders that greatly ameliorated the conditions of these people.

In another matter, a journalist, Ms. Sheela Barse, took up the plight of women prisoners who were confined in the police jails in the city of Bombay. She asserted that they were victims of custodial violence. The Court took cognizance of the matter and directions were issued to the Director of College of Social Work, Bombay. He was ordered to visit the Bombay Central Jail and conduct interviews of various women prisoners in order to ascertain whether they had been subjected to torture or ill-treatment. He was asked to submit a report to the Court in this regard. Based on his findings, the Court issued directions such as the detention of female prisoners only in designated female lock-ups guarded by female constables and that accused females could be interrogated only in the presence of a female police official.

Public interest litigation acquired a new dimension—namely that of 'epistolary jurisdiction' with the decision in the case of *Sunil Batra* v. *Delhi Administration.*[2] It was initiated by a letter that was written by a prisoner lodged in jail to a Judge of the Supreme Court. The prisoner complained of a brutal assault committed by a Head Warder on another prisoner. The

1. AIR 1979 SC 1975.
2. AIR 1978 SC 1975.

Court treated that letter as a writ petition, and, while issuing various directions, opined that :

> "...technicalities and legal niceties are no impediment to the court entertaining even an informal communication as a proceeding for habeas corpus if the basic facts are found".

In *Municipal Council, Ratlam* v. *Vardichand*,[1] the Court recognized the locus standi of a group of citizens who sought directions against the local Municipal Council for removal of open drains that caused stench as well as diseases. The Court, recognizing the right of the group of citizens, asserted that if the :

> "...centre of gravity of justice is to shift as indeed the Preamble to the Constitution mandates, from the traditional individualism of locus standi to the community orientation of public interest litigation, the court must consider the issues as there is need to focus on the ordinary men."

In *Parmanand Katara* v. *Union of India*,[2] the Supreme Court accepted an application by an advocate that highlighted a news item titled "Law Helps the Injured to Die" published in a national daily, The Hindustan Times. The petitioner brought to light the difficulties faced by persons injured in road and other accidents in availing urgent and life-saving medical treatment, since many hospitals and doctors refused to treat them unless certain procedural formalities were completed in these medico-legal cases. The Supreme Court directed medical establishments to provide instant medical aid to such injured people, notwithstanding the formalities to be followed under the procedural criminal law.

In many other instances, the Supreme Court has risen to the changing needs of society and taken proactive steps to address these needs. It was therefore the extensive liberalization of the rule of locus standi which gave birth to a flexible public interest litigation system. A powerful thrust to public interest litigation was given by a 7-judge bench in the case of *S.P. Gupta* v. *Union of India*.[3] The judgment recognized the locus standi of bar associations to file writs by way of public interest litigation. In this particular case, it was accepted that they had a legitimate interest in questioning the executive's policy of arbitrarily transferring High Court judges, which threatened the independence of the judiciary. Explaining the liberalization of the concept of locus standi, the court opined :

> "It must now be regarded as well-settled law where a person who has suffered a legal wrong or a legal injury or whose legal right or legally protected interest is violated, is unable to approach the court on account of some disability or it is not practicable for him to move the court for some other sufficient reasons, such as his socially or economically disadvantaged position, some other person can invoke the

---

1. AIR 1980 SC 1622.

2. AIR 1989 SC 2039.

3. AIR 1982 SC 149.

assistance of the court for the purpose of providing judicial redress to the person wronged or injured, so that the legal wrong or injury caused to such person does not go unredressed and justice is done to him."

The unique model of public interest litigation that has evolved in India not only looks at issues like consumer protection, gender justice, prevention of environmental pollution and ecological destruction, it is also directed towards finding social and political space for the disadvantaged and other vulnerable groups in society. The Courts have given decisions in cases pertaining to different kinds of entitlements and protections such as the availability of food, access to clean air, safe working conditions, political representation, affirmative action, anti-discrimination measures and the regulation of prison conditions among others. For instance, in *People's Union for Democratic Rights* v. *Union of India*,[1] a petition was brought against governmental agencies which questioned the employment of underage labourers and the payment of wages below the prescribed statutory minimum wage-levels to those involved in the construction of facilities for the then upcoming Asian Games in New Delhi. The Court took serious exception to these practices and ruled that they violated constitutional guarantees. The employment of children in construction-related jobs clearly fell foul of the constitutional prohibition on child labour and the non-payment of minimum wages was equated with the extraction of forced labour. Similarly, in *Bandhua Mukti Morcha* v. *Union of India*,[2] the Supreme Court's attention was drawn to the widespread incidence of the age-old practice of bonded labour which persists despite the constitutional prohibition. Among other interventions, one can refer to the *Shriram Food & Fertilizer case*,[3] where the Court issued directions to employers to check the production of hazardous chemicals and gases that endangered the life and health of workmen. It is also through the vehicle of PIL, that the Indian Courts have come to adopt the strategy of awarding monetary compensation for constitutional wrongs such as unlawful detention, custodial torture and extra-judicial killings by state agencies.

In the realm of environmental protection, many of the leading decisions have been given in actions brought by renowned environmentalist M.C. Mehta. He has been a tireless campaigner in this area and his petitions have resulted in orders placing strict liability for the leak of Oleum gas from a factory in New Delhi, directions to check pollution in and around the Ganges river,the relocation of hazardous industries from the municipal limits of Delhi, directions to state agencies to check pollution in the vicinity of the Taj Mahal and several afforestation measures. A prominent decision was made in a petition that raised the problem of extensive vehicular air pollution in Delhi. The Court was faced with considerable statistical evidence of increasing levels of hazardous emissions on account of the use of diesel as a fuel by commercial vehicles. The Supreme Court decided to make a decisive intervention in this matter and ordered government-run buses to

1. AIR 1982 SC 1473.
2. AIR 1984 SC 802.
3. AIR 1987 SC 1086.

shift to the use of Compressed Natural Gas (CNG), an environment-friendly fuel. This was followed some time later by another order that required privately-run 'autorickshaws' (three-wheeler vehicles which meet local transportational needs) to shift to the use of CNG.

At the time, this decision was criticized as an unwarranted intrusion into the functions of the pollution control authorities, but it has now come to be widely acknowledged that it is only because of this judicial intervention that air pollution in Delhi has been checked to a substantial extent. Another crucial intervention was made in *Council for Environment Legal Action* v. *Union of India*,[1] wherein a registered NGO had sought directions from the Supreme Court in order to tackle ecological degradation in coastal areas. In recent years, the Supreme Court has taken on the mantle of monitoring forest conservation measures all over India, and a special 'Green bench' has been constituted to give directions to the concerned governmental agencies. At present, I am part of this Green bench and can vouch for the need to maintain judicial supervision in order to protect our ecological resources from rampant encroachments and administrative apathy.

An important step in the area of gender justice was the decision in *Vishaka* v. *State of Rajasthan.*[2] The petition in that case originated from the gang-rape of a grassroots social worker. In that opinion, the Court invoked the text of the Convention for the Elimination of all forms of Discrimination Against Women (CEDAW) and framed guidelines for establishing redressal mechanisms to tackle sexual harassment of women at workplaces. Though the decision has come under considerable criticism for encroaching into the domain of the legislature, the fact remains that till date the legislature has not enacted any law on the point. It must be remembered that meaningful social change, like any sustained transformation, demands a long-term engagement. Even though a particular petition may fail to secure relief in a wholesome manner or be slow in its implementation, litigation is nevertheless an important step towards systemic reforms. A recent example of this approach was the decision in *People's Union for Civil Liberties* v. *Union of India*, where the Court sought to ensure compliance with the policy of supplying mid-day meals in government-run primary schools. The mid-day meal scheme had been launched with much fanfare a few years ago with the multiple objectives of encouraging the enrolment of children from low-income backgrounds in schools and also ensuring that they received adequate nutrition. However, there had been widespread reports of problems in the implementation of this scheme such as the pilferage of foodgrains. As a response to the same, the Supreme Court issued orders to the concerned governmental authorities in all States and Union Territories, while giving elaborate directions about the proper publicity and implementation of the said scheme.

In defence of 'judicial activism'

The expansion of 'judicial review' (which is often described as 'judicial

1. AIR 1996 SC 1446.
2. AIR 1997 SC 3011.

activism') has of course raised the popular profile of the higher judiciary in India. However, arguments are routinely made against the accommodation of 'aspirational' directive principles within the ambit of judicial enforcement. There are two conceptual objections against the justiciability to these positive obligations.

The first is that if judges devise strategies to enforce the directive principles, it amounts to an intrusion into the legislative and executive domain. It is reasoned that the articulation of newer fundamental rights is the legislature's task and that the judiciary should refrain from the same.

Furthermore, it is posed that executive agencies are unfairly burdened by the costs associated with these positive obligations, especially keeping in mind that these obligations were enumerated as directive principles by the framers on account of practical considerations. This criticism mirrors the familiar philosophy of 'judicial restraint' when it comes to constitutional adjudication. However, the second objection to the reading in positive obligations raises some scope for introspection amongst judges. It can be argued that the expansion of justiciability to include rights that are difficult to enforce takes away from the credibility of the judiciary in the long-run. The judicial inclusion of socio-economic objectives as fundamental rights can be criticised as an unviable textual exercise, which may have no bearing on ground-level conditions. In turn the unenforceability and inability of state agencies to protect such aspirational rights could have an adverse effect on public perceptions about the efficacy and legitimacy of the judiciary. The prescription of normative rights always carries the risk of poor enforcement. However, the question we must ask ourselves is whether poor enforcement is a sufficient reason to abandon the pursuit of rights whose fulfillment enhances social and economic welfare. At this point, one can recount Roscoe Pound's thesis on law as an agent of social change. The express inclusion of legal rights is an effective strategy to counter-act social problems in the long-run. At the level of constitutional protection, such rights have an inherent symbolic value which goes beyond empirical considerations about their actual enforcement. The colonial regime in the Indian subcontinent periodically made legislative interventions to discourage retrograde and exploitative social practices such as Sati (immolation of widows), prohibition of widow-remarriage and child marriage. Even though there have been persistent problems in the enforcement of these legislations, in the long run they have played an important part in reducing the incidence of these unjust customs. It is evident that in the short run even the coercive authority of law may not be enough of a deterrent, but in the long run the very fact of the continued existence of such authority helps in creating public opinion against the same practices. In the same way the framers of our Constitution sought to depart from the inequities of the past by enumerating a whole spectrum of rights and entitlements. While the understanding of ideas such as 'social equality' and 'religious freedom' is keenly contested in the legislative as well as judicial domains, there is no doubt that constitutional rights have been an important tool of social transformation in India. The enumeration of the various civil liberties and protections against arbitrary actions by the state are now identified as core elements of citizenship and violations provoke a high standard of scrutiny both by the judiciary as well as civil society groups. The inclusion of entitlements such as universal adult franchise have greatly reduced the coercive power of casteist and feudal social structures and empowered political parties that represent historically disadvantaged sections such as the Scheduled Castes (SC) and Scheduled Tribes (ST). Even though practices such as untouchability, forced labour and child labour have not been totally eradicated, our constitutional provisions prohibiting the same are the bedrock behind legal as well as socio-political strategies to curb the same. The Supreme Court of India has further internalized the importance of laying down clear normative standards which drive social transformation. Its interventions through strategies such as the expansion of Article 21 and the use of innovative remedies in Public Interest Litigation (PIL) cases has actually expanded the scope and efficacy of constitutional rights by applying them in previously unenumerated settings.

Furthermore, the Courts allow groups and interests with unequal bargaining power in the political sphere to present their case in an environment of due deliberation. The dilution of the rules of standing among other features has allowed the Courts to recognize and enforce rights for the most disadvantaged sections in society through an expanded notion of 'judicial review'. Even though the framers of our Constitution may not have thought of these innovations on the floor of the constituent assembly, most of them would have certainly agreed with the spirit of these judicial interventions.

Majoritarianism

Majoritarianism is probably the most frequent and, so to speak, automatic criterion used in assessing courts' activism, a kind of 'conditioned reflex' in the criticism of judicial behaviour.

The classic argument so basic as elementary suggests that when a constitutional court exercises judicial review, it substitutes another public policy for that enacted by elected representatives in legislative bodies. It is assumed that, in so doing, judges are contravening the will of the political branches and, by extension, the will of the majority itself. Such an action is often criticised from the perspective of democratic theory, wielding the sword of an alleged intrinsic 'illegitimacy' of the practice. What kind (and degree) of 'illegitimacy' are we talking about? What kind of institutional balance is shaped by the position of a hierarchically superior constitution to be enforced even against the will of the contingent majority? These questions can perhaps receive reassuring answers nowadays, at least in politically homogeneous legal orders where there are no crucial structural divergences between judicial bodies and legislatures, and when the actions of the courts do not take up any clear contrasting positions against the active politics of the moment. However, in most cases, in circumstances where tension between political actors arises, an unwelcome judgment inevitably provokes complaints of an 'invasion of the field' and accusations of misuse of a political role which is considered to be inconsistent with the constitutional jurisdiction.

This difficult, yet not precarious, balance is probably the best updated and pondered explanation of Bickel's famous and profoundly influential *counter-majoritarian difficulty.* His landmark description of the "*countermajoritarian*" and "*deviant*" role of judicial review was, in fact, the unveiling of an intrinsic *difficulty* which needs to be understood, approached and minimized, and not the denunciation of a plain inconsistency, of something presumptively at odds with democracy. Although often misconceived or taken out of context, his reflections represented the clear statement of the ontological premises of a fair analysis, and part of a preponderant *pars construens*, suggesting several interpretative paradigms and trying to balance framers' will and social change, case by case approach and principles, ultimately judicial review and democracy. The answer to the basic question of whether or not judicial review could nonetheless be democratically legitimate, at least if practised or constituted in a particular way, has seemed and seems already to be defined: being aware of this intrinsic difficulty and its consequences, judicial insulation from the *popular will* (elections) allows the judiciary to be faithful to the sovereign will (the constitution), and it is therefore an asset to be defended.

Furthermore, it is highlighted that all liberal democratic systems have other significant 'countermajoritarian' elements than courts, including bodies within the political branches themselves : "*judicial review is only one of many 'undemocratic' institutional choices*" in modern constitutional orders. This is indeed a clearly growing phenomenon, generally typical of those same 'welfare systems' described by Cappelletti and mentioned previously. In our ever increasingly complex legal orders, the structure of delegations is becoming broader, and is not limited to the judicial bodies. Few would argue that all these mechanisms are necessarily 'deviant', and such an answer seems to work well and to become typical, turning the alleged vice into a virtue: the insulated, countermajoritarian nature of institutions (including courts) can be a positive feature, because it can be a solution for them to better—and independently—perform their duties. Courts are uniquely well situated to protect the rights of individuals or disadvantaged groups against an excessively powerful majority, as well as to resolve federal disputes or inter-branch conflicts.

According to this more positive account, judicial review is clearly not a 'deviant' institution but one that upholds fundamental democratic values: not notwithstanding, but precisely because of its deviant potential. As already mentioned, not only has Bickel himself concluded that judicial review could be legitimated because the courts could serve as *'fora of principle'* and reason, which would inject higher constitutional values into the interest aggregation and bargaining process of legislative politics. But, following this line of justification, we also arrive at the most recent American debate on the *'policentric'*, and not *'juricentric'*, approach to the legitimacy of the courts, updating the debate in the light of the crisis of political representation and the transformations of democracy, and leading to a recent redefinition of the role and the "*value of judicial review in the modern era as a catalyst to debate as a polity some of the most difficult and fundamental issues" that confronts the polity as a whole, forcing it "to work to reach answers to these questions, to find solutions, often compromises, which can find broad and lasting support"*. A countermajoritarian court can make it possible for a democracy to become more deliberative, especially in light of a supposed lack of representativeness and democratic deficits, by engaging in dialogue and 'institutional comity'. *"The countermajoritarian nature of judicial review is not a 'difficulty' but an 'opportunity'"* : almost every contemporary theoretical or empirical assessment of judicial review (whether framed in positive or negative terms) seems to have moved away from the premise of treating institutions as engaged in zero-sum struggles for power.

It seems clear today that the radical underlying assumption of the 'countermajoritarian difficulty' as the only way of conceptualizing the legitimacy of judicial power distorts many aspects of the practice of judicial review, oversimplifies the relational models of inter-branch dynamics of every real legal order, and is not consistent with the original ideas that gave rise to the debate. This is not to say, again, that judicial review and other forms of judicial policymaking are normatively unproblematic. But a *difficulty* is something intrinsic and axiomatic, not to be solved once and for all: the tensions between majoritarianism and other democratic values are endemic to democratic-pluralistic constitutionalism, and the counter-majoritarian role of the courts pertains more to their constitutional *'position'* than to their action. A constitutional framework which provides for a central role of the courts is typical nowadays, in spite of the well-known continental differences. However, it is not necessitated : it is a choice, and not the only possible structural choice, as noted by strong, radical critics of judicial review. As a choice, it obviously brings with it a number of benefits, as well as a number of problems.

One has to be aware of the inherent 'countermajoritarian difficulty' in order to pursue any kind of sophisticated analysis in the field. 'Countermajoriarianism' can be understood as a heuristic, posing a stylized question—exceptional though it might be—and provoking a general inquiry into the appropriate sources of authority for judicial decision-making. However, it seems there can be no 'activism' just because of a theoretical role, of an assigned position. It would seem that if we want to try to define 'judicial activism', we must turn our attention to the other dimensions of the activity of the courts and to other dimensions of their inter-branch relations.

Substance/democratic process distinction

Another traditional line of criticism rests on considerations that seem to assess, again, more the position than the effective action of the courts, or at least both dimensions. It is often argued, with different arguments from country to country and in the wake of a historic American debate, that there is greater justification for court policymaking in some areas than in others : and that the only concrete boundary that can be traced in this regard is between judicial interventions in substantive policy areas and judicial interventions ensuring minimal "*representation reinforcement*" requirements. In this light, an activist court would be the one that directly affects substantive policies, such as those "*which make economic policy, regulate the non-political-process activities of institutions or groups, or impinge people's careers, lifestyles, morals, or religious values*".

As well as the whole debate on activism and the 'countermajoritarian' analysis, this is another lesson on the relationship between courts and political institutions that comes from the United States. In the historical *footnote four* of the *Carolene Products* case, Justice Stone offered a classic identification of those preferred areas : "*legislation which restricts those political processes which can ordinarily be expected to bring about repeal of undesirable legislation" and "(legislation) which tends seriously to curtail the operation of those political processes ordinarily to be relied upon to protect (discrete and insular minorities)*". It is notorious that, bearing in mind these suggestions, the US Supreme Court has followed an expressed "preferred position" doctrine for about a decade, subjecting laws impinging on the political process to greater judicial scrutiny. Further, it has built its complex and plural reasoning of the following years on a rhetoric reminiscent of it.

The academic debate has proposed some persuasive solutions to the countermajoritarian difficulty in light of the facilitation of the representation of minorities, of "clearing the channels of political change" and democratic participation in general. Elegant 'process-related reasons' such as that proposed by John Hart Ely, defending constitutional judicial review in its ability to open or keep open the participation processes compressed or blocked in the political sphere, are still common ground for many of the prominent contemporary theories. It would be both a countermajoritarian/competing interest and a fundamental tenet of contemporary constitutional systems that political minorities have the basic right not to suffer undue pressures in their own spheres of core freedom, and that they have an opportunity through open communication and the democratic political process to eventually become a majority. Judicial intervention protecting or enhancing these tenets, developing or even altering policies that affect the political processes, upholding, widening and equalizing basic opportunities, can be accounted as more justified than other decisions affecting other types of public policy.

Participation centred approach

Komesar's 'participation-centered approach' also rejects the underlying simplistic allocation of societal issues—"*render unto the political process that which is the political process' (substance) and render unto the courts that which is the courts' (process)*". Comparative institutional analysis teaches us here that this neat split of issues, along with the underlying idea that judicial review can take place without any judicial value judgments being made, "*is based on a basic misconception*". Courts and political branches are alternative societal decisionmakers, with different institutional features, deciding matters differently. But this does not mean, as the 'substance/ democratic process distinction' suggests, that they operate on different issues. "*Judicial review is judicial reconsideration of an issue already decided by another societal decisionmaker. When that reconsideration leads to invalidation of the governmental action, the courts are remaking societal policy*", the same societal policy already assessed by the competing institution. Ely's belief that reaction to the (various) forms of political malfunctions should be important in defining the judicial role is the first element in an analysis of the allocation of decisionmaking powers. However an appropriate analysis also requires consideration of the ability of the judiciary to make, or remake, societal decisions : and such questions of relative institutional ability cannot be hidden behind oversimplistic and falsely reassuring dichotomies. The essence of Ely's theory is therefore 'singleinstitutional': "*each institution is disqualified from a realm of activity by its imperfections without regard to the limitations of the other institution in the same realm*". Such a schematic assessment of the variety of political malfunctions and of the ability to address them cannot be an adequate substitute for institutional comparison; nor can it be a mask behind which to hide substantive judicial decisions.

Specificity of policy

According to a traditional reading, consistent with a certain formal vision of their constitutional mandate, courts step into public policy only to nullify laws, in their capacity as "*negative legislators*". Such intervention is constitutionally pre-ordained to leave legislators or administrators, as positive actors, free to pursue different approaches to a given problem, with the awareness and in light of the judicial choice. This view is the closest to the static design of a trias politica, and is coherent with Kelsen's traditional architecture. From a functional viewpoint, the division of powers seems relatively clear, calling the judiciary to a kind of *actio finium regundorum* of the discretion of the political powers. Thus, the space that is left open by the constitution for political decisions, within its framework of superior 'rules of the game', may not be filled by courts, and these are not called upon to anticipate or design any legislative measures but to review them after having been taken. A clear departure from these minimal functional rules would constitute evidence of an activist approach by the courts.

An expanded conception of judicial role was already criticized by continental scholars like Edouard Lambert in the early 1920's, studying the weight of the jurisprudential formant in the US legal order, and coining the successful, rhetorical phrase "*gouvernement des juges*". However, the original Kelsenian constitutional project, despite being the basis for a structural division of tasks and for many modern experiences of constitutional justice, is also not perfectly comparable with the becoming of contemporary 'welfare systems', from the second half of the century onwards. The change is clear in this case. As it has been noted, the classic distinction between positive and negative roles relied almost entirely on the absence, within the structural sphere of constitutional law, of enforceable human rights. Moreover, Kelsen himself explicitly warned of the 'dangers' of bestowing constitutional status on human rights, which he equated with natural law, because a rights jurisprudence would inevitably lead to the obliteration of the distinction between the negative legislator and the positive legislator. "*If in the past fundamental rights were valid only within the law, today the laws are valid only within the context of fundamental rights*"; and, in Kelsenian terms, "*Through their quest to discover the content and scope of the natural law, constitutional judges would, in effect, become super-legislators*", shattering traditional separation of powers dogmas.

Facing these historical conceptualizations and trying to update them in line with the new structural features of the debate, we inevitably blur the boundaries between *interpretation* and *creation*, as Cappelletti masterfully highlighted. Nowadays, a common perception between several scholars is that in recent years, in a wide range of legal systems (even profoundly different one from the other), courts have also increasingly played the role of positive policymakers, wielding precisely the sword of human rights. Interventions to plainly nullify unconstitutional policies still seem to be the current rule, but they are coupled with a series of more complex interventions commanding 'positive government agencies' to undertake certain policies, sometimes with attention to minute details, or specifying particular behaviours that the government agencies need to follow in pursuit of an existing policy. As Canon put it, "*(i)n some celebrated cases, courts have virtually taken over the management of school systems, prisons, and hospitals*" : an emphatic sentence that clearly refers to numerous well-known US Supreme Court's judgments on abortion, police interrogations, obscenity, which did not simply strike down laws but rewrote them "*in chapter and verse*".

"*Positive policymaking by the judiciary could be the wave of the future, but it will not arrive without considerable criticism*" : the key to activism, in this emerging facet of the debate, seems to be just that 'specificity of policy' criterion, understood as precisely the ultroneous and discretionary dimension of the judicial decision.

To what extent is this phenomenon ascribable purely to the activity (or the activism) of courts? Proponents of positive policymaking reply that constitutions contain commands as well as prohibitions and that courts are obliged to enforce the former when other agencies cannot or will not. A growing number of scholars has emphasized that the presence of elastic, open-ended clauses (which fall under the suggestive definitions of '*unbestimmte Rechtsbegriffe*' or '*incompletely theorized agreements*') is a familiar phenomenon with constitutional provisions and regulatory standards in administrative law, and is increasingly bound to lead (in the form of an excessive deontic content and 'intentional indefiniteness') to a delegation to courts of the final decisions on such issues.

In terms of the modalities of judicial intervention, a proper institutional analysis cannot be undertaken whilst ignoring that "*each claim of constitutional invalidity presents a different set of demands on the resources of the judiciary*". Through an analysis of some historical US Supreme Court's decisions, Komesar explains how cases vary in number and complexity of judicial determinations needed for their complete resolution. When a court 'declares a right', it must face "*the task of defining that right and the associated remedy*". "*In some instances, it can define the right in clear terms and offer a remedy that involves little continuing judicial action. Other instances require the court to define a right in general terms, and either clarify it gradually in future litigation or provide a remedy that involves continuing judicial supervision—even continuing appellate supervision*". This often means that less required future judicial activity can mean more judicial activism.

The transformation of our legal orders and of the modalities of public intervention has sometimes been intentional and preordained and sometimes not, but it clearly leads to an increasing shift of positive policymaking power to insulated institutions. It seems clear, from a critical perspective, that the opening of such spaces can be an opportunity to pursue intrusive, active, teleologically-oriented policies. It remains to be determined—and this is not simple—whether or not a composite body like a tribunal can have its own global policies pursued and, therefore, its ability to coherently pursue them, in the form of 'many-mind arguments'. Certainly some historical experiences have given rise to suspicion and persuasive reconstructions. On other occasions, scholars may have abused similar arguments, tracing complex dynamics back to a single fictitious rationality.

As far as the concrete case study is concerned, similar questions can only receive specific, empirical answers. This is sometimes the source of accurate casuistic, historical, behavioural analyses, while for some others it is the realm of a certain various 'courts and politics' literature which can be particularly effective in some cases, and simply seem naive in others.

Nevertheless, regardless for now of the possible responses and modalities of an empirical study, the expansion of discretionary spaces available to courts has re-ignited the theoretical debate. The popular new trends of 'judicial minimalism' are some of the last meaningful examples of this awareness, preaching a measured institutional approach by judicial bodies that minimize their own imprint on the law by meticulously assessing "*one case at a time*", ruling on narrow and shallow grounds, eschewing broader theories, and altering entrenched legal practices only incrementally.

Interpretative fidelity

Despite having started from macro-assessments of the 'judicial activism' debate, after a complex and structural analysis one arrives at a point at which an evaluation of the more internal dimensions of judicial activity is necessary. Even an inquiry on apparently remote matters such as that carried out so far, including an assessment of technical and political expertise of courts, will lead us, eventually, to the study of models of legal reasoning and interpretation employed by courts. Whether we examine technical decision-making or the value choices of courts, we need an analysis of the 'language' judges speak in taking these decisions and making these choices. By adopting an institutional perspective we discover, nonetheless, that even behind a seemingly formalist "*process of reasoned, public justification according to a set of legal and moral standard*", basic and structural choices are hidden.

Legal reasoning of Courts

A study of the legal reasoning of courts is an inquiry into the 'logic' of their judicial decision making. This concerns the kind of arguments given by judges, the relationship between the reasons and the decisions, and the adequacy of these reasons as a support for the decisions. From a critical perspective, typical of our inquiry, it is sometimes said that judges do not always reveal the real reasons for their decisions, and that the reasons they do present are no more than rationalizations for the results they reach, derived from the requirements of the constitution itself. This claim is presumably intended to suggest that it is necessary to take into account factors that lie outside explicitly given reasons, in order to explain why a case is decided in a certain way: and probably, such a realist analysis can be addressed by each of the criteria already suggested to give depth to the concept of 'judicial activism'.

In contrast, other criteria involving legal interpretation are commonly suggested as *direct expressions* of misused judicial discretion. Such criteria have been the object of a long-standing and engaging debate, probably as old as the constitutional norms to which they relate; and due to their inherent complexity.

That the 'interpretative fidelity' category comes into the discussion is no surprise, since it is part, again, of a kind of a common critical perception of the role of courts (perhaps the same that we see in the 'absolutization' of the countermajoritarian criterion discussed above). This dimension would measure courts' "*actual or inferential construction*" of constitutional provisions, and would lead to an 'activist' perception when a certain interpretation does not accord with the *ordinary meaning* of wording of the provision and/or with the *known, consensual intentions* or goals of its drafters. The use of such prudent adjectives by Canon seems very wise, in this context; it is also, however, a measure of the difficulty of establishing precise limits in the domain of constitutional interpretation, setting a clear threshold between the equally confused boundaries of *interpretation* and *creation.*

Now-traditional studies of constitutional theory tell us that there are judges and scholars who, to a greater or lesser extent, believe that it is possible to measure the interpretative fidelity of courts' decisions. John Hart Ely's milestone "Democracy and Distrust" opens with a discussion of this philosophy, renamed *'interpretivism'*, and of its common "*allure*" in the context of the American literature. I think that the comparative debate on 'judicial activism' is one of the best examples of how this *'interpretativist'* perception is common to a wide range of constitutional studies. Words and phrases, after all, do have some meaning, and drafters of constitutional provisions did have intentions and goals. When these last appear to be transgressed, dissenting justices and legal scholars often protest vigorously and engage in a considerable semantic analysis or historical research. Sometimes the issues are (and remain) hard to resolve, but sometimes a historical hindsight reveals 'interpretative infidelity'.

These are, in a nutshell, the questions at stake. It seems to me that the approach adopted here facilitates the research, because rather than looking for solutions (if they exist), an abstract inquiry into activism can limit itself to emphasizing the inner criticality of such questions and any consequent potential deviations. While conceding the necessity for discretion in applying vague phrases to specific situations, critics of activism on this dimension argue that the Constitution is not a constitution if it can be altered at the will of five or nine judges in the course of a lawsuit (to echo Bickel's emphatic words). Although it is a basic law "*intended to endure for ages to come*", it does not follow that a constitutional court can ignore the very words of the document. Special amending processes are explicitly provided, if particular provisions prove unpopular or dysfunctional. Supporters of a certain discretion argue here that a court's main function is the smooth application of a 'living' document, often framed in a distant past, to modern problems which may require new meanings for old provisions. It is the 'spirit of the law', they think, rather than the exact wording of the framers' time-bound intentions, that is important.

Comparatively, the judges' arsenal of professional techniques and legal arguments for the application of norms is often similar, while, apart from some specific contemporary experiences, constitutional texts do not normally provide specific guidance. The courts' judicial discourse is shaped through the employment of some textual methods, such as the plain literal and the contextual one, and some extra-textual methods, such as the historical and the teleological. However, such common 'language'—composed of the same 'tools'—can be used to construct rather different, sometimes contrasting, arguments. The guiding preference in this work of interpretation and application is often an institutional choice and, at the same time, is the reason for external charges of 'activism'.

With regard to wording and textual methods, the term 'activist' will be applied to "*any decision that appears to clearly contradict any constitutional provision in terms of the ordinary meaning of its wording, or any decision that is contrary to the logical implications of two or more provisions considered together*". Clearly this includes, along with gross alterations of textual meaning, those decisions that typically effectively create new constitutional provisions by finding them, through a contextual, sometimes strained or illogical interpretation of language, in preexisting provisions. This last is certainly a more realistic example, surely involving some degree of judicial discretion. Constitutional history contains a large number of such informal 'additions', which have sometimes generated little controversy for the truth, and sometimes a long critical debate: many Courts' 'amendments' are welcome, but they are not less activist for this (indeed, they share this characteristic with actual policy proposals). From an institutional perspective, constitutional theories highlighting the "*disinterested, contemplative, and neutral nature of judicial decisionmaking*", and proposing for this reason that a court should not hesitate much to 'find' a constitutional right of some kind "*if it is presented with convincing (to the judges) philosophical arguments for that right, at least if the right 'fits' with the rest of the legal fabric*", are making an (indeed simplistic) institutional argument. They suppose, *a contrario*, the legislative process as driven by passion and (unspecified) self-interest, and propose to substitute a more contemplative judiciary for the legislature. "*Societal decisionmaking thereby gains, to be sure, contemplation and reason, but it loses a basic measure of public will, desire, and reaction available in the legislative process*". Courts may not understand what 'justice' requires, or may not be good at producing justice even when they understand it. In these circumstances, their understanding of the constitution is partly a product of their evaluations about their own distinctive role as a social institution. It is reasonable to believe that judges are not well-equipped to engage in theoretically ambitious tasks, without also believing that political theory is itself problematic or useless.

Looking at the extra-textual methods, we face the tensions and challenges due to the essence of the constitution as a document with both a crucial strong source and precise, long-standing purposes. Especially at a certain stage of the American debate, some prominent authors (such as Bork, Scalia, and Rehnquist) have stressed the point of the "*framers' original intentions*" as the only canon of interpretation available for the judges to reconcile their structural lack of democratic legitimacy with reference to the "*original*" will of "*the people*". Their approaches were somewhat different, but have come to profoundly affect the global debate (perhaps more than the actual activities of the courts). Any kind of open, evolutionary interpretation would be, in their view, inevitably exposed to subjective views and, in particular, to judges' political options: while Bickel formulated the 'countermajoritarian difficulty' on the (realist, Holmesian) assumption that a creative component was inherent in the judicial function, the 'originalists' have used the argument of the lack of democratic legitimacy to raise, again, the idea that it was up to courts only to 'find' the right, as pre-existing essences. The search for an objective meaning, static in time, linked to an 'original intent theory' or rather to an 'original meaning', is in the end the expression of an explicitly felt need to limit judicial discretion. Whether agreeing or not with this urgency, a certain instrumentality in setting the criterion seems clear: because of inadequate discussion, poor records or conflict in the evidence, it is by no means always easy to ascertain a clear intention of the framers. Comparative institutional dimensions are in fact again trivialized here. Not only, through such an approach, the different kinds of delegations contained in the constitutions get confused (firstly, the purposeful delegations and the inadvertent ones, the product of mistakes, constraints on language and prediction, and the workings of aggregate decisionmakers). But also, in terms of institutional choice, no one in the present generation would need to choose among social decisionmakers, since those choices have already been made by the framers, clearly settled in their 'original position' or suggested by their 'original intent'. This fails to recognize, for example, that the framing of open-ended clauses is sometimes an intentional exclusion of certain issues from the bargaining political process in favour of the insularity of third bodies. Nonetheless, albeit to different degrees, a large number of critical commentators commonly categorize as activist those decisions seen as interpreting a provision contrary to 'their' supposed reasonably clear and consensual intentions of its writers. More specific illustrations can be found in some typical cases.

Firstly, we can consider those decisions applying a provision to a situation existing at the time of the provision's adoption, where it is clear that the drafters did not intend it to apply. The history of the US Supreme court gives us some notorious historical case studies, analysed by several scholars dealing with the question.

Secondly and more commonly, however, there are those decisions which apply constitutional norms to situations where the drafters did not and could not anticipate any application. It is easier here to exemplify, by finding hints in almost every constitutional environment. The most widely known case is, of course, the US Court's extensive interpretation of the Fourteenth Amendment's 'due process clause'.

Interpretative stability

Several supreme courts and constitutional courts hold, in addition to a '*nomopoietic*' function, a broad '*nomophylactic*' one. They are also 'guardians', of the uniform interpretation of the law and of the coherence of the legal order to which they belong. In fulfilling this function, they indirectly protect and promote equality before the law. For this reason, when examining the dimension of courts' interpretative stability, one should look both inward and outwards: at stake are both the coherence of tribunals with their own arguments, their own reasoning, their own established line of cases shaping a narrative of the legal order, and the consistency and certainty in the relations between the powers of the state and the individual citizens.

'Interpretative stability' is an important element in the debate over the merits of activism, although it is often unrecognized as such and its components are often poorly articulated. In general, from an institutionalist viewpoint, it studies the 'management' by the courts of their case-law and its development. It measures the degree to which a court decision either retains or abandons precedent or existing judicial doctrine, studying the dynamics of the relationship between the obligation to stare decisis and the legal reasoning of the court itself. After all, a common perception in reading some classics of American constitutional theory and constitutional history is that in some phases the Supreme Court (especially—but not only—the Warren Court) has been criticized more for the frequency and scope of its radical alterations of prior jurisprudence than for the antimajoritarian nature of its decisions.

The presence of previous case-law and the formal or informal tie to respect for precedents can be at the same time a constraint for the work of the courts and an opportunity for new discretionary activity. Firstly, a certain discretionary power of management of case-law seems to lie in the choice of the cases to be treated. Where a formal power of *certiorari* is not provided, courts have in any case obtained, through various techniques and different interpretations of the concepts of *standing* and *justiciability*, important spaces of discretion. An analysis of the use and misuse of such spaces, in the *ex ante* selection of the *jurisprudential narrative* of a legal order, is undoubtedly part of the debate on 'activism', given the possible instrumentality of such choices. In any case, the most dramatic *caesura*, the most dramatic instance of interpretative instability, obviously occurs when a court explicitly overrules one of its own earlier decisions. A loss of legal certainty is directly implied; in addition, several methodological questions, with strong practical consequences, arise. The first questions are in terms of transparency : judges usually are straightforward about such shifts, with explicit statements of overruling; sometimes they are indirect or reticent, creating even more uncertainty and further complicating the interpretative framework. Moreover, a court can also weaken a precedent, more or less radically, again without formally overruling it; or, conversely, it can enhance a precedent by expanding its interpretation, applying it to a new legal area, or giving it hitherto rejected or unforeseen implications. In deciding what a precedent means, it seems that a court should pay attention to comparative institutional considerations too, at least in terms of judicial fallibility ("*judges might not know what they are doing*") and dynamic effects, which courts are often not in a good position to anticipate.

"*In point of fact, precedents may also entail more freedom for the interpreter, insofar as they deflect the interpreter from the text, from the intentions of its authors, directing it towards the web of precedents*" : a court remains more or less free to depart from its own precedents or, more often, to distinguish a case, when there is a need to adapt both text and case law to a changing context. Of course, some reduction or growth in scope and reasoning naturally occurs. It is normal that, over time, subsequent decisions may put some limits on a precedent's applicability, or vice versa may find new patterns of application, perhaps by analogy. But when a precedent is drastically weakened, say by a single subsequent decision which greatly restricts its scope, possibly compromising its logic, the ideal of interpretative stability is equally weakened. And most importantly, sometimes one can find an instrumental use for such processes, which is probably one of the most frequent accusations of the discretion of the courts: for example, this can be seen in the widespread case of *step-by-step* introductions of new doctrines and policies (in the way that, somewhat banally, commonly goes by the name of 'judicial agenda').

A final, perhaps obvious, remark on this point links the dimension of 'interpretative stability' even more closely with most of the other criteria already examined, and seems to close the circle of our reflections. The parameter by which the stability in question is measured may not necessarily be a precedent, meant as a previous judicial decision on the same matter. Another baseline is the concept of the *'ongoing interpretation'* of the constitution, intended as the "*inferential interpretation of constitutional meaning drawn from longstanding and/or widespread laws and practices*". Despite the apparent vagueness of this concept, its meaning is clear, and consistent with the evolving debate on activism as a whole. The mode, degrees and acceptability of judicial discretion should be evaluated in the light of the diversity of voices within the plural constitutional community, taking into account different perspectives and different interpretations, trying to combine legal and political analysis. This also allows for a better assessment of the general external perception of the role of the court itself, fundamental ingredient of their legitimacy. The evaluation of this 'external component', its weight and its value, remains the biggest issue underlying the entire 'judicial activism' debate, and perhaps hindering the possibility of its sure dogmatic definition. However, it underlines the necessary correlation—in direct proportionality—of the constitutional justice organs with the social consensus itself on the constitution.

"Judicial Activism And Creativity of the Supreme Court—The Tools And Techniques"

"Judicium Non debet esse illusorium, suum effectum habere debet"

(A Judgment ought not to be illusory; it ought to have its proper effect)

In democratic countries the judiciary is given a place of great significance. The courts perform the key role of expounding the provisions of the Constitution. The courts act as the supreme interpreter, protector and guardian of the supremacy of the Constitution. The judiciary has to perform an important role in the interpretation and enforcement of human rights inscribed in the fundamental law of the country. Therefore, it is necessary to consider what should be the approach of the judiciary in the matter of constitutional interpretation.

The judiciary has to devise a pragmatic wisdom to adopt a creative and purposive approach in the interpretation of various rights embodied in the Constitution. The task of interpreting the constitution is a highly creative judicial function which must be in tune with the constitutional philosophy. A democratic society lives and swears by certain values such as individual *liberty, human dignity, rule of law, constitutionalism, etc.* and it is the duty of the judiciary to so interpret the constitution and the law as to constantly inculcate these values on which democracy thrives. The predominant positivist approach of interpretation followed by the Indian Judiciary emanates from the basic traditional theory that a judge does not create law but merely declares the law.

The Indian judiciary underwent a sea change in terms of discarding its traditional approach by charting out a new horizon of dynamic concept of judicial activism with many facets and dimensions which paved way for the activist liberal judicial approach to Constitutional interpretation. This assignment is about the judicial activism in India and the pro-active role played by the Supreme Court in applying judicial creativity for interpretation of the Constitution.

Judicial Activism is considered as a philosophy of administering justice whereby judges allow their personal views about Public Policy, ignoring Precedents. It is an innovative, dynamic and law making role of the court with a forward looking attitude discarding reliance on old cases and also mechanical, conservative and static view.

Judicial activism is a progressive judicial thinking, developing the law for handling constructively the contemporary problems of the Society. It is a creative thought process through which the court displays vigour, enterprise, initiative pulsating with the urge of creating new and refined principles of Law.

In fact, judicial activism is a sort of judicial creativity. It is an apparent power of judges to modify the scope and pattern of existing legal decision by application of mind and guided by law. It is also sometimes used as meaning simply the law established by judicial precedent.

Ironically, as the term "Judicial Activism" is defined in a number of desperate, even contradictory ways scholars and judges recognise this problem yet persist in speaking about the concept without defining it. Thus, the problem continues unabated people talk past one another, using the same language to convey very different concepts. To say that the idea of Judicial Activism has been around far longer than the term. Before the 20th century, Legal scholars squared off over the concept of judicial Legislation, (i.e.), Judges making positive Law.

The five core meanings of "Judicial activism" are :

(1) Invalidation of the arguably constitutional actions of other branches,
(2) Failure to adhere to precedent,
(3) Judicial "legislation",
(4) Departures from accepted interpretive methodology. and
(5) Result-oriented judging.

Origin of judicial activism in United States.—Arthur Schlesinger Jr. introduced the term "Judicial Activism" to the public in a Fortune magazine article in January 1947. Schlesinger's article profiled all nine Supreme Court justices on the Court at that time and explained the alliances and divisions among them. The article characterized Justices Black, Douglas, Murphy, and Rutlege as the "Judicial Activists" and Justices frankfurter, Jackson, and Burton as the "Champions of Self Restraint." Justice Reed and Chief Justice Vinson comprised a middle group.

The *first stage* was the Lochner era, "beginning roughly with the decision in *Lochner* v. *New York*, and continuing through the early New Deal", which "is still widely disparaged for its mobilization of personal judicial preference in opposition to state and federal social welfare legislation."

The second stage took place during the "Warren and Early Burger Courts", roughly the 1950s through the early 1970s, which "focused on finding new substantive rights in the Constitution and down played that document's structural mandates." As Judge Wilkinson sees it, "Although many of its individual decisions were overdue and salutary, when the era is considered as a whole, the states were relegated to a second-class constitutional status." *Finally, the third stage* of judicial activism "probably began with *New York* v. *United States*", and continues into the twenty-first century.

Origin of judicial activism in India

The nature of judicial process in India has undergone a metamorphosis expanding the scope of judicial review legitimately through judicial legislation. Judges have been traditional law makers. The judicial activism has flourished in India and has acquired enormous legitimacy with the Indian public.

According to Hon'ble Mr. Justice A.M. Ahmadi, the former Chief Justice of India, the initial years of the Supreme Court of India saw the adoption of an approach characterised by caution and circumspection. The expanding role of judiciary in law making in recent times has major reasons such as growth of parliamentary system and statutory intervention in the expansion of legislation has brought about a parallel expansion of judge-made law. This can be better understood by analyzing certain vital factors like degree of creativity, the modes, limits and legitimacy of law making through courts. By reason of judicial activism, much good or harm could be brought about by the Judges by resorting to innovative interpretation. Since judicial interpretation always involves some degree of law making, the creative character of judicial function and the degree of creativity depends on the most activist and dynamic nature of the judge.

Judicial activism in India has not been a spontaneous development. It is the consequence of a situation which necessitated it. When the Parliament enacted laws and the laws were intended to cover new fact situations, the judges' creativity and innovation revived in the matter of filling in the gaps. Apart from filling in the gaps in the legislation, the judges revived their creativity in all other areas which were not covered by legislation. The activist judges to an extent laid down law to fill the vacuum created by the legislature. The judges assuming an activist role applied their creative skills by introducing very many number of principles of interpretation of Constitutional provisions, especially in respect of the provisions relating to fundamental rights. In this context it is apt to quote *Justice Oliver Wendell Holmes* :

> "I recognize without hesitation the judges must and do legislate, but they do so only interstitially; they are confined from molar to molecular motions."

It is pertinent to draw the attention to a parallel statement made by *Benjamin Cardozo* while discussing the role of activist judges in his classic text the Nature of Judicial Process. Judges do and must make law but not in the manner of legislatures. Judges have power and right to make law. There is much scope for creative judicial activism in the interpretative functions of judges, on the choices inherent in their function and in the gaps in legal rules, as has been done by superior courts in several countries for many years. The law creative function of judges will be a much greater degree in a situation where there is a legislative vacuum.

The genesis of Judicial Activism in India started as an off-spring of judicial review from the mid seventies when the judiciary as an activator infused into the stream of judicial system many revolutionary changes. After

1975 the judiciary has become unelected representative of the people.

Some prominent Indian legal luminaries who adorned the bench of Supreme Court like Justice V.R. Krishna Iyer, Justice P.N. Bhagwati, Justice O. Chinnappa Reddy, Justice J.S. Verma, Justice Kuldip Singh, Justice A.S. Anand have sensitized the democratic principles in the country and played an important role by way of judicial activism and judicial creativity with their able umpiring and proactive judgments. Judicial activism earned a human face in India by liberalizing access to justice and under their leadership the Supreme Court gained in stature and legitimacy. It is pertinent to quote Rajeev Dhavan's observation on Indian judiciary who states that "Owing to indigenous pressure, the court has been mechanical in its approach to the problem on which it was called upon to adjudicate. The Supreme Court rarely exhibited any activist tendency before the eighties more precisely before emergency 1975."

Judicial creativity and precedents

Stare Decisis in Latin phrase. It means to stand by the decided cases to uphold the precedent, to maintain a former adjudication. The purpose is to have uniformity for having certainty. It is based on the public policy. Public policy as the major objectives of any legal system are certainty, predictability and stability.

The maxim is "*Stare decisis et non quieta movere*". Means—to sand by the decision and not to disturb what is settled. "Those things which have been no often adjudged ought to rest in peace."

The Supreme Court of India is not bound by its own earlier decision. It can overrule prospectively as well as retrospectively. In fact, the case law is a source of knowledge, provides basis of arguments, expounds the implications of law and sometimes even supplies the want of the legislatures.

The purpose of the judiciary is to implement the statutes in all its intents and implications. In doing so, the judges introduce their own philosophies and attitudes of life which is reflected in their judgments. The part of the judgment is called precedent which is rationale of the decision is called "*ratio decidendi*" of the case due to this ratio, a case is remembered and acknowledged as Law.

There are two theories of practices that are seen among the Judges, they are :

(1) Declaratory Theory.

(2) Constitutive Theory.

- Judges declare law that already exists incognito. They find it and apply to case before them. This view is based on the judicial process as it has been Savigny (German), Maine (English), Hugo (German), Burke (English), Bicko (Italy), Montesquieu (France) subscribe to this thought.
- The reality in law is first, decision according to the law is thereafter.

- According to constitutive theory, a judge is not a legislator and cannot be so, but laws are not made only by Legislatures.
- Article 145 of the Constitution of India empowers the Supreme Court of India to make rules for regulating practice and procedure by rules of court.
- The objections against the judge making laws are based on Separation of Power which has not been accepted in India in the way it operates in European Countries (France) and U.S.A.

Lord Becon stated that in new cases (*Unprecedented*) where statutory guidance is not available, where the constitution does not help the judge, the judges place reliance of Logic, reasoning and analogy, philosophy, custom, tradition or decide the new case. It is the permissible by judicial process. Justice Cardozo, approved these in "Judicial Process".

- The laws relating to trust, notice, fraud are creation of equity.
- Gray says "*that the power to interpret law is not different from power to make law. In fact, it is the judge who has final word to say what law on any point and this is real Law making and person doing it lawfully is true law maker.*"
- Hale held, "Judges only declare what law is, they do not make it, but, uphold rule of law, they develop law and in doing so, they make law.

Precedents

Precedent played a significant role in ensuring that ideals like creativity, stability and uniformity gave the law a garb of reasonableness and legitimacy. The pleas for judicial creativity within the precedent regime continued with Mansfield clarifying that the spirit of the case and not the letter of particular precedents make law.

According to Holmes, the need of the law to evolve and develop by defining the judges' role to be confined from 'molecular to molar motions'. He agrees that judges do, in substance, legislate, but they do interstitially that is they legislate within the gaps left by the law made by the legislature.

The judge made law may not be so perfect because of the personal thinking, attitude, and the consciousness of the judge lies the subconscious force of humanness, the likes, dislikes, prejudices, instincts, habits and convictions. For this reason it is necessary to subject judicial creativity to constant testing, revision and readjustment.

Judicial activism and creativity of the Supreme Court

Role of activist judges in judicial creativity.—The activist judges play a vital role in exhibiting their judicial creativity and they subjected the new legislation to their creative skills by introducing very many principles of interpretation. Judicial creativity requires a great skill and high creative ability. The judges evolved a number of principles while interpreting the Constitutional provisions, especially in respect of the provisions relating to fundamental rights.

The recent trend adopted by the Supreme Court has been to interpret our fundamental rights in the light of international conventions which are yet to be enacted into our domestic laws. In all these cases the judges of the Apex Court excelled in their creative skills. Anyone who analyses the judicial process of the Supreme Court and High Courts would conclude that judicial process has developed some finest principles and Courts have made tremendous contribution in establishment of a rule of law society in India and enhanced the people's quality of life.

Creativity in law through judicial process is one area that is greatly benefited by the innovative and creative interpretation of the Supreme Court and High Courts. Therefore the Creativity of the Supreme Court and High Courts shall always remain as a high benchmark of judicial creativity in India. On the contrary, it is also possible that in the process of creativity and innovation, there could sometimes be some errors, but such errors could be corrected or modified or refined either in appeal, or in a latter case, and the latter judgment would be one step more in the progress of the law. Cardozo while analyzing judicial process concludes that there is an element of creation and discovery where the judge can play a creative role in matter of constitutional interpretations. Each case coming before the judge has its own peculiarities requiring application of fresh mind and skill. The judge has constantly to be a creative artist. His work, therefore, requires constant thinking and display of talent and creativity. When judges interpret the law or a constitution by not merely giving effect to the literal meaning of the word, but trying to provide an interpretation consistent with the spirit of that statute or constitution, they are said to be activist judges. The function of the higher courts in this country has not been limited to exploring what the Constitution-makers meant when they wrote those words but also to develop and adapt the law so as to meet the challenges of contemporary problems of the society the respond to the needs of the society.

Judicial creativity of Supreme Court of India

A written constitution is not a self-executing document, and meanings of several provisions may not always be self-evident. The Courts cannot interpret a statute, much less a constitution, in a mechanistic manner. In the case of a statute, a court must determine the actual intent of the authors. In the case of a Constitution, a court must sustain the constitution's relevance to changing social, economic, and political scenarios. The courts must adopt a judicially positivist and pro-activist liberal approach in constitutional interpretation since the law-creative function of the judges is very well recognised now. Judges who interpret a written constitution cannot merely apply the law to the facts that come before them. The scope of judicial creativity expands the degree of activism when a constitution contains a bill of rights. In the words of Justice Benjamin Cardozo, a court must give to the words of a constitution "a continuity of life and expression". The judiciary at times is forging new tools, devising new strategies for the purpose of making fundamental rights meaningful for the large masses of the people. In the words of H.L.A. Hart "judges have an interstitial law-making function in so-called penumbral cases that are not clearly covered by existing law." The liberal, purposive, law-creative interpretation of the constitution must be used by the courts "with insight into social values, and with suppleness of adaptation to changing needs." It is a matter of judicial attitudes and choices as to how the judges approach the task of constitutional interpretation. The degree of necessary creativity might be well higher in constitutional adjudication than is usually the case for ordinary statutory adjudication.

The higher judiciary in India has been endowed with the onerous task of upholding the fundamental rights of the citizens. Therefore, the judicial interpretation and enforcement of social rights necessarily implies a high degree of creativity by virtue of the activist approach of higher judiciary in construing and declaring the fundamental rights. The judiciary in a constitutional democracy can play an active role through the medium of judicial review. This proposition is squarely applicable to the Indian context and it is evident from the judicial precedents that the judiciary especially the Supreme Court has started playing an activist role occasionally from its rulings in cases such as *A.K. Gopalan* v. *State of Madras*[1] and the activist role of the Indian judiciary was clearly evidence in *Golak Nath* v. *State of Punjab.*[2]

The high water mark of judicial activism in India has been reached by the Court in the landmark case of *Kesavananda Bharati* v. *State of Kerala,*[3] popularly known as Fundamental Rights case wherein the Supreme Court propounded the Doctrine of Basic Structure through its judicial creativity and activist approach.

Reformative effect of judicial creativity by Supreme Court.—A great transformation has come about in the judicial attitude towards the protection of personal liberty in the post-emergency period. The Court has re-interpreted Article 21 and practically overruled A.K. Gopalan's case in Menake Gandhi which can be regarded as a highly creative judicial pronouncement on the part of the Supreme Court. Judicial activism of the post-emergency period means liberal interpretation of constitutional provisions like Article 21 and 14, and reconceptualisation of the judicial process by making it more accessible and participatory.

The most significant aspect of Maneka Gandhi was that the Court laid down a seminal principle of constitutional interpretation. The Court held that there cannot be a mere textual construction of the words of the Constitution. Those words are significant with meanings that unfold when different situations arise. Another strategy adopted by the Supreme Court with a creative fashion to expand the ambit of Article 21 and to imply certain bundle of rights.

However, judicial activism in India has now taken on an interesting face. The courts in India pursue a form of review which can be described as

1. AIR 1950 SC 227.
2. AIR 1967 SC 1643.
3. AIR 1973 1461.

best as 'dialogic'—a term used famously by *Peter Hogg and Allison Bushell* in the context of the *canadian Supreme Court's decisions*. The Indian Supreme Court has enforced socio-economic rights, though they are not considered enforceable by the Constitution such as the right against malnutrition and the right to shelter. The judiciary has started issuing guidelines increasingly in legislative spheres, one such occasion is a landmark judgment in *Vishaka* v. *State of Rajasthan* The Supreme Court has laid down exhaustive guidelines to prevent sexual harassment of working women in work places until a suitable legislation is enacted for the purpose. The Court relied on International Conventions and made a significant interpretation of guarantee of gender equality, right to work with human dignity and safeguards against sexual harassment implicit under *Article 14, 15(3), 19(1)(a)* and *21* of the Constitution and filled the gap in legislative vacuum.

The dynamics of judicial process has a new enforcement dimension which includes 'right mobilization' without which the rights and interests of the poor and illiterate silent majority would become sterile. The Supreme Court has not confined itself to judge-made law in the traditional sense of the term, but has embarked upon legislation to fill in the gaps left by legislature. The role of judicial interpretation has to play far more active, creative and purposeful role in deciding what is according to law. The judiciary by invoking its activist approach with a camouflage of creativity laid down detailed guidelines on various spheres of law including the process of inter-country adoptions, rehabilitation of children of commercial sex workers, and the procedure to be followed by police officers prior to arrest, mildly similar to the American Miranda rights propounded 'Basu rights'. Thus, when a competent legislature fails to act legislatively and make a necessary law to met the societal needs, the courts play an active role and often indulge in judicial legislation to fill the void created by the legislature's abdication of responsibility.

While the Part IV deals with the Directive Principles of State Policy that largely enumerate objectives pertaining to socio-economic entitlements. They are the creative part of the Constitution, and fundamental to the governance of the country. However, the key feature is that the *Directive Principles* are non-justiciable. Despite the fact that the Constitution did not permit socio-economic rights to be justiciable or enforceable, the Indian judiciary taught that express constitutional provisions may not necessarily translate into social legitimacy.

The principle of harmonious construction in interpreting the relationship between Part III and Part IV of the Constitution has been reiterated in number of cases decided by the Supreme Court and consistently maintained that the Fundamental Rights and the Directive Principles of State Policy constitute the conscience of the constitution. The judiciary under our constitutional scheme has to take up a positive and creative function in securing socio-economic justice to the people.

In *State of Bihar* v. *Bal Mukund Sah*,[1] it was held that the judiciary has, therefore, a socio-economic destination and a creative function. In *S.P. Gupta* v. *President of India*,[2] it was held that the judiciary cannot remain a mere bystander or spectator but it must become an active participant in the judicial process ready to use law in the service of social justice through, a pro-active goal oriented approach. It was emphasized that the judiciary has to adopt a positive and creative approach.

The Supreme Court, in its creative role under *Article 141* and the creative elements implicit in the very process of determining *ratio decidendi*, it is not surprising the judicial process has not been crippled in the discharge of its duty to keep the law abreast of the times, by the traditionalist theory of *stare decisis*.

The Supreme Court has observed that any legal system, especially one evolving in a developing country, might permit judges to play a creative role and innovate to ensure justice without doing violence to the norms set by legislation. The role of the Court is creative rather than passive, and it assumes a more positive attitude in determining facts and circumstances of each case. The Apex Court goes to say that notwithstanding the conventional principle that the duty of judges is to expound and not to legislate. The Courts have taken the view that the judicial art of interpretation and appraisal is imbued with creativity.

Tool and techniques of creativity

Creativity must be based on principles

Judge can make law but he is not wholly free to make law as observed by *Mr. Justice Cardozo* of the U.S. Supreme Court [*as then he was*] :—

> "*The Judge is not to innovate at pleasure. He is not a knight-errant roaming at will in pursuit of his own ideal of beauty or of goodness.*"

Again, *Justice Cardozo* said that though the powers of interpretation of the Courts are narrow, yet they can fill up gaps. He said :—

> "*No doubt, the limits for the judge are narrower. He legislates only between gaps. He fills the open spaces in the law.*"

Judges have power and right to make law. In this context the following words of *Justice Holmes* are apposite. He said :—

> "*I recognize without hesitation that Judges do and must legislate, but they do so only interstitially; they are confined from molar to molecular motion.*"

Law is a social engineering and an instrument of social change evolved by a gradual and continuous process. As *Benjamin Cardozo* has put it in his "Judicial Process" life is not a logic but experience. History and customs, utility and the accepted standards of right conduct are the forms which singly or in combination shall be the progress of law.

Creativity based on changing demands of society.—In *Bengal*

1. AIR 2000 SC 1296.
2. AIR 1982 SC 149.

Immunity Company Limited v. *State of Bihar*,[1] the Supreme Court has observed that it was not bound by its earlier judgments and possessed the freedom to overrule its judgments when it thought fit to do so to keep pace with the needs of changing times. The acceptance of this principle ensured the preservation and legitimation provided to the doctrine of binding precedent, and therefore, certainly and finally the law to the changing demands of society.

In *Shah Bano's* case it is interpreted that every woman has right to live with human dignity, irrespective of her cast. In "*Mohinder Singh Gill* v. *Chief Election Commissioner, New Delhi*",[2] the Supreme Court has held that today, in our jurisprudence, the advances made by natural justice far exceed old frontiers and if judicial creativity be lights penumbral areas it is only for improving the quality of government by injecting fair play into its wheels.

Creation of Right to Education.—In case of *Unni Krishnan & others* v. *State of A.P.*,[3] the Apex Court held that the every Child/citizen has a right to free education until he completes the age of 14 years. This right flows from Article 21. This is a good example of the judicial creativity.

Creativity in open space.—There is no law on social disorder called **Sexual harassment** of a woman at work place. In *Vishaka Case*, the Supreme Court created law of the land observing that the right to be free from sexual harassment is a fundamental right under *Articles 14, 15 & 21* of the Constitution. It has been 10 years since the Hon'ble Supreme Court issued Vishaka guidelines regarding sexual harassments but still a draft bill on the subject is waiting for enactment. As per these guidelines, every organization, whether Government or Public, is to have an Internal Complaints Committee to investigate complaints regarding sexual harassment at workplace. A code of conduct is prepared for all employees and that should be incorporated in the service rules/standing instructions. Sexual harassment at work place is a criminal offence and the accused would face civil as well as criminal liabilities.

Judge made law

Duty to assign reasons is, however, a *judge made law*. There is dispute as to whether it comprises of a third pillar of natural justice.

What would be, if not permitted?

The Constitution Bench speaking through *Chief Justice Pathak* in Raghubir Singh (dead) by LRs.'s case, opined that if that was not permitted, the march of Judge-made law and the development of constitutional jurisprudence would come to a standstill.

In *T.M.A. Pai Foundation* v. *State of Karnataka*,[4] are so broadly formulated that they provide sufficient leeway to subsequent Courts in applying those principles while the lack of clarity in the judgment allows

---

1. AIR 1955 SC 661.
2. AIR 1978 SC 851.
3. AIR 1993 SC 2178.
4. AIR 2003 SC 355.

judicial creativity.

Creativity in Interpretation of Constitution.—In *Bombay Dyeing Co. Ltd.* v. *Bombay Action Group & Ors.*,[1] the Apex Court laid down the principle that the court normally would lean in favour of environmental protection in view of the Creative interpretation made by the Supreme Court in finding a right of environmental protection including right to clear water, air under Article 21 of the Constitution.

Former *C.J.I. Dr. A.S. Anand* observed that the Apex Court has given purposive liberal and creative interpretation of Article 21 of the Constitution by giving it more content, meaning and purpose. In expanding the ambit of right to life & personal liberty, the court has evolved tools and techniques of compensatory jurisprudence, implemented international conventions & treaties, and issued directions for environmental justice.

Creativity in basic structure of constitution.—The theory of basic structure of the Constitution is a result of the creative interpretation of the Supreme Court. In "*M. Nagaraj* v. *Union of India*", the Supreme Court has held that this development is the emergence of the constitutional principles in their own right. It is not based on literal wordings. These principles are part of Constitutional law even if they are not expressly stated in the form of rules. An instance is the principle of reasonableness which connects Arts. 14, 19 and 21.

In "*Minerva Mills Ltd.* v. *Union of India*",[2] the Supreme Court has held that Parliament cannot, under Art. 368, expand its amending power so as to acquire for itself the right to appeal or abrogate the Constitution or to destroy its basic and essential features. This is an example of the technique of creative interpretation of the Constitution.

Innovation of minimum rationality.—The creativity in interpreting Article 21 related its, heights when the doctrine of minimum rationality was also treated as part of Article 21 by the Supreme Court in *Mithu* v. *State of Punjab*, when *Section 303 of the I.P.C.*, was struck down on the ground that it violates Article 21.

Creation of various rights.—In *Olga Tellis* v. *B.M.C.*,[3] the creative interpretation of the Apex Court is clearly visible when it is laid down that the right to life guaranteed under Article 21 also included the right to livelihood because no person can live without the means of living that is, the means of livelihood.

Balancing technique.—In "*Lalit Narayan Mishra Institute of Economic Development and Social Change, Patna* v. *State of Bihar*,[4] the Apex Court has adopted balancing technique in holding that the provisions of the Constitution, particularly the provisions relating to the fundamental rights, should not be construed in a pedantic manner, but should be construed in a manner that would enable the citizens to enjoy the rights in the fullest

---

1. AIR 2006 SC 1489.
2. AIR 1980 SC 1789.
3. AIR 1986 SC 180.
4. AIR 1988 SC 1179.

measure. In *State of T.N.* v. *L. Abu Kavur Bai*",[1] it was held that on a careful consideration of the legal and historical aspects of the directive principles and the fundamental rights, there appears to be complete unanimity of judicial opinion of the various decisions of the Supreme Court on point that although the directive principles are not enforceable yet the court should make a real attempt at harmonising and reconciling.

Creative interpretation.—In "*Suresh Jindal* v. *BSES Rajdhani Power Ltd.*,[2] the Apex Court has observed that creative interpretation of the provisions of the statute demands that with the advance in science and technology, the Court should read the provisions of a statute in such a manner so as to give effect thereto.

Creative interpretation of Article 14.—In "*Food Corporation of India* v. *M/s. Seil Ltd.*",[3] the Apex Court has rightly admitted that Article 14 of the Constitution of India has received a liberal interpretation over the years. Its scope has also been expanded by creative interpretation of the Court. The law has developed in this field to a great extent.

Keep the law abreast of the times.——the Supreme Court, in its creative role under Article 141 and the creative elements implicit in the very process of determining *ratio decidendi*, it is not surprising the judicial process has not been crippled in the discharge of its duty to keep the law abreast of the times, by the traditionalist theory of *stare decisis*. Times and conditions change with changing society, and "*every age should be mistress of its own law*"—and era should not be hampered by outdated law.

Creation of voter's right to know.—For the first time the right to know about the candidate standing for election has been brought within the sweep of Article 19(1)(a) by the Supreme Court through its creative interpretation. The Apex Court in "*Peoples Union for Civil Liberties (PUCL)* v. *Union of India*",[4] has held that voter's right to know about the antecedents of the candidate contesting for the election falls within the realm of freedom of speech and expression guaranteed by Article 19(1)(a) and can be justified on good and substantial grounds.

Creativity in socio-economic justice.—In "*State of Bihar* v. *Bal Mukund Sah*",[5] the Supreme Court has emphasized its *creative role* in achieving the goal of socio-economic justice. The judiciary has, therefore, a socio-economic destination and a creative function. It has to use the words of *G. Austin*, "to become an arm of the socio-economic revolution and perform an active role calculated to bring social justice within the reach of the common man. It cannot remain content to act merely as an umpire but it must be functionally involved in the goal of socio-economic justice." Continuity is essential to law as a whole, but the continuity must be creative.

---

1. AIR 1984 SC 374.
2. AIR 2008 SC 280.
3. AIR 2008 SC 1101.
4. AIR 1997 SC 568.
5. AIR 2000 SC 1296.

Creativity in special situations.—In *Raj Deo Sharma case*, the Apex Court has observed that even so, leaving V.V.I.P. accused to be dealt with by the routinely procrastinating legal process is to surrender to interminable delays as an inevitable evil. Therefore, we should not be finical about absolute processual equality and must be creative in innovating procedures compelled by special situations.

Creation of right to speedy trial.—The entitlement of the accused to speedy trial has been repeatedly emphasised by the Supreme Court. Though it is not enumerated as a fundamental right in the Constitution, the Apex Court has recognized the same to be implicit in the spectrum of Article 21. In *Hussainara Khatoon* v. *Home Secretary, State of Bihar*,[1] the Court while dealing with the cases of under-trial, who had suffered long incarceration held that a procedure which keeps such large number of people behind bars without trial so long cannot possibly be regarded as reasonable, just or fair so as to be in conformity with the requirement of Article 21. The Court laid stress upon the need for enactment of law to ensure reasonable, just and fair procedure which has creative connotation after Maneka Gandhi's case,[2] in the matter of criminal trials.

Creativity needed to harmonise the law.—In "*Municipal Corporation of Greater Bombay* v. *Indian Oil Corporation Ltd.*",[3] has held that keeping in view the social, economic and political goal setting in which it is intended to operate, Judge is called upon to perform a creative function.

Iron out the creases.—It is true that one should iron out the creases and should take a creative approach as to what was intended by a particular provision. Court should take a creative, reasonable and rational approach in interpreting the statute. By way of creative approach in *Ramanna Shetty's* case, the Apex Court brought public sector corporations within the scope and ambit of Article 12 and subjected them to the discipline of fundamental rights.

Creativity is must in developing countries.—The Supreme Court in *Jagdambika Pratap Narain Singh* v. *Central Board of Direct Taxes*,[4] dealing with the question of limitation in granting a relief, has observed that any legal system, especially one evolving in a developing country, might permit judges to play a creative role and innovate to ensure justice without doing violence to the norms set by legislation. The rule of the Court is creative rather than passive, and it assumes a more positive attitude in determining facts and circumstances of each case.

In "*S.P. Gupta* v. *President of India*",[5] it was held that the judiciary has, therefore, a socio-economic destination and a creative function. The judiciary cannot remain a mere bystander or spectator but it must become an active participant in the judicial process ready to use law in the service of social

1. AIR 1979 SC 1360.
2. (1978) 1 SCC 248.
3. AIR 1991 SC 686.
4. AIR 1975 SC 1816.
5. AIR 1982 SC 149.

justice through, a pro-active goal oriented approach. It was emphasized that the judiciary has to adopt a positive and creative approach.

Creativity in the field of other wings.—The Supreme Court further cautioned itself in the S.P. Gupta case that the court must take care to see that it does not overstep the limits of its judicial function and trespass into areas which are reserved to the Executive and the Legislature by the Constitution. Judicial creativity requires a great skill and high creative ability. "Justice Cardozo approvingly quoted President T. Roosevelt's stress on the social philosophy of the Judges, who shakes and shapes the course of a nation and declares the law of the land, must be in tune with the social philosophy of the Constitution."

Purpose behind judicial creative & PIL

In "*Delhi Transport Corporation* v. *D.T.C. Mazdoor Congress*",[1] it is true that judicial jealousy of legislature in law making has long been outdrawn, but the strict construction remains still an established rule. It is generally accepted principle that Judges in interpreting statutes should give effect to the legislators' intent. By doing so, the Courts do recognize their subordinate position and their obligation to help the legislature to achieve its purpose. But in that effort, *creativity* is essential.

Demands of changing society.—In "*Union of India* v. *Raghubir Singh*",[2] it has been held that the Supreme Court is not bound by its own previous decisions while permitting necessary scope for judicial creativity and adaptability of the law to the changing demands of society becomes inevitable. In "*Mohinder Singh Gill* v. *Chief Election Commissioner, New Delhi*",[3] the apex Court has observed that if judicial creativity belights penumbral areas it is only for improving the quality of government by injecting fair play into its wheels.

Usurpation of legislative functions.—In "*Municipal Committee, Patiala* v. *Model Town Residents Association*",[4] the court cannot usurp the functions assigned to the legislative bodies under the Constitution and even indirectly require the legislature to exercise its power of law-making in particular manner. The court cannot assume to itself a supervisory role for the law-making power of the legislature under the provisions of the Constitution.

Reading fundamental rights into directive principles.—In "*State of Gujarat* v. *Mirzapur Mati Kureshi Kassab Jamat*",[5] the Apex Court has held that post Kesavananda Bharati so far as the determination of the position of Directive Principles, *vis-a-vis* Fundamental Rights are concerned, it has been an era of positivism and creativity. *Article 37* of the Constitution which while declaring the Directive Principles to be unenforceable by any

---

1. AIR 1991 SC 101.
2. AIR 1989 SC 1933.
3. AIR 1978 SC 851.
4. AIR 2003 SC 684.
5. AIR 2006 SC 212.

Court, but in "*Kesavananda Bharti* v. *State of Kerala*",[1] Court goes on to say "*that they are nevertheless fundamental in the governance of the country*". The end part of Article 37, "it shall be the duty of the State to apply these principles in making laws" is not a pariah but a constitutional mandate. Supreme Court has held that, while interpreting the interplay of rights and restrictions, Part III (*Fundamental Rights*) and Part-IV (*Directive Principles*) have to be read together.

Milestones of public interest litigation in India.—One of the earliest cases of public interest litigation was reported as *Hussainara Khatoon (I)* v. *State of Bihar.*[2] This case was concerned with a series of articles published in a prominent newspaper—the Indian Express which exposed the plight of under trial prisoners in the state of Bihar. A writ petition was filed by an advocate drawing the Court's attention to the deplorable plight of these prisoners. Many of them had been in jail for longer periods than the maximum permissible sentences for the offences they had been charged with. The Supreme Court accepted the *locus standi* of the advocate to maintain the writ petition. Thereafter, a series of cases followed in which the Court gave directions through which the *'right to speedy trial'* was deemed to be an integral and an essential part of the protection of life and personal liberty. Soon thereafter, two noted professors of law filed writ petitions in the Supreme Court highlighting various abuses of the law, which, they asserted, were a violation of Article 21 of the Constitution. These included inhuman conditions prevailing in protective homes, long pendency of trials in court, trafficking of women, importation of children for homosexual purposes, and the non-payment of wages to bonded labourers among others. The Supreme Court accepted their *locus standi* to represent the suffering masses and passed guidelines and orders that greatly ameliorated the conditions of these people. In another matter, a journalist, Ms. Sheela Barse, took up the plight of women prisoners who were confined in the police jails in the city of Bombay. She asserted that they were victims of custodial violence.

The Court took cognizance of the matter and directions were issued to the Director of College of Social Work, Bombay. He was ordered to visit the Bombay Central Jail and conduct interviews of various women prisoners in order to ascertain whether they had been subjected to torture or ill-treatment. He was asked to submit a report to the Court in this regard. Based on his findings, the Court issued directions such as the detention of female prisoners only in designated female lock-ups guarded by female constables and that accused females could be interrogated only in the presence of a female police official. Public interest litigation acquired a new dimension—namely that of *'epistolary jurisdiction'* with the decision in the case of *Sunil Batra* v. *Delhi Administration*,[3] it was initiated by a letter that was written by a prisoner lodged in jail to a Judge of the Supreme Court. The prisoner complained of a brutal assault committed by a Head Warder

1. AIR 1973 SC 1461.
2. AIR 1979 SC 1360.
3. AIR 1978 SC 1975.

on another prisoner. The Court treated that letter as a writ petition and while issuing various directions, opined that :

> "*...technicalities and legal niceties are not impediment to the court entertaining even an informal communication as a proceeding for habeas corpus if the basic facts are found.*"

In *Municipal Council, Ratlam* v. *Vardichand*, the Court recognized the *locus standi* of a group of citizens who sought directions against the local Municipal Council for removal of open drains that caused stench as well as diseases. The Court, recognizing the right of the group of citizens, asserted that if the :

> "*...centre of gravity of justice is to shift as indeed the Preamble to the Constitution mandates, from the traditional individualism of locus standi to the community orientation of public interest litigation, the court must consider the issues as there is need to focus on the ordinary men.*"

Judicial review—Is a distinctive power associated with the Supreme Court that is nowhere specifically mentioned in the Constitution. Chief Justice John Marshall in *Marbury* v. *Madison* (1803) asserted the major principle on which it rests by observing : "[i]t is emphatically the province and duty of the judicial department to say what the law is" (p. 177). Through judicial review the court most dramatically asserts its authority to determine what the Constitution means.

The power of the Court to review the law extends in two directions. The first involves decisions by other branches of the federal government. These cases include actions taken by the executive branch, like the decision by President Richard Nixon to withhold taped records of conversations in the White House, and statutes passed by Congress, such as the Missouri Compromise, which excluded slavery from northern portions of the Louisiana Purchase territory. Judicial review also expresses the authority of the federal courts over state laws and judicial decisions that involve the federal Constitution. Whether involving federal or state matters, the practice of judicial review has been marked by dynamic expansion and persistent controversy. Judicial power has been consolidated both in the superiority of the federal judiciary over the states and of the Supreme Court and the other branches of the federal government. The authority of the federal government that became centralized after the **Civil** War is one of the pillars of judicial review and *vice versa*. Justice Thurgood Marshall, in commenting on the constitutional bicentennial celebration of 1987, said that the Constitution did not survive the Civil War, but was remade following that conflict. Since the late nineteenth century, power has come to be increasingly centered in a Supreme Court that would be unrecognizable to the founding generation. Not only do the justices now have a home and no **circuit** riding responsibilities, but the power to subject the acts of other branches of the federal government and the states to judicial **scrutiny** is widely accepted. Thus, judicial review is a dynamic institution that expands with the federal authority over the nation.

Origin of judicial review

Scholars trace the origins of judicial review to *Dr. Bonham's Case* (1610). Sir Edward Coke, of England's Court of Common Pleas, stated that "when an act of parliament is against common right and reason or repugnant, or impossible to be performed, the common law will control it, and adjudge such act to be void" (p. 118a). Coke believed that the common lawyer possessed "artificial reasons of the law" and that this capacity elevated him to nearly equal footing with king and Parliament. According to Coke, special learning required to interpret the law placed it above politics.

Improper exercise of the power of judicial review

The judicial branch is invested with the power of being the final arbiter of constitutional disputes under many democratic Constitutions. India, which has modelled its Constitution, to some extent, on the US Constitution, falls in this category. One of the fundamental features of such a constitutional set-up is the judicial power to invalidate legislation on the ground of infringement of the constitutional parameters such as legislative incompetence, violation of guaranteed fundamental rights, inconsistency with an express provision or basic feature of the Constitution, etc. The power of judicial review is an exception to the principle of separation of powers, which demarcates distinct areas for the different constitutional organs to exercise their powers. The power of judicial review postulates that, in the event of a dispute as to whether the legislature or the executive has overstepped its constitutional bounds, the judiciary shall decide the dispute by application of well-established constitutional doctrines and principles of interpretation. Although the doctrine of separation of powers is not watertight or immutable, judicial interpretation must not reduce it to a nullity. Indeed, in some areas, our Constitution-framers have created evident and unambiguous barriers against judicial intervention in legislative or executive domains, but even these have been breached by the courts eager to assert their authority.

Indeed, nothing can be headier than the power to invalidate another constitutional organ's action. Such great power must of necessity bring in its wake great responsibility. The problem with judicial activism is its proclivity for excessive and legally improper use of this very great power to invalidate arguably lawful and proper legislative or executive actions. In fact, history abounds with instances where overactive Judges have jettisoned well-established principles to produce incongruous results, which they honestly thought were necessary, even if democratically elected legislatures or executive thought otherwise.

New deal legislations

During the period of the Great Depression in the 1930s in the US, the US Supreme Court invalidated a series of legislative measures taken by the Government under the so-called "New Deal" program. These legislations were intended to directly address the problems arising from the Great Depression by generating employment, obligating minimum wages, safe working conditions and other social welfare measures. However, these legislations were struck down by a majority of the Judges on the premise that they interfered with the doctrine of freedom of contract and were, therefore, contrary to the then current philosophy of *laissez faire*. The activism of the Judges in striking down such obviously valid legislation contributed to the elongation of the Great Depression leading to unavoidable loss of life and misery for millions of people. This judicial attitude led the US President Franklin Roosevelt to threaten to "pack" the Supreme Court with Judges who would show restraint and accept the legislative wisdom of the "New Deal". With this threat hanging over their heads and with the death or retirement of the activist Judges, the US Supreme Court eventually restrained its activism, leading to the famous quip about the "switch in time that saved nine"—the nine Justices!

Dred Scott v. Sandford

Judicial activism has still a darker history as seen in the infamous case of *Dred Scott* v. *Sandford* where the US Supreme Court virtually supported slavery by denying the power of the Federal Government to abolish this practice. The preposterous reasoning put forward by the Judges, ignoring clear provisions of law, was that black people were not citizens and could not, therefore, claim constitutional protections. Moreover, since slaves were chattels of the slave-owners, freeing them from slavery meant forfeiture of the slave-owner's property without compensation—something, which in the thinking of those activist Judges was unfair and unreasonable. This sort of result-oriented jurisprudence requires embarrassing legal gymnastics from Judges.

In India, disturbing trend of using the judiciary to second-guess unambiguously legislative or executive powers. Indeed, our Judges have succumbed to the temptation to interfere even with well-recognised executive powers such as treaty-making or foreign relations. A Delhi High Court judgment in 2002, made a treaty signed by India with another sovereign foreign State virtually inoperable, by striking down an administrative order connected with it, *inter alia*, on the ground that the Court did not like the policy being effectuated by it. One shudders to think whither this trend could lead—whether, for example the constitutionality of a declaration of war or peace treaty signed by India could also be questioned in a court of law? If the courts were to strike down the peace treaty as being "unconstitutional", would the armed forces be compelled to prosecute the war under a judicial mandamus? Indeed, the mind boggles at such eventualities, however improbable they may appear, given the new-found enthusiasm for judicial activism in areas that are inarguably *no pasaran* for Judges.

A.D.M., Jabalpur v. Shivakant Shukla

Improper non-exercise of the power of judicial review—"Judicial activism", has both a positive and a negative aspect. It involves both exceeding the judicial sphere as well as refusing to act within the judicial sphere. Improper non-exercise of judicial review is as dangerous as improper overuse of judicial review. Judicial activism of the former variety is best seen in the infamous *A.D.M., Jabalpur* v. *Shivakant Shukla*, better known as

Habeas Corpus case, where the Supreme Court bent backwards to support what was clearly improper executive action in detaining persons without just cause during the "phoney emergency" of the 1970s. It went to the extent of expressing its "diamond-bright, diamond-hard hope" that the powers that ought to have been clipped, would not be misused. As we all know, the executive, blessed with the Supreme Court's judgment, did precisely the opposite, confirming Lord Acton's declaration : "power tends to corrupt, absolute power corrupts absolutely". This judgment was not, however, totally unexpected because, in previous years, we had seen the spectre of the supersession of "independent" Judges in favour of more politically and ideologically "committed" ones. Often judicial independence is compromised at the altar of political or social ideology in the name of activism. Indeed, an activist Supreme Court, eager to jump into the political arena by abdicating its "counter-majoritarian" role as the guardian of the Constitution, almost brought our cherished ideal of a democratic republic to a standstill.

Liversidge v. Anderson

Similarly disingenuous was the judgment of the House of Lords in *Liversidge* v. *Anderson*, by which the British Government was given virtually unlimited powers to detain persons, even on entirely dubious grounds, during wartime. But, inevitably, there will be conscientious Judges who will not fall prey to such dubious arguments. Thus, Lord Atkin who was the sole dissenter (like Justice H.R. Khanna in *Habeas Corpus case*), went on to deplore the majority Judges who according to him : "When face to face with claims involving the liberty of the subject, show themselves more executive-minded than the executive."

This abdication of the judicial role led one Judge to later comment that from being lions under the throne, the judgment of the House of Lords had "reduced us to mice squeaking under a chair in the Home Office". Thus we have seen that judicial activism, especially the explosive admixture of law and politics, whether exceeding or abdicating the judicial function, has a thoroughly disreputable history in many parts of the world.

"Result driven" decision-making and activist interpretations of Article 14—Activist Judges have often ignored or side-stepped binding legal precedents to arrive at preconceived results, which conform to their conception of justice. However honest and *bona fide* this exercise, its legal legitimacy is open to question.

New Doctrine—Royappa view

E.P. Royappa v. *State of T.N.* is a classic example of this kind of activism in the interpretation of Article 14 of the Constitution, which, as a matter of fact, simply deals with "equality before the law or the equal protection of the laws" and nothing more. The classic formulation of the "Doctrine of reasonable classification" in *Anwar Ali Sarkar, reformulated in Ram Krishna Dalmia* and in *Special Courts Bill, 1978, In re* held the field and became formally recognised as the touchstone for testing legislative and executive violations of Article 14. However, all of a sudden, in *E.P. Royappa* the Supreme Court through the concept of "substantive due process", which had been specifically rejected by the Constituent Assembly, equated the concept of "arbitrariness" with "inequality". The Court observed :

> "Now, what is the content and reach of this great equalising principle? ... We cannot countenance any attempt to truncate its all-embracing scope and meaning, for to do so would be to violate its *activist magnitude*. Equality is a dynamic concept with many aspects and dimensions and it cannot be 'cribbed, cabined and confined' within traditional and doctrinaire limits. From a positivistic point of view, equality is antithetic to arbitrariness. In fact equality and arbitrariness are sworn enemies... *Where an act is arbitrary, it is implicit in it that it is unequal both according to political logic and constitutional law and is therefore violative of Article 14...*

Merry ride from Royappa case

From *Royappa* it was a merry ride through *Maneka Gandhi, R.D. Shetty, Ajay Hasia*, and a host of other cases where the Supreme Court freely struck down actions of the other coordinate branches of the Government on the basis that it was not "reasonable" or was "arbitrary", a standard of judicial review, neither contemplated by the framers of the Constitution nor by the plain text of Article 14. Indeed, there are numerous other problems with this "New Doctrine" as some have pejoratively dubbed it.

(I) The New Doctrine hangs in the air, because it is propounded without reference to the terms in which the guaranteed right to "the equal protection of the laws" is conferred. Indeed, by obfuscating its true meaning, the "New Doctrine" gives Judges the untrammelled power to strike down legislative and executive action at will with a bald observation that they are not "reasonable". In fact, the standard of "reasonability" is no standard at all because what is "reasonable" or "unreasonable" is in the eye of the beholder without reference to any objective examination. It is not the duty of the court to decide whether a certain statute was "reasonable" or not because that is in the policy realm of India's democratically elected representatives. The court's only duty is to examine whether the legislature had the authority to promulgate the statute and examine whether the statute violated one of the Constitution's textually enumerated fundamental rights.

(II) Secondly, the "New Doctrine" involves the logical fallacy of the undistributed middle or the fallacy of simple conversion. The "New Doctrine" purports to treat "arbitrariness" and "inequality" as the same thing. In fact, not all arbitrary actions can be termed unequal simply because some arbitrary actions are both arbitrary and unequal. If, for example, all red-haired students are expelled from a school without reason, that action is both arbitrary and unequal *vis-a-vis* non-red-haired students. If, however, all students irrespective of hair colour are expelled, it is simply arbitrary but not unequal. Hence, while "arbitrariness" and "inequality" are conceptually different, this fact is ignored by the activist mindset.

(III) Thirdly, the "New Doctrine" fails to distinguish between the violation of equality by a law and its violation by executive action. Finally, the "new Doctrine", fails to analyse certain concepts like "arbitrary", "law", "executive action" or "discretionary power" and fails to recognise the necessary implication of numerous Supreme Court decisions on classification that were arguably binding precedents and certainly settled law.

"Substantive due process" and Article 21, Gopalan and Row Cases

The Supreme Court, early in its history, in a series of judgments beginning from A.K. Gopalan, V.G. Row, and others, held that the discredited US concept of "substantive due process" could have no role in the interpretation of Article 21 because it essentially involved substituting a Judge's notion of "reasonableness" with that of the legislature's. However, from Maneka Gandhi onwards, the Supreme Court introduced into Article 21 the concept of "substantive due process", or in other words, a standard that requires executive and legislative action to be "reasonable" or "fair"—nebulous terms that are totally at the discretion of an activist Judge to use as he pleases. indeed, as we saw in the examples of the "New Deal" cases and the Slavery judgment in the US, "substantive due process" is a concept with a blackened history. With this in mind, the Drafting Committee of the Constitution of India was not in favour of using the expression "due process" in the text of Article 21 for they were familiar with its misuse in the US context. Accordingly, the Drafting Committee while debating the Draft Constitution of India decided that "due process of law" be substituted by "procedure established by law" similar to Article 30 of the Japanese Constitution of 1946. What the framers of the Constitution consciously avoided, judicial activism has brought in by the back door.

There are several problems with the use of "substantive due process" in the interpretation of Article 21. The first is the legitimacy of creating fundamental rights through judicial interpretation. With the power of "substantive due process" behind them, the courts have constantly foraged the forbidden fields by creating newer rights by treating them as flowing from the "right to life" in Article 21 of the Constitution.

Article 21; whether cornucopia

Article 21 has verily been treated as the cornucopia from which all such newly created rights flow out. Such judicial legislation is only possible by committing violence to the plain words of the article, which, as evident, is only worded in the negative. Founding new rights on Article 21 is, to say the least, debatable. The entire Constitution, in particular Part III, has been designed to provide a framework for regulation of human society in an orderly manner by providing certain *specifically enumerated* fundamental rights. The argument in favour of judicial legislation on Article 21 is that "new fundamental rights" are intricately connected with the right to life and without these "new fundamental right" life would itself become meaningless. This argument, however, has a serious flaw. In fact, if these "new fundamental rights" are premised on their intricate connection with the right to life, then the whole of Part III would be redundant, by the same token, as all rights guaranteed therein by specific enumeration would also be similarly connected. In other words, if the judicial legislation arguments were correct, the entire scheme of Part III could have been telescoped into only one provision, namely, Article 21!

Judicial legislation and international law

Polluter pays principle

Judicial activism has even extended to wholesale importation of principles of international law, which are controversial even internationally. For example, principles like "precautionary principle" and "polluter pays" have been made a part of domestic environmental law by the judicial *dicta* in *Vellore Citizens' Welfare Forum* v. *Union of India*[1] : Even otherwise once these principles are accepted as part of the customary international law there would be no difficulty in accepting them as part of the domestic law. *It is almost an accepted proposition of law that the rules of customary international law which are not contrary to the municipal law shall be deemed to have been incorporated in the domestic law and shall be followed by the courts of law*".

In fact, these principles have been the subject of much critical debate and there is no unanimity amongst scholars as to their exact content. Even the concept of "sustainable development", which the Supreme Court heavily relied upon, is an extremely nebulous concept, a fact even conceded to in the judgment itself! Sustainable development is within the realm of legislative or executive policy. The courts must properly restrain.

Further, acceptance of international norms and laws is an exclusively executive function since it is closely associated with questions of national sovereignty. Moreover, even if these particular international environmental law principles are trite for incorporation into domestic law, the Supreme Court's judgment provides for *automatic incorporation of all* customary international legal principles, whatever their content or validity, into domestic law. This is clearly a judicial overkill.

Similarly, in *M.V. Elizabeth* v. *Harwan Investment and Trading (P) Ltd.*,[2] the Court felt that where statutes are silent "it is the *duty* of the court to devise procedure by drawing analogy from other systems of law and practice". Drawing upon this rather debatable "duty", the Court read into the Merchant Shipping Act, 1958, something that was not even provided for by the said Act, but provided for in international conventions and according to the Court was a part of customary international maritime law. This was despite a *catena* of Indian precedents to the contrary. Guidance from other jurisdictions is *always* welcome, but not the wholesale incorporation of foreign principles without concern for the actual state of domestic law and the consequences of such incorporation.

---

1. AIR 1996 SC 2715.
2. AIR 1993 SC 1014.

Activism, "political questions" (Baker v. Carr) and the problem of justiciability

"Political questions" which were meant to be out-of-bounds for the courts have often been thrown into the laps of Judges. Instead of throwing them back, the courts have, with great enthusiasm, essayed into adjudication of such questions, often with unsatisfactory results.

The "political questions" exclusion" doctrine is best stated in *Baker* v. *Carr*,[1] where the US Supreme Court held that certain questions were non-justiciable in a court of law when there was : "... a textually demonstrable constitutional commitment of the issue to a coordinate political department; or a lack of judicially discoverable and manageable standards for resolving it;"

Ayodhya reference case

Ayodhya Reference case, where the President requested the Supreme Court to answer politically sensitive questions like : whether there existed a temple at Ayodhya before the construction of the Babri Mosque, fall in the second category, where the matter cannot be resolved by reference to "judicially manageable standards". It would have in fact required the Judges to opine on a point of archaeology rather than law, and thereby step on to a political minefield. The Supreme Court was perfectly correct in refusing to answer the reference. In fact, such questions have arisen merely on account of the failure of the executive or the legislature to resolve their own political problems and are attempts to pass the buck to the judiciary... The Supreme Court should stoutly refuse the temptation to crown itself with political thorns.

Jharkhand Assembly dispute

The recent Jharkhand Assembly dispute would probably fall under the first category because there is a constitutional provision, Article 212, entrusting the adjudication of such issues to a coordinate constitutional branch, namely, the legislature, which ideally should have been left free to deal with the question, the courts keeping aloof. Yet, despite the dangers of entering the political Eddystone Rocks the philosophy of judicial activism has propelled Judges to sail into uncharted waters. Judges now seem to want to engage themselves with boundless enthusiasm in complex socio-economic issues raising myriads of facts, and ideological issues, that cannot be adjudicated by "judicially manageable standards".

Sarla Mudgal case

In *Sarla Mudgal*,[2] the Supreme Court made wide-ranging observations on the need to bring in a uniform civil code and directed the State to explain the steps it had taken towards the enactment of the same. The question of a uniform civil code is undoubtedly an issue fraught with complex political fault lines involving minority rights, personal laws, women's rights and so on, and the Supreme Court's observations not unexpectedly erupted into a

1. 369 US 186 (1962).

2. AIR 1995 SC 1531.

major political issue. In a latter case, the Supreme Court was forced to back down by explaining away its controversial observations in *Sarla Mudgal* as having been "incidentally made". In other cases, Judges have sought to incorporate ideologically grounded concepts such as "Hindutva" and "Socialism" into their judgment with no credit whatsoever.

Judicial activism has also extended to the use of authorities with political overtones for deciding cases—a wholly improper approach. For instance, in *Shah Bano*, while the final order granting maintenance to a divorced Muslim woman is probably correct, the Supreme Court's approach of relying on unfamiliar non-legal sources (such as the *Holy Qur' an* itself) and making sweeping generalisations, instead of narrow legal reasoning, made the Court the target of unseemly political controversies.

BALCO case

It appears that the Supreme Court has slowly begun to realise the futility of entering upon policy issues, especially economic policy, and this culminated in the following observations in *BALCO Disinvestment case* : "Process of disinvestment is a policy decision involving complex economic factors. The courts have consistently refrained from interfering with economic decisions as it has been recognised that economic expediencies lack adjudicative disposition and unless the economic decision, based on economic expediencies, is demonstrated to be so violative of constitutional or legal limits on power or so abhorrent to reason, that the courts would decline to interfere. In matters relating to economic issues, the Government has, while taking a decision, right to 'trial and error' as long as both trial and error are *bona fide* and within limits of authority."

Judicial activism creates labels for Judges such as "pro-labour", "anti-labour", "pro-tenant", "anti-tenant", "progressive", "conservative" and so on. This is so because the scope and the extent of judicial activism ultimately depends on the personal predilections of the individual Judge and his/her own conception of what "social justice" ought to be. In effect, the result becomes personality-oriented rather than oriented towards "justice according to law", which is the duty of a Judge. Personality-driven adjudication provides avenues for "forum shopping" by lawyers and litigants. instead of "justice according to law", the courts would administer justice according to the propensities of the Judge, harking back to the days of justice at the Chancellor's foot in England.

"Judicial restraint is a 'rightist' ideology"

One of the criticisms of judicial restraint is that it is "pro-government", "pro-rich" and "anti-social justice" and hence a "rightist" ideology. It is a misconception to think that judicial activism arises from "left" or "right" oriented philosophies, two terms with hazy meanings at best. Judicial activism is nothing but jumping the fence. The fact that it is done from the "right" or "left" is hardly of significance because to an activist Judge what he considers to be the correct philosophy matters, "leftist" or "rightist" being sheer coincidence. In fact, as we have seen earlier, the "New Deal" cases, the *Habeas Corpus* judgment, the "Hindutva" judgments and the pro-slavery judgment are instances of activist Judges with a so-called "rightist" ideology.

More often than not, the individual philosophy of the Judge becomes tailored to the dominant discourse. A Judge is enjoined by the Constitution to often perform a counter-majoritarian role to prevent unjustified executive or legislative incursions into the textually enumerated fundamental rights of citizens, or to prevent abuse of representative democracy. By entering into the political thicket, as evidenced in the *Habeas Corpus case*, judicial activism can wholly erode judicial independence and run contrary to the Judge's constitutional duty to decide cases "without fear or favour".

"Judicial restraint is an activist philosophy in itself"

There can be no difficulty in accepting judicial restraint or legal centrism as a judicial philosophy in itself. But this philosophy is very different from judicial activism. Despite the high-sounding words, "judicial restraint" only means that the Judge shall stick by the law and decide legal controversies strictly in accordance with established principles of law without foraging the constitutionally forbidden territories reserved for another branch of the government. That precisely is the role a Judge is called upon to play by reason of the oath that he undertakes. A judge is not free to render justice as he thinks, but is required to render "justice according to law". "Judges are meant to act as humble interpreters of law, not pose as emperors who adjudicate on a whim. We need faceless, impassive Judges, compassionate but disciplined legislators and an executive that acknowledges the supremacy of the legislature and independence of the judiciary. Sadly, technical Judges are not easy to come by in India. Some arrange marriages between rapists and their victims. Others turn into committed municipal authorities. Courts are meant to be more serious than Bollywood makes them out to be."

Conceded that in a few cases "justice according to law" may produce less-than-perfect results, but more often than not, "justice according to law" produces an outcome that is in line with crystallised public opinion. Indeed, if "justice according to law" was so abhorrent, then we would have seen a revolution in India and a scrapping of the Constitution. the fact that this has not happened is positive proof that "justice according to law" and "justice without fear or favour" is the correct approach.

Judicial restraint would have meant no Kesavananda Bharati

There may occur occasions in judicial history, when Judges must make dramatic, sudden and even revolutionary changes to law, by marginalising the "justice according to law" principle. Exceptional situations may call for drastic steps, but that can happen only exceptionally. For example; the "Basic Structure. Doctrine" evolved by the Supreme Court in *Kesavananda Bharati* is, if at all an exercise of judicial legislation, a justifiable one, because without it there would have been no Constitution and no independent judiciary worth the name. After all, as the maxim goes, *necessitas non habet legem*.

That is a different kettle of fish from the activism of the 1980s and

1990s where judicial legislation was resorted to at the drop of a hat to address every socio-economic problem of the day, however unfortunate, but nevertheless lacking the imperative urgency facing *Kesavananda Bharati* court. The Queensberry Rules are to be strictly observed except when your own life is at stake! Fortunately, the fervour for judicial activism, which engulfed the courts during the third and fourth decades seems to be ebbing with the progressive realisation that it is preferable to tread the "highways" of justice instead of resorting to the "bye-lanes" of activism in the hope of expeditiously reaching the goal of justice. Deviation from the well-trodden path frequently leads to wholly unjust outcomes.

Judicial review and termination of the contractual jobs

The view earlier was that judicial review of termination of contractual jobs is not permissible in India. Quite recently, there is notable shift in legal position over the decade and now the termination of contractual jobs can be challenged in the court which can review the decision taken by the authority. It is no longer open to the authority passing the order to argue that the action being in realm of contract is not open to judicial review. A writ court is entitled to judicially review the action and determine whether there was any illegality, perversity, unreasonableness, unfairness or irrationality that would vitiate the action, no matter the action is in the realm of contract.

This liberty would not extend to the court substituting its own view for that taken by the decision making authority. The scope of any such review is not all pervasive. So long as the action taken by the administrator/authority is not shown to be vitiated by these or any of these infirmities or so long as the action is not demonstratively in outrageous defiance of logic the writ court would do well to respect the decision of the administrator (Honible Cyriac Joesph and T.S. Thakur JJ in *Grid Corporation of Orissa Ltd.* case reported in the Hitvada Dt. 20 Dec. 2011 at p. 9).

Rule of Law[1] and Judicial Process

Rule of law grants legitimacy and sanctity to any Government. Even dictators also seek legitimacy behind it. Human Right violators getting power by force, suppressing peaceful demonstrations and crushing legitimate peaceful demands by force, carry disapproval of this rule. In fact, it is what Coke said, Lex is Rex'.

Rule of law is a guarantee that prohibits rule of gun. Dicey analysed this rule to mean that Administrative law is no law because it concedes discretion to Administrative authorities. Twin equalities—Equality before law and equal protection of law and the statement of fact that roots of common law lies not in statute, not in Constitution, not in crown, not in Parliament but in custom and traditions of the common man. Dicey's first view no longer holds good as does the view of Austin who proclaimed International law to be 'no law' but only a comity of nations.

---

1. See Author's book on 'Indian Constitution' (2012) ALA. Faridabad (Haryana) for more specific discussion.

Rule of law is admitted reality if there is any system of law. It is the soul of legal system. Rule of law has been principles of fairness, reasonableness, decision by speaking orders, legitimate expectation, proportionality in giving punishment, doctrine of *ultra vires,* right to Information, Protection of Woman on workplace, organisation of police and reforms, handling corruption like 2G spectrum, growth of administrative law and principles of natural justice, and theories like red light and green light theories, first is fire fighting judicial review and judicial control of administrative authorities and second is fire watching; it insists on legislative measures to ensure efficiency and fairness in administrative action.

As regards judicial process herein, 'Rule of law means—

(1) Independent judiciary.—Judge should not depend on administrator, executive for his appointment, promotion or salary. His accountability should be to law and the Constitution.

(2) Independent legal profession.—Independent bar is the soul of democracy. Crush the bar, the system of law would vanish. It gets converted into one of oppression and tyranny.

(3) Standard professional ethics.—Third requisite of rule of law is well informed honest bar. Standard of profession depends on what quality does the bar possess?

Right to information or knowledge

Article 19(1) (a) includes not only right to speak and express that of the speaker, writer or performer but also that of listener, reader and viewer. Right to know is fundamental right in Article 19(1) (a).

In *S.P. Gupta* v. *Union of India,*[1] Supreme Court expressed the view that Government of India was bound to disclose the correspondence of Chief Justice of India to C.J. Delhi High Court and Law Minister. The claim of privilege of Government was disallowed. In *Dinesh Trivedi.*[2] and *P.U.C.L. case,*[3] the view that right to know is included in the ambit of Article 19(1) (a) was re-integrated, Article 19(1) (a) includes right to seek, receive and impart information to the extent it is in public domain and to the extent speaker desires or wishes. Right to Information Act, 2005 (Freedom of Information Act, 2002) has been enacted by Indian Parliament making use of views expressed by the courts on right to know, except those 10 cases wherein information can be withheld and that are enumerated in Section 8(1) of the Act.

Right not to speak

Bijoy Emmanuel case (*National Anthem case*)[4] and *Motion Picture Association case,*[5] are relevant on 'coerced speech' and right not to speak.

1. A.I.R. 1982 S.C. 149.
2. (1997) (4) S.C.C. 306.
3. A.I.R. 2003 S.C. 2363.
4. A.I.R. 1987 S.C. 748.
5. A.I.R. 1999 S.C. 2334.

Every citizen has liberty to decide; what not to speak and whether to speak or not to speak.

Right to legal aid and legal assistance (pre 1978 and post 1978).

Judicial review (prior to 1978) is represented by *Janardan Reddy*,[1] and *Tara Singh Cases.*[2] *and post 1978 view Maneka Gandhi*,[3] and *Hoskot case*,[4] Pre-1978 view was in confusion on right to legal aid.

In *Reddy and Tara Singh*, (1951) Supreme Court refused to give relief even if accused was punished by trial court while he was unrepresented by counsel. In 1976, Article 39-A was added and Maneka Gandhi view and there after *Hoskot* cases held that free legal aid was essential ingredient of fair procedure. The courts held that free legal aid was peremptory principle under Article 21. It was not merely a permissive rule under Article 22(1). *Hoskot* view was affirmed in *Hussainara Khatoon (I)*,[5] *Khatri II cases*[6] and *Sukhdas case*,[7]

Speedy trial

Speedy trial is essence of criminal justice, Delay defeats justice. Law presumes accused to be innocent until proved guilty; peers presume to be guilty until declared innocent. In between stands the accused and the court trial. Justice delayed is justice denied. Justice hurried is justice burried. Speedy trial is compromise formulae in between. As such, in all criminal prosecutions, the accused shall enjoy the right to speedy and public trial. (VIth amendment U.S., Constitution). Article 21 of our Constitution implies right to speedy trial in 'right to personal liberty'.

Right from *Husainara*,[8] to *A.R. Antulay case*,[9] much water had flown prior to it was settled that right to speedy trial is enshrined in Article 21 and no law can be said to establish a procedure which does not secure speedy trial or which is not fair, reasonable and expeditious.[10] Antulay view

---

1. (1951) 1 S.C.R. 344.
2. (1951) S.C.R. 729.
3. (1978) 1 S.C.C. 2481.
4. (1978) 3 S.C.C. 544.
5. (1980) 1 S.C.C. 98.
6. (1981) 1 S.C.C. 427.
7. (1986) 2 S.C.C. 401.
8. (1980) 1 S.C.C. 81.
9. (1992) 1 S.C.C. 225.
10. See in favour of Speedy trial *Hussainara (1)*, (1980) 1 S.C.C. 81, to *Maneka Gandhi*, (1978) 1 S.C.C. 248; *Hussainara (iv)*, (1980) 1 S.C.C. 98; See also *Madheshwardhari*, A.I.R. 1986 Pat. 324 (F.B.). In *A.R. Antulay*, Nine guidelines were issued. (1) speedy trial is primarily the right of accused, (2) Right extends from Investigation to final appeal, (3) The reasons are (i) It may increase pretrial incanceration (ii) disturb his vocation, (iii) impair defence. (4) delay may be caused by either side, (5) system itself may cause delay, (6) whether any prejudice is caused by delay, (7) accused needs not claim speedy trial, (8) No limit (maximum or outer) can be fixed after which trial is held delayed, (9) In delayed cases, conviction needs not be quashed; punishment can be reduced or trial can be expedited if continues.

has been reaffirmed in *P. Ramchandra Rao case*,[1] by 6 :1 overruling *Common cause case*[2] (two Judges Bench), *Common cause*,[3] (three Judges Bench) and *Raj Deo Sharma*,[4] and *Raj Deo Sharma*,[5] wherein *A.R. Antulay view* was sought to be modified.

Bail

'Bail' or 'jail' are two probabilities open to an undertrial prisoner; 'Bail ensues from Article 21 and presumption of innocence. Jail ensues from 'social interest'. An accused has constitutional right (1) to apply for bail and, (2) to get his bail application be considered. That is why there is no limit on how many times, an accused can move bail application? The only restriction is that subsequent bail applications has to be on new grounds keeping all these, it has been held that provisions of bail from Sections 436 to 439 of Cr.P.C. are fair and reasonable.

Regarding anticipatory bail, *Gurbaksh Singh*,[6] and *Kartar Singh*,[7] are relevant.

In first, Supreme Court observed that there is nothing in law which permits constraints and conditions like heavy surety,

Second, first surrender then apply for bail unreasonable conditions after release of accused unless special conditions exist like terrorists, naxals, dacoits wherein law may provide for reasonable limitations. Not having Section 438 Cr.P.C. type of Section is not violative of Article 21. Section 438 came in Cr.P.C. in 1973. Its non application does not violate Article 21.

Death sentence[8]

Three questions on this issue have come in judicial process.

(1) Whether Sections 302 IPC (Total 8 Sections in IPC) and 354 Cr.P.C. are unconstitutional and violate Article 14 and 21?

(2) Whether Section 303 IPC violates Article 14 and 21?

(3) Whether delay in execution violates Articles 14 and 21?

Jagmohan Singh case[9] and *Bachan Singh*,[10] deal with question no. 1. Mithu case (1983), 2. S.C.C. 277 deals with question no. 2. *T.V. Vatheeswarau*[11] to Tribeni Ben[12] deal with question No. 3.

---

1. (2002) 4 S.C.C. 578.
2. (1996) 4 S.C.C. 33.
3. (1996) 6 S.C.C. 775.
4. (1998) 7 S.C.C. 507.
5. (1999) 7 S.C.C. 604.
6. (1980) 2 S.C.C. 565.
7. (1924) 3 S.C.C. 569.
8. For more detailed discussion see Author's book on Indian Constitution, A.L.A. Faridabad, (2014).
9. (1973) 1 S.C.C. 20.
10. (1980) 2 S.C.C. 684.
11. (1983) 2 S.C.C. 68.
12. (1988) 4 S.C.C. 574.

Question No. 1

Jagmohan Singh held death sentence in circumstances prevailing in India can not be said to be given under law as it did not leave enough guidelines to the trial court as to when to give death sentence? Despite it, the court however, held judicial discretion being properly guided. Reliance was placed on 35th report of law commission which recommended retention of death sentence.

Consequent upon dissenting view of Krishna Iyer J. in *Rajendra Prasad case*,[1] and *Maneka Gandhi*,[2] a Constitutional Bench was constituted in *Bachan Singh Case*,[3] this bench had to decide constitutionality of Section 302 I.P.C. and 354 (3) Cr.P.C. in light of Article 19 and 21. Sarkaria J. wrote for Majority and Bhagwati J. for minority. The majority accepted the cleavage between abolitionists and retentionists of death sentence in the world but left it to be settled by legislature. It noted that three attempts in last three decades failed to persuade the Indian Parliament to abolish death sentence as such the court should not venture to formulate rigid standards in an area in which the legislature so varily treads.

Machhi Singh,[4] issued broad guidelines for giving death sentence like manner of murder being committed, motive, nature of crime, magnitude of crime, personality of victim.

Question 2

Mithu case,[5] held Section 303 IPC unconstitutional. Death is mandatory in Section 303 when life convict commits murder. Murders are thus, (1) Life convict murderers. (2) other murderers. This is bad for reasons :

(1) judge has no choice, no discretion even if mitigating circumstances exists,

(2) the opportunity to plead these facts is denied to category convict-accused,

(3) convict accused does not get benefit of 'rarest of rare' view of *Bachan Singh* case,

(4) Deprivation of life of convict accused under Section 303 does not provide a 'due process'. It is not fair and reasonable procedure established by law (Article 21).

Question 3

In *Vatheeswaran*, delay in execution beyond 2 years was held enough to convert death into life imprisonment, Chinnappa J's view was; benefit would be given even if convict was responsible for delaying execution. This view was accepted in *Sher Singh case*.[6] The benefit would be considered whether it is petition under Article 32 or special leave petition under Article

---

1. (1979) 3 S.C.R. 78.
2. (1978) 1 S.C.C. 248.
3. (1980) 2 S.C.C. 684.
4. (1983) 2 S.C.C. 277.
5. (1983) 2 S.C.C. 277.
6. (1983) 2 S.C.C. 344.

136. Two years delay in execution as a rule was however not affirmed. Delay caused by convict could give benefit was also not accepted. In *Javed Ahmad*,[1] Chinnappa J. protested against two year's delay rule, hence in *Tribeni Ben case*,[2] Constitutional Bench was constituted which held delay in execution violates Article 21. Delay starts since mercy appeal and executive inaction thereafter. No benefit can be given when delay is caused by convict. No rigid period in number of years delay can be fixed for counting delay in execution.

Public interest litigation and judicial process;

Litigation in interest of public is a remedy wherein *Locus standi* rule has no application. It guarantees access to justice to all; particularly vulnerable groups like poor, environmentalists, consumers, racial or ethnic minorities who can not go to court for want of money, information or knowledge. It is now constitutional remedy flowing out of Article 14 and 21. It has helped people and has brought their grievances before courts. However, it has to be taken care of that the doors of court so opened are not misused. The process supplements regular remedying process. It does not supplant it.

Natural justice (common sense justice)

Natural justice are judge made rules and insists on minimum fair procedure. It includes :

(1) Rule against Bias

(2) Rule of fair hearing, (*Audi Alteram Partem*),

(3) Post decisional hearing.

Exception are; (1) Emergency, (2) Confidentiality, (3) Purely administrative matters, (4) Impracticability, (5) Interim Preventive actions, (6) Cases of legislative action, (7) Where no right of claimant is infringed, (8) Statute provides exception, (9) Necessity, (10) Cases of contractual arrangements, (11) Policy decisions of the Government, (12) Useless formality.

Article 311(2) and Article 14 of the Constitution are relevant expositions of natural justice.

Redeeming the Supreme Court

In a span of about 45 days, the Supreme Court of India has delivered two judgments that have received diametrically opposite reactions—one will count among the Court's most poorly reasoned judgments while the other is likely to be heralded as one of its finest for its clarity and fidelity to earlier decisions. The contrast between Justice Singhvi's judgment upholding the criminalisation of homosexuality and that of Chief Justice Sathasivam affirming the rights of mercy-rejected death row prisoners could not be starker. After Justices Singhvi and Mukhopadhya upheld the constitutionality of Section 377 of the IPC in *Suresh Kumar Koushal*, the credibility of the Court as a counter-majoritarian institution had suffered a

1. (1985) 1 S.C.C. 275.
2. (1988) 4 S.C.C. 574.

serious setback. However, the Chief Justice, along with Justices Ranjan Gogoi and Shiva Kirti Singh, has done a remarkable job in partly restoring the credibility of the Court through a thoroughly reasoned judgment in *Shatrughan Chauhan* v. *Union of India.* In *Chauhan,* the Court has concluded that inordinate delay in the rejection of mercy petitions of death row convicts amounted to torture and that it is a sufficient basis, in and of itself, to commute a sentence of death to life imprisonment. It is not just about the contrast in outcomes in these two cases but the processes adopted by these two judgments will go a long way in determining the position they will occupy in the judicial history of this country.

The similarities

Any comparison between the two judgments must begin by acknowledging complexities involved in both cases. The legal response to homosexuality in India through Section 377 has been on the statute books for over 150 years. Though attitudes towards homosexuality have undergone significant changes, it would only be fair to acknowledge that it is nonetheless a deeply divisive issue in India. It would also be a fair assessment that the death penalty and treatment that must be accorded to those sentenced to death are extremely polarising issues. The case before the Supreme Court in Chauhan was particularly delicate because the President had rejected mercy to all 15 prisoners before the Court. However, all 15 prisoners had returned to the Supreme Court seeking enforcement of their right to life on the ground that their suffering on death row due to the inordinate delay by the executive (ranging between 11 to 15) years) entitled them to commutation of their death sentence. It must also be noted that the Supreme Court in both cases was being asked to intervene in situations where other organs of the state had already made certain determination. In *Koushal, the legislature had made the political determination that homosexuality would be criminalised by not repealing Section 377. Similarly, in Chauhan*, the executive, through the President of India, had rejected all the mercy petitions.

Differences

Though the challenges were similar in many ways, there is an unbelievable contrast in the manner in which the Supreme Court responded. In *Koushal*, the judgment authored by Justice Singhvi does not address the legal issues that were at the heart of the constitutional challenges to Section 377. There are the poorly argued sections on equality under Article 14 and the right to life under Article 21 while completely ignoring the arguments on the protection against discrimination under Article 15. The shortcomings of Koushal are evident when it is compared to the judgment of the Delhi High Court on Section 377 in *Naz Foundation.* There are established constitutional doctrines to test whether a provision of law is discriminatory and violates the right to equality under Articles 14 and 15 of the Constitution, none of which finds any serious engagement in *Koushal.* None of this is about whether one supports Section 377 or not. It is about adopting a sound judicial technique—it is about identifying precise and relevant questions; it is about applying constitutional doctrines to those questions in a rigorous manner; it is about reasoned conclusions. Rights adjudication is not about judges merely taking a decision and that is what distinguishes them from politicians. Unfortunately, the judgment in *Koushal* fails on all these grounds. More than the unacceptable outcome, what must worry us more is that the judgment in *Koushal* reads like a thinly veiled political decision.

However, the judgment in *Chauhan* articulates a very difficult legal issue precisely and clarifies the decision of a five-judge bench in *Triveniben* (1989) on it. While clarifying and relying on *Triveniben*, there is thorough constitutional reasoning to *Chauhan* that led the Court to come to the conclusion that inordinate delay in disposing of mercy petitions amounts to torture and that the nature of the crime must have no relevance in that determination. The issue about the nature of the crime was particularly important in the context of the Supreme Court's decision in *Bhullar*. In *Bhullar*, the Supreme Court had concluded that those sentenced to death for terrorist offences could not invoke the argument about inordinate delay in disposing of mercy petitions due to the nature of crimes. While relying on *Triveniben* to come to the conclusion that the classification of terrorist and non-terrorist offences in the context of inordinate delay in disposing of mercy petitions is constitutionally invalid, the judges, in *Chauhan*, have not created new jurisprudence and have only clarified the content and application of earlier judgments. There is tremendous judicial skill in the manner in which they have analysed earlier judgments and applied constitutional doctrines.

Challenges and responses

The most obvious difference in the two judgments is the approach to the target groups concerned. In *Koushal*, the perception that only very few homosexuals have been prosecuted under Section 377 was of tremendous significance to the judges. A numerical approach to rights enforcement is rather baffling and quite alien to the jurisprudence developed by the Indian Supreme Court. In *Chauhan*, despite dealing with a very small group of individuals (those death row prisoners whose mercy petitions have been rejected) and in particular a group which is often hated and reviled, the judges emphatically held that the protections in the Constitution are available to every individual, without exception. Perhaps the greatest merit of the decision in *Chauhan* is the rejection of the argument that retribution or strong moral disapproval of actions by death row prisoners can be used to deny them constitutionally protected rights.

As far as institutional relations between different organs of the State are concerned, the Supreme Court, in *Koushal*, ruled that Parliament was free to amend Section 377 and decriminalise homosexuality. However, if the law were to stand, the judges felt there was no constitutional infirmity. There is a palpable reluctance to meaningfully scrutinise a law on a divisive issue where the political class has made a choice. However, in *Chauhan*, the Supreme Court squarely addresses the warning that the Court might be overstepping its jurisdiction because the President had already rejected the mercy petitions of all 15 prisoners. The Court is clear that it is not questioning the power of the President to reject mercy petitions but is rather interested and competent to go into the issue of whether the executive violated the rights of the death row convicts due to the inordinate delay. The Supreme Court has taken the position that it cannot be expected to abandon its role of being the guardian of the fundamental rights of all persons within the territory of India, whoever they might be.

The Supreme Court in *Chauhan*, had the courage to undertake significant course correction by clarifying the ruling in *Triveniben*. As efforts to decriminalise homosexuality gather pace again with the scheduled review of *Koushal* this week, the Supreme Court must see the fact that critical questions about the constitutionality of Section 377 have not been addressed in *Koushal*. If the review petition does not result in correction of the errors in *Koushal*, the Chief Justice of India (due to retire in April 2014) will find himself in an interesting position. After having delivered judgment that has gone a long way to restore the credibility of the Court after *Koushal*, the Chief Justice will have to decide if he wants to refer the constitutionality of Section 377 to a larger bench. Given the intensity of his commitment to the rule of law as displayed in *Chauhan*, it would be surprising if Chief Justice Sathasivam lets the poorly reasoned judgment in Koushal be a blot on his tenure as Chief Justice of India. He only needs to look as far as the Delhi High Court's judgment on Section 377 in *Naz Foundation* to realise what an alternative legacy could look like.

❑ ❑

Chapter 3

Judicial Process and the Court Structure

Effectiveness of judicial process depends on the structure of the court. The way, the judges are selected and appointed, the circumstances wherein courts function; the procedure that these follow and quality of decisions they pronounce, the public confidence, the courts enjoy and quality of bar.

In India, judges of subordinate courts are appointed by the Governor of the State on the recommendation of State Public Service Commission of the State. The promotion and transfers are under control of the High Court. The Courts work under supervision of High Court. The Higher Judicial Service is also there. It makes recommendations for appointment on higher judicial services like appointment of Additional District Judges. In junior cadre, on the post of civil judge (junior division) fresh law graduates are allowed to compete. It does not require any experience of practice at the Bar. The examination consists of preliminary and main examination followed by interview of those who are declared successful in main examination. In H.J.S. minimum 7 years practice is essential. Written examination is held under supervision of High Court. The final selection is made by full High Court after interview.

As regards, appointments of judges in High Courts, the whole process is mysterious and non-transparent, two sources of recruitment in High Court Judges include; judicial officers who entered in judiciary through P.C.S(J) and H.J.S. Ordinarily these are on the basis of seniority-cum-merit. Screening of whole career till then is done by the High Court. The names are chosen by the collegium of High Court headed by Chief Justice wherein appointment is proposed. The second source of recruitment is; from bar. Any advocate practising anywhere in High Court or districts for minimum 10 years or above is eligible for being considered for elevation as judge in the High Court. It is here in this category that lack of transparency is felt. The collegium may, pickup any. That is why many of uncle practitioners get in as judges of High Court. First generation advocates are rarely selected. Sons and daughters of sitting or influential retired judges make their way easily to High Court. The way to bench goes through another route of Standing Counsels of the Government.

For a victim-centric approach

Court proceedings are generally held in open courtrooms to ensure transparency under the maxim, "not only must justice be done, it must also be seen to be done." The recent trend of in-camera trial has evolved contrary to this maxim to ensure confidentiality and to lessen the trauma and stigma caused to a victim. It also provides protection from voyeuristic intrusion by the media.

A judge is duty-bound to maintain the delicate balance between the rights of an accused for a fair trial and the rights of a victim for protection against the violation of her dignity. Closed door proceedings place an additional responsibility on the presiding judge to ensure this, as these proceedings are not open to public scrutiny. Within this constraint, the innovative survivor support programme of Majlis in Mumbai provides a ringside view of rape trials. It becomes an important social responsibility to share these insights with a wider readership in the hope of letting in a breath of fresh air within these cloistered spaces.

Double trauma

Apart from the actual incident of rape, what rape victims fear the most is the courtroom ordeal. What comes to mind is a slogan coined during the anti-rape campaign in the early 1980s in the context of the acquittal of two policemen. They were charged with the rape of a 16 year old tribal girl, who was poor, in a police station, and had termed her a liar as there were no marks of injury on her body. "She was raped twice, first by the police and than by the courts." This still holds true for many victims, despite the introduction of statutory changes and positive rulings of the Supreme Court. Within the hostile environment of a criminal court, the victim looks up to the judge to get the wrinkles out of what is a grueling process. It is the sensitivity displayed by the judge which alone can save the situation.

On this subject, trial court judges try to pass the buck on to defence lawyers saying that it is they who need to be sensitised. However, it is entirely up to the judge to take control of the situation. A confident judge well-versed in statutory provisions and positive rulings will be in a commanding position to maintain the dignity and decorum of the court; only those who lack in confidence will allow themselves to be cowed down by the intimidating tactics of defence lawyers.

Issue of victim's past

As an example, let me discuss the case of 16 year old *K*, a victim of gang rape which happened in the pre-amendment era. She was dragged out of her paying guest accommodation in a slum to a vacant room down the street and brutally raped by five men until she fell unconscious. The first information report (FIR) could be lodged after about a month, and after the Herculean efforts of a social worker. The plea by the defence was that *K* was the daughter of a sex worker. And as she had a boyfriend, she herself was of questionable character. This background provided ample scope for her humiliating cross-examination by five astute lawyers. However, the presiding judge remained firm, relying on the path-breaking Supreme Court ruling in *Gurmit Singh (1996)*, and did not permit any questions regarding the victim's past sexual history.

In that case, while overturning the verdict of the two lower courts, which had acquitted the accused in a case of the gang rape of a 16 year old schoolchild who had been kidnapped from her examination centre, the Supreme Court had ruled "Even in cases where there is some acceptable material on record to show that the victim was habituated to sexual intercourse, no such inference like the victim is a girl of 'loose moral character' is permissible to be drawn from the circumstances alone. No stigma, like the one as cast in the present case can be cast against such a witness, for after all, it is the accused and not the victim of sex crime who is on trial in the court."

The trial court judge ruled that questions regarding the credibility of the witness, or her past sexual history can no longer be entertained after this ruling. She further commented that it was not a case of complaint of sexual assault arising out of a love affair, but was a case of gang rape. The judge ensured that the deposition of the victim was concluded on the same day, even if it meant a sitting beyond the court timings. The case finally ended in a conviction, despite the lapses.

On child victims

Let us contrast this with the case of an eight-year old who lived in a lower class tenement, and sexually abused by a neighbour, a 26 year old man. the incident lasted barely 10 minutes as the child heard her mother calling out to her and began to scream. The girl experienced great trauma, and could not describe the incident even to her mother for two days.

During the trial, the child was cross-examined by a reputed criminal lawyer over three court dates, where her parents and she had to travel a distance of two hours each way. The busy lawyer either came late or pleaded his inability to complete the cross-examination as he had other matters to attend to. The court gave in to his request, disregarding the hardship being caused to the family of meagre means. the trial was in the designated Special Court, constituted under the Protection of Children from Sexual Offences (POCSO) Act, 2012, which stipulates special child-friendly trial procedures.

Throughout her deposition, the child, of a small build, was precariously perched on the ledge of the witness box, so that the presiding judge could see her and listen to her scared and muffled voice. This case too ended in conviction. The manner in which the two trials were conducted shows that there is a world of difference.

The Sakshi Guidelines (2004) stipulate that in cases concerning children, the defence lawyer must first submit the questions in writing to the judge, and the judge, at his/her discretion, ask only those questions which are relevant to the incident. But these guidelines are seldom followed.

We have also witnessed shocking instances of judges, under the compulsion of having to complete the trial within the stipulated time-frame, and in the absence of the defence lawyer, asking the accused to come forward and conduct the cross-examination. This is in total violation of the stipulation that the victim should never be made to face the accused during her deposition, and that a screen or a one-way mirror should be installed to shield her from the intimidating gaze of the accused.

Monitoring courts

Due to the presumption that a victim of sexual abuse would feel more at ease deposing before a lady judge, there is a stipulation that, as far as possible, only lady judges should be assigned to special courts. However, the belief that all lady judges are equally sensitive to victims, and that as a class, lady judges are more sensitive to victims of sexual crimes than men is not substantiated. It is not biology which determines sensitivity. Judges assigned to these courts must be specially exposed not only to statutory provisions but also to the mandatory protective measures that are required to be diligently followed before their assignment to these courts.

There is also a need to monitor the functioning of these courts and providing mechanisms of redress, in case of lapses. Closed-door trials cannot be construed as sacrosanct spaces beyond the scope of a social audit. Campaigners who were instrumental in bringing about these changes cannot abdicate their responsibility once the statute is enacted. The enactments are only the beginning of a long-drawn and challenging process.

Sessions courts are formidable and intimidating spaces meant for the police, criminals and their lawyers. To turn them into child-friendly spaces would require special ingenuity which those in charge of structuring these space usually lack. They need to be stripped of their high podiums, musty air and black coats and the space needs to be redesigned from the perspective of victims, especially children and those with disabilities.

Within their limitations, some judges have been using simple measures such as the setting up of a temporary screen or placing a cupboard in a manner so as to shield the victim during the deposition and allowing frequent breaks during the grueling process of cross-examination. (We have ccme across instances where victims have fainted during the deposition). Some judges also permit the victim to enter from the entrance meant for judges and allow them to wait in their own chambers until the matter is called out. These are small but significant gestures which will help ease the trauma of the victim.

Before one can understand, process operating in any system of law, the study of court structure is peremptory requirement. The legal system in the world are :

(1) Common law.—General custom, particular custom, laws affecting only the inhabitants of particular district or certain particular laws adopted and used by some particular court of U.K. and its erstwhile colonies.

(2) Civil law.—European legal systems of France, Germany, Spain etc.

(3) Islamic law.—Islamic Countries of Arab, Pakistan, Bangladesh and many new countries of erstwhile U.S.S.R. etc.

(4) Hindu law.—India, Nepal, Bhutan, Indonesia etc.

(5) Chinese law.—It applies to China, Hongkong and occupied Tibet.

(6) Soviet law.—It applies to many countries of erstwhile U.S.S.R.

Court structure throughout the world consists of highest court known as Supreme Court, High Courts and subordinate courts at local level. Court process depends on Constitution and the laws made.

The Jurisdiction, appointment procedure of the judges, independence of the judiciary, qualification and experience of those appointed in higher judiciary are regulated by law.

Court Structure in India

Supreme Court of India is the principal court of the Union Judiciary and High Courts are principal courts of State Judiciary, District judge is head of District judgeship. The entire judiciary is one. There is no distinction like federal or State judicial structure. Supreme Court is the highest court for the entire country. It hears appeals in civil and criminal matters. It has original jurisdiction. It has writ jurisdiction. Article 136 provides for special leave to appeal to Supreme Court. It has advisory jurisdiction. It is a court of record and has power to regulate its own procedure and has right to punish for contempt.

The Chief Justice and 30 judges are in Supreme Court. The door to Supreme Court is open only to lawmen, whether judges in High Courts or professors of law (jurists). The judges are elevated to Supreme Court on the recommendation of a collegium of Chief Justice and four senior judges of Supreme Court. Appointment is by President of India on the clearance of names recommended by the collegium by office of Prime Minister to satisfy the constitutional mandate that President would act on aid and advice of the cabinet. Age of retirement of a Supreme Court judge is 65 years. Appointment by collegium is being criticised on grounds of promoting inbreeding and nepotism. Judicial Commission is being advocated as substitute.

High Court judges are also appointed on the recommendation of like collegium of Chief Justice of India and two senior most judges of the Supreme Court. The names for elevation are sent by Government in the name of Governor. The recommendation is also by Chief Justice of that High Court and two senior most judges of that High Court. The Governor sends the names to Supreme Court on the aid and advice of his cabinet headed by the Chief Minister. Political interference counts much at this stage. The sources of elevation are the members of Bar and Service Judges from the Districts. The requirement is minimum 10 years' practice as an Advocate or experience as presiding officer in lower court. District Judges are elevated by seniority. The combination of Advocate and person having experience as lower court judge was expected to make High Court rich in expertise and experience. The arrangement has worked well but more unbiased elevation is required. Sons and spouses of sitting judges are getting elevation in many cases. On account of political effects in selection, it tends to damage independence of judiciary on one side and confidence of common man on the other. More transparent and merit based selection needs to be ensured. The 'collegium system' damages independence on account of wrong entries at the initial stage at the first entry point in the system.

A High Court judge retires at the age of 62 years. It is unfortunate that ex-judges of High Courts are re-appointed as Chairmen of many commissions and tribunals which does not create good impressions of these in mind of the common men. There is much race for these posts and judges in office commence lobbying for these while still in High Court. Some way out has to be found. This greed has been quite unethical in so far as many sitting judges even of the Apex Court have contested election for post of the President while still judge in Supreme Court. The Government has lobbied for sitting Supreme Court judge for a birth in ICJ. All these do not fit in well in the image of independence of judiciary that is in mind of common men.

Court structure in United Kingdom

The English legal system is organised : the two main branches of law; the personnel of the legal system and their roles; and the courts which make up the system. As court cases very often form the basis of stories, a knowledge of the system will help one to understand what is going on when we report on such stories, and will ensure that you use the right terminology when writing about court proceedings.

Types of Law

There are lots of different areas of law in terms of subject, but the most important divisions are between :

(1) Criminal and Civil Law; and

(2) Public and Private Law.

Criminal and civil law.—Criminal law deals with wrongs that are considered so serious as to be an offence against the whole community, and for this reason they are prosecuted in the name of the state (or specifically, the Queen). It is also possible to bring a private prosecution, but this happens relatively rarely.

Civil law covers everything else, from road accident victims suing for compensation or neighbours fighting over who owns a fence, to newspapers being sued for libel or companies disputing tax decisions by the HM Revenue & Customs.

In some case, the same course of action can lead to both a criminal and a civil case. For example, someone who injures another as a result of dangerous driving may be prosecuted for the crime of dangerous driving, and sued in the civil courts by the person injured.

Criminal and civil law use completely different sets of terminology, and it is important to know which terms apply to which area of law. Not only does it look ill-informed if you refer to, for example, being found guilty of negligence, it could potentially even be libellous, since you would be suggesting that someone had committed a criminal offence, when in fact negligence is a civil wrong, which is generally considered less serious.

Public and private law.—A second important distinction is between public and private law. Both public and private law are aspects of civil law.

Private law comprises disputes between individual parties, such as someone injured in an accident suing the person who caused it, or a celebrity suing a newspaper for libel.

Public law is the set of legal principles which govern the way public authorities, including the Government, use their powers. Public authorities cannot act just as they please, but can only exercise the powers given to them by law, and public law is designed to make sure these powers are not exceeded or misused. The main form of action in public law is the application for judicial review, which allows individuals (or organisations) to challenge the decisions or acts of public bodies.

Difference

Criminal Law	Civil Law
When a criminal case is brought against someone, that person is described as being charged with the offence; if the case comes to court, he/she is described as being prosecuted.	When a civil case is brought against someone that person is described as being sued.
Someone accused of committing a crime is called a defendant; the other side (acting for the Crown) is called the prosecution.	The person bringing the case is called the claimant and the person the claim is against is called the defendant.
Criminal cases are referred to in writing as *R* v. *xxxxx* (the name of the person being prosecuted), but in speech this would be read as 'The Queen against xxxxx' (R stands for Regina, Latin for queen).	Civil cases are described with the names of both parties (*e.g.*, *Smith* v. *Jones*), with the defendant's name first. In speech this would be read as 'Smith and Jones'.
If the prosecution wins its case, the defendant is described as being found guilty, or convicted.	If the claimant wins the case, the defendant can be described as having lost, or being held liable for the relevant wrong (*e.g.* libel, negligence). He or she should never be described as being found guilty of (for example) negligence or libel.
A convicted defendant is sentenced.	If the claimant wins, he or she will usually be awarded a remedy. This is most, often damages, which is a sum of money, but there are other civil remedies such as, for example, being reinstated in a job from which you have been wrongfully dismissed. You can say that the defendant had damages

awarded against him or her; you should never say that he or she was sentenced or fined.

Court System

- The Crown Court;
- The High Court;
- The Court of Appeal; and
- The Supreme Court.

The Crown Court only hears criminal cases and the country courts only civil ones, but the others hear both civil and criminal cases.

The courts form a hierarchical system, in which appeals can pass up through the courts, and decisions made in the higher courts have to be followed by those lower down. Traditionally, the House of Lords was the highest appeal court in the UK, but membership of the EU has meant the European Court of Justice is effectively the highest court for cases which concern EU law. In 2009, the House of Lords was replaced by the new Supreme Court, but for the purposes of this book, its role remains the same. The Supreme Court also hears appeals from some other countries within the Commonwealth; when it sits in such a case it is known as the Privy Council. The functions of each court, and the hierarchy of courts for appeal, are explained in Chapter 3, on criminal procedure, and Chapter 4, on civil procedure.

Supreme Court of England and Wales

Magistrate's Courts Act 1980, Supreme Court Act, County Courts Act 1984, Courts and Legal Services Act, Civil Procedure Act, 1997 and Criminal Justice Act 2000 are relevant Acts on courts in Britain.

Constitution Reforms Act, 2005 has established Supreme Court of Britain consisting of a President, Vice-President and 10 judges. House of Lords stands shorn of judicial functions. Lord Chancellor survives but only as minister of justice. Under the Act, Lord Chancellor needs not to be a lawyer.

Lord Chief Justice holds the office of the President of the Courts of England and Wales and is Head of Judiciary for these regions (except Scotland) : The independence of the judiciary is guaranteed by this Act.

Judicial Appointment Commission created by Act of 2005

The Act lays down detailed and elaborate procedure for selection and appointment of judges. The Commission provided for in the Act has started working. Baroness Usha Parashar is the first chairperson of the Commission. It is a significant step in setting up a transparent and robust method of appointing judges.

The special features of British judicial system are; organisations in constituents such as England, Wales, Scotland, Ireland are not the same, there are no administrative courts, there is no judicial review, there is jury system, High Court of justice and Supreme Court of Britain for England and Wales.

Court structure in U.S.A.

The **Law of the United States** comprises many levels of codified and uncodified forms of law, of which the most important is the United States Constitution, the foundation of the federal government of the United States. The Constitution sets out the boundaries of federal law, which consists of acts of Congress, treaties ratified by the Senate, regulations promulgated by the executive branch, and case law originating from the federal judiciary. The United States Code is the official compilation and codification of general and permanent federal statutory law.

Federal law and treaties, so long as they are in accordance with the Constitution, pre-empt conflicting state and territorial laws in the 50 U.S. States and in the territories. However, the scope of federal pre-emption is limited because the scope of federal power is not universal. In the dual-sovereign system of American federalism (actually tripartite because of the presence of Indian reservations), states are the plenary sovereigns, each with their own constitution, while the federal sovereign possesses only the limited supreme authority enumerated in the Constitution. Indeed, states may grant their citizens broader rights than the federal Constitution as long as they do not infringe on any federal constitutional rights. Thus, most U.S. law (especially the actual "living law" of contract, tort, property, criminal, and family law experienced by the majority of citizens on a day-to-day basis) consists primarily of state law, which can and does vary greatly from one state to the next.

At both the federal and state levels, the law of the United States is largely derived from the common law system of English law, which was in force at the time of the American Revolutionary War. However, American law has diverged greatly from its English ancestor both in terms of substance and procedure has incorporated a number of civil law innovations.

American common law

The United States and most Commonwealth countries are heirs to the common law legal tradition of English law. Certain practices traditionally allowed under English common law were expressly outlawed by the Constitution, such as bills of attainder and general search warrants.

As common law courts, U.S. Courts have inherited the principle of *stare decisis*. American judges, like common law judges elsewhere, not only apply the law, they also make the law, to the extent that their decisions in the cases before them become precedent for decisions in future cases.

The actual substance of English law was formally "received" into the United States in several ways. First, all U.S. states except Louisiana have enacted "reception statutes" which generally state that the common law of England (particularly judge-made law) is the law of the State to the extent that it is not repugnant to domestic law or indigenous conditions. Some reception statutes impose a specific cutoff date for reception, such as the date of a colony's founding, while others are deliberately vague. Thus, contemporary U.S. courts often cite pre-Revolution cases when discussing the evolution of an ancient judge-made common law principle into its modern form, such as the heightened duty of care traditionally imposed upon common carriers.

Second, a small number of important British statutes in effect at the time of the Revolution have been independently re-enacted by U.S. States. Two examples that many lawyers will recognize are the Statute of Frauds (still widely known in the U.S. by that name) and the Statute of Elizabeth (the ancestor of the Uniform Fraudulent Transfer Act). Such English statutes are still regularly cited in contemporary American cases interpreting their modern American descendants.

Federal Judiciary in U.S.A.

The judicial powers of the United States shall be vested in one Supreme Court and in such inferior courts as the Congress may from time to time ordain and establish. (Article 3 of U.S. Constitution). The Congress has passed Judiciary Act, 1789 which is the basis of federal judiciary in U.S.A.

Swiss Court Structure

The **federal judiciary** of Switzerland consists of the Federal Supreme Court, the Federal Criminal Court, the Federal Patent Court and the Federal Administrative Court. These Courts are charged with the application of Swiss Federal Law through the judicial process.

The Federal Supreme Court in Lausanne is established in the Swiss Federal Constitution as the supreme judicial authority of Switzerland. It is the court of appeal for all decisions of the cantonal courts of last instance, and also for most decisions of the three federal courts of first instance.

The Federal Criminal Court in Bellinzona tries the (relatively few) criminal cases subject to federal criminal jurisdiction, such as cases involving organised crime, terrorism and crimes against federal institutions. It also decides disputes between cantonal prosecuting authorities. The Federal Administrative Court in Berne reviews decisions made in application of federal administrative law that have been issued by federal and in some cases by cantonal authorities. The Federal Patent Court of Switzerland is a specialized court, which started hearing patent cases in 2012, taking jurisdiction from the cantonal courts.

It consists of 'Judges' and alternatives (Deputy Judges). This is done. No court higher, no court lower exists in Federal Judiciary. Federal Tribunal was created in 1874. The Tribunal has 30 judges and 15 alternatives (Deputy Judges). Both are elected by both Houses of Federal Assembly in Joint Session for 6 years. In practice, judges work till they like. No qualification for judges or alternatives (Deputy Judges) is prescribed. Anybody eligible for National Council of Federal Assembly may contest for judge or Alternatives in Federal Tribunal. Representation of all the three languages (German, French, Italian) has to be ensured when election is done.

The tribunal elects a President and a Vice-President for two years. The. salary of judges is 53000 yearly Swiss currency, President gets 3600 more than judges. Vice-President gets 2400 more than a judge. Deputy judges (alternatives) do not get any salary. They get allowance for each working day. After 60 years of age, pension is given to judges. The seat of Federal Tribunal is in French speaking canton Vaud's capital at Lausanne, as the seat of Federal Assembly and Federal Council is in German speaking canton at Berne.

Jurisdiction.—The tribunal has 3 divisions. Its decisions are executed by Federal Assembly.

For Civil Cases.—Conflicts amongst cantons or confederation and cantons and by private persons against these, matters of nationality, citizenship or amount exceeding 1000 Swiss Frances in between individuals, suits for debts, bankruptcy, copyright, industrial inventions, come in civil division.

For criminal cases.—For criminal cases, the tribunal holds 'assizes' at fixed centres. In one assize, three judges sit and are assisted by jury of 12 from nearby villages where it sits. Concurrence of 5 or 6 of the jury is necessary for conviction.

Four Chambers of Federal Tribunal.—For criminal cases, the court sits in 4 Chambers :

(i) Federal Criminal Court
(ii) Court of Accusation
(iii) Court of Cessation
(iv) Extraordinary Court of Cessation

For Constitutional Cases.—In conflict of competence of federal and cantonal authorities, federal contribution prevails over cantonal constitutions, the cantonal Constitutions prevail over ordinary laws, Disputes between Cantons *inter se* on public law, violation of Constitutional rights of the citizens, by federal or cantonal authorities, violations of International treaties and agreements, and political crimes.

For administrative cases.—Legal competence of public officials, Railways suits and taxation matters.

Appellate jurisdiction.—In matters upto 8000 Francs or above, the Federal Tribunal hears appeals from Cantonal Courts.

French Judiciary.—France has two separate sets of courts, ordinary and administrative.

The judicial system in Canada

Court system of Canada

The **court system of Canada** forms the judicial branch of government, formally known as **"the Queen on the Bench"**, which interprets the law and is made up of many courts differing in levels of legal superiority and separated by jurisdiction. Some of the courts are federal in nature while others are provincial or territorial.

The Canadian constitution gives the federal government the exclusive right to legislate criminal law while the provinces have exclusive control over civil law. The provinces have jurisdiction over the administration of justice in their territory. Almost all cases, whether criminal or civil, start in provincial courts and may be eventually appealed to higher level courts. The quite small system of federal courts only hears cases concerned with matters which are under exclusive federal control, such as federal taxation, federal administrative agencies, intellectual property, some portions of competition law and certain aspects of national security. The federal government appoints and pays for both the judges of the federal courts and the judges of the superior and appellate level courts of each province. The provincial governments are responsible for appointing judges of the lower provincial courts. Provincial administrative tribunals also comprise part of provincial courts. This intricate interweaving of federal and provincial powers is typical of the Canadian constitution.

Very generally speaking, Canada's court system is a four-level hierarchy from highest to lowest in terms of legal authority. Each court is bound by the rulings of the courts above them; however, they are not bound by the rulings of other courts at the same level in the hierarchy. Civil courts in Quebec, in particular, are under no obligation to apply judicial precedent—the principle of *stare decisis*—which is the general rule elsewhere in Canada. This is because Quebec's civil law is entirely codified, while civil law in the other nine provinces grew out of the English common law.

Outline of Canada's Court System

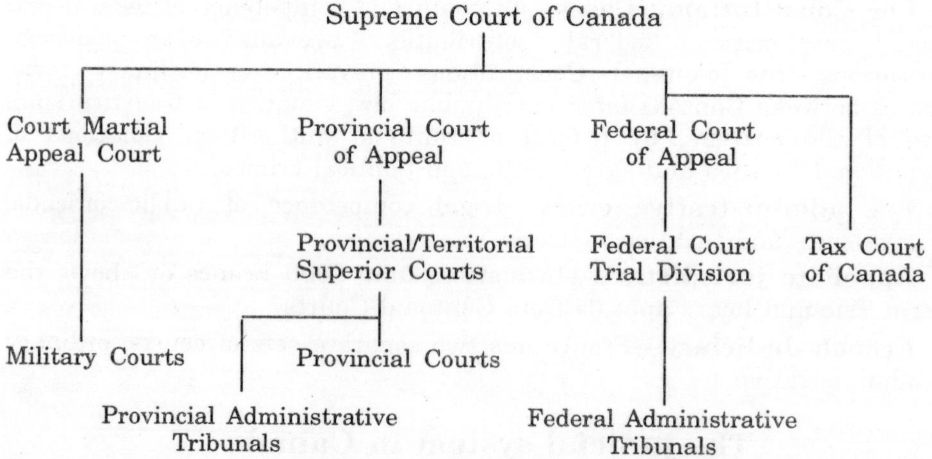

Court structure in Japan

In the **judicial system of Japan**, the Constitution of Japan guarantees that "all judges shall be independent in the exercise of their conscience and shall be bound only by this constitution and the Laws"

(Article 76). They cannot be removed from the bench "unless judicially declared mentally or physically incompetent to perform official duties", and they cannot be disciplined by executive agencies (Article 78). Supreme court judges, however, may be removed by a majority of voters in a referendum that occurs at the first general election following the judges' appointment and every ten years thereafter.

The judiciary was far more constrained under the Meiji Constitution than it is under the present Constitution and had no authority over administrative or constitutional law cases. Moreover, the Ministry of Justice had complete and direct control over the courts' administrative affairs. Nonetheless, Professor John Haley argues that the courts maintained complete independence in the adjudication of particular cases. "Judicial independence from the political branches was emphatically established as a fundamental principle of governance in Article 57 of the Meiji Constitution. Of all branches of government only the courts exercised authority "in the name of the Emperor." Haley argues that this was and remains a matter of great pride for Japanese judges and notes that "placed prominently in all courtrooms was the inscription "in the name of the Emperor" as a meaningful reminder to imperial officials and subjects alike that the Emperor's judges were not subject to political control or direction."

At the first of the four tiers of courts are the 438 summary courts (*kani saibansho*), staffed by 806 summary court judges. Summary court judges are not career judges. Qualification as a regular judge is not required. Instead, summary court judges are formally nominated for proforma cabinet appointment by a special selection committee formally comprising all Supreme Court justices, the President (*chokan*) of the Tokyo High Court, the deputy procurator general, representatives of the bar, and others "with special knowledge and experience. They mostly handle small claims civil cases (disputes not in excess of 1,400,000), as well as minor criminal offenses. They are only able to imprison defendants in a few special cases. Summary Courts are presided over by one judge. Civil cases in the Summary Court are appealed to the District Court, while criminal cases are appealed to the High Court.

At the second tier are the district courts (*chiho saibansho*), the principal courts of first instance. There are 50 district courts with additional 203 branches. Except for minor cases, which account for 80 to 90 percent of all adjudicated cases, trials require a three-judge panel. These are the courts of general jurisdiction and the principal court of first instance. District Courts have original jurisdiction in felony cases and in civil cases where the disputed amount is over 1,400,000. They also handle bankruptcy hearings. Each District Court trial is presided over by at least one judge : two associate judges are also called in for appellate cases from Summary or Family Courts, or for criminal cases where the maximum penalty would be in excess of 1 year in prison. Attorneys sit on either side of the courtroom, facing the center. In a criminal case, the accused faces the judges from the rear of the courtroom. The witness box is in the center, also facing the judges.

There are eight **High Courts** (*Koto-saiban-sho*). They (Sapporo, Sendai, Tokyo, Nagoya, Osaka, *Chiteki-zaisan-koto-saiban-sho*) in Tokyo, which is a special branch of Tokyo High Court. A High Court usually sits in the same manner as a three-judge District Court. Each court is led by a President, who is appointed by the Cabinet. An appeal to a High Court is called *koso*. The High Courts are appellate courts for either koso appeals from district court judgments, criminal judgments from summary courts, or, in civil cases tried initially in summary courts, second (jokoku) appeals limited to issues of law.

At the apex of the judicial hierarchy is the **Supreme Court** (Saiko saibansho), located adjacent to the National Diet Building. The "Grand Bench" *Daihotei*) of the Supreme Court has associate justices, who are appointed by the Cabinet with the Emperor's attestation. The Chief Justice is nominated by the Cabinet and appointed to office by the Emperor. The Grand Bench is subdivided into three "Petty Benches" (*Shohotei*) of five justices each, who hear incoming appeals and recommend them for an audience before the Grand Bench. An appeal to the Supreme Court is called *jokoku*, and requires either an error in the interpretation of the Constitution, or an error in the interpretation of case law from the Supreme Court or High Court.

In addition to these strata, there is also a **Family Court** (*Katei-saiban-sho*) tied to each District Court, as well as in over 200 branch offices throughout the country. Family Courts primarily deal with juvenile delinquency cases and divorce, although they have a broad jurisdiction that encompasses all forms of domestic disputes, including correcting koseki registration data and partitioning estates. If a settlement cannot be reached between the parties, the case is transferred to the District Court.

Court structure in China

Judiciary system of China

The judicial branch is one of three branches of government in the People's Republic of China, along with the executive and legislative branches. Strictly speaking, it refers to the activities of the People's Court system. The Chinese court system is based on civil law modeled after the legal systems of Germany and France, but with local characteristics.

Constitutionally, the court system is intended to exercise judicial power independently and free of interference from administrative organs, public organizations, and individuals. Yet the constitution simultaneously emphasizes the principle of the "leadership of the Communist Party."

Court structure

According to the Constitution of the People's Republic of China of 1982 and the Organic Law of the People's Courts that went into effect on January 1, 1980, the Chinese courts are divided into a four-level court system :

- At the highest level is the Supreme People's Court (SPC) in Beijing, the premier appellate forum of the land, which supervises the administration of justice by all subordinate "local" and "special" people's courts. It is the court of last resort for the whole People's Republic of China except for Macau and Hong Kong.

- Local people's courts—the courts of the first instance—handle criminal and civil cases. These people's courts make up the remaining three levels of the courts system and consist of "high people's courts" at the level of the provinces, autonomous regions, and special municipalities; "intermediate people's courts" at the level of prefectures, autonomous prefectures, and municipalities; and "basic people's courts" at the level of autonomous counties, towns, and municipal districts.
- Courts of Special Jurisdiction (special courts) comprises the Military Court of China (military), Railway Transport Court of China (railroad transportation) and Maritime Court of China (water transportation), and forestry.

The court system is paralleled by a hierarchy of prosecuting offices called people's procuratorates, the highest being the Supreme People's Procuratorate.

Hong Kong and Macau have separate court systems due to their historical status as British and Portuguese colonies, respectively.

Court structure in U.S.S.R.

Law of the Soviet Union

The **Law of the Soviet Union** was the law as it developed in the Soviet Union (USSR) following the October Revolution of 1917. Modified versions of the Soviet legal system operated in many Communist states following the Second World War—including Mongolia, the People's Republic of China, the Warsaw Pact countries of eastern Europe, Cuba and Vietnam.

The Soviet legal system regarded law as an arm of politics and courts as agencies of the government. Extensive extra-judiciary powers were given to the Soviet secret police agencies.

Soviet concept of law

Soviet law was rooted in pre-revolutionary Russian law and Marxism/Leninism. Pre-revolutionary influences included Byzantine law, Mongol law, Russian Orthodox Canon law, and Western law. Western law was mostly absent until the judicial reform of Alexander II in 1964, five decades before the revolution. Despite this, the supremacy of law and equality before the law were not well-known concepts, the tsar was still not bound by the law, and the "police had unlimited authority."

Marxism/Leninism viewed law as a superstructure in the base and superstructure model of society. "Capitalist" law was a tool of "bourgeois domination and a reflection of bourgeois values." Since law was a tool "to maintain class domination", in a classless society, law would inevitably disappear.

Like all other government institutions, the judiciary was officially subordinated to the Supreme Soviet of the Soviet Union.

Early Soviet law

In 1917, the Soviet authorities formally repealed all Tsarist legislation and established a socialist legal system This system abolished Western legal concepts including the rule of law, the civil liberties, the protection of law and guarantees of property. Crime was determined not as the infraction of law, but as any action which could threaten the Soviet state.

For example, profiteering could be interpreted as a counter-revolutionary activity punishable by death. The deportation of the 'Kulaks' in 1928-31 was carried out within the terms of Soviet Civil Code. Some Soviet legal scholars even asserted that "criminal repression" may be applied in the absence of guilt." Martin Latsis, chief of the Ukrainian Cheka explained :

> "Do not look in the file of incriminating evidence to see whether or not the accused rose up against the Soviets with arms or words. Ask him instead to which class he belongs, what is his background, his education, his profession. These are the questions that will determine the fate of the accused. That is the meaning and essence of the Red Terror."

The purpose of public trials was "not to demonstrate the existence or absence of a crime—that was predetermined by the appropriate party authorities—but to provide yet another forum for political agitation and propaganda for the instruction of the citizenry. Defense lawyers, who had to be party members, were required to take their client's guilt for granted..."

Post Stalin

Constitutional law

1. 1918 Soviet Russian Constitution
2. 1924 Soviet Constitution
3. 1936 Soviet Constitution
4. 1977 Soviet Constitution.

Court structure

Soviet criminal and civil cases involve trials that were "primarily official investigations of the truth of the claims and defenses presented." Soviet law is very similar in this respect to civil law of European countries like France and Germany.

Criminal cases

Criminal cases consisted of a preliminary examination before the indictment and the actual trial. In the preliminary examination, the *sledovatel* (or "investigator") "interrogated the accused and the witnesses and examined evidence." The accused was informed of his/her rights before the examination. Before 1958, counsel was only available during the trial. After 1958, counsel was available at the last stage of the preliminary examination after the accused was indicated. The examiner was prohibited from using force though the accused could be confined for long durations : up to 10 days before being charged, up to 9 months during the preliminary investigation (with the approval of the Procurator General) The testimony to be used in the trial was presented to the accused. The sledovatel was subordinate to the procurator (prokuratura) that was tasked with the prosecution, "general supervision of legality", and reporting illegal administrative actions. The indictment that included the preliminary examination was considered the "official record" at trial.

The trial court consisted of a professional judge with a 5 year term and two assessors (lay judges) from the population with a 2.5 years term. The proceedings were informal compared to United States standards. the judges first questioned accused and witnesses, then the procurator and defense counsel to corroborate the evidence in the indictment. The accused and the victim could question each other or the witnesses. The accused was presumed innocent, though not in the common law sense. The court decided by majority vote. The accused or the procurator could appeal decisions to a higher court consisting of three professional judges that reviewed the facts and the law. If the procurator appealed, the higher court could set aside the judgment and remand the case. Although the decision of the appeals court was "final", higher courts could review them as "supervision". Here, the accused or his/her counsel could submit briefs, but they could not appear in person.

During the trial, the judges had the additional responsibility of educating the people like revealing and removing the causes and conditions that led to the crime.

Judges kept legal technicalities to a minimum; the court's stated purpose was to find the truth, rather than to protect legal rights. Although most hearings were open to the public, hearings could also be held privately, if the Soviet Government deemed it necessary.

HIERARCHY OF COURTS—INDIA

'Hierarchy' is establishment of judicial set up from highest court to courts at lowest rung. In India, our Constitution establishes union judiciary (Chapter IV, Part V, Article 124 to 147) and State Judiciary (Chapter V, Part VI, Article 214-231).[1] Part V deals with three organs of Union; Executive (Chapter 1, Article 52-78), Parliament (Chapter II, Articles 78-122) and judiciary (Chapter IV, Articles 124-147). Part VI deals with three organs of State; Executive (Chapter II, Article 153-167), The State Legislature (Chapter III), Article 168-213) and the High Courts in States (Chapter V, Article 214-231).

Supreme Court

The Union judiciary consists of Supreme Court of India consisting of a

---

1. Article 231 and 232 (original) have been rewritten and included in Article 231 so there is no Article 232 now in Constitution; see 7th amendment 1956.

chief justice and of not more than 7 other judges. Parliament can prescribe a larger number of law. It has now been raised to 30. The judges shall be appointed by President by warrant under his hand and seal after consultation with such judges of Supreme Court or High Court, as President may deem necessary. There are no other courts in hierarchy as in Union Judiciary. In India, there is nothing like federal judicial structure. All courts and tribunals established by Central or State work under and are subordinate to the Supreme Court. Decisions of Supreme Court are law of the land and are binding on all.

High Courts

The High Courts of the States are highest courts of any State. In India, High Courts are : First chartered High Courts established by Separate charters issued by British Crown under Indian High Courts Act 1861, 2ndly, High Courts established under various Government of India Acts 1915, 1919, or 1935, 3rdly High Courts established under Article 214 of Constitution of India 1950.

The jurisdiction of three chartered High Courts (Kolkata, Chennai, Mumbai)[1] is regulated by Three charters that established them. All the three have identical jurisdictions; original as well as Appellate jurisdictions. In addition, they have all those jurisdictions that are conferred by Constitution of India, 1950. All High Courts established by or under Government of India Acts owe their birth to various letter patents. High Courts under Constitution of 1950 have been established by Government Notifications.

District Judiciary

District judge is constitutional position in District judiciary. Subordinate to him are various civil courts criminal courts, revenue Courts and special courts and tribunals. The constitution and jurisdiction, appointment, terms and conditions of service of the presiding officers of these courts and tribunals are regulated by separate provincial acts. For example courts in U.P. work under Agra and Oudh Civil Court's Act. The tribunals work under Acts. These are established. For example tribunals Service Tribunal (CAT or SAT) under Administration Tribunals Act, 1985. Hierarchy is helpful in study of judicial process in any country.

Common law system are represented by England and India and Civil law system by France and Germany. The main difference is that in common law, there is nothing like Administrative Courts and in civil law, these occupy the same position as is accorded to ordinary law courts, but with separate hierarchy.

Hierarchy of Courts—England.

There are civil courts and criminal courts.

(1) Civil Court

In civil system there is a county court in every district.

---

1. The names of cities are changed as above, However, High Courts retain their old names like Calcutta, Madras and Bombay.

1. County Courts and Magistrate Court.—At the bottom are *County Courts and Magistrate Courts.* County Court is court of first instance but it has a limited power within a particular district.

Magistrate Courts are essentially a criminal court but in certain minor disputes, the magistrate court tries the cases of civil nature also.

2. High Courts

(i) Single Judge.—High Courts have an unlimited jurisdiction for trying a case. It can try a case of any value. It has original as well as appellate jurisdiction. It is the appellate court after *magistrate and county courts.* Its original jurisdiction is divided among three branches :

(a) King's bench.
(b) Queen's bench.
(c) Chancery division (Probate, Divorce and Admirality divisions).

(ii) Divisional Courts.—In certain cases the appellate jurisdiction of High Court vests to the Divisional Court. It is also a branch of High Court.

3. Court of Appeal.—It has only appellate jurisdiction. It hears appeals from High Court, County Court and Divisional Courts.

4. House of Lords.—It was at the top and was called highest court of England. It had appellate jurisdiction only since 1948, House of Lords heard appeal by way of petition from the judgments of court of appeal, court of sessions in England and court of appeal in Northern Ireland. The decision of House of Lords was final. Before 1948 it heard the cases of Peers and Lords. Now by Constitution Reform Act, 2005, it is shorn of all judicial powers. The Lord Chancellor remains only a minister in the Cabinet and House of Lords an Upper Chamber in British Parliament.

5. Supreme Court of England.—By Constitution Reforms Act, 2005, Supreme Court has been established for England and Wales at the place of House of Lords, which has ceased to have judicial powers. All powers of House of Lords, have now, been transferred to the new Supreme Court, which consists of a President, Vice-President and 10 judges.

(2) Criminal Court's Hierarchy

1. Magistrate's Courts or Courts of Petty Sessions.—It is the lowest Court. The summary jurisdiction of all kinds of criminal cases are first tried by Magistrate's Court. Magistrate's Court tries cases committed by minors. It has power to punish upto *one month imprisonment and £ 100 as fine.* When two or more *magistrates sit to decide the case, it is known as the court of petty session.*

2. Court of quarter sessions.—The Court of quarter sessions has appellate and original jurisdiction. It hears appeal from Magistrate Courts. It has original jurisdiction in the offences that are *serious in nature. It sits with the jury.* It is comprised of minimum *of two judges.*

3. Assize Courts.—Assize Court is said to the part of High Court and tries very serious offences, that is, indictable offences and it is constituted by the judges of the High Court.

4. Queen's Bench division.—Queen's Bench is essentially an appellate court although it has original jurisdiction too. It hears appeals in certain cases from the quarter session.

5. The Court of Criminal Appeal.—It is essentially an appellate court and it hears appeals from Assize Courts and is constituted by a bench of *three judges*.

6. House of Lords.—It was a final court. It had only appellate jurisdiction. It heard appeals from the Court of Criminal Appeal provided requisite leave was obtained. Now Supreme Court of England has been established since 2005. The powers of Court are no longer in the House of Lords.

Doctrine of Stare Decisis (Precedents) in England.—Following rules are laid down.

I. All the Courts in England were bound by the decisions of *House of Lords till 2005*. It was held earlier by House of Lords that it is bound by its previous decisions but in 1966 in the case *Chancery Lane Safe Deposit etc. Co.* v. *Ireland Revenue Commissioner*,[1] it has been observed by the court that the House of Lords can reject its previous decision in the following circumstances.

(a) Where principle is obscure;

(b) Where decision is out of line with other authorities or established principles;

(c) Where principle is much wider than was necessary for the decision;

II. Court of appeal in both civil and criminal cases is bound by its previous decisions.

III. A division Court of Queen's bench division is bound to follow its previous decision.

IV. A High Court is *not bound* by its own decisions nor it is bound by the decision of another High Court.

V. The lower courts of first instance do not create binding precedents and all the lower courts are bound by the judgments of higher one.

Hierarchy of courts in India.

In India the following courts are working at present :—

(a) Revenue Courts

(i) Courts of Naib Tahsildar

(ii) Court of Tahsildar and Additional Tahsildars

(iii) Court of Deputy Collector/Sub-divisional officers

(iv) Court of Chief Revenue Officers

(v) Court of Ziladhikari (Collector) and Additional Collector (Deputy Commissioner)

(vi) Commissioner/Additional Commissioners

1. 1 All. E.R. 1960 at p. 1 Lord Reid and Upjohn L.J. *See* Policy statement of the House of Lords.

(vii) Board of Revenue

(b) Civil Courts

All States have separate civil courts below District judges. Civil judge (junior division) is the lowest court in U.P. It has jurisdiction upto Rs. 25000/- in U.P. This Court is established under Agra and Awadh Civil Courts Act. Above, it is civil judge (senior division) with unlimited jurisdiction. Court of District Judge is the first appellate court. High Court is second appellate court. Special appeals lie to Supreme Court under Article 136 or Section 109 of Code of Civil Procedure. Code of Civil Procedure mentions chartered High Courts (Order 49). Provincial small causes Courts (Section 7) (Order 50) and Presidency small cause Courts (Order 51) (Section 8).

(i) District Judge.—Under Agra and Awadh Civil Courts Act, District Judge is the first appellate court. This court has special jurisdiction under some special Acts. Hierarchy of Courts elsewhere are regulated by other Acts. District judge is everywhere as its establishment is controlled by the Constitution of India.

(ii) High Court.—Every State has one High Court. Many High Courts have more than one bench. Common High Court for two or more States is possible. It hears appeals from District Judge in civil and criminal cases. By Article 226 (Judicial review) Article 227 (Power of superintendence) is vested in High Courts. Section 3 of the Code of Civil Procedure deals with subordination of Courts. It provides that for purposes of C.P.C., the District Court is subordinate to the High Court and every civil court of a grade inferior to that of District Judge and every Court of small causes, is subordinate to the High Court and the District Court. District judge presides over Court of District and Sessions judge.

The expression District Judge according to Article 236 of the Constitution of India, includes judge of a city civil Court, Additional District Judge, Joint District Judge, Assistant District Judge, Chief Judge of Small Cause Court, Chief Presidency Magistrate, Additional Chief Presidency Magistrate, Sessions Judge, Additional Sessions Judge and Assistant Sessions Judge.

Civil appeals to High Court

Second Appeal (after disposal of first appeal filed before District Judge under Section 96) lies to High Court under Section 100 of Code of Civil Procedure. On satisfaction of the High Court that the appeal involves substantial question of law and on no other ground, the substantial question involved shall be precisely stated in memo of appeal. If High Court is Appellant, the High Court shall itself formulate that question. The appeal shall be heard only on the question so framed. However, with permission of Court, any other point can also be argued.

Civil Appeals to Supreme Court

Civil Appeal to Supreme Court lies only on a certificate issued by a High Court that (a) the case involves a substantial question of law of general importance; (b) in the opinion of High Court, the said question needs to be decided by the Supreme Court. No appeal against single judge decision of High Court lies to Supreme Court unless the Parliament by law provides otherwise.

(c) Criminal Courts

Petty crimes are tried by the Magistrate's court for the first time and an appeal can lie in Session's Court. Serious crimes are investigated by the Magistrate at the first instance then they are committed to the Session's Court for trial. Then appeal can lie to High Court but death sentence must be confirmed by the High Court. In certain circumstances under Article 134 of the Indian Constitution an appeal can lie to Supreme Court against a decision of a High Court in criminal matters. (when death sentence is confirmed by High court).

Hierarchy of the Criminal Courts

Subordinate Criminal Courts are—(Section 6 Cr.P.C.)

1. Courts of Magistrates
2. Courts of Session
3. High Court
4. Supreme Court

Section 6 of Criminal Procedure Code, enumerates four classes of criminal courts—

1. Court of Sessions (Sections 9 and 10).—Every State shall be a Session Division or shall consist of Session divisions; and every Session Division shall be a District or consist of Districts. Every metropolitan area, shall be a separate Session division and District.

It is open to a State Government by notification to declare any town or city whose population exceeds one million to be a metropolitan area.

One Sessions Court shall be established for every Session Division by the State Government. It shall be presided over by a judge to be appointed by High Court, Additional and Assistant Sessions Judges can also be appointed likewise.

2. Court of Judicial Magistrate (Section 11).—In every district, except Metropolitan area, the State Government with consultation of High Court may establish Courts of judicial Magistrate first class or of second class as may be thought proper. The number and place shall be worked out by State Government and High Court of that State.

3. Chief Judicial Magistrate and Additional Chief Judicial Magistrate (Section 12).—High Court shall appoint any judicial Magistrate of first Class to be Chief Judicial Magistrate for that District. Additional Chief Judicial Magistrate shall also be appointed by High Court in like manner.

4. Special Judicial Magistrate (Sections 13-15).—On request of Government, Central or State, the High Court may confer power of Magistrate first class or second class on any person in respect of particular cases or classes of cases. This power of special judicial Magistrate can be given only to a person who holds or has held any post in the Government. It is also necessary that such person possesses the qualification or experience in relation to legal affairs as rules may require. Such Magistrate can be appointed only for one year at a time. The local limit of area of Special Judicial Magistrate shall be decided by C.J.M. subject to control of High Court.

Chief Judicial Magistrate shall be subordinate to Sessions Judge and all other Magistrates shall be subordinate to C.J.M.

Metropolitan cities (Sections 16-18).—Courts of Metropolitan Magistrates shall be established by State Government in consultation with High Court. The High Court shall appoint the presiding officer in these Courts. Any out of these, shall be appointed by High Court as Chief Metropolitan Magistrate (Equivalent to C.J.M.) and additional chief metropolitan Magistrates. Special Metropolitan Magistrates can also be appointed like special judicial Magistrates.

5. Executive Magistrates (Sections 20 to 23).—Executive Magistrates (Section 20) special Executive Magistrates (Section 21) are appointed by State Government in every district and Metropolitan area and one of them shall be appointed District Magistrate. The High Court is not consulted. Any out of these executive Magistrate shall be appointed Additional District Magistrate.

State Government may appoint, any of these executive Magistrates to be Special Executive Magistrates for particular area and for performance of particular function.

High Court

There shall be a High Court for each State (Article 214). It shall be Court of Record (Article 215). Every judge of High Court shall be appointed by President. (Article 217) Article 227 gives power to every High Court to issue certain writs (226) and Article 227 vests power of superintendence in High Court over all Courts in State. Article 231 provides that common High Courts for two or more States can be established.

Power of High Courts in Criminal Cases

Confirmation of death sentence.—Section 366 Cr.P.C. provides that in case of death sentence, it shall not be executed until confirmed by High Court. All records shall be sent by Sessions Court to High Courts. The High Court may direct further enquiry to be made or additional evidence to be taken if it is to be satisfied on any point on innocence or guilt of the convicted person. It may confirm or annul conviction. (Section 368).

Appeal.—Sections 372-394 deal with appeals—

(a) Appeals from conviction (Section 374).

(b) Appeal by State—

(i) On grounds of inadequate sentence (377).

(ii) Against acquittal (378).

(c) Appeal to Supreme Court (Section 379).

Reference (Section 395).—Section 395 provides for reference in criminal cases.

Revision (Section 397).—Section 397 read with Section 401 provides for revision.

Transfer of case.—By Supreme Court (Section 406) : By High Court (Section 407), By Sessions Judge (Section 408). These provisions deal with transfer of cases.

Supreme Court.[1]—Article 124 provides that there shall be a Supreme Court of India which is the highest court in judicial system. It has original and exclusive jurisdiction in matters of Union and State disputes or inter state disputes. Article 32 provides that Supreme Court can enforce fundamental rights of the citizens and it can issue prerogative writs and orders for this purpose. A citizen can directly move to Supreme Court in case of violation of his fundamental rights. Article 32 is itself a fundamental right and remedy both at the same time.

Article 133 deals with jurisdiction of the Supreme Court in civil matters. Article 134 deals with appellate jurisdiction of the Supreme Court in criminal matters. The appeal in Supreme Court under Article 134 lies—

(a) if High Court reverses the acquittal by Sessions Court and awards death sentence.

(b) has withdrawn trial from Session to itself and has given death sentence by itself in trial.

(c) certifies that case is fit for appeal either :—

(i) on its own motion, or

(ii) on oral application of convict or on his behalf.

In its appellate jurisdiction, the Supreme Court is the final interpreter of the Constitution. It is the highest appellate court in civil and criminal matters. Under Article 136 Supreme Court possesses a special jurisdiction over all judicial and quasi-judicial tribunals except armed forces tribunals, it can hear special appeals against the decisions of such tribunals and its decisions are final in such matters. Article 143 vests in Supreme Court an advisory jurisdiction. The President may refer to it a question of law or fact which has arisen or which is likely to arise. The Court after such hearings as it thinks fit may report its opinion to the President. But such opinions are not legally binding. Besides, the Supreme Court is a Court of Record with a power to punish for contempt of itself. While overruling its previous decision in a constitutional matter, the Supreme Court can lay down that such overruling would not have retrospective operation and such decision shall apply in future cases.

Doctrine of *stare decisis* in India.[2]—Article 141 of the Constitution declares that the law declared by the Supreme Court shall be binding on all courts within territory of India. Thus no court, including High Court, in India can disregard the decisions of Supreme Court. Here we find, like

1. Constitution of India, 1950.
2. Constitution of India, 1950.

England, that decisions of the Highest Court have compulsive nature of binding force. Every court in India is bound to follow the decisions of the Supreme Court. But it may be noted that Supreme Court is not bound by its own previous decisions. In case of *Bengal Immunity Co.* v. *State of Bihar*,[1] the Supreme Court laid down that it can reconsider its own previous decision and it can reverse it. Thus, the Supreme Court has power to rectify its own previous errors. In fact Supreme Court has reversed its decisions in *Shankari Prasad*[2] and *Sajjan Singh*'s,[3] case in *Golaknath*'s[4] and the latter in *Kesavanand Bharti*'s case.

High Courts are bound by the decisions of the Supreme Court and they are also bound to follow the decisions of Privy Council (before 1949 the Privy Council was the highest appellate court for India) unless reversed by the Supreme Court or repealed by the Legislature. A bench decision of High Court is not binding on another bench. However, one bench cannot overrule decision of equal number of judges bench even if it does not agree. It needs not to follow that. But if so, the file shall go to the Chief Justice, for constituting larger bench to decide the conflict. The decisions of High Court are binding on all subordinate courts within that State. The decision of other High Courts have only persuasive force or authority.

The Supreme Court of India enjoys powers and jurisdiction wider than the British Supreme Court in England or the Federal Supreme Court of the United States. Even the appellate jurisdiction of this Court is wider than that of any of those courts. Apart from having all the jurisdiction of the Privy Council which devolved upon it through the Federal Court, the Supreme Court has also power to entertain appeals from all final orders and judgments of the High Court passed under Articles 226 and 227 of the Constitution and possesses an unlimited power under Article 136—a power which none of those Courts possess to entertain appeal, by special leave in any cause or matter determined by any Court or tribunal whatever in India save the military tribunals.

Similarly, while civil appeals from the court of appeal in England go to the House of Lords (now British Supreme Court since 2005) only *by leave* and not otherwise an appeal lies to our Supreme Court as *of right* under the provision of Article 133(1) of the Constitution. Also in criminal matters, an appeal to the House of Lords (earlier to year 2005) formerly lay only if the *Attorney-General granted a certificate* of law of exceptional public importance being involved and now lies only by leave of the court granted on the ground of some point of law of general importance being involved. Whereas in some cases as specified in Article 134(1) of our Constitution that is death sentence, an appeal lies to Indian Supreme Court as of right. The jurisdiction of Supreme Court of United States is, unlike that of Indian Supreme Court confined to causes arising out of federal jurisdiction or relating to validity of federal laws. The Supreme Court of India has on the other hand, not only

1. A.I.R. 1955 S.C. 661.
2. A.I.R. 1951 S.C. 458.
3. A.I.R. 1965 S.C. 845.
4. A.I.R. 1967 S.C. 1643.

ultimate say on question of both Central and State laws but, also review matters which the U.S.S.C. would regard as non-reviewable. Indian Supreme Court has broader powers also over subordinate courts than the Supreme Court of the U.S.A. has over the remaining courts of that country.

It is also to be noted that Supreme Court of India is not only the ultimate court of appeal but also an invincible instrument against all oppressions and stands as the guardian and sentinel of liberty and fundamental rights of the citizens. No court or tribunal ever established in this country possessed such a wide and plenary authority, commanded such a great respect and inspired so much awe in the heart of an oppressor, as the Supreme Court.

Hierarchy of Courts in France

The most distinctive feature of the French court system is its division into Regular and Administrative Courts. This division arises precisely from the fact that the French legal system distinguishes between the Administration and the judiciary. The case which affects an administrative official or in which State is a party with the exception of criminal cases are tried by administrative court but the disputes between the individual in the form of civil cases and those in which a person is accused in the form of criminal cases are tried before the regular court.

The French Constitutional Council

In France, judges are considered civil servants exercising one of the sovereign powers of the state, and, accordingly, only French citizens are eligible for judgeship. France's independent judiciary enjoys special statutory protection from the executive branch. Procedures for the appointment, promotion, and removal of judges vary depending on whether it is for the judicial, administrative, or audit court stream. Judicial appointments must be approved by a special panel, the High Court of the Judiciary, made up of other judges from the receiving court. Once appointed, judges serve for life and cannot be removed without specific disciplinary proceedings conducted before the Council with due process.

The Ministry of Justice handles the administration of courts and the judiciary, including salaries or constructing new courthouses. The Ministry also funds and administers the prison system. Lastly, it receives and processes applications for presidential pardons and proposes legislation dealing with matters of civil or criminal justice. The Minister of Justice is also the head of public prosecution, though this is controversial since it is seen to represent a conflict of interest in cases such as political corruption against politicians.

At the basic level, the courts can be seen as organized into :

- ordinary courts (*ordre judiciaire*), which handle criminal and civil litigation;
- administrative courts (*ordre administratif*), which supervise the government and handle complaints.

The structure of the French judiciary is divided into three tiers :

- Inferior courts of original and general jurisdiction
- Intermediate appellate courts which hear cases on appeal from lower courts
- Courts of last resort which hear appeals from lower appellate courts on the interpretation of law.

Procedural

While in Germanic Europe the Supreme Courts can and do tend to write more verbose opinions supported by legal reasoning, the typical Francophone court of cassation decision is short, concise and devoid of explanation or justification. There is no *stare decisis*, or principle of precedent, binding lower courts to respect superior courts' rulings (case law) on questions of law; but a line of similar case decisions, while not precedent *per se*, forms the *jurisprudence constante*.

Criminal

Public offenses are categorized as :

- *crimes*, serious felonies, which are heard by the Assize Court (*cour d'assises*);
- *delits*, less serious felonies and misdemeanors, which are heard by the Criminal Court (*tribunal correctionnel*, also called the Correctional Court);
- *contraventions*, minor offenses and violations, which are heard by the Police Court (*tribunal de police*, also called the Police Tribunal).

For petty misdemeanors like most traffic violations, suspected offenders may either plea nolo contender and pay a set fine amount (*amende forfaitaire*) or contest the charge in court. The court may then find the defendant innocent or guilty, but if found guilty, they are liable to be sentenced a higher fine.

Constitutional Council

The Constitutional Council (*Conseil Constitutionnel*) practices judicial review of legislative acts and laws. The ordinary and administrative courts have refused to perform this type of judicial review, outside of 2 exceptions in 1951. It supervises controversies of elections and performs judicial review by determining the constitutionality of parliamentary legislation.

Court of Audit

The financial courts—national Court of Audit (*cour des comptes*) and regional audit courts (*chambres régionales des comptes*)—have jurisdiction to try cases involving possible misuse of public funds, and, in some rare instances, of private funds.

They are empowered and mandated by Article 15 of the 1789, Declaration of the Rights of Man and of the Citizen which set forth that French citizens have the right to hold public officers, agents, and officials accountable for the finances they oversee and operate. The courts' roles and responsibilities are laid out in the Financial Court Code.

Ordinary Courts in France

Before the civil or criminal cases go to the regular courts for trial, the French legal system provides a means of reducing the number of cases. The system is a part of regular courts. The entire complaint is attended by members of special courts whose personnel are not magistrates. They are concerned more with the conciliation and arbitration rather than adjudication.

Court Structure in U.S.A.

The United States Court System

Supreme Court of the United States

- United States Courts of Appeals 12 Circuits
  - 94 District Courts Including 3 Territorial : Guam, Virgin Islands & Northem
  - United States Tax Court
- United States Court of Appeals for the Federal Circuits
  - United States Court of International Trade
  - United States Claims Court
  - United States Court of Veterans Appeals
- United States Court of Military Appeals
  - Army, Navy Marina, Corps Air Force and Coast Guard Courts Of Military Review

❑ ❑

Chapter 4

Creativity of the Judicial Process and Precedents

When a judge does not have any provision in constitution to assist him in deciding case before him, he does not have any statute on the point to help him in deciding the case, what he would do, where he will go, what would help him so that he not only disposes of the case before him but does it with confidence that it would not result in compromising his judgeship, his acumen as lawyer, his training and the public confidence that exists in him and the court he is called upon to preside. He should also maintain his integrity in the mind of the losing party.

Search of precedent is research

It is here that precedents come to his rescue. They may be stored in his mind or hidden in law books or law reports. Precedents are not ultimate and final determinants. These carry along with, in their background, the basic juridical conceptions which are postulates of judicial reasoning. In the background of precedent, we find life, further deep; a little more deep, we get institutions of society in which those conceptions (enshrined in precedent) had their origin and which by process of interaction, they have modified in turn.

The legislative Court

In *Koushal* v. *Naz*, a two-judge bench of the Supreme Court overturned a 2009 decision of the Delhi High Court decriminalizing sodomy by Section 377 of the Indian Penal Code. In doing so, it has recriminalised every Indian who has ever had oral or anal sex (irrespective of the gender of the person they had it with, and irrespective of consent).

Koushal represents two structural failures of the Supreme Court, at least one of which has sometimes been commended as a great success by some commentators. The first structural failure is the near-total abandonment by the Supreme Court of the principle of separation of powers, and its transformation into a populist, legislative court of governance. The second failure, one that flows from the first one, is the court's routine dereliction of its duty to give reasons for its decisions. Let me explain both of these failures in turn, and how they have facilitated the decision in *Koushal*.

Playing to the gallery

In *Koushal*, the court could barely conceal its disdain when it described lesbians, gays, bisexuals and transgendered people as "a minuscule fraction of the country's population" with "so-called rights". This may seem bizarre to those of us who believe that one of the primary functions of unelected constitutional courts is the protection of vulnerable minorities from majoritarian excesses. Clearly, a "minuscule" minority should be of particular concern to a counter-majoritarian institution.

The court's position is easier to fathom if understood in the context of its history following the Emergency imposed by Indira Gandhi. During the Emergency, the court agreed to the suspension of *Habeas Corpus*, a fundamental right against the arbitrary detention of citizens by the state. After the Emergency, the court started to reinvent itself to gain institutional legitimacy. This reinvention was, however, not in terms of pitting itself against the representative organs of the state, but by *competing* with these organs. The process, which began in the 1980s, only intensified in the 1990s which saw an end to one-party-dominance in politics. Coalition politics and weak legislatures remain a feature of our politics to this day. The court, in the meantime, became a populist institution of governance—stepping in to fill the void left by an increasingly dysfunctional Parliament. In a country where the majority of the population suffers significant disadvantage, majoritarianism can often become aligned with "progressive" politics. A majoritarian court continued to play to the gallery and wreaked havoc on the principle of separation of powers.

It should not surprise us that this majoritarian populist institution found it impossible to respect the "so-called" rights of a "minuscule" minority. Of course, our courts have sometimes stood up for minority rights. So has Parliament. What matters here is the self-image the court has been allowed to cultivate, which overwhelmingly determines its institutional course of action. This self-image is not that of a counter-majoritarian institution correcting the excesses of democracy, but one that is acutely conscious of the reception of its judgments by the people (such consciousness extends only to the outcome of a case, not its reasoning). Under this model, if representative bodies did a good job of representing the people, the courts would be unnecessary. The court is a political actor, which wants to be judged as politicians are judged. Its legitimacy rests on popular acceptance, not constitutional mandate.

This political context explains, rather than complicates, how the bench in *Koushal* suddenly discovers the joys of separation of powers. The court first extends the presumption of constitutionality to a pre-constitutional colonial law by suggesting that the democratic Parliament has "adopted" it by failing to amend it. It specifically mentions a 2013 legislation amending the law dealing with sexual assault as proof that "the legislature has chosen not to amend the law or revisit it", ignoring completely the fact that there was no need for Parliament to do so after the Delhi High Court had read down Section 377 to exclude private sex between consenting adults from its ambit. That the 2013 legislation was enacted after the hearing in *Koushal* was concluded, thereby of forbidding no opportunity to the parties to challenge its use by the court, is another matter.

This ostensible deference to democratic will is an opportunistic fig leaf of a populist court with little more than contempt for the representative institutions of democracy. In an act of concluding magnanimity to the legislature, the final sentence of the judgment grants it permission to consider the "desirability and propriety of deleting section 377". The fact that it thought such a clarification was necessary tells us that this is not a court deferential to the legislature—this is a court with unhesitant pretensions of being the legislature.

Duty to give reasons

A key feature of adjudication is the public articulation of reasons after hearing principled submissions by the parties involved, on the basis of which a judge arrives at her decisions. In this respect, adjudication differs from voting, which allows a decision maker to decide without having to articulate her reasons (or even without having any reason). The following factual inaccuracies, unsupported conclusions, and omissions in the judgment are particularly noteworthy in this regard.

(a) The court records the government of India's position on the case as one defending the criminal provision under review. This, despite the fact that the government had chosen not to appeal the High Court ruling and its top lawyer—the Attorney General of India—had clearly told the bench that the government supported the High Court's decriminalisation of adult consensual sex. Remarkably, the court describes the Attorney General as "amicus". The suggestion in the judgment that the Attorney General was simply a friend of the court appearing in his personal capacity forced him to publicly clarify that he had very much represented the government's official position in the case.

(b) The court found itself able to ignore the voluminous material placed before it to conclude that there was no evidence to show that "homosexuals, gays, *etc.*, are being subjected to discriminatory treatment either by State or its agencies or the society."

(c) Long-standing precedent is clear that Article 14 (right to equality) of the Constitution requires every legal classification to be based on an intelligible differentia and have a rational nexus with a legitimate state objective. The court, while repulsing the Article 14 challenge, finds it sufficient to say that the classification between "those who indulge in carnal intercourse in the ordinary course and those who indulge in carnal intercourse against the order of nature" is intelligible. It wastes no ink trying to identify the state objective being pursued, or asking whether the measure has any nexus with that objective.

(d) Even this half-hearted attempt to give reasons is not made when rejecting the Article 15 (right against discrimination) challenge. No reasons whatsoever are provided.

(e) The way the court deals with the challenge under Article 21 (the right to life and liberty) is even more curious. After devoting several paragraphs quoting established precedents on Article 21,

> the court makes no specific finding with respect to Article 21 After these block quotations, the court moves seamlessly to simply assert that the use of Section 377 to "perpetrate harassment, blackmail and torture" is "neither mandated by the section nor condoned by it." How the preceding six paragraphs setting out the established doctrine under Article 21 help the Court reach this conclusion, and how this conclusion repels the Article 21 challenge, is anybody's guess.

The hearing in the case concluded in March 2002, and the judgment was delivered in December 2013, the day before the senior judge on the bench was due to retire. A cavalier attitude to its duty to give reasoned judgments is not uncommon in the court's jurisprudence. Although unfortunate, this is hardly surprising. The pressure of its workload also results in the constitutional requirement that any constitutional case involving a substantial question of law must be heard by at least five judges (Article 145) being routinely ignored (including in *Koushal*). Only 0.12 per cent of all cases disposed of by the court between 2005 and 2009 were decided by a bench of five judges or more.

Given such volume, what is surprising is the respectable number of cases where our judges do manage to give reasoned judgments. The fragmentation of the court into small benches deciding thousands of cases every year had led to a situation where even a conscientious judge would find it next to impossible to respect *stare decisis*, the duty of the court to apply previous decisions (*i.e.*, precedents). For less conscientious judges, the opportunity to cherry pick precedents is limitless.

Furthermore, the academy simply cannot keep up with the judicial assembly line. Academic criticism is the real check on judicial power in a democracy. In the Indian context, academics are forced to focus on the outcome of the cases alone—only a handful of cases (like *Koushal*) that really stand out receive proper academic attention. The outrage that this judgment has inspired among politicians, activists and academics presents an opportunity to rethink the fundamental structural weaknesses of the Indian Supreme Court. Most of the recent debate on the reform of the court has focussed on changing the appointment system of judges (currently, the court appoints its own judges) and dealing with the lack of diversity in the judiciary. While who gets to be a judge is an important issue, unless these structural infirmities are addressed, even Herculean judges cannot change the situation very much. The court needs to reaffirm its central counter-majoritarian purpose in a liberal democracy. It must do less and do it well. It must stop voting and stick to adjudicating.

Precedent and case in hand.—Compare examine and apply; judicial process requires the judge to examine and compare what is before him (the case in hand) with the precedent before him. If they are plain and simple, judicial process consists of just to apply the precedent to case in hand and decide the case. It is same as he does when applies the statute to case before him.

When there is no precedent, the judge is called upon to fashion law for the litigant before him.

Not final truth but only a working hypothesis

Get a ruling from law reports; see whether it is on all four to case in hand, analyse and apply. Judicial process consists of only this job. Courts are laboratories for testing and retesting of existing ruling. After researching an applicable precedent, the courts experiment every new case and sees whether, it yields desirable result it continues being repeated and applied. If results are seen unjust the precedent is reconsidered. It does not happen in every new case but the process continues and if feeling of it creating injustice still continues, the rule is reformulated. The principle itself is re-examined if changes in society so necessitate. It may be done by superior court or the legislature.

Testing and retesting is continuous process

'Exception' may become rule and the rule may be eaten up by exception. *Donoghue* v. *Stevenson* and *Ryland* v. *Fletcher* started as exceptions to General rule of liability. These are now rules of liability. First lays down neighbour formulae and latter rule of strict liability. Custody and *animus possessendi* as elements of possession have been replaced by constructive possession. *Derry* v. *Peek* which laid down 'Deceit' is eaten up by exceptions. 'Absolute liability' is now an exception. History repeats is well established.

Finding *ratio decidendi*; a technique in judicial process

No case declares that it is *ratio* of this decision. Get and apply it whenever you are in difficulty. A case may have one *ratio* or more than one. Finding which one is relevant is the job of the judge. Likewise it is very difficult to distinguish in between ratio and *obitur* of a case. It is not layman's job. It needs expert technique and great experience. This experience comes in judicial training and experience after experiments. Finding the underlying principle (ratio) is great job that the judges do in the court.

Applying the *ratio*.—How to apply the ratio (ruling) is another difficult judicial process. The path finding is discretion of the judge. He has to decide what direction he chooses to proceed in the actual case before him. The first job (search of *ratio*) is wherein judges are quite accustomed. Too many cases are cited by the bar to help the judge to conclude either way. It creates more problems than it helps to solve. Judicial process requires to separate the accidental and non-essentials from the essential and inherent. Extracting the accurate latent principle from *ratio* sorted out is not too easy for judge in real cases before him. If he chooses one ruling, he is to say why does he choose it and also why did he not choose the other or others. He has to give reasons not only for why chosen but also for why not chosen.

What guides to choose the path

Here he gets assistance from the analogy (method of philosophy), from the history (method of Evolution) or from custom of community (method of Tradition), and from the justice, moral and welfare of the society (method of sociology).[1]

Do judges make Law?

Reply to this question in 'yes' or 'no' is not possible. The reply depends on the legal system wherein the judges develop the law. One can, call this 'developments' making law or declaring law. To a judge it does not make any difference. Admittedly his principal job is 'deciding the case before him.' He is not a legislator whose principal job is 'to legislate'. Those who start from separation of power or division of power see the difference in what legislator does and what the judges do. Both wings discharge their duties in their own way. The legislature does it by making laws and court administers. Those laws for giving justice according to law.

Judicial law making.—Judicial law making means; two things :

(firstly, laws made by the superior courts for regulating its own procedure Art. 145 of Indian Constitution)

and secondly, the legislative action of the courts in creating new law by its decisions. (Art. 141, 142).

The Judicial law making in second sense is a casualty of Blackstone and Montesqieu. The former, as he propounded the thesis that Judges do not make law, they only find and apply it, and to the latter for his doctrine of separation of powers which has caused greater injustice than the assumed injustice by despotism that it intended to do away with. The social welfare role of the State and maternal/paternal role of the Governments would have been very difficult to practice but for the modification of the separation of powers theory, in letter and spirit by the doctrine of checks and balances. The separation of powers doctrine does not work when it is needed, *i.e.*, where there is despotic ruler, a dictator, military ruler, it works to hamper the work where it is not needed, *e.g.*, when there is popular Government committed to socio-economic upliftment of the common man. In the name of separation of power, the society, pays in case like New Deal Legislation equal but separate classes (U.S.A.), Bank nationalisation case (India), Indira Gandhi election petition case (wherein single Judge held the election of Indira Gandhi illegal creating social and legal debacle all around), Golak Nath case where fundamental rights were held sacrosanct and inviolable by 6.5 majority judgment in India. The case has since been overruled in *Keshavanand Bharti* case (7 to 6) and it being superseded by constitutional amendment.

Despite these, the judicial legislation has been a reality throughout. In name of construction or interpretation of statutes, common law judges, have frequently gone the same line as their counterparts in the continent but in different direction. The continental judges legislate for giving effect to the policy of the statute, the common law judges have legislated to impose their ideologies on the society.

---

1. See 'Nature of judicial process,' B.N . Cardezo at p. 30.

The two extremes are represented at one end by Coke, Hale and Blackstone and at the other by Austin, Holland, Gray and Jethro Brown in English system itself. The older writers maintained that judges did not legislate at all. A pre-existing rule was there embedded if concealed in body of the customary law. All that the judge did was to throw off the wrappings and expose the statute to our view.

Austin and others maintained law is not made by any one else except the legislature or sovereign. Not so by the judge, in no case whatsoever customs howsoever, firmly established are not law until adopted by the courts.

Individual sentiments of the judge and fundamental interest of society—Which regulates law making by the judge. Swiss Civil Code 1907, first Article says that the statute governs all matters within the letter and the spirits of any of its mandates, In default of an applicable statute, the judge is to pronounce judgment according to customary law, and in default of a custom according to the rules, which he would establish if he were to assume, the part of the legislator however, from the situations cause created by the doctrine of the learned and the jurisprudence of the courts.

The judges even when he is free, is still not wholly free. He is not to innovate at pleasure. he is not a knight errant rocking at will in pursuit of his own ideal of beauty or of goodness. He is to draw his inspiration from cause created principles. He is not to yield to spasmodic sentiment, to vague and unregulated benevolence. He is to exercise a discretion informed by tradition, methodized by analogy, disciplined by system and subordinated to the primordial necessity of order in social life."

The truth is in between the two extremes; the "old view" and the "modern view' that is as and when social interests necessitate the court has discretion to mould the law and the relief. He is not free to legislate whether so needed or not. He has to know his limits has to decide cases keeping this warning ahead in front of him.

There are two practices that are seen among the judges :

(a) Declaratory theory.—Continental judges do make law. They do not make secret of it. The ghost of Blackstone does not hover on them, but English judges are by and large conservative. They have left law making entirely to the Parliament. May be there is some secret understanding between judiciary and British Parliament to keep hands off from each other. The judges enjoy independence and the parliament supremacy, the British crown is left with sovereignty. Sovereignty is with crown, judges are crown's mouthpiece, the crown can and does speak only through judges, the political supremacy is with British Parliament. The English Judges have been making law visibly but have never accepted, as gentlemen they are, that they have ever made law. The whole of British law is basically judge made law.

Judges declare law that already exists *incognitio*. They find it and apply to case before them. This view is based on the judicial process as it has been Savigny, (Germany), Maine (English), Hugo (Germany), Burke

(England), Bicko (Italy), Montesquien (France) who subscribe to this thought. Coke was of the view that precedent is not source of law but these are most typical and valuable evidence of what law is. Mathew Hale believed that court rulings do not make law. The reason he gave is that law can be made only either by the king or parliament. However, judges have great value in construing what is the law on the point in that country where they work. They declare what law on particular point is. They carry great weight in giving acceptance and public approval to that law. Their decisions carry weight heavier than opinion of private individuals.

Blackstone's view carries greater force on this point. He said that common law is made by customs and usages but who identified these too. He said it is judges in courts who did it. Common law came out of this recognition by judges. The customs are common law. The recognition of these customs by judges is crucial primary and authoritative evidence for existence and adoption of these usages as part of common law. He advocated that once a point has been settled by court, it should be followed if identical question arises subsequently but these can be ignored if these are found to be absurd and improper.

Carter is a U.S. based thinker who supported that judges declare law. They do not make it. The argument was; How can you apply a law which you make to facts arising prior to their being made. This would be unjust and improper. The reality is law first, decision according to that law thereafter. Decision first, law thereafter is unfair and unreasonable. It can not be accepted.

(b) Constitutive theory.—According to this, Judges constitute law. The judgments inject legality to customs and whatever they decide becomes law. Even the words of parliament have the same meaning as the judges interpret it to have. If the interpretation of some statutes is brought to the notice of the parliament that enacted it, it will cry on what the judges have done or think self immolation for having failed to convey itself properly. Some english judges like Lord Denning have tried to assert the view that judges make law but they found no support neither from his colleagues in Court of Appeal nor House of Lords nor from the Court of Appeal again when he returned back from House of Lords. House of Lords has ceased to be a law court.

A judge is not legislator, and can not be so, but laws are not made only by legislatures. There are many other sources as well through which many laws are made. Regulations are made by Executive. The President has legislative power under Article 123. The Governor makes law under Article 213. The Municipalities the Panchayats Public Corporations, Private organisations, Associations, Companies etc. make laws. Art. 145 empowers Supreme Court to make rules for regulating practice and procedure by rules of court.

All these make it clear that legislation is the primary function of legislative bodies but it is not exclusive to these alone. The objection against judge making laws are based on separation of power which has not been accepted in India in the way it operates in European Countries (France) and U.S.A.

In U.K. the issue came in light beyond proportion for the simple reason that British Parliament is Supreme Law maker. It is exclusive law maker. It is all powerful law making institution. It can make or unmake any law. The clash in between courts and parliament in U.K. resulted in compromise victory of Parliament.

So judges in England, felt shy in accepting reality of making laws. They did it under cover. Never accepted that they have tc make law. When justice and reason so necessitate. They developed principles of interpretation which were nothing else than judicial legislation. This was done to avoid head long collision with Parliament. Parliament digested, conceded and tolerated this much of liberty taken by the judges but this was taken note of by thinkers and some great judges.

Lord Bacon was one such jurist who admitted that judges do make law. He stated that in new cases (unprecedented) where statutory guidance is not available, where the constitution does not help the judge, the judges place reliance on logic, reasoning and analogy, philosophy, custom, tradition to decide the new case. It is permissible by judicial process. Justice Cardozo, approved these in "judicial process".

Prof. Dicey, Gray and Salmond stand strongly for the view that judges make law. Dicey accepted that major portion of English law rather the best part thereof consists of laws laid down by courts in deciding the cases. It consists of judge made law. Common law is judge made. It contributes to laws of England. There may be some doubts on common law but equity, the whole of it is judge made. It began as system to supplement common law but supplanted it. The laws relating to trust, notice, fraud are creation of equity.

Gray not only holds the view that judges make law but goes a step further to join issue with opponents who say that judges do not make law. He says that power to interpret laws is not different from power to make law. In fact it is judge who has final word to say what is law on any point. He states this is real law making and person doing it lawfully is true law maker.

Salmond criticises Hale as giving out a view wherein he himself is victim of utter confusion. Hale held judges only declare what law is. They do not make it. He made it clear that judges uphold Rule of law. They develop law and in doing so, they make law.

Bentham and Austin criticised declaratory theory

Bentham said declaratory theory is white lie spread intentionally. The truth is that in deciding case the judges steal law making power which they can openly not admit and certainly do not have courage to denounce it. Austin said that declaratory theory is childish fiction invented by English judges to cover up what they are doing but do not have courage to say that they are doing. This may be out of fear of Parliament or on account of judicial modesty. The whole common law is their creation but they keep it surrounded in mystery.

In *Mansa Ram Nainwal*, the Supreme Court said, a case is precedent for what it explicitly decides and no more. The words used by the judges is their judgments are not to be read as if they are words in an Act of Parliament.

'Precedent' means anything that has been done in similar situations earlier by superior courts. As the superior court has earlier decided. Further, the same law laid down earlier in identical facts. This is to bring certainty in law; to give predictability to the course of conduct to be followed by courts to bring certainty in law. It is different from *'res judicata'*, which means thing decided in between same parties cannot be re-opened in same courts in same parties or their privies and heirs. Precedent is decision of Supreme Court that binds all the courts below. It is *ratio decidendi* the *ratio* of the decision, that is binding on all courts below. Article 141 of Constitution says so for Supreme Court. Law declared by the Supreme Court shall be binding on all courts throughout the territory of India. A Decision is available on binding precedent only if it decides a question of law. If no law question is decided, it cannot be precedent. For example; when appeal is dismissed and impugned judgment is upheld.

Adherence to Precedent

***Stare decisis* and *Ratio decidendi*.**—'*Stare decisis*' means when a court is bound by its own decision. It was so with the House of Lords. Indian Supreme Court is not bound by its own earlier decision. It can overrule prospectively as well as retrospectively. The case law is very popular source of general law of the land. The study and grasp of case law is very fruitful to lawyers. It, a source of knowledge, provides basis of arguments, expounds the implications of law and sometimes even supplies the want of the legislatures. It is said to rank second among the sources of general law. The first being statute which is a formal expression of the legislative will. The purpose of judiciary is to implement the statute in all its intents and implications. In doing so, the judges introduce their own philosophies and attitudes of life which is reflected in their judgments. this takes us to the conclusion that nature of judgments, their recognition and validity differs from country to country. The difference may not be in the form of the judgment. The part of the judgment is called precedent which is rationale of the decision. This rationale is called *ratio decidendi* of the case. This is due to this ratio that a case is remembered and acknowledged as law.

'*Stare decisis*' is a Latin phrase. It means to stand by the decided cases to uphold precedent, to maintain a former adjudication. The purpose is to have uniformity for having certainty. It is based on public policy. Public policy is that the major objectives of any legal system are certainty, predictability and stability.

The maxim is "*stare decisis et non quieta movere*". To stand by the decision and not to disturb what is settled. "Those things which have been no often adjudged ought to rest in peace."

Whether doctrine is 'imprisonment' of reasons.—'No'. The underlying trend is that *stare decisis* is not a dogmatic rule allergic to logic and reason. It is flexible of law operating in the province of precedent providing room to collaborate with the demands of changing times dictated by social needs, State policy and judicial conscience.

The Relevant enquiries into case law—The following questions may be considered in this respect—

(i) *How does case law of one country differ in form from case on similar points decided by courts of other countries?* For example : continental case law and Anglo-American or Indian case law.

(ii) *Where is the case law to be found?* The cases are reported in law reports of different countries. The reports are published somewhere under the supervision of court like U.S.S.R.; somewhere by private agencies like A.I.R. and S.C.J. in India and somewhere by Government organisations like S.C.R. and S.C.A. in India and AllE.R. and W.L.R. in England and U.S.S.C.R. of U.S.A. *etc*.

(iii) *How far may the case law be treated as authoritative?* What is the difference in ratio decidendi and *obiter dicta*?

(iv) *What are the merits and demerits of doctrine of ratio decidendi* and doctrine of stare *decisis?*

Precedent 'Meaning'.—The importance of judicial precedents has always been a distinguishing characteristics of English law. The great body of the common or unwritten law is almost entirely the product of decided cases accumulated in an immense series of reports. The orthodox legal theory professed to regard common law as customary law and judicial decisions as merely evidence of custom and of the law derived therefrom. The practice, common law of England has been created by the decisions of the English judges. Neither Roman Law nor any of those modern systems which are founded upon it, allow such a degree of authority to precedent. English law unlike continental practice, draws a sharp distinction between Law Reports containing decision and law text books. A judicial precedent speaks in England with authority; it is not merely evidence of law but a source of it, and the courts are bound to follow the law that is so established. The authority of the precedents in England has historical origin. The judges of royal court enjoyed confidence of the King. They acted in harmony and the centralisation and concentration of the administration of justice in royal courts gave to the royal judges a power and prestige which would have been unattainable in any other system. The power, skill and professional reputation of the judges gave it added form. The Bench or judiciary in England had always given law to the Bar. But the position was quite reverse in Roman and other continental countries—Rome did not have permanent body of professional judges till quite recently.

Precedent means two things

(a) It means body of case law which is reported, may be cited and may probably be followed by courts. This practice is found in continental countries.

(b) Precedents must be followed. This rule was developed by common law courts in nineteenth and twentieth centuries.

The doctrine of binding precedent was adopted for the purpose of bringing certainty in law. A bad decision could be nullified only by the Parliament. Moreover, there were many other redeeming features. The process of distinguishing gave much liberty (though restricted) to the judges, however, this required acute mental gymnastics. Besides, there is a practice that a High Court judge may refuse to follow another High Court judge and a higher court may overrule a decision of an inferior court. Salmond is of the view that the strict doctrine should be retained in so far as it binds a court to follow the decision of superior courts but the court, should cease to be bound by decisions of courts of coordinate jurisdiction. The court of appeal and House of Lords should have power to refuse to follow their own previous decisions. This view of Salmond seems to have found favour with House of Lords which has recently held that it is no longer bound by its previous decisions if they are illogical, outmoded and not fitting in with the time.

Kinds of precedents.—Two

(i) Authoritative.—It is one which the judges must follow whether they approve of it or not. The general rule is that a court is bound by the decisions of all courts higher than itself. A High Court Judge cannot question a decision of the court of appeal nor can the court of appeal refuse to follow judgments of the then House of Lords (now British Supreme Court). The courts are bond only by decisions of the higher courts and not by those of equal or lower rank. A High Court judge is not bound by previous High Court decision though he will normally follow it on the principles of judicial comity, in order to avoid conflicts of authority and to secure certainty and uniformity in administration of justice. If he refuses to follow it, he cannot overrule it, both decisions stand and the resulting antimony must wait for a higher court to settle.

The decision lays down binding *ratio* only when it is given in case in which issues are framed, the arguments of both sides are heard and appreciated and the evidence of both are considered. An *ex parte* decision, as such would not operate as *ratio decidendi.*

it is also necessary to see that the *ratio* forms binding precedent only when it was necessary for the decision of that case. There can be only one *ratio* in any case. However, there may be a case which may lay down more than one *ratio* in any particular case.

There are two statements of practices which are *in nature self-imposed limitations or exceptions to the authoritative precedents* :—

(a) Courts of inferior jurisdiction do no create binding precedents for courts lower in rank. For example, the decisions of quarter sessions do not as precedent bind the magistrate's courts; nor the decisions of country court judge are binding as precedent upon country court registrar. Courts of inferior jurisdiction are bound only by decisions of courts of superior jurisdiction *i.e.* High Court of Appeal and House of Lords (now Supreme Court of England and Wales).

(b) Several courts had established that they are bound by their own decisions. The House of Lords, the Court of Appeal, the Court Criminal Appeal and Divisional Court regarded themselves bound by their own decisions. However, recently House of Lords has broken this self-imposed limitation and it feels no longer bound by its own decisions.

(ii) Persuasive precedents.—The persuasive precedent is one wherein the judges are under no obligation to follow, but which they may take into consideration and to which they will attach such weight as it seems to deserve. It depends for its influence upon its own merits, not upon legal claim which it has to recognise. The following persuasive precedents are important.

(a) Foreign Judgments,

(b) Judgments of the courts of other countries in commonwealth,

(c) Judgments of Privy Council,

(d) Judicial dicta or *obiter dicta*.

In England, the hierarchy of courts lay down a very important ruling 'stare decisis', that every court is bound to follow the decision of any court given by a court above it. In this regard, the following rules are followed by England :

(1) All the courts below are bound by the decisions of the then House of Lords (now British Supreme Court since 2005). In the case of *London Street Tramways* v. *L.C.C.*,[1] it was held that the House of Lords is bound by its previous decisions. But in the case of *Scruttones Ltd.* v. *Midland Silicones*,[2] it was observed by the Court that the House of Lords' can reject the previous decisions, where the principle is obscure or where a decision is out of line with other authorities or established principles or where principle is much wider than was necessary for the decision. In the *Chancery Lane Safe Deposit and Offices Co. Ltd.* v. *Inland Revenue Commrs. Per.*,[3] it was held :

(i) that the rule of the House of Lords not to reverse nor depart from a previous decision of the House applied to reasoning of the decision but did not bind the House to follow a previous case merely because it was indistinguishable on its facts.

(ii) The civil courts of appeal in civil cases and criminal courts of appeal for criminal cases are bound by their previous decisions in similar cases.

(iii) A divisional court of King's or Queens bench is bound to follow its previous decisions. A High Court Judge is not bound by the decisions of another High Court.

(iv) The lower court of first instance, that is the county court Magistrate court, the Court of Quarter Session and the Assize Courts,

---

1. 1 All. E.R. (1966) 1.

2. (1962) A.C. 522.

3. 1 All. E.R. 1 (1966).

do not bind any court by their decisions in other cases nor are they bound by their own previous decisions.

(v) The decision of a superior court is treated as persuasive by courts above that court in the hierarchy.

Utility of binding precedent

The doctrine of binding precedent is subject to some restriction :—

(a) Use sparingly criterion.—This view was that if any precedent is proving injurious, it is better to use it sparingly rather than to overrule it.[1]

(b) Legitimate expectation criterion.—Even if less helpful, a precedent should not be overruled. In *Re Ross Smith*,[2] and *In re Indyka*.[3]

(c) Construction criterion.—*Jones case*,[4] is authority for it as well.

(d) Unforeseable criterion.—*In re Steadman*,[5] is authority.

(e) Need for comprehensive reform.—This view found support in *Myers case*,[6]

(f) Precedent merely wrong criterion.—*Knuller case*,[7] is authority for this view.

Precedent ought to be overruled.—The precedent ought to be overruled in following situations :—

(a) Rectification of uncertainty criterion.

(b) Unjust or outmoded criterion.

Legal argument when there is a precedent

Noting the court ranking of the judge before whom the lawyer appearing and guided by the doctrine of *stare decisis*, the lawyer will then prepare his or her argument. Usually, the best position for the lawyer occurs when there is a precedent case supporting his or her client's case. The lawyer will then argue that the court is either bound, or that the court, if not actually bound, ought to be persuaded by the precedent case to find in the client's favour. In his or her research, the lawyer will therefore look for cases with results which support the client's position and the lawyer will prepare to argue that the *ratio decidendi* of those precedent cases covers the facts of the case at bar. However, just locating and evaluating the prospects of precedent cases is not easy since it is often difficult to determine and articulate the authority of a case. Moreover, skill is necessary to analyze and organize the material facts of both the precedent case and the case at bar. That said, more difficult problems of legal reasoning and legal argument occur when the lawyer is unable to find a close case or any case at all or, worse yet, when a case presents itself which appears to be unfavourable. How does the lawyer deal with these problems?

1. *Jons* v. *Secretary of State*, (1972) A.C. 944 is authority for such view.
2. (1963) A.C. 280.
3. (1969) A.C. 32 are authorities supporting this view.
4. (1972) A.C. 944.
5. (1976) A.C. 536.
6. (1965) A.C. 1001.
7. (1973) A.C. 435.

To get around an apparently unfavourable case, there are a number of tools and techniques available to the lawyer. The lawyer may not simply ignore the unfavourable case and hope that the other side does not discover the authority. This is unethical and with respect it may be submitted that it is also unethical and intellectually dishonest for a judge in deciding a case to simply ignore a precedent case which stands in the way of the decision that the judge wants to make. This is not to say that lawyers and judges must deal with every case that remotely touches on a subject but only that there should be an honest effort to play by the rules.

Stare decisis

The techniques that are available follows as a consequence of accepting and then manipulating the doctrine of *stare decisis*. The techniques and structure direct the lawyer's legal reasoning and argument. The following are generally recognized :

(1) Case cited does not stand for the proposition.—The lawyer can argue that the precedent case does not stand for the legal proposition for which it has been cited. In other words, the lawyer articulates the *ratio decidendi* of the case differently. An example of this may be found in the treatment of the case of *Rivtow Marine Ltd.* v. *Washington Iron Works*. In *The Attorney General for the Province of Ontario* v. *Fatehi*, Estey J. without resolving the difficulties associated with this case observed : Nonetheless it must be acknowledged that *Rivtow* has been variously applied or rejected by the courts of this country, some of whom find in the majority judgment recognition of economic loss and some of whom have found the opposite.

(2) Is obiter dicta.—The lawyer can argue that while the precedent case does articulate the legal proposition for which it has been cited, nevertheless the proposition was *obiter dicta* (things said by the way). Subject to an exception for considered pronouncements of the law by appellate courts, comments by the judge which are not part of the *ratio decidendi* are *obiter dicta* and are theoretically not binding in a subsequent case. The exception is that where an appellate court expresses a considered opinion on a point of law then such ruling is binding on the lower courts notwithstanding that it was not absolutely necessary to rule on the point in order to dispose of the appeal.

It should be noted that if a judge rests his decision on two different grounds neither can be characterized as *obiter dictum.*

(3) Has been effectively overruled.—The lawyer can argue that while the precedent case does stand for the legal proposition for which it has been cited, the case has been effectively overruled by a decision of a High Court or by the introduction of a new statute. Examples of this kind of legal argument will obviously occur after significant decisions of the Supreme Court of Canada. For instance that Court's decision in *Kamloops* v. *Nielsen* did away with the distinction between non-feasance and misfeasance in negligence actions against municipalities and many old cases turned on that distinction can no longer be relied upon.

(4) Facts distinguished.—The lawyer can argue that while the precedent case does stand for the legal proposition for which it has been cited, the case at bar is different; that is, the cases are factually distinguishable. Glanville Williams suggests that there are two kinds of "distinguishing" : restrictive and non-restrictive and states.

(5) Restrictive distinguishing.—Non-restrictive distinguishing occurs where a court accepts the expressed *ratio decidendi* of the earlier case, and does not seek to curtail it, but finds that the case before it does not fall within this *ratio decidendi* because of some material difference of fact. Restrictive distinguishing cuts down the expressed *ratio decidendi* of the earlier case by treating as material to the earlier decision some fact, present in the earlier case, which the earlier court regarded as immaterial.

Peabody Fund and Anns Cases

An example of restrictive distinguishing may be noted in the House of Lords decision in *Peabody Fund* v. *Sir Lindsay Parkinson Ltd.*, where the Court restricted the application of *Anns* v. *Merton London Borough*. The *Anns* case is cited as authority for the proposition that a municipality may be liable in negligence where it fails to properly inspect building plans. In the *Peabody Fund* case, by defining the duty of the municipality as being owed to owners and occupiers threatened with the possibility of injury to safety or health, the House of Lords specified and made less general, the scope of the municipality's responsibility as it had been defined in the *Anns* case. In the result, the Court did not allow a claim by the developer of a housing project who suffered damages when the municipality's drainage inspector failed to point out that the drainage system was not being installed in accordance with the approved design. Thus, in *Peabody Fund* the element of restrictive distinguishing is the introduction of the requirement of the possibility of injury to safety or health.

Town of Pas v. Parky

An example of non-restrictive distinguishing may be noted in the Supreme Court of Canada decision in *Town of the Pas* v. *Parky Packers Ltd.* In this case, the Court noted that the authority of *Hedley Byrne Co. Ltd.* v. *Heller* required the plaintiff in a negligent misrepresentation claim to show the relief on the skill and judgment of the party from whom he had received incorrect information. In the *Parky Packers* case the plaintiff had received incorrect zoning advice from municipal officials but the plaintiffs representative was a former municipal council member who had more expertise in planning matters than the officials. In these circumstances, there could be no reliance and the doctrine of authority of *Hedley Byrne* by its own criteria was not available. The plaintiff's claim was dismissed. The material fact of the plaintiff's lack of reliance provided the element for non-restrictive distinguishing of *Hedley Byrne*.

(6) Changed public policy.—Where the case being relied upon has a built in public policy factor, the lawyer who wishes to distinguish the case may argue that public policy has changed and while the legal principle of the precedent case is still good law, it is distinguishable because of the change of circumstances. The possibility of this type of argument was noted in the case of *Nordenfelt* v. *Maxim Nordenfelt Guns and Ammunition Co.*, an important case with respect to the principle that contracts in restraint of trade may be voidable on grounds of public policy. In his judgment in this case, Lord Watson noted : A series of decisions based upon grounds of public policy, however eminent the judges by whom they were delivered, cannot possess the same binding authority as decisions which deal with and formulate principles which are purely legal.

(7) Precedent of equal weight.—The lawyer can argue that while the precedent case does stand for the legal proposition for which it has been cited, there is another precedent of equal weight which stands for the opposite proposition. The lawyer then goes on to argue that it is that other case which the court should follow. This type of argument is related to but in the end result different from the "per incuriam argument" because it does not necessarily challenge either decision as having been given per incuriam. The rule is rather that the court may decide which one of the conflicting decisions to follow.

Three legal way outs when there is no binding precedent

The above seven types of legal argument are the principal techniques used to get around an apparently binding precedent and we can turn next to the problem of not being able to find a precedent case. Because there is considerable room for imagination and creativity in responding to this problem, it is more difficult to identify the main techniques. Nevertheless, some typical responses may be identified. Below we will consider three classical types of legal reasoning used in these circumstances. Again the doctrine of *stare decisis,* this time in spirit, may be noted.

(1) Reliance on non-binding precedents.—Where a lawyer cannot find a binding precedent, he or she may rely on a non-binding precedent from another jurisdiction. while not obliged to do so, the court may be impressed with or be persuaded by the reasoning and be prepared to adopt the rule established by the foreign case. However, care must be taken in employing this technique because it often necessitates reviewing the foreign law to determine whether there may be underlying differences in principles quality of which may diminish the persuasiveness of the foreign case. For example, decisions on the *American Bill of Rights* will obviously be important and helpful in interpreting our own *Charter of Rights and Freedoms*. However, it must not be lost sight of that there is no provision in the *American Constitution* comparable to the provision in our *Charter* that the rights set out "are guaranteed subject only to such reasonable limits prescribed by law as can be demonstrably justified in a free and democratic society".

(2) Articulate ratio differently.—Where a lawyer cannot find a binding precedent, he or she may form a legal argument from first principles. this approach identifies legal principles from decided cases and argues that while the factual circumstances of the cases may appear different, analytically they are the same. The kind of legal argument is often used with respect to determining the measure of damages. For example, without any reference to its particular facts, *Wertheim* v. *Chicoutimi Pulp Co.* is often cited as authority for the legal principle that where there is a breach of contract then as far as money can do so, the injured party is to be placed in as good a position as if the contract had been performed. The general principle is then applied to the particular facts of the immediate case.

Hedley v. Heller example

This type of approach may be noted also with respect to the issue of liability; for example, *Hedley Byrne & Co. Ltd.* v. *Heller, supra*, has frequently been cited as applying to fact situations which do not remotely resemble the facts of that case. This kind of argument does not purport to extend or develop the law; rather, the sense of it is just the opposite. The underlying premise is that the judge will be applying and will not be departing from decided law. The spirit of *stare decisis* may be noted here.

(3) Cases evolve general principle.—Where a lawyer cannot find a precedent he or she can go beyond first principles and instead develop an argument that the decided cases have evolved to a general principle which covers the immediate case. This is a very sophisticated and creative type of argument. It is the kind of argument in which common law lawyers and judges take particular pride. It is this type of argument that can be identified in the majority judgment of Lord Atkin in *Mc Alister (or Donoghue)* v. *Stevenson*. In that case, there were two strong dissenting judgments of Lord Buckmaster and Lord Tomlin and their legal argument was that the plaintiff's claim did not come within the reach of the established authorities but represented a new type of claim. Lord Atkin's response was that while the decided cases might each examine particular types of liability, there must be a common rationale. In his approach, we can again note the spirit of *stare decisis*. Lord Atkin did not ignore the precedents. Instead he found within them an underlying principle which he then applied. In a sense, Lord Atkin looked backward before he moved the law forward. Further, his argument was not based on any assertion that the principle he was articulating was the next logical step in the law. Indeed, an appeal to pure logic is difficult because established precedents may prevent the law from developing as a matter of logical progression. *McAlister (or Donoghue)* v. *Stevenson* does not offend the letter or spirit of the doctrine of *stare decisis* and provides a classic example of legal reasoning and legal argument in circumstances where there was no near precedent for the case.

Stare decisis is one way of legal reasoning, and argument but not all. There are substantive rules for the interpretation of statutes and there are special rules and considerations when the statute is a tax Act or a criminal code or a constitutional document. There are special and often difficult rules for the interpretation of contracts and testamentary instruments. There are unique considerations when principles of the law of equity are involved and problems caused by the evidentiary rules of onus of proof or of rebuttable and irrebuttable presumptions. Yet, while the multitude of these rules provides the lawyer with a large variety of other tools and techniques for legal reasoning and legal argument, it also has to be conceded that *stare decisis* continues to play the pivotal role.

Erosion of the principle of *stare decisis*

During the 1980s, there was a tendency to deviate from settled principles of law in the name of "innovative principles"; the objective being to render "social justice". On the other hand, Professor Roscoe Pound has stated "Law must be stable, yet it cannot stand still." Similarly, Justice Aharon Barak says, "Stability without change is degeneration. Change without stability is anarchy." These wise observations imply that changes in law brought about by judicial interpretation must, more often than not, be evolutionary and not be revolutionary or dramatic. As dramatically changed interpretations are error-prone and based only on expediency, it would be wiser to take one step at a time than a quantum leap, particularly into unknown regions. There may, however, be situations that call for dramatic or sudden changes in law, but exceptions must be few and far between and not easily resorted to, as *stare decisis* is yet one of the fundamentals of our legal system.

Judicial activists do not easily accept *stare decisis* as a fundamental principle and in the 1980s the Supreme Court gave the lead to the process of dismantling *stare decisis*. The judgment in *D.S. Nakara* is a classic example of this approach. In *D.S. Nakara*, the Court observed : "Socio-economic justice stems from the concept of social morality coupled with abhorrence for economic exploitation. And the advancing society converts in course of time moral or ethical code into enforceable legal formulations. Overemphasis on precedent furnishes an insurmountable road-block to the onward march towards promised millennium. An overdose of precedents is the bane of our system which is slowly getting stagnant, stratified and atrophied."

If the observations of the Court are right, then at any given time the Judge may do what he thinks in conformity with his conception of "social justice" by throwing to the winds established principles of law and binding judgments. Moreover, dramatic changes in law create immeasurable difficulties for the High Courts and the subordinate courts for they are left to flounder in a sea of conflicting precedents. They also create chaos and instability for citizens who have moulded their legal relationships based on the extant law but now find that the goal post has been moved in the middle of the game! Further, when the highest court in the land itself shows scant respect for precedents, it may well encourage the High Courts and the subordinate courts to follow suit, leading to judicial indiscipline and anarchy, which bodes ill for any legal system.

Precedents in continental countries

The continental lawyers see no difference of the kind between precedent and any other expression of expert legal opinion. A book of reports and text book are in the same legal category—they are both evidences of law : they are both instruments for the persuasion of the judges, but neither of them is anything more. From the standpoint of strict legal thereof, French law is not based on case law at all. The case law is called 'Law jurisprudence' which is different from 'statute law'. The civil and penal codes are theoretically complete in the sense that they are supposed to cover every situation with which the ordinary courts are concerned. In France, the case law is not a source of law because the French judge is not obliged to consider it when deciding any suit. In fact, French civil code[1] forbids the judge from laying down general rules when stating a decision. There is every probability that such attempts may lead to the whole decision being set aside by French appellate court, likewise, any judgment given on the basis of past precedent is bound to be reversed unless adequate legal basis is available to it otherwise.

Difference in Systems—why?

The above theoretical proposition does not hold good for ever. In practice in French jurisprudence, there is a substantial body of case law dealing mainly with constructions of the statutes and *droit administratiff* of the council d'etat is itself based mainly on case law. The common law and continental case law differ both in theory as well as practice. French judge does not regard himself as absolutely bound by the decision of any court in a single previous instance. The practice of the courts does not become a source of law until it is definitely fixed by the repetition of precedents which are in agreement on a single point. *The causes of the difference between these systems are fundamental. Some of these are* :

(a) Quest of certainty.—The need of certainty has always been pressing each time in every country. But the French judges had been in comfortable position since long they had it in shape of Roman law and codified customs and later on in code Napolean. This kept continental law more certain than anything else. The position was reverse in England and India. The Roman law was never received in England. Therefore, the common law was comparatively fluid and uncertain. The development of chancery courts and equity jurisdiction created more uncertainty. The principles of the equity varied with changing foot of the Chancellors. This equity sometimes supplemented the common law and sometimes supplanted it. It had auxiliary, concurrent as well as original fields of the operations. This made the whole of common law uncertain. The common law of England was applicable to India through the doctrine of justice, equity and good

1. Article 5 French Civil Code.

conscience and sometimes it was applied by judges of Privy Council which was ultimate court of appeal from all civil and criminal cases decided by higher courts in India. The quest for certainty became more acute when the problem of codification was taken up in India. It was said that the aim of codification in India was to bring about uniformity, where it could be had and to tolerate diversity, where it was bound to be had, but in all cases certainty.

(b) Hierarchy of the courts.—This is a second aspect of law that deserves to be compared as cause of different approach to precedents. In French judicial system, the whole country is divided into districts and in each district, two courts are established—firstly, the court of first instance and secondly, the court of appeal. There is right of appeal on points of law from any of the district court of appeal to *Cour de Cassation* in Paris. The serious criminal cases are tried by district assize courts. This is the final court although an application may be made for an order of retrial to Cour de Cassation on points law. This highest court is practically not a court of appeal. It is a chamber of revision. No order on merit is finally made. The legal points are explained and the case is usually referred back to district courts of appeal. As compared to this, the hierarchy of courts in common law countries is more cohesive, interlinked and uniform. The same life runs from lowest to the highest Court. This creates the need of precedents more in England and India than in continental countries.

(c) Different positions of the Judges.—The number of the judges in higher French judiciary is larger in comparison to the higher judiciary in commonwealth countries. French judiciary is constituted of personnel of civil service whereas common law judges are recruited mainly from Bar. The judges in French higher judiciary are relatively younger and less experienced in comparison to common law courts and judges. Besides, the common law is a monument to the judicial activity of the common law judge. He created the common law and not the legislator or scholars. Therefore, he still enjoys the prestige of that accomplishment.

The problem in U.S.A. is more *akin* to the English practice in comparison with continental set up. However, the United States Supreme Court and the State appellate courts in U.S.A. do not regard themselves as absolutely bound by their past decisions. The problem of precedents in U.S.A. may be considered in the following two broad outlines :

(i) *Numerous jurisdictions.*—The judicial set up in each State is independent. State judiciary is separate but co-extensive with national judiciary. This leads to the multiplicity of law reports. The result is that production of restatements on various topics has become a necessity. The case method study is another device adopted in American law schools for finding out recent judicial trend.

(ii) *Constitutional issues.*—In these cases, the written document is more important and the case law becomes of a secondary consideration. The rigid method of precedents is inappropriate to the construction of a Constitution which has to be applied to changing conditions of national life and public policy.

The English principle of *'stare decisis'* is not followed by the French courts. Thus, a French judge does not regard himself absolutely bound by decisions of any court as higher previous instance. The district courts of first instance in both civil and criminal cases are not bound by their own previous decisions and not those of any other district court of first instance. The appellate court are not bound to follow their previous decision on identical facts.

Form of Judicial Precedent

So far as the form of judicial precedent is concerned, the continental case-law consists of the reported decisions of the court and like that of common law countries, *it follows the principle of reporting the decision but the two bodies of law differ in any respects.*

(1) *Brevity.*—The characteristic feature of a continental law report is its brevity. The facts are only summarised and the arguments of lawyers are not reported. The conclusions arrived at by the courts are stated only in few sentences. On the other hand, the case law in India, England and other common law countries is reported in detail. The judges, in giving the decisions of a case, not only state the facts but also dwell upon the arguments of the counsels and state the reasons for the decisions of the case.

(2) *Minority opinion.*—A continental judgment is never personal. It is the decision of the court as a whole and the voice of the dissenting judge is never heard. In India, England and other common law countries dissenting judgment is also reported, although the decisions of the majority judges prevail and are considered for reporting the case law. Till recently the minority opinion of a member in Privy Council could not be given or reported. They have now started giving it.

(3) *Effectiveness.*—In France, past precedents are not referred to in the judgment and if it is given, they are not cited as precedents, but in common law countries the judge refers to the precedents, on which he has based his reasoning in coming to a conclusion. In France, the earlier holding of the court is referred by way of illustration only. They are treated to have no binding effect. Whereas in common law countries, the decisions of the highest court of the land or other superior courts are taken to be binding on lower courts. They cannot go beyond these even if they consider it erroneous. If they want to get rid of its binding force, they can do so only by process of distinguishing. The judgments given *'amicus curie'* (in absence of knowledge of decision of higher court on the point) is fatal to the decision.

(4) *Legal Technique.*—The continental lawyers and common law lawyers adopt different techniques. The continental lawyer is not concerned with precedent applicable to particular point in a dispute. He is concerned more with its generalised form; he may analyse the case decided earlier with enquiry whether any gėneral principle can be propounded on the basis thereof. If so, it may serve the purpose, that, the case law does in common law countries. If no general principle can be deduced from the earlier decided case, it will have no value for a continental lawyer whereas for

common law specialist, every pronouncement of higher court is binding as law.

(5) *Form of judgment.*—The French judge is bound to follow the prescribed way of judgment. It must be in writing and must comply with the formal requirements. This avoids the lengthy judgments being given by French courts. The usual form in a civil suit is the *stage of qualities* (names and description) of the parties *minutes and finalisation of motifs or issue, and deposit or operative part of judgment.* The common law judge has full freedom regarding the form and length of the judgment.

(6) *Conflicting nature.*—The continental case law has no binding force. It binds neither the court that established it, nor the lower courts subordinate to it. The result is every court has its own way and there is no difficulty in finding out two or more different chains of judicial opinions on any legal problem. The highest judicial body in France is Cour de Cassation, which is not an appellate court. It only revises the proceedings of the lower court. So its impact is not much. Uncertainty and chaos are the natural consequences if the system is given trial afresh somewhere.

(7) *Judicial Legislation.*—The continental jurists and judges are armed with a weapon which is called the process of extensive interpretation. They have full liberty to see that the codes may not bar the economic and social progress of the nation. They will interpret the statutes as the time desires. This freedom is not available to the lawyer practising common law. He is to interpret it in light of circumstances in which the statute was made. The continental judges are not fettered by narrow or formalistic interpretations. Their's is a living judiciary. This point can be illustrated with changing concepts of acquitas, *bona fides*, good morals and public order.

Precedents in India

In India, the practice like that of English courts has been in existence. In ancient Hindu law, there was a hierarchy of courts for example King's court presided over by King himself or some other well read judge (pradvivak) was the highest court. Below this, the courts of sreni, courts of pug and courts of kul were in operation. The modern English concept of the precedent was certainly not known. The previous decision was given due weight minus the rigidity it has got in English law. The Hindu concept of precedent was flexible and of absorbing nature. After Hindu regimes conceded to muslims, the whole set up was almost changed. The system of Arabia was planted in the country. The country was divided in suba, sarkars and villages. Kazi was appointed at every village or group of villages and headquarters of the Government in Sarkar and Suba. The Sultan was the chief of the whole system at the centre of the administration. It appears that doctrine of precedents had the theoretical recognition. Respect to the decisions of the superior courts was given. But it was not of much practical importance because these courts were not courts of record. They gave usually oral decisions, heard the plaintiff or complainant orally. No records were maintained.

The modern concept of precedent implies that the records must be kept.

After English regime took over the rein, many courts of records were established in due course. However, the doctrine of precedent does not appear to have been adopted, due to fluid political situations, whatever may have been the causes, the Sadar Diwani Adalat emerged as the highest court of appeal in civil matters in 1772 and Sadar Nizamat Adalat in criminal cases. The appeals from these used to go to Privy Council or King in Council. From here begins the effective application of the rules of precedent. The judgments of the Privy Council carried greater regard in all the courts of India. In 1861 Indian High Courts Act provided for the establishment of High Courts in India at the place of Sadar Adalats and Supreme Court established by Charter of 1774 issued in persuance of the power conferred by Regulating Act, 1773. The Supreme Court was a Court of record and it had manifold jurisdictions including power to issue various writs. These powers were taken over by the High Courts.

The Government of India Act, 1935 established a Federal Court, whose decisions were considered as binding on all the courts throughout the territory of British India.

The present Constitution of India came into force on 26th January, 1950. The existing High Courts have been given jurisdiction subject to the provisions of this Constitution and to the provisions of any law of the appropriate legislature made by virtue of powers conferred on that legislature by this Constitution, the jurisdiction of and the law administered in, and existing High Court, and the respective powers of the judges thereof in relation to the administration of justice in that court including any power to make rules of Court and to regulate the sittings of the courts and of members thereof sitting alone or in division courts, shall be the same as immediately before the commencement of this Constitution. In India, the present High Courts have similar jurisdictions as was hitherto being exercised by them.

(i) Precedents in civil courts.—The subordinate civil judicature has the civil judge (junior division) at the lowest rung. It creates no binding precedent. Neither one is bound by the decision of another civil judge (junior division) in like matters nor he is bound by his own prior ruling in similar case. The post of the civil judge is transferable. If the civil judge of a court takes certain view and is transferred thereafter, the new civil judge is not bound by his views. Likewise, the next higher Courts are court of civil judges (senior judge) and district judge. Neither of these creates a binding precedent nor is bound by the chains of *stare decisis*.

(ii) Precedents in subordinate criminal courts.—The position is more fluid and uncertain here. *The Magistrate's courts* are the courts of first instance. Thereafter comes *Sessions Court*. These two courts create neither binding precedents for other courts nor are these bound by their own previous judgments.

(iii) Precedents in High Courts.—The working of the High Courts is mainly in benches which are of three kinds :

(a) Single Judge.—Position of this court is clear. A single judge is not bound by his own opinion expressed on similar issues in different cases. Likewise, decision of single judge is not binding on another single judge of the same High Court, division bench or full bench. It is also not binding on single judge, division bench or full bench of any other High Court. Single judge is bound by the decision of division bench or full bench of the same High Court but division bench or full bench rulings of other High Courts have only persuasive value for him. He is not bound by them.

Can a single judge overrule earlier single judge view with which he does not agree?—The answer is 'No". What he can do is to write his opinion and the reason why does he not agree with earlier single judge view. He must refer the matter to Chief Justice with a request to constitute Division Bench to consider his opinion and earlier opinion and thus which view is correct. The Division Bench would decide the conflict and send the case back to the judge who raised the conflict. This Court would decide that case in the light of Division Bench ruling.

(b) Division Bench.—It consists of two judges hearing the case. Jointly, their judgment, if unanimous becomes final so far as High Court is concerned. If they mutually disagree, the matter is placed before the Chief Justice for nomination of the third judge. His opinion decides the issue along with any one of the two views expressed earlier. If he is of third opinion, the matter may be sent for consideration of Full Bench. The division Bench is not bound by similar decision of any other division Bench or single judge ruling of the same High Court. The rulings of division Bench or full benches of other High Courts have only persuasive value. Sometimes the decision of single judge is also quoted with approval in division bench's decisions but it is not due to precedent's command.

(c) Full Bench.—Full Bench is constituted of Chief Justice to resolve conflicts between two Division Benches of the High Court and where there is no Supreme Court decision, when any third Division Bench, so locates, the difference in earlier Bench matters. The bench so seized may place the matter before the Chief Justice for referring the matter to larger bench or Full Bench as the Chief Justice may so think proper. The rulings of the Full Bench of one High Court are binding on all single judge or division benches of that court. But they are not binding on Full Bench or others of different High Courts. Full Bench is not bound by similar rulings of the similar Full Bench of the same High Court.

The rulings of single judge of High Court are binding on all courts of subordinate judicature, unless there is contrary ruling of division bench or Full Bench. If there are conflicting rulings by single judges, the lowest courts may refer the problem for consideration and guidance of the High Court. The problem so sent is to be considered by larger bench and directions are remitted accordingly. If there is conflict in between a single judge ruling and division bench ruling, the subordinate courts are bound by the rulings of division bench. They will disregard the views of single judge. The division bench ruling binds the single judge hearings and all subordinate courts. The precedents established or acknowledged by Full Bench are binding as such on all division benches, single judge hearings and subordinate courts. The precedent is binding downward. It is persuasive in upward direction.

(iv) Precedents in Supreme Court.—Federal court was the highest court of India immediately before the present constitution and the jurisdiction of the Privy Council had just been abolished in 1949. The rulings of the Federal Court and Privy Council are still binding as existing law on all subordinate courts until they have been overruled by present Supreme Court or competent legislature. The Supreme Court is the highest Court in India. It is not bound by the precedents established in other countries. The rulings of High Courts and superior courts of other countries are only raw materials to it. It can accept and may apply them. This will give them a judicial verdict and stability as general law of the land.

Sardar S.T. Saifuddin,[1]. was a five judges decision which held by majority of 4 to 1 that Bombay Prevention of Ex Communication Act, 1948 was *ultra vires* Article 26(b) and was not saved by Article 25(2).

In *Central Board of Dawoodi Vohra Community Case,*[2]. the prayer was made before two judges bench for reconsideration of the above. The two judges bench referred itself the matter to 7 judges bench. The question was whether this reference was proper. The Court of 7 judges bench found it not proper and sent it back to Constitution bench of 5 judges.*Held* two judges bench was bound by five judges bench, right or wrong and it could not disagree with it and had no liberty to refer it direct to 7 judges bench. The matter could be disagreed only by 5 judges bench and if so, the matter should have been sent to Chief Justice by even such 5 judges bench and it was Chief Justice alone who was competent to refer it to 7 judges bench. The procedure adapted by two judges bench was wrong.

The Supreme Court of India is now 57 years old Institution. It has inherited rich traditions of Federal Court and Privy Council and has shown that it is not bound by its own decisions if these come in way of progress, prosperity and fulfilment of directive principles of State Policy which are fundamental in governance. The point becomes vivid when the cases concerning constitutional amendments are considered. In *Shankari Prasad* v. *Union of India,*[3]. the Supreme Court held that the word 'law' under Article 13 excludes the constitutional amendment. It means only legislative law. The position was dittoed in later case of *Sajjan Singh* v. *State of Rajasthan,*[4]. In fact, the then Chief Justice Gajendragadkar expressed the view that if a law point has been established and settled, the Supreme Court would be rather reluctant to upset it, on this ground he refused to re-examine the proposition established in *Shankari Prasad's* case. However, this view found a big jolt two years later in *I.C. Golak Nath* case[5]. in which Supreme Court re-examined the meaning of the word 'law' under Article 13. The Court

---

1. (1962) Supp. 2 S.C.R. 496
2. A.I.R. 2005 S.C. 752
3. A.I.R. 1950 S.C. 458
4. A.I.R. 1965 S.C. 845
5. A.I.R. 1967 S.C. 1643

refused to follow the earlier proposition and ruled that law includes legislative as well as constituent law. Both are hit by Article 13 if they abridge or abrogate any of the fundamental rights. This was an unfortunate ruling of the Supreme Court which was condemned strongly by jurists. The Parliament had to intervene. The absolute majority in Parliament helped the Government in passing unscratched, the twenty-fourth amendment nullifying the effects of Golak Nath ruling. The whole thing was put to test again and certainly for the time before the whole Supreme Court sitting as largest Full Bench. The decision in *Keshavanand Bharati's* case swings the pendulum back to 1950 position and *Shankari Prasad's* case has become a living law. The majority was of the view that *Golaknath* was not properly decided. It took wrong view of law. Every part of Constitution was amendable under Article 368 which gives power to amend and also lays down procedure for amendment. Basic features are exception. These cannot be amended. What features are basic, it shall be decided by Court from time to time in case to case. Separation of power, independence of judiciary, secularism, socialism, sovereignty are few examples.

It is, submitted that since most of the areas of legislation are covered by codes and bye-laws, the law is almost certain and *stare decisis* should not be allowed to circumscribe the judge's liberty and delimit judicial independence. The Constitution is a dynamic document. Its interpretations should allow it to accommodate the changed outlooks and changing needs of the society. The rigidity of the *stare decisis* will seldom allow this to happen. The spirit of Hindu codes should be imbibed in constitutional interpretations so that it may stand even in circumstances altogether changed.

Law declared by the Supreme Court to be binding on all Courts.—Article 141 of the Constitution provides that the law declared by the Supreme Court shall be binding on all courts within the territory of India. This article gives obligatory force to the decisions of the Supreme Court. But it leaves us nowhere as to what is the meaning of the law declared. Does it mean only the *ratio decidendi* of the Supreme Court decisions? Or does it also include the *obiter dicta* thereof? Is it possible that the advises tendered by the Supreme Court to President under Article 143 be included in the law declared? And hence binding on all the courts within the territory of India.

Every decision contains three basic postulates. *Firstly*, finding of material facts, direct and inferential. An inferential finding of fact is the inference which the judge draws from the direct or perceptible facts. *Secondly*, statements of the principles of law applicable to the legal problems disclosed by the facts; and *Thirdly*, judgment based on the combined effect of the above. A decision is an authority for what it actually decides. What is of essence in a decision is its *ratio* and not every observation made in the judgment. Words in judgment are not words of an Act of legislature; something to be read, something to be inferred. Court decision is authority for what it actually decides and no more. It is not authority for what can be logically inferred from what is actually decided.

It means *ratio* of the decision.—The rationale of the decision is always binding as 'law declared' on all courts. It means the 'cream of the case', 'the ruling' or the 'basis on which the decision is pronounced'. The courts in India are directed to be bound by it. But it is not obligatory on the Supreme Court to take its earlier ruling as binding. The phrase 'on all courts in India' excludes the Supreme Court. It is submitted that Article 141 should be suitably amended by providing that law declared by Supreme Court shall be binding on all courts in territory of India except Supreme Court so that the doubts to the contrary may be set at rest. The Supreme Court is essentially a court of appeal, so all the cases here are heard by division bench. The practice of single judge hearing a case is not followed here, in this court. The decisions of larger bench are binding on benches of smaller number and decisions of the larger full bench are given due regard by smaller full benches. This practice has got rooted in Indian judicial set up. A decision is precedent on its own facts. Each case presents its own features. It is not everything said by a judge while giving judgment that constitutes a precedent. The only thing in a judge's decision binding a party is the principle upon which the case is decided and for this reason it is important to analyse a decision and isolate from it the *ratio decidendi.*

A decision is an authority for what it actually decides. What is of the essence in a decision is its *ratio* and not every observation found therein nor what logically flows from the various observations made in the judgment. The enunciation of the reason or principle on which a question before a Court has been decided is alone binding as a precedent.[1].

Obiter of the Supreme Court whether included in law declared.—Obiter is that part of the decision that is said by the way due to valour and chivalarity of the judge for showing his academic grasp. This is expository in character and explains the law point more clearly and elaborately sometimes than does the *ratio*. It is however not binding on courts as 'law declared'. 'Law declared' is different from both the 'Law expounded' and the 'Law elaborated'. The latter two serve as guides to the subordinate courts. They are free to accept or ignore them as sound expositions of Law. An *obiter dicta* is an observation of the court on a legal question suggested in a case before it but not arising in such manner as to require a decision. It is not precedent but is of considerable weight. If a judge gives two reasons for his decision, one cannot select one as better reason and reject the other. It also does not matter which comes first. Additional reason can also be given. It is, however, in tradition that the obiters of the Supreme Court are also given much weight and respect and are taken as binding if not inconsistent with any majority view on that point.

Minority opinion is not law declared.—The practice of writing minority opinions is accepted procedure in Indian set up. They may be in the form of dissenting opinions or concurrent opinions. In whatsoever form they may be, they are not binding on subordinate courts as law declared. It however, sometimes happens that minority views in one case become

1. (2006) 6 S.C.C. 366

majority opinion in any subsequent case. In later case, they become of a binding nature.

Article 141 and 142—The difference.—In *Indian Bank* v. *A.B.S. Mariner Products Ltd*,[1]. the question clarified was that in some cases, the Supreme Court, on special facts of the case, after decision, issues certain directions to the Government by moulding the relief sought. This is by virtue of power under Article 142. But, the High Courts reading this direction on part of the decision start following and issuing identical directions and it is so repeated and as such becomes law. Therefore, it is the duty of the Supreme Court, while issuing directions, to make it clear, that it is being done under authority of Article 142 and does not form part of *ratio decidendi* of the case. These directions may even be contrary to the 'law declared'. It is at variance with it. This power is only with Supreme court; High Courts cannot exercise it under cover of 'law declared' under Article 141. It is not so under Article 141. It is not precedent. It is exemption or relaxation of law declared.

Advisory opinion is whether law declared.—The President of India has the discretion to seek the opinion of the Supreme Court on any vexed question of law or otherwise on a matter of public interest. The President is neither bound by any such opinion nor the Supreme Court is bound to give any such opinion in these cases.

Judicial decisions as a source of law in common law and civil law countries.

The role of courts in creation and development of law under the civil law system has often been compared in recent years with their role under the common law systems. The most important difference between French and Anglo-Indian system is the degree of recognition given to decided cases. In common law countries, the system rests on the principle of '*stare decisis*' which means adherence to decided cases. The courts in India, England and other common law countries are not so much concerned with doing justice to the parties in an individual case, as with the following of the precedent set by earlier decision of a similar case. Thus, in Common law system, an unwritten law and case which the judges have made and which are found in different reports and digest is as binding as the statutory law, but the position in France and other continental countries is quite different. The case law has no binding force, and the judicial decision binds neither the courts which establish it, nor the lower court. In other words, judicial decisions are not treated as a law in civil law countries.

Strictly speaking, in France, judges do not create rule of law. Their function is only to decide the dispute between the parties. Courts only apply a statute or custom and in their absence, the decisions of the court are as based on the principles of equity, justice, reasons or traditions. The French view point, that the decision *of a court can never be justified by reference to prior court decisions is based on the following reasons.*

1. A.I.R. 2006 S.C. 1899

(a) In France, it is a common belief that a judge can commit mistake in the interpretation of law or its application.

(b) Judgment of the court cannot be relied upon because of continued changes in social, political, economic and international conditions.

(c) In France, the doctrine of *stare-decisis* is not followed, because judges have no fear of reversal or adverse comment. The French judges are the members of the civil service, and they are to continue in their office for the term. As such they are in no way under the authority of the superior courts.

(d) The courts in France, are meant to dispense justice according to law and this justice can only be given, if the courts do not follow the opinion of the judges in previous cases.

Despite the absence of a formal doctrine of 'stare-decisis' there is a strong tendency on the part of French courts to follow the precedents of the higher courts. Though the French courts are free as a matter of law, to disregard precedents, but it is certain that they will not do so without sufficient reason. Not a single instance has been found where the Court of Cassation has overruled its prior decisions. Further, the attitude of lower courts towards the decision of the Court of Cassation is quite similar to that of common law countries. Normally, the lower courts follow the precedents established by the 'Court of Cassation'.

Prospective overruling

Prospective overruling is modern theory of precedent. It is exception to rule that Supreme Court decision overruling earlier wrong decision (precedent) is restricted to actions in future. Past is preserved; future is protected. Done is not undone even if done under wrong law, but wrong law would not be allowed to continue in future in name of binding precedent. In doing so, law is not declared, it is found but for future. What is done is not disturbed. This is under Articles 32, 141, 142. So the High Court has no power under Article 226 or 227 to prospectively overrule. The doctrine is basically of U.S.A. origin but has now been used in *Golak Nath* case overruling prospectively *Shankari Prasad* and *Sajjan Singh* cases and *Keshavanand Bharti* overruling *Golak Nath* view prospectively.

Judicial Activism and Self-restraint.—Of all the institutions established by the Constitution the higher judiciary seems to have acquitted itself in the last 62 years as the best in a relative sense. The most respected public institution in India is the Supreme Court, respected by the elite and the illiterate alike. If the Court has come increasingly effective in its role as the final arbiter of justice, it is because of the confidence the common man has placed in it. The Court has no army at its command. It does not hold any purse strings. Its strength lies largely in the command it has over the hearts and minds of the public and the manner in which it can influence and mould public opinion. As the distinguished French author Alexis de Toquevulle describes the power wielded by judges is the power of public opinion. Hamilton called the court system the weakest organ of government because it had control over neither the sword nor the purse. A court becomes strong only when it identifies itself with the disadvantaged minorities and they see the court as an independent institution, a bulwark against oppression and tyranny. A court gains strength only by carving a niche for itself in the minds of the people. A court must appear to the people as their protector. It must not only be, but also must appear to be impartial, principled, and capable of achieving results. There would have been no Fundamental Rights worth mentioning if Article 21 had been interpreted in its original sense.

Judges participating in judicial review of legislative action should be creative and not mechanistic in their interpretations. According to Justice Cardozo, a written constitution "states or ought to state not rules for the passing hour but principles for an expanding future". Judges who interpret a written constitution cannot merely apply the law to the facts that come before them. The scope of judicial creativity expands when a Constitution contains a bill of rights. It is one thing to consider whether a legislature has acted within its powers and another to consider whether its acts, although within its plenary powers, are violative of any of the basic rights of the people. Therefore, judges who interpret a bill of rights must expound upon the philosophy and ideology that underlies the bill of rights. When judges interpret the law or a constitution by not merely giving effect to the literal meaning of the words, but by trying to provide an interpretation consistent with the spirit of that statute or constitution, they are said to be activist judges. In this sense, the judges who developed the common law were also activist.

Justice Krishna Iyer, explained that 'A Nineteenth Century text, when applied to Twentieth-Century conditions, cannot be construed by signals from the grave. Justice Krishna Iyer in the landmark decision of *Rajendra Prasad* v. *State of U.P.* observed that, "When the legislative text is too bald to be self-acting or suffers zigzag distortion in action, the primary obligation is on Parliament to enact necessary clauses by appropriate amendments to Section 302 I.P.C. But if legislative undertaking is not in sight, judges who have to implement the Code cannot fold up their professional hands but must make the provision viable by evolution of supplementary principles, even if it may appear to posses the flavour of law-making. [He further went on to quote] Lord Dennings' observations : "Many of the Judges of England have said that they do not make law. They only interpret it. This is an illusion which they have fostered. But it is a notion which is now being discarded everywhere. Every new decision-on every new situation-is a development of the law. Law does not stand still. It moves continually. Once this is recognised, then the task of the Judge is put on a higher plane. He must consciously seek to mould the law so as to serve the needs of the time. He must not be a mere mechanic, a mere working mason, laying brick on brick, without thought to the overall design. He must be an architect-thinking of the structure as a whole, building for society a system of law which is strong, durable and just. It is on his work that civilised society itself depends".

The Supreme Court of India in Charles Sobhraj's case observed that a constitution is not to be interpreted by reference to the wishes or opinions of its framers, but by consideration of 'the evolving standards of decency and signify that marks the progress of a mature society'.

The extension of judicial review over constitutional amendments was itself an exercise in judicial activism on the part of the Supreme Court of India. The Supreme Court, in the leading case of His Holiness Kesavananda Bharati v. *State of Kerala*, held by a process of judicial interpretation that though there are no express words in Article 368 of the Indian Constitution limiting the power conferred by that Article on Parliament to amend the Constitution, that power is not an unlimited or unrestricted power and it does not entitle Parliament to amend the Constitution in such a way as to alter or affect the basic structure of the Constitution. this is undoubtedly a most remarkable instance of judicial activism, for that has gone to the farthest extent in limiting the constituent power of Parliament.

The Indian Court has emerged relatively unscathed in recent decades as a leading actor in the ordering of domestic priorities within the polity can be attributed in no small measure to a constitutional ethos that encourages all institutions, including the judiciary, to become active participants in the realization of particular ideological aspirations. In effect there exists a constitutional mandate for judicial activism.

Nevertheless it is obvious that unless the Executive and the Legislature begin to respond to the needs of the citizens and discharge their responsibilities, public interest litigation and judicial activism are bound to remain centre stage as long as courts continue to respond the way they do now.

In a country like ours more than eighty percent of people are economically backward and they are subjected to discrimination as a rule. In such an explosive situation causing adverse effect on society, when the executive and legislature are apathetic and fail to discharge their constitutional duties and deliver the goods, the apex court which is the custodian of the citizen's rights and liberties and which in that capacity acts as sentinel on the *qui vive* has no other choice but to step in and direct these constitutional functionaries to discharge their obligation. When the bureaucracy shows callous indifferences and insensitivity to its mandatory duties which affect the basic rights of the people and when the law enforcing agencies exhibit their brutality in the process of implementation of law, should the court remain a passive observer of the scenario? Will judges of the highest court be justified sitting in an ivory tower like an Olympian closing their eyes to the stress and storm that affect society and remain into cocoons or in isolated and protected cells without giving appropriate mandates and thereby protecting the Fundamental Rights and liberties of the citizens of the country,

In Gopalan's case, the Supreme Court upheld the validity of a pre-Constitution preventive detention law on the grounds that once the deprivation was supported by law, Article 21 could not be said to be infringed. One of the judges expressly referred to the debates in the Constituent Assembly (which was very recent in legislative history) to indicate that the American Due Process model had been expressly rejected by the framers of the Constitution. During the deliberations of the constituent Assembly, the due process clause was watered down in the light of American warnings. In its place, the Assembly approved an "any procedure" clause so that the life and liberty of a person could be restrained by any procedure established by law". Yet years after Gopalan, a later Constitution Bench of the Supreme Court in *Maneka Gandhi's* case held that the State could deprive any person of his life or liberty under Article 21 not only because a law so empowered it; that law had also to meet the test of being non-arbitrary, non-discriminatory and hence violative of Article 14. Due process, which was expressly rejected by the framers of the Constitution, was in substance reintroduced in *Maneka Gandhi* when interpreting the life and liberty clause of the Constitution. The decision is illustrative of the saying that a written Constitution is a 'living document' and must receive its interpretation not according to the intent of those framed it but according to 'the felt necessities of the times'. thus, the Supreme Court has declared that "the substance of American due process has been introduced into the conservative text of the Constitution."

Numerous railway passengers in India suffer from fatal injuries as a result of falling down in their anxiety to get into a moving train. In such cases, are railways liable to pay compensation? The Supreme Court rejected the railways' plea that there was no fault on its part and there was contributory negligence on the part of a deceased passenger. After an elaborate analysis and a global survey of the principle of strict liability the court has to develop new principles for fixing liability in cases like the one before it. The bench held that railways were liable to pay compensation on the principle of strict liability on the premise that "because such public bodies benefit the community it is unfair to leave the result of a non-negligent accident to lie fortuitously on a particular individual rather than to spread it among the community generally".

Whether judicial activism is an aspect of judicial review? Judicial activism is not an aberration. It is an essential aspect of the dynamics of a constitutional court. It is a counter-majoritarian check on democracy. Judicial activism, however, does not mean governance by the judiciary. It also must function within the limits of the judicial process. Within those limits, it performs the function of legitimising or, more rarely, stigmatising the actions of the other organs of government..." The judiciary is the weakest organ of the State. It becomes strong only when people repose faith in it. Such faith of the people constitutes the legitimacy of the Court and of judicial activism. Courts have to continuously strive to sustain their legitimacy. They do not have to bow to public pressure, rather they have to stand firm against any pressure.

It may be the case that such interpretation goes beyond the supposedly original intent of the Constitution makers. Even so, it captures the spirit of what was intended in a manner consistent with the human rights and social justice enterprise of the Constitution as a whole. By interpreting 'life' and 'liberty' as including the total well being of a human being, the Constitution has cast a protective umbrella around the everyday concerns of ordinary life. This definitional expansion has necessitated a transformation of the 'any process' clause into a 'due process' clause. These various quandaries over the definition of fundamental rights are strong reminders that human rights issues do not lend themselves to narrow textual interpretation. Constitutional interpretation must view the definition of human rights with an expansive wisdom to interpret the text purposively so as to preserve the right of all human beings to mutual respect and concern.

The Courts cannot interpret a statute, much less a Constitution, in a mechanistic manner. In the case of a statute, a court must determine the actual intent of the authors. In the case of a Constitution, a court must sustain the constitution's relevance to changing social, economic, and political scenarios. The court must give to the words of a Constitution "a continuity of life and expression". An apex court, besides deciding the law that birds all courts subordinate to it, also must make "vocal and audible" the ideas that otherwise might remain silent. The original intentions of the founding fathers do not bind a constitutional court. Rather, the court is free to interpret the Constitution in terms of what the framers would have intended under the circumstances that exist at the time of such interpretation. In the absence of such judicial activism, a Constitution would become stultified and devoid of the inner strength necessary to survive and provide normative order for the changing times. Further, it is strongly contended that the Constitution has to be worked. That is, it has to be acted upon by men and women in society for their requirements and purposes. Ideas, feelings, desires, change as does society, economy, and technology. What was written in one situation has to be implemented in a very different context decades, centuries, later. What is acceptable at one time may not be at another. In short, interpretation is inevitable.

Judicial intervention is legitimate when it comes within the scope of permissible judicial review. the thin dividing line demarcating appropriate and inappropriate judicial intervention is drawn on the basis of functions allocated to the different branches by the Constitution. In borderline cases, a legal question at the core determines the need for judicial intervention. Purely political questions and policy matters not involving decision of a core legal issue and outside the domain of judiciary. The US Supreme Court laid down a pragmatic test in *Baker* v. *Carr*, for judicial intervention in matter within a political hue apart from those expressly allocated to another branch. It held that the controversy before the court must have a 'justiciable cause of action' and should not suffer from a 'lack of judicially discoverable and manageable standards for resolving it' This is a pre-requisite for judicial intervention. Otherwise, the policy of 'judicial hands-off' should govern, because such a matter is required to be dealt with by another branch. Appropriate judicial intervention or legitimate judicial activism is that which is founded on an established or evolved juristic principle having precedent value and performed within judicially manageable standards. It should only compel performance of duty by the designated authority in case of its inaction or failure, while a takeover by the judiciary of the function allocated to another branch is inappropriate. Judiciary has intervened to question allotment of a particular bungalow to a judge, specific bungalows for the judge's pool, monkeys capering in colonies to stray cattle on the streets, cleaning public conveniences, and levying congestion charges at peak hours at airports with heavy traffic etc., under the threat of use of contempt power to enforce compliance of its orders [are some of the few cases in which judiciary has stepped into executives shoes]. The judiciary has stepped in, not only to direct the designated authorities to perform their duty, but it has also taken over the implementation of the programme through non-statutory committees formed by it.

The failure of the politicians to perform their duties properly and the consequent role of the judges in providing some relief from misgovernance is no reason to support the judges' expansion of their powers through creative interpretations. Whatever may be the positive results of such judicial intervention and interpretation the ends do not justify the means. But the constitutional interpretation of fundamental rights in India cannot be wholly understood without comprehending the human situation in which the demand for rights is made. The human condition speaks of poverty at levels of penury where basic needs and livelihood are not assured. Further, the main motive of democracy is to maximise mass-welfare. In India, the special features of society and its institutions, and the urgency of the problems presented to the courts, doubtless help to explain the demands for "judicial activism". Indignant critics forget that it is the Executive's failure to perform its duty and the notorious tardiness of legislatures that impels judicial activism and provides its motivation and legitimacy. When gross violations of human rights are brought to its notice, the judiciary cannot procrastinate. It must respond. In order to achieve this goal, even if one wing of Government takes upon itself the responsibility that is supposed to be carried out by the other wings, there requires no eyebrow to be raised. Therefore, it is strongly contended that judicial activism in India is justified because of its peculiar circumstances different from western countries. The judicial activism in India is justified to the extent it safeguarded basic human rights of citizens and gave a new hope to the downtrodden that judiciary is one of the organs of the state to turn to, when there is failure on the part of other organs to perform their duties. It is the creativity of the Supreme Court of India that has preserved the basic human rights of the citizens. As a guardian and watchdog of fundamental rights it is within the mandate of the Court to infuse a new life in Article 21 and broaden the scope of 'right to life' and 'personal liberty' so as to make it meaningful and cherish it for the generations to come.

The Indian Judiciary has evolved itself as a saviour of mankind by interpreting Article 21 of the Constitution in the widest possible manner. The Supreme Court has interpreted right to life to include right to live with human dignity, right to pollution free environment, right to livelihood, freedom from noise pollution etc. The Court day-by-day is enhancing the ambit of right to life and personal liberty. There is considerable scope for further expansion of the content of Article 21 by the judiciary with the objective of taking India forward towards a modern industrial society.

There are at least two types of situation in which the Court takes on an activist posture and either assumes a legislative role or attempts to directly undertake governance. The first is where gaps and ambiguities exist in the law or where the full protection of Fundamental Rights warrants enunciation of a new policy or extension of an existing policy in conformity with the Constitutional scheme and the international obligations of the state. The *Visakha judgment* and *Lakshmi Nath Pandey case* are examples of this type of judicial activism in the legislative sphere. The expansion of the right to life under Article 21, invoking Directive Principles, is another example of activism in areas legitimately belonging to the legislature. Justice J.S. Verma has cautioned the use of judicial activism. He referred to judicial activism as a sharp-edged tool which has to be used as a scalpel by a skillful surgeon to cure the malady. Not as Rampuri knife which can kill Judges now seem to want to engage themselves with boundless enthusiasm in complex socio-economic issues raising myriads of facts, and ideological issues, that cannot be adjudicated by "judicially manageable standards. Judges should be conscious of the limitations of the judicial function and the consequent need to remain within the judicial sphere. Judicial activism, however, does not mean governance by the judiciary. Judicial activism must also function within the limits of judicial process. Judicial activism should go hand in hand with judicial restraint. Though our learned judges drive safely on the established roads, they risk deviation in case of an urgent call for protecting the spirit of our Constitution. They overreach when legislatures or executives cross the line of control drawn in Constitution. But it's equally true that the judges neither represent the people's will, nor they are accountable to the people. It is argued that every single instance of judicial activism in recent memory has been a reaction to a particular malafide of the legislature in matters of public or national interest. If the legislature and executive acted in accordance with the spirit of the Constitution and not in accordance with their narrow political vote bank interest, there would have been no room for such judicial activism.

Court rulings on freebies, elections and caste-based rallies, and the CIC order on political parties are a beginning towards cleansing politics but whether they can achieve the desired result is debatable

The slew of judgments from the higher judiciary in the period of just about a month or so has been like manna from heaven on the parched earth of electoral reforms. First, the Supreme Court frowned upon freebies, which it said "shake the root of free and fair elections." Then came the verdict on Section 8(4) of the Representation of the People Act 1951 (the Act) being *ultra vires* of the Constitution and along with it the barring of jailed persons from electoral contest. For its part, the Allahabad High Court banned caste-based rallies, the staple of many a political party. Not to be left behind, the Central Information Commission added its mite by declaring that political parties came within the ambit of Right to Information Act (RTI).

Varied response

The reactions have been varied to the striking down of Section 8(4) of the Act. Two prominent politicians, one from the Congress and the other from the Bhartiya Janata Party, both eminent lawyers, were in agreement with the reasoning of the court. Some have questioned it for creating two categories of convicted legislators and some other on the competence of a two-judge bench overturning the 2005 verdict of a five-judge bench. The reactions have been sharper over the part of the verdict on the jailed not being eligible to contest elections, calling it "judicial over-reach".

Rattled perhaps by the verdict that upon conviction a legislator loses his seat, all kinds of objections have been raised. It has been faulted for discriminating by creating two categories of legislators, those who were convicted but appealed and so will continue as members and others who would hereafter immediately lose their seats. The fact is lost sight of that this so-called 'discrimination' is, in fact, a 'distinction' the court made in the larger interest of preventing chaos and confusion that might arise if many legislators lost their membership suddenly.

Another issue was that a legislator losing his membership upon conviction cannot get it back if acquitted on appeal. Those who raise it conveniently forget that a disqualified person who lost the chance to contest has no remedy either if acquitted in appeal soon thereafter. These are inevitable as no law can be made to perfectly suit every situation.

As for the barring of jailed persons from electoral contest, the verdict may perhaps not stand on further scrutiny. While the law takes away the right to vote of a person in jail, that it does not take away his eligibility to be registered as an elector seems to have escaped notice. Only those who are disqualified lose the eligibility to be electors. May be the corrective will come in a review petition.

Misplaced hype

Some have quoted legal experts to claim that a larger bench of the Supreme Court has already upheld in 2005 the provision in Section 8(4) and so the present judgment is erroneous. They have also faulted it for failing to interpret the law "bearing in mind the object of the provision for enactment" which is to protect the House. All this hype seems misplaced. The simple fact is that before the Constitution bench in 2005 the question agitated was only the duration for which the protection afforded by Section 8(4) would be valid, not its *vires*, and the court had clarified that it was available only till the term of that House and till the person continued to be a member.

If the political class is getting worried, it is just as well because with growing number of legislators with criminal cases, there is a real threat of this ruling creating problems but only if pending cases get decided. The percentage of legislators with pending criminal cases is not less than 15 to 20 per cent in most Houses and the number is not small. Uttar Pradesh is said to have a whopping 50 per cent of criminally charged legislators. According to some newspaper reports, there is one legislator with as many as 36 cases pending 14 of them for murder. Another 'gentleman' is an accused in 12 cases of murder, out of 20 pending cases. Should we shed a tear if such distinguished people lose their membership because of the operation of this judgment?

'Strict and narrow construction'

In its 2005 Order, the Supreme Court Bench said in a slightly different context "while a strict and narrow construction may not be adopted which may have the effect of shutting of any prominent and other eligible persons to contest elections but at the same time in dealing with a statutory provision which imposes disqualification on a citizen it would not be unreasonable to take merely a broad and general view." In the current context, I am sure public opinion will be overwhelmingly in favour of not a "broad and general view", but a "strict and narrow construction" to shut off such 'prominent' persons from contesting elections or continuing as legislators.

But then, from another angle, the judgment declaring Section 8(4) of the Act as *ultra vires* of the Constitution, may merely seem "all sound and fury signifying nothing." Given that the wheels of our criminal justice system grind slower than God's, the chance that these 'tainted' legislators will easily lose their eligibility to contest elections or to continue as legislators by being convicted, seems a little far-fetched. Being 'prominent', they may successfully manage to slow the system even further so that they come to no harm. That is the real danger. Interminable interlocutory proceedings or the compromising of witnesses and the like are not unknown weapons in the armoury of those who strive to slow down the judicial process.

If this verdict leads to political parties denying ticket to such 'distinguished' people, it would be a change for the good. But if the past is any guide, it does not inspire. Notwithstanding the sentiments expressed at the highest level by the two prominent national parties, before the 2009 Parliament elections, there was no substantial improvement when it came to ticket distribution. In fact, the number of MPs with criminal record actually went up by 25.78 per cent for those with criminal cases and by 36.36 per cent for those with serious criminal charges in the 15th Lok Sahba as compared to the 14th. So it is a moot point whether this verdict, though welcome as it strikes a blow for 'cleaner' legislators, will lead to a substantial reduction in the number of 'tainted' lawmakers. A legislation to bar those charge sheeted for involvement at least in heinous crimes from contesting elections combined with fast-tracking of such cases is the need of the hour if we are keen on the decriminalisation of legislatures and politics. The verdict by itself is only a case of crossing half a well.

Hollow argument

A self-serving argument that such a special provision is needed to protect that House would ring hollow in this age and time. Political parties cannot escape responsibility when they merrily distributes ticket on the grounds of winnability to tainted candidates as though in a country of a billion people they could not find untainted people to contest elections. Seeking to save this provision by asking for a review, moving a larger bench, or through an alternative enactment will only mean conferring an advantage where it is least deserved, namely on persons with criminal cases against them. Political parties should not, in the first instance, nominate such persons but should seek the fast-tracking of such cases against their tainted members. Therein lies the remedy, not in seeking a special provision.

'Institutional Integrity' is a phrase that has required much currency after the Supreme Court verdict in the CVC appointment case. If appointing a 'tainted' officer can compromise the integrity of an institution which is Parliament's creation, how can the presence of 'tainted' legislators not compromise the institutional integrity of the Parliament and Assemblies, the highest symbols of our democracy? It is time political parties considered that the country, the legislatures and the public deserve better.

Bureaucracy

In a path-breaking verdict, the Supreme Court said bureaucrats should not act on verbal orders given by political bosses as it sought an end to frequent transfers and suggested a fixed tenure to insulate them from political interference.

Suggesting sweeping reforms in the functioning of bureaucracy, a bench headed by Justice K.S. Radhakrishnan said Parliament must enact a law to regulate postings, transfers and disciplinary action against bureaucrats. Holding that much of the deterioration in bureaucracy is because of political interference, it said that civil servants should not act on verbal orders given by political executives and all actions must be taken by them on the basis of written communication. The bench also comprising justice P.C. Ghose said giving a fixed minimum tenure to a civil servant will not only promote professionalism and efficiency, but also good governance.

It asked the Centre and all State Governments along with Union Territories to issue directions within three months for providing fixed tenure to civil servants.

The bench also said Civil Services Board be constituted at the Centre and State-levels.

The verdict, which is on the line of Apex Court's earlier order on police reforms for giving fixed tenure to senior police officers in *Prakash Singh* case, will go a long way in giving freedom and independence to the functioning of bureaucracy.

❑ ❑

Chapter 5

Judicial method under statutory and codified system Application of legal reasoning

When the judge has some statute on the point which comes before him in court in any case, he is just to apply the provisions of that statute to the facts of the case and decide accordingly. Judicial process consists only of this task. But this does not mean that judge becomes a machine, or just a computer. Judging is not mechanical or perfunctory job. The statute does not decide the case. Case has to be decided by the judge. There may be ambiguities on the point in the statute. The statute may need to be read in the light of developments since it was made. Indian Contract Act, 1872 uses example of post for communication of offer and acceptance. What would happen to these provisions of communication in era of phone, cellphone, telex and internet wherein there is instant communication. Offer and acceptance in era of standard form contracts do not retain same importance for simple reason. That it is judicial process which will keep 1872 provisions abreast and in tune with 2012 developments in the world. Days of Conflict of Laws of early 17th or even 19th century could not contemplate of growth of International Trade law and International Economic Law (contracts between private corporations and the public corporations *inter se* or with Government departments).

The judicial process does not only consist of finding *sententia legis*. It extends now to ascribing intention where there may not be one or needs ascribing the intention different from one that is. Judge has to fill the gaps if any in now and then situation. He is no longer a critic trying to find fault in statute, he has to play a role of wellwisher trying to plug the loophole if any. The judicial process is not a job of adversary but it is one of cooperation and co-entreprenuership. Assist the legislator and not desist is the new mission of the judge and judging. Construct the legislature's message, not destroy it in the process. The judge fills the gap left or seen in statute. It supplements the statute. It fills the vacant space in statute. The function flourishes and persists by virtue of the human need to which the judicial process steadfastly responds and is capable of responding. The law is for the people. The people are not for law. Law is our well-wisher. It is neither our adversary nor enemy. One should not take law in image of policeman but in image of doctor, teacher or spriritual guru. Not to be feared but to be endeared and loved. Judicial process helps to create, uphold and promote it.

Mimansa rules and legal reasonings

In ancient and medieval India there was tremendous development not only in the fields of Science and Philosophy, but also in the field of law. However, the advent of British rule denied us the benefits of these developments as the alien rulers made it a policy to demoralise and denigrate us by propagating the idea that Indians were a race with no worthwhile achievement to their credit.

The principles of interpretation of statutes mainly relied on in our law courts are those dealt with in the works of Western jurists like Maxwell and Craies. However, in our country we had developed from very early times a scientific system of interpretation known as the Mimansa Principles and these were regularly followed by our renowned jurists like Vijnaneshwara (author of Mitakshara), Jimutvahana (author of Dayabhag), Nanda Pandit (author of Dattak Mimansa) *etc.* Whenever there was any conflict between the Smritis *e.g.* Manusmriti and Yagnavalkya Smriti, or ambiguity in a Shruti or Smriti, the Mimansa Principles were applied. Most of these principles are rational and scientific, and in some respects superior to the principles obtaining in Western Law. At present there is no reason why we should not apply them in appropriate cases.

In *Tribhuwannath* v. *D.I.O.S.*, Writ Petition No. 17544 of 1990 decided on 30-3-1992 : (1992) ALR 921, one of these principles was applied. In this case the petitioner, who was the seniormost teacher in an Intermediate College, had filed a writ petition in the Allahabad High Court claiming that he should have been appointed ad hoc Principal on the retirement of the previous Principal, but the management had superseded him. In the course of hearing two Division Bench decisions apparently conflicting with each other, were cited. While the Division Bench ruling written by Hon'ble R.M. Sahai, J. had held that the seniormost teacher should be appointed ad hoc Principal the Division Bench ruling delivered by Hon'ble V.N. Khare, J. had held that it is the discretion of the Management as to who is to be appointed. By way of employing the Samanjasya principle of Mimansa it was easy to reconcile the conflicting decisions by holding that the former decision should be interpreted to mean that ordinarily the seniormost teacher should be appointed Principal, while the latter decision should be interpreted to mean that in exceptional cases, *viz.*, if there are grave charges against him, he can be superseded by a reasoned order, though only after giving him a show-cause notice.

Jaimini Sutra

The Mimansa or the Purva Mimansa Rules to be exact, were laid down by Jaimini in his Sutras written around 600 B.C. That they are very ancient is proved by the fact that they are referred to in many Smritis which themselves are very old. Thus, the Apastamba Sutras copiously refer to Jaimini's principles. Since these Sutras are written in very concise form it became necessary to explain them. Many commentaries were written on them, the main ones being of Sabara, who lived around Second Century A.D., and Kumarila Bhatta and Prabhakara, who lived around the Eighth

Century A.D. Before mentioning some of the Mimansa Principles it is necessary to give a short background. Classical Hindu Philosophy has six schools (shatdarshan) all of which aim at Moksha (liberation). Purva Mimansa is one of these schools, and according to it one can achieve Moksha by performing Yagya (sacrifice) in accordance with the Shastras. The Shastras consist of Shruti and Smriti, the former being superior to the latter. Shruti consists of the four Vedas, the Brahmanas, the Aranyaks and the Upanishads. Brahmanas are treatises written in prose which prescribe methods of performing various Yagyas. To every Veda one or more Brahmanas are attached. Thus, the Aitareya Brahmana is attached to the Rig Veda, the Taitareya Brahmana to the Krisna Yajur Veda, the Shatapatha Brahmana to the White Yajur Veda, and the Tandya Brahmana to the Sama Veda.

Utilization of Mimansa Principles

Knowledge of Mimansa Principles enables one to creatively develop the law. A few examples of utilization of Mimansa Principles :

1. In *Sardar Mohammad Ansar Khan* v. *State of U.P.*, (1993) ALR 89, the controversy was as to which of two clerks appointed on the same day in an Intermediate College would be senior, and hence entitled to promotion as Head Clerk. Now there is no rule to cater to this situation. However, Chapter 2, Regulation 3 of the U.P. Intermediate Education Regulations states that where 2 teachers are appointed on the same day, the senior in age will be senior. Using the atidesh Principle of mimansa it was held that the same principle which applies to teachers should be also applied to clerks, and hence the senior in age would be senior. The atidesh principle originated in the practical difficulty of performing certain yagyas. There are some yagyas (*e.g.* agnihotra, darshapurnamani, *etc.*) whose method of performance is given in detail in the Brahmanas. These are known as prakriti yagyas. However, there are other yagyas whose rules are not given any where, and these are known as vikriti yagyas. The question arose how these latter are to be performed? The atidesh principle was created to resolve this difficulty, and according to this principle the vikriti yagya is to be performed according to the rules of the prakriti yagya belonging to the same genus.

2. In *Tribhuwan Misra* v. *D.I.O.S.*, AIR 1992 Alld. 351, the Samanjasya principle was used to reconcile 2 apparently conflicting Division Bench rulings. This technique avoided reference to a Full Bench which would have tied up 3 or more Judges for several days in resolving the conflict. No doubt this decision (as a Single Judge) curtailed the full effect of the 2 Division Bench decisions, but that was done on the authority of the maxim of the lost horse; and burnt chariot (Nasrhtashva Dagdharatha Nyaya). This is based on the story of two men travelling in their respective chariots. One of them lost his horses and the other's chariot was burnt through the out break of fire in the inn where they were spending the night. The horses that were left were harnessed to the remaining chariot, and the two men pursued their journey together. Its teaching is union for mutual advantage, which has been quoted in the 16th Vartika to Panini, and is explained by Patanjali. It is

referred to in Kumarila Bhatta's 'Tantravartika'.

3. The Anusanga Principle of Mimansa has been used in *Mahabir Prasad Dwivedi* v. *State*. The principle has been explained in great detail in this decision, which may be seen in the aforesaid journal. The conclusion reached in this decision could not have been reacted by any principle of Western Jurisprudence, and this illustrates the great use which can be made of Mimansa Principles to make the statute more democratic and equitable.

The Laghava Principle has been used in *Vinay Khare* v. *State of U.P.* The controversy in this case was that if in a competitive examination two candidates got equal marks whether the candidate who got more marks in the oral interview should be placed higher in the select list or the candidate who got more marks in the written test. It was held in this case that the candidate who got more marks in the written test should be placed higher because to interpret general suitability on the basis of marks in the written test is a short and simple interpretation and provides a clear objective test, whereas the criteria in the oral interview involves consideration of the candidate's personality, dress, physique, *etc.* which is complicated and in which there are more chances of favouritism and arbitrariness.

In *Vijay Narayana* v. *State of Maharashtra*, this appeal has been filed against the impugned judgment and order dated 21.01.2008 passed by a Division Bench of the High Court of Bombay whereby the writ petition filed by the appellants herein has been rejected.

4. The facts in brief are that a Notification under Section 4 of the Land Acquisition Act, 1894 (hereinafter for short 'the Act') was issued in respect of the land in question on 29.8.2002. Thereafter a Notification under Section 6 of the Act was issued on 18.6.2003. The said Notification under Section 6 was challenged and the writ petition filed by the appellants was allowed on 20.1.2004 and the Notification under Section 6 of the Act dated 18.06.2003 was quashed. Subsequently a second Notification under Section 6 dated 30.10.2006 was issued by the State Government.

5. The short question that arises for consideration is whether the Notification under Section 6 dated 30.10.2006 is valid. In our opinion, the said Notification was clearly barred by clause (ii) of the proviso to Section 6 of the Act which reads as under :—

> "[Provided that no declaration in respect of any particular land covered by a notification under section 4, sub-section (1),-
>
> (i) ....
>
> (ii) published after the commencement of the
>
> Land Acquisition (Amendment) Act, 1984, shall be made after the expiry of one year from the date of the publication of the notification;"

It can be seen from the aforesaid proviso to Section 6 that it is couched in negative language. It is well settled that when a Statute is couched in negative language it is ordinarily regarded as peremptory and mandatory in nature. [See Principles of Statutory Interpretation by Justice G.P. Singh 11th Edition, 2008 pages 390 to 392]. As stated by Crawford "Prohibitive or negative words can rarely, if ever, be directory. And this is so even though the statute provides no penalty for disobedience." [See Crawford : Statutory Construction P. 523; See also in this connection *Haridwar Singh* v. *Begum Sumbra*, AIR 1972 SC 1242 (1247), *Lachmi Narain* v. *Union of India*, AIR 1976 SC 714 (726), *Mannalal Khetan* v. *Kedarnath Khetan*, AIR 1977 SC 536 *etc.*]

6. In this connection we may also refer to the Mimansa Rules of Interpretation, which were our traditional principles of interpretation for over 2500 years, but which are unfortunately ignored in our Courts of law today.

7. It is deeply regrettable that in our Courts of law lawyers quote Maxwell and Craies but nobody refers to the Mimansa Principles of Interpretation. Most lawyers would not have even heard of their existence. Today our so-called educated people are largely ignorant about the great intellectual achievements of our ancestors and the intellectual treasury which they have bequeathed us. The Mimansa Principles of Interpretation is part of that great intellectual treasury, but it is distressing to note that apart from the reference to these principles in the judgment of Sir John Edge, the then Chief Justice of Allahabad High Court in Beni Prasad vs. Hardai Bibi 1892 ILR 14 All 67 (FB), a hundred years ago and in some judgments of one of us (M. Katju, J.) there has been almost no utilization of these principles even in our own country. Most of the Mimansa Principles are rational and scientific and can be utilized in the legal field (see in this connection K.L. Sarkar's 'Mimansa Rules of Interpretation' which is a collection of Tagore Law Lectures delivered in 1905 and which contains the best exposition of these principles).

8. The Mimansa Principles of Interpretation, as laid down by Jaimini in his sutras around 6th Century B.C. and as explained by Sabar, Kumarila Bhatta, Prabhakar, Mandan Mishra, etc, were regularly used by our renowned jurists like Vijnaneshwara (author of Mitakshara), Jimutvahana (author of Dayabhaga), Nanda Pandit (author of Dattaka Mimansa), *etc.* Whenever there was any conflict between two Smritis, *e.g.*, Manusmriti and Yajnavalkya Smriti, or ambiguity or absurdity in any Smriti these principles were utilized. Thus, the Mimansa Principles were our traditional system of interpretation of legal texts. Although originally they were created for interpreting religious texts pertaining to the Yagya (sacrifice), gradually they came to be utilized for interpreting legal texts also (see in this connection P.V. Kane's 'History of the Dharmashastra', Vol.V, Pt.II, Ch.XXIX and Ch.XXX, pp. 1282-1351), and also for interpreting texts on philosophy, grammar, *etc.* *i.e.* they became of universal application. Thus, Shankaracharya has used the Mimansa adhikaranas in his bhashya on the Vedanta sutras.

9. While the first edition of Maxwell's book was published in 1875, in India we have been doing interpretation for over 2500 years, as already stated above. There were hundreds of books (all in Sanskrit) written on the subject, though only a few dozens have survived the ravages of time, but even these show how deep our ancestors went into the subject of interpretation.

10. To give an example the Mimansakas examine the subject of negative Vidhis (negative injunctions such as the one in the proviso to Section 6) very searchingly and exhaustively. First of all, they distinguish between what may be called prohibitions against the whole world, and those against particular persons only. This distinction resembles that between judgments or rights in rem and judgments or rights in personam. The former prohibitions are called Pratishedha and the latter Paryudasa. For example, the prohibitory clause 'Do not eat fermented (stale) food (na kalanjam bhakshayet) is a Pratishedha; while the prohibition 'those who have taken the Prajapati vow must not see the rising sun' is a Paryudasa. In the second place, Pratishedhas are divided practically into two sub-clauses *viz.* those which prohibit a thing without any reference to the manner in which it may be used, and those which prohibit it only as regards a particular mode of using. For instance, 'Do not eat fermented food' prohibits the use of it under all circumstances, while 'Do not use the Sorasi vessel at dead of night' forbids the use of the vessel only at the dead of night.

11. Then Paryudasa is also of two kinds. In one case, it relates to a person performing some special act which is not enjoined by a Vidhi, as in the case of the Prajapati vow. In the other, it relates to a person engaged in performing a Vidhi; as for instance, when one is to do Shradh during the full moon by virtue of a Vidhi but not in the night of the full moon. In this case, the prohibition of doing Shradh in the night is a Paryudasa, which is the same as an exception or proviso as we understand these terms. For, the clause 'not in the night' is an exception to the rule 'Perform the Shradh during the full moon'. These are the four classes of negative clauses. The first class, of which the Kalanja (fermented food) clause is an example, may well be called a condemnatory prohibition. The second class consists also of absolute prohibitions of things under certain circumstances, as in the case of the Sorasi vessel. The third class consists of prohibitions in relation to persons in a given situation, as in the case of the Prajapati vow. The fourth class restricts the scope of action of persons engaged in fulfilling an injunction, as regards the time, place or manner of carrying out the substantive element of the injunction.

12. Thus we see that in the Mimansa system as regards negative injunctions (such as the one contained in the proviso to Section 6 of Land Acquisition Act) there is a much deeper discussion on the subject than that done by Western Jurists. The Western writers on the subject of interpretation (like Maxwell, Craies, *etc.*) only say that ordinarily negative words are mandatory, but there is no deeper discussion on the subject, no classification of the kinds of negative injunctions and their effects.

13. In the Mimansa system illustrations of many principles of interpretation are given in the form of maxims (nyayas). The negative injunction is illustrated by the Kalanja nyaya or Kalanja maxim.

14. The Kalanja maxim (na kalanjam bhakshayet) states that 'a general condemnatory text is to be understood not only as prohibiting an act, but also the tendency, including the intention and attempt to do it.' It is thus

mandatory.

(A) AXIOMS (Elementary rules).—Axioms are 6 :

(1) *Sarthakya.*—Means all words and sentences of veda have meaning. All are 'Sarthaka' carry sense and purpose. None is useless. Texts of vedas have to be read keeping it in mind.

(2) *Laghav.*—Means that construction wherein shorter or simpler meaning of text is possible is preferable. If one proposition is sufficient, no further search is needed.

(3) *Arth-i-Katwa.*—It means if any word or sentence is used at one place and repeated elsewhere also (it carries) only one meaning. It is read in one and the same sense everywhere.

(4) *Matsya Nyaya* (Gun Pradhan).—It is the principle of adjustment. Any word or sentence if expresses any subordinate idea but conflicts with any principal idea expressed elsewhere, its meaning has to be read and adjusted with principal idea. Bigger devours smaller.

(5) *Samanjasya* (Reconcile).—If any word or sentence is used at several places, this rule advocates all to be reconciled. No conflict can be assumed.

(6) *Vikalpa* (option).—Where texts are really contradictory only that prevails which may be opted. The other must be ignored.

(B) MAXIMS OF GENERAL PRINCIPLES (Four).—

(1) *Shruti.*—This maxim of interpretation resembles literal or grammatical construction that is in use now. According to it, the words are to be read in their ordinary natural sense. No moderation or deviation therefrom is permitted even if it leads to absurdity. The court is to behave like a horse in a carriage. The eyes of horse in carriage are closed from side. It can see things ahead but not in sides or around, so is a judge following *shruti* may of interpretation. Read as it is. No modification is permitted.

(2) *Linga.*—This maxim resembles 'Golden rule'. The golden rule is because there are no golden rules. It provides that text can be modified so as to avoid it being absurd. If ordinary grammatical or literal meaning does not fit in context, then read it as if the context justifies. In the horse example above, *linga* would not permit the horse to jump in the ditch on the read but avoid it by taking circuit road/diversion. So can a judge.

(3) *Vakya.*—Framing/arranging sentences. If words or the sentences of any text are not well arranged so as to give clear sense or meaning, it is open to the court, to rearrange these words or sentences so as to give readable or intelligible meaning to those words or those sentences. Vakya method permits re-arrangements.

(4) *Prakaran.*—This rule resembles *noscitur a socio* rule of English law. When complete picture does not come out of the clause or sentence as used in the vedic text in vedic sanskrit, it is then open to read the whole subject to find it out. A word is known by the company it keeps.

(C) MAXIMS OF ELEMENTARY PRINCIPLES (1 to 14).—

(1) Pathakrama nyaya.—According to this, the order of sequence of various acts required to be performed in a given case are to be performed in the same order in which they are mentioned in the verbal text. The principle is that if the provisions of law give sufficient indication as to the various steps to be performed to fulfil a designed purpose, then the sequence cannot be altered as it would defeat the very purpose of those steps. Sabara explains this principle thus :

> "At any one sacrifice, the acts should be performed in a definite 'Order of Sequence' : Why? because such is the very nature of actions; things are generally found to have the character of being done in a definite order; for instance, in the case of the sentence—'one should bathe, rub sandal-paste, break fact', it is understood that the acts are to be performed in this definite order of sequence.
>
> "From all this it follows that in all such cases the order of sequence is the one that is indicated by the order of the verbal texts concerned."

An illustration would bring forth the force of this principle. If the law requires that before the imposition of municipal tax in a local area, or declaring an area as coming under local authority, there should be a publication of the proposal inviting objections, consideration of representations or objections received, consultation with the specified interests and thereafter a final decision should be taken, in order that the decision be valid, the same sequence has to be followed. If the decision is taken first, and the procedure for consultation etc., is followed next, it would be illegal. However, this principle is applicable only to cases where the sequence is implicit in the rule and disobedience of it would defeat the very purpose of the law, as in the case of the aforementioned illustration. This is an accepted principle under the present rules of interpretation also.

(2) Satra Nyaya.—At a *Satra*, if there is some disqualification in one of the masters, there may be a substitute for him.

This principle has been discussed with reference to a sacrifice for which the minimum number of 'masters' prescribed was seventeen. The view taken was, if one of the masters became disqualified, the vacancy had to be filled up by a qualified person, as the performance of the function by any number less than the prescribed number (seventeen) was invalid.

This is a very important principle. In modern jurisprudence also, if a statute requires that a prescribed number of persons should perform a statutory function, if one of them dies, resigns or becomes disqualified or otherwise ceases to be a member, another has to be brought in, and an act performed by a lesser number of members would be invalid.

(3) Dvayo-pranayanti nyaya.—This was one of the most popular *Nyayas* which emphatically declared the impermissibility of an inconsistent stand being taken by a party. One and the same text should not be taken as a case of *Paryudasa* (mere exception) and again as a case of *Pratishedha* (prohibition). "Great importance is attached to it by the Hindu jurists. It lays down, however, a very elementary principle that one should not blow hot and cold at the same time.

"The effect of the *Dvyao-pranayanti* maxim is briefly this : a positive and a negative text may be either in conflict with each other or not. If there be reasons to hold that they are in conflict, you must stick to that view and *vice versa*. You cannot shift your position at pleasure."

(4) Darshapurnamasa nyaya.—This relates to the performance of a single act by several persons. The acts though separate should be regarded as 'one act' because they are related to a single purpose and because they are named by a single term.

This rule means that if a provision requires several persons to do an act, if the indication is that all of them should perform only one act, it is not correct to hold that each individual should perform the act. Sabara explains this with reference to the requirement of a text for the performance of a specific religious act called *Darshapurnamasa* by several persons.

(5) Kalanja nyaya.—This maxim flows from a *Nishedha—'Na Kalanjam Bakshyayet'*, which means, 'Do not eat fermented food'. *Kalanja nyaya* is used to indicate a prohibitory act or *Nishedha Vidhi*.

Illustration.—To say that the *Kalanja* maxim applies to the interpretation of a provision of any law, it means that the said rule, being couched in a negative language, is prohibitory in nature and therefore such a rule must not be allowed to be violated directly or circumvented indirectly. This corresponds to the modern rule of interpretation that negative expressions are rarely directory, *i.e.*, generally they should be considered mandatory.

(6) Madhyadipika nyaya.—Literally this means, 'Lamp in the centre'. This principle is useful in the interpretation of statutes. According to this, a word can be shown to throw light on the preceding as well as the succeeding clause, just as a light placed on a half partition wall throws light over both the apartments.

(7) Mandukapluti nyaya.—This maxim may be linkened to a 'frog's leap', according to which the clause lying between two clauses is skipped over in order to make a reasonable interpretation of the statute.

(8) Gobaleevardan nyaya.—This means cattle and bull maxim. According to this, when two adjoining words having almost similar meaning are used in a provision out of which one is general and the other is more specific, the latter word qualifies the former.

Kulluka has used this *Nyaya* to interpret Manu VIII 28. The king should take care of women who are barren, who have no sons, who have no family, wives who are faithful to their respective husbands, widows who are afflicted and have none to look after.

Kulluka holds that in view of the last specification, the rule means that the duty of the king is to protect all women who had none to look after. In other words, he holds that the women of whatever category, who are required to be protected by the king, are those who are destitutes.

The Nyaya is somewhat similar to the modern rule of construction indicated by the rule of *ejusdem generis* which requires that a general word which follows a specific word of the same category takes the restricted meaning of the preceding specific word. But in order to attract this rule there must be a genus or category.

(9) Ghata-pata nyaya.—This is the converse of the rule of *ejusdem generis*. The meaning is, if two words, like *ghata* (pot) and *pata* (portrait), appear one after another in a provisin, one of the words cannot be understood as qualifying the other. Therefore, in such a case, the *ejusdem generis* rule is not applicable, as the words do not belong to the same genera. Analogous to *Ghata-patanyaya* is the principle laid down by the Surpeme Court that the rule of *ejusdem generis* is not applicable for interpreting the words 'local' or 'other authority', used in Article 12 of the Constitution after the word 'State'.

(10) (i) Samanya vishesha nyaya.—This is a maxim of the general and the special.

(ii) Apavadaihiutsarga bodhyante.—According to this maxim, general rules are set aside by special ones. The purport of these two *Nyayas* is the same, namely, where there are two *Vidhis* applicable to a given case, one of them being general and the other special, the latter should prevail.

This is a well accepted rule of consruction in the present legal system incorporated in the maxim *generalia specialibus non derogant i.e.*, the special provision excludes the general provision.

(11) Roodhir yogamapa haratihi.—According to this maxim, popular usage overpowers etymological meaning.

It is a very useful maxim, and of immense use, frequently applied in the interpretation of the laws. Whenever a word used in a statute has an etymological meaning and also a popular meanign which is different from the former it is the popular meaning which prevails over the etymological meaning unless there is an indication to the contrary.

(12) 'Sandhigdhe nyaya pravartate' iti nyaya.—This maxim provides that where there is a doubt reason comes into play.

This maxim points out that whenever a doubt is created in respect of any question that arises for consideration, the same should be resolved by the application of reasoning.

(13) Sandhigdaysa vakyaseshan nirnaya.—According to this maxim, the meaning of an ambiguous expression is to be determined from the context.

This rule means that whenever the legislature has used an ambiguous expression in enacting a provision, the real meaning of the provision should be ascertained by looking into the whole scheme of the legislation and the purpose for which the provision is incorporated. In other words, the context of the provision would help to clear the ambiguity and to arrive at the correct conclusion. This is also a well known principle of construction in modern rules of interpretation.

(14) Savakasha niravakashyoh niravakasho baleeyan.—This maxim stipulates that the injunction which is clear is stronger than the one which is ambiguous or gives room for doubt. This maxim means that whenever there is a seeming conflict between two provisions of a legislation, one of which is clear and the other ambiguous, the former must prevail.

(D) MAXIMS OF GENERAL EXPERIENCE (1 TO 35)

(1) Kakadanta pareeksha nyaya.—This is a maxim which exposes the futility of seeking an explanation which may be akin to the examination of a crow's teeth. It describes a manifestly fruitless inquiry—just as it is useless to attempt to examine the teeth of a crow, which do not in reality exist.

(2) Yadashvena hritam pura that paschad gardabhaha praptum kenopayena shaknuyet.—This maxim is to overrule one explanation as against another on the principle that one riding an ass cannot overtake another riding a horse.

It means that a person who relied on a *Smriti* text cannot claim to succeed against the opposite party who was relying on the *Sruti* text, as the latter must necessarily prevail over the former. This maxim can be made use of when, out of the two parties to a case, one is relying on the provisions of a section of an enactment and the opposite party is relying on a rule framed under that Act which is *ultra vires* the enactment. In such a situation the latter cannot succeed against the former.

(3) Sundopasunda nyaya.—This is a maxim of 'two monsters'. It is derived from a mythological story, according to which two monsters, Sunda and Upasunda, fought with each other for acquiring Tilottama, a heavenly damsel, but destroyed themselves in that process.

It has its counterpart in the latin maxim *Allegans contraria monest andien.lu* *i.e.*, He is not to be heard who makes mutually destructive allegations. This maxim can be used to describe the mutually destructive pleas put forward by a party to a litigation who ultimately loses both the pleas.

(4) Arkamadhu nyaya.—This maxim states—Go not far if you can find it close at hand. If you can find in the *Arka* plant which grows in your yard, why go to the mountains in quest of a bee-hive?

The meaning is that when an object can be achieved by following a straight path, why one should resort to a circuitous procedure. The maxim applies to cases where parties raise several contentions and try to advance long arguments at the expense of much public time though the case can be got decided in one's favour by a short and clinching argument.

For instance, when a petition is liable to be dismissed on the ground of want of *locus standi*, or when a petition presented by a person who has *locus standi* has to be dismissed on the ground of limitation or when a petition has to be allowed as the act complained of cannot be sustained in view of the same being made without jurisdiction *i.e.*, by an incompetent authority, it is unnecessary to spend time in addressing or hearing arguments on the other points raised, as e.en after considering those points, the petition has to be dismissed for want of *locus standi* or on the ground of limitation, or the petition has to be allowed on the ground that the order impugned was bad for want of jurisdiction, as the case might be, irrespective of any decision on other points.

(5) 'Ekamanu sandhit satoparam prachyavate' iti nyaya.— This maxim relates to an incongruous situation when one relies on an argument which gives rise to an equally strong objection. It is like 'joining a stick at one end while breaking it at the other end' as the *Nyaya* is styled. For instance, in a case where the petitioner relies on a statutory rule and the respondent relies on an executive order (which is made in contravention of the rule), the respondent by doing so invites the objection that the executive had no jurisdiction to issue the order in contravention of the rule. In such a case, therefore, it is no use relying on such an order.

(6) Shiroveshtanena nasikasparsha' iti nyaya.—This maxim applies to a case of resorting to a circuitous and time consuming argument to bring home a point though a straight and short argument is possible. It is like moving the hand round the neck to show the nose' as the *Nyaya* implies.

(7) Upajeevya virodha nyaya.—This maxim means that one should not take up an argument which would cut at the root of one's case. It is like a person seeking benefit under the provisions of law also raising an argument that the very law is unconstitutional, because if his latter argument succeeds, the very basis of his right falls to the ground. This maxim is similar to the proverb—'Sitting on the branch of a tree and cutting its trunk'.

(8) Panka prakshalana nyaya.—This maxim is by way of caution—Better not to tread mire than to tread and then wash oneself.

It means, one should not indulge in an undesirable act and then try to get out of it. For instance, making unfounded allegations against another party in the pleadings may lead to withdrawing them therefore, being unable to substantiate them.

(9) Ardha jaratiya nyaya.—This is a maxim which disaproves half and half or 'young through old' approach. It is based on the story—A person who found that by his describing the cow meant for sale at a shandy as old and therefore good, on the first day of the shandy, did not attract any buyers. Then he began to describe it on the next day as young in spirit though old in age, and still failed to attract buyers.

This is similar to a party who after strenuously putting forward the case on the question of limitation and after having miserably failed to carry the court with him, saying that at least on merits he has a good case, which is of no consequence so long as the case is barred by limitation. This *Nyaya* may also be put in another form *viz.*, 'Cutting a hen into two halves, reserving one half for preparing soup and the other half for laying eggs.' This forcefully brings forth the futility or baselessness of two inconsistent approaches to similar cases. It can be used to criticise a judgment when a judge, on the same set of facts and evidence, acquits one of the two accused in a case and convicts the other.

(10) 'Krute Karye Kim muhurta prashnena' iti nyaya.—This maxim is to show the incongruity of enquiry for the auspicious moment after the event.

(11) Krutak shourasya nak shatra pareeksha nyaya.—It is like, "Inquiring about stars after a hair cut" (by persons who believe in not having a hair cut during an inauspicious time). It stresses the importance of timely action and the futility of a belated decision. The maxim advises that if anyone wants to do a particular act or perform a ceremony at an auspicious moment, he must select the moment before doing the act or performing the ceremony, and points out that if anyone were to do the act or perform the ceremony first and thereafter begin to inquire whether the act or ceremony was performed at an auspicious moment, such an inquiry is purposeless.

For example, a person who wants to file a suit on a pronote, does not take care to examine the question of limitation, and only after filing it before the court begins to consult on the question of limitation and finds that the date before which he should have filed it was over. This maxim impresses that such a consultation must precede the filing of a suit which should be done in good time and that belated inquiry about it is futile.

(12) Ajataputra namokirtana nyaya.—This maxim relates to premature action like "Nothing the child before it is born" which is futile. It is like approaching the court challenging an action which in fact has not at all been taken, *i.e.*, even before any cause of action has arisen.

(13) (i) Shringagrahika nyaya.—The maxim refers to anticipatory action like "seizing a bull by its horns." This means meeting the most seemingly difficult point first and showing that it is in one's favour, which renders the winning of other points easy.

(ii) Pradhanamallanir vahana nyaya.—The principle of this maxim is the destruction of the most formidable opponent first. It means that if the most formidable opponent is defeated, the rest are virtually overcome. This is similar to the preceeding rule. If one is able to dislodge the most formidable point against him, he can easily overcome the other points.

(14) Virddhimishtavato mulamapi te nashtam.—This is a maxim to show the folly of stressing an unimportant point first at the cost of losing the main point, which is like "seeking to obtain interest while losing the principal.' In the anxiety to get an interim order urgently one may file a petition without properly examining the main case and lost it.

(15) Pistapeshana nyaya.—This maxim warns against useless repetition like "grinding of that which is already ground". It means the repetition of the same point even after it is found useless, *i.e*, unwanted or fruitless repetition is not worthwhile.

(16) Kashakushavalambana nyaya.—This is a maxim to show that clinging to a useless point when all others have failed is like a drowning man catching the last straw. Hanging on to a worthless point in a case when all other important points urged have been found to be without substance will be of no avail.

(17) Ghattakutiprabhata nyaya.—This maxim exposes that addressing a roundabout argument in order to avoid being caught on a specific point not favourable to one, but ultimately finding himself caught on that point itself, is like "lading before the toll gate in the morning after attempting evasion all night." This is based on the story of a merchant who took a circuitous route in the night with the object of evading payment of toll, but having lost his way, found himself right before the toll gate in the morning.

(18) Gaganaromantha nyaya.—This is a maxim to show the worthlessness of an argument which holds no water which is like "hitting the sky with one's fist" (*Akashamushtikanana nyaya*), which produces no result but exertion. It is like filing a case even though there is absolutely no substance in it, since fighting such a case will only mean waste of money and public time, whether it is done by a private individual or the Government or a public body.

(19) Kukataliya nayaha.—This maxim of "crow and the palmyra branch" bears on the principle of association of ideas. For example, when a crow comes and sits on a dry branch of a palmyra tree and that branch happens to break and fall down at that moment for natural reasons, one who sees these simultaneous happenings gets the impression that the crow was responsible for the breaking of that branch, even though in truth it is not so. This is a case of erroneous judgment based on inference.

This *Nyaya* may be used to explain the case of a person being charged of committing an offence (by a spectator or the police) just because he was seen at the place of occurrence of the offence even though his presence there was accidental and he had no connection at all with the offence in question.

(20) Jalanayana nyaya.—This maxim of "water and the vessel" is meant to explain that when the principal purpose is expressed all incidental matters connected with it must be deemed to have been included in it. Just as "feteh me water to drink" includes and suggests that the water must be brought in a vessel, and bringing water includes bringing the vessel. This is also a well known rule of construction in modern administration, *viz.*, that whenever a power is conferred on any body or authority it must be held to include all incidental powers necessary for its effective exercise.

(21) 'Na hi drishteanupapannam nama' iti nyaya.—This maxim relates to a situation where the reason of a thing is found by perception and it is not proper to seek any other proof for it. This means, when the intention or reason behind a provision is self evident, it must be accepted as correct and one should not seek any further proof in support of it. This is the equivalent of the present rule of construction that the intention of the legislature must be gathered only from the provision of the law and not outside it.

(22) Andhasyevandhalagnasya vinipathaha pade pade.—This is a maxim to caution against a situation like "the blind leading the blind', when both may fall into a ditch. When a counsel relies on a over-ruled decision and the judge also accepts it, both being ignorant of the latest position in law, both will be falling into the same error.

(23) Swashrunirgachhokti nyaya.—This is a maxim to show the tendency of asserting one's prerogative and in the process unreasonably abusing another with a vengeance for what one would himself have done under those circumstances. It is like a mother-in-law taking her daughter-in-law to task for refusing alms to a mendicant and with a vengeance calling him back only to tell him, "I alone have the authority to refuse alms and so I now refuse to give you alms. You may go!" This is like a higher officer taking objection to the rejection of an application or claim of an individual, by his subordinate who is equally competent to do so, calling for records and then rejecting it, to the amusement of the junior officer and the utter disappointment of the party concerned.

(24) Padahtchharalunthite veshmani yamikajagaranam.—This maxim is to show the futility of exercising caution after the damage has been done, like the vigilance of a watchman after the house has been burgled. This is equivalent to the English proverb, 'closing the stables after the horse has bolted.' This is similar to a case where a judge, after making an order unsustainable in law without due care and caution, tries to find out the correct position in law, or a party or his counsel conducting the case being at first negligent and trying to find out a good point in his favour after the case has gone against him.

(25) Ashoktoham griharambhe shaktoham grihabhanjane.—This maxim brings out the idea that one who is not capable of doing a good act might be capable of doing ill, like one saying, 'I am incapable of constructing a house but I have the capacity to destroy the constructed one." This *Nyaya* explains the conduct of individuals who have no ability to do any constructive work but at the same time have the capacity to do mischief, thereby destroying what is achieved by the efforts of others.

In particular it applies to social and political organisations and institutions. Instances are not wanting which disclose such tendencies. Persons who are incapable of building an organisation or institution are quite capable of creating internal dissensions and thereby destroying the organisation built by others with great sacrifice and effort. In fact such a conduct on the part of individuals was censured by the ancient law givers. Severe punishment was prescribed to persons who, being members of a corporation or guild, indulged in such activities.

(26) Chouraparadhan mandavyanigraha nyaya.—This maxim warns against punishing the innocent merely on the basis of circumstantial evidence, like the punishment of Mandavya for the crime committed by thieves. This *Nyaya* against convicting a person for an offence merely on the basis of circumstantial evidence without proper and convincing corroboration. It is based on the story of a saint by name Mandavya who was convicted and punished for an offence of theft merely on the basis that stolen property was found at his hermitage, which had been left there by the thieves on being chased by the servants of the king, and the saint, who was observing silence, did not answer the questions put to him by the king's servants.

(27) Manadheena meyasiddhi.—This is a maxim to show that the knowledge of a thing is necessary in order to know its application like "to know a thing to be measured, you must know the measure". This maxim may be taken as an advice to judges that in order to be able to know the correctness of the arguments advanced by the parties, they must be well versed in the tests which are to be applied to decide their correctness.

(28) Ekakini pratijna hi pratijnatam na sadhayet.—This maxim implies that "bare assertion is no proof of the matter asserted". Many a time the parties to a case merely assert certain set of facts or the position in law. The maxim points out that in the absence of evidence in support of the assertion of facts or convincing arguments as regards the position in law, one cannot succeed. In other words, the maxim indicates the futility of mere assertion without proof.

(29) Ekamasiddhim pariharato dwiteeya apadyate.—This maxim is by way of of caution that "whilst avoiding one fallacy, another is likely to appear". It explains a situation in which a party in order to get over the fallacy pointed out by his opponent in the case put forward by him, brings up another case which is equally fallacious. For example, when a petition is resisted by the opponent as barred by limitation, the petitioner contents in the first instance that it was not so when his plea is found to be fallacious, contends that no period of limitation was fixed, which plea is again found to be fallacious.

(30) Yah karyati sa karotyeva.—This is a maxim to show that "he who causes an act to be done by another is himself the real doer of it." The principle here is that whenever a person gets an act done through another, it is as good as having been done by himself. This corresponds to the vicarious liability of a person in civil law for the act done by another under his authority and the liability of a person under penal law for being an abettor for the commission of a criminal offence.

(31) Sarvanashe samutpanne ardham tyajati panditaha.—According to this maxim, "when the loss of the whole is imminent, a wise man gives up half (when by so doing he can save the other half)." This is by way of advice to one and all and in particular to litigants who have a weak case. When in the course of trial or hearing of a case in which a party has legally a weak case, his opponent out of compassion makes an offer for compromise by way of giving him something less than what he had claimed, either on his own initiative or at the suggestion of the court, the former would be well advised to accept the compromise instead of insisting on his claim and losing everything.

(32) Ahridayavachasam ahridayamuttaram.—This maxim is on the principle, "heartless words get a heartless answer". This *Nyaya* justifies the rejection of a highly technical plea raised by one party by an equally technical plea put forth by the other party, just as the demand of 'the pound of flesh' by the creditor in the Shakespearnean play, *Merchant of Venice*, from his debtor as he had agreed to, was met with an equally technical plea that "he may take the pound of flesh but not a drop of blood."

(33) Ito vyaghraha itas tatee.—This maxim refers to the dilemma faced by a person, like "A tiger on one-side and a precipice on the other."

Such a situation may arise before a person who illadvisedly goes to court and finds the case going against him. If he pursues the matter defeat is certain and if he were to withdraw, he would be put to shame and loss.

(34) Koopa manduka nyaya.—This maxim refers to a person who adopts the 'frog in the well" policy. It is based on the story of a frog living in a well which says, "There is no tank, lake or sea bigger than the one in which I live." A person who has a narrow outlook or limited knowledge or experience of the world thinks and asserts that whatever he says is the correct thing and the highest truth, like the frog in the well, and is not prepared to listen to man of better knowledge and understanding.

(35) Anishiddha manumatam.—According to this maxim, "that which is not objected to is taken as agreed to." The purport of the maxim is 'silence tantamounts to consent'. This is a well accepted principle in the law of pleadings. Whenever a specific plea is raised by a party and the opposite party fails to traverse such specific plea, the silence on the part of the latter would amount to acceptance or admission of the first party's plea. In such a case, the court can proceed on the assumption that the second party has admitted the specific plea.

(E) PRINCIPLES OF BAR

Vedic texts are divided in 5 classes which determine whether any text principle is obligatory or non obligatory.

(a) Obligatory.—*Vidhi* and *Nisedh* are obligatory. Vidhi relates to what you have to do. These include positive commands. These are injunctions. These are in many categories; Mandatory, permanent or perpetual temporary injunctions, specific performances, directions or writs.

(b) Nisedh.—There are negative commands; restraint from doing anything or something. These may be absolute or qualified and are of many kinds.

(b) Non-obligatory.—*Arthavad* and *Namdheya* are non-obligatory bars. These are mere recommendations. May, or may not be done.

'*Arthvada*' means explanation or Illustration or examples added to clarify a principle. These explanations etc. neither add any thing to the principal text nor substract anything therefrom. Arthavad is distinct from 'vidhi' which is principal text laying down mandatory law. Arthvada can also be in a negative command or nisedh texts.

'*Namdheya* is a definition clause added to any Act or text of law in veda. It has general bearing on the subject.

(c) Quasi obligatory.—*Mantra* are formulae. These may be mandatory or recommendatory as the context may require.

Order of preference

1. Sruti, Linga, Vakya and Prakaranan are used to read a text of veda in descending order. First not helping, resort may be to second, third or fourth.

2. Sruti (Veda) is superior to smiriti, sruti prevails over smiriti if there is any conflict, so is case of 'smiriti' over custom, except when smiriti is contrary to vedic text or conflicts with another provision of same smiriti or another smiriti or equal authority.

3. clear proof of usage would outweigh written text of law is judicial approach to smiriti and custom in conflict.

4. When two customs conflict one that has support of 'shastra' prevails over the other that is contrary to a *shastra*.

Current position

Mimansa was set of rules of interpretation laid down for reading vedas. It no longer remains in practice for veda and smiriti are no longer law; these are sources of Ancient personal Hindu Law. Recently, in some cases, Supreme Court (specially Markande J) has referred to rules of Mimansa while deciding some cases before Supreme Court. It is encouraging sign.

Interpretation and construction of a statute.—The function of the court is to find out the intention of the legislature. The courts are to gather the legislative intent out of the words used. They are supposed to assume that legislature has said that it meant and meant what has said. This is interpretation. Judges are not at liberty to add or to take from or modify the letter of the law simply because they have reason to believe that the true *sententia legis* is not completely or correctly expressed by it. It always finds out some intention whether that one is the real intention of the legislature or not. What court construes to be the intention becomes legislative intent for all legal purposes.

The difference between construction and interpretation

Interpretation means finding out the meaning as intended and as it is expressed in the statute, construction means finding out the *purpose* which the statute means to accomplish. Letter of Act and spirit of Act and two things, to be read; interpretation and construction. Where one ends; the other begins. Where interpretation ends, construction begins but this point is very difficult to establish. Ascertainment of legislative purpose permits the evidence for policy to be admitted. In interpretation, these would not be admissible.

How does the court find out the intention?—There may be three situations before a court which is called upon to apply an Act. The Act may be clear letter and spirit or it may be clear in letter but not in spirit or it may be clear neither in letter nor in spirit.

When the courts have constitution or statutes of their guidance, there is no choice. They have to abide by these. The Constitution is supreme law of land. It prevails over statutes. The statute if constitutional prevails over judge made law. The judge made law is secondary and subordinate to constitution and legislative law.

The reading of these laws is called interpretation. The interpretation of statutes is a very important branch of general jurisprudence. Its object is to find out the legislative intent *sententia legis* as it is called. The court is to interpret the words of satute on the basis of certain well formulated principles. The interpretation has a very important role to play in modern times when statutes are passed by legislature, implemented by executive and enforced by the judiciary. The statute is formal expression of legislative will. It is a product of many brains and accommodation of many views. At the stage of policy determination, at the stage of select committee deliberations and at the time of its laying on the Parliament's table, its clause by clause discussion and motion of amendments from the opposition are different factors that make it necessary to construe the provisions of statute objectively. Indian Law was richest so far as the rules of interpretation and cannons of constructions are concerned. Mimansa rules of interpretation have been in practice for innumerable years. These are meant for the interpretation of the texts of Vedas. The lucid and brief shape had been the special feature of these rules. Besides, this branch of interpretative jurisprudence, some of the smritis contained in are themselves the rules of interpretation.

English rules of interpretation seem to be based on many rules of mimansa. Whatever may be the opinion to the contrary, it can easily be proved that the richest situation in which the English jurisprudence is in modern times, owes much to the rules of mimansa and their adaptation in English law.

Interpretation in English Courts

In English practice which is also the practice in India, the various ways of interpretation are :—

(i) Purposive interpretation.—Purposive construction or an enactment is one which gives effect to the legislative purpose—

(1) by following the literal meaning of the enactment where that meaning is in accordance with the legislative purpose. This is called '*purposive and literal construction*'.

(2) by applying a strained meaning where the literal meaning is not in accordance with the legislative purpose. It is called '*purposive and strained-construction*'.

(ii) The mischief rule.—The rule is popularly called the rule in *Heydon*'s case. It was laid down in this case that for a sure and true interpretation of all statutes in general, be they penal or beneficiary restrictive or enlarging of the common law, the following four things are to be discerned and considered.

(a) What was the common law before the making of the Act?

(b) What was the mischief and defect for which the common law had not provided?

(c) What remedy the Parliament has resolved and appointed to cure the disease of the commonwealth?

(d) The true reason of the remedy.

(iii) Grammatical or literal construction of a statute or plain meaning 'rule'.—According to this rule, the letters of the Act must be construed as and where they stand. If the precise words used are plain and unambiguous, these have to be read in their ordinary sense even if any court is of the view that plain reading would lead to a manifest injustice or absurdity. The court should not feel wiser than the legislature. The common law judge must confine himself to what the legislator has said in the statute. He can take the surrounding circumstances into account so far as they are matters of common knowledge. He must make the best of the text and give effect to any meaning which it bears which is not manifestly unjust or fantastic even though the result may be not to fulfil the intention of legislator. He may not consult the reports of the debates or, the measure in Parliament or any other record of the ministerial or Parliamentry deliberations which have led to its enactment. He must ignore the statements made in Parliament by ministers in charge of the draft bill and the reports thereon of Parliamentary or governmental committees. The statute simply means what it says in a literal sense and this is all that courts are to expound. The theory is based on the ground that the worst person to construe a statute is the person who was responsible for its drafting.

According *to this rule the first and foremost elementary step* is to assume *that the words and phrases of technical legislation* are *used in their technical meaning* if they have acquired one and otherwise in their ordinary meaning; and the second is that the *phrases and sentences are to be construed according to the rules of grammar*. The length and detail modern legislation has reinforced the claim of literal construction as the only safe rule. Where the language is plain and admits of but one meaning, task of interpretation can hardly be said to arise, because of use of clear and unequivocal language capable of only one meaning of statute enacted by the legislature. It must be enforced, however hard, absurd, or contrary to common sense the result may be.

The riders on Grammatical rule.—This rule can be accepted subject to following riders—

(a) When a statute itself gives a special meaning for a term in interpretation clause this special meaning would prevail and not the common meaning. For example, in Transfer of Property Act, 'Transfer' means sale, gift, exchange, lease or mortgage. It does not include auction sales.

(b) Technical words will mean in their technical sense unless otherwise provided by statute.

(c) No word can be inserted by implication.

(d) The ordinary meaning of any word may change in course of time.

(e) Words have meaning with reference to a context. Context may change the meaning.

Omission not to be inferred.—The corollary to the grammatical construction in this rule is that nothing is to be added to, or taken from a statute unless there are adequate grounds to justify the inference that the legislature intended something which it omitted to express. It is strong thing to read into an Act of Parliament words which are not there and in absence of clear necessity it is wrong to do. The court cannot add words to a statute or read words into it which are not there especially when the literal reading produces an intelligible result. The Court must proceed on assumption that the legislature did not make a mistake and that it intended to say what is said.

Every word in a statute to be given a meaning.—A construction, which would leave without effect, any part of the language of a statute will normally be rejected. Superfluity should not be easily conceded. Likewise, main part of a section must not be construed in such a way as to render a proviso to the section redundant.

(iv) Golden rule.—The so called 'golden rule' is really a modification of the literal rule. It is a very useful rule in the construction of a statute to adhere to the ordinary meaning of the words used and to the grammatical construction unless that is at variance with the intention of the legislature (which is to be collected from the statute itself) or leads to any manifest absurdity or repugnance, in which, the language, may be varied or modified so as to avoid such inconvenience but no further.

The correct view is that literal or ordinary meaning must be given. If meaning is clear, there is no scope for judiciary except to read it as it is.

Whenever, a court purports to depart from it and applies mischief or golden rule, there is every probability that they would do more damage by substituting their own impressions, views, prejudices or predispositions. This would create a conflict which has been long known between what the Parliament intended and what the judges assumed the Parliament to have intended.

Logical interpretation.—This method also keeps the intention of legislature at the centre. It permits departure from the letters of the law and permits the court to go behind the language of the statute for knowing its meaning. It is open only when grammatical interpretation leads to some absurdity or inconsistency. It is then the duty of the court is to give effect to *sentra legis*. It is the duty of the court to give effect to the intention of legislature. If it is clearly expressed; well and good; Read literally; plainly or grammatically. *Litera legis* is exclusive and conclusive evidence of *sententia legis*.

Exception.—Two exceptions are to *litera legis* being conclusive evidence of *sententia legis* :

(a) Where *litera legis* (letter of law) is logically defective; and as such fails to give a definite, coherent and complete idea; For example, ambiguity, inconsistency and incompleteness.

(b) Where text leads to a result which is so unreasonable that it is clear that legislature could not have meant what it has said. Such lacuna or omissions can be supplied by logical interpretation.

(v) Beneficial Construction.—Beneficial legislation is that which is enacted for the benefit of a particular class of people. The strict interpretation is relaxed in these cases. This rule permits the judge to adopt certain different course. This rule has its own limits. It applies only where the judges are faced with a choice between a wide meaning which carries out what appears to have been the object of the legislature more fully, and a narrow meaning which carries it out less fully or not at all. They will often choose the former. Beneficial construction is a tendency rather than a rule. The illustrations of the beneficial construction are found in social legislations of the welfare State; for example, labour legislations *etc.*

(vi) *Ejusdem Generis* Rule.—Lord Tenderen's Rule :—

This rule provides that where words of specific meaning are followed by general words, the general words will be construed as limited to persons or things of the same general kind or class as those enumerated by the specific words. The principle has to be applied having regard to the fitness of the matter and with restraint in view of the fact that it is a dubious yardstick. The operation is presumptive and not peremptory. The content of the statute must never be lost sight of, for to ignore the content would make the intention of the legislature subordinate to this principle.

Essential of doctrine

For application of *ejusdem generis* rule the following conditions are necessary :—

(i) The statute contains an enumeration of specific words that constitute a class;

(ii) The class aforesaid, is not exhausted by the enumeration;

(iii) The general words follow the specific words;

(iv) The legislative intention is not clearly manifest in favour of according broader meaning to the general words.

(v) There must be a distinct 'genus' or 'category', the mention of single species does not constitute a 'genus'. For example mention of 'water rate' does not constitute a genus.

Exceptions to Rule.—Following exceptions are :

(1) If the proceeding term is general as well as that which follows, the doctrine of *Ejusdem generis* does not apply;

(2) When the particular and specific words exhaust the whole genus, nothing is left for the application of this principle;

(3) The principle does not apply when specifically enumerated objects are essentially diverse in character;

(4) The doctrine does not apply if legislative intent is clearly to the contrary;

(5) The principles relate to strict construction; therefore, the Courts may relax this principle in cases of beneficial or remedial

statutes;

(6) This principle applies to resolve conflict in two different Acts but not conflicts in two different provisions of the same Act.

(vii) *Noscitur a Sociis* Rule (Associated words).—This rule provides that meaning of a word can be gathered from the content or by the company it keeps. The associated words indicate a guideline for ascertaining the meaning of a doubtful word.

Noscitur rule is broad generalised form of *ejusdem generis rule. In other words, ejusdem* rule is an example of *noscitur* principle.

Conditions for applicability

(1) *Noscitur* and *ejusdem* rules are merely rules of construction to remove ambiguity if any. If statute or words in statute are clear, these rules of construction cannot apply.

(2) The *Noscitur* rule is a maxim and is only an extended version of *ejusdem generis* rule. It implies that there may be words, which are not expressed by words 'likes', 'whatsoever' or 'otherwise' preceded by specific words, can, still their meaning be affected by other words with which they are associated; they take their colour from each other.

(viii) *Reddendo Singula Sngulis* Rule.—It means 'giving each to each'. A clause in a document is to be read when one or two provisions in one sentence is appropriated to one of the two objects in another sentence and the other provision is similarly appropriated to the other object. For example, in a will the words used are "I *devise* and *bequeath* all my *real* and personal property to *B*." 'Devise' goes for 'real' and 'bequeath' for personal property according to rule of *Reddendo Singula Sngulis* (giving each to each); Another example is 'A transfers for money' or other consideration—'paid' or 'given'. The 'paid' refers to 'money' and 'given' to consideration.

(ix) *Ex Visceribus Actus Rule* (Statute must be read as a whole).—This rule is called an 'elementary rule'. This rule applies to construction of all statutes. It means that all provisions must be read within four corners of the Act. The whole Act must be read together. If any provision of Act is not clear to the judge, it is his duty to read the whole Act to understand that provision. Its meaning is the same that the statute as a whole ascribes to it. A provision cannot mean otherwise than what the whole Act expects it to mean. It cannot be considered separately. This alone is most natural and genuine exposition of a statute to construe one part of the statute by another part of the same statute.

Expressio Unius Personae Vel Rei, Est Exclusio Alterius Rule (Express mention of one person or thing is the exclusion of another).

This cannot be regarded as a safe rule and obiligatory. It is a valuable servant but dangerous master.

Expression Facit Cessary tacitum is analogous to above. It means that express words put an end to implication. It connotes that when there is express mention of certain things, then anything not mentioned, is excluded.

For example, where a power is given to do a certain thing in a certain way, the thing must be done in that way or not at all.

This would apply where one power is given but not when more powers are given.

The Interpretation of statute in continental system

The continental judges are not bound by any formalistic interpretation. The continental law is armed with many theories of interpretation. Some of the theories have met with general acceptance and some have not found such a wide support. But in all cases they have posed a serious challenge to the existence of the grammatical and logical rules of interpretation.

Strict adherence to the doctrine of separation of power denied any power of interpretation to Civil law judges and whenever need be, the problem of interpretation was directed to be sent to legislature for interpretation. In a bid to meet the growing number of reference for interpretation a separate organ of the legislature known as Tribunal of Cassation or *acupres du Corps* legislatíve was opened. Its only function is to quash the incorrect interpretations of the judiciary and leave the matter back to Court for final decision. It does not decide the case. It does not leave any guidance to the judge on the matter. The only thing it does is 'your interpretation is quashed, decide afresh'. As against this in common law system, the higher court does two things—(i) lay down correct law; (ii) decide the case in one way or the other. Gradually the tribunal began to explain as to what was the correct interpretation and from a tribunal, it became a Court; from a Tribunal of Cassation, a Court of Cassation and full title being Supreme Court of Cassation.

Though not in any sense of common law system, even then such a judicial legislation has had existence in civil law world. Judicial legislation in civil law system takes any one of the three approaches—

(i) Unclear provisions.—The Judge is to interpret the provisions quite strictly but he has no liberty to dismiss the provisions on the plea that law is unclear.

In this interpretation, the judges are not to find out the intention of the legislature. The theory does not leave the judges with—that this is the way. It merely establishes the concept which is inconsistent with the orthodox view of judicial interpretation. In this process, the judge is not asked to decide. He is told how to state what he has.

(ii) Problem of non-existent provision.—Where there is no statutory provision bearing precisely in the form; the Judge is to reason by analogy from other statutory provisions; If this does not work, then he is to resort to the principles known as general principles of the legal order of the State.

(iii) Evolutive interpretation.—It is resorted to where the terms of statute remain the same but its meaning is changed by interpretation. An old statute, if applied in the traditional way, may produce undesirable results. This happens because the circumstances may have changed to require a different interpretation. If he applies the old law, injustice occurs to parties,nation and to his own self. If he changes the interpretation, it amounts to judicial legislation which he is not permitted to do. But the civil law system does not bother about it and terms this interpretation as something entirely different from judicial legislation.

Extensive Interpretation.—This process serves two purposes :

(a) It is used to fill up the gaps in law—Gaps in different statutes on the same subject and different provisions of the same statute, as well as different aspects of the same section. The extensive interpretation fills up the blank and interconnects and collates them.

(b) It mitigates hardships which may flow from rigid adherence to the letters of law so that it may not cause injustice or fraud. The scope of the statute is enlarged, restricted or modified by this process.

This process is similar to the equity therefore it is called 'continental equity' though Gutteridge has opposed the use of such a title. This theory has found support of the jurists including Friedmann, Walton, Amos, Schwatz.

Free law theory of Interpretation

This theory invests the judge with the widest powers in dealing with the language of the statute. The language of the Act may be disregarded if it is incomplete, ambiguous or is likely to cause injustice. This rule leaves the duty on the judges to implement the known or probable object of the Act. If the legislature could not properly express the alleged object in language of the Act, the continental judge is free to take every step for enforcing these objects without any rigid loyalty to the language. This theory had a very brief life and it has now been discarded. This theory has found support of the jurists like Ehrlich, Kantorowicz, Geny, etc.

The Social purpose theory

The practice in continental courts (for example Germany) is that social purpose of the Act must be taken as guide to the intention of the legislature where the language of the statute is ambiguous, the judges must adopt the interpretation which accords most closely with the social and economic purpose of the statute. This theory has found support of the jurists like Patonillet, Savigny, Wach, Ihering, Geny, Planioletc.

This empowers the judge to carry forward the investigation into the intention of the legislature to any extent he likes. This liberty is unlimited and it has the probability that the normal type of interpretation may easily be disregarded. The judge becomes legislature. The social purpose becomes predominant.

Statute law, whether in form of a code or of an amending statute, may give rise to the difficulties of interpretation in several ways. It may be perfect in the sense that it omits to deal or only deals in part, with the circumstances to which it is applicable *ex facie*. In this event, the judge must determine whether the omission is deliberate, or whether it is due to some oversight on the part of the legislator. If it appears that the statute is silent because the legislator intentionally refrained from any expression of his will, the judge must disregard the statute and seek elsewhere for a rule of law to be applied to the matter. If the omission is inadvertent, it becomes the duty of the judge to make good the deficiency. But in this case, he may be assisted by the possibility of reasoning by analogy to other rules contained in the same code or statute.

The problems may also arise owing to the existence of two or more conflicting statutory rules, in which case *lex generalis* must give way to *lex specialis* and if there is an antinomy or deadlock the rules must be regarded as cancelling one to another. A statutory rule may become obsolete by reason of some change in social or economic circumstances, or it may be of such a nature that its enforcement would lead to absurdity or injustice. In all these cases, the judge must disregard the rule. Finally, a difficulty of interpretation may arise because the language of the statute is defective and its meaning is ambiguous. The judge may, in such a case, go to the historical origin of the rule, he may, consult the records of the legislature including parliamentary debates.

Common law approach to the method of interpretation is different from civil law countries. But upto a certain point the two systems are identical. In interpreting the law, the judges of India, England, France and other common law and civil law countries take the intention of the legislature as dominant factor. Thus, if the language of the statute is such as to make the intention clear; the judges of both common law and civil law countries could accept as it stands, even if the interpretation does not correspond to their own views.

Interpretation in Civil and Common law system.—The following points are relevant—

(1) The most marked differences between the common law and civil law methods of interpretation, the approach in construing the meaning of 'statute' is that in India and England, much importance is given to the grammatical or literal interpretation. Thus, it has been pointed out repeatedly by the courts of India and England that if the meaning of the statute is plain and clear, it should be given ordinary and natural meaning. But in the civil law countries the courts give weight to the logical interpretation rather than grammatical interpretation.

(2) In France, a judge is required to look beyond what has been stated in the statute law and thereby to ascertain the true intention of the legislature. The language of statute could be avoided in order to avoid obvious absurdity. In common law countries, the practice is that where the language of statute is unequivocal and certain the judges are not allowed to take surrounding circumstances into account. So far they must make the best use of the matters of common knowledge, consistent with that of the text and give an effect to any meaning which it bears and which is not manifestly unjust, even though the result may be to defeat the intention of the legislature. They may not

consult the reports of the debates in Parliament or any other record of ministerial or Parliamentary deliberation in this regard but the continental method in such cases is similar to France where the consultation of the preliminary proceeding leading upto legislation has long been a favourite instrument of judicial interpretation. The judges in France will in case of doubt consult not only ministerial statements and reports of the parliamentary committee but also the reports of the committee in the Chamber of ministers and Senate. They like use of these materials by courts in cases of doubt if light may be thrown on the intention of the legislature thereby.

(3) In India, England, and in other common law countries the scope of interpretation is limited. The power of the lower court judges regarding interpretation is restricted by the decisions of the superior courts and in interpretation they cannot overrule the prior decision of a superior court. In other words, the common law countries a judge in his power of interpretation, is bound by the doctrine *ratio decidendi and stare-decisis*. On the other hand, France and civil law countries, the scope of interpretation is unlimited, for the courts are not bound to follow the decisions of other courts, or even superior courts. Thus, in France lower court judges have better freedom of action and superior court cannot impose any rule by order.

(4) In India, England and in other common law countries the judges very rarely look into the social and economic purposes of interpretation. Their method of interpretation is historical, for they are not required to trace the history of the statute and interpret the provision accordingly. On the other hand, the position in continental countries is quite different. In France and Germany, judges make interpretation by reference to the social conditions and the social needs of persons as well as effect of the statute on society. Thus, teleological interpretation is always in France and in no case can a judge isolate from the realities of social life. The historical interpretation is resorted to in civil law countries.

❑ ❑

Chapter 6

Response of the Judicial Process to the cases of first impression

How does the Court Work

First impression cases are those which come before Trial Court but traditional judicial methods like Constitution, Statutes and rulings do not help to decide. The facts come from evidence—There is jura—none of the above sources. How will court decide it? By going to logic (Philosophy), History or Sociology? The Courts work under law, it may be substantive and procedural. Substantive law provides the rights and liabilities which the Courts are to enforce. Procedural law provides how does the Court work. Justice is mission. Overall Court structure is regulated by Constitution of the country. The structure gets legitimacy by Constitution. The Constitution is supreme law of the land. If there is any provision on the point it has to apply. If the Constitution does not provide specifically for solution of the problem before Court, it would search law in statutes and precedents. Where there is no such guidance, what would the Judge do? He has four ways open. These are called methods of Judicial Process. Any of these can help him to find law for the case before him.

Judicial process depends on Constitution and Statutes. Former prevails over the latter. Third, is Precedent which is next to the first and second.

First impression

A new legal issue or interpretation that is brought before a court. In a case of first impression, the exact issue before the court has not been addressed by that court, or within that court's jurisdiction, thus there is no binding authority on that matter.

Cases of first impression often occur in connection with recently passed legislation, or when that issue has been addressed by other jurisdictions, but not in the jurisdiction of the presented court.

Courts may seek guidance from other jurisdictions, or by making analogies to related or similar issues.

TRIAL is fast approaching. Trial counsel knows a question of first impression is lurking in the background. A case of first impression is "a case that presents the court with an issue of law that has not previously been decided by any question of first impression at the right time and in the right procedural context of vital importance to trial counsel.

For example, in recent years we have encountered multiple plaintiffs' counsel in different jurisdictions who have sought a finding of liability as a matter of law based on the equitable doctrine of offensive non-mutual collateral estoppel. Under that doctrine, a plaintiff seeks to prevent a defendant from litigating an issue that the defendant had previously litigated and lost in an action with another party. The plaintiffs' counsel argued that summary judgment on the questions of negligence and defect was proper based on the fact that juries in other jurisdictions had found either that the manufacturer was negligent in the design of the product or that the product at issue, was defective under identical theories of defect.

Many courts recognize the use of that doctrine in the right circumstances, even in the negligence and products liability context. The Supreme Court in our jurisdiction had sanctioned the use of the equitable doctrine of offensive non-mutual collateral estoppel in certain contexts. The court had not, however, applied that doctrine in the context of negligence or products liability involving mass produced consumer goods.

Counsel facing a question of first impression like this should develop a strategy with appellate counsel for addressing the question before the trial court and on appeal. Considering all the options and having a strategy in place will help minimize the possibility of mistrial, waiver, or reversal on appeal.

Counsel should plan a strategy for addressing a question of first impression long before trial

A question of first impression gives trial counsel the opportunity to use the well-reasoned rationale of persuasive authority from other jurisdictions as well as public policy arguments to advocate a client's position. Even if trial counsel perceives that the trial court will not have the time or resources necessary to do an in-depth analysis, laying that foundation in the briefing at the trial court level is necessary to avoid a finding of waiver in the event of an appeal from a final judgment.

Trial counsel should not leave a question of first impression to appellate counsel to address on the fly during trial or as an afterthought on appeal. Instead, trial counsel litigating a case raising a question of first impression should recruit the assistance of appellate counsel long before trial to map out a workable strategy of when and how to raise that question, or to seek intermediate appellate review, to avoid procedural pitfalls that could result in mistrial, waiver, or reversal on appeal.

Intermediate appellate review may be allowed in certain procedural contexts

To avoid the possibility of reversal on appeal, trial counsel should consider whether intermediate appellate review is an option. Federal courts allow an immediate appeal from a "small class" of collateral orders. Many appellate courts are more inclined to exercise their discretionary mandamus jurisdiction to review a question of first impression. As a general rule, discovery orders are interlocutory orders that are not immediately appealable. Writs of *mandamus* for discovery orders can be obtained in extraordinary circumstances. Further, depending on the jurisdiction's statutes and rules, certain interlocutory orders may be immediately appealable by right.

Trial appellate counsel should review the governing law carefully as the failure to timely appeal an interlocutory order appealable by right may preclude intermediate appellate review by a writ..

Reference system

Section 113 of Code of Civil Procedure contains a guidance for Subordinate Courts. It is to the effect that if during judicial process of a case in court, any question arises regarding interpretation of the Constitution, it can frame that question and send it to High Court for reply or elucidation. After it is so replied, the rest of the case shall proceed in light of this view so given in that reference.

This procedure can be adapted even in cases of first impression. this is another way, in addition to what Cardozo discussed *e.g.*, Analogy, logic or philosophy—Tradition, Custom or History and the Sociology.

WHAT DOES THE JUDGE DO? On whom does he depend for guidance when no help is available from the three. Four paths or directions are open to him in these situations :

1. **Go to Philosophy.**—Logic or analogy; this is called method of philosophy,
2. **Go to History.**—Historical development; this is called method of evolution,
3. Custom of the community; this is called method of tradition,
4. **Go to Sociology.**—Justice, morals, social welfare and the mores of the day; this is called method of sociology.

Tradition as method; its use in judicial process

The Courts or the Judges have been seeking guidance from the traditions of people and predecessors. It later on, developed and merged into path of history (custom) and custom of realm (common law) and custom of the Court (Precedent or rulings).

The term tradition derives from the Latin *tradere*, which means "to transmit" or "to give over". Generally, it refers to beliefs, doctrines, customs, ethical and moral standards, and cultural values and attitudes which are transmitted orally or by Holy Book or Scriptures or by personal example. Under this designation, the process of transmission itself is also included. Theologically, in Judaism, Islam, Christianity and Sanatan dharma tradition is the name applied to the Code of Law given by God.

Terms of traditions

Masoret is the general name for tradition. It is found in *Ezekiel and means originally "bond" or "fetter"*. Tradition is the discipline which establishes the correct practice and interpretation of the Torah and was therefore regarded as a hedge or fetter on the Law. Since this knowledge was handed down by successive generations, it was also associated with the Hebrew word masor, denoting "to give over". In the talmudic literature, the terms *masoret* is used to include all forms of tradition, both those which relate to the Bible and those which concern custom, law, historical events, folkways, and other subjects. Different kinds of traditions were given special names. Traditions which specified the vocalization, punctuation, spelling, and correct form of the biblical text were called *masorah*. Those legal traditions which were revealed to Moses at Mount Sinai and were later preserved in writing were known as *Halakhah le-Moshe mi-Sinai* ("law given to Moses on Sinai"). A legal tradition which was handed down by word of mouth, but did not necessarily emanate from Sinai, was called *shemu'ah* ("a report"). Religious and general traditions which became binding as a result of long observance by successive generations were termed *minhag* ("custom"). Prophetic traditions described in the books of the prophets and Hagiographa were known as *Divrei Kabbalah* ("words of tradition"). Esoteric and mystical traditions concerning God and the world transmitted to the elect and then passed down through the ages were called *Kabbalah*, from *kibbel* ("to receive"). Likewise, Quran is Allah-e-hukm; hadis, izma, qiyas are other ways to know Islam; Sruti (Veda), Smiriti, Custom (Sadachar) and Justice and good conscience (what dictates the inner conscience) are ways to know Sanatan dharma (Vedic law).

Origin of traditions

It is almost not denied that many statutes are credited to Moses. However, the vast majority of laws were handed down orally by him. The Written Law did not always detail the manner and form of practice, giving rise of necessity to tradition. An instance of this kind is the law relating to fish which meet the biblical dietary requirements. Leviticus 11:9 states that a fish that has a fin and a scale in the water can be eaten. However, the minimum number of fins and scales that a fish must have to be ritually edible is not specified. The traditions relating to the Bible and Mishnah taught that a fish needs at least one fin and two scales to satisfy the biblical dietary requirements. Similarly, the Bible commands that a paschal lamb be slaughtered on the 14th day of Nisan. There is no mention in the Bible as to whether it is permissible to perform this act if the 14th day of Nisan occurs on the Sabbath when the slaughtering of animals is forbidden. In the year 31 B.C., the 14th of Nisan fell on the Sabbath. The sons of Bathyra, the heads of the High Court, forgot the precedent previously established. Hillel, a then unknown Babylonian, volunteered the information that he had heard from Shemaiah and Avtalyon, the foremost teachers of the age, that it was permissible to slaughter the paschal lamb on the Sabbath. This reported tradition of Hillel's mentors was readily accepted, and it is mentioned that because of this display of erudition with regard to tradition, Hillel was appointed *nasi*.

Tradition was also the vehicle of transmission for the rules of interpretation, of the written law, such as the laws of *hermeneutics*. Since it was impossible within the confines of writing to record all the laws and their applications in all situations, a medium was needed to preserve this information. Even today, with the availability of writing media, much of our culture is handed down orally. Tradition was the means whereby extant law was maintained and applied to life. Thus R. Joshua b. Levi declared that all teaching both the Bible, Mishnah, Talmud, and *aggadah* and those that were initiated by veteran scholars were already given to Moses on Mount Sinai.

Some traditions arose as a result of the common practice of the community. These practices were considered to emanate from eminent religious authorities and owed their binding character to having been handed down by previous generations, from father to son, a principle upheld by R. Lohanan in the Talmud. The citizens of Beth-Shean complained to him that the custom of not going from Tyre to Sidon on the eve of the Sabbath was impossible to observe. R. Johanan replied. "Your fathers have already taken it (this custom) upon themselves". As a result, this tradition could not be abrogated.

History (comes in tradition); Follow it

In rabbinic Judaism, tradition was binding and had the force of law. The divine revelation to Moses consisted of the written law and oral law with its implied exposition by the sages of Israel. *Berakhot* tells that R. Levi B. Hama said in the name of R. Simeon B. Lakish: "What is the meaning of the verse, and I will give thee the tables of stone, and the law and the Commandments, which I have written to teach them. It means as follows: 'the tables of stone are the Ten Commandments, 'the law' is the Pentateuch, 'the commandments' is the Mishnah, 'which I have written' are the prophets and the Hagiographa, 'to teach them' is the *Gemara*. This teaches us that all these things were given at Sinai. "Originally, the oral law was handed down by word of mouth. When its transmission became difficult, it was set down in writing in the Mishnah and Talmud. The validity of the oral law was attacked by the Sadducees, one of the early sects in Judaism. Josephus records that the Sadducees held that "only those observances are obligatory which are in the written word but that those which derived from the tradition of the forefathers need not be kept".

Talmudic times—Temple prayer demolished

After the destruction of the temple, the Sadducees disappeared. The body of tradition continued to grow as rites were introduced to replace the temple ritual. *Megillah* pictures the patriarch Abraham as concerned with how Israel could obtain forgiveness, once the temple ceased to exist. God assures Abraham, "I have already ordained for them the order of the sacrifices. Every time that they read them, it is considered as if they offer up a sacrifice and I forgive them all their sins." After the destruction of the temple, the system of public prayer was instituted to substitute for the temple service. The liturgical traditions were handed down verbally, through the centuries, until they were compiled in the prayer book of Amram Gaon.

Medieval times—Rabbinical traditions denied

At the end of the eighth century, rabbinic Judaism was again challenged by a new sect, the Karaites. They accepted the authority of the Bible but denied rabbinical tradition and law, which had developed further as the Mishnah and Talmud were elucidated and applied to life. Through its great exponents, Saadiah and Maimonides, rabbinic Judaism triumphed over the Karaites. The latter wrote his Code of Law. *Mishneh Torah* ("the Second Torah"), and showed the direct connection between the written law and its explanation in the oral law. As new situations arose, the talmudic, geonic, and post-geonic traditions were further amplified. They in turn were set down in writing in the Responsa and Codes. In the 16th century R. Joseph Caro produced his Definitive Code, the Shulhan Arukh. With the addition of the glosses of R. Moses, Isserles and later commentaries, it became the most comprehensive compendium of Jewish law and tradition to this day.

Modern times—Reform movement; break with tradition

At the end of the 18th century rabbinic Judaism, which had maintained an unbroken chain of tradition from the days of Moses was again challenged. A reform movement began in Germany which sought to assimilate the Jews into the general culture by modifying Jewish traditions. Among the reforms instituted were sermons in the German vernacular, hymns and chorals in German, the use of the organ, and the confirmation of boys on the Feast of Pentecost instead of the traditional bar Mitzvah. In the course of time, this movement established itself in America. Here it continued to propound its doctrine that Judaism was primarily a universalistic and moral religion. Only the moral law was binding. Ceremonial laws which could be adapted to the views of the modern environment were to be maintained. Other Mosaic and rabbinic laws which regulated diet, priestly purity, and dress could be discarded.

Conservative movement.—In reaction to the reformers' break with tradition, the Conservative movement was formed in America. At the founding meeting of its congregational organization in 1913, it declared itself "a union of congregations for the promotion of traditional Judaism." Other aims were the furtherance of Sabbath observance and dietary laws, and the maintenance of the traditional liturgy with Hebrew as the language of prayer. As the complexion of American Jewry changed, the Conservative movement incorporated some reforms externals of worship such as family pews and the use of the organ in many congregations. However, it accepted the authority of rabbinic tradition, instituting changes advocated by its scholars, with regard for the attitude of the people and the place of the observance in Jewish tradition.

Transmitters of the tradition

In rabbinic literature the chain of tradition is given as follows: Moses received the Torah on Sinai and delivered it to Joshua, who in turn delivered it to the elders, the elders to the prophets, and the prophets to the Men of the Great Synagogue. According to rabbinic Judaism, the teaching of the great sages in every generation in keeping with the *halakhah* is binding. Thus, the transmitters of tradition included the successors to the Men of the Great Synagogue down to modern times, namely: the scribes (*soferim*), the pairs (*zugot*), the *tannaim*, the *oraim*, the *savoraim*, the *geonim*, the codifiers, the world famous Torah authorities of every era, and the *rashei hayeshivah* ("heads of the academies").

Significance of the traditions

Tradition has given Judaism a continuity with its past and preserved its character as a unique faith with a distinct way of life. As the successor of rabbinic Judaism, Orthodoxy representing tradition harks back to the Sinaitic divine revelation and can only be changed within the framework of rabbinic law. In Conservative Judaism, tradition is a vital force capable of modification according to the historical evolution of Jewish law. Reform Judaism has recently displayed a greater appreciation of traditional practices but tradition remains voluntary in character.

One special feature needs to be explained. All traditions, be it that of Sanatan dharma (India), Judaism, Christianity, Islam or Hindu dharma, Buddhists, Jains or Sikhism, all have developed on almost same dotted lines. The specialities of each of them are contributions of their first thinker. The differences are; in what to worship? Whom to worship? Worship or not to worship? Rituals or matters of detail? None says, 'theft is sublime, truth is bad, do not follow dharma', do not respect your parents; the researchers and students of law need to think on these secrets as to what has kept all these paths (religions) on identical tracks?

The judicial process and history of case

The tendency of any rule, principle or idea to extend upto the maximum limit of its logic is challenged by the tendency to confine these within limits of their history. History illuminates past, in illuminating the past, it illuminates the present and in illuminating the present, it illuminates the future. The path of history and logic are not always opposed. They may be overlapping. Effect of history is to make the path of logic clear in so many cases.

The growth may be logical, whether it is consistency with past that shapes it or it is shaped by some pre-established norm or shaped by some general conception or by some indwelling and creative principle are various issues that this method may help the judicial process to solve.

Property Law and method of evolution

Property law can be one field wherein the application of method of history in judicial process can be illustrated. Property law can be read only in terms of its history. Can system of feudal tenure be created by Code of Law? How does the simple interest differ from estate for life? or estate of life from an estate for years? Restraint on alienation, contingent reminders, private trust for charities can be studied only in terms of history. In these cases too method of philosophy plays vital role. Forms of action, we have buried but they still rule as from their graves, (Maitland). If we consider law of contract, we find it full of history (Holmes). Doctrine of consideration is historical.

Two methods history and philosophy, supplement each other. Which method will predominate in any case may depend at times upon intuition of convenience or fitness too subtle to be formulated, too imponderable to be valued, too volatile to be localized, or even fully apprehended.

Chapter 7

Custom and judicial process

Creative energy of custom may not be so much today as it has been in history or tradition. From Blackstone to Pound, thoughts have undergone sea change. Custom whether what common law meant or what sociologists advocated it to be custom of Courts. The growth has been very interesting.

Whether rules laid down by judges generate custom or custom generates rules?—Custom must determine whether there has been adherence or departure. The creative energy of custom must manifest not in making thereof by judicial process but it lies in application of old ones. Judicial process whether adheres to it or has departed from the notoriety of custom is important. This should be so that courts are bound to take judicial notice of these customs (Section 57 of Indian Evidence Act, 1872).

Custom in law is the established pattern of behaviour that can be objectively verified within a particular social setting. A claim can be carried out in defense of "what has always been done and accepted by law." Related is the idea of **prescription**; a right enjoyed through long custom rather than positive law.

Customary law (also, **consuetudinary** or **unofficial law**) exists where :

1. a certain legal practice is observed; and
2. the relevant actors consider it to be law (*opinio juris*).

Most customary laws deal with *standards of community* that have been long-established in a given locale. However, the term can also apply to areas of international law where certain standards have been nearly universal in their acceptance as correct bases of action—in example, laws against piracy or slavery (see *hostis humani generis*). In many, though not all instances, customary laws will have supportive court rulings and case law that has evolved over time to give additional weight to their rule as law and also to demonstrate the trajectory of evolution (if any) in the interpretation of such law by relevant courts.

Nature, definition and sources of customary law

A central issue regarding the recognition of custom is determining the appropriate methodology to know what practices and norms actually constitute customary law. It is not immediately clear that classic Western theories of jurisprudence can be reconciled in any useful way with conceptual analyses of customary law, and thus some scholars (like John Comaroff and Simon Roberts) have characterised customary law norms in their own terms. Yet, there clearly remains some disagreement, which is seen in John Hund's critique of Comaroff and Roberts' theory, and preference for the contributions of H.L.A. Hart. Hund argues that Hart's "The Concept of Law" solves the conceptual problem with which scholars who have attempted to articulate how customary law principles may be identified, defined and how they operate in regulating social behaviour and resolving disputes.

Customary law as an indefinite repertoire of norms

Comaroff and Roberts' famous work, "Rules and Processes", attempted to detail the body of norms that constitute Tswana law in a way that was less legalistic (or rule-oriented) than had Isaac Schapera. They defined "mekgwa le melao ya Setswana" in terms of Casalis and Ellenberger definition : *melao* therefore being rules pronounced by a chief and *mekgwa* as norms that become customary law through traditional usage. Importantly, however, they noted that the Tswana seldom attempt to classify the vast array of existing norms into categories and they thus term this the 'undifferentiated nature of the normative repertoire.' Moreover, they observe the co-existence of overtly incompatible norms that may breed conflicts, either due to circumstances in a particular situation, or inherently due to their incongruous content. This lack of rule of classification and failure to eradicate internal inconsistencies between potentially conflicting norms allows for much flexibility in dispute settlement and is also viewed as a 'strategic resource' for disputants who seek to advance their own success in a case. The latter incongruities (especially of inconsistencies of norm content) are typically solved by elevating one of the norms (tacitly) from 'the literal to the symbolic'. This allows for the accommodation of both as they now theoretically exist in different realms of reality. This is highly contextual, which further illustrates that norms cannot be viewed in isolation and are open to negotiation. Thus, although there are a small number of so-called non-negotiable norms, the vast majority are viewed and given substance contexually, which is seen as fundamental to the Tswana.

Comaroff and Roberts describe how outcomes of specific cases have the ability to change the normative repertoire, as the repertoire of norms is seen to be both in a state of formation and transformation at all times. These changes are justified on the grounds that they are merely giving recognition to *de facto* observations of transformation. Furthermore, the legitimacy of a chief is a direct determinant of the legitimacy of his decisions. In the formulation of legislative pronouncements, as opposed to decisions made in dispute resolution, the chief first speaks of the proposal norm with his advisors, then council of headmen, then the public assembly debate the proposed law and may accept or reject it. A chief can proclaim the law even if the public assembly rejects it, but this is not often done; and, if the chief proclaims the legislation against the will of the public assembly, the legislation will become melao, however, it is unlikely that it will be executed because its effectiveness depends on the chief's legitimacy and the norm's consistency with the practices (and changes in social relations) and will of the people under that chief.

Paradigm of argument

Regarding the invocation of norms in disputes, Comaroff and Roberts used the term, "paradigm of argument", to refer to the linguistic and conceptual frame used by a disputant, whereby 'a coherent picture of relevant events and actions in terms of one or more implicit or explicit normative referents' is created. In their explanation, the complainant (who always speaks first) thus establishes a paradigm the defendant can either accept and therefore argue within that specific paradigm or reject and therefore introduce his or her own paradigm (usually, the facts are not contested here). If the defendant means to change the paradigm, they will refer to norms as such, where actually norms are not ordinarily explicitly referenced in Tswana dispute resolution as the audience would typically already know them and just the way one presents one's case and constructs the facts will establish one's paradigm. The headman or chief adjudicating may also do the same : accept the normative basis implied by the parties (or one of them), and thus not refer to norms using explicit language but rather isolate a factual issue in the dispute and then make a decision on it without expressly referring to any norms, or impose a new or different paradigm onto the parties.

Law as necessarily rule-governed

Hund finds Comaroff and Roberts' flexibility thesis of a 'repertoire of norms' from which litigants and adjudicators choose in the process of negotiating solutions between them uncompelling. He is therefore concerned with disproving what he calls "rule scepticism" on their part. He notes that the concept of custom generally denotes convergent behaviour, but not all customs have the force of law. Hund therefore draws from Hart's and analyses distinguishing social rules, which have internal and external aspects, from habits, which have only external aspects. Internal aspects are the reflective attitude on the part of adherents toward certain behaviours perceived to be obligatory, according to a common standard. External aspects manifest in regular, observable behaviour, but is not obligatory. In Hart's analysis, then, social rules amount to custom that has legal force.

Habits and binding social rules

Hart identifies three further differences between habits and binding social rules.

First, a social rule exists where society frowns on deviation from the habit and attempts to prevent departures by criticising such behaviour.

Second, when this criticism is seen socially as a good reason for adhering to the habit, and it is welcomed. And,

Thirdly, when members of a group behave in a common way not only out of habit or because everyone else is doing it, but because it is seen to be a common standard that should be followed, at least by some members. Hund, however, acknowledges the difficulty of an outsider knowing the dimensions of these criteria that depend on an internal point of view.

First form of rule scepticism

For Hund, the first form of rule scepticism concerns the widely held opinion that, because the content of customary law derives from practice, there are actually no objective rules, since it is only behaviour that informs their construction. On this view, it is impossible to distinguish between behaviour that is rule bound and behaviour that is not—*i.e.*, which behaviour is motivated by adherence to law (or at least done in recognition of the law) and is merely a response to other factors. Hund sees this as problematic because it makes quantifying the law almost impossible, since behaviour is obviously inconsistent. Hund argues that this is a misconception based on a failure to acknowledge the importance of the *internal element.* In his view, by using the criteria described above, there is not this problem in deciphering what constitutes "law" in a particular community.

Second form of rule scepticism

According to Hund, the second form of rule scepticism says that, though a community may have rules, those rules are not arrived at 'deductively', *i.e.*, they are not created through legal/moral reasoning only but are instead driven by the personal/political motives of those who create them. The scope for such influence is created by the loose and undefined nature of customary law, which, Hund argues, grants customary-law makers (often through traditional 'judicial processes') a wide discretion in its application. Yet, Hund contents that the fact that rules might sometimes be arrived at in the more *ad hoc* way, does not mean that this defines the system. If one requires a perfect system, where laws are created only deductively, then one is left with a system with no rules. For Hund, this cannot be so and an explanation for these kinds of law-making processes is found in Hart's conception of "secondary rules" (rules in terms of which the main body of norms are recognised). Hund therefore says that for some cultures, for instance in some sections of Tswana society, the secondary rules have developed only to the point where laws are determined with reference to politics and personal preference. This does not mean that they are not "rules". Hund argues that if we acknowledge a developmental pattern in societies' constructions of these secondary rules then we can understand how this society constructs its laws and how it differs from societies that have come to rely on an objective, stand-alone body of rules.

Customary law and codification

The modern codification of civil law developed from the tradition of medieval customs, collections of local customary law that developed in a specific manorial or borough jurisdiction, and which were slowly pieced together mainly from case law and later written down by local jurists. Customs acquired the force of law when they became the undisputed rule by which certain rights, entitlements, and obligations were regulated between members of a community. Some examples include Bracton's *De Legibus et Consuetudinibus Angliae* for England, the Coutume de Paris for the city of Paris, the Sachsenspiegel for northern Germany, and the many *fueros* of

Spain.

International law

In international law, *customary law* refers to the *Law of Nations* or the legal norms that have developed through the customary exchanges between states over time, whether based on diplomacy or aggression. Essentially, legal obligations are believed to arise between states to carry out their affairs consistently with past accepted conduct. These customs can also change based on the acceptance or rejection by states of particular acts. Some principles of customary law have achieved the force of peremptory norms, which cannot be violated or altered except by a norm of comparable strength. These norms are said to gain their strength from universal acceptance, such as the prohibitions against genocide and slavery. Customary international law can be distinguished from treaty law, which consists of explicit agreements between nations to assume obligations. However, many treaties are attempts to codify pre-existing customary law.

Customary law within contemporary legal systems

Customary law is a recognized source of law within jurisdictions of the civil law traditions, where it may be subordinate to both statutes and regulations. In addressing custom as a source of law within the civil law tradition, John Henry Merryman notes that, though the attention it is given in scholarly works is great, its importance is "slight and decreasing." On the other hand, in many countries around the world, one or more types of customary law continue to exist side by side with official law, a condition referred to as **legal pluralism.**

In the canon law of the Catholic Church, custom is a source of law. Canonical jurisprudence, however, differs from Civil law jurisprudence in requiring the express or implied consent of the legislator for a custom to obtain the force of law.

In the Common Law of England, "Long usage" must be established.

It is a broad principle of property law that, if something has gone on for a long time without objection, whether it be using a right of way or occupying land to which one has no title, the law will eventually recognise the fact and give the person doing it the legal right to continue.

It is known in case law as Customary Rights "Customary rights". Something which has been practised since time immemorial by reference to a particular locality may acquire the legal status of a custom, which is a form of local law. The legal criteria defining a custom are precise. The most common claim in recent times, is for customary rights to moor a vessel.

The mooring must have been in continuous use for "Time Immemorial" which is defined by legal precedent as 12 years (or 20 years for Crown Land) for the same purpose by people using them for that purpose.

To give two examples :—A custom of mooring which might have been established in past times for over two hundred years by the fishing fleet of local inhabitants of a coastal community will not simply transfer so as to benefit present day recreational boat owners who may hail from much further afield.

Whereas a group of houseboats on a mooring that has been in continuous use for the last 25 years with a mixture of owner occupiers and rented houseboats, may clearly continue to be used by houseboats, were the owners live in the same town or city.

Both the purpose of the moorings and the class of persons benefited by the custom must have been clear and consistent.

In Canada, customary aboriginal law has a constitutional foundation and for this reason has increasing influence.

Scandinavian Countries

In the Scandinavian countries customary law continues to exist and has great influence. Customary law is also used in some Third World countries, such as those in Africa, usually used alongside common or civil law. For example, in Ethiopia, despite the adoption of legal codes based on civil law in the 1950s according to Dolores Donovan and Getachew Assefa there are more than 60 systems of customary law currently in force, "some of them operating quite independently of the formal state legal system." They offer two reasons for the relative autonomy of these customary law systems : one is that the Ethiopian government lacks sufficient resources to enforce its legal system to every corner of Ethiopia; the other is that the Ethiopian government has made a commitment to preserve these customary systems within these boundaries.

In 1955, President of Kyrgyzstan Askar Akaev announced a decree to revitalize the *aqsaqal* courts of village elders. The courts would have jurisdiction over property, torts and family law. The *aqsaqal* courts were eventually included under Article 92 of the Kyrgyz constitution. As of 2006, there were approximately 1,000 *aqsaqal* courts throughout Kyrgyzstan, including in the capital of Bishkek. Akaev linked the development of these courts to the rekindling of Kyrgyz national identity. In a 2005 speech, he connected the courts back to the country's nomadic past and extolled how the courts expressed the Kyrgyz ability of self-governance. Similar *aqsaqal* courts exist, with varying levels of legal formality, in other countries of Central Asia.

The Somali people in the Horn of Africa follow a customary law system referred to as Xeer. It survives to a significant degree everywhere, including the Somali communities in the Ogaden. Economist Peter Leeson attributes the increase in economic activity since the fall of the Siad Barre administration to the security in life, liberty and property provided by Xeer in large parts of Somalia. The Dutch attorney Michael van Notten also draws upon his experience as a legal expert in his comprehensive study on Xeer, *The Law of the Somalis : A Stable Foundation for Economic Development in the Horn of Africa (2005).*

In India many customs are accepted by law. For example, Hindu marriage ceremonies are recognized by the Hindu Marriage Act.

Law and custom

The Custom is one normative order but is not law. It can become law if it is so incorporated in any enactment (as in Hindu Laws Acts) or when it is given recognition in Court's judgments (like Law merchant). Law has three basic features which taken together, distinguish it from other *normative orders*, such as custom or *convention*.

These features are following :—

(a) Pressures to comply with the law must come externally in the form of actions or threats of action by others regardless of whether a person wants to obey the law or does so out of habit;

(b) these external actions or threats involve coercion or force;

(c) those who implement the coercive threats are individuals whose official role is to enforce the law (*i.e.*, judges, police, etc.).

The custom is to society what law is to State. The society is mostly regulated by the customs which are veins and nerves of any society. These are called by many names like volkgeist, living law, or practice of people, (Vyavahaar) people's law, good conduct (Sadachar), etc. and differ from enacted law in the sense that they are not made at no particular point of time and not by established Legislative procedure by institution having authority to legislate. Their growth and development is hidden in the mysteries of the past.

When does a custom become law?

In English law, the custom is not law. It is source of law. It becomes law only when it satisfies the requirements of **firstly**, antiquity, certainty, continuity, consistency, not being opposed to morality, not being opposed to fundamental law, public policy or any statute and is not unreasonable. And **secondly**, when it gets either legislative or judicial stamping, *i.e.*, when it is incorporated in some enactment or when enforced in some court of law. Both conditions must be satisfied. The former alone will not make it, whether the latter alone can do it is an open question.

In **continent, custom is propric vigore law.** It is not a source of law provided it satisfies all the above requirements of antiquity, certainty, reasonableness, morality, consistency, continuity etc. No legislative or judicial stamping is essential. In Hindu law, custom is source of law but ranks much higher in recognition as compared to position where it is in muslim law. The custom ranks next to sruti (veda) and smriti but if it is clearly proved, it is powerful enough to override written texts of law. In muslim law, custom ranks much lower to quaran, hadis, ijma, qiyas. Hadis is also a kind of custom.

Kinds of custom

Customs are—legal custom, conventional custom and custom of the court.

Legal customs may be—

1. **General custom.**—It applies like general law of the land to all

persons in the area. Common law is a kind of general custom. The only difference between custom and common law is that practice of a particular place is called custom whereas common law is a general immemorial practice throughout the realm. (common law system).

2. Particular custom.—It applies to a particular entity or institution and may form part of or supersede general law of the place. It is this custom that needs to have antiquity, consistency, continuity, certainty, reasonableness, moral, not opposed to fundamental laws, or statute before it can be accepted as such. This may be of following kinds:

(a) **Family custom.**—A custom applying and limited to a particular family is family custom. For example, whether a woman can be head of a family in patriarchal system or whether rule of primogeniture applies? These are questions concerning family customs.

(b) **Tribal custom.**—Tribal customs are those that apply within a tribe or between sub-tribes. How is chief of a tribe to be appointed; by heredity, election or nomination? Whether a tribe's man can marry a girl outside tribe? Whether and how tribal customs are to be traced and enforced? These are issues relating to tribal custom.

(c) **Local custom.**—Local customs are restricted territorially to a particular locality, municipality, village, etc. They apply to all who come or reside in the locality. These are exceptions of the general custom.

(d) **Personal custom.**—These are called prescriptions also. It is personal and as such apply in most part to person. It is made in the name of certain person or his ancestors or those whose estate he has or body politique or corporate and their predecessor. It differs from local custom which is annexed to no person but to a place.

Conventional custom or usage or custom of the trade.—A conventional custom is one whose authority is conditional or on its acceptance and incorporation in agreements between the parties to be bound by it. It has independently otherwise no legal authority. These may be incorporated expressly or impliedly. It may pass through 3 stages, namely, **first**, when its existence is to be pleaded and established as a question of fact and is to be determined by jury or judge (when jury is not part of the system) upon evidence in the particular case in which it arises.

Secondly, when the courts take judicial notice of the usage in question. It needs to be just pleaded but needs not to be established.

Thirdly, the custom that had its original source in convention and secondary source in precedent is embodied into a statute.

In case of conventional custom, no specified duration is legally necessary and in fact no distinction is drawn between ancient and modern custom. What is insisted upon is notoriety of a nature that it may legally be presumed to have been incorporated as part or term of the agreement. Like legal custom, conventional custom, may also be local or general, both classes are source of law and rights within the scope of their application.

Custom of the court

The precedent is otherwise a custom of the court. It can be classified into two categories.

(1) Pre-1189 A.D. customs of the court.

(2) Post-1189 A.D. customs of the court.

The pre-1189, custom of the court are *ex proprio vigore* law and are referred to as general custom of the realm. This refers mainly to pre 1189 A.D. customs which were accepted by the judges before 1189. This means practically the same as common law. But whether custom of the realm which came into existence after 1189 A.D. and which is contrary to judge made law can be law *Ex proprio vigore* is doubtful?

Habit, convention, custom

A *habit* is a course of conduct which is regularly, though not necessarily invariably, pursued but without any sense of obligation or compulsion to do so. The main point about habits generally is; that they are regarded neither socially nor legally compulsive. Habits may be, self-regarding or other-regarding.

Customs are rules of conduct in defined situations that are of relatively long duration and are generally observed without deliberations. It is the socially obligatory element which characterises customary observance and distinguishes it from habit. Customary rules of conduct are called usages, and there is no sense of duty or obligation to follow them.

Lying somewhere between habit, usage and custom, *conventions* are rules for conduct which involve a sense of duty and obligation. Pressures of social character, which usually include expressions of disapproval, are exerted on individuals who do not conform to conventions. Unlike law, a conventional order lacks specialized personnel for the implementation of coercion. Whereas both custom and conventions are normative in the sense that they establish rules of conduct for compliance, habits and usages do not refer to or depend on norms, but simply involve regularities of behaviour which are in fact observed. Most habits never assume a *normative character*, but remain on the level of personal discretion.

The fact is, however, that habits can and do become converted into customs. It is a recognised form of human progression that practices which continue to be observed over a period tend to be *norm-creating,* especially if they appear to possess a distinct social function utility.

Custom and customary law

Customary observance has not necessarily always grown up in this kind of way the custom may result from deliberate innovations instituted by the ruling class or the example of some authoritative (*i.e.*, king, prince, chief) or highly revered (*i.e.*, high priest, Imams, judge, poet, artist) person in a community. The headman or chief in a society, for instance, may settle a dispute in a particular way, and although such a society may have no conception of *legal precedent*, either because of the authority of the chief, or because the ruling seems eminently reasonable, a *custom*, thenceforth, may be established, which will be regarded as binding in like situations and that might be a first step in the establishment of a *customary law*, based upon the custom born in the way described.

Thus, laws are a special kind of reinstitutionalised or crystallised custom. Customs are norms or rules about the ways in which people must behave if social institutions are to perform their functions and society is to endure.

Customary law is any recurring mode of interaction among individuals and groups, together with the more or less explicit acknowledgment by these individuals and groups that such pattern of interaction produce reciprocal expectations of conduct that ought to be satisfied. Customary law consists of customs accepted by members of a community as binding among them.

Originally, common law was described as that part of the law of England which was non-statutory and common to the country as a whole, rather than limited to any particular part of it. The term is also used at times as a synonym for "judge-made" law or "case law". It was, as it is, as it still remains, the product of a sophisticated legal professional tradition and technique; unwritten, in the sense of not being enacted, but contained in innumerable decisions of the judges, whose judgments are distilled and which can be applied to fresh cases as they arise. Such a system as the common law, especially in its earlier stages, is something of a bridge between genuine *customary law*, and highly developed codified system of law to be found in many modern States.

Custom and trade usage.—The term usage of trade is to be understood as referring to a particular usage to be established by evidence and is perfectly distinct from that general custom of merchants which is part of the law of the realm. The general custom is collected from decisions, legal principles and analogies and is capable of being enlarged by proof of living general usage. Such a general usage remains unaffected by the provisions of the Act even though it may be inconsistent with those provisions. As regards usage of trade and its method of examination, section 92(5) of the Indian Evidence Act, lays the relevant law. This section enacts that though a contract may be in writing, oral evidence may be adduced to prove any usage or custom by which incidents not expressly mentioned in the contract are usually annexed to contracts of that description provided that annexing of such incidents would not be repugnant to or inconstent with the express terms of the contract. The term usage of custom of trade as used in sections 190 or 211 of the Indian Contract Act, always means a particular usage as distinguished from a general or universal usage.

A general usage pervading over all trades has no binding force if it is inconsistent with the provisions of the Act. A general usage is equivalent to general law and as such equivalent to the provisions of the Contract Act, which in its own way lays down the general principles applicable to contracts. Therefore, general principles borrowed from elsewhere cannot override the provisions of the Contract Act. They would not be given effect to if inconsistent with the Contract Act and if consistent, the question of applying them in preference to the provisions of the Act, in fact, does not arise.

The distinction drawn between custom and usage, in Article 298 of Halsbury's Laws of England, is as follows:—

(1) In case of mercantile usages, their importance chiefly lies in the fact that they are imported as a term of the contract.

(2) Mercantile usages lack three of the distinguishing features of customs properly so-called,
first they need not have existed from time immemorial;
secondly, they need not be confined to a limited locality;
thirdly, usages, however, extensive if they happen to be contrary to positive law, will not be sanctioned by the courts, customs on the other hand may be inconsistent with the general law of the country.

Certain important questions arise in discussing custom or usage of trade: The questions are mainly two. They are :

(i) why is an ordinary custom distinguished from trade usage or custom of the trade?

(ii) What is the meaning and scope of the terms "reasonableness" and "against law of public policy".

From an examination of authorities we find that usage can be broadly described *as a particular course of dealing or line of conduct generally adopted by persons engaged in a particular department of business life*. It may also be described more fully as a particular, course of dealing or line of conduct which has acquired such notoriety that persons dealing in that business must be taken to have intended to follow that course of dealing or line of conduct, unless they stipulate otherwise either expressly or impliedly. A custom on the other hand is "*a particular rule which has existed either actually or presumptively from time immemorial, and has obtained the force of law in a particular locality, although contrary to or not consistent with the general common law of the realm*.

In two essential particulars custom differs from usage of the trade. They are :

(1) the necessity of the existence of a custom either actually or presumptively from time immemorial.

(2) Confinement of all customs to a definite limited locality. In other words, there cannot be a custom in one place to do something in another place. It follows as a necessary corollary from the aforesaid nature of custom that it cannot extend to the whole country nor can it be applicable to every member of the public, for, in either of these cases, it would amount to the common law of the country. In its strict legal sense, custom exclusively denotes an immemorial local custom. It is to be lamented that

some of the judges have confused between the words "custom" and 'usage', and have made indiscreet use of the concepts.

Trade usage

The essential requirements of trade usages are that it has to be :

(1) notorious; (2) certain; (3) reasonable, and, (4) must not offend against the intention of any legislative enactment.

The importance of a usage lies in the fact that it is well-known and not that it traces its origin to antiquity. The meaning of the term 'notoriety' is that it must be well-known at the place in which it applies, it needs not be known to all the world nor even that it should be known to the person against whom it is asserted. The usage must be capable of ready ascertainment by any person who wishes to enter into a contract of which that usage would form part. Every usage must be certain. It must have as much certainty as the written contract itself. The reason is obvious. The usage is read as a term of the contract and unless it is specific, it cannot be utilized for the purpose for which it is chiefly intended.

A usage must also be 'reasonable. A usage cannot be deemed reasonable unless it can be regarded as fair and proper and such as honest, right-minded and reasonable men would adopt. A usage which is founded on the general convenience of all parties engaged in a particular business can never be regarded as unreasonable. An arrangement which would not be unreasonable for individual persons to adopt by express agreement cannot be regarded as unreasonable if it be adopted as a usage.

Any usage, however, extensive will not be permitted to prevail if it be directly opposed to positive law, as it will amount to a defiance and obviously contrary to fundamental principle. Evidence of usage has been admitted as supplementing the terms of a contract relating to marine insurance, charter parties, bill of lading, sale of goods, stock exchange transactions, building, brokers and actors and even to landlords and tenants.

❑❑

Chapter 8

Ethical Reasoning Philosophy and the judicial process

The reasons, satisfy us to draw conclusions which affect people's lives, influence their behaviour, and sometimes change society's reactions to issues that govern life. These reasons are very often not supported by reasoning, leaving people confused, as a result, raising doubt over institutional wisdom and integrity. The reasoning in support of reasons is an important function in decision making process. It assures society of the quality of the decisions, promotes healthy and informed debate and clears the way of improvement of future actions. Ethical reasoning is important in all spheres of influential decision making.

Judgment writing requires skills of narration and story-telling. After giving facts and discussing admissible and relevant evidence a judge is required to give reasons for deciding the issues framed by him. The reasons convey the judicial ideas in words and sentences. The reasons convey the thoughts of a judge and are part of judicial exposition, explanation and persuasion. There is a difference between giving reasons and the reasoning, which may ultimately lead to a decision by a judge on the issue or the issues raised before him. The process adopted by a judge in arriving at a decision through the reasoning, tests the judge of his ability and integrity. He may adopt a syllogistic process, inferential process or intuitive process. 'Syllogism' means, a deductive scheme of a formal argument consisting of a major and a minor premise and a conclusion. A judge accepts an argument on a major premise, which overweighs the minor premise to draw his own conclusion. In case of inferential process a judge simply relies upon the evidence, and reaches to a conclusion. In the intuitive process, the Judge adopts psychological process, which may or may not be based by his subjective preference or biases. In this process the judge arrives at a conclusion more by intuition or emotion rather than reason. the judge may believe a witness in part (which is permissible in India) or whole and then draw a conclusion by justifying it from the reasoning supplied by him either by his own belief or experience. In all these methods the object is to arrive at the truth. If judge succeeds in finding out the truth, the methods may be justified.

Reasons are the rational explanations to the conclusion. Reasoning is the process by which we reach to the conclusion. Reasoning is the mental process of looking for reasons for beliefs, conclusions, actions or feelings. In philosophy, the study of reasoning typically focuses on what makes reasoning efficient or inefficient, appropriate or inappropriate, good or bad. This is done by either examining the form and structure of the reasoning within the argument or by considering the broader methods used to reach particular goals of reasoning.

'Homer' a Greek philosopher in eight century B.C. used mystic stories that used gods to explain the formation of the world. 'Aristotle' is the first writer, who gave an extended, systematic treatment of methods of human reasoning. He identified two methods of reasoning :

(a) Analysis : in which we try to understand the object by looking at its component parts.

(b) Synthesis : in which we try to understand a class of objects by looking at the common properties of each object in that class.

'Aristotle' developed syllogistic logic : which analyses reasoning in a way that ignores the contents of the arguments and focuses on the form or structure of the argument. He points out :

"If no pleasure is a good, neither will any good be the pleasure".

Second Premise : "*A* belongs to none of *B*'s.

Conclusion : "*B* does not belong to any of *A*'s.

Premise : "Most of the deaths on Delhi roads are caused by blue line buses."

Conclusion : "All blue line buses are driven rashly and negligently".

There are various forms of reasoning :—

Deductive Reasoning

Reasoning in an argument is valid if the argument's conclusion must be true, when the premises (the reasons that support the conclusion) are true, also known as syllogism.

Premise : Dravid, Ganguly, Tendulkar, Laxman and Dhoni have averaged 60 runs each in an inning in this season.

Conclusion : Indian team will score 300 runs in the inning.

The reasoning is valid, because there is no way that premise is not true and so the conclusion cannot be doubted.

Within the field of formal logic, a variety of different forms of deductive reasoning have developed. These forms include syllogistic logic, propositional logic and predicate logic.

Inductive Reasoning

It contrasts with deductive reasoning. Even in the best, or strongest cases of inductive reasoning, the truth of the premise does not guarantee the truth of the conclusion. Instead, the conclusion of an inductive argument follows with some degree of probability. The conclusion of the inductive argument contains more information than it is already contained in the premises.

David Hume gives an example :

Premise : the sun has risen in the east every morning up to now.

Conclusion : the sun will also rise in the east tomorrow.

Adductive Reasoning

Adductive reasoning or argument to the best explanation often involves both deductive and inductive reasoning. However, as the conclusion in the adductive argument does not follow with certainty from its premises, it is best thought of as a form of inductive reasoning. What separates them is an attempt to favour one conclusion above others, by attempting to falsify alternative explanations or by demonstrating the likelihood of the favoured conclusion, given a set of more or less disputable assumptions.

Reasoning by Analogy

It is also form of inductive reasoning. Reasoning by analogy goes from one particular thing, or category, to another particular thing or category. Even the best reasoning from analogy can only make the conclusion probable, given that the truth of the premises is not certain.

Very frequently analogical reasoning is used in common sense, science, philosophy and humanities, but it is only accepted as an auxiliary method. A refined approach is case based reasoning.

All these methods may contain formal fallacies and informal fallacies. Some of the examples of these fallacies are a red herring argument or an argument containing circular reasoning.

Rationality

Rationality is a term related to the idea of reason. It has dual aspects. One aspect associates it with comprehension, intelligence or inference. Such inference is drawn in ordered ways like syllogism. The other aspect associates rationality with explanation, understanding and justification.

A logical argument is rational if it is logically valid. Rationality is, however a broader term than logical. It also includes 'uncertain but sensible' argument based on probability, expectation, personal experience, whereas logic deals with provable facts, and demonstrably valid relations between them.

Practical syllogism

A simple philosophical definition of rationality refers to "practical syllogism".

The accused did not like the deceased.

The accused always avoided him.

The deceased came and sat besides the accused.

Therefore the accused attacked him.

Now all that is required to be rational is to believe the action.

The argument is logically valid but not necessarily sound. The premise may be incorrect.

Types of rationality

German sociologist Max Weber distinguished between four types of rationality.

(1) Purposive or instrumental rationality

(a) Expectation about the behaviour of other human beings or objects in the environment;

(b) Value/Belief oriented rationality;

(c) Action for one might call reasons intrinsic to the other; some ethical, aesthetic, religious or other motive;

(d) Effectual : Action determined by actor's specific effect, feeling or emotion, which are meaningfully oriented.

(2) Tradition

Determined by ingrained habituation.

Max Weber emphasized that it is very unusual to find any one of these orientations. Combinations are the norm. First two are significant and the third and fourth are subtypes.

(3) Bonded Rationality

Human can be reasonably approximated or described as rational entities. Some people are, however, hyper rational, and would never do anything to violate their preferences. The concept of bounded rationality assumes that perfectly rational decisions are not feasible in practice due to finite computational resources applicable to them.

(4) Perfect Rationality

Some people always act in a rational way and are capable of arbitrarily complex deductions towards that end. They are always capable of thinking through all possible outcomes and choosing the best things to do.

Superrationality

Two logical thinkers analyzing the same problem will come up with the same correct answer. If two persons are good in math's, and they are given a complicated sum to do, both will get the same answer.

Rational decisions and thoughts are based on reason rather than on emotion. A rational person is someone, who is sensible and is able to make decisions based on intelligent thinking. Equity justice and good conscience are the hallmark of judging. One who seeks to rely only on principles of law, and looks only for the decided cases to support the reasons to be given in a case or acts with bias or emotions, loses rationality in deciding the cases. The blind or strict adherence to the principles of law sometimes carries away a judge and deviates from the objectivity of judging issues brought before him.

The traditional theory of adjudication is that a judge must search for the relevant rule of law derived from settled legal principles found in precedents and then apply it to the facts of the case. The approach basically assumes that the answer to any legal problem is to be found by searching in the reports and locating the relevant case. Benjamin Cardozo likens the process of identifying a precedent to matching 'the colors of the case at hand against the colors of many sample cases. The sample nearest in shade supplies the applicable rule. Thus, the decision should be the same regardless of the identity of the judge. The traditional view is seen as 'the archetype of legal science in the practice of law'. It places 'emphasis on uniformity, consistency and predictability, on the legal form of transactions and relationships' and sometimes, on literal, rather than purposive interpretation.

the principal rationale for the theory is the notion that people rely on certainty in the law in deciding how to settle their affairs. It is said, with some justification, that the willingness of people to engage in commercial activities and transactions depends on the reliability of the rights and obligations assigned by the law. The less predictability and certainty there is, the less likely it is that parties will be able to settle disputes without litigation and this is clearly contrary to public policy. Following precedent and treating similar cases alike enhances certainty and enables formal equality to be achieved.

The truth without and the truth within

Judge Cardozo in one of his lectures delivered at Yale University in 1921, said : "There is an inescapable relation between the truth without us and the truth within. The spirit of the age, as it is revealed to each of us, is too often only the spirit of the group in which the accidents of birth or education or occupation or fellowship have given us a place. No effort or revolution of the mind will overthrow utterly and at all times the empire of these subconscious loyalties."

Recent critical legal studies

In recent times, a more radical view of decision-making has emerged, which has been given the label 'critical legal studies'. It is described as the intellectual successor of realism, though it appears to go further than realism. Perhaps unsurprisingly, the critical legal scholars seem to be exclusively academics. They have been described, variously, as self-consciously leftist, nihilist and as people who 'sincerely want to be radicals'. The central tenet of this movement is that the act of adjudication is a political function. These theorists suggest that legal thought is necessarily incoherent and indeterminate and legal doctrine can be manipulated to justify an almost infinite spectrum of possible outcomes. It is nothing more than a sophisticated vocabulary and repertoire of manipulative techniques for categorising, describing, organising and comparing. Law is viewed as being political, and legal reasoning as a technique used to rationalise, in legal jargon, the political decisions that are actually made.

Sub-conscious factors

One cannot discount the possibility that subconscious factors are at play in the decisions. In *Garcia* v. *National Australia Bank Ltd.*, a wife had given a guarantee for loans to businesses conducted by the husband. When the bank called in the loans, she sought to avoid liability, relying upon the principles in *Yerkey* v. *Jones* to the effect that married women are under a special disability and require special protection against improvident bargains. The bank countered this argument by contending that in today's society it is neither necessary nor appropriate to give special protection to married women. The High Court disagreed. The majority was bound to and did acknowledge that both Australian society and the role of women in it has changed in the last six decades. However, they went on to say that there are also things that remain unchanged. "There is still a significant number of women in Australia in relationships which are, for many and varied reasons, marked by disparities of economic and other power between the parties. Their decision was clearly influenced by what they thought was right in light of what they termed 'the disparities between the parties'. Kirby J. agreed in the orders but disagreed with the majority's underlying rationale. He said that :

Whatever may have been the position in Australian society of 1939, it is offensive to the status of women today to suggest that all married women, as such, are needful of special protection supported by a legal presumption in their favour.

What produced the difference in opinion about the position of a modern married woman? It was certainly not grounded in the evidence, as no sociologist, economist or psychologist was called. The result can only partly be explained by the application of strict legal principle. It is evident that the judge did attempt to discover in what respects the position and role of women had changed since the 1930s, although they did this without the assistance of any evidence. This notwithstanding, it is likely that the judges were also influenced by their subjective views about whether or not women require 'special protection'. The extent of this influence is something we can never know, and perhaps the judges themselves will never know.

The reasons are very often based on personal beliefs, morality, biases and prejudices harboured patently or latently. We may not even know such prejudices which shadow our judgments. They pollute our thoughts and act as a dangerous virus which corrupts our thought process. We do not try to sanitise ourselves, perhaps because there is no accepted process to do it and more because we refuse to acknowledge such biases.

In law, we know of the personal bias, pecuniary bias, and official bias. A predisposition to decide for or against one party without proper regard to the true merits of the dispute is bias. A biased decision also stands included in it the attributed and broader purview of the word "malice", which in common acceptation means and implies "spite" or "ill will". A judicial bias in common accepted norm means, that no man can be a judge of his own cause. It is a clear rule of law embodied in principles of natural justice, as well as natural equity and is rigorously enforced.

The other area of decision making is objectivity, which is a particular discipline of reasoning. The pursuit of ethical objectivity takes the form of the search for some ethical objects. The argument goes, the ethical statements that presume some known or identifiable objects rely upon a fact or a quality and its evaluation, the ethics however cannot be simple truthful description of specified objects. The real ethical questions cross over to the realm and practical questions which do not involve valuing. They involve a complex mixture of philosophical beliefs, religious beliefs, and factual beliefs as well.

Justice as fairness

John Rawls argues in presenting his ideas on objectivity of 'justice as fairness'; the first essential is that a conception of objectivity must establish a public framework of thought sufficient for the concept of judgment to apply and for conclusions to reach on the basis of reasons and evidence after discussion and due reflection.

In any argument, more so in making judgments if the persons are reasonable in taking note of other peoples points of view, and in accepting information in good faith with an open mind, the gap between rationality and reason with objectivity may narrow down. The idea here is not for a person to reinforce his views with new inputs to justify himself but to allow him to be enlightened and take a more ethical decision. A reasonable person will take advantage to interactive discussion and try to reach underlying issues with greater objectivity.

While answering a rather difficult question as to whether a person found guilty of conduct and proof of causing disharmony in relations is entitled to divorce on the ground of irretrievable breakdown of marriage, (which is still not a ground of divorce, in law and is more in realm of judge made law) where the marriage has gone dead with no signs of revival, requires rational thinking with objectivity. The applicability of common reasoning would disentitle such person the relief. The ethical reasoning would however support not to deny relief and allow dead relations to survive, rather put the party to be blamed with punitive conditions harsh enough to meet the injustice caused to the non-blaming party.

Theory of moral sentiment

Adam Smith in his 'Theory of Moral Sentiments', argues that the reasoning can be judged by viewing other people and their claims with examining different grounds for respect and tolerance. There is no room for sentiments in reasoning. The instinctive psychology and spontaneous responses may not always deviate from ethical reasoning. To that extent reasoning and feeling are deeply interrelated in all moral determination and conclusions.

The Method of Philosophy, reason :—"The judicial process is there in microcosm. We go forward with our logic, with our analogies, with our philosophies, till we reach a certain point. At first we have no trouble with our paths, they follow the same lines. Then they begin to diverge, and we must make a choice between them. History or custom, or social utility or some compelling sentiment of justice or sometimes perhaps a semi-intuitive apprehension of the pervading spirit of our law must come to the rescue of the anxious judge, and tell him where to go.

Idea of justice on ethical objectivity and reasoned scrutiny

"It is hard to see that ethical judgments demand *rahi aql*—the use of reason. The question that remains, however, is this : why should we accept that reason has to be the ultimate arbitrator of ethical beliefs? Is there some special role of reasoning—perhaps reasoning of a special kind—that must be seen as overreaching and crucial for ethical judgments? Since reasoned support can hardly be in itself a value giving quality, we have to ask : why precisely, is reasoned support so critical? Can it be claimed that reasoned scrutiny provides some kind of guarantee of reaching the truth? This would be hard to maintain, not only because the nature of truth is moral and political belief is such a difficult subject, but mainly because that rigorous searches, in ethics or in any other discipline, could still fail."

Although most judges strive diligently to avoid bias in making their decisions and firmly believe their rulings are free from extraneous influences, subconscious factors may sometimes lead a judge to make a factual determination on unacceptable grounds. Judges are not 'dehumanized vehicles of faultless, logical truth'. We are all prone to using subconscious simplifying strategies when processing significant amounts of information.

One such strategy is to create mental categories so that when we are faced with a given set of facts, we approach them with these categories in mind. If we are not careful this may result in perceived or actual bias. Stereotypes may affect judgment through their impact on processing evidence (that is, in the findings of facts).

Second, negative stereotypes about minorities may affect decision-making in a myriad of areas. Subconscious caste and religious discrimination is one area that has been the subject of a substantial degree of analysis, particularly in India. Subjective judgments about character, motivation and intellectual ability may be applied by the decision-maker to a class as a whole. These subject judgments may be rationalised by the decision maker to enable him to maintain an egalitarian self-image.

Cognitive illusions enable decision-makers to process voluminous information efficiently, though they can produce systematic errors in judgment. Common cognitive illusions include making estimates based on irrelevant starting points ('anchoring'), and perceiving past events to have been more predictable than they actually were (*'hindsight bias'*). Psychologists have identified many other cognitive illusions that are said to infect decisions, but the two serve as examples. Anchoring causes people making numerical estimates to rely on the initial value available to them, no matter how irrelevant it is. For example, claims for damages, awards or proposals for levels of penalties to be imposed by the court may tend to anchor the final determination of the amount. Hindsight bias consists of using known outcomes to assess how predictable an event was at a previous point in time, for example, reconstructing how foreseeable a car accident was to the motorist involved before the event. As judges are not always particularly enlightening when it comes to explaining how decisions were reached, it is difficult to say with any certainty that cognitive illusions infect them.

Law as interpretive concept

"Judges should decide what the law is by interpreting the practice of other judges deciding what the law is. General theories of law, for us are general interpretation of our judicial practice. We rejected conventionalism, which finds the best interpretation in the idea that judges discover and enforce special legal conventions, and pragmatism, which finds in it the different story of judges as independent architects of the best future, free from the inhibiting demand that they must act consistently in principle with one another.

The third conception, law as integrity unites jurisprudence and adjudication. It makes the content of law depend not on special conventions or independent crusades but on more refined and concrete interpretations of the same legal practice it has begun to interpret."

"In their effort to give to the social sense of justice articulate expression in rules and in principle the method of the lawfinding experts has always been experimental. The rules and principles of case law have never been treated as final truths, but has working hypothesis, continually retested in those great laboratories of the law, the Courts of justice. Every new case is an experiment, and if the accepted rule which seems applicable yields, a result which is felt to be unjust, the rule is reconsidered. It may not be modified at once, for the attempt to do absolute justice in every single case would make the development and maintenance of general rules impossible; but if a rule continues to work injustice it will eventually be reformulated. The principles themselves are continually retested, for if the rules derived from a principle do not work well, the principle itself must ultimately be re-examined."

Holmes told us, "the life of the law has not been logic, it has been experienced."

Philosophy or Analogy as method

Philosophy of law is concerned with the formulation of concepts and theories to aid in understanding the nature of Law, the sources of its authority, and its role in society. In English-speaking countries, the term "Jurisprudence" is often used synonymously and is invariably used in reference to particular sub-divisions of the field. To the extent that it implies some necessary link or coincidence with general philosophy of law is mostly untouched by the conflicts of different philosophical schools, and its practitioners may without incongruity draw on diverse philosophical outlooks-on logical positivism for some analytical problem of the structure of legal orders and simultaneously, on existentialism for a problem of sociological jurisprudence or justice, for example-without commitment in any such instance to an entire philosophical outlook.

Nor can one treat philosophical view of law as a specialized branch of philosophy such as ethical or political philosophy, epistemology, or logic, for in philosophy of law, all these branches may make contributions. Ideas that may illumine jurisprudential problems must indeed be sought not only in philosophy but in all systematic bodies of thought. Only if "philosophy" is interpreted in its least technical and broadest sense does "philosophy of law" cease to be a misnomer.

Philosophy' is ocean of principles and thoughts wherein any body may delve in and pick these up depending on one's need, skill and proficiency. There are two methods of study that are relevant for any researcher in realm of philosophy :

(i) prior method of assumption. Certain things are assumed to exist and then on the basis of that assumption principles are deduced in order. This is fool proof method of analysis. It is shaken only when assumption itself is threatened or challenged. Kelson applied it. He assumed that every system of law has a grundnorm and law flows therefrom. It is like 'Himalaya' and rivers coming down to plain. The river will not dry till Himalaya is not disturbed. So is law, continuous and never drying reality till grundnorm exists. This is quite popular for religio-legal proposition. Santandharm (vedic culture) till vedas exist and enjoy acceptance. Quran (grundnorm) of Islam and Islamic legal system, Bible for church and church law.

(ii) 'Posteriori' is method of study wherein we start from a hypothesis and induct principles in order from that hypothesis. It is logical and experimental. If *X* has done and got some particular result; *Y* can also do it and get that result. Do it and observe it. It is practical.

So happens in life of law and judges in court. When there is nothing for guidance, no beacon light on any moot point; no constitution, no statute, where will the judge go? How will he use the literature available but not directly on the point. What does the man do when all doors of normal life are shut? He surrenders to God for help and guidance. A flash is there and see the path becomes clear. Some solution comes, likewise, when there is nothing to help the judge to decide the case before him, he surrenders to logic and resorts to 'analogy' or philosophy, and he gets enough strength and confidence to decide the case.

He studies mass of particulars, a congeries of judgments on related topics, the principles that unify and rationalise them, and searches a way out to decide the case whereon there is no other authority. The path so reached may not be the best but it is certainly the 'next best possible', option.

Law whether logic.—It is not always correct and is also not totally incorrect. Law is not always logical. Logical consistency may not be supreme god but that does not mean it is not good. Holmes said life of law has not been logic, it has been experience'. True to Holmes but logic may not be always ignored where experience does not help.

A judge has to be impartial. So he has to be logical and consistent. He can not decide any case one day this way and second day, the opposite way. This will kill the system of law. People expect like to be treated alike particularly from a law court. To decide differently would generate resentment. Faith of litigants is the crux of our system, loss of faith is sure to kill or damage the system. To lawyers, it means much than to clients who do not bother about good or bad case. The client wants his work done on most favourable terms.

If case is decided against client and his counsel satisfies him that this judge has been doing so for all, the resentment subsides. We have judges who are of relief giving nature. We have judges who give relief in final hearing but are not good in interim relief cases. Counsels know it, tolerate it, because he is consistent, and logical. He may not be popular as judge but no body says him to be dishonest. It is because he is logical and consistent.

Logic and analogy do away with 'chance and favour' affairs of men are governed with impartial uniformity, which is of essence to the idea of law. This means only this much that analysis is a good tool for a lawyer but it works to produce better results if legal problem is sorted out alongwith history, traditions and other methods including sociology.

Logic does not exert on single path

'Will of deceased must be respected' is one logic. Murderers should not get share in will of one whom he has murdered. Both are logical. Both are correct. It is discretion of the court that opens one path and closes the other.

Misuse of logic

The misuse of logic or philosophy begins when its methods and its ends are treated as supreme and final. Logic can not be ignored forever. It can not banish other methods popular in continent.

Analysis of fundamental conceptions of jurisprudence

Analytical or positivist thinking consists of analysis of fundamental legal terms like possession, ownership, property, title, status or obligation.

Consistency.—Logic means being consistent. But what does the consistency mean? Consistent with what? Consistency with the origin of the rule or the course and tendency of the development? Or does it mean being consistent with logic or philosophy? Or the fundamental conceptions of jurisprudence?

❑❑

Chapter 9

Method of Sociology

'Security' is basic concern of individual; security of 'body', preservation, protection or prevention thereof. Just like concern for body, developed ayurvedic knowledge, ayurvedic medicines, unani, homeopathic or allopathic treatments for ailments in human body giving options, so is the ailments of wealth and assets of men. Natural instincts took him to sheltors available when sun tormented him, rain came in to remedy the sun burn; rain was followed by soothing winter. He developed techniques for prevention and protection to preserve (himself). Property was natural ally of the man beyond his concern for body'. so its concern or protection was addressed first, 'power' strength of body'. 'muscle power' was the instant reply. So the man found remedy in regulating the use of property.

Various approaches to constitutionalism and judicial process

Constitutionalism's belief is that a State should have arrangements, that limit the powers of the rulers and all those which give the ruling regime legitimate/moral authority to govern. Constitutinalism includes both legal and political limits on the government. It requires government machinery to be accountable to some independent body (like courts). It requires check and balance between different government departments. It ensures proper control within departments.

Social laws and pre-social laws.—The social laws are ways to regulate one's physical activities quo protection or preservation of body.

Judicial process in Ancient India

Administration of justice was not a part of the state's duties in early times. We do not find references to any judicial organisations in Vedic literature. The aggrieved party in order to get its wrong redressed used to sit before the accused house and not allow him to move till his (aggrieved party) claims were satisfied or wrong righted. Later justice was administered by the tribe and clan assemblies and the judicial procedure was very simple. But with the extension of the functions of the state and the growth of the royal powers, the king came gradually to be regarded as the origin of justice and a more or less elaborate system of judicial administration came into existence. The Dharma Shastras, Niti Shastras and the Arthashastra provide us information about the well-developed judiciary. According to these literatures the king is the fountain head of all justice and he was required to spend every day about a couple of hours in adjudication. The paramount duty of the king is the protection of his subjects which involves the punishment of the wrongdoer. The law to be administered is the Dharma Shastras subject to local and other usages which are not inconsistent with the shastras.

Types of Courts: Brihaspati speaks of four types of courts

- Movable courts
- Stationary courts
- Courts deriving authority from the king and
- Courts presided by the king himself.

He mentions three kinds of itinerant courts, one for the benefit of forest dwellers, one for the benefit of caravan serai merchants and one for the benefit of military men. According to Bhrighu there were fifteen kinds of courts. Some of the prominent courts where justice was delivered were :—

1. The Kings Court.—At the head of the judicial system stood the king's court at the capital and presided by the king himself. But more often a learned Brahmana was appointed for the purpose and he was known as Adhyaksha or Sabhapathi. Earlier the Adhyaksha was selected for each particular occasion and in course of time became a permanent officer of state and held the position of the Chief Justice (Pradvivaka). Apart from the king, this court consisted of the Pradvivaka and three or four jurors.

2. Court presided by the Chief Justice.—The court presided by the chief justice appointed by the king called Pradvivaka was the second type of court.

3. Principal Courts.—Another court of importance were the principal courts in large towns where royal officers assisted by learned persons administered justice. They were presided by Adhyakshas appointed by the central government.

4. Popular Courts.—One special feature of ancient Indian judicial system is the existence of popular courts. Yajnavalkya for the first time refers to three types of popular courts.

- **Kula.**—The Kula has been defined by the Mitakshara as consisting of a group of relations, near or distant. The Kula or joint families were often very extensive in ancient India. If there was a quarrel between two members the elders used to attempt to settle it. The Kula court was this informal body of family elders.
- **Sreni.**—When the effort at family arbitration failed, the matter was taken to Sreni court. The term Sreni was used to denote the courts of guilds which became a prominent feature of the commercial life in ancient India from 500 B.C. Sreni had their own executive committees of four or five members and it is likely that they might have functioned as the Sreni court also for settling the disputes among their members. This was an assembly of persons following a particular profession like betel sellers, weavers, shoe makers and the like.
- **Puga.**—This was an association of persons drawn from various castes and following different professions but staying in the same village or town. The Sabha or the village assembly of the Vedic

period and Gramavriddha court of the Arthasastra were the forerunner of the Puga court.

Though these courts were essentially non-official and popular, they had the royal authority behind them. The government refused to entrain any suits except in appeals against their decision. It also gave effect to their decrees.

In ancient India village panchayats and guild courts were appreciated and encouraged for several reasons like :—

- They reduced the burden of the central administration.
- The members of a village panchayat or a guild had more or less reliable knowledge of the fact in dispute as the parties belonged to their guild or locality and
- It would be difficult for a witness to tell a lie in the presence of his own people and thereby lose his respect.

There was no limit to the jurisdiction of the popular courts in civil matters. They could not however try criminal cases of a serious nature. The popular courts played a prominent part in ancient India.

The regular courts met once or twice every day usually in the morning and evenings and were open to all. Trials were always held in public.

Different kinds of laws.—Justice was administered in accordance with rules which fell under one or other of the following four heads, namely

- Sacred law (Dharma)
- Secular law (Vyavahara)
- Custom (Charitra) and
- Royal commands (Rajasasana)

Dharmashastra constituted the sacred law and secular law depended upon evidence. Custom was decided by the opinion of the people and royal edicts constituted the administrative law. Of the divisions of laws, Manu and almost all law-givers consider customs as the essential principle in the administration of justice and say that disputes should be decided according to the customs of countries and districts; of castes; of guilds and of families.

Types of law-suits.—The topics which give rise to law suits are grouped by the law-givers under 18 titles, namely

- Recovery of debt
- Deposit and pledge
- Sale without ownership
- Concerns among partners
- Resumption of gifts
- Non-payment of wages
- Non-performance of agreements
- Revoking of sale and purchase
- Dispute between owners of cattle and herdsmen
- Dispute regarding boundaries

- Assault
- Defamation
- Theft
- Robbery and violence
- Adultery
- Duties of man and wife
- Inheritance and partition and
- Gambling and betting

The list includes both civil and criminal cases.

Judicial Procedure.—The judicial proceeding in a case consisted of four stages namely

1. The statement of the Arthi/Purvapaksha (plaintiff) who had filed a complaint (Prathigna) stating precisely his case and claim.
2. The Prathyarthi/ Uttarapaksha (defendant) was summoned with a notice and was required to submit his written statement in reply.
3. Then the actual trial would begin wherein the judge would call upon the parties to cite evidence/proof (Pramana) which were of two kinds namely human (manushik) and divine (daivik). The human proof consisted of documentary evidence, oral evidence and possessions. Divine proof was of five kinds, ordeal by balance, by fire, water, poison and by drinking water. Divine proof was resorted to only in the absence of human proof.
4. When the evidence was over the judge would in consultation with Sabhyas or jurors give his decision/judgment (nirnaya). A copy of the judgment was given to the parties. The unsuccessful party could appeal to the higher courts.

Importance of Jury.—Even the king and the chief justice could not begin the trial of a case if they are not assisted by a panel of three, five or seven jurors called sabhyas. They were expected to be impartial and fearless. A juror keeping silence has been condemned. They were to express their opinion even if it was in opposition to that of the king. They were to restrain a king going astray or giving a wrong decision. A number of famous jurists maintain that the king or judge is to be guided by the verdict of the jury and only when the jurors could not come to a definite decision, the king exercised his privilege to decide the case according to his own view. These sabhyas were usually Brahmins as they were well versed in Dharmashastras. However knowledge of sacred law was not necessary when the case (the party to the dispute) concerned the disputes among the cultivators, merchants and forest dwellers. Dharmashastra writers themselves recommended that the cases should be tried with the help of the jurors selected from the castes or the professions of the parties themselves.

Pleaders rarely figure in ancient Indian judicial system. Sukra refers to the practice of appointing recognized agents in the law courts to defend a case when a party was himself unable to do so owing to his preoccupation or ignorance of the law. Such agents were known as Niyogins and they were expected to guard the interests of their parties very carefully. Their fee varied from six to half percent, according to the value of the property. If they colluded with the other party they were punished by the state.

Fines, imprisonment, banishment, mutilation and death sentence were the punishment in vogue. Fines were most common and punishment often differed with the caste of the accused. The jail department was under the charge of an official called Sannidhata and the jailor was called Bandhanagaradhyaksha. Male and female prisoners were kept in separate wards.

Administration of Justice during Mauryan times.—The king was the head of justice, but there were special tribunals of justice both in cities and country side presided over by Mahamatras and Rajukas. The chief-justice was known as Dharmadhikarin. Kautilya speaks of two types of courts,

- Dharmastheeya—Civil courts with jurisdiction over ordinary civil and criminal issues.
- Kantaka Sodhana—Courts consisting of three commissioners (Pradestaras) with jurisdiction over matters of commerce and industries and prevention of breach of peace.

According to the Greek accounts the criminal code of the Mauryas was rather severe and sternly administered. A large number of ordinary offences like giving false evidence, evasion of government taxes, causing serious hurt to artisans and workmen were punished by mutilation and death. Judicial torture was used to extort confessions. There were 18 codes of torture including seven varieties of whipping. Such a harsh criminal code had the good effect on maintenance of peace and order. According to Megasthenese there were very few crimes and thefts uncommon. As a result people left the door of their houses unlocked. Ashoka introduced reforms in the judicial administration and procedure. He ordered that a respite of three days was to be granted to person condemned to death so that his relatives might use the interval to petition for mercy to the local authorities or enable the convicts to prepare spiritually for death by giving alms or observing fasts.

Administration of Justice during Gupta times.—The king was considered to be the incarnation of justice and so justice was often administered by the sovereign himself. There was also a high official called Mahadandanayaka who probably performed the combined duties of the Great Judge and General. Another official closely associated with him must have been the Mahaksapatalika or the Great Keeper of Records. In villages justice was administered by royal officials with the help of the members of the village council or assembly. In addition to official courts at the headquarters of districts and provinces there existed a number of popular special courts of self-governing corporations or guilds which decided disputes arising among their members. The criminal laws during the Gupta rule were not as severe as it was in the time of the Mauryas. They were mild and most of the crimes were punished only by fines varying in amounts according to the gravity of the offence. Capital punishment was unknown and the highest punishment for repeated rebellions was mutilation. Still law and order were well preserved and the Chinese traveller, Fa-Hien toured all over India without molestation.

Administration of Justice during Harsha times.—The Chief Judge during Harsha's time was known as Mahapramatara and the Record Keeper was styled as the Mahaksapataladhikaranadhikrita. Judicial officers were called Nyayakarnika. Compared to the Gupta period, the criminal code during Harsha's time was very severe. For violation of the statute, law and conspiracy against the king, the offender was imprisoned for life and was socially ostracized. For breach of social mobility and filial duty, the penalty was mutilation of limbs or exile. For minor ordinary offences the penalty was payment of money. In spite of this severity in the administration of justice, highways were infested with robber gangs and the Chinese traveller Hiuen-Tsang himself fell a victim to them.

Administration of Justice in South India.—In the regions ruled by the Chalukyas of Badami and Pallavas of Kanchi, the king was the fountainhead of justice and the final court of appeal. In villages and rural tracts the village courts decided the disputes. During the Rashtrakuta rule the king's court did not entertain any cases at the first instance and only when the parties felt dissatisfied with the decision of the village courts, they could appeal to the king or his courts. There was a Chief Judge who was the final appellate authority for cases coming from the lower courts, except when the king decided them himself. The records of the Kalyani Chalukyas mention the office of Dharmadhikari or chief justice. During the times of the Cholas we have references to dharmasana in several inscriptions, probably signifying the king's court of justice. Learned Brahmins known as dharmasana-bhattas assisted the court. The village assemblies exercised large powers in matters of local interest which they settled with the help of small committees called Nyayattar or Nyayavattar. All offences-civil or criminal were tried in the first instance in village courts and in cases of disaffection the matter was taken to the officer of the king's government-in-charge of the administration of the nadu. The Chinese writer, Chou-Ju-Kua mentions about flogging or giving blows to the culprit with a stick after tying him to a wooden frame for minor offence. It is said that punishments during the Chola period was not all severe. Even for murder, the punishment meted out to the criminal was the payment of a fine to the temple. During the time of Rajendra II the assassin of a state official was asked to give 96 sheep towards the maintenance of a perpetual lamp in the temple. Hence it was remarked that the Chola administration of justice could not be charged with severity or vindictiveness, it may rather be regarded as swayed by over mercifulness.

Justice Cardozo talked abut judicial methods to decide cases of first impression and was of the view that cases of this category are or can be decided on logic drawn from philosophy or search history if any hint is traceable (custom-usage-tradition) or Courts are free to travel to sociology in search for something which may guide the court to decide cases of first impression. Cardozo was a judge by training and temperament. He knew his limits and wrote within it.

'Panchayats' are age old institutions for delivery of justice. Cardozo has not mentioned these in his lectures, but Nyaya Panchayats have played a very important role in administration of justice and their role in judicial process needs to be correctly stream lined. Such 'Adalats' have worked and are still contributing in some form or the other like Biradari Panchayats (caste Panchayat), Kul (Family Courts), Khap Panchayats, Sreni (Court of same professionals Disciplinary).

Panchayati raj and judicial process

The **Panchayati raj** is a South Asian political system found mainly in India, Pakistan, Bangladesh, Trinidad and Tobago, and Nepal. It is the oldest system of local government in the Indian subcontinent, and historians mention date to the C. 250 A.D. period. The word *raj* means "rule" and *panchayat* means "assembly" (arat) of five (*panch*). Traditionally panchayats consisted of wise and respected elders chosen and accepted by the local community. However, there were varying forms of such assemblies. Traditionally, these assemblies settled disputes between individuals and between villages.

The leader of the panchayat was often called the mukhiya or sarpanch, and elected or generally acknowledged position. The modern panchayati raj of India and its gram panchayats are not to be confused with either the traditional system nor with the extra-constitutional khap panchayats (or caste panchayats) found in northern India.

Mahatma Gandhi advocated *panchayat raj* as the foundation of India's political system. It would have been decentralised form of government where each village would be responsible for its own affairs. The term for such a vision was *Gram Swaraj* ("village self-governance"). Instead India developed a highly centralised form of government. However, this has been moderated by the decentralisation of several administrative functions to the local level, empowering elected gram panchayats. There are significant differences between the traditional panchayati raj system, as envisioned by Gandhi, and the system formalised in India in 1992.

Yaksha Prashna and judicial process

The **Yaksha Prashna** (also known as the Dharma Baka Upakhyan, the Ashkardhama) appears in the Vana Parva, Aranyaka-parva or Aranya-parva. Mahabharata Aranya Parva 311-12 : Meaning; (The Book of the Forest) of the great Hindu epic, the Mahabharat. The story is set as the Pandavas end their twelve years of exile in the forest.

Vana Parva

At the end of their 12 years of exile in the forests, time had come for the pandavas to live in Agyat Vasa (living incognito). As they were discussing their course of action the Panadava Princes came across a Brahmin who complained that a deer has taken on its antlers his Arani—a pair of wooden blocks to generate fire by friction and therefore he was not able to light the fire for the performance of Vedic rituals. The valorous Pandava Princes set out to retrieve the Brahmin's Arani and followed the hoof-marks of the deer.

In the quests of the mysterious deer, Yudhishthira, became exhausted and thirsty. His brother Nakula thus ventured out to fetch water and found a beautiful lake. the lake was devoid of any living creature except a crane (Baka). When he attempted to take water from the lake, the crane spoke, "O Nakula! The water of this lake will turn into poison if you take it without satisfactorily answering my questions." Nakula, in arrogance, did not pay heed and hurriedly took water rom the lake. Upon drinking the crystal clear water, Nakula instantly died of poisoning. Nakula's twin Sahadeva, coming in search of his brother, also found the same lake, saw Nakula dead, and was warned by the crane. But Sahadeva too ignored the crane and died after drinking the water. In the same manner, both valiant Arjuna, and powerful Bhima met the same fate.

Since none of the brothers returned with water, Yudhishthira engaged in search of them. Upon following the same path, Yudhishthira came across the lake and found his brothers lying dead Before searching for the killer of his brothers, Yudhishthira decided to drink some water from the lake. But when the crane warned him, Yudhishthira realized that the crane held the answer to the turn of events. The virtuous Yudhishthira proceeded to answer the questions put forth by the crane.

Before putting the questions to Yudhishthira, the crane revealed itself as a Yaksha. The Yaksha asked 18 questions with philosophical and metaphysical ramifications. This dialogue between the Yaksha and Yudhishthira is embodied in the Madhya Parva of the Mahabharata, and is also known as the Dharma-Baka Upakhyan (Legend of the Virtuous Crane).

Baka Prashna/Yaksha Prashna : (The Questions of the righteous Crane or the Yaksha)

Q.1. The Yaksha asked Yudhishthira, "Who makes the sun rise and ascend in the skies? Who moves the sun around? Who makes the sun set in the horizons? What is the true nature of the Sun and where is the Sun established"?

Yudhishthira answered, "Brahma makes the sun rise and ascend. The Gods perambulate about the Sun. The Dharma sets the Sun. Truth is the actual Sun and the Sun is established in Truth only."

Q.2. The Yaksha asked, "Who is Arjuna Krishna? What has he achieved"?

Yudhishthira replied, (Reply is not relevant to judicial process).

Q.3. The Yaksha asked, "What instills divinity in Kshatriyas? What is the quality of virtuosity in a Kshatriya? What is the humanity of a Kshatriya? What is the conduct akin to a non-virtuous person in a Kshatriya"?

Yudhishthira replied, "The art of archery instills divinity in a Kshatriya. Oblation is the quality of virtuosity in a Kshatriya. Fear is his humanity. Abandoning people under protection of the Kshatriya is a conduct akin to a non-virtuous person in the Kshatriya."

Q.4. The Yaksha asked, "What is that thing which is like Mantra in the performance of oblations (Yajna)? Who is the performer of rites and ceremonies during Yajna? Who accepts the offerings and oblations of a Yajna? What is that which even a Yajna cannot transgress"?

Yudhishthira replied, "Breath is like Mantra in the performance of rites. Mind is the performer of all rites in the course of Yajna. Only Shlokas of the Vedas, termed rucha or the richa accept oblation. The Yajna cannot surpass nor transgress the richas."

Q.5. The Yaksha asked, "What is heavier than Earth, higher than heavens, faster than the wind and more numerous than straws"?

Yudhishthira answered, "One's mother is heavier than the Earth, one's father is higher than the heavens, the mind is faster than the wind and our worries are more numerous than straws."

Q.6. The Yaksha asked, "Who is the friend of a traveler? Who is the friend of one who is ill and one who is dying"?

Yudhishthira's response, "The friend of a traveler is his companion. The physician is the friend of one who is sick and a dying man's friend is charity."

Q.7. The Yaksha asked, "What is that which, when renounced, makes one lovable? What is that which is renounced makes happy and wealthy"?

Yudhishthira replied, "Pride, if renounced makes one lovable, renouncing desire one becomes wealthy and to renounce avarice is to obtain happiness."

Q.8. The Yaksha asked, "What enemy is invincible? What constitutes an incurable disease? What sort of man is noble and what sort is ignoble"?

And Yudhishthira responded, "Anger is the invincible enemy, Covetousness constitutes a disease that is incurable. He is noble who desires the well-being of all creatures, and he is ignoble who is without mercy."

Q.9. The Yaksha asked, "Who is truly happy? What is the greatest wonder? What is the path? And what is the news"?

Whereupon Yudhishthira replied, "He who has no debts is truly happy. Day after day countless people die. Yet the living wish to live forever. O Lord, what can be a greater wonder? Argument leads to no certain conclusion, the Srutis are different from one another; there is not even one Rishi whose opinion can be accepted by all. The truth about Dharma and duty is hid in the cave of our hearts, therefore that alone is the path along which the great have trod. This world full of ignorance is like a pan. The sun is fire, the days and nights are fuel. The months and the seasons constitute the wooden ladle. Time is the cook that is cooking all creatures in that pan (with such aids). This is the news."

Yudhishthira could answer all the many questions put forth by the Yaksha, but although he doubted the real nature of the Yaksha, raising a question in this regard, he received no response. However, at the end of the questions the Yaksha revealed himself to be Yama-Dharma, the god of death, who was none other than Yudhishthira's father. He also admitted to Yudhishthira that it was he who had stolen the arani disguised in the form of the deer. He blessed him saying since he had adhered to Dharma (righteousness), the Dharma would protect them and no-one would recognise them during the Agyat Vasa.

Political values and approaches to Law

Howsoever, selfish man is, he is by compulsion of nature compelled to abide, some or the other of political values which may be either—

Liberalism or republicanism or communitarianism (democracy),

(1) Liberalism

It concentrates on the Individuality. Individual's interest, not interest of the community. The community protects individual interests. It advocates liberty, equality, autonomy and freedom to the individuals. Hobbes (impersonal state (Leviathan) and individualism) Locke (Individual rights and majority governments), and welfare liberalism of Hume, Utilitarianism (Bentham and Mill) and Libertarian liberalism (Robert Nozick—1938-2002), economic or market liberalism (Fredrick Hayek—1899-1992) and liberal pluralism (group liberalism) are different ways as to how liberalism has found recognition.

(2) Republicanism

Republicanism concentrates on men's 'social nature'. It requires political involvements in governance as equal citizens. The concept originated in Greece, it was revived in renaissance period and developed in propositions of Machiavelli (1469-1527), and Montesquieu (1689-1755). Republicanism builds on the ideas of positive freedoms. Its key concepts are the virtuous politically active citizens, limited and balanced governments under law, and political equality. Unlike liberalism that advocated for separation in between State from community, republicanism incorporates the community into the state.

On the liberal social contract tradition (Kant, Hobbes, Rawls).—"The chief problem with the liberal social contract tradition of Kant, Hobbes and Rawls, is that it tries to justify the modern state without regard to its democratic legitimacy." The named philosophers each contribute to the liberal social contract tradition through using various social assumptions to explain why individuals consent to a hypothetical agreement that forms the basis of legitimate state authority. This essay will outline and critique the role of democracy legitimacy in the political philosophies of Hobbes, Kant and Rawls, as well as show that the failure to give due regard to the democratic legitimacy of the state is a key problem with the liberal social contract tradition, particularly when it is applied to current political reality, given the ubiquity of democracy.

In the Hobbesian state the sovereign holds absolute power to make laws and administer the government and cannot be challenged, questioned or accused of injustice. Hobbes further states that once the contract has been formed, it cannot be changed. The authoritarian notion that the state can be vested in a single person is fundamentally at odds with democratic principle, as are the lack of ways to alter or resist the state's influence and control. Hobbes more directly criticizes democracy by connecting it to disagreement and factionalism, which would defeat the very stability that the state is instituted to provide. Legitimacy from a Kantian perspective is principally vested in the government's existence, as the formation of a government presupposes an exit from the state of nature and thereby signals move towards a normative or correct manner of living. Accordingly, there is little room for democratic legitimacy in both Hobbesian and Kantian regimes and indeed if democracy were to play a part it would be criticized for upsetting the delicately balanced stability of the liberal society and potentially inviting regression towards the undesirable state of nature.

In contrast to Hobbes and Kant, Rawls developed his theory of political liberalism at a time when democracy had attained a hegemonic status as the global state paradigm. However Rawls bases the legitimacy of a regime on his idea of civic justification, in doing so leaving little room for a freestanding idea of democratic legitimacy. In Political Liberalism Rawls applies his earlier work theorizing social justice to a political context. He proposes that the main requirement for a legitimate society is a basic structure that is just. Maintaining a structure of justice in political terms requires that political power be exercised in accordance with a political conception of justice, to be determined by public reason. The political conception of justice therefore functions as the main source of legitimacy for the state. The political conception of justice necessarily includes three basic principles, fairness, freedom and equality, determined through the exercise of practical reason. Despite applying differently to all societies, every liberal political conception of justice will share certain central features based on various interpretations of the same three fundamental ideas, fairness, freedom and equality. These features are alike to key values which democracy seeks to represent. In this way, the political conception of justice works to instantiate general democratic principles in society. Hence in a liberal society political power can only be legitimate when exercised in accordance with general principles of democracy. However the political conception of justice only indirectly gives regard to the importance of democracy as a factor legitimating the state. For Rawls the true expression of political identity is not inherent in the "vitality of local institutions" but rather exists in the constitution or the structure of the state.

A principal feature underpinning Rawls's political liberalism is the development of "public reason". Rawls describes "public reason" as the reason of equal citizens who as a collective body exercise final political power over one another in enacting law and amending the constitution. The collective decision making process that public reason represents strongly resembles deliberative models of democracy. Recognizing the similarity, Benhabib proposes that both justice and democratic legitimacy can be obtained with regard to collective decision making processes conducted rationally and fairly among free and equal individuals. However for Rawls the exercise of "public reason" primarily serves to examine the justice of institutions. This is because public reason can only determine "constitutional essentials" such as what religions are to be tolerated. In this way, the concept functions instrumentally to delimit Rawls's idea of structural justice and does not embody any meaningful substantive democratic value in itself. Additionally, public reason is a legal instrument and not a democratic one. For instance, public reason is typically exercised through the deliberation of the Supreme Court rather than at the level of the demos. As a result, Rawls's idea of public reason does not do enough to justify the state with regard to its democratic legitimacy. Even when acknowledging democracy is a concept that may be realized in a greater or lesser sense, Rawls's theory can at most identify with thin procedural conceptions of democracy rather than more meaningful substantive democratic paradigms.

If liberal contract theory is to remain relevant to contemporary society, it should regard democracy as key to the process of legitimizing the state. It is unrealistic to base the legitimacy of the state on the formation of a social contract as a single event or one-time set of affairs. In particular framing democratic value solely in principles of justice involves subordinating actual democratic politics to the results of a hypothetical agreement made by rational agents under a veil of ignorance. Wolin thereby questions whether substantive democracy can ever be effectively achieved through a "predesigned framework of equal rights as a gift to the demos". Castoriadis extends this view by arguing that the liberal society must be proactive in ensuring democratic value realized at an individual level, as democracy holds an "intrinsic worth beyond the mere aggregation of voters' preferences". Also, on such an interpretation, the inclusion of a substantive democracy in liberal social contract theory would work to consolidate and ensure the values of freedom and equality that liberal theorists uphold above all else. In this way, the liberal social contract tradition should give more regard to strong versions of democracy that prioritise the values of freedom and equality, and work to continually legitimize the state from the bottom up.

The failure of Hobbes, Kant and Rawls to give due regard to the importance of democratic legitimacy in their political philosophies should be considered as a major failing of the liberal social contract tradition. Whilst Hobbes and Kant regard the exit from the state of nature as the central source of political legitimacy and take democracy as hostile to their primary end, Rawls gives some effect to democratic value in his political philosophy. Although democratic legitimacy can be obtained through Rawls's political liberalism, it is not freestanding and can only be reached in an indirect fashion through the wider roles of the political conception of justice and public reason, and even when compared to thin models of deliberative democracy is only realized in a limited, instrumental manner.

Liberal Morality.—There is a common misconception amongst conservatives, especially the evangelical sort, that liberals are amoral. We all know that this assertion is untrue, but it is not unfounded. Liberals have a very different kind of morality than do conservatives.

I also want to make some attempts to find out how we can go about showing the legitimacy of liberal morality to conservatives. Ultimately, I think that conservative morality will not function in modern society and indeed does not function well at this point. It will only become less and less useful.

The fundamental difference between conservative morality and liberal morality is their roots. Conservative morality comes out of predetermined rules, be they religious or traditional. Liberal morality is based on reason that can be derived from pure philosophy or a religious doctrine.

Modern American conservatives fight against the homosexual agenda, because they believe that homosexual acts are sinful. Homosexual acts are sinful, because either conservatives believe that they have always been rejected by society, or they are banned by God. The conclusion is already there, and conservatives, out of necessary defense, will come up with rationales for why homosexual acts are bad for society.

Conservatives wish to defend existing social mores and tradition, because that is how they learned to be functioning members of society. They learned right from wrong by learning rules from their parents and other leaders in their community. A number of things are wrong, because that's how society has to function for conservatives. To a conservative, a child would not be able to become a good person without learning the rules. Without those rules, the person is a moral deviant or freak.

Liberal morality's basis in reason makes it very different from conservative morality. Rules can exist, but they come out of reason. It is important to note at this point that liberal morality is not necessarily moral relativism. Liberal morality is often a form of moral absolutism in that there is a fundamental belief that there is a right and a wrong. Liberals believe that murder is wrong, just like conservatives do, but for liberals, the reasoning for murder's immorality is more important. A conservative can easily tell you why murder is wrong, even outside of the need to follow rules, but that reasoning is more of an after-thought.

You cannot reason very much without basic assumptions, and liberals differ on those assumptions. I would like to give some examples of liberal morality foundations. The most obvious is Enlightenment reason. While there are different schools of thought in this founding assumption (Kant's deontology, Mill's utilitarianism, etc.), they all come out of pure thought.

Another founding assumption in American culture is Christian (or Jewish.) Liberal Christian morality differs from conservative Christian morality in that liberal Christians don't look at the Bible and see rules but instead see guidance for how to think about morality and justice. Right and wrong is not determined by God, but God's morality is based on fundamental truths of right and wrong. Conservative Christians criticize this thinking as non-Biblical, because it excludes sections of the Bible that are clearly rules-based. Liberal Christians have a number of responses, including the idea that God is constantly trying to get us to change and move beyond what we once were.

Less commonly, we can find people who base their liberal morality on other religious ideals, such as Budhism, Wicca, and the like, while they are not necessarily the mainstream, I think that such thinkers have important impact on modern liberal moralism. For example, those who prescribe to Wiccan thought often focus on nature and how we morally interact with nature. People following Eastern religions think about personal moral balance and our participation in the cycles of life and suffering.

For the most part, liberal morality and conservative morality come to the same conclusions about right and wrong, but their routes to those conclusions are different. Also, the concepts of how to get people to behave morally are very different. Conservatives have rules, so they expect there to be institutional laws dedicated to enforcing those rules. (Drug use is immoral, so we must arrest and punish all drug users.) Liberals have reasoning to get them to their conclusions, and thus their approach to the interaction of institutional laws is often very different. (Drug use is destructive to individuals, so we must take steps to prevent people from using drugs.)

How can we liberals teach our morality? I think that first of all, we can live our lives in a moral fashion, thus living as examples, but we should do that anyway. Furthermore, when conservatives perform immoral acts based on their own system of morality, we should point out the trouble. Think of the administration's condoning of torture and Alan Key's disowning of his own daughter.

I think that we should point out our own moral systems more often, and talk about its success in our own lives. We need to talk about how it works out better for our children, making them more thoughtful and moral in situations in which the pressure to follow the rules is absent. Think about all of the poor conservatives who go to college and go wild once they realize that their parents and church aren't there to police them.

(3) Democracy

Republicanism and liberalism share ideals of Democracy but these two are different versions thereof. Democracy is when the people, of a country decide the contents of laws that organise and regulate their political associations. These are decisions made by the majority. The basis is not that majority is right but it is that voting gives equality to all. Constitutionalism, rule of law and individual freedom do not exist always amicably with democracy. There is always tension.

(a) Representative democracy.—It is when public choose, call to account and remove the Government.

(b) Participatory democracy (deliberative democracy).—It promotes direct participation by individuals and the groups in decision making process which affects them. Jury system is an example. Panchayat raj system basis on participatory democracy.

(c) Market democracy (domination of political parties).—In market democracy, the system is dominated by political parties. These parties publicise and coordinate different opinions and all these are for 'common good'. Election is on party line. Voting is also on party lines. The policies of the Government go in terms of outcomes and targets rather than justice and fairness. Public and private sectors are blurred.

(d) Managed democracy.—It means nominate dummy candidates to cut the votes of opposition candidates who is otherwise strong. May be to cut the vote on caste factor or religion factor.

This is not what concept of western democracy would like to be but in communist country, it is an accepted norm. It allows even suspension of democracy for the clean governance, stability, development, economic growth and other desirable objectives. In 1975 emergency, we had this experience.

Over throwing Iraq's President *Saddam Hussain* by U.S. and U.K. forces invading Iraq was under pretext of promoting democracy. So was Musharraf throwing out Sharif's democratically elected government said to be promoting *Grass root democracy*.

Elections and Democracy

Free and fair elections may be the starting point for democracy, they are by no means "the be all and the end all" of democracy. The support of independent institutions like Election Commission, independent judiciary, free media, individuals protection and protection of the minorities is a must for democracy.

Election; free or fair or both and credible dispute resolution mechanism is a corner stone of democracy but it is only one link in the chain that guarantees democracy. Others in the chain are; independent judiciary, a free press and a vibrant civil society. Absence of any of these tends to break the chain.

James Boward a U.S.A. political commentator described democracy to be something more than two wolves and a sheep voting on what to have for dinner. Is it correct description of democracy?

English Approaches and judicial process.—The analytical questions in jurisprudence are concerned with articulating the axioms, defining the terms, and prescribing the methods that best enable one to view the legal order (or part of it) as a self-consistent system and most rigorous solutions are those which, like that of Hans Kelsen, a contemporary Austrian-American legal philosopher attempts to identify structural or relational features as being necessarily entailed in the meaning of legal norms or in lawyers' intellectual interaction with them. Alternatively, the basis for logical structuring may be found in some imputed attribute of law not itself inherently structural. The 19th century English legal philosopher, John Austin, for example, thought it an essential preliminary to his quest for a logical system in law to clarify what was involved in his assumption that law always consists of "commands". This clarification is important, but the claim that such a clarified version of a common assumption necessarily amounts to an analytical model of law seems unwarranted.

On more modest levels, the analyst may seek to infuse clarity and orderliness into some particular branch of a legal system or even into the applications of some particular rule. Such work shades over, on the one hand into ordinary legal analysis and, on the other, into jurisprudential efforts to clarify the meaning of particular legal terms. Analysis of a particular word or even a particular branch of law will usually, by necessity, be particularized in the sense that it works upon legal materials found only in one particular legal system. In between particularism and universalism lie what are sometimes called comparative approaches, in which analytical jurisprudence is applied to materials drawn from more than one (but not all formal) legal systems.

American approaches and theories of justice.—The sociological questions in jurisprudence are concerned with the actual effects of the law upon the complex of attitudes, behaviour, organization, environment, skills, and powers involved in the maintenance of a particular society. Conversely, sociological jurisprudence is also concerned with the effects of social phenomena on both the substantive and procedural aspects of law, as well as on the legislative, judicial, and other means of forming, operating, changing and disrupting the legal order. The fact that men in a given time and place hold particular ideas and values, including ideals of justice, is itself a fact, the relation of which to law must be studied; but the focus is sharply different from that in the study of theories of justice, its focus is descriptive, not normative; it is concerned with what is or with what goes on, not with what ought to be or ought to go on.

The theory of justice is concerned with the evaluation and criticism of law in terms of the ideals or goals postulated for it. This involves the identification and articulation of the values that the legal order seeks to realize. This aspect of jurisprudence is inextricably interwoven with ethical and political philosophy, and theories of justice thus tend to parallel the full image of ethical and political philosophies.

Morality of law.—A consideration of fundamental importance in the philosophy of law is that of the distinction between law and morality. The importance of the distinction is illustrated by the main questions to which it gives rise;

(1) How far and in what use should the law of community seek to give effect to its morality?

(2) Is there a moral duty to obey the law even when it does not embody morality, and, if so, are there any limits to this duty?

(3) When a legal rule directs conducts that morality forbids, which should the citizen obey?

(4) Is there ever (and, if so, when is there) a duty to overthrow an entire legal system because of its conflict with morality?

In all these questions, the word "Law" refers to the specialized form of social control familiar in modern, secular, and politically organized societies. The word "morality" in the four questions may, however, refer to any of the following :

(1) The community's relevant factual behaviour patterns (its morals);

(2) its socially approved behaviour, patterns, as sanctified by some

widely held rational or religious ideal, whether observed in practice or not (social morality); or

(3) the moral ideals accepted by each individual as binding on himself and on others, whether or not those others agree (individual morality).

All these, like law, are means of controlling human conduct by setting normative standards; and all three have constantly changing interaction with each other, as well as with law.

The fact that legal and moral norms vary from place to place and from one historical period to another lies in part behind a persistent theme in the philosophy of law: the search for unchanging norms that are universally valid. Clearly, the most certain way of establishing such norms would be to base them on widely observed facts, such as men's social propensities or the ubiquitous importance of kinship in social organization, which supposedly reveal something fundamental about the nature of man and his adjustment to the world. The attempt to base norms on some such category of facts has for two millennia been associated with the concept of natural law. This concept has many versions.

Continental approaches and justice.—The continental thinkers have utilized most of their time in finding an acceptable response to the question: What is Law? This question has been answered in all centuries by people from disciplines including sociology, philosophy, psychology, religion, theology, history and political science. The answers have come from India, Greece, Rome, Italy, France, Germany and Vienna. The answers are about the structure of law, history of law, sociology of law, anthropology of law, philosophy of law and law as pure science and law as it functions. These approaches are known as Natural law theories or Natural law school, historical school, philosophical or ethical school, pure theory of law and economic interpretations of law. Manu, Kautilya, Jaimini, Socrates, Plato, Aristotle, Augustine, Acquinas, Kant, Savigny, Stammler, Kelsen, Marx and a host of others have attempted to define "Law" in light of their training, discipline, experience and the legal system that they were seeking to uphold, justify, condemn or establish. The result is, that all these approaches that originally sought to define law have concluded into the study about law. None of these definitions is complete in the sense that they define law for all countries (legal systems) and for all times.

This leads us to question the validity of the question itself. What is law? This question is either wrongly framed or the host of the above jurists have answered it wrongly. In fact, no other subject has been subjected to such critical analysis as law. It is due to its multifarious behaviour it has in the society. What is law is a theoretical question. It is not a question of law, and the theories about law are just reactions from the sister disciplines about law. Political science views law as a system relating to government and polity, History as a process of evolution of a society. Economics as a system defining structure of economy, statistics and finance, Sociology as a system that functions in the society side by side many others, and

Anthropology looks into its biological origin. The question what is law is diluted when it is attempted to be answered by these disciplines. So, it becomes for all practical purposes an answer about the law.

The traditional approach to Law results into growth by the following schools:—

Vedic Law School and concept of justice

Law in veda; its interpretation by Mimansa, its elaboration in Smiritis and Puranas, revelation and revealed law, source of law is God. The Vedic system of home establishment and 'teaching establishments' are unique. 'People' in the entire country are known by the 'Gotra' or 'Family' of the different 'Seers' or 'Guragharana' for example; "Garg, Gautam, Shandilya are three initial 'guru'. In addition, many more 'Rishi schools' were seen. The system of 'Gurukul' developed and these the sources of all 'Grihastras' in the vedic system. Likewise on intellectual side, different branches are traceable depending on the specialisation in any particular branch of veda, for example; Rigveda school, (Rigveda shakha), Yazurveda School, Samveda and Atharvaveda Schools. In course of time, sub-schools (thoughts) developed.

Theories of justice and dharma are interwoven.

Natural Law School

1. The catholic natural law.—It owes its origin to the scheme developed by St. Thomas Acquinas and as modified by neo-thomists. It applies in the countries under the influence of the catholic church.

2. Philosophical natural law.—This form of natural law is prominent in the continent and owes its origin to Kant and is seen in shape of neo-kantianism. Thoughts of Stammler and Del Vecchio, are instances of this approach.

3. Sociological theory of natural law.—In contrast to the idealistic approach of catholic and philosophical natural law, the sociological theory of natural law adopts a more factual approach. They are concerned with primary data of man's fundamental drives, urges, needs and norms of conduct. For this, they use the scientific methods developed by social sciences. It is very popular in U.S.A. and Scandinavia.

Scientists and social scientists; their approaches to law and justice

The first answer to the question 'What is Law' comes from those who linked the law with nature. They defined law as any other natural phenomenon. The man in the beginning was just like an animal and was governed by instincts and impulses. He merely gazed at the natural phenomena, sun, moon, rain and thunder, birth and death and so on. The man enjoyed when objects and environments were pleasant and agreeable but suffered helplessly when unpleasant and disagreeable.

He never questioned about or tried to improve what he gazed on. This was the *age of gazing*. Then he developed and entered into '*age of observation*' when his intellect started reacting. He started pondering over the phenomena of nature around him. His intellect started on *causation hunting*. This was the age of superstitions. After this, the man evolved further and entered the '*age of scientific enquiry*'. He sought to discover the cause of everything happening around him. He investigated into the working of phenomenal world, collected data and facts, experimented upon them, drew intelligent and rational conclusions and formulated laws and thus systematized his knowledge.

The scientific age continues to discover more and more the secret powers of nature for the greater benefit of the society. The physicists, the chemists, the botanists and the mathematicians, the economists and the politicians are all exercising their efforts and contributions of scientists in discovering the secret law of nature which are called law of nature and of the social scientists and human scientists are called natural Law.

NATURAL LAW AND LAW OF NATURE

The central theme of natural law is law and nature. How the nature regulates, directs and adjusts behaviour? How does it react when law of nature is violated? This is the law of nature. It cannot discriminate. It cannot be unreasonable. It is consistent and uniform in its operation. Natural law is the product of reason. It is the dictate of reason. It is either the natural law of method or natural law of content. The former concerns to discover the method of which just rule may be reviewed to meet ever varying circumstances whereas the latter attempts to deduce entire body of rules from some absolute first principles. Natural rights belong to this second category, *i.e.*, natural law of contents. Natural law theory chooses to concentrate on "The Law" as it ought to be. The notable exponents include Socrates, Plato, Aristole, Kant, Acquinas, Stammler, etc.

Greek approaches

The term natural law means any of the following:—

1. Ideals which guide legal development and administration.
2. A basic moral, the quality in law which prevents a total separation of the 'is' from 'ought'.
3. The methods of discovering the perfect law.
4. The content of perfect law deducible by the reason.
5. The condition *sine qui bus non* for the existence of law.

Law of nature and natural law: the difference

These are not interchangeable. They are sometimes used as such. This is the wrong approach. In fact, they may sometimes contradict each other. They are different. Law of nature is the basic principle that governs operation of the nature. Laws of maths, physics, chemistry and biology are laws of nature. They are constant and consistent. These are mainly the concern of scientists. New and newer inventions in science and technology help to override the rigidities of the law of nature. For example, the law of heat and the law of cold. We have developed coolers and heaters to do away with their rigours. That does not mean their denial. Similarly, the Law of nature is that man cannot fly. We have aeroplanes now. But it does not mean that the man can fly.

The natural world and the human world are different, but supernatural forces direct the actions of all beings of the natural world or human world. Nature is subordinate to supernatural forces. This is the basis of early natural law thinking and the basis of supernatural entity is the assumption based on faith or belief generated by the religion. In the 19th century, a faith suffered set back due to scientific and technological advancements. The result was the growth of positivism but turmoils, wars, revolutions and barbarinism in the cover of positivism has yet led again to the revival of the natural law ideologies. Natural Law may be divided in to three categories:—

Mystical attitudes.—The history of natural law may be traced to the dawn of humanity when no distinction was maintained between the natural world and the human world. Both were directed by God and supernatural spirits. There was no difference in the laws of physical nature and decrees of Gods or their representatives on earth (King) which determined order in human society. The supernatural power could turn day into night or change the course of the moon, and stars in the same way as it could destroy nations' rulers, empires or kill people or even give life to the people. The nature was inferior to and within the control of supernatural forces.

Theological attitudes : Judiac view of Law (revelation, intuition and inspiration as source of law):

The Judiac approach established monotheism as against polytheism. The relation between God's will and nature put the nature on a pedestal. Divine capriciousness was substituted by the notion of divine purpose or pattern. The divine pattern created belief in all natural or human orders established by the decree of God. God came to be accepted as a divine law giver. The law of God's will on earth was revealed through intuition or inspiration. The laws so given were put in two categories:—

(1) Laws laid down for the fixed order of the physical world, and

(2) Laws to govern human affairs. The divine intervention became an exception. It did not interfere with the divine plan but occurred in furtherance of the divine plan.

How did the laws of the physical world originate and what was their source? This question was different from the existence and operation of these laws. The origin was left to theology and the theological operation was taken over by the science.

Pre-Socrates thinkers

Rationalism; structure of world in terms of human reason.—Pre-Socrates thinkers were concerned mainly with the principles which could explain the structure and the functioning of the universe. They did not rely on their intuition or inspiration to guide them but on power of human reason for understanding the world. To them, the universe was *governed by intelligible laws capable of being grasped by the human mind.* This was known as rationalism in western science and philosophy. Thus, by the time of the early Greeks, the structure of the world was sought in terms of nature.

The meaning of nature created difficulties. As regards the physical world, there was no much problem but in the human world, it created many complications, *e.g.*, if nature enables the strong to prevail over the weak, is it right to apply this to the human world? Or should the law protect the weaker against the stronger? Or are there no rules governing the human conduct so far as the nature is concerned? Is the law just a matter of conventional arrangement? Post-Socrates philophers like Plato and Aristole addressed themselves to such questions.

Contribution of Greece cosmological ideals about justice.—The major contribution of Greece was a body of philosophical and cosmological ideals about justice, more apt for orators' appeals to popular assemblies than for perceptual application to day to day life situations. Early Greek cosmologies embedded in some of the earliest myths, had seen the individual as held within a kind of transcending harmony of the universe, emanating from the divine Law (logos) and expressed in relation to human life in the law (nomos) of the polis, the city state. The later Sophists, however, who examined critically all assumptions relating to life in the city-state, pointed to the wide disparities in human law and morals and rejected the claim that this human law (nomos) necessarily reflected any universal law (logos).

Taking man as "the measure of all things", they rejected any claims of his law (nomos) to absolute value and saw law and justice and values generally as created by men's reasons, in their multitudes and generations, in all their individuated, relativistic, and historically changing dimensions.

Vedic approach.—Veda is ancient in origin. These are Yajurveda, Rigveda, Sam veda and Atharava veda. In Vedas, not such as we know, as man made law, not much information is contained. In Smriti's man made law is given, Law of the cosmos or of the universe is traceable in Vedas. Worship of the sun, moon, rain, air and recognition of Gods is given in Vedas. Law of nature, natural law, human law are all traceable to controller of universe. The existence of this entity is well acknowledged in revealed laws. Law has its religion *i.e.* Religion of law and religion has its laws.

Law of Religion.—The basics can be collected from the law of cosmos, Law of nature, natural law or even in human law; religion of law is love, co-existence, non-violence and live and let live. The religion of law is; 'Do not touch a female when pregnant'; 'Do not kill a kill for kill' 'common use of free air, water, sun rays and effort not to pollute these.' No law would survive without these fundamentals. Principles of natural justice, rule of law, basic features, liberty, justice, fraternity, equality are all religions of law. All these have to be preserved and protected by law religiously.

Religion of law.—It means 'Dharma'. It developed in societies established in the human world. Initially, religion would mean basics that uphold, sustain or do good and promote welfare of an individual. Later, it means one that upholds or sustains or do good to the society. The basic quality of dharma is to do good to society. Dharma was everything, law, religion, moral justice and good conduct. Law and religion, law and moral separated much later. Dharma meant principles regulating one's own conduct, providing goodwill, life and sustenance to society. Preamble of Constitution enumerates religion of law.

Vedas, smritis, good conduct and one that pleases one's self are sources of dharma. It has also been indicated that there are different Vedas, different Smritis, and opinions of jurists also differ as to which path of dharma is good, the basics of Dharma are mysterious, so practicable dharma is the way elders have gone. That is vedic approach to law and religion; of dharma; king is subordinate to dharma. Every unit, community, society, caste, individual, race, creed, has its own dharma wherein many of the values of life and existence are shared as common and some of these specially those of rituals and details may differ. Basics are almost same. Raj dharma, putra dharma, patni dharma, pati-patni dharma all help the system, to sustain and go. These are laws of religion.

CHRISTIAN APPROACH TO LAW; Law of Holy Bible; Justice is part of divine law

The christians were taught to despise all worldly things on the earth and to expect destruction of the world and ultimate right to God's Kingdom. All human constitutions as property, law and slavery were product of sin as a result of the fall of the man. They are all imperfect as compared to those in city of God. Despite this, human law is to be obeyed till this world lasts and justice is very much needed in this human world. The justice is part of the divine law to govern us till sinful existence on this earth endures. So, natural Law is equated with divine law partly miraculously revealed and partly ascertainable by reason. Natural Law now came to be accepted as part of divine law by God and was to be expounded by head of the catholic church, the Pope. St Augustine was the notable exponent of christian approach to natural law.

AUGUSTINE (354-430)—Stoic philosophy re-introduced

St. Augustine Bishop of Hipps in attempting to refute the pagan assertion that christianity was responsible for the decline of the Roman power, reintroduced Stoic philosophy alongside Judeo-Christian thought into the stream of modern jurisprudence speculation. He placed God's reason beside God's will at the highest source of the unchangeable, eternal, divine law binding directly on men and all other creatures. The divine Law was thus accessible to both man's reason and his faith and was not, as St. Paul had largely concluded, the product of his will alone and hence not rational in terms of human reason as opposed to divine reason.

At a second level, Augustine (Professor of Philosophy) placed the no less unchangeable natural law, being the divine law as man is given the reason, heart, and soul to understand it.

The third level, of temporal, or positive, law (for him, the Roman Law of the Christian Roman Empire) was warranted by the eternal divine law, even though it changed from time to time and from place to place, so long as it respected the limits laid down by the divine and natural law. This rationale of secular power, preserved the idea of government under law through the disintegration of the ancient world, in the revival of learning of the 12th and 13th centuries.

Augustine assimilated Plato's philosophy with christian legal thinking. Aristole was not known by that time to Christian Law.

'Justice' has central place in Augustine's philosophy. 'A state is a band of robbers at large without justice' is what he opined.

Unjust Law is not Law.—(*Lex injusta non est lex*) is the most problematic pronouncement of Augustine.

Is **Legal Obligation Co-terminus with justice?** This was not exactly what Augustine thought. He was of the view that in temporal (human) law, nothing is just or legitimate which human beings do not derive from the eternal law. Keeping this version in sight, it is clear that Augustine kept justice in mind and not existence of human law.

ST. THOMAS ACQUINAS (1225-1274)—Eternal law

Acquinas, like Augustine long before succeeded in quieting momentarily the competing claims of the will against the reason of God, the struggle between 'voluntarism' and 'rationalism', as the underlying basis of the eternal and natural law. Acquinas, like Augustine gave a plausible place to both natural law and temporal (or positive) law under the eternal law. Human, or positive, law is a creation of human reason for the common good, within limits that natural law prescribes, so that even this proceeds from right reason and therefore, from the eternal law. Such positive law as violated the natural and thus the eternal law "was not law" and as such was not binding "in conscience". The tendency to make reason prevail over all (as in Plato's call for philosophers to be kings or the Arab Averroes" call for philosophers to interpret what is revealed) as challenged by a voluntarist counter movement at Paris and Oxford in the quarter of a century after Acquinas' death in 1274.

A Franciscan, John Duns Scotus insisted on the uniquencess of all beings as finally traceable to the uniqueness of God's will. All precepts, even of the divine law, depends on the single precept "Love God", and, since not reason but will gives access to this, there is no natural law accessible to man's reason. All that can be required of human, or positive, law is that it must be 'consonant' with the precept "Love God",or with any other precept willed by God.

MACHIAVELLI, NICCOLO; Philosopher to be king

Machiavelli presented himself (on one interpretation, at least) as seeking to escape from both transcendent will and transcendent reason into the empirical, into life as it is, observed through the eyes of a worldly man whose mind is uncluttered with philosophical and theological preconceptions. He can be understood, in his own words, to be seeking "what a principality is, the variety of such states, how they are won, how they are held, how they are lost." This conception was the more remarkable in 1513, since such an approach had then barely been promulgated for the study of the physical world. It had still, indeed, to wait its major manifesto in that sphere until Francis Bacon's Advancement of Learning at the end of the century.

Even on the more favourable view of Machiavelli's aim, *i.e.*, as describing, rather than prescribing, political behaviour it remains true that he saw this description as ancillary to the art of maintaining the State and its ruler, so that this maintenance is a kind of end in itself. The omnipotence-unrestrained by law or morality that he both ascribes and prescribes to the prince is thus a product not so much of his scientific detachment as of his tendency to view political power as a value, as an end in itself.

Supremacy of human law giver.—The supremacy of the human lawgiver, as posited by Machiaveli and in their diverse ways also by the French and English political theorists Jean Bodin and Thomas Hobbes and others, interwove in the following centuries with continued insistence of Grotius and others on the dominance of the divine reason and man's participation in it, by which he has access to the natural law.

GROTIUS (1583-1645); Father of International law

The Dutch political and legal philosopher Hugo Grotius, amidst the political expediencies and anarchy of the Thirty years' War (1618-48), sought to introduce a degree of normative restraint among the monarchical rulers of the newly emerged sovereign states of Europe and to establish a basis in natural law for a rejection of *raison de tat* as a just cause for war, as well as for legal limits on the means and modes of violence in war even if the wills of sovereign states form the basis of the international order. Grotius argued, "the totality of the relations between states" is still "governed by law." That law he found in an updated version of the Stoic natural law, as naturalized into Roman law and christian theology.

With Grotius, as with the Stoics, the normative or moral power of the natural law derives from the fact that man's innate nature (itself part of the nature of the cosmos) and his propensities are viewed as ideal or inherently good. In Grotius' own time, however, there arose a skepticism toward such unfounded optimism, a skepticism that underlies the thought of Hobbes.

HOBBES (The impersonal state and the Individualism)

Need of Leviathan (King) Man's life is nasty, brutish and short; Hence need of Leviathan

With Hobbes (1588-1679), as with the Greek sophists, the nature of man is not the ideal nature of Grotius and the stoics. It is rather man's supposed actual nature, before sociality and authority have tempered it. Man, in a sate of nature, is motivated by desire and aversion and most of all by the desire to preserve his biological existence. This need for security is best met by all men vesting their rights of self-help in a sovereign, whether that sovereign be a single man or an assembly of men, and subjecting themselves to the laws of that sovereign, or "great Leviathan".

Hobbes did not believe that humans are inherently wicked. But, by nature man is self-seeking. All good clash with all good. All against all. Free for all. They destroy each other in the clash for self seeking.

'Family' and 'personal relations are very important in the private sphere. Beyond it men, are motivated by three impulses', competition—fear—desire of power over others. This rush needs to be regulated and controlled by some. It is 'leviathan'.

Authority to Leviathan does not come from religion, nor from God; It is surrendered by people. Power to Leviathan is gift of people, in return for security and their safety which is promised by Leviathan to them. People surrender their natural freedom to the sovereign who makes law and enforces them by virtue of power so gifted by people to Leviathan (Sovereign).

Leviathan is not party to surrender. It is a one sided promise, to obey. Leviathan may be 'Assembly' or 'Single man", Artificial man. He does not have any special feature. He represents the community. He has unlimited power to govern. He has only one purpose the preserving life. There is no other work for him. Safety of people is tie supreme law to Leviathan.

When the realm is at peace, Leviathan sleeps. There is no legal remedy when Leviathan exceeds power. Leviathan alone decides where and how to act. Hobbes did not argue for people and participation in governance. He was not worried about whether Leviathan is accountable? He believed that any government is better than no government.

Hobbes joined issue with Coke on judge made law. He was of the view that Leviathan must act through general laws and must consult Parliament. He attacked common law as it was made by judges and was born out of learning of elite group. To Hobbes, laws should be made by ordinary common sense.

The reason why men must obey the law of the sovereign state, which is the only institution capable of protecting men against each other, is thus based firmly in Hobbes's conception of man's nature, albeit a very different conception from the idealist of earlier theories of natural law. Natural law theorizing after Hobbes is thus divided into two streams.

(i) Judicial supremacy.—By the beginning of the 17th century the idea of applying natural law as a test of the validity of the positive law (the law as it is found within a jurisdiction) had passed from the province of speculative writers to courts of law. The English jurist Lord Coke, in Bonham's case in 1610, was already referring to the tradition that "when an Act of Parliament is against common right or reason or repugnant or impossible to be performed, the common law will control it, and adjudge such Act to be void." About a century before that, an English treatise known as "St. German, Doctor and Student" had already presented a three tier hierarchy of the law of God, natural law (the law of reason), and human (positive) law, obviously deriving from Augustine and Acquinas.

(ii) Secular natural law.—After renaissance, two approaches to natural law were presented. Catholic church adhered to scholastic philosophy. But another new scientific approach arose which ignored claims of theology and concentrated on observation and experiment aided by human reason. Reformation established national churches controlled by the state. This inaugurated these of secular natural law. The emphasis shifted to rational character of natural law. It was not disputed that God created the world and law was given by God, but it was added that natural *law will still apply even if God ceased to exist* because of reason in every man. The rational element is shared by every man everywhere. The human order was dictated by reason and it was followed by reason. Grotius was the exponent of this approach. His views found acceptance in International Law more than national law.

LOCKE (1632-1704) (Individual rights and majority government)

Natural Rights and Natural Law.—Locke developed the theory of natural right out of material drawn from the natural law ideology. Locke's views were adopted by the U.S. Constitution when it incorporated the bill of rights in the Constitution and gave constitutional guarantee for their enforcement in court of law. This process was followed in other countries of Asia and Africa when they drafted their own Constitutions. Doctrine of Fundamental Rights (Part III of the Indian Constitution) traces its origin to Locke's theory of natural rights.

Locke's theory of man being a social animal

Locke was the founder of modern liberalism. He was against monarchy. He was of the view that men had natural rights and the purpose thereof was to serve God. He stressed on individual conscience and self improvement by hard work. He supported the British Revolution of 1688. The natural right to Locke consisted of life-health-freedom and property. The purpose of Government was to protect all these when needed. The Government has limited powers as compared to Hobbes' Leviathan.

Locke and Hobbes

Both believe that Government depends on the consent of people. To Locke, the power of the Government was limited to the protection of natural rights. He believed in check on the power of Government. He advocated for separation of power and also that Government must be accountable. He favoured that Government holds power as trustee of the people. He said that election is a way to make the Government accountable. He accepted the right to rebel if trust is broken by the Government. He was believer in protestant religion. He advocated for toleration in life till it did not upset the political framework.

Relevance of natural law in present century.—In the United States, constitutional theory became highly infused with ideas of natural rights. The Declaration of Independence, with its assertion of the self-evident right of life, liberty, and the pursuit of happiness, marked the beginning of a continuing natural law influence on American constitutional development. The power of the judiciary to "review" legislation for consistency with a written Constitution was taken by the Supreme Court of the United States imports the power to declare it void, constitutional law being analogized to natural law. Indeed, the American Judicial statements of 1874, 1822 and 1831 asserted the power of the judiciary to strike down statutes for violation not only of explicit constitutional restraints but also of "eternal principles of justice which no government has a right to disregard." The analogy of constitutional and natural law did not necessarily require that the power to strike down legislation should be a judicial power. This was not so in ancient Rome, nor is it always so in modern civil law countries. It is arguable that such a judicial repository of the power of final review is unavoidable, since the legislature cannot be expected to annul its own Acts; and the executive, even if it were not a party to such Acts, is scarcely equipped for the tasks of objective interpretation involved. Yet there are real difficulties of policy and principle raised by giving the judiciary the final word. A distinction must first of all be made among diverse constitutional restraints. Safeguards for such rights as free speech and assembly and access to courts, which help to assure the responsibility of rulers and to prevent the fall of democracy into tyranny or demagoguery, may well be placed in the final custody of Judges. But, beyond this point, others have argued, judicial supremacy, in enforcing restraints laid down by the founding fathers of an earlier generation, may clearly constitute an obstacle to the implementation by the courts of a society's present convictions.

Human Rights and Natural Law.—The U.S. Constitution was the first to incorporate the Bill of Human Rights in 1791 and this has led the whole world including India to repeat the course in the form of a chapter invariably included as Fundamental Rights. The Human Rights movement draws much from natural law jurisprudence. The concepts of justice, reasonableness and fairness are very popular in Civil Law and can be explained only in the context of natural law jurisprudence. In criminal law, the idea of good faith has no other origin than natural law philosophy. The whole of Administrative law cannot be explained otherwise. The principles of Natural Justice owe their origin directly to Natural Law philosophy. The basic issues of the modern Jurisprudence like, should abortion be legalized? Should euthanasia be permitted? Whether capital punishment should be abolished? Does a man have a liberty not to commit suicide? Issue of corruption and tainted Minister, M.L.A. or M.P.? are issues that defy ready-made answers due to the involvement of the natural law ideology.

At the International level, we are thinking in terms of word law and the word government. Can any justification other than natural law thinking be utilized for this purpose? The modern theories have taken full advantage of the views expressed by positivists, sociologists and historians against traditional natural law. They have reverted back to the *natural law of method* rather than *natural law of content*.

Early 20th century views

At the beginning of the 20th century, a great variety of psychological hypotheses were brought to bear on law. A theory of *dynamic psychic drives*, for example, was pronounced by an American sociologist, Lester F. Ward, who argued that such drives could be utilized in social planning. Freud's exploration of psychic activity on a subconscious level, as well as studies of the non-rational and the irrational in the social process by the Italian and German sociologists Vilfredo Parato and Max Weber, were also profoundly influential.

Revival of natural-law theories.—Jus naturalism, in the sense of the assertion of an order or norms for human conduct transcending human will, to which the validity of positive law is subjected, has certainly experienced a 20th century revival. The massive human delinquencies of the century, such as those of the Nazis, have been important in stimulating these modern natural-law yearnings. The revival, indeed, has rarely overthrown dominant positivists positions, but it has certainly reopened some questions that positivists have not adequately faced.

Contributions to this re-emergence have come from varied directions, rather than from a single intellectual movement. They have often avoided explicit reference to natural law and have even expressed hostility or ridicule towards it. The German jurist Stammler and the French jurist Francois Geny were certainly among its pioneers. Geny's Methode d'interpretation (1899) displayed the inescapably creative (or Law-making) role of the judiciary even under a comprehensive code such as the Code Napoleon. It led him to the questions of what are "the sources of Law" and where does the legislator's prescription fall short. Answers to such questions must be based on the facts of each particular situation to be adjusted—the legislator cannot impose his view on the court. This line of thinking foreshadowed a variety of doctrines about "*the nature of things*' or "*the nature of facts*", all of which shared the idea that the decisive nature of a situation has its base in the facts for which men seek governing law. The properties and circumstances of these facts themselves afford immediate guidelines for just regulation. The fact situation, if only its essence will be perceived, has the superior applicable norms imminent within it.

NATURAL LAW WITH A CHANGING CONTENT—STAMMLER

In his Lehre von dem richtigen Recht (1902), Stammler sought, the priori social principles of just law concerning respect for and participation by all members. His call for "natural law with a changing content" based on these *a priori* principles quickly became a 20th century slogan.

SOCIAL SOLIDARITY (INTERDEPENDENCE)—DUGUIT

Even as this express reinvocation of natural law was proceeding, the French public lawyer Leon Duguit was expressly denouncing it. Duguit's concern was to place law and lawyers within what he saw to be the correct frame. This be found in Emile Durkheim's positivist sociology. This led him, with some paradox for a condemner of natural law, to insist that law is but "*le produit spontane des faits*" ("the immediate result of the facts"). The observed "facts" of social solidarity arising from economic specialization of functions generated, Duguit argued for the society's norms. Breach of these norms causes social disorder and a spontaneous movement towards readjustment. Even a supreme legislator was bound (Duguit affirmed) by this objective "rule of law", so that his acts violating it are void, even apart from any other constitutional restraint. All this bears the clear, Jusnaturalist mark of the assumed imminence in observed facts of a transcending and overriding order. It pays cryptic homage to natural law, which Duguit denied. Social solidarity means my need is your need and your need is my need, you quench my need, I do yours, Inter dependence, promotes social solidarity.

DEMOCRATIC LEGAL RELATIVISM—RADBRUCH

The German legal philosopher Gustav Radbruch's turn towards natural law at the end of a life of great contribution to democratic legal relativism and positivism was very different. Positivism, Radbruch argued, had encouraged German lawyers to stand by at Nazi barbarism, declaring "Gesetz its Gesetz" ("Law is Law"). Nor was Radbruch's turn to natural law in any way cryptic. He came to declare quite openly that where justice is not even striven for, where equality which is the core of justice is constantly denied in the enactment of positive law, there the law is not only "unjust law" but lacks the nature of law altogether.

LEGAL INSTITUTIONALISM—HAURIOU

The linkage with the revived natural law of the legal institutionalism of the French legal philosopher Maurice Hauriou and the writer and historian George Renard is different again. As with Duguit, the linkage is not proclaimed, but no overt hostility disguised their obvious sympathy for thomist positions. Theirs is a catholic version of institutionalism (which regards social institutions such as the family or the corporation as expressing the social reality underlying the law). The natural law assumptions are apparent in the insistence on "the principles of organization", the "communion" of members in realizing "durable ideals", and the placing of men's powers of organization into the service of such ideals, as essential elements of any institution. For them as for Duguit, the principles of justice were principles of social organization, immanent and self-evident.

NATURAL LAW AND EXISTENTIALISM—MAIHOFER

It has been tempting for many to seek kinships between Natural Law and Existentialism, as was attempted by the German legal philosopher Werner Maihofer. Such efforts seem, however, destined to denature either Existentialism or natural law itself. Even in all their varieties, Existentialist positions approach no nearer to natural law than to assert that the traumas, anxieties, and demands of mere "existence" confront men with fateful value choices. Yet this is far short of asserting that any transcending principles of harmony may be discoverable.

Abstract symbols such as "social solidarity", "the principles of social organization" or "immanence in the facts of social life" are by virtue of their ambiguity susceptible to misappropriation by absolutist governments. The same may be said of Savigny's Volksgeist notion, as witness its affinity to the racialism of Nazi Law. Thus, while the modern revival of natural law has been in part a revulsion from totalitarianism, it can also be exploited to rationalize totalitarianism.

RESTATEMENT OF NATURAL LAW TRADITIONS

There is another paradox also: The growth of the social sciences has invited restatement of natural law traditions in terms of social ideals. Yet the very complexity of the social and economic orders and of their attendant sciences has placed forbidden barriers before the aspiration to base justice or other values on "objective" knowledge. Some have been tempted to hope that natural law may somehow overleap such barriers.

Neo-Thomist.—These Jurists accept the description of reality provided by the scientists but maintain that full explanation of the reality can only be given through reason and reflection. Humanism of Acquinas is also accepted by Neo-Thomists for steering a way out somewhere between individualist view of man and totalitarian view of the society. Nature to these Jurists is both anterior and superior to Positive Law.

Jean Dabin attempted to harmonise the restoration of natural law with the variability of human societies and at the same time to follow the new emphasis on society. His thesis was that the law of nature was deduced from the nature of man as it reveals itself in the basic inclinations of that nature under the control of reason. Since human nature is identical in people everywhere, the precepts of natural law are universal despite historical, geographical, cultural and other variations.

GERMAN APPROACH (PHILOSOPHICAL)

The Philosophical school deals with the ideals of law. What are the juristic principles on which the actual law should be based. Are the principles themselves sound? What is the purpose and mission of law? The naturalists are different from philosophical approach in the sense that they are confined to the Law as it ought to be. They are not concerned with philosophical qualities of law. This school examines the actual law in light of the ideal law and keeps on suggesting improvements in actual law. Natural law school works on materialistic standards and adopts inductive approach. Notable exponents are Kant (German), Hegel (German) and Stammler (German).

Decline of Natural Law.—If man is the measure of all things, as the sophists taught, then a given society of men is the measure of its culture including its moral and legal standards. In the modern period the French jurist and political philosopher *Montesquieu's De l'esprit des lois* (1748) and Lettre persanes (1721) offered the thesis that a people's law and justice is determined by the particular factors and environment that operate upon them. They thus could not, as the natural law theory of the time held, be unchanging from age to age and from people to people. The French sociologist August Comte's Systeme de philosophie positive (1851-54), which set out to explain positive laws, like other social facts, by reference to verified hypotheses concerning cause and effect and interaction, was similarly antithetical to natural law theory as it had so far developed. To Comte, metaphysical concepts about such abstractions as ideal essences belonged to a past stage in man's intellectual development. Darwin's on the origin of Species by means of Natural Selection, (1859), the English Philosopher Herbert Spencer's positivism, and other related thinking of the period provided a biological model of self-development of organisms and institutions through a struggle in which survival was a function of challenge and response in the given environment. Change and adoption, rather than constancy and inviolability, were thus at the heart of their system.

REACTION OF ANTHROPOLOGISTS TO NATURAL LAW

Under the leadership of anthropologists, analysis of man's internal process of response to the exigencies of existence within a particular culture-to conscious and subconscious and subconscious psychic drives and motivations—deeply affected the jurisprudential study of law and society and helped to bring natural law thinking to a 19th century nadir. In the anthropologist Bronis law Malinowski's most mature statement on the matter he distinguished four major meanings of the word Law as important in understanding the growth of civilization. They included "law of nature' in the scientific sense of ruler governing men's conscious adaptations to the environment; rules of "efficiency" and "convenience" according to which the group lives; rules for 'conflict adjustment; and rules about enforcement' of the last two. No conception of natural law, which had engaged earlier thinkers for two millennia and more, was included.

REACTION OF CONTINENTAL JURISTS TO NATURAL LAW

—Historical School;

Reaction of the continental jurists against natural law in 19th century can be explained through historical school. Savigny (German), Gierke (German), Hegel (German), and Maine (Britain) are notable exponents of historical approach.

They are concerned with history of law. The initial hypothesis before them is as to *how far the 'Oughts' of the contemporary Law have been fashioned by the past?* Their concern is the analysis of Law as it has been, as it evolved. This would help to know and define the content of Law.

This school believes that laws are not made. They are found in the society. They are born in the society, grow in the society and die in the society like language and culture. This conclusion is based on the analysis of the process of the evolution of the society. They discuss history of law-law as it has been. This school maintains that nature of any particular system of law was a reflection of the spirit of the people who evolved it. It was called *Volkgeist* and means that all law is the manifestation of common consciousness. To these Jurists, custom is proprio vigour law.

Historical school started with Savigny in 19th century but the ground for such an approach was prepared by many historical events right since 11th century in France and Italy. The most significant event in the story of the study and reception of Roman Law in Europe, was adoption of Roman Law and it is this that checked the Roman Law from disappearance after the dissolution of Roman Empire.

Glossators (Commentary Writers).—The French and Italian Jurists started by writing explanatory notes and commentaries on Justinian Code and other works in Roman Law. Their aim was to reconcile away many conflicts that undoubtedly existed despite claim of king Justinian that his code has eliminated all conflicts. Another thing that French and Italian Jurists tried was to fit the problems of their feudal society into Roman terminology. The climax of glassators came when *Glossa Ordinaria of Accursius* was complied in early 12th century.

Post glossators or commentators.—The scholars who followed Glossa ordinaria were called post-glossators or commentators. These jurists used the Roman Law as contained in glosses for solving contemporary problems; And it was this diluted Roman law that was received in Europe in the 15th and 16th centuries.

Thibaut's proposal for codification.—By the 19th century, the problems of Europe had changed a lot and Roman law whether classical or diluted was not very helpful to the practicing lawyers. Thiabaut proposed a code for Germany on patterns of Code Napolean. And this proposal was contradicted by Savigny through his essay, "On the vocation of our age for Legislation and Jurisprudence." This heralded the beginning of new jurisprudence which was known as historical jurisprudence.

COMMUNIST APPROACHES

SOVIET JURISPRUDENCE

This deals with content of law, and regards the nature of Law as reflex of an economic substrata. The theory believes that just like the physical world is governed by the universal principle of causation so is the case with social phenomenon. It is governed by the economic principles as sole motivating factor. This theory considers law to be instrument of economic domination and should be done away with rather than developed and elaborated. So, they did not specifically elaborate the concept of Law. They do not see any difference like public law or private law. Every law is public law. They also do not see anything like separation of power. There is no question of Judicial independence. Judges are instruments of policy. They must give effect to the policy. The notable exponents are Karl Marx, Engels, Nenin, Pashukanis, Tito (Yugoslavia) and Mao (China). The system is being experimented in Soviet Russia, China, Yugoslavia, Hungary, Czechoslovakia and Tanzania (Africa).

Certain residues of the Marxist economic interpretation of history have won a central place in sociological jurisprudence as indeed in most branches of social sciences. One such persistent trend of thought is the close inter relatedness of legal, ethical economic and psychological inquiries, another is the pre-eminence among those of economic factors.

Marxist doctrine—Law is super structure to perpetuate injustice through it.—According to Marxism, the political and judicial systems-the State and the law-represent the superstructure of society, their nature being determined by the economic base-the mode of production and exchange. The state and its repressive laws are but instruments of class domination, becoming redundant under communism, which has no need of coercion. During the transition to full communism, they would wither away. There were, of course, softening of this bold doctrine in its original authors, with admissions that the ethical or legal superstructure should not be seen as a merely passive effect; and Lenin himself pressed to extremes both the passion of the original thesis and its qualifications. Lenin, indeed, saw state power as an essential weapon of the proletarian dictatorship of majority (Labour) over minority (capitalist) until the movement to a full communist society would be completed.

Withering away of law.—Communism means conversion of the lowest rung of society (poors) into proletariat dictatorship. The poverty, poors or oppression on poor disappears. Crush the middle class (bourgeois) it also appears. Replace prolatariate (interim management) with administration of things; Full communism comes. State and Law disappear or wither away.

The first half-century of the Soviet Union, with its steady consolidation of state power and its attendant law, has imposed the severest strains on the withering-away prediction. The general message of the explanation is that the 'law', the disappearance of which is prophesied refers only to the kind of coercive order manifest in such instrumentalities as the courts, police, and jails of capitalist countries.

Within these sweeping theses of Marxist thinking, more modest sub theses have played a valuable part. The socialist jurist Karl Renner, for example, in his Rechts-institute des Privatrechts and Ihre Soziale Funktion (1929), was concerned to show that the legal conception of ownership, formulated in early economies, had profound new effects when continued as an institution of the 19th century economy. It then, through the law of property and contract, alienated into private hands, great segments of what should be in the public domain.

Even more notable are the German sociologist Max Weber's studies of the correlations of socio-economic and ethico juristic change, freed of the strait jacket of economic deleminism. In these, the impact of unique factors or combinations of factors in particular civilizations is taken into account, including the existence of accepted systems of values, immediate and ultimate, which may (and in Weber's view did) have a decisive effect on the emergence of the western capitalist system.

Continental jurisprudence and English jurisprudence

English jurisprudence is mainly a study of the fundamental legal principles and does not bother much about moral philosophy; but continental jurisprudence leans heavily on moral philosophy of law. British jurisprudence deals mainly with analytical aspect whereas continental jurisprudence deals mainly with ethical aspects. Continental jurisprudence is concerned with philosophical aspect of law and justice whereas British jurisprudence is concerned with practical aspect, *e.g.*, Law as it is. Emphasis in continental jurisprudence is law as it ought to be or law as it has been. Continental jurisprudence has made significant contribution to jurisprudence through natural law ideology, historical approach and sociological approach whereas British jurisprudence confines clinged mainly to positivist approach.

ENGLISH JURISPRUDENCE

In modern jurisprudence, positivism means the following:—

1. Laws are commands of human beings.
2. There is no connection between law and morals or law as it is and as it ought to be.—(Separation Thesis—The quintessence of legal positivism).
3. The analysis of legal concepts (study of meaning) (a) is worth pursuing and (b) is to be distinguished from historical enquiries into the causes or the origin of laws (c) is to be distinguished from sociological enquiries into the relation of law and other social phenomena and from criticism or appraisal of law whether in terms of morals, social aims, functions or otherwise.
4. Legal system is a closed logical system in which correct legal decisions can be deduced by logical means from pre-determined legal rules without reference to social aims, policies and moral standards.
5. Moral judgments cannot be established or defended, as statements of facts can be by rational arguments, evidence or proof (non-cognitivism in ethics).

Bentham and Austin held the views described in (1) to (3) but not those in (4) and (5).

POSITIVISM

The close of the 18th century witnesses a reaction against both Kantian Idealism and Jus-naturalism (natural-law-theorizing). The scientific temper of the age, reflected in the practical achievements of the early decades of the industrial revolution, was felt not conducive to deductive reasoning from *a priori* hypotheses, which appeared as an impractical method of solving the problems of complex societies. Such problems might better be approached via a thorough analysis of existing law and institutions. This new climate of opinion came to be known as positivism.

Among the chief meanings of positivism in the legal analytical sphere are the separation of law as it is and law as it ought to be, *stress on the analysis of legal concepts*, reliance *on logical reasoning in the search for applicable* law, and denial that moral judgments can be based on observation and rational proof. Anglo-Saxon analytical positivism has directed itself mainly to the *logical dissection, appraisal, and clarification of the precept, element of law, ignoring the elements* consisting of *lawyers' traditional techniques* and *received ideals*. By the nature of its tasks, analytical jurisprudence does not concern itself with either the facts surrounding or the consequences flowing from legal precepts or with their ethical evaluation, though particular analysts may also be interested in these matters.

Analytical positivism in England began with the work of the philosopher and legal reformer Jeremy Bentham. His work influenced John Austin, the most outstanding figure in English Jurisprudence, who set out to analyse the notions pervading English Law. In order to delimit this subject, he defined positive law as the commands of a sovereign addressed to political inferior and backed by threats of evil in the event of disobedience. Positive law might well be derived from moral precepts and other sources, but such precepts become law only when commanded by a sovereign.

The analytical positivist attitude has continued to influence thinkers, although the particular approach of Austin is now of historical interest only. Logical analysis is clearly a tool that may be employed in many spheres of Jurisprudence, and its importance thus transcends the limits of any one school. Analysis means little in itself; its value depends largely on the validity of the premises from which the argument is made and on the relevance of the subject-matter that is chosen for analysis. The paramountcy for the analytical Positivist of questions of logical order and consistency represents a permissible deviation, yet still a deviation, from the wider concerns of ordinary lawyers and students of law and society generally. This is not to say that there is a necessary conflict between the requirements of justice among changing social facts and those of logical consistency of precepts. It means only that there is surely no necessary (nor indeed usual) coincidence between them.

19th century was the age of science and technology. The science made the method of experiment and observation very popular and acceptable. The empirical studies had spectacular success in pure sciences and were tried to be made use of in all branches of life including even art and literate and landscape painting. The law could not be an exception. Locke attempted to base philosophical speculations on a more solid and empirical basis which had got success in the realm of pure sciences. David Hume carried this movement further and the outcome of it proved to be of much significance to legal and moral philosophy and established a clear demarcation between laws of physical world where law of causation operated and laws of human world where normative laws applied which laid down norms of human conduct.

Natural Law theories and Positivist approaches.—Both deal with the 'Laws as posited by God; Revealed to prophets, seers or divine incarnations, divinities and discernible to believers by faith, beliefs, values, reasons, virtues and the opinions. The basic cult of these naturalists are religion, philosophy, ethics and morality and basic issues addressed to are; relation between law and moral; legality of moral or morality of law; whether law prevails over moral or moral prevails over law. What is the role of these two in the justice, liberty, virtue and property; what is the role of one in deciding the content of the other? Validity of one or the other *quo* the one?

The reply to these come in different ways by naturalists mainly from the Continents. The basic idea is whether absolute moral knowledge is possible? Plato faced this problem.

The replies are on the basis of duty. These may be based on religion or may be based on other than religion. Religion says God has revealed truth in holy books, to prophets or transcendental experience (self-realisation). This is for believers. The problem for these is whether what God says is 'Good' or God says only 'good' things. Whether god is source of 'good' or God is source or recognition of 'good'.

Duty based on other than religion.—Kant is an example. Goodwill' is absolutely and unconditionally good. Good and bad are decided by pre-existing moral laws. Human reason can identify 'good' out of pre-existing moral laws by applying reason' with which he is gifted by the nature. This universal moral law is Categorical Imperative (commands obedience being absolute and unconditional).

Consequential alternative.—To Duty, whether under religion or universal moral law; consequence is another alternative. It holds that morality (moral quality) depends on consequences. See the consequences and decide what is good. Good consequence carries moral quality. Bad consequence means immorality.

Virtue; The third alternative morality depends on values, qualities and activities which enable human beings to flourish. If so, it is moral; if not so, it is immoral. Aristotle's Nichomachean ethics resembles virtue theory but John Finnis's theory of natural law is its working approach.

Emotivism (Boo hurray theory.—It rejects moral knowledge totally. Morality is nothing more than emotion of the man to those favouring sati, child marriage, dowry, slavery. These are moral. Those opposed to these are immoral. Emotivism as such is personal approval or disapproval. It does not solve the issue of relation in law and moral. It is evasion and not the solution.

Relativism—no absolute : moral knowledge

There is nothing like morality or immorality in absolute sense. What is moral or immoral depends on how and in which society the question is asked. The morality is what that particular society so approves. Bigamy is moral for Muslims; not so for Christians and may or may not be for tribals. The Central idea is that what is right or wrong depends on the society.

To positivists, law is ordinance, Act, statutes, rules, regulations and bye laws. These are formal expressions of the legislative will; Law may be legislation or Precedent. Whether custom is law or not is debatable to positivists. Positivist has the law maker in mind, formal expression of will is there; the subject and object of law are there. Law is law whether good or bad. It can not be good for everybody or bad for everybody. So 'goodness' or 'badness' is not an element or constituent of law.

Internal sub-division of positivists theories

These may be:

1. Strict positivism (strong or exclusive)
2. Soft positivism (Incorporationism) or (inclusive soft positivism)

The former insists on separation thesis (difference in law and moral) at all times. Soft positivism accepts the possibility of taking moral factors into account.

Soft positivism may extend to—

(1) Existence of valid law or

(2) Content of law or meaning of law.

Is it law or Is it good law; The controversy wherein naturalists are challenged by positivists narrows down to :

(a) Whether law is law irrespective of it being just or unjust, good or bad?

(b) Whether moral is moral even if it contravenes any law or any provision of law?

Factually speaking every formal expression of legislative will is law irrespective of it being good or bad. The reason is obvious. There is nothing which is good to every body or bad to every body. It can be good to some and bad to many but if it is bad to many and good to some, it can still be law but obedience to it would be adversely affected or would be badly damaged.

Any law, if approved by morality would be effective and would command general obedience; would be meaningful but if it runs counter to morality its effectiveness would be shaky and may be open to question.

Law has to adjust with morality. Since morality is an issue connected with society and likes and dislikes in each society are not the same or even similar, law has to take a decision sometimes, this or that way. The morality of one society runs counter to the same in the other. The law can choose one and restrict the other. Law and morality are not always opposed to each other they complement and supplement each other. Where it is not possible to co-exist, both go their own way. The conceptual conflict does not come in the way of actual working.

Hume distinguished between 'Is' and 'Ought'

The distinction between 'Is' and 'Ought' has been much debated by naturalists and positivists. To Hume, there are two realms of human enquiry:

1. **Field of facts.**—which is concerned with what is actually the case. Propositions of fact can be treated either true or false. For example, law of nature, pure science.

2. **Field of Ought.**—what ought to be the case. It can never be demonstrated. These do not state facts but lay down what ought to be done. These are normative propositions and lay down norms.

Human Law shares with morals. It lays down rules of conduct. Such a law does not state any facts as such. Neither is it in any way refuted (as is physical law) by its breach or non-observance. Law differs from moral norms as it calls for certain degree of regularity of observance. A moral rule may nevertheless be still valid even if it is never or scarcely ever observed.

Chief exponents of positivism include Hume, Bentham, Austin, Holland and Hart. This school concentrates on law as it is. Law as it is laid down or posited. It includes man made law alone. Natural Law to positivists (Bentham) is nothing but a phrase. They concentrate on formal characteristics of law, and bother very little or almost do not bother on the content of law which may be just or unjust, good or bad. It is law if it is laid down in accordance with the form prescribed. It cannot be challenged on the grounds of immorality or unjustness.

This movement started in the beginning of the 19th century and sought to locate the basis of law in some intelligible corner. Natural Law explanations were based on unverified hypotheses. So the positivism came as intellectual reactions against such approaches. The main contention of the positivists are that law and moral are separate.

How much there is separation (separation thesis)

Separation between 'is' and 'ought' (law and moral) is good in the present time frame that is to begin with the morality as a criteria of the validity of a law is more acceptable but moral considerations should not hamper it. There can be no separation in continuum. For continuity, the law must fulfil the requirement of morality. (soft positivism).

Whether separation between is and ought desirable?

The positivists contend it to be desirable. Law is concerned with practical things. It needs certainty. Morality is a diffused idea. Formal (legal) tests are easy to apply as compared to moral tests of validity. The court has no time, no training to apply moral test. Separation helps to criticise positive law which can be evaluated if separation is maintained.

AMERICAN JURISPRUDENCE

Sociological approaches

This school concentrates on law as it functions in the society. It is also called functional school. These studies concern law in relation to society, and the theme is law and sociology, that is the sociology of law.

Sociology of law and legal sociology

Social statics and social dynamics.—Sociology means the study of society of which law is but a part. It is the science of social order and progress. It includes two compartments (social statics and social dynamics). The former is a theory of social order and the latter is a theory of social progress. Society is a developing organism whose progress is marked by the specialization of functions within it. Its distinctive feature is its capacity for improvement and development if guided by proper scientific principles. The task of sociology is to discover and work out these principles. Sociology deals with patterns which do occur as a matter of the observations which are not prescriptions, but which can be described as 'is'. All instruments of control in the society like law, morality, religion or public opinion are prescriptions alone. They would form part of sociological study. The sociology is not concerned with these mere propositions but only when these are regularly followed and they produce uniformity of behaviour and recur with some degree of probability.

Norms of decision and norms of conduct.—Legal sociologists look at law as the sum total of legal administration and as a given phenomenon of society. A Sociological jurist is a lawyer who looks at the operation of the laws and conceptual tools of a lawyer's equipment in their social and functional setting. A Legal sociologist regards the society as a whole including the part played by the legal administration in bringing about an observable pattern of behaviour. A Legal sociologist is interested in the fact of the regular application of the force and the facts of regular use of the guides for determining disputes (norms of decision), both of which help to shape patterns of social behaviour (norms of conduct). The concept of law to a legal sociologist tends to be an ideal one, a model of the totality of the legal administration which can be fitted into model of the society.

The sociologist jurist is primarily concerned with laws and the tools of the lawyer's trade. He accepts the laws as prescriptive in nature and considers their function and functioning in society. If the sociology of law is thought to be concerned with the manner in which laws work in the society, then it is the same as sociological jurisprudence. But if it is concerned with the society and how legal administration as a whole fits into it, then it is synonymous with legal sociology. Exponents of American sociological school and later on realist school also come from bench and faculties both. Common law jurisprudence is bench dominated. The American jurists enjoy the same status as do the continental jurists and are superior to one enjoyed by the jurists of common law countries.

Whether Newtonian model of natural science holds good for social science too?—The historical jurisprudence of the earlier part of the 19th century became subject to the influence of the developing social sciences, which attempted to explain law in its social context. The result was the emergence of a sociological school of jurisprudence. The early decades of sociological jurisprudence combined 19th century faith in progress, social evolution, rationalism, humanitarianism, and political pluralism with a sanguine belief that the Newtonian model of natural science would also hold for the social sciences. It was affected by questions of whether the social sciences are truly sciences, what their mutual boundaries are, and whether they can be inaugurated or somehow transcended by some subject such as sociology or anthropology.

An outstanding figure of the early sociological school was a German, Rudolf Von Ihering, who in the 1860s contributed to the intellectual stream a theory of justice predicated on a view of law as a social phenomenon. He saw law as an outcome of the struggle of men to fulfil their purposes and of the force that they marshal behind this.

Another historical jurist, the German Otto Von Gierke, stirred a related interest with his emphasis on the importance of the inner life and activities of groups and associations as sources of binding social norms. This opened up jurisprudence to some psychological issues. Gierke's work also contributed to the later American neo-realism through its influence on Oliver Wendell Holmes, Jr. and to the theory of the "living law" of the Austrian jurists Eugen Ehrlich, in the first decade of the 20th century. Ehrlich insisted on the profuse norm-creating activities of the countless associations in which men are involved.

Growth of the sociological school—Pound (U.S.A.) and Kanlorwixz (Europe)

The most eminent pioneers and champions of modern sociological jurisprudence were Roscoe Pound in the United States and Hermann Kantorowixz in Europe. For both, the task of sociological jurisprudence, though orientated mainly to practical administrative or legislative problems, included that of framing hypotheses (as to the limits of effective legal action, for example) on which to base general laws of the operation of law in society.

Staples of sociological jurisprudence.—As with the social sciences, the principal methods available to sociological jurisprudence are those of *survey, statistical analysis, comparative observation, and experimentation.* The control and corrections available usually fall far short of those of the natural science models. Much work in sociological jurisprudence has merely brought to bear upon the law and relevant findings from other social sciences. But it may also generate its own findings, as it has done in relation to traffic laws, control of money-lending, credit unions, bankruptcy laws, the effect of antitrust practices or of poverty on legal rights,the theory of appellate judicial decision making, and a host of other matters. Examinations of the pre-history and after-careers of convicted criminals and of persons on probation or parole, probings of family and environmental influences bearing on potential deviance, and attempts to identify decisive factors predictive of future deviance are among the staples of sociological jurisprudence.

Sociological jurisprudence is confronted by the questions whether (and, if so, how and how far) it is possible through empirical methods to approach central issues of social action that involve value judgments. The fact that lawyers are necessarily involved with ideas of obligation, values, and norms sharpens this confrontation. A second group of problems arises from the high level of individuality of men, groups, and societies, from the unending variety of their emotions, roles, expectations, and from the feedback effects on human behaviour that the empirical observation and the testing of that behaviour brings about.

These problems give central importance to efforts to develop frames of social knowledge that give due place to both facts and values. Such inquiries show the great complexities of values held and their intricate and dynamic relation to the physical and cultural environments.

The study of law in society thus shares with anthropology and other social sciences a central interest in roles and functions as basic meaningful categories and in certain mechanisms and channels whereby conduct is thought to become socially meaningful. These notions are thought to permit the analysis of complex social situations into more refined terms, such as constituent goals, tasks, expectations, allocated rights, powers and duties.

As to the mechanisms or channels through which conduct becomes socially meaningful, earlier thought tended to explain social norms as built up from individual instances through group usages and mores that then crystallize in institutions such as law. In so far as this suggests a cumulative movement or process, and the current thoughts would regard it as oversimplified. The growth of socio-ethical convictions is rather to be seen in terms of symbolic interaction between individuals. A particular society may be seen, in this light, as a collection of individuals with a culture that has been learnt by symbolic communication from other individuals back through time, enabling members to gauge their behaviour to each other and to the society as a whole.

Pound's programme of practical objectives.—In his famous programme of 1911-12, Pound formulated a series of rather practical objectives for the movement, including studies of the law in action, of the means of more effective legislation and law enforcement (by creation of ministries of justice, for example), of legal and judicial reasoning, of legal history in its social context, and of the role of the legal profession. An early quip against the sociological school was that it was like a great orchestra constantly tuning its instruments but never actually playing. Yet, many practical tasks have been performed,and the school continued to show a gathering momentum and a widening range of concerns.

The mal-adjustments and inadequacies of the law gave to early sociological jurisprudence an intensely activist drive, directed to *ad hoc* remedies, and a great deal of the relevant work is still of this nature. Especially since 1945, however, juristic work on the relations of law and society has come into more fruitful contact with other social sciences, leading in turn to greater stress on cognition of the social and economic orders in their complex unity. Whatever the difficulties of designs for an overall analysis of the social system, some adjustment towards them is inevitable for sociological jurisprudence. This is in part, no doubt, as a result of the waning of interest in many of the kinds of *ad hoc* problems with which it was initially concerned. But the interest in sociological theory also results from growing awareness that some problems require to be approached on a wider basis. This has created new stirrings of the turn-of-the-century ambition that the study of law in society become a specific branch of social science, concerned with framing and testing general laws governing law as a social phenomenon.

Realist approaches

American realists are mostly lawyers. They argue that in reality, law is not what is in code, court decisions or statute books. These are in no case more decisive sources of law as the psychological elements; For example, likes and dislikes of the judge, mood of the judge, his family background, etc. According to these, law is that the courts actually do. Like positivists, they also believe that law is expression of the will of the State but the former takes it when expressed through the legislature whereas realists, when expressed through the courts. They concentrate on the fact what the courts actually do. They are also known as experimentalists, or constructive skeptics.

This approach is of two kinds. American realism and Scandinavian realism. The only difference is that American realists are mostly the lawyers, judges or law teachers whereas in Scandinavia, these are mostly philosophers. American realists have practical and empirical approach and Scandinavian realists deal with psychic reality and transcendentalism in law. The notable exponents of American realism are Frank, Holmes and Llewellyn and of Scandinavian approach notable exponents are Hagerstrom, Lundstedt, Olivecrone and Ross.

Pure theory approach

In part, at least, the influence that the distinguished legal philosopher Hans Kelsen's "pure theory of law" reflects early 20th century skepticism about natural law and sociology, to both of which Kelsen opposed his claimed purity of method, *i.e.* a method free from contamination by values of any sort. He asserted first, that legal theory was properly a science in the sense of an uncommitted, value-free, methodical concern with a determined object of knowledge.

Second, he argued, legal theory must be isolated from psychological, sociological and ethical matters. Third, purity of method permits the analyst to see that every legal system is in essence a hierarchy of norms in which every proposition is dependent for its validity on another proposition. The justification for describing any particular rule as law thus depends on whether there is some other proposition standing behind it, imparting to it the quality of law. This regression is continued until the Grundnorm or "basic norm", is arrived at. The basic norm derives its validity from the fact that it has been accepted by some sufficient minimum number of people in the community.

Kelsen's assertion that norms can spring only from other norms seems but another way of stating his rejection of the relevance of facts to values and, therefore, of Jus naturalism and sociology to his pure science of law. Yet finally it seems to many dubious whether the Kelsenite theory itself escaped the liaison fatal between facts and norms; for, if all legal norms must finally hang on the basic norm, then whatever, it is that the basic norm hangs on "habitual obedience to determinate person", as the English legal philosopher John Austin in effect proposed a century before, or on "efficaciousness", as Kelsen proposed, what it hands on is fact rather than norm. Critics have complained that, at most points in the creation of norms in Kelsen';s system, what is decisive is the intervention of *acts of will of persons* endowed by higher norms with norm making authority. The determination whether such *acts of will* have occurred is a factual inquiry, to the decisiveness of which Kelsen's pure theory gave little weight.

The American jurist, Oliver Wendell Homes's description of law in 1897 as "what the courts will do in fact" and of the "real ground" of decisions as rests often on some "inarticulate major premise" rather than on expressed reasons such as it gave 20th century legal realism its central theme.

Common feature

Certain features are common to the 'realist' jurists. They include (besides concern with "the law in action") stress on the social purposiveness of law on *the endless flux in both society and law,* on the need to divorce the "*is*" and the "*ought*" for purposes of study and to question all *orthodox assumptions* made by lawyers, and in particular on the *need to substitute more realistic working categories for current lawyers generalities*. Among the orthodoxies thus challenged, these writers tended to include the works of early sociological jurisprudence. Yet it is clear, from the present perceptive, that the concerns common to the realist and the more orthodox sociological jurists were far more important than the conflicts that it first flared up between them. The American realists in their important surviving contributions have for the most part reinforced, clarified and elaborated a number of men in insights, notably *about rule uncertainty and fact uncertainty*, which they shared with sociological jurisprudence.

Scandinavian realists, while temperamentally akin to their American colleagues, were rather different in intellectual concerns. Methodologically, they invoked a somewhat gross empiricism, leading them to *deny that the law* could *be the subject of scientific inquiry at all, since in concepts and principles are not founded on spatial* and *temporal data of experience*. Taking lawyers' talk of the will of the sovereign very literally, they were concerned to show that there is no such *will of common content* and that even legislators who enact a code are merely rubber stamping that others drafted.

The Swedish jurist Axel Hagerstrom insisted that the idea of rules of law as commands is an idea not corresponding with facts. His disciple Karl Olivecrona added that this false idea results from the syntactical imperative form used in modern legislation. Such rules, he urged were commands only in a depersonalized sense. He preferred to describe them as "independent imperative". Such "imperative statements about imaginary actions, rights, duties" may not be directed to any particular persons. Yet, even if some legal rules are directed "so to say, into the air", others are certainly directed to particular persons. If any form of imperative notion is to be preserved, it should be one that accommodates both situations.

Some of the problems that these writings address are rather tied to the special experience of their authors' own legal cultures. Others reach out independently towards truths already reached earlier in Anglo-American jurisprudential scholarship, especially as to the merely noetic and conceptual (rather than physical or psychological) nature of rights, duties, and liabilities.

The contemporary jurisprudence

By the middle of the 20th century, serious scholars no longer argu for or against the exclusive imperium of either the analytical logical, the justice-ethical, or the sociological approach. Whether jurisprudence is a single field in some scientific sense or whether its unity lies in the need to serve the intellectual needs of those concerned with making, applying, improving, or generally understanding law, all the above areas are included within it.

A characteristic feature of contemporary jurisprudence is what has come to be known as "the revolt against formalism"; that is, against preoccupation with the technical and logical aspects of law. It can be traced back to Savigny's early 19th century reaction against natural law, to Ihering's attacks on the German I' andectists (commentators on Roman Law), and to Maine and the work of the anthropologists and early sociological jurists. Its early pressure was towards broader and deeper history, towards recognition of the organic nature of the processes of cultural growth, and towards problems of social action and the value choices therein entailed.

In the United States, the legal philosopher Morton White identified five contributing strains of thought, including the pragmatism of John Dewey; the economist Thorstein Veblen's institutionalism, rejecting both the abstractions of classical political economy and the fatalism of the Marxist interpretation of history; the revolt within jurisprudence of the American legal realists; and the approach to history as no mere chronicle of kings and battles but rather as a product of underlying economic forces and a guide to present and future civilizations.

The sometimes-overhasty criticisms of this revolt have proved less important than its positive affirmations. It has affirmed, for example, that the evaluating activities of justice must somehow move alongside the describing activities of sociological jurisprudence, that the choices of ethics, social policy, and justice still remain to be made when all the empirics of social science are done. The central question includes not merely what are the facts but also what should be done about the facts. These affirmations reject any regression to simple amoralism, stirring new temptations to return to natural law or other intuitive absolutes.

There are important advantages in the drive, characteristics of much contemporary social science, for an overall cognition of the social and legal orders and the identification of key points for social action within them. But there are also dangers, for, especially with subject-matters such as the law, systematic theory and overall cognition can rarely be of aid save in the rather long run, for which present decision makers cannot usually wait.

❑❑

Chapter 10

Comparison as an Aid to the Judicial Method

When saturation point reaches on any point before any court or when no light is seen or is available for guidance or any moot issue, when Constitution of the country does not prove to be of assistance, when statutes of the country are non-existent, the analogy, philosophy, custom, usages or precedent fail to help to solve, comparative method is a sure sought method open to the judicial process to do its job. How that problem has been solved in sister systems can that experience be of some help to the judge before whom identical issue has come for decision. For proper comparison every thing or any thing would be relevant. Comparison knows no limit and would seldom fail for any issue on any point.

Major virtue of comparative method is that it is kind of mental travelling. In the course of such an exercise one is able to disengage from local and national prejudices by passing in review the usage of the other communities.

This problem has been very complicated since the legal acumen knew something of looking around. The personnel of law may be divided into four groups; namely, law students, lawyers, judges and professors of law. The students of law are beginners. They are busy with the subjects prescribed in syllabus. The comparative study to them, only means the process of writing good answers *etc.* They may compare one topic of the same subject to another related topic of the same subject, for example; they may compare divorce with judicial separation or void and voidable contracts. They may compare Hindu wife's powers, with powers enjoyed the muslim and christian wives. They may compare any two topics and analyse heir similarities and dissimilarities. They may study the course prescribed in paper on comparative law. Beyond some of these, the students of law cannot proceed nor the time so permits them to proceed.

The second class covers the lawyers or advocates. Most of the advocates in India are busy in money making. They have no access or very little concern with extra municipal laws. Their limitations compel them to take a different line of approach which is of meagre importance so far as comparative study is concerned. They confine themselves to the rulings of the Board of Revenue, High Court or to the rulings of Supreme Court. This gives them enough literature suited to their task. An average lawyer has nothing to go beyond. It is concern of a very few lawyers who have creative brain and who are apt to adopt a new and novel argument. They are benefitted by the comparative method. They may consult provisions of parallel law and adopt the reasoning advanced in those countries. For example, in the *Keshavanand Bharti* case the corresponding provisions of American, British and Canadian Constitutions were exhaustively quoted, and pressed for being accepted as meaning of the word 'amendment'.

Coming to the judges, the comparative method helps them much. The task of the judge is almost coextensive with the expositions of the lawyers. So the utility is the same or similar. The judge may, with the help of comparison, sort out the meaning acceptable in local situations. For professors of law, comparison is almost a necessity. He cannot feel satisfied unless he has specialised in his subject vertically as well as horizontally. The former is possible within the framework of municipal law. But the latter, comparison with other parallel laws and systems is the only process available. These techniques are not new to India or Indian legal system; But a tendency is developing now a days of studying this technique from a different angle. The technique is given a new name. It is called comparative method. It consists for a particular mission. It knows only one object. The mission is comparison. The object is comparison. It is not yet clear as to what is to be compared. Compare anything you like; compare at any point you like, but comparison must be there. This comparison in field of law gives it a new name of comparative law. So this is the method of study or branch of legal science where too concepts of law or elements of law are taken together, collected, examined and collated in order to find out the similarities or dissimilarities between them. All the legal notions, doctrines, rules and Institutions can be compared. There is no limit on area or scope. The comparative method collects and tabulates the legal Institutions of the various countries. The material so collected is then handed over to the jurists who would set forth an orderly view of the ideas and methods which have been variously realised in actual systems. The area of the comparative lawyers is undefined. He has no prohibited zone. He can enter any place, collect material from any place and draw any conclusion he may like. The comparative lawyers are kings without countries. They are monarchs of the field they cultivate and tread upon. The reason is that no delineation of the space or territory for it has ever been attempted. The comparative lawyer enjoys complete freedom when he sets out on a voyage of discovery. He can select topic for the purpose of comparison. Its merit lies till comparison is going on. The worth ceases when the process of the comparison is over. This merit of the process has raised confusion regarding the nature of this branch of legal study. Whether it is science or method of study? The jurists are divided. Some of them accept it as a branch of legal science. According to them, comparative law is an independent branch of jurisprudence as is Legal Theory, Legal History, Private International Law, Public International Law. Transfer of Property, Contract, Constitution, Criminal Law and Criminology.

Such jurists will have to explore new avenues for the subject if they want to see it prosperous and growing. The comparison alone will not be able to give it a long life as durable as other branches of legal science have got. It will have to establish a territory of its own. It can no longer be a permanent guest dining forever at another's table. Unless comparative lawyers are in a position to explore new sites, they will be sailing in an unchartered vessel rowing in the open sea. Their subject may have ready reception and standing ovation in the beginning but the time will come when this would leave nothing within their power. This could happen immediately if comparative study of each subject is started for example: Instead of legal history of India, the comparative legal history of selected legal systems is introduced in syllabus; likewise the study of Comparative labour law, Comparative penal law, Comparative jurisprudence, Comparative personal laws, Comparative law of obligations and Comparative commercial law or Comparative procedure is equally possible. The wide recognition of the Comparative method and its universal application is bound to cause its extinction for ever. It may then no longer claim its independent existence as separate branch of legal science.

Some of the writers on law treat the comparative study as method of study. They call it Science in application. This is safer side to adopt. This branch is still struggling for independent existence as branch of legal science. Its solidarity exists in comparison. It is a craft which may be made use of by specialists. If the lawyer knows the laws, their contents, their applications and the reactions of the mass and interpretations made by courts of his own country and at the same time, if he is aware of corresponding laws of other countries, he may make use of the failures and successes experienced there. The comparative study, therefore, is a craft or method of study which may assume a status of independent branch, if new avenues are opened after researches. It is premature to extend it recognition as branch of legal science.

Methodology of Comparative Legal Research

Researchers get easily lost when embarking on comparative legal research. The main reason being that there is no agreement on the kind of methodology to be followed, nor even on the methodologies that could be followed. Moreover, almost everything that was more or less established in the area of comparative law over the last century has been increasingly criticized during the last few decades : the concept of 'legal family', the possibility of comparison itself, the object of comparison, *etc.*

On the other hand, comparing domestic law with the way the same area has been regulated in one or more countries has become almost compulsory in doctrinal legal research. Also in legal practice, globalization and most notably Europeanization involve comparative research. How should a comparative researcher cope with this apparent paradox?

In this paper, an attempt is made to work out a methodology for comparative legal research, which goes beyond the 'functional method' or methodological scepticism.The starting point is the idea that we need a 'toolbox', not a fixed methodological road map, and that a lot of published, but largely unnoticed, research outside rule and case oriented comparative law offers varying approaches, which could usefully be applied in comparative research. Basically, it is the aim of the research and the research question that will determine which methods could be useful. Moreover, different methods may be combined, as they are complementary and not mutually exclusive. This paper focuses on scholarly comparative legal research, not on the use of foreign law by legislators or courts, but, of course, the methodological questions and answers will largely overlap.

Why compare?

At the end of the nineteenth century and early twentieth century, in France, Raymond Saleilles and others saw comparative law mainly as an instrument for improving domestic law and legal doctrine, as a way to renovating the fossilized approach of the still dominating Exegetic School to the Civil Code and its interpretation. By the end of the twentieth century, many legal scholars in Europe considered comparative law to be the necessary instrument for a (desirable) harmonization of law within the EU. Hence, according to the circumstances, there may be different aims and diverging reasons for comparing legal systems.

In a general way, Patrick Glenn has answered this question under the heading 'Aims of Comparative Law'. He lists (a) comparative law as an instrument of learning and knowledge (information on the law elsewhere and a better understanding thereof), (b) comparative law as an instrument of evolutionary and taxonomic science (common evolutions, diachronic changes, legal families), (c) contributing to one's own legal system (understanding it better, including the resistance of its traditions, improving it, using it as a means for interpreting the constitution), and (d) harmonization of law. However, Glenn strongly criticizes much of the ideology that underlies traditional comparative law and largely still does today. There is the constructivist belief in the use of foreign law for one's own, otherwise nicely protected, national legal system, or in harmonizing law being just a technical matter, or in taxonomies of coherent 'legal families'. There is also a lot of Western imperialism in what William Twining has called the 'Country and Western approach' of comparative law. Nevertheless, even in a more open, pluralist and less constructivist comparative research, the mentioned aims are still largely valid, Glenn concludes.

In concrete comparative research projects, it is the aim of the research and the research questions that will imply some form of comparative law (or not). If the aim of the research is making some part of the domestic law more coherent one may well do without any external comparison. If the aim is to harmonize the law, e.g., within the EU, comparing the legal systems involved is already implied by this aim, but also the approach to be followed is partly determined by it, as the focus will be on the commonalities, on the common core of the compared legal systems and on the possible ways of erasing differences.

When one tries to improve one's own legal system, be it as a legislator or as a scholar, it has become obvious to look at the other side of the borders. However, importing rules and solutions from abroad may not work because of a difference in context. Hence, a more thorough contextual approach may be required.

One may also want to inquire to what extent a legal evolution in one's own country finds parallel developments in other countries. A paramount example is the developments in family law, mainly in Europe, over the last half century.

When comparing official state law in African countries with local customary law, one will notice that they show a tension between tradition and modernity, between Western law only followed by an elite and African law as the large majority of the population perceive it. Hence, an anthropological approach that puts the law in context will be necessary for explaining this tension, for understanding it and for finding solutions for it.

If one's research question would be whether the position of the notary public in some continental European country could be abolished and replaced by a civil officer or by a practising lawyer (advocate), it seems rather obvious to have a look at the common-law countries where such a specific profession doesn't exist.

All scholarly research implies comparisons. Scholarly legal research often requires comparing one's own legal system to another one. Here, we will focus on comparing national legal systems, as this is the most common geographical level of comparison.

Choice of legal systems to be compared

Comparative research is still mainly about comparing national legal systems, even if different forms of globalization, such as Europeanization, and an increasing recognition of non-state law, such as customary law, religious law or unofficial law-making by international companies are challenging the very concept of 'legal system'. Here, we are not entering into that discussion. In practice, when choosing national legal systems to compare with, most (individual) researchers will make a choice on the basis of their knowledge of languages, which explains why most comparative research in the Anglo-Saxon world is focusing on comparing common-law countries that still use English as their (main) official language. This makes comparative research in most areas of the law quite easy, as the whole conceptual framework and the older history of the common law is also the same for all legal systems compared. However, such research may be useful at the informative level, for businessmen for instance, but is not entirely useful in the context of broader scientific research.

Increasingly, some translations of legal texts in English are available for most countries all over the world. However, they tend to cover only legislation and do not always follow changes made to the law, so that they may rapidly be outdated. The same goes for general introductions in English, to the law or a specific area of it, of individual countries. It may be desirable to use such information in some cases, for instance as a confirmation of what has been found elsewhere, but for a thorough comparative research a good reading knowledge of the local language is an absolute requirement. Even for a limited use of English language publications on the law of a country of which the researcher cannot read the local language, it is highly recommended to check whether one's own interpretation is correct and whether there have been any recent changes in that law, by contacting a local scholar who speaks English or another language the researcher masters. For this, a well-elaborated network of colleagues in the same area of law is very valuable.

Even when one's knowledge of languages will be the prime reason for choosing or eliminating some country, the researcher should be able to give good reasons why her choice is acceptable from a scholarly point of view. For instance, when studying the division between public law and private law, it makes sense to focus on France and on the UK, as they may well have the most opposed views on the matter. This may be used as a strong argument, so that the researcher may leave aside her initial problem that French and English may be the only two languages she knows.

For larger projects, an international team, that masters together all required languages, may be the solution, on the condition that the internal communication within the group is sufficiently intense and qualitatively good. Every member of the team should be able to detect the relevant commonalities and differences between the studied legal systems and their contexts, and, moreover, be able to explain them clearly to the other members of the team. In the case of such teams the choice of legal systems to be compared may be based on more relevant criteria than the accidental (lack of) knowledge of languages of individual researchers. However, one has to be aware that lack of sufficient understanding of foreign legal systems may arise from an imperfect communication within the team.

It is also risky to involve legal systems with legal cultures one is not familiar with, at least to some extent, at the start of the research project. Assume that a research team wants to set up a worldwide research project on divorce. For this, they draft a lengthy questionnaire with all kinds of questions on the grounds for divorce, on the procedure and on the legal consequences of each type of divorce. After this, they contact their network for answering those questions. However, the response will be largely biased if they based the questionnaire on Western law only. Indeed, it will not take into account the 'repudiation' of a wife under Islamic law, which sometimes has been equated to 'divorce by mutual consent' in Europe. It will not take into account traditional marriage in African countries, where legislation only regulates 'official' (and monogamous) marriage, even if traditional marriage, concluded according to customary law, is accepted. This customary marriage largely doesn't include the concept of divorce, nor is there a need to do so in view of the (unlimited) polygamy set-up. This means that, before setting up a large comparative research project of this kind, one has to define different levels of comparison, on the basis of such elements and their correct understanding. One cannot study divorce inter-culturally without a broader understanding of marriage, of the role of families, of the general attitude to divorce in each of the compared societies.

The wording of the research question will be the main criterion for the choice of legal systems to be compared. If, for instance, one wants to inquire to what extent the law on contracts for renting houses or flats could be harmonized within the European Union, the law of the 28 member states will have to be studied. However, if the working hypothesis would be that such harmonization is not possible, it may suffice to study two legal systems, such as the French and the English one, if one may prove that harmonization between those two legal systems would be impossible and, hence, any harmonization within the whole of the EU.

If one would like to study the role of the king or queen in kingdoms worldwide, or the way federal states are organized, one should in principle involve all legal systems that are relevant for this topic. In practice, however, a much more limited selection of countries may still be quite relevant and, hence, suffice. Comparing, for instance, just the US and Germany may allow to go deeper into the historical developments which explain the current situation and into the way these federal structures work in practice. If one wants to challenge the concept of 'federal state' itself, a comparison with the structure of the European Union may look quite attractive.

Another approach may be to look first at the reasons for a more decentralized organization of a country : historical coincidence, making the practical organization of a large state feasible, living together of various communities with different languages, religions, and/or cultures within the same state, *etc.* If one wants to inquire how, for instance a federal structure, or some specific parts of it, has contributed to a peaceful living together of people within the same state, it may be more relevant to compare, for instance, Belgium, Canada, and Nigeria than the US and Germany.

What has to be compared?

In the nineteenth century, associations and journals were founded on 'comparative legislation'. At that time, there was a focus on comparing rules in different societies. Later on, more attention was paid to judicial decisions and the way legal problems were solved in practice. Meanwhile, many authors on comparative law emphasize also the importance of taking into account the socio-economic and historical context of the law when carrying out comparative legal research.

Where has the comparative researcher to look for in foreign legal systems : legislation, and/or case law and/or their entire context? Relevant legislation and (published) case law may be found relatively easily. In the first place, in doctrinal books and articles (much less in Italy, however, where legislation is often discussed without direct references to case law) and, for more recent months and years, through electronic databases. But what to do with the context of the law? Occasionally, some explanations may be found in doctrinal legal writings, but until now this has been rather exceptional. Sometimes it was explained widely in the international press, such as the financial crisis as the context and explanation for some domestic and European changes in regulations of the financial sector. Sometimes, the researcher may discover historical, sociological, and/or economic literature on her topic for a country included in the comparison, but that is not obvious either. Whereas some limited social science research may be feasible within the context of one's own legal system, for foreign countries this will, as a rule, be excluded within the frame of research in law carried out individually. Much will depend on the focus of one's research and on the available sources. A good balance between both will guarantee the feasibility of the research design. An overly ambitious law-in-context approach for a topic where there are insufficient available sources will make the research plan unrealistic within the context of comparative legal scholarship.

In short, comparing only legislation is risky when there is no information available on how it works in practice, and such a limited comparison is only acceptable for countries which are not at the core of one's comparative research. For instance, when comparing one's domestic law with German law, the researcher may add that the legislation is the same in Switzerland and/or in Austria, without making a thorough analysis of those legal systems in relation to this point.

Comparing case law (and legislation) will require some knowledge of the historical and socio-economic context that transpires from the available sources. When comparing neighbouring countries, the researcher may have a general idea of historical and/or socio-economic similarities and differences. For differences, some better insight into that context will be required. Also, focusing on practical solutions to legal problems should not dissociate the legal solutions from their doctrinal context, as some solutions may be accidentally similar, which may hide more important differences at the level of the concepts used and the systemic building of that area of the law.

Fully comparing law-in-context within individual research will only be possible if one is lucky to find sufficient relevant sources and literature for each of the legal systems to be compared. Otherwise, team research will be required, preferably with an interdisciplinary team. Again, some rough understanding of differences and similarities between the legal systems, and of the relevant context for explaining them, will be a prerequisite for setting up the research project and selecting not only the legal systems to be compared, but also the disciplines relevant for the context research. When comparing banking law, for instance, one may assume that economics is most relevant for explaining similarities and differences, but maybe history and/or psychology would eventually appear to be even more relevant for the specific research question. With inter-cultural comparisons, apparent similarity of (imported) legislation, e.g., on the equality of men and women, may hide a completely different reality. Only (legal) anthropological research may reveal and adequately explain this. In all cases, however, comparison should never stop at the level of legislation, and even not at the level of case law, as the social reality may be more different than similar rules suggest (and sometimes more similar than different rules would suggest). Rules may exist on paper, but are not applied in practice. Absence of case law on the matter may have diverging explanations : (a) everybody follows the law; (b) the matter has been settled for a long time (e.g., unchanged legislation as to real estate for many decades, if not centuries) and, hence, there are nowadays few disputes that end up in court and/or the judicial decisions are not interesting from a doctrinal point of view and are, therefore, not published; (c) victims of illegal practices don't dare to go to court because of strong social pressure (e.g., in cases of rape); (d) problems and conflicts are (almost) always solved outside the law or outside its institutions; *etc.* In all those cases, lack of sociological inquiries may lead to a completely distorted view on the law in a foreign country. Lawyers generally will have a basic understanding on these points as to their own law, but mostly not, or at least not to the same extent, as to foreign legal systems.

How does one compare?

Comparative law has often been criticized for not following any method when carrying out comparative research. Indeed, comparatists often act like tourists who visit a foreign city and notice that things are different, be it to some extent similar too, compared to their home-town. After their visit they will be able to describe what they have seen to their family and friends at home, but they will lack a more general framework used, for instance, by specialists in architecture or art historians to describe the same sights in a (very) different way. Comparative researchers should become professionals rather than be tourists. However, the theoretical framework historians and architects may dispose of is still largely lacking for comparative law. Whereas legal scholars have been educated with a firm doctrinal framework for their own legal system, they lack such an overarching framework for comparative research.

Sometimes 'comparing' is considered to be a 'method' in its own right and called 'the comparative method' without further explanation or concrete guidelines. The only 'method' proposed in comparative literature, which goes one step further, is the so-called 'functional method'. It offers one concrete guideline in that it suggests to focus on (common) legal problems and legal solutions in the compared legal systems, rather than on the (diverging) rules and doctrinal frameworks. However, some elements for other comparative methods may be found in the literature, mainly in the area of legal theory. On the basis of these writings, we may distinguish six different methods for comparative research : the functional method, the structural method, the analytical method, the law-in-context method, the historical method and the common-core method. Probably they constitute together the whole toolbox for comparative research.

Following Berthelot, Geoffrey Samuel has distinguished six different 'schemes of intelligibility' : causal, functional, structural, hermeneutical, actional and dialectical. They are, according to Berthelot and Samuel, to be identified as separate epistemological readings in that not one of the six can be reduced, in terms of its fundamental logical relations, to one of the others.

Hereafter, we will discuss the functional method and the structural method in the context of comparative research, next to the analytical method, the historical method, the law-in-context method and the common-core method. The latter methods are not mentioned among the six distinct schemes of intelligibility in the context of the social sciences in general, but we may see them as combinations of two or more of them. Causal understanding, for instance, has a pivotal role to play within the law-in-context approach and the historical method. Hermeneutics, in its turn, is vital to all comparative methods.

The different 'methods' discussed hereafter are not mutually exclusive. It is even possible to combine all of them in one and the same research. The name of the method points to the specific feature of that approach, without excluding its combination with another method.

The functional method

Following Zweigert and Kötz and their popular introductory book on comparative law, it is often taught at universities that 'the' method of comparative law is the 'functional method', optimistically supported by the alleged conclusion that rules and concepts may be different, but that most legal systems will eventually solve legal problems in a similar way. Apart from the conclusion that both authors never seem to have elaborated, or even applied, this 'method' themselves, the 'functional method' and its underlying 'praesumptio similitudinis' have increasingly been criticized in recent years.

Ralf Michaels, summarises his critical analysis as follows :

'In short, "the functional method" is a triple misnomer. First, there is not one ("the") functional method, but many. Second, not all allegedly functional methods are "functional" at all. Third, some projects claiming adherence to it do not even follow any recognizable "method"'.

Indeed, 'functionalism' is used in quite diverging meanings, serving rather different goals : understanding law, comparing (*tertium comparationis*), focusing on similarities (*praesumptio similitudinis*), building a system (of 'legal families', for instance), determining the 'better law', unifying law, critical appraisal of the legal orders. This variety of 'functional methods' points to the importance of the research aim and research question for choosing an appropriate comparative method. Basically, what the researcher will compare and how, largely depends on the research question(s) and research interest. The method followed should serve that goal. The idea behind functionalism is to look at the way practical problems of solving conflicts of interest are dealt with in different societies according to different legal systems. This allows us to perceive those problems (largely) independently from the doctrinal framework of each of the compared legal systems. Many societal problems, such as accidents, family problems, theft, murder, quarrels between neighbours, *etc.*, are to be found in most, if not all, societies. All societies have some form of 'law' which helps to solve those problems. Legal concept, legal rules and legal procedures may sometimes rather diverge, but still the solutions given to some problems may be similar or even identical. In other words, the legal solution may be the same, notwithstanding the diverging roads used to reach that solution. The functional method is looking for such 'functional equivalents' at the level of the solutions. If, in view of the research question, such as 'Which solution is given in countries A, B and C to legal problem P?' or 'Which institution in system B performs an equivalent function to the one under survey in system A?' Only the result counts and if this legal solution is the same in the compared countries, then the researcher may conclude that the law is 'the same' in those countries. However, if the focus is on the way in which the legal rules and doctrinal constructions of the respective legal systems solve that legal problem, the functional method is not very relevant. Moreover, in some cases similar or identical rules in two compared legal systems lead to diverging results. This is a kind of functional 'dis-equivalence'. Here, focusing on the rules only would not be very useful.

In the same chapter, Ralf Michaels rightly points to the conclusion that 'at least three main current approaches other than functionalism remain : comparative legal history, the study of legal transplants, and the comparative study of legal cultures'. However, the first one has a strong historical dimension, the latter an anthropological one, and the study of legal transplants a sociological one, as it studies how rules and concepts may (not) work in a different socio-economic environment (apart from a different doctrinal environment). Functionalism, for its part, is often used with the (implicit) assumption that problems are the same everywhere (theft, car accident, failure of executing a contract, *etc.*). This may be true in many cases in countries with a similar historical and socio-economic background (the Western European countries, for instance), but even then not in all cases and certainly not in all countries and legal cultures worldwide. Moreover, different doctrinal structures may 'create' different problems, complicate or facilitate them being solved. Hence, proponents of the functional method try to limit the comparison to 'universal facts', like two cars hitting each other at a crossroad, leaving aside whatever is determined by the local law or legal culture. However, in this way not much may be left for a functional comparison. Indeed, functionalism cannot isolate the solutions to practical problems from their doctrinal legal framework (including procedural rules), and it cannot separate those problems from their socio-economic and historical context.

In its most common understanding, the functional method doesn't compare primarily rules, but solutions to practical problems with conflicting interests. It is true that there are relatively universal human attitudes to certain situations, such as taking care of children, respecting property rights, executing contractual obligations, compensating in one way or another damages caused by one's wrongful conduct, and so on. Hence, practical solutions to similar problems in those areas in different legal systems will often more converge than the legal roads used to reach those results. Canon law, for instance, doesn't encompass divorce. Nowadays, all countries with a Christian tradition offer the possibility of divorce in their legislation. In practice however, the Roman-Catholic Church is quite flexible as to declaring a marriage void, whereas this is much more difficult in the state legal systems. There are still important differences between state laws and canon law, but the practical answers to problematic marriages diverge less than the differences in divorce legislation would suggest. As a result, the functional method helps the researcher to broaden the scope of her research. Indeed, similar results are often reached following different roads, or too harsh consequences of too strict rules are attenuated by other means. By focusing on practical problems and their solutions, one may discover those different legal roads. Actually, law is a way to structure reality. Different cultures may use different ways to structure similar realities, but partly they also create different realities. Hence, the functional method has to be complemented by other methods.

What makes functionalism easier than the other 'methods' listed, is that it requires a less thorough analysis of the broader cultural context, if any, and, hence, is more accessible to the average legal researcher. It reduces the complexity of comparing legal systems in a very attractive way for most researchers

The price paid for it is that the explanatory force of research using the functional method is more reduced and that more creative work can be done, e.g., in comparative legal history, or using the law-in-context method.

The structural method

Functionalism typically applies at the level of micro-comparison. From a broader perspective a more structural analysis of (parts of) legal systems may be used. When discussing this approach in social sciences in general, but presenting it as an alternative to the functional method in comparative law, Geoffrey Samuel notes :

> *'This is a grille de lecture whereby the observer focuses on the structures hidden within the phenomenon being observed. These structures can be loose in the way they interrelate (for example plot structures in literature) or they can be a collection of elements that form a system, this latter notion being characterised by the creative interaction of the elements within a totality that can be identified as having frontiers and thus being independent'.*

When elaborating classifications of 'legal families', a structural approach has been underlying them. Differences between legal systems at the level of concrete rules become irrelevant if they share enough structural commonalities, such as Roman law principles and concepts in private law, to classify them as members of the same 'legal family', as opposed to other legal systems and families which do not share those commonalities. Of course, the selection of the most relevant criteria for determining 'similar structures' partly determines the outcome.

Example : assume one wants to compare land law worldwide and to try to classify them into 'legal families'. The obvious starting point will be to follow the traditional distinction between the 'Anglo-Saxon' and the 'Romano-Germanic' legal families. However, one may prefer to start from the distinction between public or rather private law governing the matter : in the so-called 'socialist' or 'communist' regimes in Eastern Europe during several decades in the twentieth century disposing of means of production (ownership) was a matter of public law, whereas in most other countries it was a matter of private law (mainly ownership or rent). From another point of view, one might consider that a basic distinction is the one where the state owns all the land and citizens have more limited rights than full ownership, even if they may be the proprietor of the house they have built on it. When using this criterion, it would bring together countries such as the United Kingdom ('The Queen owns all land'), the Democratic Republic of Congo (citizens may obtain an 'eternal' concession on the land, companies and foreigners only a concession for 25 years), and the People's Republic of China (the state owns all land, but not necessarily the buildings built on it). Nevertheless the legal systems of those countries wouldn't be considered to belong to one and the same legal family, when looked at from almost any other perspective. However, there is no 'objective' reason why this criterion would be less relevant compared to other criteria.

Everything depends on the underlying theory. If the worldwide dominant paradigm accepts the distinction between the Romano-Germanic family and the Anglo-Saxon family as the most vital one, the criterion of the state ownership of land as opposed to full private ownership may still be useful for the selection of legal systems for some micro-comparison, but it will not be accepted for classifying legal systems worldwide.

Also, the traditional 'legal families' classifications assume that one specific criterion or structure may be considered decisive for classifying the totality of each legal system into one and the same family. However, as all these classifications are based on private law only, it is obvious that a public law classification may lead to quite different results, again depending on the criteria used (kingdom or republic, federal or centralized state, direct elections of the key governing bodies or not, states with or without a constitutional court, degree of respect of human rights, *etc.*). Within private law, one may also argue that it is not possible to make one overall classification, but that a further distinction has to be made (family law, land law, inheritance law, labour law, *etc.*). If this would be accepted, it would throw a different light on our example of the ownership of land. Suddenly, bringing together the UK, Congo and China into one legal 'land law' family, wouldn't only sound reasonable but even quite convincing.

Structural analyses may be made in many different ways, on the basis of a large variety of distinctions and criteria. At the most basic level one could actually argue that all legal systems structurally have a common core, which is linked to the definition of law as an identifiable system in any society. One such basic distinction typical for all legal systems is the presence of (primary) rules of behaviour and, in addition, secondary rules that govern the coming into being and the application of those primary rules. Joseph Raz has argued that, at the level of the secondary rules, there is some minimum content which is common to all legal systems :

> *'The minimum content and the minimum complexity of all legal systems, together with the principles of individuation, determine the necessary internal relations existing in every legal system, that is the internal structure which is necessarily common to all legal systems'.*

As a result, it should be possible to identify those secondary rules in every legal system and compare them as to the competence for law making (who has the power to make law or to change the law?) or for legal adjudication (who has the power to (finally) decide about the application of the law?). Moreover, in developed legal systems, all this has to happen through specific procedures. So, the question as to the procedures for law making and for the adjudication of the law are also relevant for all legal systems. Of course, in more primitive legal systems those functions may be mixed up (e.g., the chief of the tribe being both competent for making law and applying it) and the procedures may be very limited. Hence, the degree of development of such procedures and the degree of separation between law making and the adjudication of the law may offer a comparative criterion for classifying legal systems at the level of their secondary rules.

The analytical method

Well known in the Anglo-Saxon legal world, but less in the rest of the world, is the analysis of the concept of 'right' by the American law professor Wesley Newcomb Hohfeld (Hohfeld 1919). He noticed that the concept of 'right' is used in several different meanings. It may mean a 'claim', a 'power', a 'liberty', or some other legal concepts, which he calls 'immunity' (escaping from someone else's legal power) and 'privilege' (an exception to a more general prohibition). This refinement of the concept of 'right' was an important step forward in analysing the 'deep structure' of the concept of 'right' and in clarifying the actual meaning of this word, as used in several different contexts. Moreover, and most importantly, he studied the logical relation between the different sub-concepts of 'right' and other concepts, such as 'duty' or 'liability'. For example, if one has the right to do A, there can be no duty not to do A. Hohfeld distinguished 'legal opposites' (one cannot have at the same time a right and non-right on the same object, or a privilege and a duty as to the same behaviour) and 'legal correlatives' (when A has a right against B, then B has a correlative duty towards A).

Here, we are mainly interested in the analytical force of such a distinction for comparative law. Many legal concepts, in all legal systems, contain a bundle of 'rights' of a different kind. 'Property', for instance, includes a claim (of non-interference), a liberty (to use) and a power (to transfer the property rights partly or fully). By looking at this deeper level we may better distinguish differences and commonalities between legal systems as to apparently similar or different concepts (*e.g.*, 'ownership' of land v. 'fee simple absolute in possession', 'easement' v. 'servitude', 'mortgage' v. *'hypothhque'*) used in each legal language. A broad concept such as 'trust' in the Anglo-Saxon tradition is unknown in Continental Europe. However, upon a closer look, it appears that, depending on the context, rather similar constructions may sometimes be discovered and clear differences at other times (*e.g.*, the power of the creditor in some cases to seize money directly with a third person, as if it were his property ('imposed trust'), which is impossible on the Continent). Only at the deeper 'Hohfeldian' level, adequate comparison between the 'trust' and continental legal concepts and constructions become possible.

Brouwer and Hage believe that, by using the Hohfeldian analysis, or another of that kind, 'the private law of the different European countries can be reconstructed in terms of a limited set of the same basic concepts'. According to them, such a set of basic concepts should allow for correct representations of the contents of private law and render it comprehensive and non-redundant. Characteristic of a basic concept is, moreover, that it cannot be specified in terms of other, more elementary concepts. For Brouwer and Hage there are only two basic legal concepts in private law : 'duty' and 'competence'.

The above mentioned examples also point to the conclusion that it is not possible to disconnect concepts from the rules of the legal system to which they belong. The content of a legal concept is defined by the actual rules governing the field covered by the concept, within a particular legal system at a specific moment of time. However, sometimes these are minor differences, and some common core may be detected, with concepts such as 'will', 'ownership', 'state', *etc.* For this reason, Eke Frdndberg made a distinction between concepts that are 'system-dependent' and concepts that are (relatively) 'system-independent'. He proposed to work with 'ideal types' of such concepts. According to Hedenius, as noted by Frdndberg, a system-independent definition of 'ownership' contains two elements : 'protection of possession' and 'freedom of disposal'. The 'ideal type' of 'ownership' (in a technical sense, not a normative one) is one with a total protection of possession and an absolute freedom of disposal. All actual concepts of ownership in the different legal systems may be defined on a scale of more or less protection of possession and more or less freedom of disposal. Combined with a Hohfeldian analysis, this approach may probably be refined, but the idea of using 'ideal types' in comparative law should certainly be fruitful.

A thorough analytical approach may, eventually, offer in its turn building blocks for a structural comparison of legal systems.

In 1973, Andri-Jean Arnaud published his *Essai d'analyse structurale du Code civil frangais.* In this book, Arnaud aimed at 'decoding' the *Code Napolion*, at drawing its 'eucledian geometry'. As regards, for instance, the law of obligations, he discerns 'jural opposites', such as voluntary/involuntary, action based on the law (legislation) or on an act (*e.g.*, a contract), a duty to give or to do (including not to do), a duty to give a thing or to give money, equilibrium or not, reciprocity or not, *etc.*. When revealing the deep structure of the (French) law of obligations, he finds a taxonomy with, as a grand total, 32 possible or even imaginable relations. Arnaud concludes that his opposites do not exactly correspond to the 'official' opposites, as used in the Code (for example : synallagmatic/unilateral, aleatory/commutative), but that they offer a conceptual framework which is fundamentally valid for the law of (civil) obligations in any legal system. Whether this is correct has still to be checked, but at least it has the advantage of offering a structure built on the basis of an analytical research in one legal system with, as a working hypothesis, its validity for any legal system. If this were true, even only partially, this might be an important building block for the methodology of comparative law, as it is not just offering concepts, but a whole structure covering a whole field of law, a kind of Table of Mendeleev for the law of obligations.

The most ambitious attempt to determine the 'legal grammar' of legal systems in view of their analytical and structural comparison is to be found in the work of Leopold Pospisil (1971). As an anthropologist of law, he tried to work out a model that could be used for cross-cultural comparison, valid for both primitive societies and developed modern legal systems. Being well aware of the important role of ideology in law, which is most visible in cross-cultural comparison, he emphasizes the need for 'a comparative analysis of basic "jural postulates", derived from the culture and its institutions in general, on the one hand, and legal values, abstracted from the ius as implied in legal decisions, on the other'.

At a second stage, he worked out an analysis in terms of 'legal correlates', which should present the subdivisions of a legal concept or field in a logical, systematic, succinct and complete way. Again, the aim is to get a better understanding, at this deeper level, of the similarities and differences amongst different legal concepts and regulations. Pospisil, for example, has thus structured all different forms of terrain ownership amongst the Kapauku tribe in Papua New Guinea in the 1960s. For this, he used opposites, such as 'owned by an individual' or 'owned by a group', more or less exempt from control by others, limitations or not of rights to trespass. Some of the opposites he described, however, are clearly culture bound, such as the right to gather frogs or hunt 'non rats'. Pospisil called the systematic set of such jural opposites the 'legal grammar' of the analysed systems.

One may doubt whether such a complete model may be worked out for comparing legal systems in quite different cultural contexts, but combined with the methods discussed in this paper it may be useful for understanding very different legal relations and conceptual frameworks in other cultures and for determining the most adequate level for comparing rather different legal systems.

The law-in-context method

All legal scholars will agree that comparative research cannot be limited to pure black-letter comparison of legal rules, concepts or systems. Even domestic legal doctrine will at least take into account the way the law works in practice, as far as it transpires from judicial decisions. On the other hand, law-in-context as a method cannot be isolated from the other methods. They are complementary and interdependent for an adequate understanding of the law. Whereas some forms of the analytical method could be carried out at a more abstract, conceptual level, rather disconnected from the underlying social reality, this is not the case with the other ways of comparison. The functional method refers already by definition to a context : which societal problem is solved with what kind of legal construction? If a society wants its citizens to act responsibly and carefully, so as to avoid to create damages to others, it may use tort law, contract law, statutory obligations, 'subjective' or 'objective' liability, accept 'pure economic loss' or not, *etc.* In different legal systems and situations legislators (or judges) may have chosen diverging means to reach such an end. In order to guarantee the payment of damages they may have introduced compulsory insurance or other ways that should lead to a balanced redistributive justice, as conceived in the world view of (the majority in) that society. Hence, the functional method is at least to some extent including a law-in-context method.

From several examples above, it appears that the structural method and most of the analytical method cannot be carried out without some minimum law-in-context approach, even if in practice it is often more hidden than made explicit.

There is a whole range of possible law-in-context methods of research. One may just point to some generally known context element, such as the liberal economic world view underlying the European Union; one may use data from historical, sociological, anthropological, psychological, *etc.* research, or even carry out such research oneself; one may set up a large interdisciplinary comparative project in which several non-legal disciplines are brought together. Much will depend on the focus of the research and on the available knowledge with the involved researchers, time and financial means when choosing the type and size of the law-in-context approach. In his law-in-context approach, Rodolfo Sacco has been focusing on the 'legal formants', on what has made the law as it is. In this approach it is notably the legal context which seems to be most important : constitutional and legislative rules, case law, and legal doctrine, but also 'implied patterns' and other hidden elements, such as world views, influencing the way law is interpreted and handled. He calls them 'cryptotypes'. 'Some cryptotypes are more specific, others more general. The more general they are, the harder they are to identify. In extreme cases they may form the conceptual framework for the whole system'. This 'conceptual framework', which I have called the 'paradigmatical framework' indeed plays a decisive role in the way law is perceived, interpreted and applied.

Putting law in context aims at *understanding* the law, as a foreigner to that legal system and, hence, explaining why the law is as it is. Inevitably, this implies empirical observation. This may lead to general explanatory propositions, as emphasized by John Henry Merryman, such as 'developed legal systems contain procedures for controlling administrative legality'. These are hypotheses about more universal characteristics of (sets of) legal systems. They should and can be tested against empirical data.

The (different) institutional contexts in the compared countries or societies play an important role in explaining apparent differences in law and legal practice. For instance, Adams, Weyers, and Griffiths showed to what extent the different health care systems influence the legal practice concerning euthanasia (or more exactly, 'medical behaviour that potentially shortens life'). Referring to Koen Raes, Koen Lemmens pointed to the importance of tax law as an explanation for non-pecuniary losses being widely covered in Belgian law.

It should be clear that case law is not always offering a correct picture of the living law in a society. When, for instance, no case law can be found at all in some country, it may mean that the law has become obsolete, that the underlying societal problem has disappeared, but also that earlier problems as to the interpretation of the law have meanwhile been settled, so that cases are no longer brought to court, as everybody (or at least their counsellors) knows perfectly how to apply the law. It may also mean that a parallel ordering is governing the case, rather than the law (mafia for instance). Courts are the hospitals of social ordering. Only 'ill' cases come to court. The healthy ones remain invisible in the records of judicial decisions. For an overall account of legal reality, an analysis of court decisions in comparative research should be complemented by some legal sociological research.

Legal sociology, in turn, cannot cover all aspects of reality and should, as far as needed according to the research questions, be supplemented by law and economics, and/or legal psychology and/or other disciplines. Researchers will always have to find a balance between the ideal research design, on the one hand, and what is feasible under the current circumstances, taking into account the restraints as to time, money and available knowledge, on the other.

The current 'empirical legal research' approach, which has become popular in the US and is slowly gaining ground in Europe as well, is a kind of modest legal sociology, without the ambition of creating grand theories, but just aiming at checking implicit assumptions of the law or the effect and efficiency of legislation. It should be obvious that such empirical testing is not only useful but very desirable or even necessary. In some cases a broader comparative scale, that transcends the borders of one single legal system, may offer more reliable information, compared to purely domestic research.

Empirical investigations in comparative research will be carried out using one or more of the varying methods known in the social sciences. Mainly qualitative methods will be used, but increasingly attempts are made to use quantitative methods in legal research. Here we cannot go into detail on this point.

The historical method

Actually, the historical method is just one part of the 'law-in-context method', the context being here the historical origins of the present-day laws, which are compared. A specific feature of this historical approach is that its use cannot be avoided in any comparative research. Fully understanding the law as it functions today in some society, is only possible when one knows where it comes from and why it is as it is today. It is not accidental that also among legal historians 'comparative legal history' has become quite popular over the last decade or so.

For the comparatist, information and sources on legal history are generally more readily available than for other forms of law-in-context approaches. In traditional legal doctrine, many books will include some historical chapter or at least historical references to the origins of some legal concepts, legal rules, legal construction, *etc.* A historical study will inevitably also use sociological, economic, psychological, and/or other context data. In this way it may encompass, on occasion, a full law-in-context approach.

Historical comparisons may not only explain the origins and reasons for the law as it is today in that society, in some cases they may reveal that similar rules or approaches to law we find in one legal system have been present in another in the past, whereas the current law or views in the latter are different today. Differences may then appear to be just differences in stages of development of legal systems, or differences as to the outcome of ongoing tensions between two opposite views which remain latent in the compared societies, one view taking priority in one society, at least for some time, whereas the other view has become dominant in another legal system (a little like the victories and losses of 'right wing' and 'left wing' political parties in parliamentary elections in the Western world).

Example : In contract interpretation it looks like England, France and Germany are taking rather diverging positions as to what determines the meaning of the contract. In England it is (only) the text of the agreement that counts, in France the subjective will of the contracting parties, and in Germany an 'objectivated' will (what each party could reasonably have understood the intention of the other contracting party was). A historical research, however, reveals that the (French) subjective will theory was dominant in Germany in the second half of nineteenth century and obtained a central position in English law in about the same period, whilst a more objective approach to interpretation became popular among French lawyers by the end of eighteenth century. Actually, each of those approaches to contract law happens to have held a strong position in each of those countries at some time in history. It is mainly a matter of historical coincidence, which 'explains' the differences among the compared legal systems in a more recent past.

The historical method may, thus, as it appears from this example, reveal other similarities and/or differences at a deeper level, compared to what transpires from an analysis at the surface level.

The common-core method

By the end of nineteenth century and early twentieth century, under the influence of the positive sciences, comparative lawyers wanted to find out which legal concepts, legal rules and legal institutions all societies had in common. This ambition was soon reduced to the 'civilized countries' at the 'same level of development', but even that proved to be not very realistic. Hence, not much research results came out.

In the second half of the twentieth century, new initiatives were taken with the aim of finding a common core among legal systems in some area. New was the focus on how the different legal systems were solving cases rather than on their legal rules and concepts. The largest research project was carried out at Cornell University between 1957 and 1967, in the area of the formation of contracts.

In Europe, the creation and development of the European Union together with tendencies to harmonize law within the EU stimulated research into the common core of law in Europe, to be identified within each of the member states. As a kind of follow-up of the Cornell project, the 'Trento Common Core Project' was set up in Italy by Ugo Mattei and Mauro Bussani. It was more ambitious : 'The ambition of the work in which we are engaged here in Trento is a considerable broadening of the scope of the Cornell project. We are seeking the common core of the bulk of European private law, as divided in the general categories of contract, tort and property.'

The 'Ius Commune Casebooks for the Common Law of Europe' were also set up in the nineties, in view of 'uncovering common principles already underlying existing laws' and to 'enable students from across Europe and beyond to study the same leading cases and materials'.

Also in judicial and legislative practice at the European level, some common-core comparative research has been carried out (Pescatore 1980; Van Der Mensbrugghe 2003). So, looking for the common core of many areas of law is done in legal practice (European administration, legislation and court practice), in legal education and in legal scholarship. Of course, looking for a common core also ends up in pointing to differences. Moreover, the increase in member states, most notably after 2004, when it jumped from 15 to 25 states, made it increasingly difficult to encompass all member states in such a research, so that for instance the Ius Commune Casebooks are mainly focusing on the three main legal systems for private law, England, France, and Germany.

The common-core method is largely based on the functional method, to some extent combined with the law-in-context method. What is specific to the common-core method is that one looks for a common core in view of the (possible) harmonization of a certain part of the law. In Europe this is a dynamic process, both top-down through European rules and judicial decisions and bottom-up through legal education and legal scholarship.

The common-core method looks for commonalities and differences between legal systems in view of the question to what extent harmonization on certain points would be possible among the compared legal systems or the question how a European rule, for instance, could be interpreted in such a way that it fits best the different national traditions.

Levels of comparison

'Levels of comparison' may be distinguished in various ways, comparing law from different perspectives. The levels on which the law is made and practised geographically (e.g., international, European, state, sub-state) will as such also influence the possible, or at least most evident, levels of comparison.

Macro and micro level

The most classical one is the distinction between macro and micro level, comparing legal systems as distinguished from comparing more concrete rules and legal solutions to societal problems in different legal systems.

A peculiar case is the comparison of EU law with national laws. As the structure of both types of legal system, and also their underlying objectives, are different, this will influence the methods for comparison.

Renaud Dehousse gave as an example the disintegrative impact of EU law on national insurance policies, caused mainly by the diverging regulatory objectives pursued at each level : market integration for the EU, regulation of the insurance market at the national level. This implies that the functional, structural and analytical method should be carried out at a deeper level, where those mcre fundamental differences between the compared legal systems and regulations are taken into account. Also, the structural interdependence of both legal systems prevents the researcher from comparing them as if they were separate and independent units. 'Cross-level comparisons', argues Dehousse, 'should be explicitly concerned with their interaction, and try to encompass the two levels within one single analysis' and 'the exercise is indispensable : in a complex situation, the analyst cannot simply assume a degree of simplicity that no longer exists'.

Hence, this will often lead to a combination of different methods to be used in such a cross-level comparison. A typical example is the comparison of the EU institutions and decision-making processes with the traditional separation of powers structures in the nation states : parliament, government, courts. In order to understand the differences one will have to analyse the diverging functions of those institutions at both levels (functional method), analysing the different competences of each body in order to draw a full picture of similarities and differences (analytical method) whilst also analysing the whole framework and the relations among the different bodies (structural method) and, finally, putting all this in a historical perspective (historical method).

Underlying general and professional legal cultures (or traditions)

Also, located at a deeper level are comparisons as to legal culture, legal argumentation (Bomhoff 2012), judicial decision making (Lasser 2004), styles of legal writing, diverging approaches to legal sources and to statutory interpretation (*e.g.*, the use of travaux priparatoires), the role of legal doctrine, the respective role of the legal professions (*e.g.*, Van Caenegem 1987), the role of form in law in relation to substance. Such comparative research has a strong theoretical dimension and tries to draw the background against which legal systems are understood and applied by those working in those legal cultures.

The methods used for comparison at this level will mainly be analytical and historical, often revealing hidden world views, which strongly orientate the attitude towards the law. Even if such underlying legal cultures and world views are not part of the positive law as such, they mostly have a decisive influence on the final content of the law as applied in practice.

Law in action v. law in the books

Indeed, law in action may be (quite) different from law in the books. Most lawyers are well aware of this conclusion. That is why a comparison at the level of rules has to be complemented by, or in some cases started with, a comparison of judicial decisions. In some cases, such as very recent legislation or unavailability of other sources in a language one has access to, comparison will be limited to the level of legislation. However, in any substantive research in comparative law, both legislation and case law will have to be studied, as, in all legal systems, common law and civil law alike, they are both of decisive importance for knowing the law. This may show how diverging rules and doctrinal constructions may lead to similar decisions or ~~how~~ similar rules and/or doctrinal constructions may lead to diverging practical solutions. The main reason for this is that, especially in hard cases, judges first see a desirable solution for the case at hand, which, afterwards, they try to construct on the basis of the legal tools available within their legal system.

However, the specific doctrinal constructions of a legal system and/or underlying paradigmatic views may block certain outcomes and facilitate other ones, as appears, for instance, from the example of the interpretation of contracts.

Surface level v. deep level

A more thorough look at superficial similarities and/or differences among legal systems may reveal that adequate comparison has, indeed, to take place at a deeper level of doctrinal construction or paradigmatic framework. Actually, Ernst Rabel considered it to be the aim of comparative law to go to that deeper level in order to get a true understanding of the law.

Example 1 : International private law rules on jurisdiction

Ralf Michaels has shown how not only rules are different in the US and Europe as to deciding which courts have jurisdiction when several countries may be involved, but moreover *'they think differently about how to apply jurisdiction and they even think differently about what jurisdiction is. Americans and Europeans disagree on the answers because they disagree on the relevant questions'*. For example, *'although territoriality and state boundaries are central to both U.S. and European thinking about jurisdiction, they play different roles in each paradigm. In the domestic U.S. paradigm, the role of boundaries is one of delimitation. The power of a court goes to the state's boundaries, not beyond them. It is fair to force a defendant into a court in the state with minimum contacts, but not beyond its boundaries. (...) By contrast, the role of state boundaries in the international European paradigm is one of allocation : the locus of an event or a party defines the place that has jurisdiction in a multilateral fashion'*.

This means that an adequate comparison has to take place at the level of the underlying paradigms and not only at the levels of legislation or case law.

Example 2 : The interpretation of contracts

In France, the *Cour de cassation* has, for more than two centuries, considered the interpretation of contracts a matter of 'fact' not of law and, hence, left this to the lower courts. As a result, it escapes the control of the Cour de cassation, which only controls the correct application of the law, not the reality of facts. However, in order to be able to control such interpretations this court worked out a theory of 'dinaturation de l'acte', which assumes that texts may have a 'clear meaning' on their own, so that any 'diverging' interpretation would be incompatible with the 'real meaning' of this text. If judges depart from this 'obvious meaning' the Cour de cassation will quash the decision. French doctrinal legal writing concentrates on this problem rather than on the interpretation methods and reasoning by lower courts outside the realm of an alleged 'dinaturation de l'acte'. No other legal system seems to have a comparable approach, due to the lack of 'cassation' and full reconsideration of the case or to different theories (there is no 'denaturation' theory in any of the other countries where the Napoleonic code was introduced).

In Germany, discussions are focusing on the, rather diverging, articles in the civil code on the interpretation of contracts and of the 'declaration of will' for any legal act.

In England, the interpretation of contracts is not a subject in its own right, but is discussed in other contexts such as the question on whether there was 'consideration'. However, the concept of 'consideration' is unknown in civil-law countries and typically linked to the common-law (business) conception of 'contract'.

This means that any comparison at the surface level of legislation, case law and legal doctrine is virtually impossible or meaningless. Comparison will have to be carried out at a deeper (paradigmatic) level of underlying views and theories on meaning and on interpretation.

When comparing the law in radically different legal cultures, it is obvious that meaningful comparison will only be possible at the deeper level of the underlying cultures and not at the surface level of rules and concepts. Here, surface level comparative law inevitably turns into deep level comparative law and becomes mainly legal anthropology.

Doctrinal framework v. underlying legal culture—Three basic conceptual frameworks in the world

In private law, three conceptual legal frameworks have been very influential worldwide : the common law, the French *Code civil* and the German *Bürgerliches Gesetzbuch.* Virtually all legal systems of nation states use one of them or a combination of two or more of them.

Through colonization, the English common law was spread over North America, Australia and New-Zealand, parts of Africa and Asia. In Europe, its influence has been limited to Wales, Ireland and, to a lesser extent, Scotland. After independence, the legal systems of the Latin American states were largely based on Roman law and French civil law. As from the twentieth century, this continent has seen a growing influence of the common law. *'The result of this is a mosaic of highly diverse legal systems which, even if located in the circle of the "civil law" family, show a special coloration with its own and particular characteristics'.*

It has not led to conceptually rebuilding the legal framework of civil law in the Latin American countries, but to transplanting practical legal solutions from other legal traditions wherever it seemed useful.

In Africa, the former French, Belgian and Portuguese colonies largely inherited the Code Napolion. Only South Africa takes a special position with its inheritance of Roman-Dutch law, combined with common law.

In the Islamic countries, parts of the civil law principles are derived from the Quran, but otherwise, former colonizers have been influential, such as France in the Maghreb countries. Other countries, such as Turkey, largely imported a European Code (the German BGB in this case).

In Russia, after 1991, legal doctrine had to a large extent to make a new start, within a new paradigmatic framework. The need for rapid legislative changes made the Russian draftsmen look for inspiration in the Western European Codes (Reid 1998, p. 43). Before the Russian revolution, until the mid-nineteenth century, most law professors were German, the language of education being Latin or German. The legal doctrine, which developed during the nineteenth and early twentieth century had been eradicated by the 1917 communist Revolution. Until the early nineties of the twentieth century, the civil law was first completely dominated by communist ideology and, later on, increasingly tried to combine these ideological premises with some degree of meeting the needs of social reality. This has led to an incoherent legal doctrine. Moreover, parts of the traditional civilian matters, such as granting a flat or eviction of a flat (by the public authorities) were governed by administrative law, hence limiting the scope of civil law.

As for East Asia, *'the modern legal systems of Japan, Korea and China were once all shaped by the reception of Western legal models, albeit to varying degrees and in a variety of ways'*.

These Western legal models were mainly German. The first Chinese Civil Code was enacted under the Qin Dynasty, in 1911. It was drafted by Japanese experts, who took over the German Civil Code. Recent codes on Contract Law (1999), Property Law (2007) and the Law of Obligations (2009) were all mainly influenced by German law, with some elements of the common law. The common law has spread over parts of Asia too, most importantly in India. Central and Eastern European countries took up the Roman law tradition again, after a few decades of communism in the second half of twentieth century. Moreover, in the 1990s, in their desire to join the European Union, they were keen to adopt, as much as possible, Western European law for modernizing their own private law.

The Nordic countries in Europe never took over French, German or English law, but their doctrinal framework has largely been influenced by German legal scholarship.

In Europe today, all legal systems are mixed ones. The Netherlands, for instance, started with the *Code Napolion* in 1804 and basically kept it in 1838, when enacting their *Burgerlijk Wetboek*. Later on, German legal doctrine has been more influential than in the other countries that followed the *Code civil tradition*. This resulted in a new *Burgerlijk Wetboek* in force as from 1992 (most parts having been finished many years before). In the course of the last few decades there is, in The Netherlands, a notable influence of Anglo-Saxon doctrine, both English and American.

Through EU law, but also European Human Rights law, concepts from French and German legal doctrine have entered the other legal systems, such as the (continental) good faith principle in the UK and Ireland, or the (German) proportionality principle in the other member states. Of course, this doesn't necessarily imply a similar use or interpretation of these principles in the countries to which they travel.

With varying application according to the local legal culture

Conceptual frameworks are one thing, the content of the law (values, principles, rules) and the attitude towards the law are another.

Of course, concepts cannot be completely isolated from rules or from their underlying principles. Property, marriage, leasing, contract, servitude or easement, have some common core of meaning all over the world, even if differences may be sometimes quite important (e.g., acceptance or not of homosexual marriage or of polygamous marriage). However, the larger cultural framework may give a quite different content, for instance, to a rule in Congo, which had been literally copied from the Belgian Civil code (e.g., rejecting monogamy). Japanese civil law is not German, notwithstanding the use of German doctrine, as informal rules still play an important role when it comes to (not) applying the law.

Also, within the same legal system, old traditions may make new law to be interpreted in such a way that it blocks all change.

This deeper level of the underlying cultural differences is of utmost importance for correctly judging similarities and differences at the surface level, most notably, but not exclusively, when legal systems from states belonging to rather different cultural traditions are compared.

Tertium comparationis

In order to compare, it has been emphasized, we need a *tertium comparationis*. We should not look at a foreign legal system with the eyes and doctrinal framework of our own legal system, but try to transcend it, by using external 'neutral' elements for comparing legal systems : 'the comparatist must eradicate the preconceptions of his native legal system'. Indeed, describing law is not an 'objective' activity, it doesn't offer 'pure facts' everybody would see in the same way, like a flower as compared to a tree, or a dog as compared to a cat. Looking at concepts, rules, institutions, and the like in other societies will, at least at a first stage, always happen at the background of one's own legal system and doctrinal framework. What comparatists mainly wanted to emphasize with the *tertium comparationis* is the need to be aware of this bias and to try to get out of one's own conceptual framework. What this *'tertium comparationis'* could be and how to find it, remains less clear. Should one compare apples with oranges by reference to banana's, or to pears and lemons? Or to an abstract concept of 'fruit'? What could be the *tertium comparationis* when comparing the repudiation of a wife in Islamic law with divorce in Western law?

Actually, what has initially been a well-founded warning against biases in comparative research has, erroneously, been perceived as part of comparative method. There is no reason why comparative research should be limited to legal phenomena with common characteristics or to legal systems 'at the same stage of development', as Esin Örücü has rightly claimed. As comparative law has largely developed with the aim of improving one's own legal system, it is understandable that this kind of research required some level of comparability in order to be useful. However, comparative research carried out with other aims, such as understanding quite different legal cultures, cannot and should not use such conditions.

Nils Jansen analysed the concepts and methods of comparison in historical linguistics and comparative religion and concluded, as for the latter :

> *'Thus, tertia comparationis cannot be defined as part of the method; comparison must remain open for new insights. Nevertheless, as a result of successful comparisons, the discipline has—perhaps unconsciously—developed a comparative second-order language describing the concepts that constitute the different religions' beliefs. It has become highly useful for analysing the complex commonalities and differences of religion; all in all it represents a large body of comparative knowledge'.*

Above, when discussing the methods of comparative legal research, we have seen how, in most cases, comparatists focusing on methodology have tried to develop such a, relatively neutral, second-order language describing the concepts that constitute the different legal systems, even if in applied comparative research mostly first-order languages are used. Instead of looking for tertia comparationis, legal comparatists should, indeed, through their research, develop such a comparative second-order language. Actually, what is presented as tertium comparationis is sometimes in fact such a second-order language. It is true that legal systems can only be correctly understood in their own language, from their own internal perspective, but in order for comparative law to develop as a discipline some kind of second-order language(s) will have to be worked out. Only in case of harmonization of law a new common (first-order) legal language has to be developed.

The comparatist disposes of a pluralist toolbox containing the following methodological opportunities :

- The functional method is looking at the actual societal problem (e.g., a train accident) and the way this is solved in different jurisdictions (most notably compensating the victims for their damage) along similar or different roads (e.g., contract liability or tort liability) and with similar or different results (e.g., compensation or not for pure economic loss). The focus is on the societal problem and the actual result of the legal approach to that problem.
- The analytical method is analysing (complex) legal concepts and

rules (*e.g.*, ownership) in different legal systems in such a way that common parts and differences are detected (claims, liberties, competences, *etc.*). The use of 'ideal types' makes it possible to rank those legal concepts, rules, institutions, on a scale according to the degree of fitting with the core characteristics of the 'ideal type'.

- The structural method is focusing on the framework of the law or of the elements reconstructed through an analytical approach. This is not the structure of each of the compared legal systems, but just one way of looking at them, which proves to be revealing for answering the research question.
- The historical method will almost always be a necessary part of the methods used, for understanding differences and commonalities among legal systems and for determining their degree of belonging to a deeply rooted tradition or rather to accidental historical events.
- The law-in-context method has inevitably also a historical dimension but focuses on the law's current societal context, including, where appropriate, culture, economy, psychology, religion, *etc.* It studies a much broader context when compared to the functional or analytical method and implies the use of (results from) other disciplines.

Most of those methods will make the researcher move from a surface level of comparison to a deeper level : diverging types of 'right' included in complex legal concepts, rules and institutions, underlying world views, a detected common structural framework behind apparent differences, elements in history that are weakening the strength of seemingly opposed and irreconcilable approaches, *etc.*

One may also distinguish other levels of comparison, each of them implying the use of some method(s) rather than other ones.

A first distinction is the one between micro and macro comparison : studying concrete legal problems or concrete legal concepts, rules or institutions, as compared to a broader approach as to, for instance, the overall organization of the state, or the organization of social security. A second distinction is the one between comparing the content of the law versus comparing doctrinal frameworks relatively independently from that content (a more 'technical' comparison).

It has to be repeated : the choice of method or level for comparison will mainly depend on the research question(s) guiding the research project.

Different aims often imply different methods, be it not always. For instance, the different aims mentioned above, in section 1, of improving domestic law in France by the end of the nineteenth century when compared to harmonization initiatives in the EU by the end of the twentieth century, basically have led to the use of similar methods. In both cases, legal scholars have been looking for the 'better solution'. According to Lambert, scholarly research should be able to prove the superiority of some legislation over others and should, hence, be chosen as *'droit commun ligislatif.'* Today the better solution approach is, explicitly or implicitly, underlying many comparative law research projects. This is most notably the case when economic analysis of law is used within a comparative law context.

Are the methods listed above the only possible ones? For instance, what about legal transplants? Legal transplants are rather an aim or a result, not a comparative method in its own right.43 Successful legal transplants will require a law-in-context method. What seems to work well in another legal system may indeed fail to do so in one's own legal system because of a different context. The import of European family law in most African countries during colonization times, and kept after that, is a clear example of failed transplants because of a quite different cultural context. Hence, just copying foreign law could hardly be considered to be a 'method'. It is rather the typical example of lack of method in comparative law.

What about social-sciences methodology? A law-in-context approach may require the use of at least some methods of the used social sciences (historical, economic, political, sociological, anthropological,...) unless the relevant information is already available in published research results. The social-science methods will then be an instrument within the context of one of the chosen comparative methods. Even at the level of the sheer description of foreign law one may, for instance, want to get a full and correct view of the law as it works in practice by taking interviews of relevant stakeholders and not limit oneself to consulting legislation, published case law and legal doctrine (or in case one doesn't master sufficiently the local language). However, it still will remain part of a description of foreign law, which in turn will be part of some of the mentioned methods within the context of scholarly comparative legal research.

Social purpose mission of law

Law is still predominantly considered to be bread and butter subject. The contribution of law and lawyers in freedom movement changed this deep rooted feeling of common man about legal profession. It is only comparative studies that have compelled the lawyer community to move beyond court work. Legal aid and advice has been taken as a challenge. The law college are out to do their duties to society by organising legal aid camps and legal literacy extension programs. The lawyers out of court are contributing their might in this mission. Lawyers in court are giving legal aid to needy and poor. Public interest litigations are coming up to superior courts consequence to awakening of lawyer to do their job as part of their duty to society. This change is cent per cent to their knowledge obtained by comparative studies.

Whether it is Cinderella of legal science?

Comparative law has been so described. Cinderella was a heroin of a fairy tale, who when left at home in the kitchen by her step mother an step sister was sent by her fairy god-mother to the court hall, on the understanding that at midnight her fancy dress would change back into rags, her coach into pumpkin and attendants into rats and mice; She would thus remain a person of unrecognised merit or beauty. Is comparative law so? Has its merit remained unrecognised? Some of the jurists give this title to the method of comparative study because it was not known as separate branch few decades ago. At that time, the use of the process was confined only to the task of preparing a general scheme for the preparation of code but recently its use is quite obvious in processes of law reform and law making; In field of law of International Trade, in fields of Public and Private International law *etc.*, its value and potentials are now well recognised. To give a title of Cinderella of legal sciences' to this method of study is not a gentleman's treatment to the subject. In fact, this tile shows that comparison is new to the field of law whereas such a conclusion is denied by the facts. It is human nature to compare one thing with the other, if there is any. The fast increasing intimacy and means of communication and transport have thrown the mass at such a critical juncture where either conflict is possible or mutual give and take is desirable. Both of these tend to give new life and re-orientation to the systems compromising. Cinderalla remained unacknowledged because her step-mother and step-sisters neglected and tortured, whereas comparative approach remained lagging behind because the need thereof presupposes a minimum standard of growth of the legal systems. Till they are below that minimum, the comparative study has very little use for them. Once they come upto the mark, the comparative study thereof starts as usual. The norm is that the system must be in a position to be called as 'civilised one'. The potentials of comparative study have always been recognised though the extent of the emphasis has frequently been changing. Comparative law has just gained a foothold in the domain of law but even today its position is by no means secure and such studies are carried on in an atmosphere of hostility or at best in a chilly environment of indifference.

The scope of comparative law is undefined. Any two things: rules, doctrines, concepts, principles, Constitution, Governments, Legislatures, Judiciary, Executives may be taken and compared. They may be similar or dissimilar but comparison is always possible. After all, it is only face to face study or comparison of the two that will ultimately give a verdict whether they are similar or dissimilar. No such conclusion is possible without making comparative studies of the two. So it is rather very difficult to say as to what is studied in comparative law.

Really speaking, the subject matter of comparative law is two or more legal systems or parts, branches or aspects of two or more legal systems. In other words, subject matter may be divided into—macro comparison and micro-comparison. The former is concerned with two or more entire legal systems, whereas the latter is limited to aspects or topics of two or more legal systems.

The Comparative method of study requires selection

'What to Compare' is the first problem in this method of comparative study. The comparison always bases itself on selection. It is selection which prescribes the scope of the comparative study. The inquisitive researcher may adopt self-imposed restrictions or limitations. He may choose that the Common law and civil law systems are to be studied comparatively (because these are broad sub-divisions of the legal world). But this will not help the researcher, because he was, before it, sailing in unchartered vessel thrown in open sea. He tried to delimit the area of study but again further delimitation is necessary. He will have to make further narrower selection whether he will make Comparative Study of penal law, legal history, commercial law, or he will confine his research to the comparative investigation of the juristic concepts like precedents, interpretation, custom *etc.*, or he will select the hierarchy of the courts for comparative survey or anything else that he may like. But this selection must be narrow. In fact, his research is bound to be of greatest utility if it is narrowest in area. Nobody can make a comparative survey of Indian law and French law. This will take many centuries and even then may not yield the desired fruit. Therefore, the prime quality of the comparative surveyor is that he succeeds in narrowing down the scope of his research. It is very useful that the terms like "comparative jurisprudence' and "comparative legislation" may be used as substitutes to comparative law as their use is entirely with merit. For example, in Oxford, there is a post of professor in Historical and comparative Jurisprudence. In France and England 'Societies of comparative legislation' are well known societies engaged in promotion of comparative studies. The method of study is 'comparison'. The material for the comparison is 'law' and the literature so produced after comparison is 'comparative jurisprudence.'

What law means with reference to this method

Does it mean body of rules? The nature of the enquiry as is normally undertaken is such that rules are seldom involved. It deals with body of rules at no stage. The method neither lays down any rule nor formulate any set of rules for anybody's guidance. In fact, no such result is ever aimed at before, during or even after comparison. In this 'Law' therefore, does not mean body of rules. The rules are method raw material for studies; as any other concept may be. Purpose is not knowledge of rules.

No Separate Comparative branch of Law

We hear of 'Family law', 'Mercantile law', 'Maritime law', and 'Commercial law'. Each signifies as a branch of law which deals with a particular subject matter. There is nothing like this in Comparative law. Comparative law of marriage, for example, does not mean that the Comparative lawyer has developed a new set of rules governing the relationship of husband and wife. It only means that marriage laws drawn from two or more municipal laws have been compared with a view to ascertain as to how far and in what respects do these differ or are similar to each other. How can shortcomings of one be removed by the experience of the other?

German equivalent more specific.—English law uses the term Comparative law. Its equivalent term in German law is Rechtsvergliechung. It means only a process of comparison. The nature of the subject is better described by the German equivalent.

Comparative legislation; can these be substituted for the term Comparative law?—In order to obviate the confusion arising out of the use of the term 'law' in this method comparative jurisprudence and comparative legislation are used. The main idea behind comparative jurisprudence is to emphasise the role as an aid to historical or analytical jurists in tracing out the origin and development of concepts common to all the systems of law. As regards the term comparative legislation, the main idea behind it is to lay emphasis on the practical use of the legal research. The comparison is the process of the study. It is a method of the study and research. The material for the comparison is drawn from two sources; may be from one and same system of law or from two different or many different systems of law. The process of study and analysis is comparison. The result arrived at in consequence thereof is or does not belong to either.

Comparative study feeding on others.—The **comparative method of study feeds itself on others.** It has no pedestal of its own; it has no specific field of operation for it. Its purpose is not to solve any specific issue in any legal proceeding. It provides an incentive for collection of raw material for legal research and helps in the establishment of uniform legal thought in all the countries around the world. The lawyer of one country may be benefited by achievements and failures, experiences and conclusions reached on specific matters in sister systems in like problems. He may adopt the kernel and reject the chaff thereof. This is done by the process of adaptation, analysis, thesis, antithesis and synthesis. This mode is called comparison and the science that deals with nature of this process is known as comparative law. The resort to provisions of foreign law is not for copying or imitation. It is usually seen that lawyers in higher courts (High Court and Supreme Court) frequently cite English, American, Canadian, Australian case laws and references from legal writings and treatises in support of their arguments. The reports of the Supreme Court have abundant examples of this practice. The higher courts may accept these elaborations or may accept them with modifications and reservations or may even reject them altogether when it has solid arguments otherwise. This is all that is permitted and studied by comparative method.

If we do not indulge in logomachies, and avoid tautological expression, comparative law, in the most simple and ordinary sense of the term, denotes a method of study and research by which rules and institutions of different systems of law are compared. In other words, it concerns with the examination of the contents of various legal systems in their application to different legal problems.

The comparative law is as old as law itself. It has always been in existence throughout in one form or the other in all the legal world. All legal education and attempts of jurists started with comparative method and ended with the same method. There is not any statute passed by any competent legislature in the name of comparative law. The meaning of the term, 'comparative law,' has been explained by many distinguished lawyers and jurists. Prof. Wigmore has pointed out, "It is a convenient but a loose term."[1] According to him, it serves to embrace all those studies which, characteristically do not confine their attention to domestic law.

Does comparison mean a cut paste and scissors affair?—Comparative method always aims at a fruitful comparison. Comparison of legal precepts is definitely so important but besides, the discipline insists on a comparison of systems. The task of a comparative lawyer is quite different from that of Robinhood or Lord Bramwell's pick-pocket.[2] It avoids empty logics and over-concern with particular methodology. The task of a comparative lawyer is formulation of fruitful philosophy of law or practical theory.

Is a comparative lawyer a comparative physiologist or comparative anatomist?—To be fair, the task of the comparative lawyer is nearer to the former rather than the latter. True comparison must take into account the physiognomy of the legal systems to which the study extends. If comparison is restricted to legal phenomenon alone, the approach is unscientific and results would be less convincing. A legal system is a unity the whole of which expresses itself in each part; the same blood runs in the whole organism. Hence each part must be read in relation to whole of moral, economic, religious and many other factors; as such all these should be taken into account by the comparative lawyer and must be weighed in process of comparison.

Comparative method feeds the intellectual hunger

The intelligentia group always wants to know something more. It leads to research. New things may be invented by the original thinkers. But their task becomes easy when they have knowledge of all around. Who are working in the same or similar fields? What have been their findings and conclusions? How much newness are they bound to give to their work? All this is possible only when he maintains a close touch and makes frank observation of all these. This is comparison. It keeps him busy throughout his life with his researches. Something achieved, more still to be achieved. This is what the comparison leads to the guiding factor is not 'what', but it is 'why'. Why are the jurisprudence of the two divergent, and what are the reasons for the divergence?

Whether comparative method is professional tool or academic toy?—'No'. It is none of the two. It has a higher purpose. The purpose is to provide an insight into social purpose of law. It is to evolve a better science of law. Its view is that without comparison, legal science cannot be more than empirical craft or provincial casuistry. The comparison is, therefore, central to study of law.

Purely descriptive observation is not in the province of comparative law.—Descriptive material might be indispensable as the tool for research in comparative law but it by itself, cannot be called comparative

1. Journal of the Society of Public Teachers of law 6 (1926).
2. The story goes that the pick-pocket went to a charity sermon. He was so moved by the preacher's eloquence that he picked the pockets of everyone in reach and put the contents in the plate.

law.[1] For example: An Indian author may write a book, essay or describe the Family law or court structures in Pakistan, Russia or China and the authors of these countries may describe about the system in India. But it will not be a work on the comparative law. For example, Derret's Modern Hindu Law, Maine's Hindu Law and Usage, Halhad's Gentoo Code are the works by foreign authors on Indian law. They are purely descriptive in nature. They are not works on comparative law, though comparative lawyer may base his analysis entirely on them.

Literary treatments are not within the province.—The monographic or synoptic observations may do much in promotion of mutual understanding and goodwill. The persons doing similar works on the country's art, poetry, philosophy or pottery do the same service in promotion of goodwill and trust. But these are not in province of comparative law.

Comparative study in traditional fields.—Comparative study in traditional fields like public law, labour law, property law, succession, administrative law, law of obligations, in money and banking can be of much use.

Questions underlying entire legal order and comparative method.—Questions are: How specific or universal is the western idea of law; what premises are basic to the western thinking about the manner in which the disputes are resolved. How universally are these premises shared. Likewise, how far are Indian ways of settlement of dispute relevant to western ways. How far are rules of interpretation given in mimama relevant in interpreting legislature enactments. What relevance can one see in the application of these rules to vedic texts and to texts of the modern enactments.

Comparative method and non-legal matters.—Comparative method is not confined strictly to legal matters. Such method can be of much use to studies of control of community designs, regulation of land use, the provisions of public services, securing improvements and developments, policing, quality standards, in construction and maintenance, price control and consumer benefits. Comparative study can yield good results in these areas.

Scientific treatment of law is within province.—The term comparative law should be reserved to demonstrate those kinds of scientific treatments of law which go beyond taxonomic or analytical description of technical application of one or more systems of positive law.

It helps all the systems of law

There can be no branch of legal science which may not take the substantial help of comparative law. Comparative law has always helped the other systems of law, knowingly or unknowingly. It is very difficult for any branch to arrive at a definite and universal conclusion without taking into consideration the method of comparative law. Comparative law is the process of comparison.

---

1. See *Surpa* pp. 9-12 Chapter 1.

It is process of comparing rules of law

In fact the province of comparative method is much more wider than the other branches of law in the legal field. Undoubtedly the province is the process of comparing rules of law taken from different legal systems. It does not result in formulation of any independent rule for the regulation of human relationship or transactions. The comparison may start with rules but does not end with rules. It is so because rules are law. But these alone are not law. Law goes forward after including rules within its fold. Rules may form the subject of comparison. Along with these or quite independent to these, something else may equally form the subject of comparison. There is no branch or independent department of comparative law as such.

The province of comparative method is not clear and is very strange. How strange it is, becomes manifest, when attempts are made to define it or when attempt is made to ascertain its relations with other forms of learning. Much of the doubt will disappear if this fact be consistently recognised that the phrase 'comparative law' denotes a method of study and research and it is not a distinct branch or department of law. If, by law, the body of rules is implied, the comparative law can have nothing like rules of its own. Comparative method can be used for creating better laws and lawyers and promotion of understanding between nations so as to reduce world tensions.

Scope and Province of Comparative Study.—It may be easy to explain comparative law but it is a bit difficult to define the term in the sense we define other laws like civil law, personal law, public law or private law. The reason is that since the subject matter is non-existent, it defies definitions. We have employed the phrase to describe a process or a method by which two or more legal system or parts thereof are compared with some definite aim. The area of the comparison may extend from comparison of the doctrines, customs, practices, structures, systems, and rules to any other field of choice. The area of investigation is limitless, because it is king without kingdom.

No one can say what can be compared or what cannot be compared. Any two things are chosen. Similarities are searched. Dissimilarities are seen. Causes are seen. Effect is realised. A possibility is worked out to get experience and make use of it for something new or newer to establish. The exercise should have some purpose.

Apart from the practical and theoretical difficulties, certain useful efforts have been made by the jurists and lawyers since middle ages to define the comparative law but they have not arrived at any positive conclusion so far. Some of these definitions are as follows:

Early narrow view

Vacabulaire Juridique.—"Comparative law is a branch of legal science, whose object is to bring about systematically the establishment of closer relations between the legal institutions of the different countries."

Holland.[1]—To Holland, comparative philology collects and tabulates similarities and differences in growth of different languages which ultimately become the foundation of abstract grammar. So is the function of comparative law. "Comparative law collects and tabulates the legal institutions of various countries and from the results thus prepared, an abstract science of jurisprudence is enabled to set forth an orderly view of the ideas and methods which have been variously realised in actual systems."

Holland's statement regarding function of comparative law is shared by Allen.

Allen.[2]—Comparative jurisprudence is identified with the study of racial origins and early social institutions as an aid to analytical jurisprudence. His views were similar to the ones expressed by Holland.

Science of Legislation

Maine's[3] attitude was different from Holland. He describes—"the chief function of comparative jurisprudence is to facilitate legislation and the practical improvement of law."

These definitions give a very restricted view of the discipline. These do not in fact, deal with the nature of comparative law but only with its objects. Every author has concentrated on specified function which according to him characterises, the employment of the process of comparison. These definitions regard the comparative research as of little importance except as one tending to help to establish uniformity of law is wide scale. These early comparative lawyers either identified comparative law with comparative legal history or treated it as ancillary to analytical jurisprudence.

Wider view

The comparative law gradually got gradual recognition either as a branch of Analytical Jurisprudence or Legal History, but in the process it established its many-sided character. This compelled its areas to broaden and it gave good-bye to restricted views as to its nature.

Bryce.—Bryce wrote for the first time in 1901. He realised the difficulty of giving a suitable definition to this discipline and therefore, he adopted a new way to encounter the problem. He recognised this subject in its two broad aspects—scientific and practical. To the former, he gave the title of the comparative science of jurisprudence which deals with the "Historical study of law in general." The latter sets out to know the rules actually in force in modern civilised countries and how do these solve the actual problems in these countries. What is the difference in rules of the countries selected and what difference remains when these are pressed into service to solve actual problems Rules and actual solutions of one civilised country is compared with those of others selected or proposed to be studied.

Comparative jurisprudence is the study of the resemblances and

1. Jurisprudence (9th ed.) at p. 8.
2. Law in the making, 3rd ed. pp. 21-22.
3. Village communities, (3rd ed.) at p. 3.

differences between different legal systems. It is not a separate branch of jurisprudence". Salmond said further that comparative law serves its purpose when one compares, for example, English law with Roman law, either for purposes of analytical jurisprudence, so that the conceptions and principles thereof may more comprehensively be examined in one with the help of the other, likewise, for purpose of historical jurisprudence, it is utilised for better understanding of the course of development of each country, and, for ethical jurisprudence, the comparative study helps to judge in better way all the practical merits and demerits of each of them.

But these definitions do not give the full meaning of comparative law. The reasons are as follows:—

(i) Process of Law.—Comparative law is not a law, in the real sense, but it is *process in the study of law.*

(ii) Growing affair.—The process of the study of law is never static, it is always a *growing state of affairs.*

(iii) No demarcation.—*No serious efforts have been made to demarcate* comparative law with other existing laws of the land.

Aforesaid legal definitions are notoriously unsatisfactory. The controversies regarding these are often barren of results. These complicate the problems rather than solving them. There is nothing like comparative law. Since it may be everything except law. As law, the subject is non-existent and therefore it is one which defies any definition.

Divisions of Comparative method.—Modern jurists seem to have readily realised the difficulty in giving definition and its barrenness both with the result, present day writers sub-divide the subject before defining it. It serves the purpose, succeeds in giving a broad picture of the discipline and saves the readers from the fruitless labours and barren controversies. The comparative law is divided into following by many jurists as given below. The division makes the scope wider and facilitates in giving it concrete definition—

To Wigmore Comparative method means *Comparative nomoscopy* that is the description of other systems of law. It may be—

(a) *comparative nomothetics.*—It is an assessment of the relative merits of the rules under comparison;

(b) *comparative nomogenetics.*—It deals with the study of the development of the systems of law in relation to one another.

Rabel divides comparative law into (a) ethnological jurisprudence; (b) historical comparison; (c) systematic—dogmatic comparative law.

(iii) Bryce.—He divides:—

(a) *the comparative science of jurisprudence.*—It concerns with purely scientific aspect of the subject from its more practical side;

(b) *practical aim of comparison.*—This aspect, as printed out by Bryce, has the practical aim of ascertaining and examining the rules actually in force in modern civilised countries with a view to project the similarities.

Kaden distinguished formal comparison from dogmatic comparison.

Formal comparison means, the comparative investigation of the sources of law *i.e.*, statutes, cases, and custom. What weight do these get is studied as formal comparison. Dogmatic comparison is concerned with the various solutions which have been found for the same legal problem in different systems of law.

Lambert classifies the subject into (i) comparative legal history; (ii) comparative legislation; (iii) descriptive comparative law.

To Lambert, comparative law had two purposes—purely cenotaphic *i.e.*, comparative legal history. In it those various causes extending to both time and space are studied comparatively which underlie the origin, development and extinction of legal institutions. The second is purely practical *i.e.* comparative legislation. It is not a science but a form of legal technique. Its purpose is to create an international common law.

To Gutteridge, the essential problem is not what is comparative law. The problem is what is its purpose? So he divides and then defines the comparative law. He makes a broad distinction between descriptive comparative law and applied comparative law.

What is descriptive comparative law? It is a process pressed into service to collect information. It is of no concern to an investigator as to what use will be made of the result of his investigations. It is rather sometimes employed loosely to embrace any enquiry into foreign law but it is unfortunate extension because enquiry into lone foreign legal system can seldom qualify as a comparative one. Mere compilation of parallel or tabular statements relating to several legal systems is not within descriptive comparative law.

However, if any statement dwells upon the divergences between two legal systems, it would come within descriptive comparative law irrespective of its merit and character. A typical example of descriptive comparative literature is enquiry undertaken by League of Nations into civil status of women in 1937. The committee was to collect data from different legal systems. It was not to formulate any project of law reform or to comment upon efficiencies or deficiencies calling for urgent amendment in law of any country.

Applied comparative law.—Comparison with any definite aim other than collection of data or information as to foreign law would very well come within the province of applied comparative law. The aim may be purely scientific, practical, abstract or utilitarian. It may be to enable legal philosophers to construct abstract theories of law, to assist historians in tracing origin and evolution of legal concepts and institutions. But the most popular use of this discipline is practical such as to prepare a brief for law reform and unification of divergent laws. The applied comparative law does not require mere description of the differences which exist between the concepts, rules, or institutions of laws under examination.

Function of applied comparative lawyer

An applied comparative work must aim to discover the following three:—

(a) To ascertain as to how far these differences are fundamental and how far merely accidental.

(b) To find out those various causes which are responsible for these differences and how far these differences are related to the general structures of the system in which they arise.

(c) He must examine the operation of the rules in practice having regard to the legal and social environment in which each of the systems is called upon to function.

This classification serves a purpose. It distinguishes purely descriptive side of comparative law from its utilitarian side. Nomoscopy (Wigmore), Descriptive (Gutteridge), Synoptic (Rheinstein) come under the former whereas Nomothetics, applied and functional comparisons come under the latter. This latter could be either jurisprudence in purpose or practical.

Foreign law in comparison with local law.—Comparative law is not concerned with the study of foreign laws as they are, nor it has anything to do, regarding the compilation of any factual information regarding a foreign legal system. It only provides a method of study of foreign law in comparison with local laws.

The task of comparative lawyer does not consist in giving information alone about different legal systems. But his object should be to have insight into their practice, procedure, the structure of government and judiciary and substance so that he may give his own version of the processes of growth, development and habits of thought. The task of comparative lawyer is one of comparative physiologist rather than that of a comparative anatomist.

Comparative method—whether science or method of study

Comparative law is regarded by some writers as a branch of legal science and, therefore, it has been included in the study of jurisprudence. It is said to be a systematized study of different legal systems in comparative way, to ascertain the likenesses and distinctions and to analyse objectively the solutions which various systems offer for any legal problems. Further, comparative law is also associated with comparative jurisprudence and early writers did not make any difference between the two. A comparative lawyer is concerned with "why" during his investigations and not with the problems of "what". He should inquire as to why the alleged differences between principles of jurisprudence exist and what process should be adopted for correcting them.

The comparative law is, therefore, neither a professional tool nor an academic toy.[1] It has a higher purpose of providing an insight into the social purposes of law and of evolving a better science of law. Any legal science, without comparison could scarcely rise about level of provincial casuistry and empirical craft.

1. O.K. Freund : Comparative Law as an Academic Subject 82 LQR 45.

Systematized study of foreign laws with local laws.—Opinions of the writers are sharply divided on this vexed question, whether comparative law is a science or the method of study? Some of the writers consider comparative law a science as it is regarded as the branch of jurisprudence, while others treat it as the method of study.

According to Munroe, Smith, Allen, Rabel, Lambart, the comparative law is studied like that of other branch of positive law and therefore, it should be treated as a science. They maintain that comparative law is a systematized study of foreign law in comparison with local law and therefore its main function is to ascertain, similarities and differences in various legal systems and thereby analyse the solutions which such legal systems offer for any legal problems. Thus Munroe Smith says:

> "Comparison is pre-eminently scientific; a science of English law or of American law is conceivable as a science of Anglo-American ethics."

Comparative law should, it is submitted not be called a science,in formation stage. The reason is that its use remains till the process of comparison goes on. During this period it is not science but method of legal research. But once the process of comparison is over, the resultant product is in no way inferior to any other branch of law or jurisprudence. Thus, it is method of study in beginning and assumes the status of science of law after crossing over this stage *i.e.* comparison of marriage law of Hindus and English people is part of legal technique but the thesis submitted after process is over becomes part of legal science.

Method of Study.—In the words of Allen, "comparative law is not a body of law in a positive sense but a method and technique of scientific enquiry."

On the other hand, Holland, C.K. Jenks, Gutteridge, Bryce are of the opinion that: "comparative law is a method of study and not the branch of legal science."

They point to the fact that the technique of different legal system can be employed in almost every branch of law and comparative law, unlike other doctrine of law, provides that technique. It does not make comparison for scientific enquiry, but lays down a method by which two or more legal systems are compared.

Thus Gutteridge says, "the fundamental characteristic feature of comparative law used as a method lies in the fact that it is applicable to any form of legal research. This method is equally at the service of the legal historians, the analytical jurists, the judge, the practitioner and the teacher of law."

Schlesinger pointed out, "Unlike other subjects in law school's curriculum, comparative law is not a body of rules and principles. It is a method, a way of looking at the legal problem. Strictly speaking the term comparative law is such a term by misnomer, it would be more logical to speak of the term as comparative method."[1]

Schmithoff makes the remark in answer to the question, whether comparative law is a science or a method of study. "It seems to be a moot point whether comparative law is a method or a science." The answer depends entirely on the interpretation of the term 'method' and 'the science'. How vague and interchangeable are these expressions, so far as legal terminology is concerned? It may be seen from the fact that there is an essay entitled 'the methods of legal science' as well as a book styled 'the science of legal methods'. It may well be left to philology to unravel the tangled skein of the problem. It is submitted that one answer for all circumstances is never possible. The science or method of study? It is one, when considered from one angle and it is the other, when examined from opposite angle. Every science is a method of study, and every method of study is by itself a science. So the distinction is not relevant so far as practical utility of the subject is concerned.

The province of comparison includes any juristic analysis which pays some attentin to one or more laws other than that of the observer's own country. This attention to foreign law might be occasional, and haphazard, or it may be systematic. The systematic observation may be of two kinds:—

(a) *Monographic*.—When it is focused upon one particular foreign legal system (*i.e.*, Canada, Russia, England or U.S.A.).

(b) *Synoptic*.—When it is directed to more than one foreign law (*i.e.*, German and French Law, Latin-American Laws, Anglo-American Legal System, Continental Legal System—British Commonwealth of Nations).

Methods of comparison.—Comparative law in its form can be classified under two heads to indicate the method of comparing different laws:—

(1) Pure comparison

The pure comparison is descriptive in nature. It is concerned with the analysis of the variations between the law of two or more countries. Pure comparison consists in examining the reactions of a number of legal systems too and individual legal problems. The pure comparison has two important elements:—

(a) The *subject of comparison and the problem therein all possible forms should be more or less the same*. Due regard must be had to the legal and social background of every topic of comparison. In other words, comparison must be to a lot strength governed by *sociological tendencies* because law is a social fact and it exists in society.

(b) An analytical classification of an *impartial and purely scientific character must be applied* to the matter under investigation. There should be classification of different topics and the comparison should be according to the laws.

---

1. Science of Comparative Law, 7 Cambridge L.J. 109, (1939).

(2) Subsequent utilization of results

After the different legal systems have been compared, the conclusion drawn should be utilized in some form or the other. Without utilization, the method of comparative study will not give scientific results. According to Schmithoff, 'the result gained in the description may be utilised in different modes.'

The following modes are possible:—

(a) Utilization may be made for the improvement of the general knowledge of law.

(b) Utilization may be made for the improvement of one's own legal system.

(c) Utilization may be made for the avoidance of conflict in different legal systems.

Comparative law, Distinguished from some other form of learning

Comparative Jurisprudence

Comparative jurisprudence has received recognition as a science. For practical purposes, the science of comparative jurisprudence has an extreme value. Gutteridge observes "Legal institutions are called upon to function in so many different environments and in such different conditions, that it is extremely dangerous if not fallacious, to deduce the universality of a rule of law from its existence in all systems." Thus it collects and examines the legal systems and seeks thereby to construct a system, which shall be natural. The comparative jurisprudence is an expression of the belief that the main purpose of the comparative method of study is to aid the historians or analytical jurists in tracing the origin and development of concepts common to all systems of law. For example, the process through which the concepts of possession, ownership and personality have gone. What have been the factors common in more than two different systems? Likewise, rules as to marriage and their analysis as prevailing in one country may be studied in light of rules in any other or more countries. These are studies that are fundamental in Legal theory or Jurisprudence as it is popularly called. If one is read along with the other the process passes into the field known to be within the control of comparative law. The whole of it is called comparative jurisprudence. The term signifies the use of the device of comparison as an aid to analytical jurisprudence. What fruits will it yield is the matter with which researcher or analysis maker should not bother about.

Use of Comparative Study in Legal History

Legal history is very much associated with comparative law. The research on historical lines is one of the indispensable tools for a comparative lawyer. Legal historians of all countries and of all schools of thought employ the method freely. The terms comparative jurisprudence, Comparative legal history, Historical jurisprudence and General history of law have often been used interchangeably. However, in some quarters, there is tendency to confine Comparative legal history to research into the early institutions of mankind, for example Salmond regards it as the history of the first principles and conceptions of legal systems. Schmithoff and Maine go the same way. This tendency is however not good in all respects. The application of Comparative method to the study of legal history does not necessarily involve research of an ancient character. For example, the modern Commercial law was developed not much before. It does not claim antiquarian character. Nevertheless its course of development is to be examined for its proper evaluation. Likewise, many new trends in law of obligations including doctrines of unjustifiable enrichment and abuse of rights and frustration cannot successfully be read without considering their historical background.

Use of the Comparative Study in Penal Law.—It is of course true, that the historical development of the law of crime has not been the same in all countries and that standards of wrong doing and of the means to be adopted for its prevention and repression are by no means uniform in character. But comparison cannot be excluded so as to learn about the law of other nations. The futility of such comparison is the opinion held by jurists who give only one subject to comparative law. That is to furnish materials for the drafting of the unified codes of law. Such draft in criminal law is neither possible nor desirable. These jurists stand on wrong footing. Every legal system has something to learn from the other, howsoever complete it may apparently seem to be. The International crimes for example hijacking, smuggling, piracy, genocide etc. can successfully be checked if the records of failings and scores in various countries are thoroughly checked and examined. These offences have one thing or the other in common. The study of specific cases in light of penal law of that country is bound to awaken the other countries. The comparison of penal laws of different countries serves the purpose of fixing the maximum target of criminal justice. It also saves the vigilant lawyer and his country from the perils of undue complacency. The fast means of transport and communication, internet services and the rate of growth of international crimes and cyber crimes and the sense of security that the modern public demands are some of the factors that will compel the systematic comparative study of the penal laws; including definition, mode and extent of crimes, the punishment and its efficiency, the criminal courts and procedures.

Use of Comparative Study in Labour Law.—In labour law, comparative method is always used. Labour problems of India do not differ from the labour problem of America and England *etc.* In an international age, we can solve the diverse labour problems by applying the methods of comparative process. The comparative study of labour problems and labour legislation is being made since 1900 when the International Association for labour legislation was founded. In 1919 the International Labour office was established at Geneva for the same purpose where the Government agencies and private organisations are doing research into the field of comparative labour law. The utility of these researches are two fold: (i) How has country is similarly circumstanced; (ii) It is desirable to have similar standard in International sphere, otherwise, unfair competition is bound to arise in International trade. Fast growing International Trade Law and International Economic Law need comparative study more than conventional relations in International cooperation.

Use of comparative study in Personal Laws.—In personal laws, the comparative study gives encouraging result, as the family laws can be ameliorated according to varying circumstances. It is however certain that the business of comparative lawyer is dim in the field of family law, property and succession because avenues of comparison are few and far between. The two origin to race, religion and politics which defy any comparative analysis. Nevertheless the aspects like sale and pledges of moveabls *etc.* admit the comparison because they are nearer to commercial law. Concept of limping marriages, growing sense and activities in area of adoption by foreign couples, expanding areas of marriage, live in relation, unwed couples, single parenthood are instances which would compel comparative study in personal law field. Inter caste, inter sect, inter religious inter country marriages create situations which throw challenges to comparative law. The studies so made would be literature on comparative jurisprudence.

Use of comparative method in the Law of obligations.—Breach of contracts and torts give rise to almost the same problem in all civilized communities and this gives a peculiar interest to comparison in these branches of law. With comparative study and research, the laws may be modified in the light of changing social, political and economic conditions. The law of contract and torts appears to provide one of the most promising field for comparative study and research because it deals with the mobile elements in human relationships. Law of obligations is law of everyday life. The use of comparative research has the glaring examples in English law in shape of statute of frauds, doctrine of consideration *etc.* In torts, the popular examples are the torts arising due to growth of motor traffic; defamation and newspaper libels.

Use of Comparative Study in Commercial Law.—In this sphere, the comparative study is very valuable; the reason being that diversity of laws affect the commerce more seriously than any other form of human activity. The conflict of law fails to give remedy in these cases which remain fluctuating. Therefore, traders are left to secure remedies for themselves in shape of gold clauses, gold value clauses and gold bullion clauses and the protection of standard contracts. The comparative research into the problems of commercial law is of much use in these circumstances.

Use of Comparative Study in Law of Procedure.—This varies from one country to another and comparative study helps a lot in tailoring their legal system to suit a particular set-up. The comparative approach to procedure is peculiar phenomena of Swiss, German and Italian legal systems. *Lex fori, lex situs, lex loci contractus, lex domicilli* are very clear in their application and utility in matters involving foreign elements. Comparative law is very useful in these areas.

Use of Comparative method in Legislation and Law Reform.—The main purpose of comparative law is to facilitate legislation and the practical improvement of law. By the examination and comparison of different laws, the most valuable material are obtained for legal improvement; there is no branch of judicial enquiry more important than this. Thus, the comparative method is employed for the formation of a unified and universal civil right. It is a fact that legislator is mainly concerned with whatever law is in existence. But new rights and new duties are emerging daily. The legislation is bound to provide protection and enforcement thereof. The material for legislation can be borrowed from neighbouring countries. Likewise, techniques of legislation may also contain much to derive from comparative analysis. Foreign legislation is a new and emerging topic for research and study in various degree courses in Europe and U.S.A. The intimacy with the legislation and comparative law is so well-established in that the growth of comparative legislation is taking place. Comparative legislation seems to have been devised in order to emphasise the practical as opposed to academic aspect of comparative legal research, which tends to give two results; one, is the collection and distribution of information as to foreign law, two, to make its use for Law Reform.

The Sources of Foreign Law for Comparison.—A comparative lawyer can get the materials for comparison from the following sources:—

(1) The Codes.—The Code is the collection of all statutes or a statute collecting all laws in the particular sphere. In the process of comparison, the most important source of foreign law is codified law. The comparative lawyer's first step is to study and examine the provisions of the Code. The form, structure and the draftsmanship of the codes are different in different countries and one should study them carefully. The Indian and English Codes may be compared with French Codes and the Codes of other civil law countries:—

(i) An Indian or English Code or a Code of common law country is based on the rules of common law which were existing in England before the code was adopted. Thus, most of the codified laws in India that is Contract Act, Indian Penal Code, T.P. Act *etc.* have been made on the basis of laws prevalent in England. On the other hand, a continental code is intended to lay down the new rules of law and is not conceived as resting on a pre-existing body of law.

(ii) The English and Indian codes are classified under different heads, although, they deal with the general principles of law, but the different sections, therein follow more or less accepted lines and group the topics under different headings but a continental code is not arranged in accordance with the classification as found in common law countries.

(iii) The Indian and English codes are more detailed and adoptive in comparison to French or German codes. It is the aim of continental legislature to express a rule of law in form as concise as possible. The result is that the continental judges have wider powers of interpretation in comparison to those enjoyed by Indian and English judges.

(2) Other forms of statute law and regulations.—Codified Law cannot be self-sufficient and all pervasive. New situations always arise, which were not contemplated by the codifying authority and further, a legislation making rules and regulations becomes necessary. Thus, in all countries of codified law we find statutes, which amend or supplement the decisions of the court. Further, there is a mass of delegated legislation as the subsidiary which is designed to fill up the gap in law.

(3) Customs.—In a system of codified law there should in theory be no room for custom. The code displaces legal sources of law and can only be employed and modified by legislation. But in practice the continental lawyers admit the existence of customary law, although, they may not agree as to what is to be included in the term custom or how its relationship may be ascertained with codified law. The Swiss Civil Code recognises custom as subsidiary source of law. The German Civil Code is silent on this question. In France, the civil code abolishes all general or local customs, but some of them are still existing therein.

As regards the place of custom in civil law countries two important things are to be considered:—

(1) In the first place, the term 'customary' law may be employed to indicate unwritten law of Romanistic origin which often serves the purpose of supplying the gap left in the provisions of the code.

(2) So far as, usages and customs are concerned the question depends on the interpretation of terms in continental countries. Evidence for the purpose are more readily admitted on the continent than in India and England and commercial usages can be adopted to the changing needs of the times.

(4) Opinions of the legal writers or jurists.—In France and other continental countries, the writings of the jurists and opinions of the professors enjoy a high degree of prestige and they are regarded as important sources of law. They can be submitted to the court as correct interpretation of law and may form the basis of the decision of court. Even the law declared and interpreted by the teachers in the university in the lecture room is considered and followed by the court. On the other hand, in India and England, the opinions of the writers, jurists, professors and academic lawyers are not held in high esteem. They are regarded as the subsidiary sources of law, and can only be considered by the court, if other sources do not supply the rule in a particular case.

Further, in civil law countries, the legal writers are authorised to criticize the decisions of the courts with much greater freedom than in India and England. They can place criticisms against the decisions of the court in any way and they are not amenable to the proceedings for the contempt of court.

(5) Bibliographies.—In India, there are no bibliographies so far published either in Hindi or in English which can help in the study of comparative law. In France, they have not published such types of Bibliographies. *Some Bibliographies in English language have been published in America. Kelsen's Bibliography of Comparative Law is the only work of the kind specially designed to meet the requirements of Comparative Law and contains much useful and valuable materials.* The Bibliographies contained in the publications of the Institute Desultude Legislative of Rome, must not be overlooked as they furnish a valuable guide to publication of recent date but we should keep in mind the following observation of Gutteridge that Bibliographies, however well planned and exhaustive they may be cannot always meet the requirements of an English reader who may need more detailed and explicit information. In this event he can consult the Society of Comparative Legislation which is prepared either to furnish the information or to put the inquirer to some one who can do so.

(6) Certain works of an encyclopaedia type.—*Burge's colonial and foreign law* is the only publication of this type. It is also remarkable that this work has never been completed. It includes summaries of the detailed provisions of foreign law and very useful bibliographies. The *Repertoire Droit* international, by Niboyet contains much valuable material for the comparison of the rules of Private International Law. Encyclopaedia is of great assistance to a comparative lawyer: Encyclopaedia of social science, Encyclopaedia Britannica, Encyclopaedia Americana are some of these that are being used by the comparative lawyers throughout the world.

(7) Introductory works.—There are many treatises of a genesis character designed to serve as an introduction to the study of Comparative Law. None exists in the English language in India or anywhere else. That *is only one work in Germany* which is well known and widely read.

(8) Law reports.—Next in sequence come the law reports. They exist only in some *countries and not in all countries*. In fact, the only legal systems which can claim to be well equipped with law reports are those of *U.S.A., U.K., France, Germany, Italy, Belgium, Switzerland and India.* Language is a great problem in continent wherein reports are in French German, and foreign researcher who wants to utilise these may find handicapped. The Common Law countries have no such problem among themselves. Digests of case law are of great value as they exist in England or in the continent. But their place has been taken by the summaries of table of cases which are as a rule, of much assistance to comparative law students. This is however, not a matter of concern because the standard commentaries and text books give references to case law or important values.

(9) Foreign commentaries.—Comparative law student will find that he must as a general rule base his readings on foreign commentaries and text books. It will suffice for the present to observe that sufficient matter can be obtained in country for many types of comparative study and that foundations have been laid down for the building up, at some future date and adequate facilities for research in the foreign legal system.

(10) Legal periodicals.—Legal periodicals published on the continent are most numerous and enjoy a wider circulation than those issued and published in India. They are valuable to comparative lawyers because that often contain articles of considerable importance by distinguished foreign lawyers. They also supply the best means available of keeping up with changes in foreign law.

(11) Internet.—The Information Technology has advanced much. Now many law reports and judgments of Superior courts are 'on line' and can be made use of and known on internets.

(12) Foreign case.—Foreign case is good when there is no Indian case law on the point. If Indian case law is available on any point but takes a narrow view on any question, any foreign case law taking wider view cannot be pressed into service.[1]

Values and Utilities of Comparative Method

Method of comparative study keeps on marching onward due to its inherent qualities which had to be recognised though gradually and cautiously. Comparison is a natural instinct of a man. A saying is that 'one's child and neighbour's wife look prettier'. This conclusion is pointer to comparison. In field of legal research, the only way to improve upon one's structure with a view to keep it abreast of and with time, the seekers of knowledge comparative studies are being carried in all branches. Fundamental rights chapter in Indian Constitution is quite like the documents Bill of Rights in English and American Constitution, Part IV. Directive Principle, Part XI Distribution of Power in Union and States find parallel in many other Constitutions. The concept of secularism, socialism are borrowed objectives being tried in Indian polity. Cabinet, Parliamentary form of Government, privilege of the members of Parliament and State Legislature are findings of comparative analysis, and are open fields for academic researches which would add new literature of comparative jurisprudence. Material for comparison is taken from two or more different areas or system, but after project is over, the work belongs to third discipline of comparative jurisprudence. It severs it connection from both disciplines from which raw material was taken, leaving both free to utilise the findings of comparative study. The value of the comparative study may lie in following ways:—

1. Cultural utility of comparative study.

By cultural study is meant the comparison of cultural background, evolution, heritage, failure and achievements of the personnel forming Government's machinery, judiciary and many those affecting morality, religion, or economy of the country and of the legal system concerned. A legal system is a unity, the whole of which expresses itself in each part, the same blood runs in whole organism. Hence, each part must be seen in relation to the whole.

---

1. *Reliance Energy Case*, AIR 2006 SC 1148.

2. Aesthetic utility of the discipline.

Such a utility of any discipline is seldom disputed. Intellectual hunger may not know the limitation of time and space. People learn and adopt the comparative method for simple reason that here is an irresistible current in making towards knowledge. The present discipline as such serves as the vehicle for the legal, sociological and other political comprehension of foreign societies. The comparison is the chief weapon in the armoury of jurists. Thus this discipline serves the aesthetic satisfaction of the special genius of any legal system.

3. Sociological utility of comparative method.

A substantial section of people concerned with legal education believe that comparative method is a mere superficial adornment of mere bread and butter matters, others regard it as a purely cultural subject. As a matter of fact, the utility of a subject very much depends upon the development of society. To take the American experience, for generations ago the subjects regularly taught in leading American Law School consisted substantially of contract, torts, property, criminal law and procedure. With passage of time, conflict of law, bankruptcy, corporate law, Administrative Law, Taxation, Labour Law, *etc.* have become standard offerings. The newest entrant is comparative law which has found place not only in American law schools but in addition many independent institutions are also devoted to the mode of study as a subject.

Besides the nature of needs of the society dictate the course of the school. In America, for instance, the comparative law grew up in metropolitan cities on the sea coast with large commercial interests. The trading communities in these coastal cities looked for lawyers who knew foreign law to help them in international litigations.

In the words of Rheinstein 'comparative law' means 'Sociology of Law' ought to be part of general study not only of sociologists and political scientists but of every educated man desirous of understanding our civilisation.

Aesthetic pleasure helps in producing lawyers who have a better understanding of their own law. The study is often compared to that of learning foreign languages which helps on to appreciate the beauty of one's own language and one's own literature. Likewise, an adequate foundation for legal reasoning is not laid only when the principles of one system of law alone are taught. The student does not have sufficient relative criteria from which to reason and exercise his imagination. The comparison would also enrich the cultural values of a legal education.

Immigrant's problems is another social factor that has made the sociological importance of this discipline being felt. Individual immigrants who were well versed in the legal system of the countries of their origin helped to build up comparative law studies. Some important jurists of this category included Rabel at Michigan University, Rheinstein at Chicago, and Ehrenzweig at California.

4. Anthropological utility of the discipline.

Rabel divided comparative law into Ethnological jurisprudence, historical comparison and systematic-dogmatic comparative law. This has been emphasised by Hug and Sarfatti. Ethnological Jurisprudence deals with the laws of the past and compare with primitive laws. Allen's law in the making, Maine's 'Ancient Law' and village communities, 'Pollocks' Studies in History and jurisprudence prove the anthropological utility of the comparative method of treatment.

5. Practical utilities of comparative method.

The following may be studied in this connection:—

(a) Utility for students

The object of comparative law is *that it increases the understanding of the students* of the legal rules of their own country, comparison forces the students to consider what a rule is designed to achieve or whether, it is the best possible answer to the social problem to which it is addressed. Comparative law *tends to bring uniformity* in law and legal institutions of the world. Its aim and function is to avoid conflict of territorial legal systems and thereby unify the laws. The most dramatic appeal of comparative law lies in the possibility of developing a 'world common law' based on the analysis of conflicting national rules and an appropriate synthesis thereof. The comparative law brings uniformity in the International Economic Relations.

Much of it depends upon as to what society wants of a lawyer. During faculty days, the law student may be trained accordingly. Until such specification, the general training of a law student requires him to apprise himself fully not with the general culture of the profession he is to practice later on, but along with it he is expected to acquaint himself with culture of the vocation as a whole. This legal culture keeps the comparative study to appreciate the technique of applying and interpreting legal precepts in law courts. In case the law student opts for faculty, thorough grounding in law for him is the basic need of the profession.

Apart from creating legal technicians and importance of comparative law in that field legal education does not end only with this. Its purpose is to develop a psychology in law students to take upon themselves the duties of securing peace and welfare in the communities in which they live. The ideas and projects befitting one's country may be known and adopted conveniently if foreign law is open to law students. Legal Aid, Legal Advice, Legal literacy extension programmes are areas in which comparative studies are of much use to faculties of law.

Comparative Study at LL.B. Stage

Comparative law has been included as addition to the course on the jurisprudence in Indian Universities. However, it should be taught and at the same time it should be encouraged that method be used intending other subject in LL.B. classes.

At this stage, horizons of the students need to be broadened by awakening their interests in history, philosophy and comparative law. At this stage one may begin with illustrations drawn from foreign laws or even selecting the nearest system in condensed and teachable form. For example, Indian law may be taught with reference to corresponding position in English law or American law. One thing needs to be mentioned about LL.B. teaching schedule in law colleges. Over weightage is being given to law courses as preparatory for courts of law. Too much emphasis on practical training has been given. This needs reconsideration. Legal education prepares not only Advocate. The interest of non-law practitioners is not given due weight. Over burdened syllabi leaves no time for the extra legal studies which every lawyer must have. Law courses need slashing so as to leave more time with law students for general studies. Law is no more a lawyer's hegemony. His relation with sociology, economics, history, political science, trade, commerce medicine need more specific place in legal education.

Comparative Study at LL.M. stage.—At LL.M. level, the teaching is always open and broad. Alongwith Indian Constitution the relevant aspects of U.K., U.S.A., Canada, Australia may also be taught. The teaching may be done comparatively rather than separately in separate classes. In LL.M., writing of a dissertion is almost required in all universities. It is for students and teachers to suggest areas which need comparative studies. Specialisation in LL.M., has to be re-scheduled and if so proper, the syllabi needs to be re-considered.

Comparative Research.—In this field, team work is a method which may be given a fair trial and along with it comparative efforts in research and proper co-ordination are the minimum things which may be used with profit in comparative researches. In legal research, table work has to be discouraged. Socio legal field work based researches are more useful for specialists in law.

(b) Utility for lawyers

Comparative law is of great *utility to practising lawyers*. A well trained lawyer should be more than a technician. He must be a resourceful social engineer in working out the pacific adjustments of controversies in a world which is growing smaller daily due to the expansion of communication and transport. The knowledge of foreign law and legal institutions can be of direct assistance to practising lawyers in the following ways:

(a) In a *conflict of law-cases,* where foreign law is involved, effective examination and cross-examination of witnesses presumes at least a minimum acquaintance with the laws and techniques of foreign countries in question.

(b) An eminent lawyer of standing can be engaged in foreign countries by a *foreign client.*

(c) In order to handle legal problems in a foreign country with regard to *foreign trade or business*, a lawyer conversant with foreign laws is bound to be helpful to a client.

(d) A lawyer who knows about foreign law can quote the *various references* of foreign laws, and it may be helpful in his case. This would be of much use in cases of first impression.

(e) Comparative law also enables lawyers to *argue the cases before International Tribunals* who looks to the general principles of law recognised by civilized nations as source of law.

(c) Utility for legislature

Comparative law *supplies materials to the legislatures* to make different laws and to repeal the undesirable rules therein and to effect the improvement in the legal system. The comparative law is indispensable in the preparation of international legislation. Promotion of International peace and security is direction to State. So is preparation of uniform civil code; separation of judiciary from the executive. Drafting of law on these areas would definitely require comparative studies, comparative analysis and reference. As such the utility of this method even to legislature is crystal clear. Every day, we see delegations of Parliamentarians or legislators visiting systems outside the country. These visits are planned to get on the spot knowledge of how sister organisations work in countries elsewhere.

The legislator gets a torch in his hands in shape of comparative law and its practical utility in field of law reform is beyond question. The working of any law in another country may be scrutinised and analysed before any legislation on such topic is proposed to be enacted. This will save time and introduce expertisation in legislative field; what is needed is that agency for law reforms in various countries be brought together for international co-operation in legal fields so that one may remain abreast of not only what is going elsewhere in other parts of the world, but also as to that which was not yet happening but was in contemplation.

(d) Utility for Law Reform Agencies

Agencies and Institutions committed to law reform and legal research may do much with the help of this method. They can give a comparative assessment of the problems, their probable solutions attempted in various foreign legal systems and thus help the law making machineries in both ways; by guiding them with necessary particulars and keeping their eyes and vision clean and clear to probable pitfalls. Science of comparative law would thus be a positive science like physics and chemistry and the main task of the legislator would be to verify a hypothesis by successive observations of the same phenomena from different angles.

Comparative chart before the legislator would thus enable him to know that thing that ought to be avoided. In this endless process of law reform, the comparative law remains truly in action. The academies of law committed to law reforms may thus rapidly furnish requisite and relevant information from foreign laws on given points to specialists and experts with an exact documentation. Some notable academies working at present are society of comparative legislation (Paris, founded in 1869 and of London, founded in 1894), Belgian Institute of comparative law (founded in 1907).

(e) For Courts and Judges

Comparative law sometimes *guides a judge in arriving* at the decision of a case. It often happens that the local law may not make any provision for a definite set of facts and, therefore, the judges look into a foreign authority to come to a decision. The judges are really assisted by this discipline in two ways:—

(a) New problems.—In cases which are new or raise a novel issue, which has never been decided by the court of superior jurisdiction and is left untouched by statutes or when no custom is discernible, the judge may seek guidance from any other legal system and may decide the case accordingly. It is only comparative jurisprudence which may take him out of the woods.

(b) Unpalatable precedent.—It may sometimes happen that the court wishes to cut a new path than what is known because this is out moded, unreasonable and unfortunate. It may do so only when alternative way out is available to it. This can only be possible by looking into foreign legal systems through comparative law.

6. Comparative Study and International understanding

This is another way of using the comparative method for the peace and welfare of the community besides its practical use to courts, lawyers, judges, legislators and students of law. The comparative method is of much use in promotion of International understanding. It can be to promote transcendental value by unearthing general principles of law recognised by civilised nations, promoting International commercial contacts, helping UNESCO and other U.N. Agencies to accomplish their missions more effectively,, developing world common law, and common core of legal principles. As such comparative method may be made use of in the following:—

(a) Promotion of transcendental values

This may be done either through effective enforcement of international law or by evolution of a unified law with universal application. It is in this latter respect that opportunity and need for the comparative study of law is unprecedented. The cry for common values crossing over State boundaries in getting momentum in modern world, wider political co-operation and affective use of conjoined community power is claimed for securing cherished goals of human welfare. The comparative law has its own role to play in accomplishment of this demand.

Terrorism, is becoming a world wide phenomenon. These can be controlled only by international co-operation. This can be only when comparative study of the problem is made and ways are worked out to contain it. Genocide is International crime. Private citizens are becoming subjects of International Law. Establishment of the International Criminal Court is mooted. The discipline would be quite useful in these areas.

(b) International Commercial Contracts

Increasing contracts of individuals, corporations and groups of people across international borders has given rise to new situations to which international trade and commerce have added another dimension. Comparative analysis has a very vital role to play in matters like law of bills, notes, and immigration rules.

(c) UNESCO, W.T.O., W.H.O., I.L.O., F.A.O. and Comparative method

A challenge has been thrown by UNESCO *etc.* as to how far can law professors through their research contribute to an easing of tension throughout the world.

In this context researches in the following fields may be useful—

1. Problems of claimed sovereign immunity arising from East-West trade through Government controlled trading organizations;
2. Differences in legal systems and procedures that have given rise to misunderstanding and mutual distrust;
3. Arbitration of international trade dispute;
4. Selected problems in field of family law and succession;
5. The impact of State trading upon commercial treaties;
6. Protection of industrial property in the trade between East and West;
7. Assistance to civil litigants across State boundaries *etc.*;
8. Principle of non-intervention;
9. Principles of sovereignty.

(d) Contribution of Comparative method Scholars

Comparative method conveying the message of each national genius may shape *Jus gentium* and thus cross fertilize the various spontaneous national growths. By activating everywhere there catalytic agents of legal civilization, it may perform a real service for the mankind within the strictly scientific ambit of relevant descriptive comparison. Besides, the inter-relationship between legal education through comparative method and world peace is an established factor.

7. World Common Law and Comparative method

The most dramatic appeal of Comparative method is—World Common Law. It means unification of laws. This goal in its own term has given way to movements such as co-ordination, harmonisation and minimum standards.

8. Common core of legal principles

This is the latest movement and proposes an alternate to the idea of one Code. It is known as 'common core of legal principle'. The starting point of the common core theory is Article 38(1)(c) of statute of International Court of Justice which enjoins general principles of law recognised by civilized nations as rule of decision in that court.

What are these general principles? This problem falls in comparatists field. Their ascertainment would contribute as an important landmark in the development of International law.

Weaknesses or demerits of comparative method

(i) Only specialists can utilize.—Every system of law has some overt or covert lapses and, comparative law cannot claim total immunity from it. The method of comparative law and legal systems is a difficult process, which cannot be undertaken by an ordinary man. It requires a special type of attitude and training; those who are specialists can do the work of comparison with ease.

(ii) Very extensive field of comparison.—The potential field of comparison is very extensive and also its purposes are too many; as such no standardised technique of comparison is possible.

(iii) Vast differences.—The method of comparison differs from one system to another and also from one person to another. Thus, a method which could give good results to a particular system of law or to a particular purpose may prove to be a failure if applied in other directions.

(iv) Misleading result.—Comparative method sometimes gives misleading results because it is undertaken in the presence of different social, economic and political conditions. Such a study is always incompatible so far as the systems under comparative study are concerned.

(v) Result differs on methodology of research adopted.—The law permits every method of research. It is social science. It is based on human behaviour. It uses modern technology. It deals with problem which are and which may be. So different research methodologies can be used in legal comparison and so would be the result that it would yield.

❑ ❑

Chapter 11

Application of Theories of Justice and Judicial Process

Test of the judicial process is the extent of Justice, it delivers according to law, the contentment it gives to people, the discontentment it removes, the faith it creates and carries in justice delivery system. Howsoever strong law any country may have, its effect depends on how it is interpreted, how it is enforced?

Relation between Law and Justice.—Law always need to be related to the system of values recognised in the particular community in which it operates. Such a system of values may and in fact does differ from place to place and from period to period. Though it may be impossible to prove the absolute superiority of any particular system over all otners, actual or possible, nevertheless if a community believes that its values are the highest attainable, it will clearly judge the existing law in accordance with those values and try to amend or adapt it where it falls short of them. It should, however, be remembered that what values we care to affirm are a matter not of logical necessity, but of choice. Two of the most important values to which law is often related are *justice* and *freedom*.

JUSTICE

Justice has a moral connotation. It is a concept that injects life in a society, and gives meaning to the legal system. The society survives because it has a system of justice whether human or divine. Dissenters against any system plead absence of justice as one ground to dissent and promise justice to all.

In fact there can be no system or society in absence of some or other system of justice, and no society can be based on the denial of justice. This concept therefore, has many connotation and with changing contents, what is just to one may be at the cost of the other, unjust to him, and *vice versa*; which is just to day may become less forcefully just afterwards and quite unjust sometime after. Even at the same time, the border line between just and unjust may sometime be very difficult to define in specific situations.

It would not be unfair to maintain that law for its existence owes much to its capacity to administer justice. The law has adopted the concept of justice from morality and morality from religion. The religion is experience and thus principles of justice are based on experience of the people in the society.

Micro and macro justice

Concept of justice functions at two very different levels. Firstly, justice at the level of decision in individual cases; this is called justice at Micro-level. Secondly, justice operating at the level of the legal system as a whole. This is called Macro-level justice. The justice at Micro level and Macro level may conflict with each other. Because for justice, courts must have discretion (specially in individual cases). Whereas it is also desirable, that legal outcome should be predictable. The latter would definitely reduce the former. Discretion and predictability can not go together.

Real dispute justice and academic question

Courts always insist on real disputes for giving justice. Facts underlying particular disputes provide a context for the administration of justice. The court is happy only when it is dealing with real dispute based on real facts wherein the outcome would actually matter to some one in real terms.

Hypothetical cases.—The court would not hear such matters even if parties so press. Academic questions are not open for argument in actual courts of law. 'stating a case' or 'Reference' constitute exceptions.

Infructuous cases.—Expiry of time or matters like out of court settlements, alternate dispute resolutions, arbitration, conciliation, mediation, Panchayat, Lok Adalat, where parties have been overtaken by events. No decision on merit in such cases is needed.

Justice and early settlement

Justice is a concept linked to Law. It is not whole truth. Interests of the justice are served better by promotion of early settlements. This is true in all cases; contentious matters to non-contentious matters (like will, or execution of deeds, conveyancing matters). Settlement of issues by agreement is one way of doing or getting justice. Alternative dispute resolution systems like Arbitration etc. are justice delivery mechanism and part of legal system.

Lawyers are necessary evils and part of justice delivery system. To recall the famous punch cartoon, two farmer's were arguing over the ownership of a cow. One was pulling at the head and the other at the tail and where was the lawyer? Sitting happily in middle milking the cow. In fact, the cartoonist was cynical on the role of lawyer in dispute settlement mechanism. Another story goes about. Two monkies were fighting for a bread. They approached a lot for decision. The cat called for a balance and broke the bread in two parts; kept the two in balance. One was heavier. The cat broke it and ate it. So for proper balancing, the whole bread was eaten,. Nothing was left for the monkies. That happens in real cases.

So the earlier the parties settle, the better it is. Senior lawyers encourage such settlements. It always adds to their work. I have personal experience. I used to send 'say five cases' out of ten that came to me when I was in practice. "I told them frankly that there is no chance to win. Some of these went back; few went to other lawyers; paid heavy fee just to lose in first hearing. A news went assured that if this counsel says 'no' accept it. If 'yes' proceed. The number of briefs swelled to thousands very soon.

So lawyer's as community need not be blamed.

Form of legal reasoning—major premises and minor premises.—Legal reasoning has three forms: Major and minor premises and the conclusion. How Major premises and minor premises are formulated? It is not so clear in the process of legal reasoning but it is there. Major premises are 'statements of law' and minor premises are 'statements of facts'. When 'major premises' are applied to 'minor premises' what comes into being (result) is called 'conclusion'. Statement of facts (minor premises) have to be pleaded and proved to the satisfaction of the court or must be agreed by the parties.

Major premises are formulated by sources of law; Act or statutes precedent or delegated legislation.

The job of lawyer's reasoning is to fix up his client's case in any of the major premises and get result (conclusion) in his favour.

Justice means justice delivery instantly; justice then and there; no prolonged trial; open hearing open punishment and execution forthwith; For example in kidnapping, abduction or rape cases physical punishment, banishment, exile, fine, anything, approved or opposed by law.

Justice means submitting to power or centre of power.—One can do justice or injustice when he is the centre of power and others submit to it. Defiance to power or centre of power cannot deliver justice. When power itself is made use of unjustly, it creates reaction and then power has to be used to curve this creation.

Meaning of justice

Justice is value cherished by a society. It can never be absolute either in nature or in content. The values differ from place to place, society to society and from time to time. So does the meaning of Justice.

Moral justice

Religion is strictly private in character to an individual, so is morality. So the concept of justice tends to be individualistic in nature. Justice is what one feels to be just. The feelings are influenced by one's upbringing, conditioning and the environment in society all around. When the individual becomes part of a society, his private morality is transformed into group morality or social morality. The strictly private morality broadens to social morality but the character does not undergo any revolutionary transformation if the composition of the society is homogenous or tribal in character. In heterogeneous society, the grip of morality slackens and its scope broadens. When it becomes broad, it religiosity changes into secular shape and moral justice gets transformed into legal justice. It happens only in very few and broad categories of the cases when law, and moral join hands on justice, but fairly a large area is either left out or new areas crop up where morality alone reigns supreme.

Justice, in the hands of a lawyer and law courts become legal, *i.e.*, justice according to law. The law has its limitations, so legal justice must be understood within those limitations.

The tragedy is that human being is moral in his basic framework. He takes justice in the sense of moral justice. He seeks this moral justice even from the courts of law which call themselves courts of justice. The common man fails to appreciate that courts of law even as court of Justice are not to do the job he excepts them to do as institution of moral justice. The courts are structured to give legal justice. Moral justice is beyond their purview. If he goes to law courts, he will get justice according to law. In some cases, it may fall in line to his own concept of moral justice, but there may be circumstances when legal justice runs counter to moral justice. Here the common man is bewildered, and his faith in justice according to law is badly shaken. The fault lies neither with the courts of law nor with the common man. The expectations of common man from courts of law are illusion, false and misdirected. If one wants drugs, he should go to a druggist or chemist shop. How can he expect to get drug in a book shop. If he hopes, it is due to his misunderstanding either of what he wants or where he can get the things he wants.

The confusion is added in most of the cases by the courts or the legislatures as well. These use justice without doing justice to the word. The courts have quite often tried to demonstrate that they are the organs of the state where one can get justice but to their own surprise, justice they give is not the justice the common man wants. He wants something else, the courts give quite different thing though resembling somewhat in appearance, but quite different in taste. Sometimes, this fact is appreciated by the courts and quite often it goes unappreciated.

Law is for the man and justice is the cause, why the law is needed. If law fails to do justice, the whole legal system is put on trial as is presently the position.

Moral justice means practically one without content. It means vague and confused categories of treatments that have been prevalent in a particular society at a particular time. Some of these have been studied whereas many have remained analysed.

From Plato, if one is to start, the justice to him and in the *society of his time meant ideal justice.* He was of the view that everything or every person has its proper *sphere* and justice means conforming to that sphere, *e.g.*, knife; what is its proper sphere. It is to cut. In the hands of a butcher, its proper sphere is to kill; in hands of surgeon, its proper sphere is to operate. If it does so, it is just. If it behaves otherwise, it is unjust. In a just society, only a wiseman is fit to rule, if it is like that, the society is just, if otherwise, it is unjust.

Plato was of the view that every free man is to do some specific function in the society, if he behaves and behaves according to it, he is just, if he changes and behaves otherwise, he is unjust, and in most of the cases, the function of a man is decided by his birth, *e.g.*, a child born in a muslim family will be conditioned to avoid eating pork, a child born in a brahmin family will avoid even touching beef, but for a child brought up as a christian, it will never come in his mind that there may be some difference in pork and beef. To him all meat is meat, and it is all fair whether beef is eaten or pork is eaten. So, Plato's concept of justice boils down to moral justice or justice according to religion.

Administration of justice

Men and animals have common basic instincts like food, sleep, fear and sex. The only difference is that the animal moves on impulses, men on intellect. Intellect requires either of the two for keeping them united first one reason in all or one power over them. Each man moves by his own interests and passions, therefore, having one reason, in all is impracticable, 'one power' is possible. For example 'kings' but king is also a human therefore it is his interest or passion that becomes the interest and passion of all around to king. King is repository of power and force. Force is the ultima *ratio* of king as well as the whole mankind without force, the civilisation is unattainable, injustice is unchecked and triumphant and 'life of man' would be 'solitary, poor nasty brutish and short'.

Law of reason and Law of force

Law of reason is ideal situation whereas force is reality. Likewise public opinion is also counted as force to keep the people on right path. 'Peer justice' and 'mob justice' are equally noticiable features of keeping people of just path. These are supports but no system can be wholly based on these or either of these. Legal system can definitely not. It is true, reason is important, public opinion (of those around), courts much than the opinion of whole world. The censure of tens of thousands may be outweighed by the approval of ten.

Social sanction is effective only untill the force of the community supplements it. Force is a must to take care of dissenters may be in minority. Institutionalised law enforcement is a must of any legal system. If it is strong. The law and order is satisfactory and faith of people is system sustains and as such system remains. One's this faith disappears or becomes weak, the system collapses. Private vengeance comes up when system is strong, this private vengeance is transmuted into administration of criminal justice. Self help is outcome when civil justice system falters.

Purpose of criminal justice

Study of purpose of criminal justice can be from two angles (1) punishment being end in itself; (2) It is method of protecting the society by reducing criminal behaviour.

Theories of punishment

These may be:

(1) Deterrent theory.

Why one commits the crime? One of the reasons may be that there is conflict in between his interests and that who is victim of that crime. May be an individual or may be the society. I may kill person who tries to kill me or who comes to usurp my property or who comes to harm my wife, son or daughter. Deter him by punishment. Tell him not to do that so that he would not fulfil his interests. Effort to injure the other would be injury to doer. The crime does not pay. The criminal loses much in committing crime. He would be hanged for killing or jailed for that crime. His ill gotten property would be confiscated.

The criminal in deterrent theory is bad example to would be offenders. It warns the men not in dock by punishing man in dock. It creates terror in heart of potential crime doer. Who has not committed the crime but may think of doing those crimes. The punishment to the man in dock teaches lesson to those thinking alike.

Hanging on cross road, whipping in public making family of criminal State slave arresting wife, brother or children of naxal or terrorists are deterrent.

(2) Preventive theory.

Men in dock are punished by disablement or prevention. Tit for tat, blood for blood, tooth for tooth, eye for eye, life for life, cut the hand of thief for theft is example of disablement. Take life of murderer by giving death penalty.

'Prevention' includes suspension or cancellation of driving licence prevents that man from repeating rash driving or identical crimes on road by vehicles, taking security for good behaviour, preventive detention; transportation of life, Life imprisonment or any period jail term are examples wherein one who is punished is prevented from committing that crime during punishment period and gets lesson for future as well. He may not be made lesson for others, but he takes lesson for his own self by either disablement or being prevented.

How does preventive theory differ from deterrent?—Deterrent acts on motive of the offender. Man in the dock is punished to scare men not in the dock but who have tendency of the type, preventive consists of physical restraint.

(3) Retributive theory.

The punishment according to their thinkers is based on revenge against the doer of the crime. It is based on the motive to take revenge of victim or society. A crime may be crime against the victim and also crime against community or society. The victim may be aggrieved that much as is the society. A crime creates a ripple in the society by which many more are sufferers, so let the doer be punished. So that a message goes to all that crime never pays. 'Private revenge' is replaced by revenge by the community or the society of which the victim was member when that crime took place.

It is retaliation. The punishment discourages the tendency to take law in one's own hands. The system promises private revenge by saying to victim that the whole society is for him, with him and misconduct against him is offence against all. Hence the victim need not worry for revenge. The law will take it by awarding and executing punishment on doer of that crime.

This explanation is old and needs to be reviewed otherwise. Retribution ensures peace to victim and satisfies his ego which is also injured with physical injuries. The wound on body heals up but wounded feeling survives for long. Punishment heals it up forever. Punishment is not the end but it is a means to the end. The end is restoration of peace disturbed by commission of that crime.

A girl is raped, the brothers' uncles and her father commit rape on all women folks of the family of the rapist. Honour killings are the revenge of the wounded feelings, of injured family reputation, the revenge may finish the families but restores the injured ego. Dropadi of Mahabharat insulted 'karna', He avenged by putting her on thigh of 'Duryadhana', Bheem broke the thigh in revenge.

(4) Expiation.

Why do we punish? The one explanation is *Prayaschit*' or '*Penance*'. The theory is called expiatory theory. It accepts guilt and punishment is equivalent to innocence. Expiation is self-inflicted punishment on the doer by the doer (offender) himself. In offences involving morality expiation is not bad. Marrying the woman raped by the accused is an example of expiation. Returning the stolen property, by the thief to the person entitled is expiation. In all offences which are also 'sins' expiation works. Expiation cleans self, soul. The balance created by crime is set off by expiation. '*Panchatap*' or '*Prayaschit*' is self purification process of self inflicted punishment.

(5) Reformatory theory

A view finding good support of law and moralists both is that criminals are like ill persons. No child is born criminal. Criminality is the gift of community. We make criminals. He is a product of situations. No crime is pre-meditated or pre-planned. Exceptions are there but these do not become general rules of human conduct. All crimes are product of circumstances. Remove those circumstances crime rate would go down. Do we kill our diseased? No is the reply. We get them treated till last day, last moment. So is a crime. It is a product of sick mind. It is curable. The cure does not lie in his being hanged. In fact, death sentence is failure of law and system of law. It is not victory of law. The law has to ensure life and not death of individual who may be accused of having committed a crime. Article 21 or even more the civil law guarantees life and works to save it. Life means life worth living. Law is very clear we can not kill all criminals. 'Death' is given as penalty only for few crimes in Penal law (Section 34, 149, 121, 302, 303, 307, 396 IPC). It is given in some cases under Army law and so on so forth. Criminal Procedure Code (Section 367(5) stands changed in 1955. 'Death is not mandatory in any case except Sections 303, 307 I.P.C. Section 303 has already been declared constitutional (*Dina* case). IPC provides 'Death or Life Imprisonment'. It needs to be amended, let there be 'Death or Life imprisonment' or 'Life Imprisonment' or 'death'. Let us give clear signal to own Trial Courts. It has been taken care of by judicial process. Life imprisonment is rule, death penalty is an exception. State aggravating circumstances to justify why life imprisonment is not proper? What special is there that calls for death penalty? The judicial process has cleared air on this point as well. 'Death' can be given as punishment only and only in 'rare of the rarest cases', the cases that are shocking to judicial conscience. (*Bechan Singh* case).

In addition, rather in case of above, we have procedure established by law. The procedure of trial and also of punishment and its execution are reasonable, fair and impartial.

Who is to be reformed

Reformation is possible only for those who desire to be reformed. Who are capable of reform. We can not reform those who are beyond reformation.

Juveniles.—Juvenile is one who committed the crime when below 18 yrs. of age. Complete exemption from punishment is to a child below 7 yrs. of age. qualified exemption is to a child of 7 years and above but below 12 years in age.

A person below 15 yrs. in age is 'child' under Factories Act in between 15 plus to 18 years, he is called 'adolescent', on 18 years or above, he is called 'adult'. Young person means a person who is either a child (not completed 15 yrs. of age) or an adolescent (completed) 15 but not 18 years of age). All juveniles are all these and also those who are 18 plus but below 21 years of age.

Juvenile Justice Act.—Juveniles are tried in juvenile courts. The moment plea of juvenile is taken, the file is transferred to juvenile court and his trial takes place there. During trial, such accused is kept in 'children homes'. He is not to mix up with adult criminals.

Probation of First Offenders Act

First offenders.—Section 360 of Code of Criminal Procedure provides for benefit of first offender rule being given to young convicts. They are released on bond or bail and are kept under observation during probation period. The requirement is, he should be below 21 years on day of conviction. He is punished for offence punishable with fine only or imprisonment for less than 7 years. His age, character, antecedents and the circumstances in which offence was committed are considered by the court. He may not be punished after conviction and can be released on probation of 3 years. Power to grant probation can be exercised by any court at any stage of appeal or revision.

As follow up of reformatory view we have named erstwhile 'jails' into 'sudhar griha'. We have introduced 'open jails' wherein prisoners can pass some time with their families. Different crafts and avocations are going on in jails and part of income so coming is shared by prison inmates. Fear was that hardened criminals may not yield to reform measures but this confusion is getting removed and dreaded dacoits too have responded well to the liberty conceded by reform measures.

Come what may, the theories are explanations justifying punishments. Time changes and so do the views. One explanation may not always explain all cases of punishment but they all taken together prove one thing beyond doubt that system of law and administration of criminal delivery justice needs punishment, though we have need to reform the justice delivery system to meet the three enemeis of cost, corruption and delay.

Administration of justice is one of the basic functions of the law. Jurists from Acquinas to Salmond regard administration of justice as a logical part of the every motion of law. Acquinas following Augustine, maintained that unjust law is no law whereas to Salmond, law is set of rules recognised and acted upon by courts of justice. Even to positivists,who may deny any logical connection between law and justice, justice is highly relevant for a critical evaluation of law.

Justice in broad sense is synonymous with morality whereas in narrow sense it is only one area of morality.

Justice and morality

Justice has a moral content, but they are not the same. An unjust act is automatically immoral but an immoral act is not automatically unjust, *e.g.*, rape is hated as an act. It is immoral, but can one say in first instance that it is unjust. Similarly, wickedness may take any form other than injustice, for example, cruelties of Hitler, Mussolini and Stalin, murders of innocent Kashmiries by extremists in Kashmir and by naxalities in Chhattisgarh. U.S.A. and U.K., invading Iraq are shocking, but are these unjust?

Injustice is treating one or more persons more harshly or more favourably than others in the same situation, *e.g.*, father treating one of his children more than the rest is unjust father. Treating likes as unlike and unlike as like, is unjust.

Distributive and corrective justice

Distributive justice is the main job of the legislature and executive organs of the state. It works to ensure fair divisions of social benefits and burdens among the members of the community, *e.g.*, right to vote is benefit and taxation is burden. These should be fairly distributed. Distributive justice thus serves to establish a balance or equilibrium among the members of the society. When this balance is upset, the corrective justice intervenes. The distributive justice *serves to secure* and corrective justice to *redress* the balance of benefits and burdens in a society.

Legal justice or justice according to law

Justice according to law means that like cases be treated alike. Whether it is distribution of social benefits and social burdens or it is at the stage of correcting the balance. In legal language, it means equality before the law, and equal protection of law. Equality before law means that right from the prime minister down to the police constable all shall face the same court, be tried under same law and shall have end accordingly. Equal protection involves due process whether substantive due process or procedural due process.

Justice and equality

Inequality is natural, Equality is an ideal. Justice does not aim to make all men equal in size, brain, height, colour, creed, social benefits and social burdens, to make all rich or all poor. This is impossible and no law can ever accomplish it. What equality in law means, is that it will not create new forms and new avenues of inequality. It will not protect or promote an institution that secures or preserves inequality. It may at the most try honestly to remove inequalities preserved by human institutions.

Justice in hearing and Justice in finding

Existence of rules, their generality and impartial application tries to secure corrective justice at the stage of hearing but equality and its notion being crux of justice go further. What would happen if the courts give one finding today in one case, and give different finding the other day in a case that is on all fours the same or at least similar to one decided on the first day? What would be the reaction of justice if courts in Plateau State decide an issue in favour of the plaintiff and the court to Bauchi state decides in favour of the defendant though both the cases are similar. The former type of cases are taken care of by the broad principles of codes and precedent, whereas latter type of cases are met by having appeals to the highest court. This is equality at the stage of finding. Major discrepancies in finding mean in fact inequality before law.

Palm tree justice

The legal system has tried at its level to do away with the subjective elements in decision making. If individual case is decided on its merits according to what the Judge thinks fit it is a palm tree justice. The codes, precedents and computerisation of decision making is all that is being tried to make administration of justice as free from individual whims as possible.

Justice and Interests

The equal distribution of benefits and burden between actual members of the society goes on more or less satisfactorily when rules of substantive law appear on the scene, then justice gets new challenges wherein inequality may crop up. It is the field of interest. The possibility of the clash between different categories of the interests in society, *e.g.*, individual interests, social interests, public interests, interests of groups and associations, etc. The justice here consists of maximum fulfilment of the maximum interests of each and promotion of the smooth running of the society.

Content of legal justice

Equality is no doubt one of the well established content of legal justice. Like should be treated alike, equals should be treated equally but unequals should not be treated equally; otherwise, it would result in injustice.

Political Justice.—The Contents and the legal meaning of Political Justice is that even in matters of principles and policies, fair treatment should be maintained. All institutions that create inequality should be abolished *e.g.* slavery, untouchability should not be tolerated in any form whatsoever. There should be no victimisation on political grounds, and people should have voice in choosing the type of political system that they want for their country. Promotion of national integration, cultural affinities and creating the feeling of belonging to the country, nationalism and patriotism are some of the political objectives that tend to establish political justice.

Economic Contents and the Justice.—Economic justice means eradication of all institutions that foster economic inequalities or obstruct the progress of the society on economic fronts. War on poverty, indebtedness, promotion of agro-industries, small scale industries, abolition of feudal tenures, ceiling on agricultural land, ceiling on income fair wage legislation employment guarantee or payment of unemployment allowance etc. are steps to establish economic justice in the society. It includes promotion of planned and balanced economic development, harnessing and efficient distribution of the material resources of the community and guarantee of active participation in activities of promoting national economy and social welfare.

Social justice.—Social justice means removal of inequalities nurtured by social institutions, *e.g.*, caste system. Promotion of social justice includes reservations for socially, educationally and economically backward sections of society in public services, including women, children and landless labourers. Tribalism is a social evil and needs curtailment in the interest of the society and natural integration. Language and dialect also create social prejudices. Promotion of social justice includes, independent judiciary, guarantee of access to court, legal aid, right to work, education and fraternity. The idea of law has always been associated with the idea of justice, and this represented the ultimate goal to which the law should strive. In India, reservation to women has been done at the level of village Pradhan, block and district level elective offices and there is strong move for reservation in Parliament and State Assemblies.

Formal Justice.—Formal justice requires equality of treatment in accordance with the qualifications laid down by the rules, but it tells us nothing about how people should or should not be classified or treated. The classification between human beings remains of necessity, a mere formality, until we have proceeded to indicate how we are going to divide people up into further sub-groups according to what are regarded as the moral or social needs of the particular society. Moreover, even treating people equally may involve special arrangements in favour of the poorer or humble sections of the community, to enable them to seek justice on an equal footing with those who possess natural, social, or economic advantages, which otherwise would weigh heavily in their favour, for example, legal aid.

Substantial or concrete justice.—Modern legal systems draw a sharp distinction between *formal* and *substantial* or *concrete justice* with the aim to fill the gap between them. The criterion of equality, as related to formal justice, operates in this idea purely as a logical and formal principle and not as an ultimate value to which society must be directed, in spite of the fact that equality in general takes an important place in the scale of values operating at present in the society. The general nature of the rules means that not every situation can be foreseen or provided for adequately and formal justice therefore, may press hard in individual case. This is why all legal systems are introducing certain discretionary powers to interpret the laws in the spirit of equality rather than insisting on their strict letters and to limit or control their operation in cases of hardships.

Features of legal justice.—The three features of *legal justice* are: (i) the existence of rules, (ii) their generality, (iii) their impartial application.

Legal rules cannot be truly "neutral" or "fair". They only can be relatively "neutral" or "fair", within some value conception, or measured against some standard, usually of a particular society. *What is fair and just in one society, does not necessarily mean the same in other*. The law controls and regulates, but it also supports this state of affairs. To this extent, law itself is not and cannot be "fair", cannot be neutral, between classes and strata of the population. It favours those who have, even when it does nothing more than let them keep what they have.

Even if all legal systems fall short to some extent of achieving complete *impartiality*, we cannot regard the universal preservation of impartiality as an essential attribute of law itself. A certain measure of coherence and regularity is a vital feature of any legal system, but no exact standard can be laid down by which this measure is to be judged. In addition to the above mentioned features which are common, both to law and justice, equitable element should be added.

Legal Injustice

Legal injustice is opposed to legal justice. Most people distinguish following three types of cases in which injustice in relation to law may arise:

(i) Legal injustice may be done when a case is decided in a sense contrary to what the law itself lays down. Of course, whether what the law lays down coincides with what is regarded as substantial justice is quite another matter.

(ii) Legal injustice is perpetrated when the law is not duly administered in that spirit of impartiality which it requires.

(iii) Legal injustice will arise when the law, though perfectly impartially administered is itself unjust, if judged by, whatever value system, may be applied to test substantial justice of the legal rule.

Obedience, disobedience, law and society

To very idea of law implies rules that are more often obeyed than violated, because if this were not the case, we would have to speak of lawless behaviour rather than a legal order. In the same sense, we could not speak of society unless there were a tendency to conform to general social norms.

Obedience

There are many explanations of man's *obedience to law*. Some insist that man obeys law simply because he is forced to, others argue that man sees in law that reflection of natural order that morally compels obedience. In between these extremes are theories citing such factors as an internationalisation of norms, habit, a sense of the need for reciprocity and fair play, a "social contract" among members of the society through which public order is attained, the rational acceptance of law as desirable and so on. The immediate and simplest answer is that law is binding because most people in society consider it to be. The awareness and consciousness of law by most people serve as the foundation for its existence. People generally submit their behaviour to its regulations, although they may have many different reasons for doing so. Some may believe that in obeying the law, they obey the higher authority of the law: God, nature, or simply the will of other people: the kings, chief and so on. Others acknowledge the context of the law to command obedience which, in turn, is seen as an obligation. Even when laws go against generally accepted morality they are often obeyed (Nazi Germany, apartheid laws). Another reason for obeying law may be that people rather prefer order over disorder. Sanctions for disobedience to law are surely among the strongest reasons why laws have binding force.

Civil disobedience

If substantial obedience to law represented by legitimate authority are key features of the legal system, so also is *civil disobedience*. Disobedience to law may be: (i) intentional or non-intentional, (ii) individual or collective; (iii) haphazard or systematic; (iv) violent or non-violent, it may be directed against particular legal rules or against an entire legal order, and may on occasion, of course, be part of a broader rebellion. Such practices are usually defined by the legal term of "*civil disobedience*".

Civil disobedience may attempt direct interference with some official act considered unjust, or it may instead simply have indirect impact upon legal processes. But invariably, it goes beyond private law-violation, because it involves an attempt to dramatise publicly what is considered major injustice within the legal order. Thus, the term "civil disobedience" should apply only to a principled act of objection and cnallenge.

The "right to resist" in a society which flagrantly and generally flouts the most elemental principles of legality is frequently asserted by philosophers in democracy. But even within a generally democratic order, the persistent inability to correct flagrant injustice through ordinary legal processes, and the need to tame a majority into recognising its obligations to justice, may sometimes be said to justify civil disobedience.

It should however be strongly emphasised that "the legal order, by definition, cannot provide for its own violation." Those who civilly disobey must be prepared to accept penalties for such action. Indeed, sometimes such acceptance of punishment is viewed as a central aspect of achieving the goal of dramatising a legal wrong. In words of Martin Luther King.

> "One has not only a legal but moral responsibility to obey just laws. Conversely, one has a moral responsibility to disobey unjust laws. It would agree with Saint Augustine that 'An unjust law is no law at all.'

..... An unjust law is a code that is out of harmony with the moral law. To put it in the terms of Saint Thomas Aquinas, "an unjust law is a human law that is not rooted in eternal and natural law. Any law that uplifts human personality is just. any law that degrades human personality is unjust. All segregation statutes are unjust because segregation distorts the soul and damages the personality."

Mob Law and Mob Justice (INSTANT JUSTICE)

'Mob law' 'pressure of the society' is one of the notable factors on which the Rule of law survives. Whenever Rule of law fails or fails to react at the opportune time, the mob inter venes; takes law in its own hands, acts as the accuser, judge and executioner. This is 'mob law' and the justice is mob justice or instant justice.

It may be called 'brute' non-cultural, Inhuman (rude and cruel by many current societies but it is a fact that existed, exists and would exist. The working of a system of law (criminal law) in Southia (Arabia) upholds the view. There is need to study such systems of law by the researchers as to what it is; what is its secret. Does it uphold rule of law' by preventing its 'mass destruction by violating the law. The mob does the justice, feels that the justice has been done giving a signal to rule of law' to the effect that justice delayed is justice denied. Why mob beats a thief to death or lynches a rapist to die; is a mystery which can be analised to the advantage of the rule of the law. It serves a timely warning to act more expeditiously. However, it needs to take guard against justice hurried is justice buried. Balancing has to be there.

The International Criminal Court and Mass Crimes

On July 17, 1998, the Rome Statute for establishing a permanent International criminal Court (ICC) was adopted : 120 countries voted it in, the United States, Iraq, China, Israel, Qatar, Yemen and Libya voted against, and 21 countries abstained, India among them. It was a dramatic movement, when governments spanning continents and political cultures acknowledged that the criminal laws of states were not bringing the perpetrators of mass crimes to justice. The word "impunity" had acquired a significance that was no longer possible to ignore. Where states are "unable or unwilling" to investigate and prosecute perpetrators of mass crimes, the ICC could step in, breaching the structures of impunity that had set in over the years. The Court would try individuals and not states.

On July 1, 2002, the Statute came into force. By now, 122 countries have signed and ratified the Rome Statute, testimony to the anxiety over the escalation and pervasiveness of large-scale atrocities across the world. Thirty-one countries have signed up but not yet ratified it. Of these, the U.S., Israel and Sudan have withdrawn as signatories to the Statute a process not known to international law—intending to communicate that they will not be moving towards its adoption, and may even now act in ways contrary to its "object and purpose."

India's stance

The ICC challenges impunity. It is striking that when the issue of impunity was raised in discussions on the Rome Statute in India during 1997-98, there were very few who were acquainted with the term. Half-a-decade later, the word had entered common parlance. The events in Gujarat helped. When discussions were held with civil liberties groups, there was little interest in the ICC which was, in 1997, seen as irrelevant for India; in 2002, this changed.

India has been hostile to the idea of internationalising criminal justice and is not a party to the ICC. What's more, in December 2002, India inked a Bilateral Immunity Agreement with the U.S.—which has signed over a 100 such agreements to nullify the ICC's impact as far as U.S. personnel are concerned—with an eagerness that was embarrassing. the stodgy silence that India has maintained on the role and functioning of international criminal tribunals investigating mass crimes in Rwanda and Yugoslavia, and the cases before the ICC itself, belies the Indian claim for a permanent seat on the Security Council.

The Indian position, that India does not need the ICC because it is perfectly capable of dealing with mass crimes, is misleading. The ICC only steps in when the state does not act, or acts in ways that shield perpetrators. In line with its founding principle of "complementarity" between national courts and international tribunals, the ICC refers to the former's role in the domestic criminal justice system. But the responsibility for developing criminal jurisprudence in relation to mass crimes rests with the ICC, and the role of the states parties, the prosecutor, the judges and the states that cooperate with the court is not negligible; India has abdicated this space altogether.

Theories of Justice

The topic of justice has been raised since the emergence of social organisation and has been a matter of policy prescriptions at least since Aristotle. In the last three decades theoretical reflection has taken new interesting directions with reference to both autonomous analytic developments and practical reasons, such as the (founded or unfounded) need to reshape the welfare state. A reflection on existing theories of justice can be useful for both theoretical and practical purposes.

The concepts of social conditioning and individual (personal) responsibility play an important role in theories of justice. They are an essential junction of social sciences since Montesquieu.

The former has been the concern of social scientists, at least after the first appearance of modern socialism and then Engels' and Marx's scientific socialism.

As to the concept of personal responsibility eurbaey argues that economists have long since understood that unless one is willing to accept big efficiency losses, equality cannot be achieved because the agents have some influence over their own outcomes. The Political philosophers argue that equality is not desirable in the first place for exactly the same reason the equality would deny responsibility'.

However, it was not until the beginning of the eighties that the concept of personal responsibility assumed an explicit and central role in theories of justice. It was Dworkin who brought this concept to the fore in the discussion of theories of justice, reaching the conclusion that individuals must be 'compensated' only for aspects of their situation for which they are not responsible, not for those (including preferences) for which they can be held responsible.

Roemer's principle, apparently very ingenious, leads to critical considerations that may be interesting not only from an economic viewpoint but also in other areas, *e.g.*, with respect to the current debate on guilt and penalty, which has gained new momentum under the influence of neo-determinism and tends to underscore not only social but also biological conditioning of human actions.

As far as practical economic questions are concerned, the principle of equality of opportunity can have important implications with respect to the reform of the welfare state. The welfare state has been the object of heavy criticism since its establishment precisely with regard to its inconsistency with the principle of personal responsibility. Under the pressure of financial constraints this criticism has recently acquired new emphasis, and a shift from universal supply of benefits to benefits calibrated on the basis of some indicator of personal responsibility (*e.g.*, workfare) has been advocated.

Theories of justice and impact of vision.

Theories of justice differ essentially because of different visions, *i.e.*, the intertwining of value judgments and analytic elements concerning the way human 'systems' work (from an economic, social, psychological and biological point of view).

Value judgments differences

Differences in the system of value judgments are thus one of the two causes of divergences in theories of justice. This seems to be the focus of both Bobbio (1999) and Hayek (1960). Without falling into an unfounded and sterile relativism, we can however think that the difference in value judgments is not such as to lead someone to be egalitarian and another to be anti-egalitarian. All ethical theories tend to be egalitarian in some 'space', at least in order to gain social plausibility and acceptance. Differences in value judgments-and analytic models as well-tend to lead to a difference in 'focal' variables, *i.e.* the 'space' in which equality is advocated (income, wealth, 'success', happiness, capability, liberty, rights, etc.). Because of the diversity of personal characteristics, equality in one space would tend to imply inequality in another space. Therefore, different views, all supporting equality, but in different spaces, will have practical consequences that are very different : very unequal positions in one space can be associated with equal positions in another space.

Different models of economic systems

A second reason for diversity in concepts of equality derives from the different models of economic systems (more generally, of human behaviour) that one relies on : any such model emphasises different causes and/or effects of inequality. Diversity in analytic models of human behaviour interacts with each person's final value judgments, thus leading us to choose different spaces for equality.

Since we are specifically interested in questions of personal responsibility and social conditioning, we will limit our analysis to the set of spaces of 'outcomes', neglecting other aspects of individual positions such as rights and liberties. With reference to outcomes, different visions about equality will then imply different income, wealth, 'success', happiness or capability for different people.

Utilitarianism (Hedonism) (largest happiness of largest number)

A society, according to Utilitarianism, is just to the extent that its laws and institutions are such as to promote the greatest overall or average happiness of its members. How do we determine the aggregate, or overall, happiness of the members of a society? This would seem to present a real problem. For happiness is not, like temperature or weight, directly measurable by any means that we have available. So utilitarians must approach the matter indirectly. They will have to rely on indirect measures, in other words. What would these be, and how can they be identified? The traditional idea at this point is to rely upon (a) a theory of the human good (*i.e.*, of what is good for human beings, of what is required for them to flourish) and (b) an account of the social conditions and forms of organization essential to the realization of that good.

People, of course, do not agree on what kind of life would be the most desirable. Intellectuals, artists, ministers, politicians, corporate bureaucrats, financiers, soldiers, athletes, salespersons, workers : all these different types of people, and more besides, will certainly not agree completely on what is a happy, satisfying, or desirable life. Very likely they will disagree on some quite important points. All is not lost, however. For there may yet be substantial agreement—enough, anyway, for the purposes of a theory of justice-about the general conditions requisite to human flourishing in all these otherwise disparate kinds of life. First of all there are at minimum certain basic needs that must be satisfied in any desirable kind of life. Basic needs, says James Sterba, are those needs "that must be satisfied in order not to seriously endanger a person's mental or physical well-being".

Basic needs, if not satisfied, lead to lacks and deficiencies with respect to a standard of mental and physical well-being. A person's needs for food, shelter, medical care, protection, companionship, and self-development are, at least in part, needs of this sort. A basic-needs minimum, then, is the minimum wherewithal required for a person to meet his or her basic needs. Such needs are universal. People will be alike in having such needs, however much they diverge in regard to the other needs, desires, or ends that they may have.

Nature of happy satisfied life—Aristotle

We may develop this common ground further by resorting to some of Aristotle's ideas on this question of the nature of a happy and satisfying life. Aristotle holds that humans are rational beings and that a human life is essentially rational activity, by which he means that human beings live their lives by making choices on the basis of reasons and then acting on those choices. All reasoning about what to do proceeds from premises relating to the agent's beliefs and desires. Desire is the motive for action and the practical syllogism (Aristotle's label for the reasoning by which people decide what to do) is its translation into choice. Your choices are dictated by your beliefs and desires—provided you are rational. Such choices, the reasoning that leads to them, and the actions that result from them are what Aristotle chiefly means by the sort of rational activity that makes up a human life. We may fairly sum up this point of view by saying that people are "rational end-choosers". If Aristotle is at all on the right track, then it is clear that a basic-needs minimum is a prerequisite to any desirable kind of life, and further that to live a desirable kind of life a person must be free to determine his or her own ends and have the wherewithal—the means, the opportunities—to have a realistic chance of achieving those ends. (Some of these Aristotelian points are perhaps implicitly included in Sterba's list of basic needs, under the head of self-development).

So what does all this do for Utilitarianism? Quite a lot. The theory of the human good, the general conditions essential to a happy or desirable life. The Utilitarian may plausibly claim to be trying to promote the overall happiness of people in his society, therefore, when he tries to improve such things as rate of employment, per capita income, distribution of wealth and opportunity, the amount of leisure, general availability and level of education, poverty rates, social mobility, and the like. The justification for thinking these things relevant should be pretty plain. They are measures of the amount and the distribution of the means and opportunities by which people can realize their various conception of a desirable life. With these things clearly in mind the Utilitarian is in a position to argue about item (b), the sorts of social arrangements that will deliver the means and opportunities for people to achieve their conception of a desirable life.

Stuart Mill

John Stuart Mill, one of the three most important 19th century Utilitarians (the other two were Jeremy Bentham and Henry Sidgwick), argued that freedom or liberty, both political and economic, were indispensable requisites for happiness. Basing his view upon much the same interpretation of human beings and human life as Aristotle, Mill argued that democracy and the basic political liberties—freedom of speech (and the press), of assembly, of worship—were essential to the happiness of rational end-choosers; for without them they would be prevented from effectively pursuing their own conception of a good and satisfying life. Similarly he argued that some degree of economic prosperity—wealth—was indispensable to having a realistic chance of living such a life, of realizing one's ends.

So, according to Utilitarianism, the just society should be so organized in its institutions—its government, its laws, and its economy—that as many people as possible shall have the means and opportunity to achieve their chosen conception of a desirable life. To reform the institutions of one's society toward this goal, in the utilitarian view, is to pursue greater justice.

The institutions that utilitarians have championed—These are :

(1) **A public education system** open to all and funded by public money, *i.e.*, taxes.

(2) **A competitive, "free" market economy**. In the 19th century utilitarians often argued for a *laissez faire* capitalist economy. More recently some of them have argued for a "mixed" economy, *i.e.*, a state regulated market system. Mill, interestingly, argued at the beginning of the 19th century for an unregulated capitalist economy, but at the end argued for a socialist economy (which is not the same thing as a "mixed economy").

(3) **The protection of the sorts** of liberties that were guaranteed in the United States by the Bill of Rights in our Constitution.

(4) **Democratic forms** of government generally.

Utilitarianism and Competitive Capitalism

The key claim about market capitalism for the utilitarian is that free, unregulated markets efficiently allocate resources—chiefly labour and capital—in the production of goods. By a market is meant only any pattern of economic activity in which buyers do business with sellers. In the classical system of economics competition is presupposed among producers or sellers. Toward the end of the nineteenth century writers began to make explicit...that competition required that there by a considerable number of sellers in any trade or industry in informed communication with each others. In more recent times this have been crystallized into the notion of many sellers doing business with many buyers. Each is well informed as to the prices at which others are selling and buying—there is a going price of which everyone is aware. Most important of all, no buyer or seller is large enough to control or exercise an appreciable influence on the common price...

The notion of efficiency as applied to an economic system is many-sided. It can be viewed merely as a matter of getting the most for the least...There is also the problem of getting the particular things that are wanted by the community in the particular amounts in which they re wanted. In addition, if an economy is to be efficient some reasonably full use must be made of the available, or at least the willing, labor supply. There must be some satisfactory allocation of resources between present and future production—between what is produced for consumption and what is invested in new plant and processes to enlarge future consumption. There must also be appropriate incentive to change; the adoption of new and more efficient methods of production must be encouraged. Finally—a somewhat different requirement and one that went long unrecognized—there must be adequate provision for the research and technological development which brings new methods and new products into existence. All this makes a large bill of requirements.

The peculiar fascination of the competitive model was that, given its particular form of competition—that of many sellers, none of whom was large enough to influence the price—all the requirements for efficiency, with the exception of the very last, were met. No producer...could gain additional revenue for himself by raising or otherwise manipulating his price. This opportunity was denied to him by the kind of competition which was assumed, the competition of producers no one of whom was large enough in relation to all to influence the common price. He could gain an advantage only y reducing costs. Were there even a few ambitious men in the business he would have to do so to survive, for if he neglected his opportunities others would seize them. If there are already many in a business it can be assumed that there is no serious bar to others entering it. Given an opportunity for improving efficiency of production, those who seized it, and the imitators they would attract from within and without [the industry in question], would expand production and lower prices. The rest, to survive at the these lower prices, would have to conform to the best and most efficient practices. In such a manner a Darwinian struggle for business survival concentrated all energies on the reduction of costs and prices.

In this model, producer effort and consumer wants were also effectively related by the price that no producer and no consumer controlled or influenced. The price that would just compensate some producer for added labor, or justify some other cost, was also the one which it was just worth the while of some consumer to pay for the product in question. Any diminution in consumer desire for the item would be impersonally communicated through lower price to producers. By no longer paying for marginal labor or other productive resources the consumer would free these resources for other employment on more wanted products. Thus energies were also efficiently concentrated on producing what was most desired :...When the taste of the consumer waned for one product it waxed for another; the higher price for the second product communicated to the producers in that industry the information that they could profitably expand their production and employment. They took in the slack that had been created in the first industry.

Pure competitions; Conditions needed;

Idealisation (1 to 3)

(1) There are sufficient numbers of buyers and sellers so that no single firm by itself can affect the prices it pays suppliers or the prices it charges its buyers, regardless of how much or little it produces.

(2) There are no entry or exit barriers to the market, *i.e.*, the market is one into which new firms can move with ease and out of which unsuccessful firms can easily exit.

(3) The outputs or products of the firms competing in the market

are undifferentiated. When pure competition exists in a market, when, that is, the market meets conditions (1)-(3), then the following important consequences will follow :

Yield beneficent consequences (4 to 6)

(4) Resources—chiefly capital and labor—will be efficiently employed : they will be used to produce good at the lowest possible prices, and there will be adequate incentive for producers to do this and to seek more efficient (cheaper) methods of production.

(5) Resources will be efficiently allocated : the "particular things that are wanted by the community" will be provided "in the particular amounts in which they are wanted". For, again, producers have adequate incentives to accommodate to consumer demand.

(6) Reasonably full employment for all willing workers will be maintained.

Objections to the Utilitarian Argument for Unregulated Competition

It should be noted that the conditions (1)-(3) for pure competition are an idealization. They have rarely been jointly met in fact. But where they are not all realized, it cannot be argued that the operation of the market is guaranteed to yield the beneficent consequences (4)-(6). Writing in the mid-nineteen fifties, Galbraith noted that "in the production of motor vehicles, agricultural machinery, rubber tires, cigarettes, aluminum, liquor, meat products, copper, tin containers and office machinery the largest three firms in 1947 did two thirds or more of all business". For other products, "steel, glass industrial chemicals, and dairy products, the largest six accounted for two thirds" (*ibid.*). The situation has changed somewhat over the intervening half century; you would not find the same list of firms at the top of these industries now, as then. There have been mergers and buyouts, and international competition has increased. But the basic fact of a few large firms dominating the market has not changed in these industries.

When there is great consolidation within an industry, condition (1) is obviously violated : there will no longer be sufficiently many sellers doing business will sufficiently many sellers. But condition (2) typically is not longer satisfied either. Very large firms in an industry will have been able to take advantage of economies of scale; production, to be competitive, will have to proceed on a comparable scale. These objections merely touch on much larger issues about the nature of the modern economy. which in its main parts does not fit the classical picture.

Problems for Utilitarianism

The objections, to the Utilitarian Argument in favor of competitive markets are not objections to Utilitarianism itself. They reveal no fault in Utilitarianism but only with a certain argument that presupposes Utilitarianism. the fault revealed is in the argument's assumption that the modern economy consists of markets in which there is pure competition. It want now to consider an objection to Utilitarianism itself as a theory of justice.

Utilitarians look at the means or opportunities available to people to achieve the kinds of lives they find desirable. Let us introduce the term "utility" for all of the things—such as income—that people might desire for the pursuit of their happiness. What the utilitarian aims at directly, then, is an overall increase of utility or utilities. the utilitarian looks to increase the *average* utility, i.e., the aggregate amount of utility created in the society, divided by the number of people in the society. the utilitarian thinks a just society should seek to maximize average utility in order to promote the happiness of its members or at least to enable its members, with increasing success, to achieve their own happiness.

But this way of evaluating forms of social organization is arguably defective because it may lead to unjust institutional arrangements. John Rawls famously stated the objection in his *A Theory of Justice*. There is...a way of thinking of society which makes it very easy to suppose that the most rational conception of justice is utilitarian. For consider : each man in realizing his own interests is certainly free to balance his own losses against his own gains. We may impose a sacrifice on ourselves now for the sake of a greater advantage later. a person quite properly acts, at least when others are not affected, to achieve his own greatest good, to advance his rational ends as far as possible. Now why should not a society act on precisely the same principle applied to the group and therefore regard that [decision-making procedure] which is rational for one man as right for an association of men? Just as the well-being of a person is constructed from the series of satisfactions that are experienced at different moments in the course of his life, so in very much the same way the well-being of society is to be constructed from the fulfillment of the systems of desires of the many individuals who belong to it. Since the principle for an individual is to advance as far as possible his own welfare, his own system of desires, the principle for society is to advance as far as possible the welfare of the group, to realize to the greatest extent the comprehensive system of desire arrived at from the desires of its members. Just as an individual balances present and future against present and future losses, so a society may balance satisfactions and dissatisfactions between different individuals. And so by these reflections one reaches the principle of utility in a natural way : a society is properly arranged when its institutions maximize the net balance of satisfaction.

Critical difference in cases of individuals and social groups

The critical difference, between the cases of an individual and of a social group attempting to maximize their welfare. In the case of an individual it will always be the same person who experiences both the losses and the gains. In the case of the social group it may not be the same people who experience both the losses and the gains. Some may experience the losses and others the gains, or the losses may fall disproportionately on some and the gains go disproportionately to others. Thus, Rawls argues, questions of fairness or justice arise in the case of the social group that do not arise in the case of the single individual, and utilitarianism is unprepared to address these. The problem, as Rawls puts it, is that Utilitarianism does not properly recognize "the separateness of persons"—the fact that the losses and gains may be experienced by separate—and hence different—persons. The striking feature of the utilitarian view of justice is that it does not matter, except indirectly, how this sum of satisfactions is distributed among individuals any more than it matters, except indirectly, how one man distributes his satisfactions over time. The correct distribution in either case is that which yields the maximum fulfillment. Society must allocate its means of satisfaction whatever these are, rights and duties, opportunities and privileges, and various forms of wealth, so as to achieve this maximum if it can...Thus there is no reason in principle why the greater gains of some should not compensate for the lesser losses of others or more importantly, why the violation of the liberty of a few might not be made right by the greater good shared by many...For just as it is rational for one man to maximize the fulfillment of his system of desires, it is right for a society to maximize the net balance of satisfaction taken over all its members.

It should be becoming clearer what the problem here is. There are two aspects to the problem.

First, Utilitarianism, in the light of Rawls's objection may appear to permit or, in some circumstances, even require that a society adopt unfair, exploitative forms of organization to promote its overall welfare, the average utility. If the welfare or happiness can be maximized by a form of social organization in which some few are exploited—if no other form of social organization can produce greater overall welfare or happiness—then adoption of the exploitative form of organization would be justified according to Utilitarianism. To this most utilitarians respond that "under most conditions, at least in a reasonably advanced stage of civilization, the greatest sum of advantages is not attained in this way," *i.e.*, by exploitation. This may or may not be so.

The second aspect of the problem raised by Rawls has to do with the inappropriateness of the kinds of arguments by which Utilitarians reject various discriminatory or exploitative forms of social organization. The utilitarians reject such forms of organization, as we have just seen, on the ground that they don't in fact succeed in maximizing the happiness or welfare of the social group. But what if they did succeed in maximizing the happiness or welfare of the social group? Would that show that they really were just? Rawls argues that it clearly would not. Consider the institution of slavery, which is as clearly unjust as an institution can be. It is never an excuse or justification for slavery. Rawls says, "that it is sufficiently advantageous to the slaveholder to outweight the disadvantages to the slave and to society. A person who argues in this way is not perhaps making a wildly irrelevant remark; but he is guilty of a moral fallacy. But Utilitarianism, Rawls points out,"permits one to argue that slavery is unjust on the grounds that the advantages to the slaveholder as slaveholder do not counterbalance the disadvantages to the slave and to society at large,

Rawls's Theory of Justice as Fairness—Reformulation of utilitarianism

The reformulation of Utilitarianism we just saw comes from John Rawls, who did not present it as a version of Utilitarianism at all. He presented it as a first approximation to a quite distinct conception of justice from Utilitarianism, a conception that he calls "Justice as Fairness". Which is a reformulation of Utilitarianism, anyway, because it seems to me to be greatly clarifying of what's wrong with Utilitarianism to have an alternative to compare it to, an alternative that blocks the kinds of fairness objections that are typically raised against Utilitarianism.

In Utilitarianism everyone, in a way, is given equal consideration at the outset inasmuch as everyone's happiness is taken into consideration and is given the same weight in the reasoning by which a form of social organization is settled on as the one that, in the circumstances, yields the greatest average utility. But, as we saw, Utilitarianism may in some circumstances settle on a form of social organization that treats some people unfairly, by imposing undue burdens on them for the sake of the greater average utility or happiness of the whole social group. In the light of this fact it is reasonable to conclude that something is wrong with the Utilitarian procedure for weighing the interests of the individual members of the social group in deciding on what forms of social organization best serve those interests. The procedure puts individuals at and undesirable and unfair risk of being sacrificed for the overall social good. In the principle that we suggested as a revision of Utilitarianism, people would not be put at quite the same risk.

Rawls in fact argues for a more elaborate principle of justice in social organization, one that we haven't seen yet, and he does so by employing a hypothetical model of a situation requiring people to choose the fundamental principles by which the basic institutions of their society are to be evaluated and organized. He argues that in the hypothetical conditions under which the choice of principles is to be made, only fair or just principles can be chosen. He argues that this is so because of the hypothetical conditions he imposes on the situation of the people making the choice. Then he argues that under those conditions people would choose the following conjunction of principles :

(1) The Equal Liberty Principle by Rawls—Each person is to have the maximum civil liberties compatible with the same liberty for all.

(2) The Difference Principle by Rawls—Inequalities are permissible only if (a) they can be expected to work to everyone's advantage, especially to the advantage of the least well off, and (b) the positions, offices, roles, to which the inequalities attach are open to all under conditions of fair equality of opportunity.

Rawls argues for these principles by showing that they would be chosen in a certain hypothetical situation that he defines. This hypothetical situation he calls the Original Position (OP, for short). In the OP people are stipulated to be in a rather peculiar state that could never be realized in actuality. They are imagined to have simpler motivation than people in fact have and to be ignorant of certain facts about themselves that no rational person in fact could be ignorant of; they are imagined to be simply self-interested in motivation and to have no knowledge of their own particular interests. They are assumed to know that they have to choose the fundamental principles of organization for the basic institutions of their society, and given the risks posed by the choice, they are assumed to have adopted a cautious rule for choosing among the alternative principles put up for consideration. The rule by which they shall choose is often called the rule of choice. According to this rule one should choose that alternative whose worst possible outcome will be no worse than the worst possible outcomes of any other alternative.

These conditions are purely hypothetical; no one could actually meet these conditions. But this is irrelevant. For Rawls's argument does not require that you or I or anyone should actually make a choice of principles of justice under these conditions. It only requires that we be able to tell what choice we would make if we were to choose under such conditions. (Compare : We are told that nothing can travel at a velocity greater than than of light. But we can still determine what would happen if something did travel faster than light, and it is on the basis of what we thus determine that we conclude that nothing can in fact travel at a velocity greater than that of light.).

Original Position (O.P.)—conditions that define it;

1. The people in the original position are self-interested in motivation.

2. But they do not know what their particular interests are—not their inclinations, nor their plan of life, abilities, social and economic position, or even gender. (This important condition is called *the veil of ignorance.*)

3. They do know the general conditions of human life—what people are like generally, what social life is like.

4. They know that they are to choose the fundamental principles by which, ever after, the basic institutions of their society are to be organized and evaluated.

5. They are to choose among the alternative principles by the rule of maximin (a decision-making rule that says you should choose the alternative whose worst possible outcome is at least as good as the worst possible outcome of any other alternative). The rule applies, in this case, as follows. The choice is among alternative fundamental principles of justice or alternative sets of such. The relevant outcomes of each such choice are the resulting positions of advantage and disadvantage of individuals in the societies that accord with the chosen principles of justice. Let us suppose that you are one of the people in the original position. Since in the original position you are behind "the veil of ignorance", you don't know at all whether you might be one of the least favoured (least well-off) individuals or one of the most favoured in the society, and you have to take seriously the possibility that you will find yourself among the least well-off when the "veil

of ignorance" is lifted. This possibility, of course, is the worst possible outcome for you with regard to a choice of principle of justice. So by the maximin rule you should compare principles of justice by looking at the situation of the least well-off individuals under the various principles. For each principle of justice you should look at what things would be like for you if you were one of the least well-off individuals in any society that complied with that principle. Then you should choose the principle under which the least well-off individuals fare at least as well as the least well-off individuals under any alternative principle.

Rawls argues that only fair principle could be chosen by people in the OP (Original Position). Why? as Rawls argues, each person in the OP knows that he or she has some particular abilities and interests and so on; but, being behind the veil of ignorance, none of them knows what any of these are. Thus the only way that each can look out for him-or herself is to look out for everyone alike. One can look out for oneself only by choosing principles that do not favour any type of person over any other; for there is no type of person that one might not turn out to be, and so it is only in this way that one can guarantee that one will not be disadvantaged by the principles chosen. All forms of invidious discrimination will obviously be ruled out by the principles chosen in the original position; fairness therefore seems certain to be a trait of all of them. Thus, in outline, goes Rawls's argument that only fair principles would be chosen by people in the OP.

How does Rawls argue that the Equal Liberty and Difference principles would be the principles chosen in the OP (Original Position)?—There are certain liberties or rights that everyone would want to be respected by the forms of social organization or institutions of their society. Every one would want these rights to be so respected regardless of who he or she turned out to be or whatever specific interests and abilities he or she turned out to have. There may be called collectively as civil liberties or personal liberties.

These would include freedom of thought, speech, worship, and assembly, plus freedom from physical and psychological coercion, freedom of movement. These would also include *basic* property rights : the basic right to exclusive use of personal property (where this would not include the full capitalist rights to acquire and own the means of production, or full rights of bequeathal; these latter "capitalist" rights are subject to further negotiation. Everyone, whatever his interests or desires, would want the maximum of these liberties to pursue his interests; he would want this whatever else he wanted. Everyone in the OP (Original Position) would see this point; hence everyone in the OP (Original Position) would choose to have maximum of these liberties granted to everyone. Thus goes the argument for the Equal Liberty Principle.

The CHOICE OF THE DIFFERENCE PRINCIPLE is a little more difficult to explain. Initially one might expect the parties in the OP to prefer a social arrangement permitting no inequalities within society, or in other words to prefer absolute equality across the board, since obviously on one could be disadvantaged by such an arrangement. But Rawls argues that if it could be shown that some forms of inequality in income or property contributed to the improvement of everyone's circumstances, including those of the least well-off—by functioning, say, as incentives to socially productive work—then everyone in the OP would consent to allow them. Everyone in the OP (Original Position), that is, would consent to a social scheme permitting economic inequalities if those inequalities could be expected to improve everyone's lot over what it would be is the situation of absolute equality. Such an arrangement would then be supplemented, upon further reflection, by an additional protection of liberty : equality of opportunity. If an unequal distribution of wealth and property is to be allowed, everyone must, so far as possible, have an equal opportunity to attain the more desirable positions; otherwise such an arrangement might arbitrarily favour some people over others, by their social position, race, gender, or the like.

To those in the original position it would be an unacceptable risk to choose principles of justice that would permit any such serious inequality of opportunity to be built into the very institutional structure of society; for, though under such a scheme one might be in a position of advantage, one might also be seriously disadvantaged. This last is a possibility that, behind the veil of ignorance, one would be obliged to take seriously. For these reasons people in the OP (Original Position) would require that the positions or offices associated with greater income or property or prestige (or whatever) must be open to everyone alike, under conditions of equality of opportunity. This adumbrates the reasoning by which people in the OP would deliberate to a choice of the Difference Principal.

Why people in the OP (Original Position) would not choose Utilitarianism. It would be too risky. Utilitarianism, as we have seen, may permit institutional arrangements that disadvantage the few for the sake of the greater advantages that would be enjoyed by the many. Using the maximin rule, the people in the OP would have to compare the position of the least well-off persons living under such a Utilitarian scheme with the position of the least well-off persons living under the combined Equal Liberty and Difference Principles. In this comparison the Equal Liberty and Difference Principles are preferable to Utilitarianism.

Libertarianism—(Individual liberty)

The Libertarianism, emphasizes individual liberty as the central and indeed exclusive concern of social justice. A just society, according to the Libertarian, must grant and protect the liberty or freedom of each individual to pursue his desired ends. In the Libertarian view people are essentially rational end-choosers, to use our earlier term, and the kind of life appropriate to rational end-choosers requires them to be free to choose their own ends and free to pursue them without interference from others. This may seem to imply that the Libertarian holds that everyone should be able to do whatever he or she wants, but really the Libertarian holds no such view.

The Libertarian view is that each person should have the same freedom to pursue his chosen ends, that each is therefore obligated to refrain from interfering with others in their freedom to pursue their ends, and that the functions of the state is solely to protect each individual's freedom to pursue his chosen ends. The Libertarian therefore conceives of everyone as having certain rights, which protect his or her liberty to pursue a desirable kind of life. What is distinctive about Libertarianism is its conception of the rights that each individual has.

Fundamental libertarian principles—Hospers

The libertarian philosopher John Hospers states the fundamental libertarian principle in a variety of ways—

(1) Every person is the owner of his own life[;] and not the owner of any one else's life, and...consequently every human being has the right to act in accordance with his own choices, unless those actions infringe on the equal liberty of other human beings to act in accordance with their choices.

(2) No one is anyone else's master and no one is anyone else's slave.

(3) Other men's lives are not yours to dispose of.

(4) The rights recognized by the Libertarian include all the rights we called civil or personal liberties of Rawls, but in regard to property the Libertarian favours a scheme in which each person has a quite unrestricted right to acquire property, including full "capitalist" rights to acquire ownership of the means of production and full rights of bequeathal. Libertarians emphasize property rights as essential to the liberty, essential to the life of a rational end-chooser.

(5) Property does not mean only real estate; it includes anything that you can call your own—clothing, your car, your jewelry, your books and papers.

(6) The right of property is not the right to just *take* it from others, for this would interfere with *their* property rights. It is rather the right to work for it, to obtain non-coercively the money or services which you can present in voluntary exchanges.

(7) Depriving people of property is *sin. It is the means by which they live*—the freedom of the individual citizen to do what he wishes with his own life and to plan for the future...*Property rights are what makes long-range planning possible*—the kind of planning which is a distinctively human endeavor, as opposed to the day-to-day activity of [nonrational] animals. Without the right to property, the right to life itself amounts to little: how can you sustain your life if you cannot plan ahead? and how can you plan ahead if the fruits of your labour can at any moment be confiscated by [other persons or particularly by] government? So the package of rights recognized as genuine by Libertarians define and protect the freedom of choice and action that Libertarians hold to be requisite to the life desired by rational end-choosers. And property rights—the rights to acquire, use, and

transfer property—are held to be absolutely essential to effective freedom of choice and action.

Two ways to acquire property

There are two ways of acquiring property, broadly speaking. We can best see what the Libertarian position comes to by seeing what rights and duties a person has in regard to each of these ways of acquiring property.

(I) **By transfer if owned.**—Property may be acquired through its transfer from one person (who owns it) to another, or from one group of persons to another group. The transfer will be "just", and the person who acquires the property through the exchange will have just claim to the property if the exchange involves no coercion and no fraud, and if the initial owner is the legitimate owner of the property.

(II) **By mixing one's labour with the thing if unowned.**—One may acquire property by acquiring previously unowned things. In this case one does not acquire ownership through transfer from another owner; for it is an unowned thing that one acquires. How does one acquire ownership of a previously unowned thing? Can I claim ownership of the stars? If so, how? Libertarians often hold that one acquires ownership over previously unowned things by "mixing one's labour with the thing". The phrase is due to John Locke, a 17th century English philosopher. By applying one's efforts or labour to a thing, altering its condition, one can acquire ownership of the thing. Given his time and place, Locke was predictably interested in ownership of land. He thought that by planting crops on previously unowned land and tending to them, one could acquire ownership over both crops and land.

It is clear that ownership must be acquired either by means (I) or (II), and in most cases there will be a chain of transfers leading up to one's acquisition of some item of property, beginning with the initial acquisition of the item as previously unowned and then proceeding through a series of exchanges that ends with one's acquisition of the item by exchange. If there is nothing objectionable in the initial acquisition and if each of the transfers involves no force or fraud, then one will have a just claim to the item; one will be entitled by right to exclusive ownership of the item. If all property holdings have been acquired by such just means, then according to the Libertarian the distribution of property (which includes all forms of wealth) will be just, and it doesn't matter how ownership is distributed throughout the society: it doesn't matter whether everyone has significant wealth or whether all or most of the wealth is concentrated in a few hands.

Unregulated capitalist economy

Libertarians typically hold that a completely unregulated capitalist economy is the only form of economic organization that respects individuals' property rights. Individuals have the right of free association, the right to trade with one another freely, without coercion or fraud. Regulating—restricting—such rights for the sake of promoting the well-being of the community or social group would amount to an unjust interference with individual liberty. Notice the difference with 19th century Utilitarianism. The Utilitarians then favored a capitalist economy because they thought it efficiently promoted the well-being of the social group. The Libertarian does not favour a capitalist form of economic organization for that reason. He favours it because it respects individual liberty. Libertarians think that the state in particular cannot legitimately intervene in the operation of markets except to prevent fraud or coercion.

Unacceptables to libertarians

The welfare system, social security, medicare and medicaid, anti-trust laws, laws against racial, religious, and gender discrimination in hiring and promotion are one and all unacceptable to Libertarians. For each involves an unjust interference with individual liberty as the Libertarian understands individual liberty. People should be free to dispose of their property as they see fit and to associate with whomever they choose. If an employer irrationally prefers to hire only men or only white men, then that is his right and he must be permitted to do so according to Libertarianism; for he owns the property—the business—and may dispose of it as he sees fit, provided that he does not violate anyone else's Libertarian rights. If a homeowner wishes to discriminate by selling his home only to other members of his racial group, then that too is just. Again he owns the property and should be free to dispose of it as he desires, provided again that he does not violate anyone else's Libertarian rights. It is the peculiarity of Libertarianism that in discriminating in these ways one would not be violating anyone's rights. To require a person to practice racial fairness in hiring and promotion would be to recognize some positive right on the part of others that the person provide them with a job or a promotion. Libertarians recognize no such positive rights. No one is obligated to provide anyone with a job, just as no one is obligated to work for any particular employer. An employer may hire whomever he chooses and for any reason at all. It would be an impermissible restriction on his liberty to force him to hire certain types of people or to employ certain types of criteria in making the decision to hire.

In a society organized along Libertarian lines people will have to compete for the material means of survival. They will have to compete even to secure a basic needs minimum. The winners of the competition will gain control of resources and the means of production, the means by which the society provides for the material needs of its members. Thus private individuals are allowed to compete, in effect, for the power to make decisions that affect the welfare of whole communities. The very wealthy minority, by virtue of the control they have won over the community's resources and means of production, will be in a position to run the society, to make all the important decisions about the character of work and investments. And there is nothing to require that those decisions be made in the interest of the community or even that they must not be harmful in their effects on the community. The wealthy in control of economic resources are free to decide on the basis of their own interests alone. It is amazing, though true, that Libertarians see no significant loss of liberty for anyone in such a form of social organization.

Dependency Theory—Rawl Prebisch

Dependency theory is the notion that resources flow from a "periphery" of poor and underdeveloped states to a "core" of wealthy states, enriching the latter at the expense of the former. It is a central contention of dependency theory that poor states are impoverished and rich ones enriched by the way poor states are integrated into the "world system".

The theory arose as a reaction to modernization theory, an earlier theory of development which held that all societies progress through similar stages of development, that today's underdeveloped areas are thus in a similar situation to that of today's developed areas at some time in the past, and that, therefore, the task of helping the underdeveloped areas out of poverty is to accelerate them along this supposed common path of development, by various means such as investment, technology transfers, and closer integration into the world market. Dependency theory rejected this view, arguing that underdeveloped countries are not merely primitive versions of developed countries, but have unique features and structures of their own; and, importantly, are in the situation of being the weaker members in a world market economy.

Dependency theory no longer has many proponents as an overall theory, but some writers have argued for its continuing relevance as a conceptual orientation to the global division of wealth.

Dependency theory originates with two papers published in 1949—one by Hans Singer, one by Raul Prebisch—in which the authors observe that the terms of trade for underdeveloped countries relative to the developed countries had deteriorated overtime : the underdeveloped countries were able to purchase fewer and fewer manufactured goods from the developed countries in exchange for a given quantity of their raw materials exports. This idea is known as the Prebisch—Singer thesis. Prebisch, an Argentine economist at the United Nations Commission for Latin America (UNCLA), went on to conclude that the underdeveloped nations must employ some degree of protectionism in trade if they were to enter a self-sustaining development path. He argued that import-substitution industrialisation (ISI), not a trade and export orientation, was the best strategy for underdeveloped countries. the theory was developed from a Marxian perspective by Paul A. Baran in 1957 with the publication of his *the Political Economy of Growth.* Dependency theory shares many points with earlier, Marxist, theories of imperialism by Rosa Luxemburg and Vladimir Lenin, and has attracted continued interest from Marxists. Matias Vernengo, a Bucknell University economist, identifies two main streams in dependency theory : the Latin American Structuralist, typified by the work of Prebisch, Celso Furtado, and Anibal Pinto at the United Natons Economic Commission for Latin America (ECLAC, or, in Spanish, CEPAL); and the American Marxist, developed by Paul A. Baran, Paul A. Baran, Paul Sweezy, and Andre Gunder Frank.

Using the Latin American dependency model, the Guyanese Marxist historian Walter Rodney, in his book *How Europe Underdeveloped Africa*, described in 1972 an African that had been consciously exploited by European imperialists, leading directly to the modern underdevelopment of most of the continent.

The theory was popular in the 1960s and 1970s as a criticism of modernization theory, which was falling increasingly out of favour because of continued widespread poverty in much of the world. It was used to explain the causes of overurbanization, a theory that urbanization rates outpaced industrial growth in several developing countries.

According to Vernengo, the Latin American Structuralist and the American Marxist schools had significant differences but agreed on some basic points :

Both groups would agree that at the core of the dependency relation between center and periphery lays [lies] the inability of the periphery to develop an autonomous and dynamic process of technological innovation. Technology—the Promethean force unleashed by the Industrial Revolution—is at the center of stage. The Center countries controlled the technology and the systems for generating technology. Foreign capital could not solve the problem, since it only led to limited transmission of technology, but not the process of innovation itself.

Baran and others frequently spoke of the international division of labour—skilled workers in the center; unskilled in the periphery—when discussing key features of dependency.

Baran placed surplus extraction and capital accumulation at the center of his analysis. Development depends on a population's producing more than it needs for bare subsistence (a surplus). Further, some of that surplus must be used for capital accumulation—the purchase of new means of production—if development is to occur; spending the surplus on things like luxury consumption does not produce development. Baran noted two predominant kinds of economic activity in poor countries. In the older of the two, plantation agriculture, which originated in colonial times, most of the surplus goes to the landowners, who use it to emulate the consumption patterns of wealthy people in the developed world; much of it thus goes to purchase foreign-produced luxury items—automobiles, clothes, *etc.*—and little is accumulated for investing in development. The more recent kind of economic activity in the periphery is industry—but of a particular kind. It is usually carried out by foreigners, although often in conjunction with local interests. It is often under special tariff protection or other government concessions. The surplus from this production mostly goes to two places : part of it is sent back to the foreign shareholders as profit; the other part is spent on conspicuous consumption in a similar fashion to that of the plantation aristocracy. Again, little is used for development. Baran thought that political revolution was necessary to break this pattern.

In the 1960s, members of the Latin American Structuralist school argued that there is more latitude in the system than the Marxists believed. They argued that it allows for partial development or "dependent development"—development, but still under the control of outside decision makers. They cited the partly successful attempts at industrialisation in Latin America around that time (Argentina, Brazil, Mexico) as evidence for this hypothesis. They were led to the position that dependency is not a relation between commodity exporters and industrialised countries, but between countries with different degrees of industrialisation. In their approach, there is a distinction made between the economic and political spheres : economically, one may be developed or underdeveloped; but even if (somewhat) economically developed, one may be politically autonomous or dependent. More recently, Guillermo O'Donnell has argued that constraints placed on development by neoliberalism were lifted by "the military coups in Latin America that came to promote development in authoritarian guise" (Vernengo's words, summarising O'Donnell, 1982).

The importance of multinational corporations and state promotion of technology were emphasized by the Latin American Structuralists.

Fajnzybler has made a distinction between systemic or authentic competitiveness, which is the ability to compete based on higher productivity, and spurious competitiveness, which is based on low wages.

The third-world debt crisis of the 1980s and continued stagnation in Africa and Latin America in the 1990s caused some doubt as to the feasibility or desirability of "dependent development".

Vernengo (2004) has suggested that the *sine qua non* of the dependency relationship is not the difference in technological sophistication, as traditional dependency theorists believe, but rather the difference in financial strength between core and peripheral countries-particularly the inability of peripheral countries to borrow in their own currency. He believes that the hegemonic position of the United States is very strong because of the importance of its financial markets and because it controls the international reserve currency—the US dollar. He believes that the end of the Bretton Woods international financial agreements in the early 1970s considerably strengthened the United States' position because it removed some constraints on their financial actions.

"Standard" dependency theory differs from Marxism, in arguing against internationalism and any hope of progress in less developed nations towards industrialization and a liberating revolution. Theotonio dos Santos described a "new dependency", which focused on both the internal and external relations of less-developed countries of the periphery, derived from a Marxian analysis. Former Brazilian President Fernando Henrique Cardoso (in office 1995-2002) wrote extensively on dependency theory while in political exile during the 1960s, arguing that it was an approach to studying the economic disparities between the centre and periphery. Cardoso summarized his version of dependency theory as follows :

- there is a financial and technological penetration by the developed capitalist centers of the countries of the periphery and semi-periphery;
- this produces an unbalanced economic structure both within the peripheral societies and between them and the centers;
- this leads to limitations on self-sustained growth in the periphery;
- this favors the appearance of specific patterns of class relations;
- these require modifications in the role of the state to guarantee both the functioning of the economy and the political articulation of a society, which contains, within itself, foci of inarticulateness and structural imbalance.

The analysis of development patterns in the 1990s and beyond is complicated by the fact that capitalism develops not smoothly, but with very strong and self-repeating ups and downs, called cycles. Relevant results are given in studies by Joshua Goldstein, Volker Bornschier, and Luigi Scandella.

With the economic growth of India and some East Asian economies, dependency theory has lost some of its former influence. It still influences some NGO campaigns, such as Make Poverty History and the fair trade movement.

Other theorists and related theories

Two other early writers relevant to dependency theory were Francois Perroux and Kurt Rothschild. Other leading dependency theorists include Herb Addo, Walden Bello, Ruy Mauro Marini, Enzo Faletto, Armando Cordova, Ernest Feder, Pablo González Casanova, Keith Griffin, Kunibert Raffer, Paul Israel Singer, and Osvaldo Sunkel. Many of these authors focused their attention on Latin America; the leading dependency theorist in the Islamic world is the Egyptian economist Samir Amin.

Tausch, based on works of Amin from 1973 to 1997, lists the following main characteristics of periphery capitalism :

1. Regression in both agriculture and small scale industry characterizes the period after the onslaught of foreign domination and colonialism.
2. Unequal international specialization of the periphery leads to the concentration of activities in export-oriented agriculture and or mining. Some industrialization of the periphery is possible under the condition of low wages, which, together with rising productivity, determine that unequal exchange sets in (double factorial terms of trade).
3. These structures determine in the long run a rapidly growing tertiary sector with hidden unemployment and the rising importance of rent in the overall social and economic system.
4. Chronic current account balance deficits, re-exported profits of foreign investments, and deficient business cycles at the periphery that provide important markets for the centers during

world economic upswings.

5. Structural imbalances in the political and social relationships, *inter alia* a strong 'compradore' element and the rising importance of state capitalism and an indebted state class.

The American sociologist Immanuel Wallerstein refined the Marxist aspect of the theory and expanded on it, to form world-systems theory. This postulates a third category of countries, the *semi-periphery*, intermediate between the core and periphery. Wallerstein believed in a trial-modal rather than a bi-modal system because he viewed the world-systems as more complicated than a simplistic classification as either core or periphery nations. To Wallerstein, many nations do not fit into one of these two categories, so he proposed the idea of a semi-periphery as an in between state within his model. In this model, the semi-periphery is industrialized, but with less sophistication of technology than in the core; and it does not control finances. The rise of one group of semi-peripheries tends to be at the cost of another group, but the unequal structure of the world economy based on unequal exchange tends to remain stable. Tausch traces the beginnings of world-systems theory to the writings of the Austro-Hungarian socialist Karl Polanyi after the First World War, but its present form is usually associated with the work of Wallerstein.

Dependency theory has also been associated with Johan Galtung's structural theory of imperialism.

Dependency theorists hold that short-term spurts of growth notwithstanding, long-term growth in the periphery will be imbalanced and unequal, and will tend towards high negative current account balances. Cyclical fluctuations also have a profound effect on cross-national comparisons of economic growth and societal development in the medium and long run. What seemed like spectacular long-run growth may in the end turn out to be just a short run cyclical spurt after a long recession. Cycle time plays an important role. Giovani Arrighi believed that the logic of accumulation on a world scale shifts over time, and that the 1980s and beyond once more showed a deregulated phase of world capitalism with a logic, characterized—in contrast to earlier regulatory cycles—by the dominance of financial capital.

It is argued that, at this stage, the role of unequal exchange in the entire relationship of dependency cannot be underestimated. Unequal exchange is given if double factorial terms of trade of the respective country.

Criticism

Dependency theory has been criticized by free-market economists such as Peter Bauer and Martin Wolf and others :

- **Lack of competition.**—By subsidizing in-country industries and preventing outside imports, these companies may have less incentive to improve their products, to try to become more efficient in their processes, to please customers, or to research new innovations.
- **Sustainability.**—Industries reliant on government support may

not be sustainable for very long, particularly in poorer countries and countries which largely depend on foreign aid from more developed countries.

- **Domestic opportunity costs.**—Subsidies on domestic industries come out of state coffers and therefore represent money not spent in other ways, like development of domestic infrastructure, seed capital or need-based social welfare programs. At the same time, the higher prices caused by tariffs and restrictions on imports require the people either to forgo these goods altogether or buy them at higher prices, foregoing other goods.
- Market economists cite a number of examples in their arguments against dependency theory. The improvement of India's economy after it moved from state-controlled business to open trade is one of the most often cited (*see also* economy of India, *The Commanding Heights*). India's example seems to contradict dependency theorists' claims concerning comparative advantage and mobility, as much as its economic growth originated from movements such as outsourcing—one of the most mobile forms of capital transfer. South Korea and North Korea provide another example of trade-based development vs autocratic self-sufficiency. When the two states were divided at the end of the Korean War, they possessed roughly identical populations, resources and infrastructure and were at similar levels of development. North Korea pursued a policy of import substitution industrialization as suggested by dependency theory, while South Korea pursued a policy of export-oriented industrialization as suggested by comparative advantage theory. In 2013, South Korea's per capita GDP was 18 times that of North Korea. In Africa, states which have emphasized import-substitution development, such as Zimbabwe, have typically been among the worst performers, while the continent's most successful non-oil based economies, such as Egypt, South Africa, and Tunisia, have pursued trade-based development.

Dependency Theory developed in the late 1950s under the guidance of the Director of the United Nations Economic Commission for Latin America, Raul Prebisch. Prebisch and his colleagues were troubled by the fact that economic growth in the advanced industrialized countries did not necessarily lead to growth in the poorer countries. Indeed, their studies suggested that economic activity in the richer countries often led to serious economic problems in the poorer countries. Such a possibility was not predicted by neoclassical theory, which had assumed that economic growth was beneficial to all (Pareto optimal) even if the benefits were not always equally shared.

Conclusions contrary to neo-classical theory

Prebisch's initial explanation for the phenomenon was very straightforward: *poor countries exported primary commodities to the rich countries who then manufactured products out of those commodities and sold them back to the poorer countries.* The "Value Added" by manufacturing a usable product always costs more than the primary products used to create those products. Therefore, poorer countries would never be earning enough from their export earnings to pay for their imports. Prebisch's solution was similarly straightforward: poorer countries should embark on programmes of import substitution so that they need not purchase the manufactured products from the richer countries. The poorer countries would still sell their primary products on the world market, but their foreign exchange reserves would not be used to purchase their manufactures from abroad.

Three issues made this policy difficult to follow :

- The first is that the internal markets of the poorer countries were not large enough to support the economies of scale used by the richer countries to keep their prices low.
- The second issue concerned the political will of the poorer countries as to whether a transformation for being primary products producers was possible or desirable.
- The final issue revolved around the extent to which the poorer countries actually had control of their primary products, particularly in the area of selling those products abroad.

These obstacles to the import substitution policy led others to think a little more creatively and historically at the relationship between rich and poor countries.

At this point dependency theory was viewed as a possible way of explaining the persistent poverty of the poorer countries. The traditional neoclassical approach said virtually nothing on this question except to assert that the poorer countries were late in coming to solid economic practices and that as soon as they learned the techniques of modern economics, then the poverty would begin to subside.

However, Marxists theorists viewed the persistent poverty as a consequence of capitalist exploitation. And a new body of thought, called the *word systems approach*, argued that the poverty was a direct consequence of the evolution of the international political economy into a fairly rigid division of labour which favoured the rich and penalized the poor.

Dependency theory—Definition and history (LED vs MEDC)

Dependency theory posits that the cause of the low levels of development in less economically developed countries (LEDC's) is caused by their reliance and dependence on more economically developed countries (MEDC's) *i.e.* the LEDC's are undeveloped because they rely on the MEDC's. Some proponents of dependency theory assert that LEDC's will remain less developed because the surplus that they produce will be siphoned off by MEDC's—under the guise of multinational corporations. There is, as such, no profit left for reinvestment and development. As a corollary of this theory, LEDC's should cut off ties with MEDC's retain their surplus production, and follow economically independent and socialistic ideas in order to further develop their economies, as the Soviet Union had done to great effect. Additionally, it also emphasises the virtuous circle of self-perpetuating benefits that the MEDC's gain from their existing prosperity.

Dependency theory, as a theory based on materialist and structuralist theories, has been criticised for placing too much emphasis on material and economic factors. The development of many Asian economies that developed alone capitalistic, open lines, also serves as an empirical contradiction to dependency theory. (This is not to say that many Asian "tiger economies" did not follow the ideas propounded by development theory, for indeed many did—South Korea, Taiwan and others developed through a process of import-subsitution -backed up with heavy investment of American capital.)

Alternative to dependency theory

Development Theory—Frank

Development theory is a conglomeration or a collective vision of theories about how desirable change in society is best achieved. Such theories draw on a variety of social science disciplines and approaches. In this article, multiple theories are discussed, as are recent developments with regard to these theories. Depending on which theory that is being looked at, there are different explanations to the process of development and their inequalities.

Frank proposed an alternative to dependency theory—"Development theory".

Dependency vs Development theory

How does Frank's "dependency theory" differ from the traditional "development theory"? The conventional view of the undeveloped countries denies them a history: "To classify these countries as "traditional societies: implies either that the underdeveloped countries have no history or that it is unimportant." But it is increasingly clear that the history of the post-colonial countries has been crucially important in shaping their present underdevelopment. The most influential proponent of the thesis that European expansion and colonialism created the underdevelopment of these countries has been Andre Gubder Frank. Frank's thesis is that underdevelopment is not basically a consequence of traditionalism. Rather, he argues that underdevelopment in Latin America-and by extension, parts of Africa and Asia-has been systematically created by colonist exploitation. Frank has documented "the development of underdevelopment" in Chile, Brazil, Mexico and Cuba.

(1) What was wrong with the "top-down" approach?

It is widely agreed that the "top-down" approach which many agencies took to development was partly to blame. The assumption that experts, notably economists, can diagnose problems and devise plans for Governments to implement to improve people's lives is questioned. The arrogance, the ignorance of the needs and aspirations of the poor, did great damage.

(2) What does he mean by the "participatory" approach?

Agencies consulting more closely with their "target beneficiaries"-*i.e.* involving the poor themselves in problem identification and decision-making process, rather than trying to impose outsider-devised interventions on them.

(3) How does indigenous knowledge differ from scientific knowledge?

Indigenous knowledge is what "ordinary" folk know. This is local in geographical extent and cultural context. It is fragmentarily distributed, exists nowhere as a totality. although more widely shared locally than specialised scientific knowledge, no one person, institution, or authority encompasses it all.

Equivalence Theory

The deal with State is that we the citizens, agree not to kill each other over disputes or just for fun, and in return the government agrees to enforce the law equitably and promptly. A reciprocal arrangement that has enabled the freakish success of Western civilization.

In essence, we grant the government a monopoly on the use of force for all circumstances aside from self-defense. But what happens when one side or the other fails to uphold their part of the bargain?

Well, if it is the citizen who violates the rule, he is subjected to the full power and force of the government until he complies.

If it is the government that fails, the citizens determine if it is simply bad policy, or a deliberate abuse of power. If the former, then reforms are adopted to rectify the mistake. If the latter, then heads must roll and the violators are replaced and punished.

But what do we do when the latter scenario becomes the norm, not the exception? When the abuse of power is standard operating procedure, not a rare and aberrant circumstance?

The same remedy applies, but when it must occur on such a massive scale as would be necessary to cleanse the government of today, we have a different name for it—we call it a revolution.

No, I'm not calling for the violent overthrow of our government, so put down your phone. You don't know the number to the FBI anyway.

I'm simply pointing out the scale of the task before us, as we attempt to retain the republic that Benjamin Franklin warned us would be so difficult to keep.

So, aside from the typical corruption born of greed and lust for power, what threats to the social contract stand out from the crowd? I would say that misguided "equivalence theory" represents the most dangerous threat to liberal democratic society since the "targeting" rule in NCAA football.

Ok, I'm joking about the "targeting" rule. It's bad, but only in an annoying way, not like "equivalence theory" which is bad in a "we-won't-survive-it" sort of way.

Equivalence theory holds that all cultures, all societies, all ethics, religions, norms and mores are equally valid.

For those who can name the cast of "Dancing with the Stars," but not their Congressman or Senator, you can distill Equivalence theory down to a single phrase—"*who am I to judge?*"

Equivalence theory has bastard children as well, demon-spawn with names like "multiculturalism" and "political correctness," both of which have progeny of their own, such as "victimhood" and "race-baiting."

The number of offspring is nearly limitless now, after several decades of rabbit-like reproduction in the bordellos of academia. Where you find a trumped-up grievance (or even a legitimate one that has been dramatically overblown) you will find at its root an equivalence argument that precludes rational discussion.

Equivalence theory is the mental perversion that permits otherwise sane people to accept insanity, as long as someone, somewhere can say that this particular insanity will redress a grievance, no matter how old, no matter how slight.

It is also how the government has managed to turn the social contract on its head. As you recall, we citizens agreed not to kill each other in return for the government defending us individually against attacks, whether those be physical, or criminal.

However, equivalence theory places certain aggrieved groups above the law, allowing them to behave in a lawless fashion with virtual impunity. Worse yet, if the citizen attempts to interdict this behavior themselves, they are set upon by the government with a zeal reserved only for the most despicable of miscreants.

It's a simple thing really. People have made foolish self-serving arguments from the dawn of time, however in most societies, these arguments were met with the laughter and derision they deserved.

Eventually though, politicians of the left realized that championing the aims of the fundamentally foolish was an easy ticket to electoral success, and identity-politics was born.

Rather than strangling this perversion in the crib, spineless opposition gave in to nearly every demand in order to keep from being labeled as "racist, sexist, homophobic," etc. You know the drill.

Now we watch as criminals break into homes, are shot by the homeowner, and the homeowner is led away in cuffs. If he is lucky enough to avoid criminal prosecution, he still faces the specter of a civil suit for depriving the deceased criminal of his right to the homeowner's stuff.

Equivalence theory makes the ridiculous commonplace and the obscene mundane.

So how does it kill? The modern expression of base evil can be found in the perverted ethos known as Islamism. ISIS is merely the most honest expression of this stunted, flea-bitten ideology.

Throughout Europe, Muslims have declared neighborhoods, and in some cases entire cities to be autonomous Islamic enclaves, not subject to the laws of the host nation.

In Malmo Sweden, the entire city is no longer under the control of Swedish authorities. Sharia law, applied by Islamic courts is enforced against Muslim and Swede alike.

More than twelve cities in England have "no-go" areas, where even the police will not enter without a militarized presence. Crimes are committed regularly, but not reported to British authorities because the local Sharia court metes out justice.

Worse still, even cases of known child abuse and sexual exploitation are ignored by British authorities, dismissed as "cultural" issues. In one most recent case, police in Rotherham, England arrested the parents of underage British girls when the parents attempted to rescue their own children from the houses of Muslim pimps who had forced their children into prostitution.

Heinous crimes are ignored by those charged with the enforcement of the law, all to avoid possible rioting and "cultural unrest," by the Muslim perpetrators.

Being "above-all-that" here in America one may recall the supine behavior on the part of law enforcement that occurred while "aggrieved justice-seekers" helped themselves to televisions, cellphones and booze in Ferguson, Missouri. Nothing says PROTEST like a new pair of free Air Jordan's!)

Multiple attempts were made by honest social services workers to bring this illegal behavior to the attention of their supervisors, but in at least one case, the whistleblower was told to ignore it, and was sent to mandatory sensitivity training for having the temerity to mention it in the first place.

At last count, more than 1400 underage British girls were raped, beaten and forced to turn tricks by a cadre of Muslim men, operating largely in the open, protected by government-sanctioned blindness, all in the name of multiculturalism.

Who are we to judge

One may have witnessed the intimidation of Sharia gangs roaming the streets, ordering non-Muslim women to wear hijab and non-Muslim men to abstain from alcohol while offering veiled threats of violence. The call to prayer rings out loudly and triumphantly from East-End mosques while churches throughout the city have been forbidden to ring their bells by. Politically correct local councils for fear of giving offence to Muslims. Increasingly confident and aggressive men with long beards harass ordinary citizens, blocking pavements with noisy, anti-democracy demonstrations and forcing pedestrians to walk in the gutter. The ugly face of political Islam is now seen daily on the streets of London and it seems to have reached a point of high-profile prominence that is terrifying. No one is doing anything. What is the citizen supposed to do? Any protest is likely to land him or her in court on charges of hate-speech. Where is all this going?

Modernization theory

Modernization theory is used to analyze in which modernization processes in societies take place. The theory looks at which aspects of countries are beneficial and which constitute obstacles for economic development. The idea is that development assistance targeted at those particular aspects can lead to modernization of 'traditional' or 'backward' societies. Scientists from various research disciplines have contributed to modernization theory.

Sociological and anthropological modernization theory

The earliest principles of modernization theory can be derived from the idea of progress, which stated that people can develop and change their society themselves. Marquis de Condorcet was involved in the origins of this theory. This theory also states that technological advancements and economic changes can lead to changes in moral and cultural values. The French sociologist Imile Durkheim stressed the interdependence of institutions in a society and the way in which they interact with cultural and social unity. His work 'The Division of Labor in Society' was very influential. It described how social order is maintained in society and ways in which primitive societies can make the transition to more advanced societies.

Other scientists who have contributed to the development of modernization theory are : David Apter, who did research on the political system and history of democracy; Seymour Martin Lipset, who argued that economic development leads to social changes which tend to lead to democracy; David McClelland, who approached modernization from the psychological side with his motivations theory; and Talcott Parsons who used his pattern variables to compare backwardness to modernity.

Linear stages of growth model

The linear stages of growth model is an economic model which is heavily inspired by the Marshall Plan which was used to revitalize Europe's economy after World War II. It assumes that economic growth can only be achieved by industrialization. Growth can be restricted by local institutions and social attitudes, especially if these aspects influence the savings rate and investments. The constraints impeding economic growth are thus considered by this model to be internal to society.

According to the linear stages of growth model, a correctly designed massive injection of capital coupled with intervention by the public sector would ultimately lead to industrialization and economic development of a developing nation.

The Rostow's stages of growth model is the most well-known example of the linear stages of growth model. Walt W. Rostow identified five stages through which developing countries had to pass to reach an advanced economy status : (1) Traditional society, (2) Preconditions for take-off, (3) Take-off, (4) Drive to maturity, (5) Age of high mass consumption. He argued that economic development could be led by certain strong sectors;

this is in contrast to for instance Marxism which states that sectors should develop equally. According to Rostow's model, a country needed to follow some rules of development to reach the take-off : (1) The investment rate of a country needs to be increased to at least 10% of its GDP, (2) One or two manufacturing sectors with a high rate of growth need to be established, (3) An institutional, political and social framework has to exist or be created in order to promote the expansion of those sectors.

The Rostow model has serious flaws, of which the most serious are : (1) The model assumes that development can be achieved through a basic sequence of stages which are the same for all countries, a doubtful assumption; (2) The model measures development solely by means of the increase of GDP per capita; (3) The model focuses on characteristics of development, but does not identify the causal factors which lead development to occur. As such, it neglects the social structures that have to be present to foster development.

Economic modernization theories such as Rostow's stages model have been heavily inspired by the Harrod-Domar model which explains in a mathematical way the growth rate of a country in terms of the savings rate and the productivity of capital. Heavy state involvement has often been considered necessary for successful development in economic modernization theory; Paul Rosenstein-Rodan, Ragnar Nurkse and Kurt Mandelbaum argued that a big push model in infrastructure investment and planning was necessary for the stimulation of industrialization, and that the private sector would not be able to provide the resources for this on its own. Another influential theory of modernization is the dual-sector model by Arthur Lewis. In this model Lewis explained how the traditional stagnant rural sector is gradually replaced by a growing modern and dynamic manufacturing and service economy.

Because of the focus on the need for investments in capital, the Linear Stages of Growth Models are sometimes referred to as suffering from 'capital fundamentalism'.

Critics of modernization theory

Modernization theory observes traditions and pre-existing institutions of so-called "primitive" societies as obstacles to modern economic growth. Modernization which is forced from outside upon a society might induce violent and radical change, but according to modernization theorists it is generally worth this side effect. Critics point to traditional societies as being destroyed and slipping away to a modern form of poverty withou. ever gaining the promised advantages of modernization.

Structuralism

Structuralism is a development theory which focuses on structural aspects which impede the economic growth of developing countries. The unit of analysis is the transformation of a country's economy from, mainly, a subsistence agriculture to a modern, urbanized manufacturing and service economy. Policy prescriptions resulting from structuralist thinking include major government intervention in the economy to fuel the industrial sector, known as import substitution industrialization (ISI). This structural transformation of the developing country is pursued in order to create an economy which in the end enjoys self-sustaining growth. This can only be reached by ending the reliance of the underdeveloped country on exports of primary goods (agricultural and mining products), and pursuing inward-oriented development by shielding the domestic economy from that of the developed economies. Trade with advanced economies is minimized through the erection of all kinds of trade barriers and an overvaluation of the domestic exchange rate; in this way the production of domestic substitutes of formerly imported industrial products is encouraged. The logic of the strategy rests on the infant industry argument, which states that young industries initially do not have the economies of scale and experience to be able to compete with foreign competitors and thus need to be protected until they are able to compete in the free market. The Prebisch—Singer hypothesis states that over time the terms of trade for commodities deteriorate compared to those for manufactured goods, because the income elasticity of demand of manufactured goods is greater than that of primary products. If true, this would also support the ISI strategy.

Structuralists argue that the only way Third World countries can develop is through action by the state. Third world countries have to push industrialization and have to reduce their dependency on trade with the First World, and trade among themselves.

The roots of structuralism lie in South America, and particularly Chile. In 1950, Raul Prebisch went to Chile to become the first director of the Economic Commission for Latin America. In Chile, he cooperated with Celso Furtado, Anibal Pinto, Osvaldo Sunkel, and Dudley Seers, who all became influential structuralists.

Dependency theory is essentially a follow up to structuralist thinking, and shares many of its core ideas. Whereas structuralists did not consider that development would be possible at all unless a strategy of delinking and rigorous ISI was pursued, dependency thinking could allow development with external links with the developed parts of the globe. However, this kind of development is considered to be "dependent development", i.e., it does not have an internal domestic dynamic in the developing country and thus remains highly vulnerable to the economic vagaries of the world market. Dependency thinking starts from the notion that resources flow from the 'periphery' of poor and underdeveloped states to a 'core' of wealthy countries, which leads to accumulation of wealth in the rich states at the expense of the poor states. Contrary to modernization theory, dependency theory states that not all societies progress through similar stages of development. Periphery states have unique features, structures and institutions of their own and are considered weaker with regards to the world market economy, while the developed nations have never been in this colonized position in the past. Dependency theorists argue that underdeveloped countries remain economically vulnerable unless they reduce their connections to the world market.

Dependency theory states that poor nations provide natural resources and cheap labor for developed nations, without which the developed nations could not have the standard of living which they enjoy. When underdeveloped countries try to remove the Core's influence, the developed countries hinder their attempts to keep control. This means that poverty of developing nations is not the result of the disintegration of these countries in the world system, but because of the way in which they are integrated into this system.

In addition to its structuralist roots, dependency theory has much overlapping with Neo-Marxism and World Systems Theory, which is also reflected in the work of Immanuel Wallerstein, a famous dependency theorist. Wallerstein rejects the notion of a Third World, claiming that there is only one world which is connected by economic relations (World Systems Theory). He argues that this system inherently leads to a division of the world in core, semi-periphery and periphery. One of the results of expansion of the world-system is the commodification of things, like natural resources, labor and human relationships.

Basic needs

The basic needs model was introduced by the International Labour Organization in 1976, mainly in reaction to prevalent modernization—and structuralism—inspired development approaches, which were not achieving satisfactory results in terms of poverty alleviation and combating inequality in developing countries. It tried to define an absolute minimum of resources necessary for long-term physical well-being. The poverty line which follows from this, is the amount of income needed to satisfy those basic needs. The approach has been applied in the sphere of development assistance, to determine what a society needs for subsistence, and for poor population groups to rise above the poverty line. Basic needs theory does not focus on investing in economically productive activities. Basic needs can be used as an indicator of the absolute minimum an individual needs to survive.

Proponents of basic needs have argued that elimination of absolute poverty is a good way to make people active in society so that they can provide labor more easily and act as consumers and savers. There have been also many critics of the basic needs approach. It would lack theoretical rigour, practical precision, be in conflict with growth promotion policies, and run the risk of leaving developing countries in permanent.

Neoclassical theory

Neoclassical development theory has its origins in its predecessor : classical economics. Classical economics was developed in the 18th and 19th centuries and dealt with the value of products and on which production factors it depends. Early contributors to this theory are Adam Smith and David Ricardo. Classical economists argued—as do the neoclassical ones—in favor of the free market, and against government intervention in those markets. The 'invisible hand' of Adam Smith makes sure that free trade will ultimately benefit all of society. John Maynard Keynes was a very influential classical economist as well, having written his General Theory of

Employment, Interest, and Money in 1936.

Neoclassical development theory became influential towards the end of the 1970s, fired by the election of Margaret Thatcher in the UK and Ronald Reagan in the USA. Also, the World Bank shifted from its Basic Needs approach to a neoclassical approach in 1980. From the beginning of the 1980s, neoclassical development theory really began to roll out.

Structural adjustment

One of the implications of the neoclassical development theory for developing countries were the Structural Adjustment Programmes (SAPs) which the World Bank and the International Monetary Fund wanted them to adapt. Important aspects of those SAPs include :

- Fiscal austerity (reduction in government spending)
- Privatization (which should both raise money for governments and improve efficiency and financial performance of the firms involved)
- Trade liberalization, currency devaluation and the abolition of marketing boards (to maximize the static comparative advantage the developing country has on the global market)
- Retrenchment of the government and deregulation (in order to stimulate the free market)

These measures are more or less reflected by the themes which were identified by the Institute of International Economics which were believed to be necessary for the recovery of Latin America from the economic and financial crises of the 1980s. These themes are known as the Washington consensus, a termed coined in 1989 by the economist John Williamson.

Recent trends

Post-development theory

Postdevelopment theory is a school of thought which questions the idea of national economic development altogether. According to postdevelopment scholars, the goal of improving living standards leans on arbitrary claims as to the desirability and possibility of that goal. Postdevelopment theory arose in the 1980s and 1990s.

According to postdevelopment theorists, the idea of development is just a 'mental structure' (Wolfgang Sachs) which has resulted in an hierarchy of developed and underdeveloped nations, of which the underdeveloped nations desire to be like developed nations. Development thinking has been dominated by the West and is very ethnocentric, according to Sachs. The Western lifestyle may neither be a realistic nor a desirable goal for the world's population, postdevelopment theorists argue. Development is being seen as a loss of a country's own culture, people's perception of themselves and modes of life. According to Majid Rahnema, another leading postdevelopment scholar, things like notions of poverty are very culturally embedded and can differ a lot among cultures. The institutes which voice the concern over underdevelopment are very Western-oriented, and postdevelopment calls for a broader cultural involvement in development thinking.

Postdevelopment proposes a vision of society which removes itself from the ideas which currently dominate it. According to Arturo Escobar, postdevelopment is interested instead in local culture and knowledge, a critical view against established sciences and the promotion of local grassroots movements. Also, postdevelopment argues for structural change in order to reach solidarity, reciprocity, and a larger involvement of traditional knowledge.

Progressive Utilization Theory

According to a description by Terry Irving and Rowan Cahill, PROUT "envisages a decentralized, community-based world economy of self-sufficiency for the poor; economic democracy; small business; and limits on the accumulation of wealth." Sohail Inayatullah stated that the philosophy "attempts to balance the need for societies to create wealth and grow with the requirements for distribution." David Skrbina characterized PROUT as a "model of social development... which advocates a 'small is beautiful' approach to society." Economics instructor Mark Friedman places Sarkar's economic thought in the tradition of Monsignor John A. Ryan, E.F. Schumacher and Herman Daly in Sarkar's incorporation of spiritual values into economic goals.

Sarkar positioned it as an alternative to communism and capitalism. It has been characterized as a form of "progressive socialism" as well as a "socialist theory". PROUT recognizes all material goods as common property and seeks the rational and equitable distribution of that property to maximize the physical, mental, and spiritual development of all people. It seeks to guarantee what it recognizes as the five minimum requirements of life for human beings : food, clothing, shelter, education, and medical care.

PROUT describes a social order consisting of four classes of people that cyclically dominate society : shudras (labourers), kshatriyas (military—minded individuals), vipra (intellectuals) and vaishyas (capitalists). To prevent any social class from clinging to political power and exploiting the others, he proposed the concept of "spiritual elite" sadvipras (etymologically sad—true, vipra—intellectual) who would determine who held political leadership. Sarkar thought that the first sadvipras would be created from disgruntled middle class intellectuals and military-minded people. He called for sadvipras to be organized into executive, legislative, and judicial boards which would be governed by a Supreme Board. They, according to Sarkar, would be responsible for the application of force necessary to change the order of dominance within the social order, with large amounts of force akin to revolution.

PROUT's economic model advocates a three-tiered approach to industrial organization where key industries or public utilities are non—profit, a decentralized industry run by sociolinguistic unions provide people's bare minimum necessities, and most of the economic transactions are through producers' and consumers' cooperatives. It distinguishes itself from communism by proposing an incentive based economy where surplus in the society is distributed to people who serve the society.

At the political level, PROUT rejects nationalism and seeks the formation of a world government. Sarkar also supported the concept of a world army.

Cooperative communities have been established by Ananda Marga in an attempt to provide ideal models for the society outlined in PROUT. A few intellectuals support the philosophy, but it has not achieved widespread implementation.

PROUTist Universal

Sarkar founded the Ananda Marga organization in 1955 and four years later founded PROUTist Universal to advance his social, political and economic ideas. While the organizations have separate goals, members of each interviewed by researcher Helen Crovetto "considered themselves to be members of a large family" headed by Sarkar and could be assigned to either organization. At its peak, PROUTist Universal had several international chapters.

Criticism

Professor Narasingha P. Sil describes Sarkar's ideas of the social cycles that underlie PROUT as having "little originality or historical validity", having been derived "with some feeble adjustments" from traditional Hindu caste structure. Ravi Batra used the ideas of PROUT in his bestseller *The Great Depression of 1990* and other books. In reviewing the book for the *Los Angeles Times*, economist Paul Erdman described the work as "a strange mixture of voodoo historical theories and sound economic analysis"

The Political Theory of an Independent Judiciary.—Where does the root of judicial review lie namely; in corporate law (Prof. Bilder) or in political theory (Scott D. Gerber).

Many of the nation's most influential constitutional law scholars have argued recently that judicial review should be sharply limited or eliminated altogether. The list includes such notable thinkers as Larry D. Kramer, Cass R. Sunstein, William M. Treanor, and Mark V. Tushnet.

Mary Sarah Bilder's is a powerful corrective to this mounting opposition to the doctrine made famous by Chief Justice John Marshall in *Marbury* v. *Madison*. Professor Bilder concludes that judicial review is an integral part of the American constitutional order with deep historical roots. She traces the origins of judicial review to corporate law, or in political theory.

Professor Bilder marshals considerable historical evidence in support of her provocative thesis that "judicial review was the continuation of a longstanding English practice of constraining corporate ordinances by requiring that they not be repugnant to the laws of the nation." Unfortunately, she misses the mark when she claims that judicial review was a shifting "cultural practice" rather than a new "intellectual doctrine." After all, the Founders of the American regime were steeped in the history of ideas, and the Constitution they created expressed their commitment to the power of ideas.

John Adams was the American Founding's most sophisticated political theorist and when he modified Montesquieu's conception of the separation of powers by developing what can be fairly termed the political architecture of an independent judiciary, he articulated an idea that helped make judicial review possible. In fact, Adams's contribution to political theory is arguably as significant as that of the French baron whose work inspired him and the other American Founders.

It is well known that Montesquieu's seminal contribution to the history of ideas is that political power should be divided among the legislative, executive, and judicial branches of government so as to ensure the people's liberty. What is largely overlooked, however, is that Montesquieu's characterization of the judicial power differs dramatically from the American view : the preferred scheme of checks and balances Montesquieu describes in The Spirit of the Laws is not the three famous powers but the established English scheme of king, lords, and commons. "Among the three powers of which we have spoken," he writes, "that of judging is in some fashion, null." He maintains that "only two" powers truly matter—the legislative and the executive—and that the "part of the legislative body composed of the nobles is quite appropriate" for checking legislative abuse.

Likewise overlooked is that Montesquieu associates the judicial power with petit juries, rather than with a judge in a robe. "In England," Montesquieu proclaims in a much-neglected passage, "the jury decides whether the accused is guilty or not of the deed brought before it; and, if he is declared guilty, the judge pronounces the penalty imposed by law for this deed; and he needs only his eyes for that."

It would be left to John Adams to suggest that judges, and not simply temporary juries, need to be independent from the executive and legislative branches of government. Adams had been writing about the need for an independent judiciary since at least January and February of 1773, when he engaged in a series of exchanges on the matter in the Boston press with William Brattle. Brattle, a Tory, insisted that the proposed payment of judicial salaries by the Crown should not concern the people of Massachusetts Bay, as the judges of the colony's superior court, like their brethren in England, enjoyed life tenure so long as they behaved well. Adams, after conducting an extensive historical review of the subject, countered that Brattle was wrong to claim that judges in England, let alone in America, held their offices during good behavior. Consequently, the proposed control by the Crown over judicial salaries was perceived by Adams as an additional threat to the independence of the Massachusetts judiciary.

Adams revisited the matter of an independent judiciary in Thoughts on Government,published in 1776. The pamphlet—a clarion call for the separation of powers written in response to Thomas Paine's recommendation in Common Sense that all government power be vested in a unicameral legislature—explains in no uncertain terms how important an independent judiciary is to any form of government dedicated to the preservation of liberty. Adams writes,

The dignity and stability of government in all its branches, the morals of the people, and every blessing of society depend so much upon an upright and skillful administration of justice, that the judicial power ought to be distinct from both the legislative and executive, and independent upon both, that so it may be a check upon both, as both should be checks upon that.Adams argues in his pamphlet for more than merely making the judiciary a separate branch of government. He also calls for stable judicial compensation and tenure so long as judges maintain good behavior : "they should hold estates for life in their offices; or, in other words, their commissions should be during good behavior, and their salaries ascertained and established by law." Judges who misuse their offices should be impeached by the "house of representatives... before the governor and council" and, "if convicted, should be removed."

The Federal Constitution of 1787 excluded the executive from participating in the impeachment process, but otherwise contained principles identical to Adams's proposal. As David McCullough put it in his biography of Adams, "[l]ittle that Adams ever wrote had such effect as his Thoughts on Government."

Judicial review fits into the political theory of an independent judiciary in at least two ways. First, judicial review is a core component of the Constitution's system of checks and balances, a system in which each branch of the federal government is endowed with, in the words of The Federalist No. 48, "a constitutional control over the others." The President has, among other checks, a veto over congressional bills and the power to nominate federal judges. Congress has, among other checks, the power to override presidential vetoes and to control the size and jurisdiction of the federal courts, as well as the power to impeach all federal officials. Without the power of judicial review, what check—what "constitutional control"—would the federal judiciary have on the President or Congress? The answer is none. As a consequence, judicial review is an inevitable component of the Constitution's commitment to checks and balances.

Judicial review also fits into the political theory of an independent judiciary in another, equally straightforward, fashion : judicial review is the ultimate expression of judicial independence, because without judicial independence no court could safely void an act of a coordinate political branch. Bluntly stated, the risk to a judge who exercises judicial review when he or she is not independent of the executive and the legislature is either removal from the bench or a reduction in salary. John Adams knew this, and so did the Framers who met in Philadelphia during the summer of 1787 when they wrote Adams's theory of judicial independence into Article III of the Constitution.

What all of this means for Professor Bilder's project is this : it suggests that she errs by emphasizing as much as she does what might be called the "vertical" origins of judicial review—the notion that there exists a hierarchy of laws, and that when a court finds an inferior law is repugnant to a superior law, the court ought to invalidate the inferior law. An investigation into the origins of judicial review that concludes that habituation to vertical review by the Privy Council and colonial judiciaries was sufficient to give rise to judicial review by the federal judiciary turns a blind eye to the Founders' political theory—a political theory that suggests that the origins of judicial review are more accurately traced to the "horizontal" idea of separation of powers.

Of course it is difficult to fault Professor Bilder too much for her emphasis on the implications of hierarchies of law in the origins of judicial review. Chief Justice Marshall evinced a similar emphasis when he declared in Marbury itself that a statute that is inconsistent with the Constitution is void. However, the absence from Professor Bilder's article of any discussion of the role political theory played in the origins of judicial review has the unfortunate consequence of causing her to sidestep the most important question of all : how judicial review should be exercised. Because Professor Bilder locates the origins of judicial review in corporate law, and because corporate law is agnostic on the "how" question, she can only say that "the how question cannot be as convincingly answered based on early history as the whether and why questions."

An examination of the origins of judicial review that takes political theory seriously reveals that the *raison d'etre* for judicial review is to protect individual rights from overreaching by the political process. The pre-Marbury state precedents that Professor Bilder discusses—*Holmes* v. *Walton, Commonwealth* v. *Caton*, *Trevett* v. *Weeden*, the *Ten Pound Act Cases*, and *Bayard* v. *Singleton*—make it clear beyond cavil how early American judges thought the doctrine should be exercised : to protect individual rights. *Holmes* v. *Walton*, *Trevett* v. *Weeden*, the *Ten Pound Act Cases*, and *Bayard* v. *Singleton*, involved securing the individual right of trial by jury. *Commonwealth* v. *Caton*, concerned the most sacred right of all : the right not to be executed without the benefit of appropriate structural safeguards.

Revealingly, Judge George Wythe opens his opinion in Caton in a fashion that illustrates that the judges in these cases were well versed in political theory generally and in separation of powers theory specifically :Among all the advantages, which have arisen to mankind, from the study of letters, and the universal diffusion of knowledge, there is none of more importance, than the tendency they have had to produce discussions upon the respective rights of the sovereign and the subject; and, upon the powers which the different branches of government may exercise. For, by this means, tyranny has been sapped, the departments kept within their own spheres, the citizens protected, and general liberty promoted.

Judge Wythe, who was John Marshall's law teacher, also indicates that it is a judge's responsibility to check overreaching by the political branches. He writes,

[I]f the whole legislature, an event to be deprecated, should attempt to overleap the bounds, prescribed to them by the people, I, in administering the public justice of the country, will meet the united powers, at my seat in this tribunal; and, pointing to the constitution, will say, to them, here is the limit of your authority; and, hither, shall you go, but no further.

After reading these excerpts from Judge Wythe's opinion, it should come as no surprise to learn that the Virginia Constitution of 1776 was the first of the early state constitutions to establish an independent judiciary in the federal conception of the institution and that John Adams's Thoughts on Government provided the blueprint for doing so. In fact, George Mason, who is generally credited with being the principal author of Virginia's initial state constitution, borrowed heavily from Adams's pamphlet, and Patrick Henry was so taken with it that he wrote Adams a letter that said "Would to God you and your Sam Adams were here!"

Professor Bilder has made a major contribution to constitutional law scholarship with The Corporate Origins of Judicial Review. Her intriguing thesis that judicial review developed from a heretofore neglected corner of the English legal tradition demonstrates it is still possible to bring fresh insights to a subject about which scholars have been opining for generations. But any discussion of the origins of judicial review that declines to resolve how judicial review should be practiced overlooks why we have a constitution in the first place. To borrow a famous phrase from the Declaration of Independence—the document that announces the official statement of the political theory of the American regime—"to secure these rights, Governments are instituted among Men."

❑ ❑

Chapter 12

Judicial Process and the Administrative Structure

Part XIV-A (Articles 323-A and 323-B provide for tribunals. Art. 323-A authorises establishment of Administrative Tribunals and Art. 323-B provides for tribunals for other 10 matters, like tax, custom Industrial and Labour, Land reforms, Urban Ceiling, Elections, food, Rent and offences or other matters incidental to any of the above. All these tribunals shall be subject to jurisdiction of the High Court under Article 226 and 227 and of the Supreme Court under Article 136.

Administrative Tribunals

These may be for Central Government employees or for State Government employees or for employees of local authorities or other authorities or corporation owned or controlled by Government.

Administrative Tribunals Act, 1985 has been enacted and Central Administrative Tribunal (CAT) and Public Service Tribunal (SAT) have been established. These decide disputes on complaints by Government Servants arising out of recruitment and conditions of service on any post or public services.

Other Tribunals

Rent Central Tribunals, Industrial Tribunals, labour courts, Election Tribunals etc. have been established under various laws in country. The jurisdiction, power (including contempt, procedure, limitation, rule of evidence, bar of jurisdiction to other courts, transfer for a sending cases etc.) of these tribunals have been spelt out by these Acts providing for establishment of these tribunals.

Administrative Courts are tried and tested systems of adjudication in civil law. Systems of France, Germany and other European systems. Regular Court systems and administrative systems have worked together harmoniously under codified laws of European Countries. Judges in regular law courts and presiding officers in administrative courts are both Government servants committed to implement the Government policies. There is no antagonism in their working. Government formulates policies and they all work to ensure that these policies yield desired fruits. Laws are made to give effect to this policy. The judicial and administrative officials work together to give effect to these policies on the ground. The Franco German doctrine rests upon the absolute sovereignty of the written law. The legal principles are deduced from the law laid down by the legislator. The judiciary has the task of interpretation and gap filling role. However, this practice was peculiar to the field of private law where most of the early codifications took place. The field of the public law remained to be developed at later stage. The birth of State made it obligatory that the relationship between State and its citizens be defined and this was to be done without legislative intervention. The judiciary had to take the responsibility and the French judges started giving it shape on the basis of Anglo-American system, which was practically a creation of judiciary and custom. This was the genesis of the Administrative Law.

The French and Anglo American Administrative Law became different due to the fact that French Administrative Law was developed by specialized Courts whereas the Anglo American Administrative Law was framed by judges of the ordinary Law Courts. The doctrine of separation of power got different interpretations in French and Anglo American Common Law. The American Courts have consistently held that the powers of the Government must be divided into three organs—Executive, legislative and judicial. They have held it, to be less, a doctrine of separation and more a doctrine of specialisation of powers. In France also, the doctrine of the separation of powers forms a cornerstone of constitutionalism. In England, the Parliament and the Crown struggled for power. The Judiciary sided with the Parliament. The Crown lost and Parliament won. Judiciary was siding with Parliament therefore it also established its supremacy over executive. In France, similar conflicts have led to opposite results. The Executive became predominant and judiciary subordinate.

Administrative judgments and decisions of the ordinary Court.—These differ on following four counts:

(a) How the case is presented by the parties to the dispute.

(b) How the fact is ascertained with the help of evidence adduced.

(c) The method of arguments and submissions on the question of Law.

(d) The fact finding and the disposal of case *etc.*

In modern French legal system, there are in reality two distinct sets of the courts. One to dispose of disputes between individual citizens, the other to deal with cases in which the administration is involved. The former Courts are older. They are concerned with cases cognizable by judicial tribunals. The latter are more recent. They are justified due to expanding activities and roles of modern States. In other words, the former deals with the private cases and the latter with public Law cases.

Administrative Courts in France

(i) Council of State

The Council of State's origin can be historically traced to ancient regime of French monarchy. But its present reorganisation was made by the ordinance and decree of July 31, 1945 as amended by the law of February 11, 1950. It consists of 161 judges as members including one Vice-President (who is its actual head), five section Presidents, 46 Councillors of State in ordinary service, 12 Councillors of State in extraordinary service, 49 *maitres des requetes*, 38 first class auditors, 10 second class auditors. The number seems to be large in comparison to Indian, English or American highest judicial institutions. For example, Indian Supreme Court consists of Chief Justice and 30 judges only and the U.S.S. court consists of Chief Justice and 8 judges. But it should not be taken like this due to the fact that this French highest administrative court is less a court than an administrative body, and as a consultant council, it is chief advisory body of French Administration.

Members.—The Council of State consists of three types of members; (1) The Councillors of States; (b) The *Maitres des requestes*; and (c) the auditors: These indicate three tiers of the Council. The councilors are at the top and auditors at the lowest echelon. Auditors were originally 'listeners' in the council without any effective voice. The second class auditors were originally appointed on the basis of competitive examinations. But now it has been done away with and the selection is made from amongst the graduates of National School of Administration, in which the admissions are made on merits in competitive examinations. The freshers in admission must be university graduates of the less than 26 years of age and there is a second category of those who are already in administrative services. They may take up the examinations upto 30 years of age. The appointment thus is the result of (i) open competitive examination, and (ii) closed competitive selection after three years study in the National School.

In France, the judiciary on the whole is considered as a part of the civil service. The method of recruitment is highly praiseworthy since it attracts the youngmen who have training in law as well as have knowledge of social sciences including economics, public health, business administration *etc*. The promotions are almost automatic on the basis of seniority alone.

Outside members.—The Council of State consists not only of these members so recruited. There are outsiders who are made its members as councillor and *maitres des requestes*. For example 3/4 of *maitres* must be chosen from amongst first class auditors, 1/4 must be from amongst the other Government employees of ten years' service or more service experience and over thirty years of age. Likewise 2/3 of the councillors may be from amongst *maitres*, the remainder 1/3 are chosen by the Government at its discretion. Extraordinary members are appointed for one year (renewable to any period) amongst qualified persons in different domains of national activity, Law professors may also be appointed. They take part only in administrative sections and not in judicial sections.

The councillors hold office for life. They are removable only by a decree of French cabinet rendered on the initiative of the Minister of Justice. The *maitres* and auditors can be removed by Vice-President acting on the consultation of section presidents.

President of the Council.—The Prime Minister of the French republic is the *ex-officio* President. In his absence, the minister of justice will act as President of the Council. But it has become a custom that minister of justice presides over the opening session and the Council is left in the hands of Vice-President thereafter.

Administrative work for the Council.—In this capacity, the role of the Council is that of a consultative organ. It gives advice to the Government regarding draft bills of proposed Acts, or promulgation of some administrative regulation,or it has the authority to call the attention of the Government to those reforms that appear to be desirable to the Council; The *Administrative work is managed by the following sections*:

(a) Interior Section;

(b) Finance Section;

(c) Public Works Section; and

(d) Social Problems Section.

Each section is composed of a President and 6 Councillors of State, some *maitres* and auditors. The advisory function of the Council prevents the necessity of judicial consultation like Article 143 of the Indian Constitution.

Judicial Work.—Here the Council works like a true administrative court in matters concerning the public and the administration. The judicial work is done only by one section but half members of the Council are engaged in it. However, the judicial section is divided into nine sub-sections. Each sub-section consists of a president, two councillors of State, 28 auditors and 30 *maitres de requests*. The sub-sections are designated by numbers. The first four are preparatory organs and the last five have the power to decide cases by themselves. They decide ordinary cases. Cases of higher amount or novel type are referred to and decided by the judicial section as entity, and if the problem involved is of greater difficulty and importance, it is referred to the plenary assembly of the judicial section. It consists of the vice-president of the council of State, the president of the judicial section, the presidents of its sub-sections and four councillors from administrative section election by their colleagues.

Procedure.—The work is done by division of labour. The work of auditors and *maitres* is essentially to prepare the record for the decision and duty of the councillors of State is wholly to decide. But final decision is taken by majority and all are equal within the House. Each member has an equal vote. The procedure is inquisitorial type rather than of adversary type as in India.

Jurisdiction.—The French Council of State has been neither exclusively nor even primarily a court of first instance or a Court of appeal. It has been entrusted with both original and appellate jurisdiction. The original jurisdiction of the council was established in an important decision of 1889 in which the council laid down the principle that it was thenceforth the tribunal of general jurisdiction in the field of administrative law. It means that it has jurisdiction in every case except where some other administrative tribunal may have been given jurisdiction otherwise.

The decision of every other administrative tribunal is subject to appeal to the Council of State—either full appeal on the law and the facts or appeal more or less limited to points of law.

(ii) Prefecture Council.—*Administrative Courts.*

In common law system, the jurisdiction of the courts is defined on territorial basis. This practice is followed in these cases of Inter departmental Prefecture Councils. Such courts were established by a law passed in 1800. These were given limited jurisdictions in administrative law cases. They were originally connected with prefects or heads of the active administration in the departments. In 1887, a detailed judicial procedure was prescribed for these courts which was similar to that of the Council of State. In 1926, the Prefecture Councils were abolished and twenty-two Inter departmental Prefecture Councils, were established with jurisdiction over several contiguous departments. In 1953, they were re-named as 'Administrative courts'.

Composition.—The 'administrative courts' consists of a president and four councillors. Two second class councillors (law school graduate) and two first class councillors (civil servants). There are only first class councillors and second class councillors in administrative courts. The second class councillors are chosen from amongst the graduates of National School of Administration and first class councillors are chosen from amongst civil servants or members slightly below in seniority to those that are appointed 'auditors' in Council of State.

Jurisdiction.—Their jurisdiction is strictly confined to those given by the statute. These are courts of first instance. Their decisions have never been final. Appeal may be taken from their decisions in every case, however small the amount involved may be. Their jurisdiction has been essentially territorial. They are competent to see cases within their departments.

(iii) Colonial Councils

Besides Administrative courts as courts of first instance and Council of States as court of appeal there are many other courts included in French Administrative system. Colonial Councils are one of them. They have jurisdiction similar to Prefecture Councils in the overseas territories and colonies of the French Union.

(iv) Court of Accounts

This court looks into the expenditure of public funds like one exercised by court of exchequer in early common law system.

(v) Special Councils

(a) Superior Council of National Education.—It decides appeals in fields of education.

(b) Review Councils.—They work under compulsory military service laws.

(c) Assistant Commissions.—They hear appeals in field of National Assistance.

Administrative Law in U.K. and U.S.A.—In Anglo American legal system, rule of law or supremacy of law is a crucial factor. Everybody, right from a police constable upto the British Prime Minister, is subordinate to general law of the land and jurisdiction of ordinary law courts. Rule of law is peculiar to England and those countries which like India and United States of America have inherited English traditions. The supremacy of law means that no man is punishable or can lawfully be made to suffer in body or goods except for a distinct breach of law established in the ordinary legal manner before the ordinary courts of the land. This view stands in sharp contrast to the French concept of Administrative Law. The exercise of the 'judicial functions by Administrative organs saps the foundation of the rule of law which had been for generations a leading feature of the English Constitution.

Has the development of administrative process tended to weaken the rule of law as the dominant constitutional principle of the common law world? In fact it is not; because what rule of law requires is, that everybody must be subordinate to ordinary courts of the land and this is exercised by judicial review of administrative adjudications. In Anglo-American system, such a review exists as part of the constitutional scheme. In French legal system, no such possibility exists. Ordinary law courts in France have no control over administrative actions. That is why administrative law in England is possible and is studied but French administrative law is foreign to English administrative law. In fact Droit Administratif of France and rule of law in England are fundamentally opposed to each other. In former, executive is all powerful. Public officers are answerable only to special administrative courts. The ordinary law courts have no jurisdiction in cases of wrongs done by public officers while engaged in public duty.

Administrative Structures in India.—The modern Indian law is mainly based on common law. So doctrine of rule of law holds good here. Article 14 of the Constitution proclaims 'equality before law' and 'equal protection of laws' guaranteed as fundamental rights to every person within the territory of India. The root of the modern Indian administrative law lies in few articles of the Constitution for example, Articles 32, 226, 246, 311 and Articles 299 and 300 and Section 197 Cr.P.C. Sections 133, 135, 135-A of Code of civil Procedure. The rest of the topic of administrative law are based on English Administrative Law. We do not have administrative courts separately working as in France. The ordinary law courts deal with all the legalities and illegalities of the administrative actions. The administrations of Mauryas and Guptas knew something akin to administrative adjudications but that does not help at present.

Administrative Court and Service Tribunals

Service matters go to High Courts under Article 226. Looking into the rush of service cases, Administrative Tribunal Act, 1985 was passed in India. It provides for establishment of the Central Administrative Tribunals (CAT) for Central Government employees and Public Services Tribunals (SAT or P.S.T.) for State employees, for disputes like suspension, termination, regularisation, payment of salary, pension *etc.* Serious matters like dismissal, removal from service and reduction in rank (major penalty matters) can go direct to the High Court after finishing the remedies given in service rules of that department. Railway Rates Tribunals, Railways

Claims Tribunal, Labour Courts, Industrial Tribunal and others of the same type are constituted to deliver administrative justice subject to control of High Court under its power of judicial review under Article 226.

Ombudsman in India.—The corruption in administration is not peculiar only to India. But still in order to check it and stop delays, the Parliament has passed Lokpal and Lokayukta Act. It is concerned with central administration. It provides for appointments of one Lokpal and one or more Lokayuktas. The President of India will make the appointments after consultation with Chief Justice of India and leader of the opposition in Lok Sabha. Lokyauktas will be appointed after consultation with Lokpal. They will hold office for five years. They cannot seek reappointment in any office, public company or government authority, they enjoy the security of a Supreme Court judge. They will have authority to investigate any action taken by any minister or secretary or other public servant except Prime Minister, if a complaint of maladministration is lodged by aggrieved individual with it. The judicial establishment shall remain completely immune from their jurisdiction. They have powers and privileges of ordinary law courts. Right to Information Act, 2005 lays open every information to public. A hierarchy of officers from Chief Information Commissioner to Information Commissioners in centre as well as States has been created to safeguard the right to information. Supreme Court has held this right to be part of freedom of speech and expression guaranteed as fundamental right under Article 19(1) (a) of the Indian Constitution.

Comparative study of Administrative Law.—The following aspects from above legal systems are selected for comparative study :

(i) Rule of Law.—'Rule of law', is not conducive for development of Administrative Law and Justice; 'separation of power' is useful for it. Separation of power is speciality of civil law; Rule of law is speciality of common law. In India, rule of law is the basic feature of Indian Constitution. At the place of Separation of Power, India provides for division of power.

(ii) Proceedings for Judicial Review.—Anglo American Administrative law has been very much influenced with common law's concern with forms of action. This has made the procedure more complicated whereas the simplicity was needed in administrative law cases. As compared to this, the Droit Administratif has a simpler and clear cut procedure of review in administrative law problems. Anglo American legal systems have also abolished the extra-ordinary remedies and other forms of actions. They have adopted now a non-technical and uniform procedure. The legality of administrative actions can now be challenged by a simple petition in all systems whether French, English or American. This procedure has been, adopted in India also under Articles 226 and 227 of the Constitution.

(iii) Cost of litigation.—The litigation is more costly in U.K. U.S.A. and India. In French Droit Administratiff it is less costly. The exhorbitant costs for judicial review of governmental actions precludes the possibility of review itself. In French Droit Administrtiff inquisitorial method is adopted in these cases. No counsel is needed in these proceedings. The reviewing court itself plays a vital role in thrashing out the realities of the case. The court develops the case from both sides. In common law system, the procedure of investigation is adversary. A person is presumed to be innocent unless otherwise proved guilty. He cannot be compelled to speak throughout the whole proceeding except of his defence. It leaves heavy onus on the prosecution. The common law systems must find out some ways for cutting short the cost of litigation. The principle is that let hundreds guilty go unpunished rather than one innocent be punished. Now, the position is reserved by what goes on in Courts. Principle of strict liability is introduced in many cases. The trend is shifting to inquisitorial system, a bit.

(iv) Delay.—Delay in Indian Courts in civil and criminal matters is a major problem. Large pendency in courts is amounting to denial of justice and causing corruption and also disappointment. This is causing rise in tendency to establish separate courts and tribunals to solve administrative problems. Lok adalats, Consumer Forum Adalats, Departmental camps for settlement of public grievance cells, like police and thana day. Tehsil day, Telephone Adalats, Pension Adalats, are coming up to provide reliefs to victims of department's casualties and harassments.

(v) Trial by Battle.—In adversary system of trial, it is by battle. One has to prove his stand from all the corners. He has no help from opposite side. The law is that one cannot win on the weakness of the opposite party. A case has to be won on one's merit and quality of evidence. The droit administratif differs radically from common law court at this place. In French system, the justice in administrative courts in all cases is dominated by *sporting theory of justice*. The Anglo American system imposes a maximum restraint on the trial judge. He is a sheer spectator in the whole proceeding. The common law theory of litigation is that of a fair first fight according to canons of the manly art with a court to see fair play and prevent interference. The French droit administratif widely differs. The adversary elements are almost nil. The 'gifhting method of trial' is never adopted. In French system, the courts do not leave the lawyers on their own. It considers the aspects they have overlooked. The State takes the initiative to see that all relevant evidence is presented before the court. The French courts take help of *expertises*. They are selected by the court. Their duty is to make an impartial evaluation of the facts. These may go to some extent in minimising the domination of fighting method or trial by battle as it prevails in Anglo American law including India.

(vi) Locus Standi.—In Anglo American or Indian legal system, the *locus standi* of the parties is immediately inquired before any step in review proceeding is taken. The petitioner is put to explain his interest in seeking the judicial review of the administrative action. Much depends upon it. But in French droit administratif no such requirement is insisted. No personal interest of the petitioner is necessary before the review petition is entertained. In Anglo American and Indian legal system collective interest like consumer or taxpayer does not confer *locus standi* but in french system, even these are not required. Any body, howsoever unconcerned, may come and petition for a judicial review. In Anglo American system *locus standi* is essential but in French system, *actio popularis* may also be entertained. The *locus standi* has been recently relaxed in cases of public interest. In public interest cases, anybody having interest in public welfare, any non-government organisation can come to High Court under Article 226 or to Supreme Court under Article 32 and invoke its jurisdiction under these. No *locus* shall be insisted. However, concern should be genuine and *bona fide*. Public interest litigation cannot be allowed to get cheap popularity or to vindicate frivolous private vengeance.

(vii) Abuse of power.—Why was the impugned Administrative Act made? What was the motive behind? This is a pertinent question in French droit administratif in every case challenging the *bona fides* of any administrative action. But in Anglo American system no such inquiry into the motive is ordinarily held. The reviewing court of France will annul an administrative action if it has gone beyond aim and object of the Act that authorised it. If the framers of the statute had shown any disrespect to established law in making the impugned Act, it will be struck down. The French review, therefore, can check the abuse of legislative power more effectively and from wider circles than is possible in an Anglo American legal system. In India, Article 246 read with Schedule Seven, distributes legislative powers in Union and States. This divides legislative competence. Article 123 deals with legislative power of the President and Article 213 deals with legislative powers of the Governors. Article 53 read with Article 73 provides that executive power of the union shall extend to the matters with respect to which Parliament has power to make laws. Executive power of Governors is in Article 162 read with Article 154. Rule making power of the Supreme Court is in Article 145 and that of the High Courts in Article 229(2) and Articles 227 and 235.

(viii) Scope of Review.—The Anglo administrative action enjoys greater immunity from judicial review particularly in issues concerning jurisdiction and in mixed questions of law and fact. But the French council of States has gone to the other extreme of permitting review on all matters of law and fact. The scope of review is wider in France and narrower in Anglo American system. In India, the scope of review is neither too narrow as in U.S.A. nor too wide as in France. Power of judicial review is in Articles 226 and 227 in High Courts and Article 32 in Supreme Court. Power of High Court is wider. It is for enforcement or protection of fundamental rights or for 'any other purpose'. A bulk of work in High Court consists of writ petitions under Article 226. Several self imposed limitations have come up; for example; No judicial review is allowed if alternative departmental remedy is not exhausted or is available like appeal, revision or representation in services matters; no judicial review is allowed on grounds of delay or laches. The judicial orders of civil courts do not come ordinarily under judicial review, appellate orders or revisional orders cannot be prayed to be reviewed. No judicial review of any order of High Court judge is allowed under Article 226.

(ix) Liability of Public Officers.—The English courts follow the practice that King can do no wrong. So if a British subject has suffered the wrong due to action or omission of some public servant the servant is personally liable. The state is not responsible. The common law rule is one of wholesale personal liability. American Courts no longer follow the common law rule of strict personal liability of the officers. The United States Courts apply the principles of immunity. The public offices are immune from personal responsibility in many cases. In France, the officers were wholly unanswerable for acts done in public capacity. They are being gradually made liable for personal faults including malice, negligence, or extra official works.

(x) Liability of the State.—In France, the rule of State liability is accepted, while in Anglo American system the rule of 'No Responsibility' is rigidly followed. The State in France is being held liable not only on grounds of fault, but it is made liable on grounds of risk causing injury to the petitioner.

(c) Contractual liability.—Article 299 says that all contracts made in exercise of the executive powers of State or Union shall be expressed to be made in the name of Governors or the President, as the case may be, and all such contracts and all assurances of property shall be executed on behalf of Governors or President by such persons and in such manners as he may direct or authorise. Any contract made in violation of Article 229 or rules or directions made or issued thereunder shall not bind the State or the Union of India. The Governors or the President shall not be, personally or by official status, be liable for any such contract or assurance of property.

Tortious liability.—Article 30 provides how suits or proceedings against Union or State can be filed. Sections 79 to 81 of Code of Civil Procedure would apply in these matters. Article 300 says that Government of India may sue or be sued in the name of Union of India and States in the name of that State.

The vicarious liability rule in Article 30 started with *Peninsular and Oriental State Navigation case*. The Court made distinction between sovereign and non-sovereign functions. The State is not liable for the first; it is liable for the second. In *Hari Bhanji*, the difference between sovereign and non-sovereign function was rejected. The difference between State Act and non-State Acts was made. The State is exempt only for State acts. In *State* v. *Vidyawati*, the Supreme Court held the State liable for death of the husband of Vidyawati. He was crushed to death by the jeep that was in use of Collector but was driven back after repair from the workshop. The death was caused by Government servant during course of employment. The law became most unsatisfactory after *Kasturi Lal*, decision in which State was not held liable when the gold confiscated by police and kept in police custody was lost on account of police negligence, the incharge of treasury having run away with all gold to Pakistan. P. and O. Steam Navigation view of sovereign and non-sovereign function was applied. The negligence was proved but it was said to be in doing sovereign function.

❑ ❑

Chapter 13

Judicial process and Private Personal Laws

Most of the personal laws are gifts of God to the humanity. All are revealed. Many are contained in Holy books. Many are spread in religious scriptures. Law is in garb of morals. It is very difficult to decipher as to what part of a text contains 'Law' (Prohibition) what contain (Prohibition)? What are recommendatory and what are mandatory. Sources of all these is God or the Messenger of God. All messengers are accepted by all. The clash is as to which is the last prophet (Paigambar). The texts of these Holy books are not easily intelligible and in 'class' language not 'mass language'. Many of these messengers are 'Kings'. Few are commoners claiming to be son of God. Epilepsy of one is explained as receiving direct message of God and handing for blasphemy of the other is explained as "sacrifice" by the other, 'Charisma' was made use of to give identity to many of these. So holy books have stories describing 'charisma' of the prophets. The leaders like Indira Gandhi were called India is Indira and Indira is India by Psychophants. This did not work as she failed to prove it otherwise but Jesus and 'Muhammad' succeeded and established themselves. Was 'Baghdadi' not the same to his followers in ISIS? Crores made Supreme Sacrifices on clarion call given by Baghdadi. This is 'Charisma' to blind fanatics. Not many few have it and their followers continue. Followers of Vishnu (God) are called 'Vaishnav', of 'Shiv' Shaiva, of Krishna 'Krishna Bhakta', of Muhammad Mussalman, of Jesus 'Christians' of Nanak 'Sikh' of Buddha, Buddhists or 'Baudha', of Mahabir 'Jains or Jins" so of Ramanuja, Vishita dvait, by Madhavacharya—Dvait, Dualism or Bhed vada (soul and God separate) by Shankaracharya Advait (soul and God one).

Personal laws are those that are exceptions to law of land, are observed by persons of a particular sect like Mussalman Islam, 'Hindu' is a cult not a religion. It is 'sanatana' Dharma, rather 'Code of Dharma'. Different sects of those who call themselves 'Hindu' are religions : Sikhism, buddhism, jainism are religions, offshoot of 'sanatana dharma'.

When Mughals (not muslims) settled down in India, they applied Islam to Muhammedans and Law of Shastras to Hindus. By Hindus they meant non-mohammedans'. The Christians did not exist in India when Islam came. It came to India through Christian traders with effect from 1612-13 through decree promulgated by Emperor Jehangir known as Sir Thomas Roe grant.

Association of Privy Council with India effectively started when 'Mayor Court's were established by and under 1726 Royal Charter and 1774 Supreme Court Charter issued under Regulating Act, 1773 followed by Bombay Supreme Court and Madras Supreme Court; Recorder Courts 1797 and by High Courts under High Court Act, 1861.

Some famous judgments of Privy Council on Hindu law

Hanuman Prasad Pande v. *Babuc Munrajkunwari* Hindu is born not made; on Rights of natural Guardian (Section 6 Hindu Succession Act, 1956); *Tagore* v. *Tagore* (1827); Indian Appeals (Supp) 47, 9 Beng L.R. 377 on rule of perpetuity; *Collector of Madras* v. *Moottoo Ramlinga Satpathy*, (1968) 12 MIA 397 (clear proof of usage will outweigh written text of law).

Muhammedan law is applied by courts in India not to all muslims in all cases. As regards India, rules fall under three divisions. Expressly directed (Rules of Succession and Inheritance); As justice, equity and good conscience (Pre-emption); Where parties are both Muslims (Shariat Act, Evidence, Cr. Law); Shia, Sunni Sects and Motazila.

1. Shia are; Athna Asariya, Ismailiya (Khoja, Bohra, Akhabir and Usuli) and Zaidas.
2. Sunni are; Hanafi, Maliki, Shafie and Hanbali.
3. Motazila : They form an independent sect of Muslims.

Role of Privy Council

The Privy Council has contributed a lot in development of Indian Legal System. It served a cause of justice for more than two hundred years for Indian Courts before independence. As far as the judicial institution is concerned, the Privy Council was unique and unparallel among all the Courts round the world. It set the task of ascertaining the law, formulating legal principles, molding and shaping the substantive laws in India. It also helped in introduction of the concept of 'Rule of Law', on which we have setup the whole philosophy of our 'Democratic Constitution'. Besides the Privy Council also lead to the introduction of Common Law in India, which forms the basis of almost all present Indian laws.

The contribution of Privy Council in personal laws like Hindu Law and Muslim Law is also noteworthy. It acted as a channel, through which English legal concepts came to be assimilated with the body and fabric of the Indian law. It always insisted on the maintenance of the highest standards of just and judicial procedure, especially in the field of criminal justice. In this way; the decisions of Privy Council have enriched the Indian jurisprudence in many respects. Its contribution to the statute law, personal laws, and commercial laws is of great importance. Thus during the period of 1726-1949 and specifically after 1833 and onwards, the Privy Council has played a magnificent role in making a unique contribution to Indian laws and the Indian Legal System. The fundamental principles of laws as laid down by the Privy Council are considered as path finder for the Indian Courts still today.

At present also, the Privy Council commands a great respect among Indian lawyers, judges as well as Indian public as the highest judicial institution. Some of the principles laid down by the Privy Council are still followed by the Supreme Court of India. The view taken by the Privy Council is binding on the High Courts in India till the Supreme Court has decided otherwise. One of such instance can be given in the form of 'principle of absolute liability' as propounded by the Supreme Court in the historical olieum gas leak case. Thus, as a whole, the contribution of Privy Council is considered as remarkable for the development of Indian Legal System and Indian Judicial Administration. It has played a great unifying role in shaping divergent laws in India.

The common law is wholly judge made law. The role of rulings of the courts can not be underated. The system has taken case of it. Law Commission of India is constituted every three years. It does not have statutory foundation. The Constitution of Law Commission is by Government notification.

All law commissions have worked very hard so far. Over 262 reports are awaiting action in archives. Very few of these have been utilised in making new Acts in amending existing ones.

These reports are good material for research. The judges have referred to many of these in their judgments. The major portion of Modern Hindu law owes to court rulings. So is the effect of these on Muslim law which is rigid and defies alterations. The whole of common law is fathered by English judges who have done it but are not prepared to own it as having done. May be the respect they have for British Parliament which is Supreme Power in English legal system. May be they are timid and cowards and remain frightened of repulsions by Parliament. Former argument seems better where as the other bitter but those who are students of British legal History know the civil war type struggle from 1215 (Magna Carta) to 1688 (Bill of Right and Petition of Right) in which British Parliament was born and consolidated. The British Courts fought bravely with Parliament supporters against kings but fell mercilessly in their fight against British Parliament of which many of these judges were senior members in House of Lords.

The problem still remains; do Judges make law? The judge made law is struggling for legitimacy on account of this shy nature of judges making law but not acknowledging it that they do it. The judges in England have been very powerful by their being members of British Parliament (in House of Lords). They must leave this attitude and acknowledge paternity to give legitimacy to laws they have fathered. Everybody knows it, what is there to conceal? In fact, this conduct has given birth to hearing judges', not speaking judges. We have some good brains in the judiciary. We can not make them dumbs for the whole life. The judges do not speak till they are in subordinate courts wherein they operate within dotted lines (Lakshman rekha) and by the time they reach higher, they forget to speak. Do we need such judges? Do they not deserve freedom to speak? Let us liberate our judges from British created shakles in the interest of changed judiciary.

When the English came to India, the Hindu law was the personal law of the Hindus. Muslim law was the law of Courts. There was hardly any law relating to civil and criminal procedure. There was only a little of the law of torts. Some departments in the Law of property, contracts and crimes were either wanting or in a rudimentary state. There was no law dealing with public and constitutional rights because such rights did not exist. The rule of Warren Hastings, reserving the personal law in certain matters, did not remove the uncertainty of law on the matters specified in the rule because there were different schools of Hindu and Mohammedan laws having conflicting provisions. Moreover, the Hindu and Mohammedan law officers scarcely followed a particular method of interpreting them. The Hindu and Mohammedan law givers did not deal with certain branches of law, and further, they were silent on certain questions of law. In such cases the doctrine of justice, equity and good conscience was applied, but this doctrine instead of reducing the evils of uncertainty of law, increased thereby resorting to judicial legislation. Meanwhile, East India Company established a Court system. The crown established royal courts for Europeans living in India. So two parallel system of Courts, one by the Company and the other by the crown came in existence at the place of Muslim Court structure.

Existence of different Courts independent of each other, further increased the uncertainty. The decisions of different courts rendered the law, not only bulky, but uncertain and contradictory. Each of the Chief Courts, established by the Crown and the Company, was perfectly independent of the others. Every one of them was at liberty to put its own construction on the law; and it was not to be expected that they would always adopt the same construction. Under so inconvenient a system there inevitably was, in the course of a few years large collection of decisions diametrically opposed to each other, and all of equal authority.

Policy of Codification

Uniformity, where we can have it. Diversity where we must have it, but in all cases certainty.

Then the existence of different statute laws was also a great cause of uncertainty. They were : (i) English statute law as it existed in 1726; (ii) English statute law as expressly extended to India passed after 1726; (iii) Regulations of the Governor-General-in-Council from 1793 to 1843; (iv) Regulations of the Governor-in-Council of Madras from 1802 to 1834; (v) Regulations of the Bombay Council from 1827; and (vi) The Acts of the Indian Legislature passed under the authority of the Charter Act of 1833.

Codification, that is the conversion of all law into a written and systematically arranged code, was the only answer to the vices of, and problems created by, the existence of the heterogenous laws in this country. That was the only method : (i) to make the laws cognizable both to the administrators of justice and the people; (ii) to remove uncertinty of law; (iii) to check the introduction of the technical rules of English law; (iv) to avoid the evils of judicial legislation; and (v) to preserve the customs suited to the people of the country.

Section 53 of the Charter Act, 1833 has been described as "the legislative mainspring of law reform in India so far as regards policy though principles and ideas were still to come.

Principles of codification in India

Lord Macaulay formulated the principles to be followed in codifying the laws which were : We must know that respect must be paid to feelings generated by differences of religion, of nation and caste. Much may be done to assimilate the different systems of law without wounding those feelings. But whether we assimilate those systems, or not, let us ascertain them, let us digest them. We propose no rash innovation, we wish to give no shock to the prejudices of any part of our subjects. Our principle is simply this uniformity where you can have it—diversity where you must have it—but in all cases certainty.

First Law Commission (Central Law Commission)

In pursuance of the provision of the Charter Act of 1833, the First Law Commission was appointed in India in 1834. Lord Macaulay, the Law Member, became its Chairman. It submitted four reports including on Penal Code and limitation.

None of the systems of penal law existing in British India at the time of drafting the Penal Code could furnish the First Law Commission with a groundwork. The French Code, of course, was of much valuable assistance as a model and upon many questions of form, and on specific points it provided useful suggestions. Livingstone's Code of Louisiana was also of same on certain points, particularly upon the subject of offences against the human body. But the Penal Code is substantially English. According to Whitely Stokes, as in the case of the other Codes its basis is the law of England strip of technically and local peculiarities, shortened, simplified, made intelligible and precise. The Code has been taken as reproducing in a concise and even beautiful form the spirit of the law of England; the most technical, the most clumsy, and the most bewildering of all systems of criminal law; though if its principles are fully understood, it is the most rational. *Lex Loci* Report 1840 is main work of Ist Commission.

Second Law Commission.—In pursuance of the power conferred by the Charter Act of 1853, Her Majesty appointed a Law Commission in England with Sir John Romilly, a distinguished English Judge, as its chairman, on November 9, 1853. The Commission, in fulfilment of the duties devolved on it, presented four reports, the last one being dated May 20, 1856. The First Report was sent out to India in December, 1855 the Second in February 1856, and the Third and Fourth in June, 1856, for consideration of the Indian Legislature.

Third Law Commission.—During a short period of three years, the members of the Second Law Commission could not find it possible to complete such an edifice as they projected or even to lay its foundations, but they did a great work when they laid out the scheme. On December 14, 1861, the Third Law Commission with Mr. J. Romilly as its head was appointed for the purpose of preparing a body of substantive law for India, based on the principles laid down by the Second Commission in the Second Report. By appointing the Third Commission, the Government thus accepted the policy laid down by the preceding Commission. The Commission might also be required to consider and report on other matters relating to law reform.

The Commissioners were requested to report the result of their labours on one branch of civil law before they took up another branch for consideration, as the plan of successive reports on various departments of law would greatly facilitate the necessary measures which must be adopted for giving effect to their recommendations.

The appointment of the Third Commission set on foot the work of drafting and may be taken as the end of the discussion on policy and as closing—if not a chapter—at least a paragraph of British Indian history which may be entitled. 'The Codes are coming.'

In all, the Commission submitted seven reports.

Fourth Law Commission.—Many important branches of law had been codified so far, still some remained uncodified. In 1875, Lord Salisbury, the Secretary of State for India, called the attention of the Government of India to the fact that the statutory provision for the appointment of a Law Commission was designedly left in force by the Indian Councils Act and to the subsequent legislation; and intimated his intention to entrust to a small body of eminent draftsmen, the task of preparing the remaining branches of the Indian Code for the Legislative Council. After some hesitation, the Government of India proposed, in 1877, that the following branches of substantive law might be codified : Trusts, Easements, Alluvion and Diluvion, Master and Servant, Negotiable Instruments and Transfer of Immovable Property. The Government also suggested that their codification should be carried out in India in the above order. The Secretary of State accepted these proposals in the same year. The work of preparing Bills dealing with Private Trusts, Easements, Alluvion and Diluvion, and Master and Servant, was entrusted to Dr. Whitley Stokes, who completed the Bills within two years. Bills dealing with Negotiable Instruments and Transfer of Property were remodelled and redrafted. These Bills were referred for report, to a Law Commission appointed by the Government of India on February 11, 1879. This was the Fourth Law Commission. Whitley Stokes was on the Commission which submitted the Report dated November 15, 1871.

The first four Commissions deserve all compliments for their having completed a difficult, though extremely important, task. The labour of these Commissions, consisting of eminent English jurists, spread over half a century, gave to India a system of codes dealing with important parts of substantive and procedural civil and criminal law. The Commission and the codes compiled by them, "became powerful instruments which injected English common and statute law and equitable principles into the expanding structure of Indian jurisprudence."

Fifth Law Commission—Constituted every three year by notification.

During the pre-independence era, the need for creating a body designed to bring about revision of law was constantly emphasised, and some attempts were made in that direction. After Independence, on December 2, 1947, Mr. Hari Singh Gour moved a resolution in the Constituent Assembly (Legislative) recommending the establishment of a Statutory Law Revision Committee with a view to clarify and settle questions of law which required elucidation. The resolution was, however, withdrawn on an assurance given by the then law Minister, Mr. B.R. Ambedkar, that the Government would try to create some other suitable machinery for law revision. One of the methods for this purpose, proposed by him, was the creation of a permanent Commission entrusted solely with the work of revising and codifying the laws. On June 27, 1952, in the Lok Sabha. Sri N.C. Chatterjee again stressed the need of creating a Law Commission. The then Law Minister, Sri C.C. Biswar, stated during the course of his speech on this point that the Government recognised that the work of keeping the law up-to-date was of great importance, and he assured the member that the Government would examine the matter and take necessary steps. On July 26, 1954, the All India Congress Committee resolved that a Law Commission should be appointed to revise existing laws and to advise on current legislation from time to time.

The terms of reference to the Commission were :

(1) To review the system of judicial administration in all its aspects and suggest ways and means for improving it and making it speedy and less expensive.

(2) To examine the Central Acts of general application and importance, and to recommend the lines on which they should be amended, revised, consolidated, or otherwise brought up-to-date.

With regard to the first term, the inquiry of the Commission into the system of judicial administration was to be comprehensive and thorough including in its scope;

(a) the operation and effect of laws, substantive as well as procedural, with a view to eliminate unnecessary litigation, speeding up the disposal of cases and making justice less expensive;

(b) the organisation of courts, both civil and criminal;

(c) recruitment of the judiciary; and

(d) level of the bar and of legal education.

With regard to the second term, the principal objectives of the Commission in the revision of existing legislation were to be

(a) to simplify the laws in general, and the procedural laws in particular;

(b) to ascertain if any provisions are inconsistent with the Commission and suggest the necessary alterations or omissions;

(c) to remove anomalies and ambiguities brought to light by conflicting decisions of High Courts or otherwise; (d) to consider local variations introduced by State legislation in the concurrent field, with a view to reintroduce and maintain uniformity;

(e) to consolidate Acts pertaining to the same subject with necessary technical revision; and

(f) to suggest modification wherever necessary for implementing the directive principles of State policy laid down in the Constitution.

Law Commission has been constituted every three years and recently it has been decided to reconstitute it for another three years till 2009. The Commission was to consist of a Chairman and two regular members. The Commission can co-opt three more members. The Chairman is a retired Supreme Court judge. The members could be retired judges of the Supreme Court. The members can be retired judges of the Supreme Court or High Court or member of a law faculty. The Law Commission submitted 158 reports. The reports were not public but now after Right to Information Act, 2005, it is now open to public access. The unfortunate thing is that action on these reports by the government is not obligatory. The Commission is constituted by Government notification every three year. It does not have any statutory foundation.

State Law Commissions

For new legislation and the revision of State Acts, the State Commissions have also been constituted on patterns of Central Law Commission under Chairmanship of Retired High Court judges.

Continental Codes

The codification in continental countries has been as follows :

Justinian Code and Corpus Juris Civilis of Rome etc.—The whole of Roman Law was embodied in this great work at the close of ancient period. The Roman Law has a previous history of great length and great importance. It can be traced to *Code of Twelve Tables* which was compiled 450 years before Christ. The process of transformation in Roman Law has been slow but steady. The *Corpus Juris Civilis* is the later phase of that long development. The *Corpus Juris* is a product of the Eastern Roman Empire. The western had ceased to exist, even in name, a half century before the accession of Justinian. This happened just like Germanic tribes established as conquerors and sovereign in all provinces of the West and the Anglo Saxon's in Britain, the Frances and Burgundians in Gaul, the Visigoths in Spain, the Ostrogoths in Italy, the Vandals in Northern Africa.

Justinian afterwards crushed the powers of Vandals and the Ostrogoths and brought Africa and Italy into his empire. He came on throne in 529 B.C. at the age of 45. In 528 B.C. he entered upon the work of collecting, revising and systematizing the whole body of Roman Law. The whole work was done under the supervision of Tribonian. The book consists of two principal parts. The first part deals with Constitutions of the Roman Emperors and the second part deals with the treatises of the Roman lawyers.

(*i*) *Constitutions*.—This included the following :

(a) *Orationes*.—These were the proposals of laws submitted to the Senate for their actions.

(b) *Edicta.*—These were the laws put forth by the Emperor himself in his character as highest magistrate.

(c) *Mandata.*—These were the directions addressed by the Emperor to the prefect of the city or to prefects of practorium or legatus in the provinces.

(d) Decreta.—These were the decisions given by the Emperor in law cases brought before him either by way of appeal or petition.

(e) *Rescripta.*—These were the answers given by King on consultations.

(ii) Digest.—The second work was very complicated and difficult. The preparation of the Digest required the huge literature to be examined. The works to be digested were by 39 authors and consisted of about 200 books. A series of Imperial ordinances under name of decisions were issued by the King for guidance of the compilers. The changes in old law were made according to these decisions. The Digest was prepared with the help of 16 associates including four Law Professors. This digest was issued in December 533 B.C. within a short span of three years. This was also called Pandects (all receiving). It is divided into 50 Books and each book is divided into number of titles (tituli). Under these titles stand the extracts, each one preceded by the name of the author and the treatise from which it is taken. The aggregate of the extracts is about 9,000. The half of the digest is taken from the works of Ulpian and Paulus. The digest is in fact the soul of the corpus. The digest contains the definitions, maxims, principles, applications, distinctions and illustrations.

(iii) Codex Constitutionum.—In order to make it in conformity with the principles of Digest the Codex Constitutionum was revised in 534 B.C. and issued in present form as amended. It was divided into 12 books and these into titles with the same general arrangement as the digest. The Codex contains some topics not included in the Digest *i.e.* Church and Christianity. It contains much more public law than Digest.

(iv) Institutes.—These are elementary text books founded on the Institutions of Gaius. It was prepared by Tribonian Theophilus and Dorctheus. It was issued with the Digest in 533 B.C.

The Institutes, Codex and Digest were given to law schools for being taught within five years as full body of law. The law schools were at Rome, Constantionple, Berytus, Alexandria, Caesarea. No commentaries could be written on these except translation into Greece.

(v) Novels.—This was the last part of the *Corpus Juris.* It includes the latter statutes in proper arrangements. They were also called *Novellae Constitutiones.*

(vi) The XII Tables.—The Greater part of the text had perished, completely. The original bronze tables are said to have been destroyed when the Gauls burnt Rome in 399 B.C. Since then the reference to its contents are found sometimes in private notes, reference in works of Cicero and Guius etc. The arrangement of the whole Code is unascertainable except in

few tables where the numbers are still discernible. The style is characterised with extreme brevity and simplicity and the language is always careful and exact. Procedure is dealt in detail. Whereas mansipation is dismissed with simple recognition. The subject is frequently changing. No consistency of subject-matter is maintained. For example, whole property law is not at one place and in one sequence. The Romans did not regard the Twelve Tables as Code but as source of all public and private law. It was accepted even as sacred law.

FRENCH CODES

The corpus of the French law consists of the five Codes and separate statutes and regulations. The five codes are :

(i) Civil Code enacted in 1804.

(ii) Code of Civil Procedure enacted in 1806.

(iii) The Code of Commerce enacted in 1808.

(iv) The Code of Criminal Procedure enacted in 1811.

(v) The Penal Code enacted in 1811.

All Codes have been frequently amended, for example Code of Criminal Procedure was superseded in 1959 by Code of Penal Procedure.

Other Codes

Other important codes include Forest Code, 1826, Highway Code, 1839, Code of Nationality, 1945, Code of 1948, Comprehensive Acts dealing with Insurance, (1930), Cheques (1935), Industrial Accidents (1946) etc.

Civil Codes

It is composed of preliminary titles, treating of publication, the effects and application of laws in general. Besides there are three books each of which is divided into several titles, these again into chapters, in several instances, into sections and articles. Originally there were 2281 articles in civil code. They are very short sometimes containing eight or ten words in length. Civil Code consists of :—

(a) *Book First.*—It is called *Des Personnes.* It deals with matters like marriage, divorce, status of minors, guardianship, domicile *etc.*

(b) *Book two.*—It is called *Des biens, et des differentes, modifications de la propriete.* It deals with property, usufruct and servitudes.

(c) *Book three.*—It is called *Des Differentes manieres donton acquiert la propriete.* It is a curious medley consisting of twenty titles. It covers three-fourth of the whole Civil Code. It deals with different matters including gift, will, intestate succession, contract, quasi contracts, tort, sale, lease, mortgage, partnership, pledge, prescription and marriage settlements.

The codification in India has been practically done by British people. Before the birth of Anglo Indian Code the Institutes of Manu, Yagnyavalkya and Narad, the Artha Sastra of Kautilya *etc.* were of such a comprehensive nature that they stand far superior in comparison to Roman Codes. They contained the recommendatory and mandatory rules interwoven together with common thread of religion and secularism. The modern Codes in India are neither wholly similar to English law nor are they purely of an Indian origin. As compared to French Codes, they are more in number, more comprehensive and fragmentary. They neither pretend to be wholly self-contained nor exhaustive. Many Codes suffer from the vice of superfluity and repetition. No link exists between different Codes on same subject or on different subjects. The attempt in the direction of uniform Civil Code for India is going on. The first attempt in shape of Hindu Law of marriage, succession, divorce, maintenance, guardianship has been successful. Likewise, is the dissolution of Muslim Marriage Act, Shariat Act, Musalman Wakf Validation Act. The Indian Constitution provides that it shall be the duty of the State to enact a uniform Civil Code for India based on secularism.

French Code and Code Justinian

In France, the ideology of codification reflects the event of French revolution. That is why a French Code repealed all prior law in the areas covered by the Codes. The idea of glorifying the nation-state compelled the French Codes to make a fresh start and write the history afresh for getting away every thing of the pre-revolution France. Thus, effect of law was delimited to new Code. If any thing from old law was permitted to continue, it was not because of their previous existence but due to their incorporation and re-enactment in codified form. Exactly this practice was adopted when Justinian promulgated *Corpus Juris Civilis*. He also abolished all prior law. But both these differed in one essential particular. Justinian and the French codifiers sought to destroy prior law for different but analogous reasons; Justinian sought to re-establish power law of earlier time. The French aimed to establish an entirely new legal order. In both, the aims were essentially utopian.

To write off history.—The French Code was intended to write off the history of law because a major portion of it was borrowed from European common law. They drafted their codes under a belief that history could be abolished by a repealing statute. The codes could not succeed hundred per cent in discarding history prior to revolution but this definitely gave birth to a fiction for French jurists that history was irrelevant to interpretation and application of code.

To do away with lawyers.—The French Revolution had another object also. It aimed to do away with lawyers. Probably for this reason, the codes were intended to state law in simple, non-technical and straight forward manner. Thus, French Civil Code was envisioned as a kind of popular book that could be put on the shelf next to family Bible.

Complete separation of power Advocated.—In French system, a complete separation of power was advocated with all law making power lodged in a representative legislature and the task of judiciary would only be to interpret and apply these to actual cases. This rigidity compelled the codes to be complete, coherent and clear. Prussian landrecht of 1794 enacted under Frederick the Great is an example of such an attempt. It contained

16 thousand detailed provisions setting out precise rules to govern specific fact situations. But its failure cautioned the French codifiers to go on such lines.

Tribunal of Cassation established.—The French, therefore, adopted a new way out for avoiding the incorrect interpretations of courts and it is with this aim the Tribunal of Cassation or "*aupres du corps legis latiff*" was established with power to quash incorrect interpretations of the courts. This tribunal though in garb a part of judicial system, was in fact a special instrument created by the legislature to protect legislature's supremacy from judicial usurpation.

Position in Germany

In contrast to the essentially revolutionary, rationalistic and non-technical character of Code Napoleon, the German Civil Code of 1896 was historically oriented, scientific and professional. The credit for this difference goes to Savigny who opposed codification of the then German laws in absence of thorough study of existing German law in its historical perspective.

Regarding role of lawyers, the Germans were convinced that it was neither desirable nor possible to get rid of the lawyers. The application of law by ordinary readers did not find favour of the German codifiers. Therefore, the codes in Germany were drafted with care so as to be capable of being handled by lawyers. Moreover, German Code did not intend to abolish prior law and substitute a new legal system. The raw material for French Codes was mainly collected from assumptions about man's nature whereas in Germany these were drawn from careful and scientific study of the German law. In India, the materials for codes were drawn from English law.

Codes in Non-European Countries

Regarding Codes in Non-European countries, the typical example may be California Civil Code or Uniform Commercial Code. These differ ideologically and do not express anything like the same cultural reality. These codes do not pretend to be complete in all forms. The judge is not compelled to find a basis for deciding a given case within the code. These are neither based on rejections of history nor do these purport to abolish all prior law in their field. These on the contrary, attempt to perfect or supplement the existing law in the field.

Civil and Common law tendencies.—Thus, the tendencies of the common law are conservative and civil law codification owes its origin to ideology of revolution. That is the reason why these are quite different. Sometimes this ideological difference becomes more important than the form of codification in common law and civil law systems.

The Continental law and the Common Law.—The following points may be selected for comparison :

(i) The sources.

The common source in both the counties are :

Legislation.—In England, legislation has always been in the form of the Act of the King acting since many centuries with the cooperation of both the Houses of the Parliament. But in Rome, the legislative power shifted in much more striking ways.

Republics.—During Republics, it was in the hands of assemblies of the people. These were not like British Parliament consisting of people's representatives, but they were bodies in which all male citizens sat and voted. These were *group assemblies* which later on conceded to *Tribunal Assembly* organised on much more democratic lines. The presiding officer of these assemblies used to be elected magistrates. All the bills were required to be proposed by the chair. 'Private member's Bill' was unknown. No amendments could be proposed. The motion was to be accepted or rejected in the form it was proposed. No measure could become law without approval of a body known as '*Auctoritas patrum*' which consisted of the partition members of the Senate.

Senate.—By the end of the Republic, the work of legislation had passed to Senate which was a body nominated by the Emperor. The Senate used to direct the legislation to presiding magistrates which used to be Kings' nominees. Thus, legislation in Rome passed from popular assemblies into the hands of the Head of State whereas in England it passed from Head of State to popular assemblies ultimately known as British Parliament.

Edicts.—There was another method of legislation in Rome of which no paralled is found in common law countries. The magistrates, consuls, praetors, Aediles etc. used to proclaim the policies they intended to follow. These after a long run constituted the bulk of the Roman Law. The Ordinances so issued were collected in *Edict* which is popular Code of Rome. This process was called as Roman Equity which was quite different from English Equity. These are incidental resemblances in Roman Praetors and English Chancellors.

(b) *Case Law.*—Romans had in principle no case law. The Roman Judge 'Judex' was not a lawyer; so no question of binding precedents could arise. However, decisions by Emperor constituted an exception to it and it was accepted to be binding throughout the Empire. Emperor was a legislator with free hands and he could lay down the law in any way he thought fit. The continuous decisions on like facts and like circumstances in different cases is taken like an evidence of expert opinion on that legal point. The regard for the precedent in Roman Law is similar to one accorded in France.

(c) *Juristic Writings.*—In English law, such writings are sometimes considered valuable on any legal point but not as of authority, but in Roman Law, the juristic writing speaks with authority as it does in France. The English writers like Bracton and Littleton get less recognition as authority in English Court as does Gaius in Roman Law. In U.S.A. the respect for legal and juristic writings is on increase.

(d) *Custom.*—The Common law is customary. But this view has been challenged by Mcnaire as erroneous. According to him, Common Law was brought into existence by King's Justices all over the country precisely because there was no general custom in the country. But the Roman Law *i.e., Jus Civilis* has a better claim to be called as based on general custom of the realm. for example Twelve Tables was based on existing Latin customs.

(ii) Originality

The English law and Roman law, both are original creations. Both developed from their basic and fundamental works. English law from Blackstone's commentaries and Roman law from Gaius's Institute.

❑ ❑

Chapter 14

Judicial Process and Procedure

Procedural law or adjective law comprises the rules by which a court hears and determines what happens in civil, lawsuit, criminal or administrative proceedings. The rules are designed to ensure a fair and consistent application of due process (in the U.S.) or fundamental justice (in other common law countries) to all cases that come before a court.

Substantive law, which refers to the actual claims and defenses whose validity is tested through the procedures of procedural law, is different from procedural law.

In context of procedural law; procedural *rights* may also refer not exhaustively to rights to Information, rights to justice, rights to participation which those rights encompassing, general Civil and Political rights. In environmental law, these procedural Rights have been reflected within the UNECE Convention on "Access to Information, Public Participation in Decision-making and Access to Justice in Environmental Matters" known as the Aarhus Convention (1998).

Legal procedure

Although different legal processes aim to resolve many kinds of legal disputes, the legal procedures share some common features. All legal procedure, for example, is concerned with due process. Absent very special conditions, a court can not impose a penalty—civil or criminal—against an individual who has not received notice of a lawsuit being brought against them, or who has not received a fair opportunity to present evidence for themselves.

The standardization for the means by which cases are brought, parties are informed, evidence is presented, and facts are determined is intended to maximize the fairness of any proceeding. Nevertheless, strict procedural rules have certain drawbacks. For example, they impose specific time limitations upon the parties that may either hasten or (more frequently) slow down the pace of proceedings. Furthermore, a party who is unfamiliar with procedural rules may run afoul of guidelines that have nothing to do with the merits of the case, and yet the failure to follow these guidelines may severely damage the party's chances. Procedural systems are constantly torn between arguments that judges should have greater discretion in order to avoid the rigidity of the rules, and arguments that judges should have less discretion in order to avoid an outcome based more on the personal preferences of the judge than on the law or the facts.

Legal procedure, in a larger sense, is also designed to effect the best distribution of judicial resources. For example, in most courts of general jurisdiction in the United States, criminal cases are given priority over civil cases, because criminal defendants stand to lose their freedom, and should therefore be accorded the first opportunity to have their case heard.

"Procedural law" and "substantive law" in various languages

"Procedural law" in contrast to "substantive law" is a concept available in various legal systems and languages. Similar to the English expressions are the Spanish words *derecho adjetivo* and *derecho material* or *derecho sustantivo*, as well as the Portuguese terms for them, *direito adjetivo* and *direito substantivo.* as well as the Portuguese terms for them, *direito adjetivo* and *direito substantivo.* Other ideas are behind the German expressions *formelles Recht* (or *Verfahrensrecht) and materielles Recht* as well as the French *droit formel/droit matériel*, the Italian *diritto formale/diritto materiale* and the Swedish *formell rätt/materiell rätt*; all of which, taken literally, mean "formal" and "material" law. The same opposition can be found in the Russian legal vocabulary, with *MamepuarbHoe npabo* for substantive law and *npoueccyarbHoe npabo* for procedural. Similar to Russian, in Bulgarian *MamepuarHo npabo* means substantive law and npouecyarHo npabo is used for procedural. In Chinese, "procedural law" and "substantive law" are represented by these characters : "***" and "***"

In Germany, the expressions *formelles Recht* and *materielles Recht* were developed in the 19th century, because only during that time was the Roman *actio* split into procedural and substantive components.

The substance of "Procedural law"/"Substantive law" in Europe

In the European legal systems the Roman law had been of great influence. In ancient times the Roman civil procedure applied to many countries. One of the main issues of the procedure has been the *actio* (similar to the English word "act"). In the procedure of the *legis actiones* the *actio* included both procedural and substantive elements. Because during this procedure the Praetor had granted, or denied, litigation by granting or denying, respectively, an *actio.* By granting the *actio* the *praetor* in the end has created claims *i.e.*, a procedural act caused substantive claims to exist. Such priority (procedure over substance) is contrary to what we think of the relationship nowadays. But it has not only been an issue of priority and whether the one serves the other. Since the *actio* had been composed of elements of procedure and substance it was difficult to separate both parts again.

Even the scientific handling of law, which developed during medieval times in the new universities in Italy (in particular in Bologna, Mantua), did not come to a full and clear separation. (The English system of "writs" in the Middle Ages had a similar problem to the Roman tradition with the *actio.*)

The general rule is that all the rules of procedure are the hand maid of justice. The language of a Code may be liberal or stringent but the fact is that the object of procedure is to advance the cause of justice. In an adversarial system, no party should ordinarily be denied the opportunity of participating in the process of justice dispensation. The mortality of the justice at the hands of law troubles the conscience of a judge, procedural law is not to be a tyrant but a servant; not an obstruction but an aid to justice. Procedural prescriptions are the hand maid and not the mistress, a lubricant, not a restraint in the administration of justice.

The substantive criminal law in civil law countries does not differ much from common law countries. The same kind of actions are considered criminal and the same approaches to punishment are seen throughout. There are however many significant operational differences in Criminal Procedure. The typical criminal proceeding in civil law countries may be divided into three basic parts :—

(i) *The investigative phase.*—It comes under the direction of public prosecutor who also participates actively in examination stage of the case.

(ii) *The examining phase.*—This is supervised by the judge. It is primarily written and is not public. The examining judge controls the nature and scope of this phase of proceeding. The examining judge is required to conclude :—

1. Whether the crime was committed; and
2. Whether the accused is the perpetrator; If the answer is negative, the matter is dropped. If it is in affirmative, the case goes to trial.

(iii) *The trial stage.*—The civil law system has a criminal trial which is quite different in character from common law trial. The evidence is complete well before trial. The records of evidence are sent to the accused, his counsel and to the prosecution. At trial stage, the case is explained to the judge and counsels argue their law points. The arguments are public.

These three stages are known to common law but the extent of these is very much different. This may be examined in the following ways :—

Who is to prosecute?—According to English Law any citizen can, as a general rule and in the absence of some provision to the contrary bring a criminal prosecution, whether or not he has suffered any special harm over and above other members of the public. As a member of public, he has an interest in the enforcement of the criminal law. For example, *A* steals *B*'s watch. *B* may prosecute him and likewise *C, D, E, F* each one of them can prosecute. In practice, vast majority of the prosecutions are carried on by police or other public officers who have no personal interest in the outcome. The Director of the Public Prosecutions institutes and carries on the proceedings in the case of any offence punishable with death, in certain other cases referred to it by Government Departments and in some other cases which appear to him to require his intervention.

Regulations provide for Chief Officers of Police for reporting to the Director of Public Prosecutions cases of certain classes. The Chief Officer of the Police is always entitled to ask for the advice or assistance of the Director. Formerly it was necessary for police to make report about murder cases. But after the abolition of capital punishment since 1966, no such regulation has been passed that makes such a report compulsory. The police officer appears to prosecute as a member of the public even if he is in police uniform and it is on this belief that a man may be put to trial in any case. As compared to this, in Scotland, there is no private prosecution. The prosecution of the crime is in the hands of the ministers of the Crown, Her Majesty's Advocate, known as Lord Advocate. The Lord Advocate and Solicitor-General are the law officers of the Crown. The offices of Lord Advocate and Attorney-General in India are almost similar but in criminal the former carries greater and wider responsibility. The Lord Advocate has five Crown Counsels as subordinate to them. They have offices in Edinburgh and conduct cases in High Court there. Exclusive right of audience is granted to these Crown Counsels in the High Courts. In each county of Scotland, there is a Sheriff Court staffed by full time professional judges known as Sheriffs. All criminal cases come to these sheriff courts sometimes *en route* to the High Court. The sheriff exercises the widest criminal jurisdiction in Scotland. Besides him, Burgh magistrates, and County Justices also share some criminal jurisdiction.

To each Sheriff court, a public prosecutor is attached. Besides the procurator fiscal is also appointed with each Sheriff court. These persons do the job as local representatives of the Lord Advocate. In Sheriff Court, the public prosecutor or his deputy conducts the case but when the matter goes to High Court they prepare the briefs for the Crown Counsels. If the Lord Advocate declines to proceed with the prosecution, any aggrieved citizen may start a private prosecution by *Criminal Letters*. It can never be by *Indictment*. But the concurrence of the Lord Advocate must be obtained. If the concurrence is also withheld, then prosecutions may go on if the High Court so permits.

In French Criminal Procedure, the prosecutions are to be initiated and conducted by the magistrates and officials in whom the power is vested by law. Public Prosecution is a rule in France as in Scotland. Nevertheless at the same time a civil action may be pursued at the same time and before the same court as the prosecution by the party aggrieved. It may include all heads of damages, mental as well as physical or even moral which flow from the acts which are objects of the prosecution. The civil action and prosecution are independent and renunciation of civil action does not terminate or suspend the prosecution. The civil party to a criminal action has his place in procedural rules throughout the investigation and trial. In America also, generally speaking private prosecutions are not permitted. The criminal trial is conducted by a state paid professional.

The conclusion is that, in England, a prosecution may be initiated by anyone, in Scotland by an official Public Prosecutor, in France and Germany by an official Public Prosecutor with whom may be associated directly the injured private party.

Committal for Trial.—In England, the committal proceeding is preceded by information *ex-officio*, presentments by coroner's juries and historical position of the grand juries. Thereafter criminal trial is handled by justices or magistrates. The criminal trial in England takes place in public except those concerning the security of nation, decency or protection of witnesses from unnecessary and cruel embarrassment. However, as the law stands, the Examining Justices shall not be obliged to sit in open court. Even if the proceeding is public, the press and public may be excluded if the justices so decide. They do so rarely. The proceeding is opened by a speech of the prosecutor followed by the examination and cross-examination of his witnesses. The accused is asked if he wants to make a statement, whether he wants to give sworn evidence and whether he wants to call any evidence. He or his advocate is entitled to address the court. The court then decides on whether the evidence is such that the accused ought to be committed for trial. If that is decided affirmatively then in all but exceptional cases the court proceeds to consider bail.

In U.S.A. also, the committal proceedings are in public, the procedure is similar to one prevailing in England.

Immediately after a person is arrested, the law requires that he should be produced before a magistrate who will inquire about whether the State's evidence is true or whether there is any chance of conviction. If there is probability of conviction, the magistrate must accept the bail and if there is no chance and State's case is weaker, the accused is entitled to his immediate liberty. Theoretically speaking, the preliminary examinations are held as a way to get information about the State's case. But in practice, it is avoided so that an impartial jury may be available who have not made up their minds before the trial begins.

In Scotland, the preliminary proceedings upto the opening of the trial itself are kept private. A crime is first reported by the police to Procurator fiscal. The police has general power of arrest in serious crimes. This is similar to one in England. The prosecutor in every case will apply to the Sheriff for a warrant, so that the person may be arrested and brought before the Sheriff, or his person and premises may be searched, witnesses may be arranged and to set the accused on bail or put him in police custody. The second stage in a Scottish procedure is one known as Precognition. This gives authority to prosecutor so that he may examine the witnesses of his own and may record their statements. Third stage is that the precognition is examined by the Sheriff. No inquiry is held and committal is made on the basis of the enquiry so held and concluded.

The French Procedure is more interesting. The most important process of French procedure is "*L'instruction criminelle*". According to this process all the proofs against the accused must be collected before a prosecution is started. He may not be put to public ignonimity before the facts are carefully and impartialy investigated and screened by a judicial magistrate. He may not be put to a public trial simply on the basis of a police report. That is why the verdict of *judged instruction* is secured before committal. The special features of the French criminal procedure include—

(a) privacy of proceedings,

(b) the essential role of the Independent Judge,

(c) the careful separation of duties between the police, prosecutor and the examining magistrates.

The Criminal Procedure in India.—The Criminal Procedure in India is regulated by Criminal Code (Act No. 2 of 1973). It contains 484 sections and two schedules. Section 6 of the Code enumerates 4 classes of criminal courts *i.e.*, Courts of Session, Judicial Magistrate of First Class. Judicial Magistrate of Second Class, Metropolitan Magistrates and Executive Magistrates, Chief Judicial Magistrate and Additional Chief Judicial Magistrate, Special Judicial Magistrates; Metropolitan Magistrate includes Chief Metropolitan Magistrate and special Metropolitan Magistrates.

Executive Magistrate includes District Magistrate and Additional District Magistrates and Special Executive Magistrates. There is no magistrate of third class now in current criminal procedure code.

The Procedure of Arrest.—The arrest can be made by Police Officer or other persons. Arrest is detailed in Sections 41 to 60 of Cr. P.C., 1973. It may be :

(a) By police (Section 41).

Arrest by police may be without order of any magistrate or without warrant : (i) who has been concerned in any cognizable offence; (ii) on reasonable complaint; (iii) on credible information; (iv) reasonable suspicion. Section 41 enumerates such situations.

(b) Arrest by Private Person (Section 43).

Anybody who :—

(i) commits non-bailable and cognizable offence; or

(ii) is proclaimed offender.

(c) Arrest by Magistrate (Section 44).

Any magistrate (Judicial or executive) (i) in whose presence; (ii) within whose local jurisdiction any offence is committed may arrest or order to arrest the offender. They can-touch the body or confine the body of the person to be arrested if the accused does not submit either by word or action. If forcible resistance is made or attempt to evade the arrest is made, the Police Officer or other person may use all means necessary to effect the arrest. But this does not empower to kill the person to be arrested unless the offence for which he is wanted and evading arrest is punishable with death or life imprisonment. If such a wanted person enters any house or place belonging to others, the owner of that place is bound to assist the Police Officer *etc.* by all means in making search. If no such ingress is obtainable, the Police Officer with warrant may enter the place and break open any outer or inner door and window. This power is to be exercised only after notification of the authority, purpose and demand of admittance duly made, the ingress is not permitted.

Procedure to compel appearance

The persons accused of having committed some case are summoned after complaint. (Sections 61-69). Every summons issued by a court shall be in writing, in duplicate, signed and sealed by the Presiding Officer of the Court issuing it or by such other Officer as the High Court may direct. Such summons shall be served by police officer, or by an Officer of the Court issuing it or other public servant, as the State Government may provide.

The second way of compelling appearance is; warrant of arrest (Sections 70-81). Every warrant shall be in writing signed by presiding Officer or in case of a Bench of Magistrate, by any member of such Bench and it shall bear the seal of the Court. Every such warrant shall remain in force until it is cancelled by the Court which issued it or until it is executed. The Court may direct security to be taken in case of warrant and these security bonds are to be forwarded to the Court if taken.

The third way is; proclamation and attachment (Sections 82-86). If any Court has reason to believe that any person against whom the warrant has been issued by it has absconded or is concealing himself to avoid the execution of warrant, the Court may publish a written proclamation requiring him to appear at a specified place and at specified time not less than thirty days from the date of proclamation. After proclamation, the Court issuing it at any time may order the attachment of any property, moveable or immoveable or both belonging to the proclaimed person.

The fourth way is, issue of warrant in lieu of or in addition to summons. (Section 87).

The fifth way possible is, the power to take bond for appearance. (Section 88).

Investigation

The police officer moves to find out the realities of the situation; collects evidence and formulates the specific charges against the accused. After close of the investigation, a charge-sheet is submitted to the magistrate's court. The period of Investigation in India is unduly longer. The corrupt police officers and unwilling public co-operation are mainly responsible for it.

Section 154 provides for First Information Report in cognizable offence. Section 155 provides for First Information Report in non-cognizable cases (N.C.R.). Here starts the provision for investigation. Investigation is entirely within the authority of police. The Court has no jurisdiction to interfere in the investigation. If police is not investigating any case or is not registering the report, the aggrieved person can move an application under Section 156(5) for appropriate direction. Arrest is implied in every F.I.R. of a cognizable nature but it should be kept in mind that Section 41 says that arrest by police can be made where there is reasonable complaint or reasonable suspicion or credible information. Liberty to arrest has to be exercised by police keeping these provisions of Section 41 Cr.P.C. in mind. Article 226 is also utilised for arrest stay against false, *mala fide* and those

F.I.R. which do not constitute any offence; particularly where Section 438 of Cr.P.C. does not come to assist innocent persons. It is repealed in State of U.P. Investigation is given in Sections 154 to 172 Cr.P.C.

Inquiry

Inquiry is a proceeding before the Magistrate. Any investigation may end either in terms of Section 169 where final report is made by police or in terms of Section 173 Cr.P.C. when chargesheet or police report or challani report is filed. The Magistrate may accept the report under Section 169 or may reject it and may ask the police to make re-investigation or the Magistrate may himself take cognizance of the case under Section 190 Cr.P.C. and may proceed under Section 200 as complaint case. When magistrate decides to accept the final report, notice to complainant is must. Without notice to complainant, final report under Section 169 cannot be accepted. Hearing of accused is not necessary. In fact, accused has no right of hearing at this stage. When notice is issued to the complainant; he appears and files 'protest application', 'against final report and gives some evidence' in addition to what has been recorded by police under Sections 161 to 164, the Magistrate may issue 'summoning process' under Section 204 if satisfied of some offence being disclosed.

On Challani Report (173).—Section 173 proceeds in 8 clauses—All providing different steps that are required after the Magistrate takes cognizance of the charge-sheet. The investigation has to be completed within the period specified under Section 167 that is 90 days in serious matters and 60 days in non-serious cases or as soon as possible. Further, investigation even after challani report is permitted and supplementary charge-sheet or further report or reports can be filed.

Private complaint.—If F.I.R. is lodged but the police dos not investigate and order of magistrate under Section 156(c) Cr.P.C. is not given or even in writ petition under Article 226, no direction is obtained, it is still open to the complainant to file application as private complaint before the magistrate who would take cognizance on merit under Section 190. The Magistrate shall record statement of the complainant under Section 200 and his witnesses. He would dismiss the application if no case is made out even *prima facie* tentatively.—would proceed under Section 204 if case is made out.

Committal to Session

Section 209 provides for the commitment of the case to Court of Session when offence is exclusively triable by it. When accused appears or is brought out before Magistrate and case is triable by session; the Magistrate :

(a) shall comply with Section 207, in case of police cases;

(b) shall comply with Section 208, other than police case;

(c) shall remand the accused to judicial custody

  (i) till commitment;

  (ii) till trial; or

(iii) bail

(d) commit the case to session;

(e) send the record to session and notify public prosecutor.

Trial

Trial begins with framing of a charge. Trial may be—

(i) Session Trial (Sections 225-237). The Offences Triable by Session Court are in—

Sections 121, 121-A, 128, 130-132, 194, 201, 211, 222, 225, 232, 234, 235, 238, 240, 251, 255, 272-276, 302-304, 304-B, 308, 311-316, 328, 329, 331, 333, 363-A, 366-367, 371, 372-373, 376-376-A, B, C, D, 395-400, 402, 412-413, 436-439, 449-450, 459, 489-A, B, C, D, 500, 501-a, 502(a) Indian Penal Code.

(ii) Warrant case Trial by Magistrate (Sections 238 to 250) means punishable (i) by death (ii) life imprisonment, (iii) Exceeding 3 years.

By Magistrate of First Class : Sections 120-B, 129, 133, 134, 148, 152, 153-A, B, 161-169, 171-E to 171-I, 181, 193, 201, 204-205, 208-216-A, 218-222, 225, 225-A, 231, 233, 235, 237, 239, 242-250, 260, 263, 281, 295-A, 304-A, 312, 317-318, 326-327, 330, 332, 335, 345, 346, 363, 363-A, 365, 369, 370, 377, 382, 386-94, 401, 404-409, 420, 429, 433, 435, 440, 454, 465-477-A, 493-497.

(iii) Any Magistrate : Sections 135-147, 151, 153, 154-160, 170-171, 172-180, 182-190, 202, 203, 206-207, 223-225, 225-B, 227, 228-A, 229, 233, 241, 254, 262, 263-A-280, 282-295, 296-298, 309, 323-325, 334, 336-344, 347-358, 374, 379-381, 384, 385, 403, 411, 414-419, 421-428, 434, 451-454, 456, 461, 482-489, 489-E, 491, 498, 504-506-510 of Indian Penal Code.

The general principle is that if any offence is cognizable non-bailable and punishable with death, life imprisonment or rigorous imprisonment of 7 years or above, it is triable by Sessions Court. Punishable by 3 years or above but below 7 years, it is triable by Judicial Magistrate First Class and punishable by less than 3 years or fine, it shall be triable by any magistrate.

Summary trial—(Section 260-265) : and All Summon Cases.

By any Court or Magistrate. Maximum punishment is 6 months jail or Rs. 3000/- fine or both.

379, 381, 411, 414 (property below Rs. 200), 454, 456, 504, 506, the attempt and abetment of these.

System of trial

The following systems are selected for comparative study :

(i) Adversary System

In common law system, the trial is *Adversary*, or accusatorial. This system prevails in U.S.A., England, India and Scotland. It is based on the presentation by advocates for the prosecution on one hand and for the defence on the other, of such evidence as in their judgment is relevant to the only question before the Court, namely, did the accused commit this crime? This they do in such a way as they calculate will be most likely to persuade the tribunal, be it judge or jury that their side is right. The contest is presided over and controlled by an impartial judge who takes no part in the proceedings other than supervisory until the time comes when he has either to declare his decision or to give instruction to the jury who have to do so. In Scotland, the procedure is similar and the judge remains aloof likewise except in that a copy of indictment and other relevant documents is sent to him before the trial begins. These documents are sent to jury also.

Accusatorial or accusational system is the first substitute for private vengeance; originally the 'power to institute the action was only to person wronged but gradually it extended to his relatives and with development of the concept of social solidarity, it now extends to all members of the society. The criminal trial is predominantly as yet, a contest between the accuser and the accused with the judge as a referee. The proceedings take place publicly and orally and are not preceded by any official in investigation (Judicial or police) or preparation of evidence. In India, adversary system and inquisitorial system both operate. Adversary as general and inquisitorial as an exception. A move in direction of strict liability is coming up; In bride burning related dowry crimes, if it is proved that death took place within 7 years after marriage and the victim was tortured for the dowry related demands, the burden of proof shifts on accused to prove that death was not dowry death. Likewise, in custom, excise and others, strict liability is rule.

There is no 'jury' in use in India. 'Judge' has to infer facts from evidence and has to select and apply law to facts. Court is jury and judge both in a case.

(ii) Inquisitorial System

The justice delivery system in France is the best. If imitation can be regarded as indication of approval, the popularity and acceptance of French Judicial System presents such an approval in the higher degree.

Courts in France like any other Court which follows inquisitorial system moves on the presumption of "Guilty until proven innocent". The presiding Judge actively, often vehemently and acidly, participate in the court room questioning of witnesses as well as the accused—who cannot invoke the Anglo Saxon privilege of refusing to take the stands on the grounds of possible self incrimination *i.e.*, he does not have a right to maintain silence which is given in adversarial system. The judge of the court combines the power of the prosecutor and a magistrate but he is not a member of a prosecution per se. His function is to determine truth on behalf of the state, with the aid of the police. The powers of the judge are very broad which help him to reveal the truth. He may call witnesses and pester them. The whole process, from the starting of trial, investigation, examination of witnesses, their testimony judges play a very important role because they themselves assist in all the procedures.

Therefore, it can be said that criminal court in France is investigative rather than the battle between two opposing parties, which happens in adversarial system. According to one legal authority such battles denote a bitter adversary duel rather than a disinvested investigation.

Administrative Justice in France : in administrative Courts such as *Counseil d'Etate* at litigation, the proceedings are markedly more inquisitorial. Mcst of the procedure is conducted in writing, the plaintiff writes to the court, which asks explanations from the concerned administration or public service, which answers; the court then may ask further details from the plaintiff. When the case is sufficiently complete, the law suits open in courts; however, parties are not required to attend the court in appearance.

French justice delivery system has become envy of the world. As the Sanskrit Sholka goes "yukti uktam" which means "useful idea can come from anywhere". Then a question arises, what's wrong in taking the idea from France?

Continental trial is Inquisitional or inquisitorial. Amongst others, France and Germany adapt this system. In inquisitorial trial, the figure of a private accuser is altogether eliminated and public officials take up that role. The Judge does not remain a referee but becomes active inquisitoric who is free to seek evidence and to control the nature and objective of the inquiry. The equality of the accuser and accused is not seen and contest goes on between the state and the accused. These are secret and written rather than public and oral. It is mostly like starchamber court in common law system. In this system, the legal profession is divided into three parts, the judge, public prosecutor and attorney. They have separate functions. The function of public prosecutor is to present to the judicial authority those whom he believes to be guilty of crime and to supply the judge with the materials collected for investigation. He is an independent and impartial officer. He is master of his decision. If he concludes that a particular person ought to be put to trial, he will refer the matter to judicial magistrate for preliminary inquiries and at public trial. The Attorney looks after the interests of the accused from the earliest stage. He sees that the accused is not deprived of any procedural opportunity. The examination of witnesses are done by the presiding judge. The public prosecutor, or attorney may put supplementary questions alone. The cross-examination of the witness may be allowed by the judge on the joint motion of the parties which is seldom made. In this system, the prosecutor and accused do not just oppose each other as parties. They do not engage in battle before the Court; they do not introduce evidence to the Court; they do not necessarily even represent opposing interests.

The time element in the adversary and inquisitorial systems.— The French Code makes the provision for bail but it is rarely granted. In Scotland, the trial must be completed within 110 days if the accused is in custody. After that the accused must be set at liberty and he cannot be charged for that offence again. In France, it is more and in England it may be lesser than 110 days. In Germany, preliminary detention is allowed only on certain specified grounds. The reason for delay in France is judicial investigation as compared to police investigation in other countries including

England and India. In France, acquittals are quite rare but in common law countries they are quite often.

Delay and cost are the two major problems of Indian judiciary. Delay may occur during investigation; for this Criminal Code provides in Section 167, the charge-sheet must be filed within 90 days in grievous or heinous crime and within 60 days in others. The police that investigates sticks to the Schedule barring exceptions. Delayed charge-sheet gives a right to the accused of being considered for bail. For inquiry, no Schedule is fixed by Code but not much delay is involved at this stage barring petitions under Section 482 Cr.P.C. (Inherent power) of High Court. There is no such power in subordinate criminal courts, and revisions. At trial stage, the Court is under heavy duty to complete quota of disposal every month, so Court ensures the disposal at the earliest. Pendency of criminal appeals in High Court is a great problem. The courts are very busy in disposal of the fresh case filed everyday. More so, very few judges are keen to decide old cases. At this stage, much is done, more needs to be done in India. 'Free Legal Aid' to accused by state is a great addition to criminal trial system in India. Right of speedy trial is recognised as part of Article 21 of the Constitution.

The judicial office in adversary and inquisitional systems.—The standing of the judge differs in these two systems. The common law judge enjoys greater respect. It is to them that the whole community looks for justice and protection against State, whereas in continental system the judges do not enjoy greater respect than any other public servant.

Recent Trends.—In common law countries, the development of professional police force and of a public prosecutor to investigate the commission of the crime, lead evidence, with the authority to prosecute and actually conduct the cases on behalf of the State *etc.* show a shift from the accusatorial to inquisitorial system. But the public nature of trial, the oral proceeding, existence of Jury and limitation on power of Judge, presumption of innocence of the accused are the reminiscents of the system.

So is the position in civil law system. During and after revolution criminal procedure became one of the main targets of attack, demolition and substitution on English model. Institution of jury, oral and public trial rather than secret and written procedure, accused's right to be defended by counsel of his choice, requirement of accused to testify on oath, have been demanded and some of these otherwise conceded in changed forms. This has resulted in mixed system composed partly of pre-revolution concepts and partly of post-revolution reforms.

The evolution of criminal procedure in last two centuries in civil law countries has been away from extremes and abuses of inquisitorial system and in common law system, the evolution of criminal proceeding has been away from abuses and excesses of accusatorial system. The two systems, though historically different, are now converging from different directions towards roughly equivalent mixed systems of Criminal Procedure.

Dealing with relative justice of the two systems, it can be pertinent to remark that an accused if he were innocent, would prefer to be tried by a civil law Court. But that if he were guilty, he would prefer to be tried by a common law Court. The practice is, that when law is in favour, hammer the court, when fact is in favour, hammer the jury, when nothing is in favour, hammer the table. This is 'advocacy' in common law system.

Ex Debito Justitiae

Article 21 virtually says, life depends on law, so does personal liberty. These can be taken by law if the law lays down fair and reasonable procedure; therefore, CPC and Cr.P.C. are the two laws laying down procedure for taking away the liberty and the life. Liberty includes person and the property. Both these CPC/CrP.C. are fair and reasonable as such are law under article 21. Cr.P.C. lays down procedure saving life and CPC saves our property and liberty. Life without liberty is slavery and liberty alone is savagery, combined together constitutes meaningful personality.

Section 205 Cr.P.C. deals with discretion of the magistrate to exempt an accused from personal attendance. Whether it is guided and as such under supervision of High Court under section 482/483 Cr.P.C. or Article 226/227 of the constitution or it is unbriddled within complete control of the magistrate court. There are two views on the point.

Another interesting area is whether lower courts exercising criminal jurisdiction have inherent powers? The Privy Council says there is no denial and this is by *ex debito justitiae*. The Supreme Court says no such inherent power inheres; but it did not consider the Privy Council decision on the point. There is as such a possibility of Supreme Court view getting reviewed.

Whether any order passed by the Magistrate under section 205 granting exemption from personal appearance or refusing to grant exemption from personal appearance is revisable under section 397(2) of Cr.P.C.? Whether any order passed under revision by Session Judge can be set aside by the High Court under section 482 Cr.P.C. It is clear that Law does not provide for the revision of revisional order. Is it open to High Court to revise the revisional order under section 482 Cr.P.C. which itself is in nature of revision. It is clear that Article 136 applies to all such cases wherein if any party is aggrieved either by order under Section 205 or under section 397(2) or section 482/483 Cr.P.C. or Article 226/227 of constitution anybody can go to the Apex Court in Article 136 direct against order under section 205 Cr.P.C.

Section 205 Cr.P.C. confers a discretion on the court to exempt an accused from personal appearance till such time his personal appearance is considered by the court to be not necessary during the trial. While considering an application under section 205, the Magistrate has to bear only two things in his mind (1) nature of the case (2) as also the conduct of the person summoned but the magistrate cannot stay arrest of a person named in F.I.R. that too, when investigation is going on. It is for I.O. to see whether arrest is desirable. The High Courts give arrest stay orders under Article 226 but whether they can do it under section 482 Cr.P.C. is debatable.

Is the discretion of the Magistrate independent? Is it judicial and has to be exercised judiciously on well settled principles of law? Can High Court be approached under section 482 for any discretion to the magistrate to grant general exemption to any accused from personal appearance? Can the High Court issue direction to the Magistrate court to accept appearance through counsel? Does this application lie to the High Court after F.I.R. or after filing of challani report (charge sheet)? Or when summoning order is issued under section 204 Cr.P.C.? What is the stage when the High Court can intervene?

What is the relevance of Article 226/227 quo section 205 Cr.P.C.? Can such intervention be made only in those cases wherein summoning order is in a case of technical nature (section 138 of Negotiable Instruments Act) or do not involve any moral turpitude?

"To prevent abuse of process of any court"

Ordinarily High Court will not interfere at an interlocutory stage of criminal proceeding in subordinate court but, High Court is under an obligation to interfere if there is harassment of any person by illegal prosecution. It would also do so when there is any exceptional or extraordinary reason for doing so. *Shyam Sachev* v. *State* and *Shiv Prasad* v. *State of Rajasthan*, hold contrary views.

Test to determine whether there has been an abuse of any court. The court would—

(a) See whether a bare statement of facts of case would be sufficient to convince High Court if it is a fit case for interference at intermediate stage.

(b) Whether in the admitted circumstances it would be a mock trial if case is allowed to proceed.

(c) Reasons why the High Courts can interfere :

  (i) Long lapse of time

  (ii) Failure or impossibility to supply to accused, copies of police statements and other relevant documents-grounds for other relevant documents-grounds for HC to quash proceedings against accused.

"To secure ends of justice"—what does it mean?

When a clear statutory provision of law is violated High Court can interfere. It is of vital importance in the administration of justice and ensures proper freedom and independence.

When a clear statutory provision of law is violated-High Court can interfere.

It is of vital importance in the administration of justice, and ensures that proper freedom and independence of Judges must be maintained and allowed to perform their functions freely and fearlessly without undue influence of anyone, even Supreme Court. At the same time Judges and Magistrates should act with a certain amount of justice and fair play.

The Supreme Court in *Madhu Limaye* v. *Maharashtra* and also in

Amarnath v. *Haryana* and *Jadhav* v. *Shankarrao Pawar* has held that the following principles would govern the exercise of inherent jurisdiction of the High Court :

A. Power is not to be resorted to if there is specific provision in code for redress of grievances of aggrieved party.

B. It should be exercised sparingly to prevent abuse of process of any Court or otherwise to secure ends of justice.

C. It should not be exercised against the express bar of the law engrafted in any other provision of the code.

It is neither feasible nor practicable to lay down exhaustively as to on what ground the jurisdiction of the High Court under Section 482 of the Code of Criminal Procedure should be exercised. But some attempts have been made in that behalf in some of the decisions of Supreme Court as for example *State of Haryana* v. *Bhajan Lal, Janata Dal* v. *H.S. Chowdhary and others, Rupan Deol Bajaj (Mrs.) and Another* v. *Kanwar Pal Singh GIl and Another, Indian Oil Corp.* v. *NEPC India Ltd. and Others.*

What is prohibited.—No inherent power exists in cases wherein it is clearly prohibited by code. For example Order XX rule 3; Section 9.[1] limitation law, or Arbitration and Conciliation Act, 1996. One may make an application under Section 151 but the courts have like jurisdiction to refuse relief prayed therein if there are adequate reasons like unexplained delay or relief prayed for being prohibited by law. Section 151 applies in all civil courts from court of first instance to Supreme Court. It does not apply in criminal courts or revenue courts or tribunals even if some principles of Code of Civil Procedure may apply on any point to these. Section 482 Cr.P.C. preserves identical powers to High Courts.[2] Section 482 does not give any inherent power to subordinate criminal courts. The reason is that High Courts were initially established under Indian High Courts Act 1861 by merger of Supreme Courts established under Regulating Act, 1773 and company's superior courts, Sadar Diwani Adalat and Sadar Nizamat Adalats established by Warren Hastings Plan of 1772.[3]

---

1. "Code" includes Rules : "The Code of Civil Procedure has been divided into two parts—Sections and Rules. The word 'Code' includes not only Sections, but also 'Rules' contained in the First Schedule. The rules should be deemed to be enacted in the body of the Code itself. The body of the Code, which is fundamental and unalterable except by the legislature, creates jurisdiction and the rules, which are concerned with the details and machinery, indicate the mode in which it (jurisdiction) is to be exercised. And that construction should be adopted which would reconcile both, the body of the Act and rules, however in cases of conflict, the former must prevail.

2. Section 482 : **Saving of inherent powers of High Court**—Nothing in this Code shall be deemed to limit or affect the inherent powers of the High Court to make such orders as may be necessary to give effect to any order under this Code, or to prevent abuse of the process of any Court or otherwise to secure the ends of justice.

3. See Authors Book History and Growth of Courts and legislatures Published by Central Law Publications Allahabad (2010) and Bharat Ka Vaidhanika and Samvaidhanik Itihas, Published by CLP Allahabad in 1969 latest edition 2011.

When the matter is pending before Court?

The presiding officer of the court wherein the case is pending has all powers in law that are essential for discharge of his judicial duties. It can pass any order or recall any order till it is seized with the matter. The only expectation of law is that order would be just and proper. Section 148 concedes jurisdiction to fix any period for compliance of the order passed by the court. This period can be extended as and when it thinks proper and the parties or any party so prays. Only limitation is that no such order shall be passed behind the back of anybody who is adversely affected by that order. Another thing to be seen is that there should be proper applications by proper party and it should have been moved within the period of limitation, if any. An order can be passed if the application is moved within time. The order may be passed much after, does not matter. The court can do it as and when it gets time and the case is taken up. The application, if it is for enlargement of time the order may be passed even after expiry of the period fixed for performance of the act. It will be effective from the date it should have been passed that is the last date till the period for performance was in time. Passing order on extension of period subsequent to and after expiry will not have any adverse effect on extension order.

When the matter has been finally disposed of by that court

In these cases, the court becomes *functus officio*, as it is no longer seized with the matter. If the effect of the order is that in the event of non-compliance of that order, it becomes operative automatically without any further intervention of the court, then in that case no extension can be granted under Section 148. For example, the order in question is that court fee shall be paid within one week, otherwise the suit shall stand dismissed or the application to set aside *exparte* decree will stand dismissed if cost is not paid within ten days, that suit shall stand dismissed if balance of unpaid purchase money is not paid within one week or the amendment application shall stand dismissed if cost were not paid by 10th of this month. No extension in these cases of period for performance is possible under Section 148.

Time prescribed or allowed by C.P.C.

In *Bhagwan Das* v. *Hazi Abu Ahmed*,[1] the court held that the court was competent to extend the time fixed under Section 54 of C.P.C. 1882 (Now order 7 rule 11).[2]

---

1. (1891) ILR 16 Bom 263, See also *Dewan Amir* v. *Nanak Chand*, (1910) 61-c-424 in which Bombay view was endorsed by Privy Council.
2. Q 7, r 11 deals with rejection of plaint in 6 cases; wherein no cause of action is disclosed, when relief claimed is undervalued and plaintiff fails to correct the valuation within the date fixed by the court, or where plaint is insufficiently stamped and it is not done despite order of the court to do it within time fixed or suit is barred by Law or when it is not filed in duplicate or provisions of rule 9 are not complied with time may be extended if proper cause for failure is shown to the satisfaction of the court.

Code of Civil Procedure prescribes time (1) under Order 6 rule 18 (failure to amend pleading after order) (2) Order 7 rule 11 (b) correct valuation of suit, (3) Order 7 rule 11, (c) requisite stamp, (4) order 8 rule 9 (order requiring written statement or additional written statement not complied within time fixed or (5) Order 21 rule 17 (amendment of execution application) (6) Order 25 rule 2 (security for cost of suit) (7) Order 41 rule 10 (security for cost of appeal).

Whether Extension is matter of right?

'No' not as such, it is discretion of the court but discretion is that of judiciary. It is not arbitrary. It can enlarge time or may reject the application seeking extension of time, either way, the order can be but the parties have to be heard, Both must be given opportunity of hearing. The order either way, the reasons have to be given. The order cannot be cryptic. It has to be a reasoned order. Why if time enlarged, why not if not enlarged.

Extension of time in cases of final decree[1]

Section 148 is very clear. The court may exercise the power under Section 148 when the case is before it. It can be by same court till final decision. After final decree, the liberty ends. Execution court is regulated by order XX. Section 148 does not apply to court executing the final decree. The reasons for non application of Section 148 to judgment and final decree are that order XX Rule 3 and 6 do not permit execution court to extend time for payment of decree money or alter mode of payment under Section 148.

Such extension amounts to modification of final decree. There are specific provisions for any such difficulty in order XX. Discretion in Section 148 is not open.

Rejection of plaint is decree so is determinations under Section 144. However, appealable orders are not decree. Order for dismissal in default is also not a decree.

Preliminary Decree

Preliminary decree remains fully within trial court's discretionary jurisdiction. A decree is preliminary when further proceedings have to be taken before the suit can be completely disposed of. It is final when such adjudication completely disposes of the suit. It may be partly preliminary and partly final.[2]

Conditional Orders

In cases of conditional orders, Section 148 applies and enlargement of period can be considered. In *D.V. Paul* v. *Manisha Lalwani*,[3] D.V. Paul was tenant. The case was under Section 12 of M.P. Accommodation Control Act,

---

1. Decree means the formal expression of an adjudication which so far as regards, the court expressing it conclusively determines the rights of the parties with regard to all or any of the matters in controversy in the suit and may be either preliminary or final Section 2(2) Code of Civil Procedure.
2. *ibid*, Explanation f.n. 14.
3. AIR 2010 S.C. 3356 dated 18th August 2010.

1961. Suit for eviction was filed by Manisha Lalwani. The trial court dismissed the suit. High Court modified the order of trial court and passed conditional decree. The condition was that D.V. Paul (tenant) shall deposit Rs. 10000/- in trial court as compensation within 4 months from the date of judgment for payment to Manisha Lalwani : In case, the tenant failed to deposit the amount within the period specified the decree shall be executed and eviction shall follow. If payment is made within specified period, the suit of landlady shall stand dismissed.

The applicant tenant sent a draft of Rs. 10,000/- within specified date on the registered address of the landlady instead of depositing Rs. 10000/- in the trial court. The question was whether there was compliance of the conditional decree or there was no compliance? Whether application of applicant moved after expiry of period seeking further time for deposit could be considered? Whether application of applicant moved after expiry of period seeking further time for deposit could be considered? Whether it was a case of inadvertent mistake in deposit of amount? Whether mistake was *bona fide*? Whether trial court could extend time for deposit as stipulated by High Court? Whether executing court could go behind the decree?

Regarding the extension of time, the Supreme Court raised two questions, first whether extension could legally be granted where non-deposit as per High Court order created civil consequences like eviction decree against tenant? Secondly, whether extension of time was justified. The court observed that it is evident from the language that power given to court (under section 148) is discretionary and is intended to be exercised only to meet the ends of justice.

The Supreme Court observed, that power to fix time for doing something includes power to extend the time for doing that thing if adequate reasons to the satisfaction of court are shown for non-performance within stipulated time. There is nothing in Section 148 of CPC or in any other provision of that Code to suggest that such a power of extension cannot be exercised in case where there is bonafide mistake in mode of compliance, where compliance is not literally in mode fixed by court but is a mode which is logical and practical.

It makes no difference, the Court observed, whether it is a case of conditional order or conditional decree. The heart of matter is, observed Supreme Court, that where the court has power to fix time and that power is not regulated by any statutory limits, it has in appropriate cases, power to extend the time fixed by it.

Regarding D.V. Paul's conduct, the Supreme Court observed that, there may not be strict compliance of the direction of High Court to deposit money in the trial court but there was no doubt a *bonafide* mistake of the tenant D.V. Paul, the applicant. The denial of receipt of Demand Draft is not relevant. What is relevant is whether a case for extension of time is made out? The Court held in totality that a case for extension of time for payment was made out and accordingly time was allowed[1] D.V. Paul cannot be faulted in its conclusion but many things can be said against law laid down by it.[2]

❑ ❑

1. The court relied on *Mahanth Ram Das* v. *Ganga Das*, AIR 1961 SC 882 (Three Judges Bench Case) and *Chinnamarkarthian* v. *Ayyavoo* AIR 1982 SC 137 (Another Three Judges Bench Case) "These cases related to conditional procedure order. Shri S.M. Dekka the learned Director N.E.J.O. It has pointed it out in his note published in AIR 2010 journal Section Page 91. Which means to suggest that D.V. Paul case did not correctly appreciate Mahant Ram Das and Chinnamarkarthian rulings. His view is that D.V. Paul has to be read as confined to on its particular facts. The author of this paper does not join issue on learned submission of Mr. Dekka. The only view is that it makes clear that Section 148 may be open whether it is conditional order or conditional decree. Order XX rule 3 and 6 are restricted only to final decrees in execution suits.
2. *Ibid*, Dekka's view in AIR 2010 Journal 91, Mr. Dekka has criticized D.V. Paul ruling on the ground that it has referred *Mahant Ram and Chinnamarkarthian* v. *Ayyavoo* views which are not cases on conditional order. These are referred to in D.V. Paul case as authority. In fact these are not on facts identical. These are three judges bench decision where as D.V. Paul is two judges bench decision. He seems to be of view that D.V. Paul case does not follow the *Mahant and Chinnamarkarthian* v. *Ayyavoo* views. The reality is that in Supreme Court a two judges bench and three judges bench are not constituted on any technical grounds. The cases are sent in routine in the roaster whether it is two judges bench or three judges bench except in those cases where there are conflicting full bench decisions of different High Courts on any points or two judges bench of the Supreme Court differ and recommend the matter to be sent to third judge for deciding the point on which there is difference of opinion. Therefore it does not appear to be of much importance whether in Mahanth Ram Das v. *Ganga Das* and *Chinnamarkarthian* v. *Ayyavoo*, are by three judges bench and D.V. Paul is by two judges bench. The ruling of D.V. Paul is not weakened on account of the above.

Chapter 15

Judicial Process and the Legislation (Legislative Process)

In fact, legislation is none of the concern of the courts so far as its making is concerned. Law making or legislative process is the exclusive area reserved for law makers. They are king in parliament (President and Parliament) at the centre, Governor and Legislature in states; the other three units wherein people sit are municipalities for urban areas and Panchayats for villages. For union territories, some have assemblies with Lt Governors whereas others do not have assemblies; Autonomous areas are also wherein people have a say. The English system had province (Indian states), British States (Part A, B, C and D). At District level they had Pargana and then Tehsils and lowest administrative unit was revenue villages.

Parliament can make law for the whole country or any part thereof. It is Bicameral in India. Upper House is Rajya Sabha (Council of States) and Lok Sabha. Some of States are Bicameral (Vidhan Parishad and Vidhan Sabha) whereas others are Unicamerals (Vidhan Sabha).

Three aspects; Theory of legislation, and Introduction to the principles of morals and legislations are two great works of Bentham wherein his fundamental ideas may be located. First enunciates his moral and legal philosophy (Utilitarianism). The second is manual of instructions to legislators. Both taken together lay down central ideas of the Sociology of Law.

Legal Process includes legislative process and judicial process both. Legislative process is how laws are made in parliament or state legislatures. Bentham was supporter of codification. He was opposed to judicial legislation. We start from Bentham. Marx was against law and against state. He advocated withering away of state and law.

Laws by the people, for the people

We should all celebrate the recent decision taken by a Cabinet Secretary-led committee which seeks to institutionalise public participation in the law-making process. The decision requires every Central government department to publicise the details of a proposed legislation on the Internet and other media before being introduced in Parliament. Under the decision, draft bills must be accompanied with an explanatory note outlining the essential provisions of the bill and its impact on the environment and lives of affected people. The public must then be given at least 30 days to comment. Following publication, these comments are to be submitted to the relevant parliamentary standing committee examining the bill. Although this is a good start, good practice from Kerala has the potential to significantly strengthen the process.

Reflecting public will

It is uncontroversial that pre-legislative scrutiny enhances democratic governance. It has been done in a number of other countries well accustomed to transparent legislative processes. Common sense dictates that people who are potentially affected by a proposed legislation—whether adversely or favourably—should be able to have a say in the law-making process at an early stage. Appropriate subject-matter experts should also have an opportunity to inform and refine draft bills. Especially in a country as diverse as India, transparent and inclusive law-making is more likely to reflect the will of the people.

That said, while India has seen some good examples including the Right to Information Act, often the only forum for inputs for legislation is behind the closed doors of a parliamentary committee. Too often, laws are made in haste to please a particular interest group or as knee-jerk reactions to public outcry, without the balance of competing views. Too often, the impact on the lives of the vulnerable is thrown out of the window.

The Kerala police law model

While the decision to introduce pre-legislative consultation is the first step in the right direction, the procedures to be followed to make this happen require careful thought. The mode of consultation must be made well-known, and the instruments for consultation will have to go beyond the Internet and electronic media. Needless to say, in a country where Internet penetration and literacy rates are low, publicising information through written and electronic means will effectively shut out a large percent of the population. Effective consultation will require far more in the way of resources and goodwill.

A robust model of pre-legislative consultation might resemble that carried out by Kerala in relation to police legislation. In 2011, the State Government went all out to ensure true public participation in drafting its police law. The draft Bill was first placed on the Kerala police's website with an email address inviting feedback from the public at large. Some of the suggestions that were received were incorporated into the draft.

At this stage, different groups began lobbying MLAs on the contents of the Bill and its possible impact on people. As a result, when the draft Bill was introduced in the House, many MLAs knew about it and acknowledged that, being a law of such wide public importance, it needed to be referred to a select committee.

Sensibly, from October to November 2011, the 19 member Select Committee, headed by the then Home Minister and comprising MLAs from almost every party, decided to tour the State and hold district-wide town hall meetings. Notices were placed in leading newspapers publicising the committee, its visit and its mandate. In the end, town hall meetings were held in all 14 districts of the State. At least 400-500 people attended every meeting.

The upshot of this process was that the select committee suggested 790 amendments to the original Bill introduced in the House. The Bill was then debated for almost four hours and 240 amendments—many based on the public's feedback—were accepted and passed. Public consultation ensured that the legislation, while by no means perfect, included many people-friendly provisions related to police service delivery, and responses which are unique only to Kerala's Police Act.

In formulating the most effective and inclusive procedures for pre-legislative consultation, the Central Government should study and draw inspiration from Kerala's example. Although this decision was limited to the Centre, the principles of pre-legislative scrutiny equally apply to States, which should follow the Centre's lead.

When the Congress' National Advisory Council recommended in 2013 that mandatory pre-legislative consultation be introduced for all proposal laws, it said that this would take India from a "representative democracy to a participatory, deliberate democracy." Now that we have a framework in place, it is time to consider the best ways and means to make public consultation in law-making a tangible reality. Given the current climate of public discontent, now is the time to breathe new life into political engagement with the people.

Pre-legislative scrutiny is a first step towards greater transparency in law-making.—The committee of secretaries of India, chaired by the cabinet secretary has decided that all bills proposed by the government should go through a process of pre-legislative scrutiny. This follows the recommendation of the National Advisory Council, which had suggested that all bills be taken through this process in order to garner public feed-back at an early stage.

Let us quickly review the process by which government bills are passed. Each bill is drafted by the concerned administrative ministry in consultation with the law ministry and other relevant ministries. During this process, the ministry may consult experts and various stake holders—this is not mandatory. In some cases, the ministry published a draft bill for public feedback (as, for example, in the cases of the right to education and land acquisition bills). Then the bill is taken to the cabinet for approval. The minister introduces the bill in Parliament, when it may be referred to a standing committee for examination. This is not a mandatory step, and as for now about two-thirds of all bills are referred to the committee. Then the bill is taken up for consideration and passing in each House, where there is detailed discussion and amendments are made. Finally, the bill is sent to the President for his assent, and thereafter deemed to be an act of Parliament.

The process of pre-legislative scrutiny decided by the committee of secretaries adds a mandatory step at the initial stage. It requires the administrative ministry to proactively publish proposed legislation on the internet and other media. This publication should include the draft bill as well as a brief justification for such legislation, essential elements, broad financial implications and an assessment on environment, fundamental rights, lives and livelihoods of affected people, *etc.* This note should be made available for at least 30 days for public feedback. The summary of the feedback should be published for public commends, and made available to the standing committee of Parliament when it examines the bill after introduction. There may be exceptional circumstances when this process cannot be followed, and in such cases, the ministry must record the reasons for not doing so.

This is an excellent first step to increase transparency in the law-making process and increasing public participation in it. This recognises the fact that it is much easier to make changes to a proposed law at an early stage than at a later stage in Parliament, when various political parties have taken a stance and may find it difficult to change their positions. That said, the government can make more changes to strengthen the process.

The key fact to recognise is that it is Parliament that makes law. The government only proposes any new law—and in theory, any MP may do so through a private member's bill. That this system is not used—the last such bill was passed in 1970—is the subject of another article. The pre-legislative process can be extended to Parliament, as has been done in the UK.

In Britain, the government publishes a list of all bills it proposes to introduce at the beginning of each year. (Note that a parliamentary session lasts a year in the UK, and we follow a similar system of publishing a list at the beginning of each session of Parliament). The draft versions of bills are then sent to a parliamentary committee, which takes public comments and consults experts. Its report is the same available to the government, which may make suitable changes before introducing the bill in Parliament. The pre-legislative scrutiny is not done for every bill, and there is a demand by several British MPs that it should be taken up for all bills other than those that make minor changes. It is also important to note that each bill, including those that went through the pre-legislative scrutiny by a parliamentary committee, has to be examined by a parliamentary committee in each House of Parliament. This is a mandatory step before the bill is taken up for discussion in the House.

It may be useful to include two steps in our process of enacting a new law. First, there should be pre-legislative scrutiny by standing committees of draft bills. A start could be made by taking up this process only for bills seen to have a significant social or economic impact. Second, the process of scrutiny by standing committees could be made mandatory for all bills.

In order to strengthen the process, a few other changes are required. Committees need to be provided with specialised research staff. With many new laws being technical in nature, it is important that parliamentarians be provided with research support that helps them understand the nuances of various issues and enables them to take informed decisions in order to balance conflicting interests.

It is also important that MPs judge each issue on its merits and according to their conscience, and that they are not bound by party diktat. While most standing committees have followed this principle, we have seen instances where they have chosen to abide by the party line. The public accounts committee and joint parliamentary committee that examined the allocation of 2G spectrum come to mind. For the process of examination and recommendation by the committee, it is essential that each MP on the committee takes an independent view.

Laws enacted by Parliament can have a major impact on the lives of citizens. It should be made incumbent on the government to explain the gaps it is trying to fill and how the proposed legislation does so, and engage with the public in the drafting process. Close parliamentary scrutiny and debate are also essential for ensuring that the objectives and proposals have wide acceptance. The proposed pre-legislative process is a good step in this direction, but Parliament needs to do more to strengthen its processes.

Nature of Legislation

To, legislate means declaration of legal rules by competent authority. It includes all methods of law making. To legislate is to make new law in any fashion. A Statute or Act is a formal expression of legislative will. Legislators lay down rules for future without reference to any actual dispute. It is the central function of the legislators who do so many acts including making of law, Impeachment of Chief executive, judges of Superior Courts, Punishing for contempt. The job of legislation as such may be to enact law or it may be otherwise than enacting law.

Supreme and Subordinate Legislation

Supreme legislations are those bodies of enacted law which is made by sovereign in Parliament. It cannot be repealed, annulled or controlled by any other legislative authority except that by court under judicial review wherein it can be struck down on grounds of being unconstitutional, violating fundamental rights, being *ultra vires* etc. The Parliament can make law on any item in List I, state legislatures can make law on any item in List II. Both can legislate on any subject in List III. In case of inconsistency, Law made by Parliament prevails except only in that case wherein State Act has got assent of President. Parliament makes law for whole country. States make law only for that state.

Subordinate Legislation

Subordinate legislations include : Colonial (by colonial legislatures), Executive (Regulations in Regulation Provinces), Judicial (Law made by Judges), Municipal and Autonomous (Corporate Law, Railways, University, or Conventional law made by Contract or Agreement).

Laws made by Municipalities (under Municipality Act), Town Area Committee (Under Town Areas Act), Panchayats (Under Panchayat Raj Act) are Subordinate Legislations. As these have to be under the Supreme legislations made by Parliament or State Legislatures, Statutes, Rules, Regulations and bye laws fall under this category of the subordinate legislations.

Delegated Legislations

Delegated legislation is sub category of subordinate legislation. When the function of legislation is entrusted to organs other than the legislature by the legislature itself, the legislation made by such organ is called delegated legislation. It is also called Executive or Administrative legislation. The reasons for growth of this class are; Police State changing into welfare sate and as such increase in functions of state, Pressure upon Parliamentary time, Technical nature of enactment, need of flexibility and complexity. These may be title based (Rules, regulations, Bye laws, notifications, schemes, orders, ordinances, directions), Discretion based (conditional and contingent legislations), Purpose based (Date of enforcement, Appointment day, Extension of act to other areas, or include or exclude areas, Territories, persons, industries or commodities from provisions of Act) or to suspend or modify provisions of the Act, or Authority based legislation (sub-delegation).

Legislation and Judicial Process

Legislation is a very powerful instrument of social change. It may lead social change or may follow the social change. In both ways its effectiveness is beyond doubt. It is however clear that if it leads and society favours the law, it is very powerful to giving effect to the change. If society is against the change, the effect of law takes time in producing desired result. If legislation follows social change, it is always a welcome measure.

Judicial process is silent, imperceptible and quite incognito in leaving its effect on the society. It gets added force if it is incorporated in legislation. If legislation disapproves it, the decision stands abrogated. Any Act if declared unconstitutional can be re-enacted or amended and as such may remain on statute book if objections or infirmities pointed out by court are removed or if it can be removed in accordance with law and is so removed.

From Benthamite utopia (to Love the laws) to "Communist utopia" (of withering away of State and Laws)

Bentham dreamt of love the laws and Marx's dream was that state will ultimately wither away and law will disappear if Marxism comes. Study from Bentham to Marx is study of March of Law—from one extreme to the other extreme.

MANDATE THEORY OR INSTRUMENT THEORY, BENTHAM, JEREMY (1748-1832 A.D.)

Bentham, an English Jurist, was born on Feb. 15, 1748 in London and died on June 6, 1832. Although a qualified barrister, he became more interested in legal theory than practice. In 1776 he published "*Fragment on Government*" which was an attack on Sir William Blackstone's *Commentaries on the laws of England*. This book outlined his philosophical radicalism. While visiting his brother in Russia, Bentham produced the *Defence of Usury* (1787) which embraced the Laissez faire economic theories of Adam Smith and applied them logically. In an introduction to the *Principles of Morals and legislation*, he explained that the object of law is to achieve the greatest happiness of the greatest number.

Bentham stressed the social consequences of Legal acts. He despised common law which he felt was harsh and feudal.

Bentham is known mainly as a great utilitarian and champion of law reforms through codification. While writing an introduction to his book "*Introduction to the Principles of Morals and Legislation*", he addressed two questions to himself—

Namely, what is a *penal code of Laws?* and what is a *civil code?* For answering these, he investigated the nature of a law and this resulted into *limits of Jurisprudence Defined*" published in 1945 and later on in 1970 enlarged into "*Of Laws in General*' edited by Professor Hart, he was of the view that a man by his nature was ruled by passions. Anything which encourages happiness should be encouraged and that reduces it should be discouraged. The function of law should be promotion of greatest happiness of greatest number.

Definition of law by Bentham.—"A law may be defined as an assemblage of signs, declarative of a volition, conceived or adopted by the Sovereign in a state concerning the conduct to be observed in a certain case, by a certain person or class of persons, who in the case in question are or are supposed to be subject to his power."

(1) Concept of Sovereign

Bentham's Sovereign is any person or assemblage of persons to whose will a whole political community are supposed to be in disposition to pay obedience and that, in preference to the will of any other person. The powers of the sovereign are indefinite unless limited by express convention or by religious or political motivations. The sovereign may consist of more than one body, each of which is obeyed in different respects. Habitual obedience may thus be divided and partial and thus the power of one is limited by the other and each has a limited power to prescribe for the other. Thus law may be of two kinds.

(*i*) *Ordinary Laws.*—These prescribe what ordinary people shall or shall not do.

(*ii*) *Transcendental laws.*—These prescribe what the Sovereign shall or shall not do.

(2) Concept of political society

Where a number of persons (subjects) are used to be in the *habit of paying obedience to a person* or assemblage of persons known and possess certain descriptions (Governor) such persons are said in state of political community. All laws regulate, conduct positively or negatively, by imposing duties or granting permissions impassively or de-impassively. The *reactions of the sovereign to these act-situations are called Aspects.*

(3) Aspects

Every Law has a directive or sanctional part. The former concerns the aspects of the Sovereign's will towards an act-situation whereas the latter concerns the force of a law. There are four aspects of the Sovereign's command, prohibition, permission and non-prohibition and non-command.

(i) Command is in nature of "Do X" and can co-exist with non-prohibition (permission to "do X") and cannot co-exist with non-command.

(ii) Prohibition is in nature of "Do not do X" and can co-exist with non-command and cannot co-exist with command.

(iii) Non-command means permission "not to do X". It cannot co-exist with command and can co-exist with prohibition.

(iv) Non-Prohibition means "Permission to do X" and cannot co-exist with prohibition and can co-exist with either command or non-command.

(4) Extent

It may be direct or indirect. Direct when a law covers a portion of land on which acts have their termination and indirect refers to the relation of an actor to a thing, *e.g.*, being in a certain place at the time of the act (the circumstance).

(5) Force of a law

A law is dependent upon motivations for obedience. Motivation may be physical, political, religious or moral, comprising threats of punishment or reward. Regulation of conduct and stipulation of sanction govern different act-situations, so they require separate laws. Non prohibitions (Permission to do X) and Non-commands (permission not to do X) are unobligative aspects of the Sovereign's will and are supported by sanctions affecting not the subjects of the laws (persons or things) but others who are subjects of corroborative laws are not to interfere. Actual punishment is outside the province of the legislator to carry out. He is to direct the Judge by issuing subsidiary laws that he must verify that the accused is guilty. The Judge in turn is assisted by various officials all of whom are likewise under subsidiary laws. If no one obeys these subsidiary laws, the principal law is a dead letter.

(6) Remedial appendages

Sanctions are provided by the subsidiary laws. These laws address the Judge to inflict punishment with a view to cure the evil, stop the evil or prevent the future evil. These by Bentham, are called remedial appendages.

(7) Expressions

Sovereign's will may be expressed in various forms and this will is to be discovered from the expression. Expression may be of two kinds—

(a) Complete.—When the matter to be regulated coincides with one law. In all such cases, the Judge should adopt literal interpretation.

(b) Incomplete.—The completeness is needed in 3 respects if these are not present, expression is incomplete—

(i) complete in expression
(ii) complete in Connection
(iii) complete in Design.

Concept of law as mandate.—There are two essential features—Integrality and utility.

What is integrality.—Integrality means that the law should be complete in expression, connection and design. *As regards Expression*, the standard of the reference is whether the actual will of the legislature has been completely expressed. If the provision is unqualified and unexpounded, it is complete as regards the expression. If it is qualified or expounded, it is incomplete without these.

Completeness in connection is needed in those cases when parts of a law lie scattered up and down at random. These are brought into existence by different bodies at different times. For example, in case of murder, police force, court, judge, procedure, advocate, doctor and so many are involved and all these are by different laws brought out into existence at different times. These are coordinated before a *law can be said to be complete in connection*.

Law is *incomplete in design* when the legislator's idea of mischief from that which in the light of the particular case, he should and have formed. Incompleteness in design may be—

(a) in point of amplitude.
(b) in point of discrimination.

The former is when the deviation does not go far enough and the latter when goes too far.

Principle of Utility

Public good ought to be the object of the legislator. General utility ought to be the foundation of his reasoning. To know the true good of the community is what constitutes, 'science of legislation', the art consists in finding the means to realize that good.

Utility principle is not contradicted but for making it the foundation of a system of reasonings, three conditions are necessary—

(1) Utility should have a clear and precise idea to those who employ it,
(2) Every other principle should be excluded so that utility principle gets unity and sovereignty.
(3) For uniform results some process of moral arithmetic needs to be found.

Utility is an abstract term. It expresses tendency of a thing to prevent some evil or to procure some good. Evil is pain or cause of pain. Good is pleasure or the cause of some pleasure.

One that augments total sum of happiness of the individual and conforms to his interests is utility for individuals and the utility which tends to augment interest of the community and its sum total of happiness of that community carries approval of utility principle.

Opponents of utility principle

Ascetic Principle and Arbitrary principle (Principle of Sympathy and Antipathy) are two adversary principles—

Ascetic Principle

It signifies one who exercises. It was applied to monks. It indicates practice of devotion and penitence. This principle is rival to utility principle. To the supporters of ascetic principle everything which gratifies the sense is odious and criminal. They approve everything which tends to diminish enjoyment. They blame everything which tends to augment enjoyments. Philosophers and Devotees are two classes that follow ascetic principle.

Ascetic philosophers despise vulgar pleasures and for it they get reputation and glory in return. Devotees feel that every instant of voluntary pain here in this world will procure them an age of happiness in next world.

Arbitrary Principle

It is also known as principle of Sympathy and Antipathy. It consists in applying or blaming by sentiments without giving any other reason for the decision except the decision itself. An action is judged to be good or bad because it pleases or displeases him who judges. He behaves as sovereign. He admits no appeal. He needs not to justify the decision. It is his interior persuasion, it is his intimate conviction, he feels it, he consults no body.

The Ascetic principle attacks utility principle in front, the principle of sympathy neither rejects it nor admits it. It pays no attention to it. It floats at hazard between good and evil.

Contribution of Bentham to Sociology of Law

These are five—

(1) Law and Public opinion

(2) Law and Social control

(3) Law and Expectation

(4) Law and Social change

(5) Sanctions.—These are four

(A) Theory of Sanction

(B) Conditions of good law

(C) Analysis of Punishment

(D) Indirect means of Preventing offence.

Theory of Sanction.—"Pain or pleasure are sanctions of law. Sanction may be positive (Reward) and Negative (Punishment).

Pleasure and pain may be distinguished into four classes—(1) Physical, (2) Moral, (3) Political, (4) Religious.

(A) **Physical (Natural) Sanction** are pleasure and pains which may be expected in ordinary course of nature without human interventions.

(B) **Moral Sanctions** are pains and pleasure expected from the action of our fellowmen, whether it, may be out of their friendship or hatred, or esteem or contempt Bentham calls it as popular sanction, 'Sanction of Public opinion', or Sanction of honour or Sanction of Sympathy'.

(C) **Legal Sanction.**—These are pleasure and pains expected from the action of magistrate in virtue of law. These are also called 'Political Sanction'. The Magistrate means entire, court system. The punishment includes many diverse actions creating consequences; will, Divorce, contract void etc. are included in punishment.

(D) **Religious Sanctions.**—Pleasure and Pain arising from religious orientation are religious sanctions.

Pleasure and Pain

According to Bentham, humankind is subject to two 'sovereign masters Pain and Pleasure'. The utility ranks actions according to their tendency to augment or diminish the happiness of party whose interest is in question.

Utility is a capacity to produce benefit, advantage, pleasure, good or happiness or to prevent the happening of mischief, pain, evil or unhappiness to individual, party or the community as a whole. Interest of the community means, 'sum of the interests of its members.'

Any action is one which ought to be done or which ought not to be done conforms to the principle of utility. In other words, the principle requires, that if any act is right, it should be done or at least it should not be wrong; Any right action should not be wrong action.

'Ought' Right or wrong get specific content by principle of utility.

Whether principle of utility can be proved directly? 'No'.

The reason is, that one that is used to prove everything else cannot itself be proved, a chain of proofs must have their commencement somewhere. To give such proof is as impossible as it is needless.

Just like grundnorm, logical necessity for pure theory of Kelsen so is Bentham's proposition that chains of proofs must have their commencement somewhere.

Different kinds of pleasure and pain

Pleasure and Pains can be divided into two classes;

1. Pleasure and Pains which relate to others, For example, those of benevolence and malevolence.
2. Pleasure and Pains which are purely personal; Barring above two examples rest all belong to this class.

Bentham has enumerated simple pleasures (total 15) and simple pains (total 11).

SIMPLE PLEASURES

(1) **Pleasure of Sense** like Pleasure of taste, of smell, of sight, of hearing, of touch. It also includes pleasure of health and pleasure of novelty.

(2) **Pleasure of Riches** Possession of things which are means of enjoyment or security.

(3) **Pleasure of address** For example music enjoyed through mechanical instruments like touching a harpsichord.

(4) **Pleasure of friendship** the pleasure that arises out of goodwill of those around.

(5) **Pleasure of good reputation**

(6) **Pleasure of power**

(7) **Pleasure of Piety** (Favour of God),

(8) **Pleasure of Benevolence** (Pleasure of Sympathy and Pleasure of social affection.

(9) **Pleasure of Malevolence** pleasure of irascible passions, pleasure of antipathy or pleasure of the anti-social affections,

(10) **Pleasure of knowledge** (New research, New idea in Science).

(11) Pleasure of memory

(12) Pleasure of imagination

(13) Pleasure of hope

(14) Pleasure of Association and

(15) **Pleasure founded on Pain** (Pleasure of relief or of deliverance).

SIMPLE PAINS

(1) **Pains of privation (Pain of desire or unsatisfied desire).—** Pain of disappointment—Regrets.)

(2) **Pains of sense**—Nine kinds—hunger and thirst, taste, smell, touch, hearing, sight, excess of cold, or heat, diseases of all kinds and fatigue.

(3) Pains of Mal-address (fruitless efforts, tools or instruments, experiences of failure,

(4) Pains of Enmity,

(5) **Pains of Bad reputation** (Pains of dishonour—Pains of popular sanction,

(6) **Pains of Piety** (Religions fears—superstitious fears),

(7) **Pains of Benevolence** (Pains of Sympathy—Pains of social affections,

(8) **Pains of Malevolence** Pains of antipathy—pains of antisocial affections,

(9) Pains of memory,

(10) Pains of imagination and

(11) Pains of fear.

Felicific Calculus : basis of Utilitarianism

Felicific Calculus is a process developed by Bentham by which he calculates (quantify) the amount of pleasure and pain that arises out of any specific action.

Basis of felicific calculus

Intensity, Duration, Certainty Proprinquity, Fecundity, purity and extent are various qualities to assess the utility of an act. Utilitarianism is—

(1) An act utilitarianism and,

(2) rule utilitarianism

Objections against felicific calculus

1. In reality felicific calculus is usually unworkable,

(a) Pleasure and pain cannot be quantified,

(b) Consequences can not be predicted even if such calculations could be undertaken with precision.

2. Utilitarianism is suited more for evaluation of past conduct but not prescribing future conduct.

CRITICISMS

(i) *Law of Contract and Property.*—Excluded if an act situation is the object of every law, contract and property are not covered. These neither impose duties nor grant permission. Bentham answered that these are not laws but parts of a law. Bentham's answer is not convincing. His contention that all laws are either commands or permission takes no note of power to make contract or create title, etc.

(ii) *Civil and Crime-Distinction not tenable.*—The characteristics of criminal offences lie not in their intrinsic nature, but in the degree of mischief they occasion, the degree of displeasure they evoke and the degree or punishment meted out. To the category of civil offences belong, such offences as it is not judged necessary to punish with any extraordinary degree or species of punishment. To the crime such offences as it is judged necessary to punish with any extraordinary degree or species of punishment to the criminal.

Can such a distinction apply to the gradation of treatment, penal, reformative and curative meted out to criminals? The distinction breaks down in cases of those torts where the exemplary damages may be awarded.

(iii) Bentham's theory of the utility of laws is wholly subjective. No rigid test has been proposed any where by which pleasure and pain can be measured.

(iv) Bentham assumes that happiness of the majority (greatest number) would ensure happiness of the whole society. In practice it is seen that active minority rules over passive majority. Law is thus what active minority decides.

(v) Howsoever, innocuous and well meaning a law may be, aggrieved minority in the society is natural phenomena. The force of powerful minority and its effect on law cannot be ignored. Bentham did it.

(vi) Bentham's utilitarianism as test of law presents another extreme of Savigny's Volkgiest. Savigny reduced law as mere follower of custom and history. Bentham has totally ignored history and favours too much legislation.

Marxist theories; (dialectical materialism)

Marxism-Leninism—The Economic forces of Society.—Hegel attempted to give a new turn to the study of logic by his 'dialectic method'. Instead of two contradictory propositions being reconcilable only by deducing that one at least was false, he asserted that contradiction could form a thesis and anti thesis from which new synthesis might emerge.

Karl Marx turned it to good account. He began as follower of Hegel. The main change that he introduced was to turn Hegel right way up by asserting that it was not the ideas that ruled the world but material forces, specifically economic one which created not only the social conditions of a particular period but also its basic philosophy or ideology. Marx called it 'dialectical materialism' and used it to show how inherent contradictions in the capitalist system of his day must result in revolutionary upheavals out of which a new socialist society would emerge.

Marx expressed that law was distilled out of economic order which gave rise to it and was institutionalised form of prevailing ideology whereby the dominant section of the society coerced the masses into obedience.

Marxism rests on two basic ideas :

First, Progressive view of History,

Second, An insistence that economic relations are inevitably the driving force behind that progression

Marx argued that History is and always has been moving inexorably towards the emergence of a communist society with the historical phenomena of—

—Primitive Communalism,

—Slavery,

—Feudalism, and

—Capitalism.

All these are provisional stages on way to communism.

Two sides of Marxian thought :

(i) Prophetic and historist side.—It foretells a period of doom and destruction and looks for a brighter tomorrow in immediate near future. He believed that after revolution, when class conflict is resolved and institution of private property is replaced by communist regime, law and state will wither away. Coercion will not be needed. Harmony will prevail.

(ii) Attempt to apply scientific principles to the study of human society.—Marx studied closely the features of existing economic and class system and brought out an entirely new way of interrelationship between the economic ordering of a society and its dominant ideology. In this way, he launched a most constructive attack on social studies and it became increasingly clear that society could not be understood without exploring its institutional and economic foundation and assessing their impact on prevailing ideas. It was one-sided traffic between economic arrangement and ideology as he maintained that latter was wholly dependent on the former.

Current of mutual influence is even now admitted. The different stream of Idealism moving from Hegel's philosophy of history was fed into jurisprudence by Josef Kohler, Stammler's close predecessor in that subject in the Berlin University. His work is still another effort to relate social facts and the norms of justice by exposing the immanence of values in facts is "civilisation" in Kohler's case.

Marx-Karl (1818-1883)

According to Marx, the State is a class institution which becomes a tool in the hands of capitalists for the exploitation of proletariat or working class.

. Marx Karl (Heinrich)_ was born on May 5, 1818 in Trier, now in West Germany and died on March 14, 1883 in London. Marxism derives its name from him. Together with his friend, Friedrich Engels, he published manifest derkommaunistischen Partei 1848 commonly known as the communist manifesto declaring that all history hitherto been history of class struggles but that would end with the coming victory of the working class.

Expelled from Prussia and France, Marx went to London in 1848. He spent most of the remainder of his life there reading in the British museum. His most important theoratorical work was Das Kapital (1887), an analysis of the economics of the capitalism. He also became the leading spirit of the International Working Men's Association, subsequently known as first international. Most of his life was spent in poverty that was only partially alleviated by the benefactions of the friends and relatives. After his death, his unpublished writings were edited by Engels. His works are the intellectual basis of 19th century European socialism.

Karl Marx (a German) and Frederick Engels (English) are the two exponents of economic approach to law. Legal theory is just an appendage to social and political outlook. It is due to this reason they have not proposed any elaborate treatment of the concept of law. They have sought to unfold a pattern of evolution just as historians did but their conclusions are different.

They also talk about the content of law but it has nothing to do with any ideas or otherwise as Kant or Thomas Acquinas did. The law to them *is reflex economic substrata*. Law to these scholars means not a concept but administration. As such, they seem to adopt the functional approach to law and are nearer to sociological approach though sociological school was not properly elaborated when Marx and Engels wrote. Comte, father of sociology is just 20 years older to Marx and Ihering was born in the same year when Marx was born. Rest of other sociological jurists are junior to Marx. The Marxism was experimented in U.S.S.R. but the Soviet Jurisprudence embodied Marxism in actual practice.

Soviet Jurisprudence.—The study of Soviet Jurisprudence may conveniently be made by dividing it into following periods :

(i) First Period.—From Karl Marx to the established proletarian government in U.S.S.R. in 1920. War Communism and formulation of a Marxist theory are notable features of this period.

(ii) Second Period.—From New Economic policy (1921-1929) till its replacement by construction of socialism (1930-1937).

(iii) Third Period.—Consolidation of Socialism (1938-1953) (when Stalin died).

(iv) Fourth Period.—Construction of Communism (1981-till present)

MARXISM : The background.

Marx was influenced by the universal principle of causation prevalent in physical world. He proposed that social phenomena were likewise governed by the universal principle and this was the Economic Principle.

Hegel's dialectic philosophy also influenced Marx but this philosophy stood on its head with Hegel. Marx turned right side again. Hegel believed that reality (history) was unfolding of an idea but to Marx "idea" is reflection of reality. Marx pleaded that utopian socialism of Hegel should be replaced with "scientific socialism". They adopted the dialectic thesis of Hegel in terms of thesis, anti-thesis and synthesis but substituted economic and material forces as determinants of development at the place of ideals.

Thesis.—Marx starts with primitive society and believes that there was no anti-thesis in such society. There was equal distribution of the commodities. To Marx, this was a communist order. When distribution became unequal, the society was destroyed and got split into two classes of capital and labour. The value of the commodities in such a society was governed by the cost of the labour required to produce them. The state entered into the shoes of the primitive society. State became instrument of the stronger class in all forms whether as a slave-owner's state or a feudal state or bourgeois state. Legal and political order is a superstructure erected upon the economic base of the man, that is. Infrastructure and it keeps on changing with the changes in the base that is, Economic structure takes place due to the conflict between the factors of production, namely, labour and capital. In modern state, capitalist minority dominated labouring majority, and the workers are exploited by minority through the instrumentality of law.

Base and Superstructure

Marxists divide the whole social enterprise into two components.

The BASE AND SUPERSTRUCTURE Base of any human society lies in the conditions of production and economic relationship of those engaged in production.

This base gives rise to and determines the nature of a whole range of social institutions which together constitute superstructure.

Law is in superstructure category.

Conflict Theory and Marx's classless and stateless society

Class conflict, according to Marx, lies at the very heart of societal structures. The alignment of interests brings the workers together and the capitalists too come together in order to protect their interests. And a class struggle ensues. The class struggle is fundamentally to control the means of production. While the bourgeoisie feels that it simply owes the wages it pays to the workers, workers think they must have some share in the profit as well because it is on account of their labour that the profit is earned. A deadlock is not in the interest of either of the sides. Therefore, reconciliation is sought. However, neither of the parties are either willing to permanently forego their claim to the profit or let go of their desire to control the means of production. This is primarily because the worker class sees huge disparity between their standard of life and that of the bourgeoisie. Since the comfortable life of the bourgeoisie comes from the profits the proletariat sees itself producing, it thinks it is justified to ask for a piece of cake.

Marx saw this conflict originating in individual factories, but since the concerns are common, the workers join forces to have better bargaining power. In response to this coming together of workers, the bourgeoisie also feels obliged to unite. This divides the society into two broad groups and these two groups vie for political power because the group that controls political power would also control the regulations. And it is the State regulations that could tip the scale for either of the classes. State, therefore, is part of the class struggle and is not an impartial referee or maker of rules.

The political power is acquired, retained and used to have greater control of the means of production. State, according to Marx, is a tool in the hands of the bourgeoisie for the purpose of protecting their property and exercising control over it. However, the more the State works to protect the interests of the bourgeoisie, the greater cohesion it inspires within the proletariat, which unifies the proletariat across a region and then beyond.

The division between the classes widens and as the working conditions and the standard of life of the worker class deteriorate, the disquiet among its members intensifies making the social structure creak and tumble. The class struggle thus culminates in a proletarian revolution. And the revolution would result in the demolition of all such social structures that support and promote bourgeoisie interests against the interests of the proletariat. The means of production would be publicly controlled and no longer privately owned. The very basis of the class division would be, thus, wiped out. This way a classless society will come into being. And since State exists to preserve and promote class interest, in the absence of class division it would also wither away. And thus, a classless, stateless society would come into existence.

To summarize, there are seven basic elements in the Marx's conception of class conflict, how it operates and what its final outcome is. These are :

1. Classes are defined in terms of property ownership. And that does not necessarily mean that only when a class owns property it is considered a class. Even if a group of people do not own a property, it is also a class by virtue of not having any property at all. But it is the property that determines whether it is a class or not. Therefore, people who smoke or those who believe in God are not a class for the purpose of Marx's conflict theory though they otherwise might be considered two distinct classes

of people.

2. People belonging to a particular Marxian class share the same life situations and circumstances,which translates into common interests.
3. Marxian classes are essentially antagonistic because there is an inherent clash of interests.
4. Industrialized, capitalist society gives rise to two antagonistic classes, and social relations are defined on the basis of identification with one of the classes. In other words, society is broadly divided into two large groups.
5. State and political power are instrumentalities of class dominance and are part of class conflict. Therefore, there is always a struggle to take control of the apparatus of the State.
6. Change in social structures is the reflection of class struggle. Therefore, social structures are modified and rebuilt according to the wishes of and in line with the interests of the dominant class.
7. The class struggle culminates in the proletarian revolution and dismantling of the class divisions followed by the formation of a classless and stateless society.

Prophecy.—Tension between majority and minority will break into a conflict. The majority (labour) will revolt against the minority (capital) and these control of economic resources and will seek to eliminate the majority. This will usher in the establishment of 'proletarian (connected with ordinary people who earn money by working especially those who do not own any property) dictatorship. And this is, according to Marx, highest form of democracy possible in a class society. It is dictatorship of a party which would effectively guide the proletarian Government. The distribution of commodities at this stage will follow the maxim "From each according to his ability, to each according to his need." Inequality will still be there. The class struggle will take a different form. The Exploiters (Capitalists) would oppose the socialism with more frenzy and ferocity. Out of this struggle will ultimately emerge classless society of communism. In a classless society, there would be no domination, there would be no inequality and state and law both will disappear. Proletariat dictatorship will give way to the Administration of thing. The middle order (Bourgeos) has to be smashed by the proletariat prior to it being replaced by administration of things (communist order) No Separation of power, No rule of law, No private and public law distinction; only rule by law are the specialities of communism.

Inferences from Marxism

(a) Economic determination of law.—Law is superstructure on an economic system. Economic facts are independent of and antecedent to law. Law is reflex of economic substrata is a Maxim that accords with reality. Bourgeois theories of law are just distortions. Religion is another superstructure like law but all have their ultimate reality in the economic background. (infrastructure).

(b) Class character of law.—Law is an instrument used by the economic ruler to keep the masses in subjection. After proletarian Governments, this instrument would be used by the majority to crush and eliminate the capitalists city. Law will continue to be the instrument of domination.

(c) Identity of the Law and State.—The need and origin of state is due to unequal distribution of the commodities and class distinction in the society. The reflects an essentially unequal condition of affairs, and law is used to preserve and protect it. Law and state are identical. State may be called by any name republic or otherwise, it is nevertheless to do the same job, *i.e.*, *otion of the interests of dominant class (minority) against oppressed city. As such it should go yielding administration of things to people.

(d) Doctrine of the withering away of the state.—When communism or classless society arrives, the unequal distribution of wealth will disappear and there will be no domination and inequality. The instruments of domination and inequality, law and state will wither away and these would be replaced by ministration of things. The bourgeois state will have to be smashed and destroyed it cannot wither away.

The various aspects of law reflect these relationships. Law regulates the conflicting interest of equals. Marx was of the view that law was an instrument of domination. According to Pushukanis commodity exchange theory, law was : wither away before state.

Construction of socialism.—New Economic Policy was withdrawn in 1930 and concessions given to private enterprise also went with it, and the second revolution to eliminate the capitalism began from above. Private capital and private enterprise became illegal on the plea that ultimate interest of the proletarian rose superior to its own prior law. Marxist concept of law needed to be adjusted in following three respects—

(a) Sociological concept of law of Marx, Engels and Pashukanis that law is a product of economic structure of the society had to give in to law as normative concept.

(b) Capitalists were no more but law was still there. So the concept of law is wish of the people.

(c) Law continued as determined to be an instrument of policy but it also started being used as means of providing security as per the expectations as determined by the policy.

Consolidation of Socialism (1938-1953).—Socialism consolidated in form of a monolithic state. The legal theory was completely subordinate to political expediency. The State was represented by Supreme Soviet and was held superior to all its laws. Stalin believed in complete centralisation. Only Soviet interpretation of Marxism was propagated to be the correct. Yugoslavia under Tito pleaded that every communist country was free to interpret Marxism in its own way. Tito termed Stalin regime as a state which had replaced a bourgeois state with bureaucratic state. Personality cult was fostered in this period.

Legislative Procedure (Article 107-111)

Provisions as to introduction and passing of Bills

Subject to the provisions of articles 109 and 117 with respect to Money Bills and other Financial Bills, a Bill may originate in either House of Parliament. [Article 107(1)].

Subject to the provisions of articles 108 and 109, a Bill shall not be deemed to have been passed by the Houses of Parliament unless it has been agreed to by both Houses, either without amendment or with such amendments only as are agreed to by both Houses. [Article 107(2)].

A Bill pending in Parliament shall not lapse by reason of the prorogation of the Houses. [Article 107(3)].

A Bill pending in the Council of States which has not been passed by the House of the People shall not lapse on a dissolution of the House of the People. [Article 107(4)].

A Bill which is pending in the House of the People, or which having been passed by the House of the People is pending in the Council of States, shall, subject to the provisions of article 108, lapse on a dissolution of the House of the People. [Article 107(5)].

Joint sitting of both Houses in certain cases

If after a Bill has been passed by one House and transmitted to other House—

(a) the Bill is rejected by the other House; or

(b) the Houses have finally disagreed as to the amendments to be made in the Bill; or

(c) More than six months elapse from the date of the reception of the Bill by the other House without the Bill being passed by it, the President may, unless the Bill has elapsed by reason of a dissolution of the House of the People, notify to the houses by message if they are sitting or by public notification if they are not sitting, his intention to summon them to meet in a joint sitting for the purpose of deliberating and voting on the Bill :

Provided that nothing in this clause shall apply to a Money Bill. [Article 108(1)].

In reckoning any such period of six months as is referred to in clause (1), no account shall be taken of any period during which the House referred to in sub-clause (c) of that clause is prorogued or adjourned for more than four consecutive days. [Article 108(2)].

Where the President has under clause (1` notified his intention of summoning the Houses to meet in a joint sitting, neither House shall proceed further with the Bill but the President may at any time after the date of his notification summon the Houses to met in a joint sitting for the purpose specified in the notification and, if he does so, the Houses shall meet accordingly. [Article 108(3)].

If at the joint sitting of the two Houses the Bill, with such amendments, if any, as are agreed to in joint sitting, is passed by a majority of the total number of members of both Houses present and voting, it shall be deemed for the purposes of this Constitution to have been passed by both Houses :

Provided that at a joint sitting :—

(a) if the Bill, having been passed by one House, has not been passed by the other House with amendments and returned to the House in which it originated, no amendment shall be proposed to the Bill other than such amendments (if any) as are made necessary by the delay in the passage of the Bill;

(b) if the Bill has been so passed and returned, only such amendments as aforesaid shall be proposed to the Bill and such other amendments as are relevant to the matters with respect to which the Houses have not agreed;

and the decision of the person presiding as to the amendments which are admissible under this clause shall be final. [Article 108(3)].

A joint sitting may be held under this article and a Bill passed thereat, notwithstanding that a dissolution of the House of the People has intervened since the President notified his intention to summon the Houses to meet therein. [Article 108(5)].

Special procedure in respect of Money Bills

A Money Bill shall not be introduced in the Council of States. [Article 109(1)].

After a Money Bill has been passed by the House of the People it shall be transmitted to the Council of States for its recommendations and the Council of States shall within a period of fourteen days from the date of its receipt of the Bill return the Bill to the House of the People with its recommendations and the House of the People may thereupon either accept or reject all or any of the recommendations of the Council of States. [Article 109(2)].

If the House of the People accepts any of the recommendations of the Council of States, the Money Bill shall be deemed to have been passed by both Houses with the amendments recommended by the Council of States and accepted by the House of the People. [Article 109(3)].

If the House of the People does not accept any of the recommendations of the Council of States, the Money Bill shall be deemed to have been passed by both Houses in the form in which it was passed by the House of the People without any of the amendments recommended by the Council of States. [Article 109(4)].

If a Money Bill passed by the House of the People and transmitted to the Council of States for its recommendations is not returned to the House of the People within the said period of fourteen days, it shall be deemed to have been passed by both Houses at the expiration of the said period in the form in which it was passed by the House of the People. [Article 109(5)].

Definition of 'Money Bills'

For the purposes of this Chapter, a Bill shall be deemed to be a Money Bill if it contains only provisions dealing with all or any of the following matters, namely,

(a) the imposition, abolition, remission, alteration or regulation of any tax;

(b) the regulation of the borrowing of money or the giving of any guarantee by the Government of India, or the amendment of the law with respect to any financial obligations undertaken or to be undertaken by the Government of India;

(c) the custody of the Consolidated Fund or the Contingency Fund of India, the payment of moneys into or the withdrawal of moneys from any such fund.

(d) the appropriation of moneys out of the consolidated Fund of India;

(e) the declaring of any expenditure to be expenditure charged on the Consolidated Fund of India or the increasing of the amount of any such expenditure;

(f) the receipt of money on account of the Consolidated FUnd of India or the public account of India or the custody or issue of such money or the audit of the accounts of the Union or of a State; or

(g) any matter incidental to any of the matters specified in sub-clauses (a) to (f). [Article 110(1)].

A Bill shall not be deemed to be a Money Bill by reason only that it provides for the imposition of fines or other pecuniary penalties, or for the demands or payment of fee for licences or fees for services rendered, or by reason that it provides for the imposition, abolition, remission, alteration or regulation of any tax by any local authority or body for local purposes. [Article 110(2)].

If any question arises whether a Bill is a Money Bill or not, the decision of the Speaker of the House of the People thereon shall be final. [Article 110(3)].

There shall be endorsed on every Money Bill, when it is transmitted to the Council of States under article 109, and when it is presented to the President for assent under article 111, the certificate of the Speaker of the House of the People signed by him that it is a Money Bill. [Article 110(4)].

Assent to Bills

When a Bill has been passed by the Houses of Parliament, it shall be presented to the President, and the President shall declare either that he assents to the Bill, or that he withholds assent therefrom :

Provided that the President may, as soon as possible after the presentation to him of a Bill for assent, return the Bill if it is not a Money Bill to the Houses with a message requesting that they will reconsider the

Bill or any specified provisions thereof and, in particular, will reconsider the desirability of introducing any such amendments as he may recommend in his message, and when a Bill is so returned, the Houses shall reconsider the Bill accordingly, and if the Bill is passed again by the Houses with or without amendment and presented to the President for assent, the President shall not withhold assent therefrom. (Article 111).

Procedure in Financial Matters (Articles 112-117)

Annual financial statement

The President shall in respect of every financial year cause to be laid before both the Houses of Parliament a statement of the estimated receipts and expenditure of the Government of India for that year, in this Part referred to as the 'annual financial statement'. [Article 112(1)].

The estimates of expenditure embodied in the annual financial statement shall show separately—

(a) the sums required to meet expenditure described by this Constitution as expenditure charged upon the Consolidated Fund of India; and

(b) the sums required to meet other expenditure proposed to be made from the Consolidated Fund of India,

and shall distinguish expenditure on revenue account from other expenditure. [Article 112(2)].

The following expenditure shall be expenditure charged on the Consolidated Fund of India—

(a) the emoluments and allowances of the President and other expenditure relating to his office;

(b) the salaries and allowances of the Chairman and the Deputy Chairman of the Council of States and the Speaker and the Deputy Speaker of the House of the People;

(c) debt charges for which the Government of India is liable including interest, sinking fund charges and redemption charges, and other expenditure relating to the raising of loans and the service and redemption of debt;

(d) (i) the salaries, allowances and pensions payable to or in respect of judges of the Supreme Court,

(ii) the pensions payable to or in respect of Judges of the Federal Court,

(iii) the pensions payable to or in respect of Judges of any High Court which exercises jurisdiction in relation to any area included in the territory of India or which at any time before the commencement of this Constitution exercised jurisdiction in relation to any area included in a Governor's Province of the Dominion of India;

(e) the salary, allowances and pensions payable to or in respect of the Comptroller and Auditor-General of India;

(f) any sums required to satisfy any judgment, decree or award of any court or arbitral tribunal.

(g) any other expenditure declared by this Constitution or by Parliament by law to be so charged. [Article 112(3)].

Procedure in Parliament with respect to estimates

So much of the estimates as relates to expenditure charged upon the Consolidated Fund of India shall not be submitted to the vote of Parliament but nothing in this clause shall be construed as preventing the discussion in either House of Parliament of any of those estimates. [Article 113(1)].

So much of the said estimates as relates to other expenditure shall be submitted in the form of demands for grants to the House of the People, and the House of the People shall have power to assent, or to refuse to assent, to any demand, or to assent to any demand subject to a reduction of the amount specified therein. [Article 113(2)].

No demand for a grant shall be made except on the recommendation of the President. [Article 113(3)].

Appropriation Bills

As soon as may be after the grants under article 113 have been made by the House of the People, there shall be introduced a Bill to provide for the appropriation out of the Consolidated Fund of India of all moneys required to meet—

(a) the grants so made by the House of the People; and

(b) the expenditure charged on the Consolidated Fund of India but not exceeding in any case the amount shown in the statement previously laid before Parliament. [Article 114(1)].

No amendment shall be proposed to any such Bill in either House of Parliament which will have the effect of varying the amount or altering the destination of any grant so made or of varying the amount of any expenditure charged on the Consolidated Fund of India, and the decision of the person presiding as to whether an amendment is inadmissible under this clause shall be final. [Article 114(2)].

Subject to the provisions of articles 115 and 116, no money shall be withdrawn from the Consolidated Fund of India except under appropriation made by law passed in accordance with the provisions of this article. [Article 114(3)].

Supplementary, additional or excess grants

The President shall—

(a) if the amount authorised by any law made in accordance with the provisions of article 114 to be expended for a particular service for the current financial year is found to be insufficient for the purposes of that year or when a need has arisen during the current financial year for supplementary or additional expenditure upon some new service not contemplated in the annual financial statement for that year, or

(b) if any money has been spent on any service during a financial year in excess of the amount granted for that service and for that year,

cause to be laid before both the Houses of Parliament another statement showing the estimated amount of that expenditure or cause to be presented to the House of the People a demand for such excess, as the case may be. [Article 115(1)].

The provisions of articles 112, 113 and 114 shall have effect in relation to any such statement and expenditure or demand and also to any law to be made authorising the appropriation of moneys out of the Consolidated Fund of India to meet such expenditure or the grant in respect of such demand as they have effect in relation to the annual financial statement and the expenditure mentioned therein or to a demand for a grant and the law to be made for the authorisation of appropriation of money out of the Consolidated Fund of India to meet such expenditure or grant. [Article 115(2)].

Votes on account, votes of credit and exceptional grants

Notwithstanding anything in the foregoing provisions of this Chapter, the House of the People shall have power—

(a) to make any grant in advance in respect of the estimated expenditure for a part of any financial year pending the completion of the procedure prescribed in article 113 for the voting of such grant and the passing of the law in accordance with the provisions of article 114 in relation to that expenditure;

(b) to make a grant for meeting an unexpected demand upon the resources of India when on account of the magnitude or the indefinite character of the service the demand cannot be stated with the details ordinarily given in an annual financial statement;

(c) to make an exceptional grant which forms no part of the current service of any financial year;

and Parliament shall have power to authorise by law the withdrawal of moneys from the Consolidated Fund of India for the purposes for which the said grants are made. [Article 116(1)].

The provisions of articles 113 and 114 shall have effect in relation to the making of any grant under clause (1) and to any law to be made under that clause as they have effect in relation to the making of a grant with regard to any expenditure mentioned in the annual financial statement and the law to be made for the authorisation of appropriation of moneys out of the Consolidated Fund of India to meet such expenditure. [Article 116(2)].

Special provisions as to financial Bills

A Bill or amendment making provision for any of the matters specified in sub-clauses (a) to (f) of clause (1) of article 110 shall not be introduced or moved except on the recommendation of the President and a Bill making such provision shall not be introduced in the Council of States :

Provided that no recommendation shall be required under this clause for the moving of an amendment making provision for the reduction or abolition of any tax. [Article 117(1)].

A Bill or amendment shall not be deemed to make provision for any of the matters aforesaid by reason only that it provides for the imposition of fines or other pecuniary penalties or for the demand or payment of fees for licences or fees for services rendered, or by reason that it provides for the imposition, abolition, remission, alteration or regulation of any tax by any local authority or body for local purposes. [Article 117(2)]

A bill which, if enacted and brought into operation, would involve expenditure from the Consolidated Fund of India shall not be passed by either House of Parliament unless the President has recommended to that House the consideration of the Bill. [Article 117(3)].

Procedure Generally in Indian Parliament (Articles 118-122)

Rules of procedure

Each House of Parliament may make rules for regulating, subject to the provisions of this Constitution, its procedure and the conduct of its business. [Article 118(1)]

Until rules are made under clause (1) the rules of procedure and standing orders in force immediately before the commencement of this Constitution with respect to the Legislature of the Dominion of India shall have effect in relation to Parliament subject to such modifications and adaptations as may be made therein by the Chairman of the Council of States or the Speaker of the House of the People, as the case may be. [Article 118(2)].

The President, after consultation with the Chairman of the Council of States and the Speaker of the House of the People may make rules as to the procedure with respect of joint sittings of, and communications between the two Houses. [Article 118(3)]

At a joint sitting of the two Houses the Speaker of the House of the People, or in his absence such person as may be determined by rules of procedure made under clause (3), shall preside. [Article 118(4)].

Regulation by law of procedure in Parliament in relation to financial business

Parliament may, for the purpose of the timely completion of financial business regulate by law the procedure or, and the conduct of business in, each House of Parliament in relation to any financial matter or to any Bill for the appropriation of money out of the Consolidated Fund of India, and if and so far as any provision of any law so made is inconsistent with any rule made by a House of Parliament under clause (1) of article 118 or with any rule or standing order having effect in relation to Parliament under clause (2) of that article, such provision shall prevail. (Article 119).

Language to be used in Parliament

Notwithstanding anything in Part XVII, but subject to the provisions o article 348, business in Parliament shall be transacted in Hindi or in

English :

Provided that the Chairman of the Council of States or Speaker of the House of the People, or person acting as such, as the case may be, may permit any member who cannot adequately express himself in Hindi or in English to address the House in his mother-tongue. [Article 120(1)].

Unless Parliament by law otherwise provides, this article shall, after expiration of a period of 15 years from the commencement of this Constitution, have effect as if the words "or in English" were omitted therefrom.

British Parliament

British Parliament means Speaker, House of Commons and the House of Lords. It is supreme. Its powers are unlimited. There is nothing like judicial review of Acts passed by it. It can do everything except that of making a man a woman and a woman a man. The supremacy is consequent to events like Magna Carta, Petition of rights, Bill of rights, execution of Charles I, abolishing monarchy and declaring England as Commonwealth, restoration of monarchy to Charles II, glorious revolution of 1688 and abdication of James II, invitation to William and Mary to throne by Parliament, Act of Settlement, 1701 determining Succession to throne and Prime Ministership of Pitt the younger (Dismissal of Minister not by King but by Prime Minister) gave substantial control to Parliament over finance, legislation and administration. During all these, courts were with Parliament. Lex is Rex and not Rex is Lex was established as Rule of Law. From 1781 onward; it is Parliament versus court that is interesting after 1689 in British Constitutional history.

House of Commons.—House of Commons is the most remarkable public meeting in the world. Its venerable antiquity, its inspiring history, its splendid traditions, its youthful spirit and energy, the unrivalled influence it has exercised as the model of Parliament, its inseparableness with the vitality of English nation, its place as the visible centre and working motor of (British) Constitution have given unique place to it in England. It is purely an elective body. The electorates are determined by census every 10 years. Everybody of 18 years of age or above is voter except lunatics, bankrupts and criminals. Clergymen of 3 historic churches, Peers of England, Scotland and Wales, persons holding Government contracts and officers under the Crown cannot contest elections. The age for contesting eligibility is 21 years. The present number of House of Commons is 659.

Life of House of Commons is 5 years unless sooner dissolved by the King. It can also be extended during emergency. A member cannot resign from the membership. Membership is duty to Crown. A member loses membership if he accepts any paid public office under the Crown; for example one of Steward under the children hundreds or of Manor of Northstead. Speaker presides over House of Commons.

House of Lords.—It is the oldest second chamber in the world. It is successor of 'Great Council' which succeeded to 'Watan' of Anglo-Saxon period. Its membership is 1100 at the moment. Maximum number is not fixed. Seven distinct categories of members exist; mamely, *All princes of royal blood* (Duke of Cornwal, Duke of York and Dukes) *all hereditary peers representative peers of Scotland* (60) and *Ireland* (28), *Life Peers* (all retired high officials), *Lords of Appeal* (21) and *Lords spiritual* (26). Peerage is heritable. Fresh peerage can be created. Lord Chancellor presides over House of Lords, but in 2006, centuries old convention has been changed. House of Lords elects its own President. This change has been introduced under changes made by Blair Government (Mrs.) B.H. Heyman (Baronejus Hellene Heyman) is first elected President of House of Lords.

It has been shorn of judicial power by *Constitution Reforms Act, 2005*. Supreme Court of England and Wales takes place of judicial responsibilities hitherto having been discharged by House of Lords. Lord Chancellor now remains a minister like others in Cabinet.

The Federal Parliament—Australia

The six State Parliaments have been established on model of British Parliament and Federal Parliament of Australia is modelled on State Parliaments with modifications required by Federation of Australia. Crown (Governor-General), the Senate and the House of Representatives (all three) constitute federal Parliament. Parliament meets once a year at Canberra (Headquarter).

The Senate.—Para 2 of Constitution provides for the Senate; 12 members are elected by people in equal (total 76) from all six States. Two each are from capital territory and Northern territory. The term is 6 years. Half retire every three years. Those from two territories serve for three years. Eligibility for re-election exists. The Senate represents the interest of States.

President.—Senate elects the President of Senate. He has a vote as a Senator but does not have casting vote. Equality in votes means negative result. The quorum is 1/3 of 76. Senate is also dissolved by Governor-General if dead lock exists between two Houses on any matter. In the consequential vacancy the Houses of Parliament of State involved may choose a person as senator for remaining period or till successor is elected. If State Parliament is not in session at the relevant moment, it is Governor of State who will nominate Senator on advice of State Executive Council. Until expiration of 14 days on the date State Parliament meets. in by-election, thus people do not elect the senator. The qualification for members of Senate and House of Representatives is same; 21 years age, residence in State concerned for 3 years or above and must be a British subject. Voting age is 18 years. Voting is compulsory. Voting is by secret ballot. The voting system is by proportionate representation.

House of Representatives.—It is the lower chamber or 'People's House'. This house represents national interests. The number of members in lower House must be twice more than Senate. (Section 24). It is 150 at present. Population is the basis of seats to States in House of Representatives. The term is 3 years. The members are elected directly by people. Section 24 lays down a formulae for seat to each State (quota). It decides population of Australia in latest census divided by number of senators (double thereof). This is seat for House of Representatives from each State. For State Parliament (lower house) the formulae is : Population of State divided by double number of senators in Senate. Remainder more than half shall be counted one full.

Speaker.—Members of House of Representatives, elect the Speaker. Each member has one vote. Majority of votes decides the matter. Speaker of House of Representatives has casting vote; President of Senate does not have it. Procedure in each House is regulated by House itself. Power, privileges and immunities are similar to those of British M.P.

Federal Assembly of Russia

Federal Assembly means, Federal Council (upper chamber) and State Duma (lower chamber). It is the supreme representative and legislative body of the federation.

State Duma.—It consists of 450 members. The election is from party vote list (225 members) and single member constituencies (225 members). Anybody of 21 years age can vote. Nobody can be member of both houses simultaneously. The members are called 'Deputy'. A deputy cannot accept paid assignment. He can accept teaching, research or other creative activity. Duma is for 4 years. Article 103 describes jurisdiction of Duma. Duma can be dissolved under Article 111 and 117.

Federal Council.—It consists of 178 deputies (members). Section 103 describes the function of the Federal Council.

National People's Congress (N.P.C.)—China

It is the highest organ of State power and all authority of the people's Republic of China flows from it. It is unicameral central legislature. There is no second chamber. How is this body constituted and what is its membership; the constitution of 1982, nowhere prescribes. The congress is elected for 5 years. Elections are to be completed two months before expiry of term of current congress. There is no Election Commission. The Standing Committee of N.P.C. conducts the election to congress. It meets once a year unless Standing Committee decides to call special session or 1/5 members of congress (NPC) so propose.

Article 62 enumerates the functions of National People's Congress. It is the sole law making body of China. When it is not in session, the Standing Committee makes the law. President, Vice-Presidents, Prime Minister and members of State Council (Executive) and members of Standing Committee, Auditor General and the Secretary-General of State Council, and Chairman of Central Military Commission are elected by N.P.C. Its members are called deputies. 2/3 majority of N.P.C. can amend any part of constitution. It is only under the control of Communist Party of China. The privileges, duties and immunities of the members of National Peoples Congress (N.P.C.) are given in (73-75) of the 1982 Constitution.

Standing Committee of National People's Congress (N.P.C.).—This Committee consists of a Chairman, Vice-Chairman, Secretary-General and the members. The number is not fixed by the Constitution. The National People's Congress decides the number. The Committee is responsible to and is elected by N.P.C. The Chairman of Committee presides over the meetings. Its tenure is co-terminus with that of N.P.C. It is constituted every time afresh after election of N.P.C. Its functions are legislative, relating to elections, executive and judicial and financial. It does everything that N.P.C. can do.

The Diet—Japan

Japanese Parliament is called 'Diet'. It is bicameral; House of Councillors is upper Chamber, House of Representatives is lower house.

House of Representatives (lower Chamber).—The members of this house are elected for 4 years directly by adult franchise. The age is 20 years and above. By Political Reforms Bill, 1994, each 274 district would elect one legislator to the Diet. The members have to be citizens of Japan, not less than 25 years in age, and resident of district for 3 months and should not be mentally incompetent and convict of serious crime; one cannot be member of both houses at the same time.

House of Councillors.—It is elected. The number is 247. The election is direct by same electorates as of the lower house. Two types of constituencies exist, local and national. As such two votes are given by each voter. The tenure is 6 years; 1/2 retire every three years. The house is never dissolved. The minimum age for a member is 30. The quorum is 1/3 of total membership. 'Gicho' is the name of the presiding officer of House of Councillors. Gicho is elected by the House by Secret Ballot at the start of session and continues with House.

U.S. Congress

"All legislative powers herein granted shall be vested in a Congress of the United States which shall consist of a Senate and House of Representatives." (Article 1 of U.S. Constitution).

House of Representatives.—It is the lower house of the Congress. The term of a member in this House is 2 years and the number is fixed on the basis of population of each state. The larger the population of a state, the larger is number of representatives it sends to House of Representatives. Its membership as such varies according to census carried every 10 years after. At present, it is 435. A U.S. citizen of 25 years age or above, and of not less than 7 years as such and inhabitant of the state from which he seeks election, can be a member of house. The majority in house constitutes minimum quorum as compared to 10% (India), 40 members (U.K.), 20 members (Canada) and 1/3 (Australia). A member is paid one lakh fifty-four thousand taxable U.S. dollars as annual salary. After 62 years proportionate pension is given. Speaker presides over House of Representatives.

The Senate.—Senate is the upper chamber of the U.S. Congress consisting of two Senators from each state by direct election irrespective of size or population of the states. Total number as such is 100 in the Senate. The Senate represents area and the House represents numbers. For Senator, the requisite qualification is, 30 years of age, citizen of 9 years or more standing and inhabitant of same state from which he is chosen. The term of a Senator is 6 years, 1/3 retire every 2 years by rotation. Re-election is permissible. It is a continuous body subject to no dissolution. It holds regular session each year. Special sessions can be called. Vice-President of U.S.A. is *ex officio* Chairman of the Senate. The Senate elects a President who takes over when Vice-President of U.S.A. is not available to preside for one reason or the other. The deliberations is Senate are free and unrestricted. House of Representatives is the most shackled deliberative body in the world whereas the Senate is the freest. However, recently, closure rule has been adopted by the Senate. Any long speech can be stopped by resolution of 2/3 Senators present and voting and irrelevant speech has to stop one hour after such resolution. It is said that U.S. Senate is the strongest and the House of Lords, the weakest of all upper houses in the world today.

Federal Assembly—Switzerland

Swish Federal Assembly is bicameral—The supreme constitutional power vests in Assembly subject only to people and cantons. Laws passed by Federal Assembly can neither be vetoed by executive (Federal Council) nor subject to judicial review by Federal Tribunal.

The National Council.—It is the lower house. Its number is not fixed. It changes with the growth of the population. It is 200 at the moment. After 10 years, census is done and number of members from each canton is adjusted. Voting eligibility is age of 18 years. Women have voting right since 1971.

The house is elected for 4 years. It cannot be dissolved by executive. It gets dissolved in case of total revision of the Constitution when houses do not agree with each other. After 4 years, election is held on last sunday of October. Generally, elections take place in churches. The house sits 4 times regularly every year in March, June, September and December. The quorum of National Council is 101. The decisions are by majority of members present. National Council elects its own President and Vice-President for a year. No consecutive term is allowed. Vice-President succeeds President. President does not get any salary. There is no official opposition in National Council.

Council of States.—It is the upper chamber. It is on account of cantons sovereignty. All cantons have equal seats in Council of States. Area or population of canton is irrelevant. Every full canton sends 2 representatives and half canton, one representative, in council of States. Total members are 46, from 23 cantons. The members are called Deputy. The Council meets once a year unless special session is convened by the Federal Council or Deputies of five Cantons. The house elects Chairman and Vice-Chairman for two years. The majority decision is final in business matters. Both the Chambers have equal role. None is superior to the other, Legislation has to be passed by both houses. Both enjoy parity even in financial matters. There are no 'whips'. The members vote on conscience. There are no treasury or the opposition benches.

The Houses meet separately. However joint session is held for appointments to Federal Council (Executive), Federal Tribunal Judges (Judiciary), Chancellor of the Confederation and General in Chief of Federal army and for resolving conflict in executive and judiciary and also for granting pardon.

French Parliament

French Parliament consists of two Chambers :

The National Assembly.—It is the lower house. Its members are called Deputies', the number of deputies is 577. Deputies are elected through two ballot systems in single member constituency. Each has to get absolute majority of votes cast in first ballot and simple majority of such votes in second ballot. The election is by direct suffrage which is universal, equal and secret. The life of Assembly is five years. It can be dissolved earlier. Voters are from both sex of majority age. Minimum age for Deputies is 23 years.

The Senate.—Election to Senate is by indirect suffrage. It consists of representatives of the territorial entities of the Republic. Its number is 321. Metropolitan France (Seats 255), overseas departments, overseas territories and French citizens living abroad are four such entities represented in the Senate. The, electorate college is composed of local Deputies, members of department Councils (local unit) and representatives of the municipalities. The term of Senate is nine years. Minimum age for Senator is 35 years.

Article 26 deals with privileges of the members of Parliament. Article 27 makes the right to vote personal. Voting by proxy is not allowed. However, power to vote can be delegated by any member on grounds of illness, accident, family circumstances, on Government duty or Military service or absence from France provided notice in advance is given. Attendance bonus is given. Non-attendance is penalised.

Parliament meets twice a year. First session is budget session. The second is for legislative business. In October (second session) Session, each House elects the bureau. It consists of Presidents; 10 Vice-Presidents (6 for Assembly and 4 for Senate), 20 secretaries (12 for Assembly, 8 for Senate) and 3 Questeurs for each house. The bureau organises and supervises different services in houses and particularly discipline and admissibility of bills and resolutions.

Dominion Parliament—Canada

It is bicameral; the Senate and House of Commons (lower House).

The Senate.—The number of Senators must not exceed 118. The seats are divided amongst states; there is no equal representation. The senator is appointed on recommendation of Prime Minister. The Governor-General appoints. They hold office till age of 75 years. In a way, it is reward of service to the party in old age. Senator is appointed on party basis. The minimum age for senator is 30 years; must be natural or naturalized subject of the queen. Senate is presided over by Speaker. He is appointed by Governor-General. Speaker has right to vote. Tie in voting negative decision. Speaker does not have casting vote. 15 members constitute quorum.

House of commons.—The British North America Act, 1867 fixed 181 members for House of Commons. In 37th election, the number was 172. The number is adjusted after census every 10 years after. No province can have lesser number of members in House of Commons than it has in the Senate. Every person of 18 years or above can be voter. He should be citizen of Canada and he must have residence in preceding 12 months in province concerned. The member eligible to contest must be 21 years or above in age. All are single membered Constituencies. The tenure of House is five years, the term can be extended by 2/3 votes of commons during war, invasion or insurrection. House is presided by speaker.

The expiration of a period of fifteen years from the commencement of this constitution, have effect as if the words 'or in English' were omitted therefrom. [Article 120(2)].

Restriction on discussion in Parliament.—No discussion shall take place in Parliament with respect to the conduct of any Judge of the Supreme Court or of a High Court in the discharge of his duties except upon a motion for presenting an address to the President praying for the removal of the Judge as hereinafter provided. (Article 121)

Courts not to inquire into proceedings of Parliament.—The validity of any proceedings in Parliament shall not be called in question on the ground of any alleged irregularity of procedure. [Article 32(1)].

No officer or member of Parliament in whom powers are vested by or under this Constitution for regulating procedure or the conduct of business, or for maintaining order, in Parliament shall be subject to the jurisdiction of any court in respect of the exercise by him of those powers. [Article 122 (2)].

❑ ❑

Chapter 16

Rule of Law and Judicial Process

The **rule of law** is the legal principle that law should govern a nation, as opposed to being governed by arbitrary decisions of individualgovernment officials. It primarily refers to the influence and authority of law within society, particularly as a constraint upon behaviour, including behaviour of government officials. The phrase can be traced back to 16th century Britain, and in the following century the Scottish theologian Samuel Rutherford used the phrase in his argument against the divine right of kings. John Locke defined freedom under the rule of law as follows :

"Freedom is constrained by laws in both the state of nature and political society. Freedom of nature is to be under no other restraint but the law of nature. Freedom of people under government is to be under no restraint apart from standing rules to live by that are common to everyone in the society and made by the lawmaking power established in it. Persons have a right or liberty to (1) follow their own will in all things that the law has not prohibited and (2) not be subject to the inconstant, uncertain, unknown, and arbitrary wills of others."

The rule of law was further popularized in the 19th century by British jurist A. V. Dicey. The concept, if not the phrase, was familiar to ancient philosophers such as Aristotle, who wrote "Law should govern".

Rule of law implies that every citizen is subject to the law, including lawmakers themselves. In this sense, it stands in contrast to an autocracy, dictatorship, or oligarchy where the rulers are held above the law. Lack of the rule of law can be found in both democracies and dictatorships, for example because of neglect or ignorance of the law, and the rule of law is more apt to decay if a government has insufficient corrective mechanisms for restoring it. Government based upon the rule of law is called nomocracy.

History

Although credit for popularizing the expression "the rule of law" in modern times is usually given to A. V. Dicey, development of the legal concept can be traced through history to many ancient civilizations, including ancient Greece, China, Mesopotamia, India, and Rome.

Antiquity

In the West, the ancient Greeks initially regarded the best form of government as rule by the best men. Plato advocated a benevolent monarchy ruled by an idealized philosopher king, who was above the law. Plato nevertheless hoped that the best men would be good at respecting established laws, explaining that "Where the law is subject to some other authority and has none of its own, the collapse of the state, in my view, is not far off; but if law is the master of the government and the government is its slave, then the situation is full of promise and men enjoy all the blessings that the gods shower on a state." More than Plato attempted to do, Aristotle flatly opposed letting the highest officials wield power beyond guarding and serving the laws. In other words, Aristotle advocated the rule of law :

It is more proper that law should govern than any one of the citizens : upon the same principle, if it is advantageous to place the supreme power in some particular persons, they should be appointed to be only guardians, and the servants of the laws.

According to the Roman statesman Cicero, "We are all servants of the laws in order that we may be free." During the Roman Republic, controversial magistrates might be put on trial when their terms of office expired. Under the Roman Empire, the sovereign was personally immune (*legibus solutus*), but those with grievances could sue the treasury.

In China, members of the school of legalism during the 3rd century BC argued for using law as a tool of governance, but they promoted "rule *by law*" as opposed to "rule *of law*", meaning that they placed the aristocrats and emperor above the law. In contrast, the Huang-Lao school of Daoism rejected legal positivism in favor of a natural law that even the ruler would be subject to.

There has recently been an effort to reevaluate the influence of the Bible on Western constitutional law. In the Old Testament, there was some language in Deuteronomy imposing restrictions on the Jewish king, regarding such things as how many wives he could have, and how many horses he could own for his personal use. According to Professor Bernard M. Levinson, "This legislation was so utopian in its own time that it seems never to have been implemented...." The Deuteronomic social vision may have influenced opponents of the divine right of kings, including Bishop John Ponet in sixteenth-century England.

Middle Ages

In Islamic jurisprudence rule of law was formulated in the seventh century, so that no official could claim to be above the law, not even the caliph. However, this was not a reference to secular law, but to Islamic religious law in the form of Sharia law.

Alfred the Great, Anglo-Saxon King of the 9th century, reformed the law of his kingdom and created a law code (see Doom Book) with the biblical Mosaic law and Christian commandments as its basis. He ruled that justice had to be equal between people, whether rich or poor, friends or enemies. This was likely inspired from Leviticus 19 : "You shall do no injustice in judgment! You shall not be partial to the poor; nor defer to the great! But you are to judge your neighbour fairly!".

In 1215, Archbishop Stephen Langton gathered the Barons in England and forced King John and future sovereigns and magistrates back under the rule of law, preserving ancient liberties by Magna Carta in return for exacting taxes. This foundation for a constitution was carried into the United States Constitution.

In 1481, during the reign of Ferdinand II of Aragon, the *Constitucis de l'Observanga* was approved by the General Court of Catalonia, establishing the submission of royal power (included its officers) to the laws of the Principality of Catalonia.

Early modern period

The first known use of this English phrase occurred around AD 1500 Another early example of the phrase "rule of law" is found in a petition to James I of England in 1610, from the House of Commons :

Amongst many other points of happiness and freedom which your majesty's subjects of this kingdom have enjoyed under your royal progenitors, kings and queens of this realm, there is none which they have accounted more dear and precious than this, to be guided and governed by the certain *rule of the law* which giveth both to the head and members that which of right belongeth to them, and not by any uncertain or arbitrary form of government....

In 1607, English Chief Justice Sir Edward Coke said in the *Case of Prohibitions* (according to his own report) "that the law was the golden met-wand and measure to try the causes of the subjects; and which protected His Majesty in safety and peace : with which the King was greatly offended, and said, that then he should be under the law, which was treason to affirm, as he said; to which I said, that Bracton saith, *quod Rex non debed esse sub homine, sed sub Deo et lege* (That the King ought not to be under any man but under God and the law)."

Among the first modern authors to use the term and give the principle theoretical foundations was Samuel Rutherford in *Lex, Rex* (1644). The title, Latin for "the law is king", subverts the traditional formulation *rex lex* ("the king is law"). John Locke also discussed this issue in his *Second Treatise of Government* (1690). The principle was also discussed by Montesquieu in *The Spirit of the Laws* (1748). The phrase "rule of law" appears in Samuel Johnson's *Dictionary* (1755).

In 1776, the notion that no one is above the law was popular during the founding of the United States. For example, Thomas Paine wrote in his pamphlet *Common Sense* that "in America, *the law is king*. For as in absolute governments the King is law, so in free countries the law *ought* to be king; and there ought to be no other." In 1780, John Adams enshrined this principle in the Massachusetts Constitution by seeking to establish "a government of laws and not of men."

The influence of Britain, France and the United States contributed to spreading the principle of the rule of law to other countries around the world.

Status in various jurisdictions

The rule of law has been considered as one of the key dimensions that determine the quality and good governance of a country. Research, like the Worldwide Governance Indicators, defines the rule of law as : "the extent to which agents have confidence and abide by the rules of society, and in particular the quality of contract enforcement, the police and the courts, as well as the likelihood of crime or violence." Based on this definition the Worldwide Governance Indicators project has developed aggregate measurements for the rule of law in more than 200 countries, as seen in the map below. A government based on the rule of law can be called a "nomocracy", from the Greek *nomos* (law) and *kratos* (power or rule).

Europe

The preamble of the European Convention for the Protection of Human Rights and Fundamental Freedoms says "the governments of European countries which are like-minded and have a common heritage of political traditions, ideals, freedom and the rule of law".

In France and Germany the concepts of rule of law (*Etat de droit* and *Rechtsstaat* respectively) are analogous to the principles of constitutional supremacy and protection of fundamental rights from public authorities (see public law), particularly the legislature. France was one of the early pioneers of the ideas of the rule of law. The German interpretation is more "rigid" but similar to that of France and the United Kingdom.

Finland's constitution explicitly requires rule of law by stipulating that "the exercise of public powers shall be based on an Act. In all public activity, the law shall be strictly observed."

United Kingdom

In the United Kingdom the rule of law is a long-standing principle of the way the country is governed, dating from Magna Carta in 1215 and the Bill of Rights 1689. In the 19th century, A. V. Dicey, a constitutional scholar and lawyer, wrote of the twin pillars of the British constitution in his classic work *Introduction to the Study of the Law of the Constitution* (1885); these two pillars are the rule of law and parliamentary sovereignty.

United States

All government officers of the United States, including the President, the Justices of the Supreme Court, state judges and legislators, and all members of Congress, pledge first and foremost to uphold the Constitution. These oaths affirm that the rule of law is superior to the rule of any human leader. At the same time, the federal government has considerable discretion : the legislative branch is free to decide what statutes it will write, as long as it stays within its enumerated powers and respects the constitutionally protected rights of individuals. Likewise, the judicial branch has a degree of judicial discretion, and the executive branch also has various discretionary powers including prosecutorial discretion.

Scholars continue to debate whether the U.S. Constitution adopted a particular interpretation of the "rule of law," and if so, which one. For example, John Harrison asserts that the word "law" in the Constitution is simply defined as that which is legally binding, rather than being "defined by formal or substantive criteria," and therefore judges do not have discretion to decide that laws fail to satisfy such unwritten and vague criteria. Law Professor Frederick Mark Gedicks disagrees, writing that Cicero, Augustine, Thomas Aquinas, and the framers of the U.S. Constitution believed that an unjust law was not really a law at all.

Meaning of rule

The rule of law in its tangible shape means.—Three clear principles of rule of law (against rule of men or rule of bullet). Three principles mean—

(1) Administrative law is no law;

(2) Equality before law and equal protection of law are its basics;

(3) All Laws owe their origin to common men.

Dicey made history and history keeps Dicey as original Shaper of rule of Law.

The "rule of law" (like partially concurrent expressions such as *Rechsstaat, etat de droit*, or *estado de derecho*) is a disputed term. Its minimal (and historically original) meaning is that whatever law exists is written down and publicly promulgated by an appropriate authority before the events meant to be regulated by it, and is fairly applied by relevant State institutions including the judiciary (though other state institutions can be involved as well). "Fairly applied" mean" that the administrative application or judicial adjudication of legal rules is consistent across equivalent cases; is made without taking into consideration the class, status, or relative amounts of power held by the parties in such cases; and applies procedures that are pre-established, knowable, and allow a fair chance for the views and interests at stake in each case to be properly voiced. The Minimal significant criterion is that if A is attributed the same generic rights (and, at least implicitly, the same legal personhood and agency) as the more powerful B with whom A enters into a crop-sharing arrangement, employment contract, or marriage, then it stands to reason that A has the right to expect equal treatment from the State institutions that have, or may acquire, jurisdiction over such acts.

This implies formal equality, in two senses.

First, it is established in and by legal rules that are valid (at least) in that they have been sanctioned following previously and carefully dictated procedures, often ultimately regulated by constitutional rules.

Second, the rights and obligations specified are universal, in that they attach to each individual considered as a legal person, irrespective of social position, with the sole requirement that the individual in question has reached competent legal adulthood and has not been proven to suffer from some (narrowly defined and legally prescribed) disqualification.

These rights support the claim of equal treatment in the legally defined situations that underlie and may ensue from the kind of acts above exemplified. "Equality [of all] before the law" is the expectation tendentially inscribed in this kind of equality.

Another important point is that the rights and obligations attached to political citizenship by a democratic regime are a subset of the more general civil rights and obligations attached to a legal person as a member of a given society.

In addition to the well-known participatory rights to vote and run for office in fair elections, the freedoms of expression, association, movement, and the like are usually considered necessary to the existence of a democratic regime. In many highly developed countries, these and similar freedoms became legally sanctioned civil rights well before becoming political freedoms.

Strict meaning.—Strictly speaking, there is no "rule of law." or "rule by laws, not men." All is individuals in various capacities interpreting rules which, according to some pre-established criteria, meet the condition of being generally considered law. Such a situation is clearly superior to a Hobbesian state of nature or the creation and application of rules at the whim of a despot. Yet it is not enough that certain actions, whether of public or private actors, are *secundum legem*, that is, in conformity with what a given law prescribes.

An act that is formally according to law may nonetheless entail the application of a rule that is invidiously discriminatory or violates basic rights. Or such an act may involve the selective use of a law against some, even as privileged sectors are enjoying arbitrary exemptions.

The first possibility entails the violation of moral standards that most countries write into their constitutions and that nowadays, usually under the rubric of human rights, countries have the internationally acquired obligation to respect.

The second possibility entails the violation of a crucial principle of fairness—that like cases be treated alike.

Still another possibility is that in a given case the law is applied properly, but by an authority that does not feel obligated to proceed in the same manner on future equivalent occasions.

These cases may be construed as being "ruled by law," but they do not meet the criteria of the "rule of law." Rather, these possibilities indicate the absence, or at least serious breaches, of a reasonable application of what the rule of law is supposed to be.

Whether a Positive Definition of rule of law feasible ? Difficulties.

A first complication is that the concepts of the rule of law and of *estado de derecho* (or *Rechsstaat*, or *etat de droit*, or equivalents in other languages of countries belonging to the Roman-originated civil-law tradition) are not synonymous. Furthermore, each of these terms is subject to various definitional and normative disputations.

First, in both the civil-law and common-law traditions, most definitions have at their core the view that under the rule of law, the legal system is a hierarchical one (usually crowned by constitutional norms) that aims at yet never fully achieves completeness. This means that the relationships among legal rules are themselves legally ruled, and that there is no moment in which the whim of a given actor may justifiably cancel or suspend the rules that govern his or her actions. No one, including the most highly placed official, is above the law. In contrast, the hallmark of all forms of authoritarian rule, even those that are highly institutionalized and legally formalized, is that at their apex sits some person or entity (a king, a junta, a party committee) that is sovereign in the classic sense of being able to make decisions unconstrained by law when the sovereign judges that there is a need to do so.

Second, "the government shall be ruled by law and subject to it" and that "the creation of law is itself legally regulated" is to imply that the legal system is an aspect of the overall social order that in principle "brings definition, specificity, clarity, and thus predictability into human interactions. Achieving this situation though not necessarily an unmixed blessing, is a great public good. A necessary condition for this is that the laws have certain characteristics. Many lists of such characteristics are available *e.g.*. Joseph Raz espouses :

1. All laws should be prospective, open, and clear;
2. Laws should be relatively stable;
3. The making of particular laws... must be guided by open stable, clear, and general rules;
4. The independence of the judiciary must be guaranteed;
5. The principles of natural justice must be observed (*i.e.*, open and fair hearing and absence of bias);
6. The courts should have review powers... to ensure conformity to the rule of law.
7. The courts should be easily accessible; and
8. The discretion of crime preventing agencies should not be allowed to pervert the law.

The first three points refer to general characteristics of the laws themselves. Each point pertains to the proper enactment and content of the laws, as well as to a fact that Raz and others stress : The laws must be possible to follow, and should not place unreasonable cognitive or behavioral demands on the addressees. The other points of Raz's listing refer to the courts and only indirectly to other State agencies. Point four requires specification : The value of independent courts (itself a murky idea) is shown, *a contrario*, by the often-servile behavior of the judiciary in relation to authoritarian rulers. But this independence may be misused—and has been misused with some frequency in democratized-countries —to foster the sectoral privileges of judicial personnel or to allow unchallenged, arbitrary interpretations of the law. Consequently, it also seems required "that those charged with interpreting and enforcing the laws [must] take them with primary seriousness.

The stewards of the law must hold themselves ready to support and expand that very democracy which, in contrast to the old authoritarian order, confers upon them such independence. This is a tall order everywhere, where a long roll of institutional innovations has shown scant success in striking a proper balance between judicial subjection and excessive judicial independence. In this area another difficult accomplishment is implied by point six, especially with respect to overseeing the legality of acts performed by presidents who feel themselves electorally empowered to do whatever they think best while in office. The denial of redress to many of the poor and the vulnerable (points five and seven). The same goes for the eighth point, particularly as regards the impunity enjoyed by police and other (so-called) security agencies, as well as violence perpetrated by private agents who often take advantage of police forces and courts that are culpably indifferent towards or even complicit in such unjust acts.

Origin and Evolution of Rule of Law.

The concept of rule of law is of old origin. It is an ancient ideal, and was discussed by Ancient Greek philosophers such as Plato and Aristotle around 350 B.C. Plato wrote : "Where the law is subject to some other authority and has none of its own, the collapse of the State, in my view, is not far off; but if law is the master of the Government and the Government is its slave then the situation is full of promise and men enjoy all the blessings that the gods shower on a State". Likewise, Aristotle also endorsed the concept of rule of law by writing that "law should govern and those in power should be servants of the laws."

Rule of Law and other values : Relation

In considering the relation between the rule of law and the other values that the law should serve it is of particular importance to remember that the rule of law is essentially a negative value. It is merely designed to minimise the harm to freedom and dignity which the law may cause in its pursuit of its goals however laudable these may be. Finally, regarding the rule of law as the inherent excellence of the law means that it fulfills essentially a subservient role. Conformity to it makes the law a good instrument for achieving certain goals, but conformity to the rule of law is not itself an ultimate goal. This subservient role of the doctrine shows both its power and its limitations. On the one hand, if the pursuit of certain goals is entirely incompatible with the rule of law, then these goals should not be pursued by legal means. But on the other hand one should be wary of disqualifying the legal pursuit of major social goals in the name of the rule of law. After all, the rule of law is meant to enable the law to promote social good, and should not be lightly used to show that it should not do so. Sacrificing too many social goals on the altar of the rule of law may make the law barren and empty.

Features of Rule of Law

The essential characteristic of the rule of law are :

(i) The supremacy of law, which means that all persons (individuals and Government) are subject to law.

(ii) Equality before law.

(iii) A concept of justice which emphasises interpersonal adjudication, law based on standards and the importance of procedures.

(iv) Restrictions on the exercise of discretionary power.

(v) The doctrine of judicial precedent.

(vi) Legislation should be prospective and not retrospective.

(vii) A formal and rational system of adjudication which provides for adequate opportunity for correction of error through appeal and review processes.

(viii) An independent judiciary.

(ix) The exercise by Parliament of the legislative power and restrictions on exercise of legislative power by the executive.

Comparative Analysis of Rule of Law in India & U.K.

Development of the concept of rule of law in U.K.

The rule of law in U.K. was developed over the centuries as a brake on arbitrary power. The modern concept of Rule of law owes much to the great battles between the English kings and their subjects, the struggle for supremacy between parliament and Stuart kings, and finally the war between the British Empire and its American Colonies.

The Great Charter : Magna Carta

On June 15, 1215 in the meadows of Runnymede, King John and his rebellious barons agreed to the great charter known as Magna Carta. The great charter was the first significant written instrument limiting the power of the king and confining him to what the barons regarded as good governance. These promises were a bargain between the king and the feudal lords dictated by the force of arms.

James the first and Chief Justice Coke

The role of Sir Edward Coke, Lord Chief Justice of England in the fight against the absolute power of Stuart kings, is epic in its dimensions. James I was bent on establishing his absolute power claiming the divine right of the king. Parliament and the royal courts of Justice stood in his way.

Under the leadership of Chief Justice Coke the Courts had started interfering in the matter of prerogative powers, seizures and detentions and were issuing writs to review the decisions of local feudal and ecclesiastical courts. As a result Coke was dismissed from his position as Chief Justice of the King's Bench. It was only after the Glorious Revolution and Act of Settlement (1701) that parliamentary powers became ascendant and the independence of the judges' tenure was firmly secured.

Wilkes v. Wood : rule of law applied

In England, the doctrine of rule of law was applied in concrete cases. If a man is wrongfully arrested by the police, he can file a suit for damages against them as if the police were private individuals. In *Wilkes* v. *Wood* it was held that an action for damages for trespass was maintainable even if the action complained of was taken in pursuance of the order of the minister. In the leading case of *Entick* v. *Carrington* a publisher's house was ransacked by the King's messengers sent by the Secretary of State. In an action for trespass, £ 300 were awarded to the publisher as damages. In the same matter, if a man's land is compulsorily acquired under an illegal order, he can bring an action for trespass against any person who tries to disturb his possession or attempts to execute the said order. Dicey's formulation of the rule of law has played a significant role in the development of constitutional law of United Kingdom.

Rule of Law in India

India has a written Constitution; a body of laws, subordinate to the Constitution, dealing with various subjects; rules and regulations, executive instructions & Conventions. All these may be broadly termed as 'law' and their operation to subject population is the 'rule of law.'

These fundamental rights guaranteed by the Constitution take precedence over any other law of the land. They include individual rights common to most liberal democracies, such as equality before the law, freedom of speech and expression, freedom of association and peaceful assembly, freedom of religion, and right to constitutional remedies, such as *Habeas Corpus*, for the protection of civil rights. Furthermore, they act as bulwark against various forms of exploitation which take place against women, children and minority communities.

Human Rights Abuse

At first sight, it seems that the rule of law and the respect for human rights and human dignity prevail but there exists significant human rights abuses, despite the extensive constitutional and statutory safeguards. Many of these abuses are generated by intense social tensions, violent secessionist movements and the authorities' attempts to repress them, and deficient police methods and training. Serious human rights abuses include extra-judicial executions and other political killings, torture, and excessive use of force by security forces and separatists militants, as well as kidnapping and extortion by militants, especially in Kashmir and north east India; torture, rape, and deaths of suspects in police custody throughout India; arbitrary arrest and incommunicado detention in Kashmir and in the north-east; continued detention throughout the country of thousands arrested under special security legislation; long delays in criminal trials; widespread inter-caste and inter-communal violence, both societal and by the police and other agents of Government, against women; discrimination and violence against indigenous people; and widespread exploitation of indentured, bonded, and child Labour.

Maladministration

Unsatisfactory functioning of municipal administrative organs also impacts very negatively on the rule of law. It is not surprising, therefore, that an overwhelming number of complaints are directly related to the work of public administrative bodies. Administrative organs still do not apply principles of good administration. Good administration is based on a high level of courtesy to be shown to citizens, free access to all information in the possession of the authorities, strengthening of supervision, especially of municipal systems of Government, de-politicization of the public administration, etc. the recent enactment of a law guaranteeing a right to public information is a step towards good governance.

Judiciary & Rule of Law

The Hon'ble Supreme Court and the various High Courts through Judicial activism and public interest litigation, other bodies such as the National Human Rights Commission and State Human Rights Commissions and various non-Governmental organizations have made significant contributions towards protecting freedoms and preventing human rights violations and abuses, thereby ensuring that the Rule of Law and respect for citizens' rights do not remain only on paper but are incorporated in practice too.

Rule of Law as Basic Feature

In *Sub-Committee on Judicial Accountability* v. *Union of India* the Supreme Court has held that rule of law is a basic feature of the Constitutional fabric and is an integral part of the constitutional structure.

The Rule of Law ; few aspects, Reflections

Unlike *estado de derecho* and equivalent terms, the English-language phrase "rule of law," defined as above, does not refer directly to any State agencies other than courts. This is not surprising given various countries' respective traditions, including the particularly strong role that the courts have played in the political history of any country. Nevertheless, the whole State apparatus and its agents are supposed to submit to the rule of law.

If the legal system is supposed to texture, stabilize, and order manifold social relations, then when State agents or even private actors violate the law with impunity, the rule of law is truncated. Whether State agents perpetrate unlawful acts on their own or give private actors *de facto* license to do so does not make much difference, either to the victims of such actions or to the ineffectiveness of the rule of law.

Rule of Law and democracy ; Three Senses

The corollary of these reflections is that, when discussed in relation to the theory of democracy, the rule of law—or *estado de derecho*—should be conceived not only as a generic characteristic of the legal system and the performance of the courts, but also, and mostly, as the legally based rule of a democratic State. This entails that there exists a legal system that is itself democratic, in three senses.

(1) It upholds the political rights, freedoms, and guarantees of a democratic regime;

(2) It upholds the civil rights of the whole population; and

(3) It establishes networks of responsibility and accountability which entail that all public and private agents, including the highest

State officials, are subject to appropriate, legally established controls on the lawfulness of their acts.

As long as it fulfills these three conditions, such a State is not just a state ruled by law or a state that enacts the rule of law : it is a State that enacts a democratic rule of law, or an *estado democratico de derecho*.

State Institutions and Rule of Law.

In addition to the legal system itself, there are a number of state institutions that are directly related to a democratic regime. Thus the legal system is not just a set of rules but a system properly so called, which interlaces legal rules with legally regulated State institutions. In turn, a democratic legal system is a species of this genus, with two main features : It enacts and backs the rights attached to a democratic regime; and it holds all officials and institutions in the state (and indeed in society) at large answerable to the law—no one is *de legibus solutus*. In an *estado democratico de derecho*, everyone is subject to the legal authority of one or more institutions—the legal system closes, in the sense that no one is supposed to be above or beyond its rules. In turn, this characteristic is intimately related (as the tradition of liberal constitutionalism recognized early) to the protection of political and other rights. Absent the safeguard of universal answerability to the law, there would exist some ultimately uncontrollable power or powers that could unilaterally curtail or simply take rights away.

Accountability; rule of Law and democracy.

In a democracy, rulers are supposed to submit to three kinds of accountability.

One, vertical electoral accountability, results from fair and institutionalized elections, through which citizens may change the party and officers in Government.

Another kind of vertical accountability, of a societal kind.

Is exercised by groups and even individuals who seek to mobilize the legal system to place demands on the State and the Government aimed at preventing, redressing, or punishing presumably illegal actions (or inactions) perpetrated by public officials. Still a third kind of accountability, horizontal. It results when some properly authorized State institutions act to prevent, redress, or punish the presumably illegal actions (or inactions) of public officials.

Ways how these accountabilities differ

These types of accountability differ in an important way. Vertical or electoral accountability must by definition exist in a democracy. The degree and effectiveness of societal and horizontal accountability, by contrast, vary across cases and time periods. These variations are relevant to attempts to assess democratic quality. The lack of a vigorous and self-assertive society, for instance, or the incapacity or unwillingness of certain State institutions to exercise their prescribed authority over other State institutions (especially elected officials) is a telltale sign of low-quality democracy.

Another important measure is the effectiveness of the legal system at actually bringing a beneficial degree of order to social relations. This is a function of the interactions among the elements that compose this system. At one level, *i.e.* "inter institutional." the authority of a judge dealing with a criminal case would be nil were it not joined, at several stages, by that of police officers, prosecutors, defense attorneys, and so on, as well as by, eventually, higher courts and prisons. Horizontally, in a democratic legal system no State institutions or officers are supposed to escape from legal controls regarding the lawfulness of their actions.

In a third, territorial, dimension, the legal system is supposed to extend homogenously across the space delimited by the State—there must be no place where the law's writ does not run.

In a fourth dimension—that of social stratification—the legal system must treat like cases alike irrespective of the class, gender, ethnicity, or other attributes of the respective actors.

In all these dimensions, the legal system presupposes what Juan J. Linz and Alfred Stepan call an "effective State," it is not just a matter of appropriate legislation but also of a network of State institutions that is itself democratic. The weakness of this kind of State is one of the most disturbing characteristics of most countries.

Flaws in the existing law

In spite of progress recently made, there still exist laws, judicial criteria, and administrative regulations that discriminate against women, members of indigenous peoples, and various other minorities, and which often force defendants, detainees and prison inmates to endure conditions that are repugnant to any sense of fair process.

Flaws in the application of the law

"For my friends, everything; for my enemies, the law." This sentence, attributed to Brazil's President Getulio Vargas (1930-45, 1950-54), expresses an attitude typical of dictatorships. The discretionary, and often exactingly severe, use of the law against the political enemy or the vulnerable can be an efficient means of oppression. The other side of this is the manifold ways in which, even in a democracy, the privileged manage to exempt themselves from the law. There is an old Latin American tradition of ignoring or twisting the law in order to favour the strong and repress the weak. When a shady businessman said in Argentina. "To be powerful is to have [legal] impunity," he expressed a presumably widespread feeling that to follow the law voluntarily is something that only morons do and that to be subject to the law is not to be the carrier of enforceable rights but rather a sure signal of social weakness. This is particularly true—and dangerous—in encounters that may unleash the violence of the State or powerful private agents, but an attentive eye can also detect it in the stubborn refusal of the privileged to submit themselves to regular administrative procedures, to say nothing of the legal impunity that they too often obtain.

Flaws in access to the judiciary and to fair process.

This has proved quite vexing even in highly developed countries. Across most countries the judiciary is too distant cumbersome, expensive, and slow for the poor and vulnerable even to attempt to access it. And if they do manage to obtain judicial access, the available evidence often points to severe and systematic discrimination. Criminal procedures in particular often tend to disregard the rights of the accused before, during, and after trial.

Flaws due to sheer lawlessness.

It is a mistake to conflate the State with its bureaucratic apparatus insofar as most of the formally enacted law existing in a territory is issued and backed by the State, and as the State institutions themselves are supposed to act according to legal rules. The legal system is a constitutive part of the State. As such, "the legal State" (that is, the part of the State that is embodied in a legal system) penetrates and textures society, furnishing a basic element of stability to social relations. In many countries however, the reach of the legal State is limited. In many regions, not only those geographically distant from the political centers but also the peripheries of large cities, the bureaucratic State may be present in the form of buildings and officials paid out of public budgets, but the legal State is absent : Whatever formally sanctioned law exists is applied intermittently, if at all.

More importantly, this intermittent law is encompassed by the informal law enacted by the privatized—patrimonial, sultanistic, or simply gangsterlike—powers that actually rule those places. This leads to complex situations involving a continuous renegotiation of the boundaries between formal and informal legalities, situations in which it is vital to understand the interplay between both kinds of law and the uneven power relations that develop.

The resulting informal legal system, punctuated by temporary reintroductions of the formal one, supports a world of extreme violence, as abundant data from both rural and urban regions show. These "brown areas" are subnational systems of power that have a territorial basis and an informal but quite effective legal system, yet they co-exist with a regime that, at least at the national political center, is democratic.

The problems indicate a severe incompleteness of the state, especially its legal dimension. In many cases this incompleteness has increased during democratization, thanks to economic crises and the sternly antistatist economic policies that have prevailed over the past two decades. There is evidence, too, that this deficiency has been fostered by the desire of national politicians to shape winning electoral coalitions by including candidates from the perversely privatized areas. These local politicians use the votes they command and the institutional positions they attain at the center in order to reproduce the systems of privatized power they represent. In Argentina and Brazil, legislators from these "brown" areas have shown a keen interest (with frequent success) in dominating the legislative committees and do not permit legal State to function effectively.

Points of Ruptures in formal legal systems.

In many new (and not so new) democracies, and in other regions, there exist numerous points of rupture in formal legal systems. To the extent that this is true, the rule of law has only intermittent existence. In addition, this observation at the level of the legal State is mirrored by numerous violations of the law at the social level, which jointly amount to a truncated, or low-intensity, citizenship. In these countries, many individuals are citizens with respect to political rights but not in terms of civil rights. Indeed, they are as poor legally as they are materially.

Agencies Supporting rule of Law.

At present, many international and domestic agencies support the expansion of the rule of law as they conceive it, and legions of experts are busy with various aspects of this task. In principle this is not bad news, but there is a danger due to the strong orientation of the resulting legal and judicial reforms towards the perceived interests of the dominant sectors. Typical areas of reform include domestic and international commercial law, some aspects of civil law, and the more purely repressive aspeccs of criminal law. This may be useful for attracting investment, but it tends to produce a "dualistic development of the justice system." centered on those aspects that concern the modernizing sectors of the economic elite in matters of an economic, business, or financial nature—while other areas of litigation and access to justice remain untouched, corrupted, and persistently lacking in infrastructure and resources.

For societies that are profoundly unequal, these trends may reinforce the exclusion of many from the rule of law, while further exaggerating the advantages that the privileged enjoy by means of laws and courts favoring their interests.

Legal status

The CBI was set up by a Government Resolution in April, 1963. It acquired a legal cover under the Delhi Special Police Establishment Act, 1946—"a special police force" to be called "the DSPE". On May 20, 1988, the Union Minister of State for Home and Personnel, P. Chidambaram, told a CBI Officers' conference that the Centre was examining conferment of a legal status on the CBI. "Should it not get legal status to investigate or should we beg State Governments to give us consent to investigate?"

Section 6 of the [DSPE] Act of 1946 bars the CBI from exercising any of its powers in a State "without the consent of the Government of the State." The Constitution makes "police" a State subject exclusively while the CBI is a Union subject. Unlike in the United States, all offences, whether under a Central or State law, are enforced by the State police. The Estimates Committee 1991-92 recommended in its 13th Report to the Lok Sahba on April 6, 1992, the "enactment of a new law laying down the organizational structure of the CBI, functions to be discharged by it, types of offences which it can investigate and providing for conferment of power of

Police laid down in Criminal Procedure Code, 1973, on the members of the CBI." Also recommended was a constitutional amendment to provide for extension of the CBI to any State without the consent of its government. A drat Constitution Amendment Bill and a draft Bill on the CBI were sent to the Home Ministry on June 12, 1990.

Need to respect autonomy

It is unlikely that the States or political parties would consent to a Constitutional amendment. That is no reason for not giving the CBI a charter, to replace the archaic Act of 1946, delete the curbs imposed since, codify its status as a police force and define precisely the powers of "superintendence" which properly belong to the Union. Section 6A was introduced in 2003 to override the Supreme Court's ruling in the *hawala* case. The CBI cannot conduct even a preliminary inquiry into an offence committed by Joint Secretaries "and above". It must be deleted.

The government's affidavit of July 3, 2013 in the Supreme Court offers to bar directions "to investigate or dispose of any case in a particular way." This should be amplified in the light of the past record. The affidavit does not propose deletion of Section 6A. It proposes an Accountability Commission to probe into allegations of misbehaviour against a CBI official. State Police Acts should emulate this and also draw on the model of the Police Complaints Authority set up by Section 83 of the U.K's Police and Criminal Evidence Act, 1984.

Amend the law we must. But unless the political elite respects autonomy, we shall have a spectacle which drew Roy Campbell's withering lines. "They use the snaffle and the bit all right. But where's the bloody horse?"

Special Courts

A stark example of change in the disposal of cases is the impact of additional CBI special courts. About five years ago, the CJI had written to the Union government for the creation of additional special courts for dealing with CBI corruption cases. A figure of 50 cases per court was proposed. The government accepted this figure and proceeded to coordinate with states to have 71 new courts, of which most are operational. Later, another 22 were sought to be added. the impact of this addition has been quite astounding. The disposal of cases since the courts were added is 50 per cent more than it was on an annual basis.

Trials in a number of such special courts proceed on a weekly basis and are concluded within months. And this is after we take into account that abuse of authority and disproportionate assets cases have a large number of witnesses and documentary evidence. These figures show that there needs to be a concerted drive to add to court numbers on an all-India basis.

Fast track Courts

Creating or nominating short-term fast-track courts is not the answer, although it is part of the solution. It is time we studied the "court/case/disposal" ratio for different kinds of cases and added up the numbers to buffer the criminal justice system by creating courts at the trial level and adding judges at the high-court level to ensure that the constitutional imperative of speedy justice is met.

And this planning must be futuristic, with annual or biennial reviews, with the study of the added numbers and disposal rates to ensure adequate infrastructure for the future.

Dimensions of a Democratic Rule of Law

The relevant question concerning the rule of law and democracy should address the various dimensions and degrees along which the attributes of a democratic rule of law, or *estado democratico de derecho*, are present or absent in a given case. This requires convenient analytical disaggregations of the various aspects that the rule of law in general, and the democratic rule of law in particular, include. The next step is to identify the empirical indicators (variables or standards) that may allow a mapping of levels and variations along the various dimensions that have been defined. These tasks, of course, are fraught with difficulties.

Full democratic rule of law has not been reached in any country—and arguably it might be undesirable to do so. Against the somewhat positivistic inclinations of earlier legal views, today practically all theories about law—despite their differences in other respects-hold that, like any other rule, the actual meaning or intent of the laws are defined by the dominant or authorized interpretations. The "proper" interpretation of laws and, indeed, constitutions is one of the great topics around which political battles are fought. Contrary to technocratic and positivistic views, we should never forget that the law, in its content and application, is largely (like the State of which it is a part) a dynamic condensation of power relations, not just a rationalized technique for the ordering of social relations. Societal change, as well as unending struggles for the acquisition of new rights and the reinterpretation of old ones, makes the rule of law, especially the democratic rule of law, a moving horizon.

The dimensions of a democratic rule of law

(1) In relation to the legal system

First, we may look at the degree to which the legal system extends homogeneously across the entire territory of the State—the "brown" areas discussed above in reference in Latin America are clear signs of gaps. In addition, there is the degree to which the legal system behaves uniformly relative to various classes, economic sectors, and other societal groupings. Also, the rule of law entails the enactment and application of rules that prohibit and eventually punish discrimination against the poor, women, foreigners, and various minorities. Especially of concern in many Latin American countries is the degree to which the legal system deals in a respectful and considerate manner with indigenous communities and their legal systems and cultures. Finally, there should be generalized recognition of the supremacy of the Constitution, and a supreme or constitutional court that effectively interprets and protects it.

(2) In relation to the State and the Government

First, we must examine the extent to which there exists a State that exercises effective and law-bound control over its whole territory. Second, there should exist adequately authorized and empowered State institutions for the exercise of horizontal accountability, including in relation to cases of presumed illegal actions (or inactions) by elected officials. Finally, State institutions should treat all individuals with due consideration and respect, and there must be adequate mechanisms for the prevention and redress of situations that ignore this requirement.

(3) In relation to the courts and their auziliary institutions.

The judiciary must be free of undue influences from executive, legislative, and private interests, and if this is the case, the judiciary must not abuse its autonomy for the pursuit of narrowly defined corporate interests. There should be reasonably fair and expeditious access to courts, differentiating by kind of courts. We should also examine the degree to which courts recognize, and to what extent and in what kind of cases, international covenants and treaties, including those on human, gender, childhood, economic, social, and cultural rights. A democratic rule of law should also entail reasonably effective arrangements for ensuring that the poor, the illiterate, and otherwise deprived persons and groups have access to courts and to competent legal counsel. The police and other security forces must respect the rights of all individuals, and individuals should not be held in prison or subject to other ills in violation of basic rules of procedural fairness. Finally, the prisons should be in conditions adequate to the human dignity of the inmates.

(4) In relation to state institutions in general.

A democratic rule of law requires that all state institutions beyond merely the courts treat every-one with fairness, consideration, and respect. The rules that regulate State institutions should be clear, publicly available, and properly enacted. Finally, prompt and effective mechanisms must be in place to prevent, stop, or redress State violations of citizens rights.

(5) In relation to the social context.

Beyond the right to associate in directly political organizations, the right of participation must exist, with at least the civil rights (and eventually the labour rights) of members being upheld. Furthermore, adequate rights and guarantees must exist for the functioning of diverse social organizations and for the exercise of vertical societal accountability.

(6) In relation to civil and human rights.

In terms of assessing the extent to which rights are violated, one should investigate the numbers, social position, gender, age, and geographical location of individuals who are victimized by physical violence, including domestic and police-perpetrated violence. Furthermore, data could be collected on the number and geographical locations of various crimes, especially homicides, armed robberies, and sexual and family violence. Finally, foreigners should be assigned the same civil rights as citizens, should be allowed at least at the local level to participate in political affairs and should be treated by State agents and citizens with due consideration and respect.

Much has been said and written lately concerning the rule of law. To this large amount of discourse I would like to add the regretful observation that at times the rule of law (or at any rate, the rhetoric of the rule of law) has been employed in the service of authoritarian ideologies. In earlier times, in countries ridden by severe inequality as so many in Latin America have been (and too often still are), practices associated with the law were not used in the service of fairness, but rather to entrench sharp inequalities and the manifold social ills associated with them.

'Rule of law must for good governance'

Adherence to the rule of law is the fundamental prerequisite to good governance.

Grids of good government

"Good governance is critically dependent on existence of some fundamental prerequisites. At the core is the inviolable adherence to the rule of law. From it would emanate critical need for participatory decision-making structure, transparency, responsiveness, accountability, equity and inclusiveness". "It is important to ensure speedy and thorough investigation of allegations. The prosecution should also be speedy so that the guilty are punished without delay. This would enhance the deterrent value of punishment."

Lack of good governance, "robs the citizenry of their security, and their social and economic rights."

While remarkable progress in "several grids" of good governance had been achieved since Independence, country needed to improve participatory decision making, the application of rule of law, enhance transparency, increase accountability and promote greater equity and inclusiveness.

"CBI of today has the foundation of a world class enforcement agency, we need to take not of the dynamic changes in the environment. There are growing grassroots voices against corruption. The public expects it to act with greater effectiveness and speed. the advances in information technology are increasingly encompassing most areas of work. New age cyber and economic crimes need new skills and upgradation of existing knowledge."

"Anti corruption is moving to the mainstream of international economic relations. The increasing engagement of Indian economy with ASEAN, EU and SAARC member countries is expected to have major implications on the nature of our work...In short, CBI has to prepare to work across the globe. This can only be done by putting in place the requisite human and systems capacity backed with a clear vision for the future."

❑ ❑

Chapter 17

Independent Judiciary and Judicial Process

Judicial independence is the concept that the judiciary needs to be kept away rom the other branches of government. That is, courts should not be subject to improper influence from the other branches of government, or from private or partisan interests. Judicial Independence is vital and important to the idea of separation of powers.

Different countries deal with the idea of judicial independence through different means of judicial selection, or choosing judges. One way to promote judicial independence is by granting life tenure or long tenure for judges, which ideally frees them to decide cases and make rulings according to the rule of law and judicial discretion, even if those decisions are politically unpopular or opposed by powerful interests. This concept can be traced back to 18th century England.

In some countries, the ability of the judiciary to check the legislature is enhanced by the power of judicial review. This power can be used, for example, by mandating certain action when the judiciary perceives that a branch of government is refusing to perform a constitutional duty, or by declaring laws passed by the legislature unconstitutional.

Economic basis

Constitutional economics studies issues such as the proper distribution of natural wealth including government spending on the judiciary. In transitional and developing countries, spending on the judiciary may be controlled by the executive. This undermines the principle of judicial independence because it creates a financial dependence of the judiciary on the executive. It is important to distinguish between two methods of corruption of the judiciary : the state (through budget planning and privileges) being the most dangerous, and private. State corruption of the judiciary can impede the ability of business to optimally facilitate the growth and development of a market economy.

In some countries, the constitution also prohibits the legislative branch from reducing salaries of sitting judges.

Development of the concept

National and international developments

The development of judicial independence has been argued to involve a cycle of national law having an impact on international law, and international law subsequently impacting national laws. This is said to occur in three phases : the first phase is characterized by the domestic development of the concept of judicial independence, the second by the spread of these concepts internationally and their implementation in international law, and the third by the implementation in national law of these newly formulated international principles of judicial independence.

A notable example illustrating this cycle is the United Kingdom. The first phase occurred in England with the original conception of judicial independence in the Act of Settlement 1701. the second phase was evident when England's concepts regarding judicial independence spread internationally, and were adopted into the domestic law of other countries; for instance, England served as the model for Montesquieu's separation of powers doctrine, and the Founding Fathers of the US Constitution used England as their dominant model in formulating the Constitution's Article III, which is the foundation of American judicial independence. Other common law countries, including Canada, Australia, and India, also adopted the British model of judicial independence.

In recent decades the third phase of judicial independence has been evident in the U.K., as it has been significantly influenced by judicial independence principles developed by international human rights constitutional documents. The European Court of Human Rights (ECtHR) has had a significant impact on the conceptual analysis of judicial independence in England and Scotland. This process began in the 1990s with the ECtHR hearing UK cases and, more significantly, in the application of the European Convention on Human Rights in British law through the Human Rights Act, 1998. which came into force in the UK in 2000.

Where British national law had previously impacted the international development of judicial independence, the British Constitutional Reform Act, 2005 marked a shift, with international law now impacting British domestic law. The Constitutional Reform Act dramatically reformed government control over the administration of justice in England and Wales; importantly, it discontinued the position of the Lord Chancellor, one of the country's oldest constitutional offices, who was entrusted with a combination of legislative, executive, and judicial capacities. The Lord Chancellor served as speaker of the Upper House of Parliament, the House of Lords; as a member of the executive branch and member of the senior cabinet; and as the head of the judiciary. Historically, the appellate function had a connection with the executive branch due to the types of cases typically heard—impeachment and the hearing of felony charges against peers. The Constitutional Reforms Act established new lines of demarcation between the Lord Chancellor and the judiciary, transferring all the judicial functions to the judiciary and entrusting the Lord Chancellor only with what are considered administrative and executive matters. In addition, the Constitutional Reform Act replaced the Lord Chancellor by the Lord Chief Justice as head of the judiciary, separated the judicial Appellate Committee of the House of Lords from the legislative parliament, reforming it as the Supreme Court, and creating a Judicial Appointments Commission. The creation of the Supreme Court was important, for it finally separated the highest court of appeal from the House of Lords.

Thus, the United Kingdom, where judicial independence began over three hundred years ago, illustrates the interaction over time of national and international law and jurisprudence in the area of judicial independence. In this process, concepts and ideas have become enriched as they have been implemented in successive judicial and political systems, as each system has enhanced and deepened the concepts and ideas it actualized. In addition to the UK, similar developments of conceptual cross-fertilization can be seen internationally, for example in European Union law, in civil law countries such as Austria, and in other common law jurisdictions including Canada.

International standards

The International Association of Judicial Independence and World Peace produced the Mt. Scopus International Standards of Judicial Independence between 2007 and 2012. These built on the same association's New Delhi Minimum Standards on Judicial independence adopted in 1982 and their Montreal Universal Declaration on the Independence of Justice in 1983. Other influences they cite for the standards include the UN Basis Principles of Judicial Independence from 1985, the Burgh House Principles of Judicial Independence in International Law (for the international judiciary), Tokyo Law Asia Principles, Council of Europe Statements on judicial independence (particularly the Recommendation of the Committee of Ministers to Member States on the independence, efficiency and role of judges), the Bangalore Principles of Judicial Conduct 2002, and the American Bar Association's revision of its ethical standards for judges.

The justice system

In recent years, the principle of judicial independence has been described as one of the core values of the justice system.

Canada

Canada has a level of judicial independence entrenched in its Constitution, awarding superior court justices various guarantees to independence under Section 96 to 100 of the Constitution Act, 1867. These include rights to tenure (although the Constitution has since been amended to introduce mandatory retirement at age 75) and the right to a salary determined by the Parliament of Canada (as opposed to the executive). In 1982 a measure of judicial independence was extended to inferior courts specializing in criminal law (but not civil law) by Section 11 of the Canadian Charter of Rights and Freedoms, although in the 1986 case *Valente* v. *The Queen*, it was found these rights are limited. They do, however, involve tenure, financial security and some administrative control.

The year 1997 saw a major shift towards judicial independence, as the Supreme Court of canada in the Provincial Judges Reference found an unwritten constitutional norm guaranteeing judicial independence to all judges, including civil law inferior court judges. The unwritten norm is said to be implied by the preamble to the Constitution Act, 1867. Consequently, judicial compensation committees such as the Judicial Compensation and

Benefits Commission now recommend judicial salaries in Canada. There are two types of judicial independence : institutional independence and decisional independence. Institutional independence means the judicial branch is independent from the executive and legislative branches. Decisional independence is the idea that judges should be able to decide cases solely based on the law and facts, without letting the media, politics or other concerns sway their decisions, and without fearing penalty in their careers for their decisions.

Hong Kong

In Hong Kong, independence of the judiciary has been the tradition since the territory became a British crown colony in 1842. After the 1997 transfer of sovereignty of Hong Kong to the People's Republic of China pursuant to the Sino-British Joint Declaration, an international treaty registered with the United Nations, independence of the judiciary, along with continuation of English common law, has been enshrined in the territory's constitutional document, the Basic Law. In recent years, this independence has been put into question after a number of interventions from China on several cases which swayed rulings in the Executive's favour, most notably the Hong Kong Legislative Council oath-taking controversy of 2016.

United Kingdom

History

During the middle ages, under the Normal monarchy of the Kingdom of England, the king and his Curia Regis held judicial power. Judicial independence began to emerge during the early modern period; more courts were created and a judicial profession grew. By the fifteenth century, the king's role in this feature of government became small. Nevertheless, kings could still influence courts and dismiss judges. The Stuart dynasty used this power frequently in order to overpower the Parliament of England. After the Stuarts were removed in the Glorious Revolution of 1688, some advocated guarding against royal manipulation of the judiciary. King William III approved the Act of Settlement 1701, which established tenure for judges unless Parliament removed them.

Contemporary usage

Under the uncodified British Constitution, there are two important conventions which help to preserve judicial independence. The first is that the Parliament of the United Kingdom does not comment on the cases which are before the court. The second is the principle of parliamentary privilege : that Members of Parliament are protected from prosecution in certain circumstances by the courts.

Furthermore, the independence of the judiciary is guaranteed by the Constitutional Reform Act, 2005. In order to try to promote the independence of the judiciary, the selection process is designed to minimize political interference. The process focuses on senior members of the judiciary rather than on politicians. Part 2 of the Tribunals, Courts and Enforcement Act, 2007 aims to increase diversity among the judiciary.

The pay of judges is determined by an independent pay review body. It makes recommendations to the government after taking evidence from a variety of sources. The government accepts these recommendations and will traditionally implement them fully. As long as judges hold their positions in "good order", they remain in post until they wish to retire or until they reach the mandatory retirement age of 70.

As of March 2008, the legal profession is self-regulating; it is responsible for implementating and enforcing its own professional standards and disciplining its own members. The bodies which perform this function are the Bar Council and the Law Society. However, this self-regulation will come to an end when these bodies come under the regulation of the Legal Services Board, composed of non-lawyers, under the Legal Services Act, 2007.

United States of America

Federal courts

Article III of the United States Constitution establishes the federal courts as part of the federal government.

The Constitution provides that federal judges, including judges of the Supreme Court of the United States, are appointed by the President "by and with the advice and consent of the Senate." Once appointed, federal judges :

...both the Supreme and inferior Courts, shall hold their Office during good Behaviour, and shall, at stated times, receive for their Services a Compensation which shall not be diminished during their Continuance in Office.

Federal judges vacate office only upon death, resignation, or impeachment and removal from office by Congress; only 13 federal judges have ever been impeached. The phrase "during good behaviour" predates the Declaration of Independence. John Adams equated it with *quamdiu se bene gesserint* in a letter to the Boston Gazette published on 11th January, 1773, a phrase that first appeared in Section 3 of the Act of Settlement 1701 in England.

The President is free to appoint any person to the federal bench, yet typically he consults with the American Bar Association, whose Standing Committee on the Federal Judiciary rates each nominee "Well Qualified", "Qualified" or "Not Qualified".

State courts

State courts deal with independence of the judiciary in may ways, and several forms of judicial selection are used for both trial courts and appellate courts (including state supreme courts), varying between states and sometimes within states. In some states, judges are elected (sometime on a partisan ballot, other times on a non-partisan one), while in others they are appointed by the governor or State Legislature.

Independence of judiciary means it is free from other organs of the State, especially executive, and legislative body. It must be from power pressure or other undue thing. Independence means "the state or condition of being free from dependence, subjection, or control. Political independence is the attribute of a nation or State which is entirely autonomous, and not subject to the Government, control, or dictation of any exterior power." The word judiciary means "that branch of Government invested with the judicial power; the system of court in a country; the body of judge, the bench that branch of Government which is intended to interpret, construe and apply the law."

Judicial independence is the doctrine that decisions of the judiciary should be impartial and not subject to influence from the other branch of Government or from private or political interests. In most cases, judicial independence is secured by giving judges long, and sometimes lifetime, tenure and making them not easily removeable. "Judicial independence means that judges are free to decide cases fairly and impartially relying only on the facts and law.' Dr. Laxmimal Sindhawi clears that "concept of independence of judiciary is also relative and not absolute. Judicial independence is not yet a finished product and there is no perfect model anywhere in the world.

The concept of independence of judiciary has two aspects—functional and structural independence. Functional independence means the freedom of the individual judges or the judiciary to decide the issues before it. The judiciary shall decide matters before them impartially, on the basis of fact and in accordance with the law without any restrictions, improper influences, pressures, threats on interferences, direct or indirect from any quarter or for any reason. The judiciary shall have jurisdiction over all issues of a judicial nature and shall have exclusive authority to decision within its competence as defined by law. There shall not be any inappropriate unwarranted interference with the judicial process, nor shall judicial decisions by the courts be subject to revision. The principle is without prejudice to judicial review or to mitigation or commutation by competent authorities of sentences imposed by the judiciary, in accordance with the law. Beside these the court must be impartial and competent. Structural independence of the judiciary denotes mainly the autonomy of the judiciary or it is free from other organs of the state so that all probable interference can be exclusive. "It is the duty of each member State to provide adequate resources to enable the judiciary to properly perform its functions". It is the duty of the State to provide adequate financial resources to allow for the due administration of justice. In this way, judicial independence means freedom from direction, control or interference in the exercise of judicial power by either the executive or legislature. Independent judiciary is backbone of the democratic State. In the beginning of the development of the concept functional independence of the judiciary was regarded as sufficient requisite. But in modern era both structural and functional independence are equally important for independence of the judiciary.

Development of the independence of judiciary

Judiciary independence emerged slowly in the United Kingdom and later in Europe. Under the Norman Monarchy, the King and his Curia Regis held judicial power. Later, however, more courts were created and a judicial profession grew. In the fifteenth century, the king's role in this feature of Government thus becomes small. Nevertheless, kings could still influence courts, and could dismiss a judge. The Stuart dynasty used this power frequently in order to overpower parliament. After the Stuarts were removed in the glorious revolution of 1688, some advocated guarding against royal manipulation of the judiciary. Thus, King William III finally approved the Act of settlement 1701, which established tenure for judges unless parliament removed them. The Supreme Court Judicature Act, 1925 was introduced as a first step towards the independent judiciary.

The concept of independence of judiciary was introduced in 18th century when the doctrine of separation of power was formulated in the political and legal field. After the American independence, the Constitution of USA accepted the notion of the independent judiciary. They incorporated independent judiciary in Art 3 of the U.S. Constitution, in this Constitution various provisions like criteria of appointment, tenure, court jurisdiction etc. have been mentioned. The U.S. court developed the doctrine of *ultra vires* on the ground when ordinary law is inconsistent with the constitution. The conceptual development of independence of judiciary in Nepal is not so long before the restoration of democracy though the Constitution did not prioritize the judicial independence. The Constitution of Kingdom of Nepal, 2017 laid the milestone for the independence of the judiciary in Nepal.

Importance of independent judiciary

Independent and competent judiciary is necessary for the protection of civil liberties in the democratic State. Judicial functions are always subject to public scrutiny. The primary beneficiary of judicial independence is not the judiciary itself but the society at large, the structural and functional independence of the judiciary has unique importance.

"The Constitution guarantees the three basic principles of the modern concept of constitutionalism-justice, liberty and equality in addition to attempting to establish a framework for the achievement of economic prosperity and national unity. For achieving the objectives, various organs of the State and specialized agencies are created by the Constitution to work towards them one of which is the judiciary. In many ways the judiciary is the main institution on which the responsibility of a free Government rests." Without justice being freely, fully and impartially administered, therefore, neither individuals, nor rights, nor the property of any person, could be protected." The doctrine of separation of power, which was pronounced by Moresque, insists on the exercise of the power of the Government by three separate organs-executive, legislature and judiciary. An independent judiciary plays a vital role to check the power of executive and legislature. Only the independent judiciary can protect the rights of the minorities and the indigenous communities. Independent judiciary maintains the supremacy of the Constitution. Independence of judiciary helps to ensure rule of law in the country and protects the country from entering into anarchy. It is universally accepted that without an independent judiciary safeguard of the right of the people is impossible. "The judiciary plays an important role in the transitional justice initiatives such as reconciliation, rehabilitation, and reconstruction and in ensuring respect for human rights, combating impunity, building sense of confidence in the rule of law enhancing effectiveness of the State institution."

Basic components of independence of judiciary

There are different models of the judiciary in the world so that no single country can claim its judiciary is perfect. There are some basic norms, which are accepted by the international community through conferences, symposium workshop etc. They are accepted as basic components of judicial independence, which are selection or appointment, transfer, tenure, salary and privileges, security of office, process of removal etc. if these components are fully incorporated in national law judiciary will certainly be more independent. An independent judiciary requires the following basic minimum.

(1) adequate constitutional and legal provisions to insulate judges from illegal pressures and influences from non judicial authorities
(2) adequate physical infrastructure for discharge of judicial functions
(3) well educated and well trained judges
(4) well trained and competent court staff
(5) secured and adequate resources for court administration, and
(6) proper mechanism for disciplining judges and ensuring their accountability.

Basic principles of independence of judiciary were

Adopted by seventh United Nations Congress on the prevention of crime and treatment of offenders held at Milan from 26 August to September 1985 and endorsed by General Assembly resolution 40/32 of 29 November 1985 and 40/146 of 13 December 1985. These include;

1. Legal authority

The independence of judiciary should be guaranteed by the Constitution or law of the country. The judiciary shall decide matters before them impartially based on facts and in accordance with the law without any restrictions, improper influences, inducements, pressures, threats or interferences, direct or indirect, from any quarter or for any reason. All issues of judicial nature must come into the ambit of jurisdiction of the court. The judiciary must be free from any improper and unwarranted interference and the decisions of the court should not be the subject of review, everyone has the right to be produced in an ordinary court or tribunal for trial and there should not be any encroachment on the jurisdiction of the court.

2. Freedom of expression and association

According to Sections 8 and 9 the basic of the independence of judiciary is freedom of expression, belief, association and assembly of the members of the judiciary like other ordinary citizens. The judge should exercise this freedom in such a manner as to preserve the dignity of their office and the impartiality and independence of the judiciary. This freedom for the judge is to promote their professional training and to protect their judicial independence.

3. Qualification, selection and training

Persons selected for judicial office shall be individuals of integrity and ability with appropriate training or qualification in law. Any method of judicial selection shall safeguard against judicial appointments for improper motives. In the selection of judge, there shall be no discrimination against a person on the grounds of race, colour, sex, religion, political and other opinion, national or social origin, property, birth or status, except that a requirement, that he must be a national of the country concerned, shall not be considered discriminatory.

4. Condition of service and tenure

The term of the office of judge, their independence, security, adequate remuneration and conditions of service, pensions and the age of retirement must be adequately secured by law. The tenure of the judges except their voluntary retirement must be fixed by the law. Promotion of judge should be based on objective factor, in particular ability, integrity and experience. The promotion proceedings should be in the initiation of the judiciary itself or of a board or commission where there is a majority of judicial persons. The judges should maintain professional secrecy and immunity in the course of their duty. There must be an atmosphere for the judges to enjoy personal immunity from civil suits for monetary damages, for improper acts or ommissions in the exercise of their judicial functions.

5. Discipline, suspension and removal

Judges have a right for fair hearing when a charge is against him. The examination of the matter at its initial stage shall be kept confidential, unless otherwise requested by the judge. All disciplinary, suspension or removal proceedings shall be determined in accordance with established standards of judicial conduct."

Decisions in disciplinary, suspension or removal proceedings should be subject to an independent review. This principle may not apply to the decisions of the highest court and those of the legislature in impeachment or similar proceedings.

6. Transfer of judge

Improper transfer of the judge may affect the independence of the judiciary though timely transfer is essential sometimes for fair and impartial justice. Judge must not be transferred by the executive from one jurisdiction or functions to another without their consent, but when a transfer is in pursuance of an uniform policy formulated by the executive after due consultation with the judiciary, such consent shall not be unreasonably withheld by an individual judge.

7. Professional immunity

The judges should enjoy personal immunity from civil suits for monetary damages for improper acts or omission in the exercise of their judicial duty. A judge should enjoy immunity from legal action and the obligation to testify concerning matters arising in the exercise of his official functions. The judiciary has also the power to punish in the case of contempt of court, this power of the judiciary helps it to enjoy professional immunity.

8. Autonomy; Judicial as well as financial

Unless there is judicial autonomy there can be no judicial independence. Judicial autonomy has various dimensions *i.e.* financial autonomy, administrative autonomy and rule making autonomy.

Financial autonomy includes the self-regulatory right of the judiciary for its annual budget. The judiciary must have right to submit its budget directly to the Legislature. It must be able to allocate its budget internally within the judiciary. Administrative autonomy means right to regular organizational structures, improvement of its staffing and remuneration system, filling up of positions, disciplinary actions of the employers subject to the personal management policies and civil service rules.

The provisions about the judiciary in the Constitution express full commitment to independence of the judiciary and concepts of the rule of law. It shows that the Constitution reflects the commitment of the nation towards an independent judiciary and the concept of rule of law. The chief justice has the ultimate responsibility to make the administration of justice.

The Constitution has clear provision for the appointment of judge. Qualifications are fixed. Constitution provided the tenure of the office of the chief justice and judges. Salary of the judges is fixed and remuneration and privilege of the judge of the Supreme Court are chargeable on the consolidated fund. There is restriction for discussion of the conduct of the judges. Courts have power to punish for the contempt of court. Supreme Court has power to judicial review and to issue writs and necessary order. Orders and decisions of court are binding. The collegium of the judges is responsible for the appointment, transfer and disciplinary action of judges of all courts. Provision of the judiciary service commission. Judiciary should be separated from the executive and legislature. Separation of power is necessary for independent judiciary. Theory of separation of power seems to be incorporated in the Constitution.

The Constitutional provision contradicts with international standards *i.e.* the provision that the Chief Justice can be assigned to another work than his regular job. The provision of appointment of *ad hoc* and additional judge. The judiciary must realize the spirit of the people's movement. The judges serving in the Supreme Court and High Courts take an oath of commitment to Constitution in such form as determined. Any judge who refuses to take an oath shall *ipso facto* be relieved of his or her office.

Independence of a judge

The Constitution focuses on the individual independence of the judge.

Lack of functional autonomy *i.e.* determining the jurisdiction of the court, selecting its support staff, and financial autonomy. Fundamental freedom of judge is the means to protect the judicial independence but the Constitution has not spoken about the freedom of expression and association of the judges. Constitutional arrangements for the independence of the judiciary adequately meet the international standards. Judiciary is one of the organs of the State. The independence of the judiciary is the cornerstone of a democratic system. Without independent judiciary, people cannot get justice. Only the independent, impartial and accountable judiciary can protect the rights of the minorities and the indigenous communities. Independent judiciary can maintain the delicate balance between the three major organs of the State. Some of internationally recognized principles have been incorporated in our present Constitution. But basic principle *i.e.* judicial autonomy, freedom of expression and association, professional immunity are not incorporated. Our judiciary lacks functional autonomy to determining the jurisdiction of the court, selecting its support staff. Another issue is concerning the financial independence of judiciary which is a must for an independent judiciary. Judiciary training, judicial education is necessary for independence of judiciary. Role of national judicial academic is satisfactory in this regard.

Independence of Judiciary—Some latent dangers

The Constitution has tried to insulate the Judiciary from outside influence both from the Executive and the Legislature. Independence of the judiciary constitutes the foundation on which rests the edifice of Democratic Polity. The general concept of Judicial Independence is that a judge should be free from any pressure from the Government or anyone else as to how to decide any particular case; for that reason, a judges salary is not dependent on the Executive decision and his conditions of service are secured and not to be varied at the whim of the Executives.

No financial independence

Thing have changed in the recent past, particularly in the last 40 years. There has been a great upsurge in crime and criminal litigation, and equally in the number of civil disputes. So to say, there is unmanageable docket explosion in every court. To meet this challenge there has to be a large increase in the number of judges, courts, court staff and other infrastructure. But no such increase has been made. Even in the existing courts, the working conditions in most of them are unsatisfactory. The courts do not have financial independence, since finance falls under the Executive control. The judges are not provided with the up-to-date statutes or law books. They are generally under the mercy of lawyers to provide copies of the decisions or enactments relied during the course of arguments. The judges are not given proper training either at the induction level or periodical refresher courses. Commenting on the similar conditions in the British Justice System which existed at one time, Lord Delvin opined : "If our business methods were as antiquated as our legal system, we would have become a bankrupt nation long back."

Judges are not civil servants

These deficiencies are indeed, subtle threat to the Independence of Judicial System. The independence of legal system depends upon the manner in which the system is operated, and how Judges are provided for : "........The service conditions of the Judges should not be linked to those of the Executive and the service conditions of the Judges have to be revised to meet the special needs of the judicial service"......"The Judicial Officers throughout the country perform the work of the same nature and, therefore, their service conditions have to be uniform and it should be examined by separate Commission and the State should not make a grievance if their service conditions are improved,"....... "The exertion involved in the duties of the Judge cannot be compared with the duties of other services and the judicial service by its very nature stand on a different footing and should be treated as such."

Periodic raise in salary

The Judiciary's reliance upon Government for periodic increase in remuneration entails an obvious potential for impairment of judicial independence. As the Chief Justice of Australia has noted : "Those who control the purse strings will always have some capacity to influence the actions of those who are dependent upon the content of the purse..... There can be no doubt that executive Government control over judicial salary fixation is always at least an incipient threat to judicial independence."

As a Canadian Judge puts it more bluntly : "When you are reduced to begging for a decent salary, how can you be truly independent?" The devastating effects of inadequate remuneration of the judges in the long run can only lead to worsening morale and eroding commitment to service. The losers are, however, not the judges in the ultimate analysis, rather it is the pubic. The public have to go before the courts for critical decisions in cases effecting law and order, cases that affect their civil and legal rights, involving their lives and liberties, their welfare. Public cannot afford to entrust such cases in the hands of dissatisfied judges.

Service conditions

Senator Henry Clay during the debate in the House of Representatives warned : "The labourer is worthy of his hire; and if you do not give him the wages of honesty, it is to be apprehended the wages of corruption may, in the process of time, come to be sought." Therefore, improving the service conditions of our judges is not in the interest of the judges alone, but in the interest of the sound and efficient administration of justice as well. "If Judges have to live in mean houses, wear cheap clothes..... not only would their work suffer by reason of their mental discomfort but the present high estimation in which the judiciary is everywhere held would also suffer. If the members of the judiciary are not regarded with respect, their impartiality will, such is human nature, come to be doubted...."

In the words of Churchill : "Our aim is not to make our judges wealthy men, but to satisfy their needs and to maintain a modest and a dignified way of life suited to the gravity, and indeed, the majesty, of the duties they discharge."

Cost of living rising

In the Commentary 'Justice for Judges : The road blocks on the path to Judicial Compensation Reform' by Kristen A. Holt : In 2005, Chief Justice John G. Roberts, Jr. warned that, "Our system of justice suffers as the real salary of the judges continues to decline, if Congress give judges a raise of 30% tomorrow, judges would after adjusting for inflation be making about what judges made in 1969." Between 1990-2005, "92 judges...left the bench and 59 of them stepped down to enter the private practice of law."

These developments are disturbing in the light of dramatically increasing case loads and constantly rising cost of living. Through United States Constitution's Compensation Clause, salaries are guaranteed to all judges under Article III, "which shall not be diminished during their continuance of office." For over 30 years, judicial compensation has been inherently unreliable. This financial uncertainty directly relates to a steady stream of attrition of capable Judges from the bench. The loss of judges is having a deleterious impact on the fabric of our Judiciary. As qualified an experienced judge's leave, current judges overextend themselves to bear an increasing number of complex cases until replacements are found. As a result, not only is there a problem of retention, but there is a decreasing pool of capable individuals willing to be considered for judgeship. Moreover, concerns exist regarding the number of applicants for federal judgeships, as well as the quality of those individuals. The fiscal reality of current judicial compensation threatens this diversity because only economically well situated lawyers can afford to accept an appointment as Judges. Anecdotal evidence suggests that part of the judicial compensation grid clock problem relates to a basic political reality. Members of Congress must run for re-election every 2 or 6 years and, therefore, are continually fundraising and campaigning. In contrast, federal judges receive life time appointments and a generous retirement package.

Therefore, members of Congress may hesitate to approve any judicial compensation plan, whether temporary or long term, to increase judicial salaries to a level above their own. This political reality may call for more creative solutions to the judicial compensation dilemma. Article III, Section 1 of the U.S. Constitution establishes that "the judges, both of the Supreme and inferior Courts, shall hold their offices during good behaviour, and shall, at stated times, receive for their services, a compensation, which shall not be diminished during their continuance in office." Alexander Hamilton emphasized the proper balance of power between the legislative and judicial branches of Government, stating that "in the general course of human nature, a power over a man's subsistence amounts to a power over his will." He asserted that in order to specifically protect the vulnerability of the judiciary, "next to permanency in office, nothing can contribute more to the independence of the judges, than a fixed provision for their support." Thus, the framers acknowledge the importance of an independent judiciary in structure of United States Government while further recognizing that in order to preserve judicial independence, it would be imperative to preserve a secure means of financial support for judges.

Public criticism

The other aspect relates to the public criticism regarding the functioning of judiciary. The public criticism includes among others, the delay in disposal of cases; unsatisfactory judgments and creeping corruptions in some quarters. The judiciary cannot afford to be indifferent to these criticisms. The cost of providing justice is like other calls on the public revenues. All persons and departments who utilize the public revenue are accountable to the public. The judges cannot be an exception to this recognized principle. They are equally accountable for their acts and omissions both on the Bench and off the Bench. It is therefore, necessary for the judges, individually and collectively, to ensure that no criticism is levelled against them or against the system.

Misbehaviour by judges increasing

"Misbehaviour by any Judge, whether it takes place on the Bench or off the Bench, undermines public confidence in the administration of justice and also damages public respect for the law of the land, if nothing is seen to be done about it, the damage goes unrepaired."

Corruption

According to a new Transparency International report : Corruption undermines judicial systems worldwide, released on 25-5-07, the majority of people in nearly all Southest European countries consider their judicial and legal system corrupt. "When courts are corrupted by the greed or political expediency, the scales of justice are tipped, and ordinary people suffer. Judicial corruption means the voice of the innocent goes unheard, while the guilty act with impunity."

Global Corruption Report 2007 : Corruption in Judicial Systems distinguishes two categories of judicial corruption :

(i) political interference by the legislative or executive branch, and

(ii) bribery.

According to a survey conducted between June and September 2006, the group said that the majority of respondents in 33 of the 62 countries polled described their national judiciary and legal system as corrupt. The report also stated that of the 8,263 people who had been in contact with the judicial system recently more than one in ten had paid a bribe. The situation appears to be worst in Paraguay, where nearly 90% of the respondents have described their judiciary and legal system as corrupt. With less than 10% of Danes perceiving their judiciary as corrupt, Denmark is the cleanest of the 62 countries. In the SEE region, the percentage of people describing their country's judicial and legal system as corrupt ranges between 54% in Greece and slightly over 80% in Macedonia, which is 4th on the list. About 78% of

Croats consider their judiciary to be corrupt, placing the country 7th on the list. Bulgaria is 9th, Turkey is 16th and Albania is 26th. Next comes Romania, then Serbia as 29th and Greece is 31st. Within the region, Kosovo is the only territory where fewer than 50% of the respondents described the judiciary and legal system as corrupt.

It also stated that while 23% of people in North America and 19% of those living in EU or other Western European nations had contact with the judiciary in the past year, the figure for the SEE countries for the period was only 9%. However, 9% of those who had contact with the judiciary reportedly paid a bribe. In North America and in the EU and in other Western European nations only 2% and 1%, respectively paid bribes. It offers a number of recommendations to improve judicial independence and combat corruption. These includes judicial appointments made by the independent panels, making judges' appointments based on merits, and making salaries in the sector reflect Magistrates' experience and performance. Furthermore, judges should receive limited immunity for actions related to judicial duties and allegations against them should be rigorously investigated by an independent panel.

Former Chief Justice of Supreme Court, J.S. Verma said regarding the accountability of the judges. "There is no point in saying that there is no corruption in the judiciary. No one is going to say it much less accepted. One cannot go on sweeping it under the carpet and not accept it to show"........ "When moral sanction doesn't work, then legal sanction is required."

Citing the example of Shiv Prasad Sinha, a judge of Allahabad High Court, he said, "There were allegations against him and the finding was that some judgments of his appeared to be made for extraneous considerations....." At a meeting of the Supreme Court on May 7th, 1997 two resolutions were adopted.

One, that the Chief Justice should devise an 'in-house procedure' for enforcing accountability.

And two, all judges should declare their assets. The 'in-house procedure' is also stuck now because there is no mode of enforcement.

"Judicial independence means independence from your own infirmities. Latent dangers are more lethal. Unless you have fearless and independent judges, judicial independence is a myth..... If in a court of 20 there are 2 judges whose integrity for good reason is doubtful." In a recent decision, the Supreme Court has reiterated the high standard of moral and ethical behaviour expected from a judge, and the desirability of a suitable 'in-house procedure' to maintain discipline among judges by self-regulation. Justice Karnan's conduct is unprecedented (2017).

'In most present-day Western political systems the authority of Governmental institutions is no longer self-evident. The role of modern judiciaries has substantially changed over the years; its bearing and weight as a law maker has increased *vis-a-vis* the administration and the Legislature due to the growing complexity of society. The original legitimization of judicial action lies in the independent role of judge as an arbiter operating under the rule of law, judging conflicts, supervising and reviewing State actions, this new judiciary is activist, with new responsibilities in the field of law making and even policy making. New judiciaries like this, partly performing on the political platform, can no longer be totally shielded by judicial independence from public control and public accountability. If we want the rule of law values to be effective in a new setting, new forms of control and accountability for the judiciary may be warranted. Transparency, openness, a more efficient delivery of justice, and new forms of interaction between politics and judiciary are the modern buzzwords in debates on the accountability and legitimacy of non-elected organisations.

Accountability.—Hard accountability for the judiciary entails that judges can only be scrutinized and held answerable indirectly for their professional functioning. This method traditionally is aloof in order not to compromise judicial independence. These methods of accountability evidently provide legitimacy to judicial authority. Soft accountability, on the other hand, is not indirect, but deals with the openness and representation of the judiciary in a more direct way. This type of accountability demands procedural transparency, representation and sensitivity as regards different interests and needs of a changing social environment.

Credibility.—"A basic postulate of the rule of law is that 'justice should not only be done but it must also be seen to be done'.... Credibility in the functioning of the justice delivery system and the reasonable perception of the affected parties are relevant considerations to ensure the continuance of public confidence in the credibility and impartiality of the judiciary. This is necessary not only for doing justice but also for ensuring that justice is seen to be done." The review of all the Judicial Officers at the age of 50, 55 and 60 years for compulsory retirement by the procedure prescribed by the respective Service Rules should be undertaken regularly.

There should be continuing Committee of senior Judges of the High Court headed by the Chief Justice for this purpose of review. "It is incumbent for each occupant of every high office to be constantly aware that the power invested in the high office he holds is meant to be exercised in public interest and only for public good, and that it is not meant to be used for any personal benefit or merely to elevate the personal status of the current holder of that office. Constant awareness of the nature of this power and the purpose for which it is meant would prevent situations leading to clash of egos and the resultant fall out is detrimental to public interest."

According to the Charter of the United Nations the peoples of the world affirm, *inter alia*, their determination to establish conditions under which justice can be maintained to achieve International co-operation in promoting and encouraging respect for human rights and fundamental freedoms without any discrimination. Whereas Universal Declaration of human Rights enshrines in particular the principles of equality before the law, of the presumption of innocence and of the right to a fair and public hearing by a competent, independent and impartial tribunal established by law. International Covenant on Economic and Cultural Rights and on Civil and

Political Rights both guarantee the exercise of those rights, and addition, the Covenant on Civil and Political Rights further guarantees the right to be tried without undue delay. The sixth United Nations Congress on Prevention of Crime and the Treatment of Offenders, by its Resolution 16, called upon the Committee on Crime Prevention and Control to include among its priorities the elaboration of guidelines relating to the independence of judges and the selection, professional training and the status of judges and the prosecutors.

Independence of Judiciary whether truncated by the Judicial Standards and Accountability Bill, 2010

Some notable features—

(1) The Judicial Standards and Accountability Bill, 2010 was introduced in the Lok Sabha on December 1, 2010. The Bill was introduced by Shri M. Veerappa Moily, the Minister of Law and Justice.

(2) The Bill seeks to (a) lay down judicial standards, (b) provide for the accountability of judges, and (c) establish mechanisms for investigating individual complaints for misbehaviour or incapacity of a judge of the Supreme Court or High Courts. It also provides a mechanism for the removal of judges.

(3) The procedure of removal of judges is presently regulated by the Judges (Inquiry) Act, 1968. The Bill seeks to repeal the Act.

(4) The Bill requires judges to practise universally accepted values of judicial life. These include a prohibition on : (a) close association with individual members of the Bar who practice in the same court as the judge, (b) allowing family members who are members of the Bar to use the judge's residence for professional work, (c) hearing or deciding matters in which a member of the judge's family or relative or friend is concerned, (d) entering into public debate on political matters or matters which the judge is likely to decide, and (e) engaging in trade or business and speculation in securities.

(5) Judges will also be required to declare their assets and liabilities, and also that of their spouse and children. Such declaration has to take place within 30 days of the judge taking his oath to enter his office. Every judge will also have to file an annual report of his assets and liabilities. The assets and liabilities of the judge will be displayed on the website of the court to which he belongs.

(6) The Bill establishes two authorities to investigate complaints against judges. The two authorities are :

1. National Judicial Oversight Committee; and
2. Scrutiny Panel.

(a) Initial complaints will be made to the Oversight Committee, and they will be referred to the Scrutiny Panel.

(b) A Scrutiny Panel will be constituted in the Supreme Court and every High Court. It shall consist of a former Chief Justice and two sitting judges of that court. If the Scrutiny Panel feels there are sufficient grounds for proceeding against the judge, it shall report on its findings to the Oversight Committee. If it finds that the complaint is frivolous, or that there is not sufficient grounds for inquiring against into the complaint, it shall submit a report to the Oversight Committee giving its findings for not proceeding with the complaint.

(7) Frivolous or vexatious complaints may be penalised by the Oversight Committee.

(8) The Oversight Committee will consist of a retired Chief Justice of India as the Chairperson, a judge of the Supreme Court nominated by the sitting Chief Justice of India, a Chief Justice of the High Court, the Attorney General for India, and an eminent person appointed by the President.

(9) If the Scrutiny Panel recommends investigation into a complaint against a judge, the Oversight Committee will constitute an investigation committee to investigate into the complaint. The inquiry committee will consists of not more than three members. It will have some powers of a civil court and also the power to seize documents and keep them in its custody.

(10) The investigation committee will frame definite charges against the judge and shall communicate the same to the judge. The judge shall be given an opportunity to present his case, but if he chooses not to be heard, the proceedings may be heard without him being present.

(11) If the charges against a judge are proved, the Oversight Committee may recommend that judicial work shall not be assigned to the judge. It may also issue advisories and warnings if it feels that the charges proved do not warrant the removal of the judge. If the Committee feels that the charges proved merit the removal of the judge, it shall (a) request the judge to resign voluntarily, and if he fails to do so, (b) advise the President to proceed with the removal of the Judge. In such a case, the President shall refer the matter to Parliament.

(12) A motion for removal of a judge can also be introduced in Parliament by members of Parliament. In such a case, the Speaker or the Chairman can either admit the notice, or refuse to admit it. If the notice is admitted, the matter shall be referred to the Oversight Committee for inquiry.

(13) The Bill exempts documents and records of proceedings related to a complaint from the purview of the Right to Information Act, 2005. The reports of the investigation committee and the order of the Oversight Committee shall be made public.

Judicial Independence.—Some ideas—

(1) State should provide adequate resource for the due administration of justice. The judiciary should be allocated a fixed percentage of the national budget by law.

(2) The provision of appointment of *ad hoc* and additional judge and the chief justice assigned to another work than his regular job are against the international standards of independent judiciary. So it should be revised by the constitutional provision.

(3) State should provide reasonable remuneration and other privileges for the judge and it would be subject to periodic change.

(4) Separate judicial service Act should be formulated and implemented.

(5) There should not be any inappropriate interference with the judicial process by public official of other branches of Government or private individuals.

(6) Judges should perform their duties free from improper influences and without undue delay, cost and corruption.

(7) Judges should ensure that judicial proceedings are conducted fairly and that the rights of parties are respected.

(8) Fundamental freedom of judge *i.e.* freedom of expression and association should be expressed incorporated in constitution.

(9) Judges must have guaranteed tenure until retirement of the expiration of their term of office; No fresh engagement under Government thereafter.

(10) The Constitution should provide the judges immunity from all risks that come in the course of carrying their official duty.

(11) Judges shall not be subject to suspension or removal only for reason of incapacity or behaviour that render them unfit to discharge their duties.

(12) Judicial information and court decisions should be made available to the public.

(13) The composition of judicial council must be redesigned by the majority members of the judiciary.

(14) Decision solely based on the law and facts, without influence of political figure, and media; No media trial.

(15) The process of appointment of judge should be transparent.

(16) Special types of courts, judicial institutions and tribunals should not be created to displace the jurisdictions of the ordinary court.

(17) Decisions of the court should be enforced fairly and effectively.

(18) The judges must be accountable and responsible.

❑ ❑

Chapter 18

Democracy : Expectation from Judiciary

In the preamble of Constitution people have resolved to Constitute India into a Democratic Republic which shall be sovereign socialist and secular. In preamble lies the message of Constitution to its functionaries be it, the three organs of the Government or other bodies or authority or the officers. The advent of Political Democracy in India was unique and distinct. The Constitution of India as adopted on 26th November 1949, created a democratic republic and pledged to secure justice, liberty, equality and fraternity for all its citizens.

Universal adult franchise was provided at one go, compared to the very limited franchise under which the elections of 1937 and 1945-46 were conducted. Provisions were built in the Constitution of affirmative action in favour of the historically disadvantaged sections; and secularism to guarantee the pluralism of society, culture, civilization, religion and polity. Of the hundred or more countries that came to liberation in the years following 1947, India was the only one to translate Independence for the country into freedom of her people. India has since strengthened the Political Democracy by giving constitutional sanctity to the Panchayati Raj in Rural and Municipal Bodies in Urban area, creating 3 lakhs elected units of local self Government to which have been elected no less than 32 lakhs members as many as 12 lakhs of whom are women, and 86000 of whom hold office as President and Vice-President of their respective local bodies.

The way democracy was brought about in India by a Constituent Assembly constituted through a limited franchise, would reflect that it was constructed by an enlightened elite in accordance with its conception of a modern State. It was a democracy from above provided to the people and was not as claimed by the people from below. Possibly, there was a grain of expectation of this happening because of the participation of people from below in the Freedom Movement led by the elite leadership. So stage was set for the State to assume the role of mediator in reconciling the conflict among different groups and classes having equal political rights. The leadership had pledged on the eve of Independence of wiping tear from each eye and the Nation would dedicate itself to the service of millions of poor who suffer. Gandhi had envisioned India of his dreams in which the poorest shall feel that it is their country.

The leadership had adopted resolutions before independence towards the goal of deliberately state-led development; it was axiomatic that development process must set in.

In fact development process had been conceived and schemes executed in pre-independence administration as well and also in the areas administered by Native States who were somewhat autonomous for devising schemes of development for their subjects. The degree of efforts and achievement was dependent upon the vision of the Ruler, Dewan and Civil Servants of the Native State who were among the elitist Chandan Gowda has studied the motivation of such an elite group to undertake development and the model adopted. Gowda concludes that through developmental efforts, the objective was to seek civilisational recognition with respect to India's capacity for development and in the process become heroes in the eyes of nationalists throughout India since they provided evidence of how splendidly Indians could govern themselves.

Such elites were educated in Western thought and were at the receiving end of the orientalists negative impressions of India. Therefore, they were out to dispel their negative impressions by adopting their developmental models without caring to go into the vitality of the models. West had progressed through Industrial Revolution and the Great-Britain's achievements were by far more remarkable than France and Germany. These elitist also took a leaf on the protectionist policies as adopted by those countries to protect their industries.

Thus in keeping with the 19th century European evolutist view of history, the Mysore State elite also understood industrialization as development and the great need to stir-up industrial enterprise and progress was felt. It was remarked by the Dewan of the State "If we want to know in what direction to move, we must compare ourselves with, and be guided by the experience of, progressive countries". "Agriculture was viewed as a sector sure to become marginal in future."

In this background and the leadership being with the elites, economic development at the dawn of independence was shaped by the colonial past and the nationalist present. Thus State was to play dominant role in the process of development and the upcoming industries would need protection and there would be conscious effort to limit the degree of openness and of integration with the world economy. This approach had the consensus of the time. A view was adopted, in consonance with the elitist approach of the colonial period, that agricultural was subject to diminishing return whereas industrialization promised not only increasing return but also productive employment for surplus labour from the rural sector.

At this juncture, a dye was cast for the concept that industrialization was synonymous with development. In this scenario, scarce investible resources were preferentially developed for industry to the relative neglect of agriculture. This approach not only reflected consensus on the strategy of development but also included in itself the political consensus as well because of the dominance of Congress Party, which represented within itself coalition of interests. Conflicts on approach were resolved within the party after debating the issues. People at large were not vocal enough at this stage of evolution. They had implicit faith in the leadership. Thus public interest and national interest were congruent. While the strategy of Industrial Development took primacy, there were certain actions to address the exclusion of the poor and exploited. Land Reforms Legislation were adopted, community development programmes for the rural areas were initiated and Panchayat institutions were encouraged. There were affirmative legislations for bringing about reservation for the disadvantaged sections in Government employment and admissions to the institutions of learning.

In this era, while political leadership within the Congress Party was in the hands of elites who came from Industrialist capital class, the land owning class and the educated class. The debates within the party would accommodate interests of these classes by way of appropriate tradeoffs in the economy by the alignments of subsidies and concession. In the absence of vocal spoke persons for their causes, the poor had to settle for with the phrases such as "Socialistic Pattern of Society" and commanding heights of economy". A policy of building up industrial capitalism with accompanying rhetoric was emerging with the objective of eradicating poverty of the people and put the country to industrialization.

Sooner or later, the democratic process which were set in motion through Universal Suffrage of franchise were to assert.

The pro-poor rhetoric did not deceive the people. It became evident that the strategy adopted by the Government had by-passed the poor and the economic growth accrued to the rich. In fact the number of poor and the number of those below the poverty line increased significantly. Still worse was the explosive of the inability of Government to tackle drought situation accentuating not only the miseries of the poor but also driving the nation to a stage of dependency on imported food grains. Such a situation was bound to affect the process of industrialization and economy in general so much so that even economic planning had to be suspended for a period of three years.

Democracy v. Capitalism

Over the last few months, India has been going through an experience well known to the historically inclined students of political economy : namely, a clash between democracy and capitalism. Most wealthy democracies have had this experience at a certain stage of development, and one might even argue that the clash has not yet fully disappeared. By looking at the matter comparatively, we can perhaps get a surer perspective on India's current economic malaise.

Let us begin with a deceptively simple question : what produces the clash between democracy and capitalism? Fundamentally, the building blocks of the two systems—democracy and capitalism—are different. Democracy is premised on the idea of political equality. Capitalism is not about equality, political or economic. It is fundamentally about economic freedoms : freedom to buy and sell, freedom to invest and make a profit, freedom to invest, freedom to reap the rewards of one's work, capacity or luck. It does not matter whether one is rich or poor; each person has only one vote in a democracy. A person ten times richer than his neighbour would still have one vote, but in the marketplace, the same person would undoubtedly have greater clout. The rich matters more in the economic market; the poor, especially if they are numerous, count for ore in the market for votes. Even if the rich finance election campaigns, the vote of the poor must be won.

By giving the right to vote to the subaltern, democracy inevitably tends to put restrictions on economic freedoms. When such restrictions are viewed as excessive, capitalism often punishes democracy. The term "investment strike" best expresses this phenomenon. Faced with a government going supposedly too far in the direction of the poor, the capitalist can simply refuse to invest.

This has well-known consequences for democracy. Without investment, the democratic project of welfare or redistribution begins to falter. One must, therefore, enlarge the cake in order to split it. Where the balance between the democratic desire to provide mass welfare and the capitalist impulse towards economic freedom lies has been a concern for all democracies.

Let us now turn to India. The external origins of India's macroeconomic fragility are undeniable : as capital leaves emerging markets, the economic recovery of the US is a problem for them to begin with, and a blessing only later. But the domestic origins of India's economic problems are firmly anchored in the clash described above. As Indian democracy moves towards presenting access to food, education and partial rural employment as a right to the masses, the investment rates have fallen, capital has begun to move out, and the currency has come under enormous pressure.

Only 66 years old, India is a new democracy. How have the older democracies handled the problem? Three things ought to be noted.

First, older democracies instituted universal franchise—the right to vote without any distinction of gender, race, ethnicity or income—only after they had become rich.

Universal franchise became a Western institutional practice in the 1910s and 1920s. The West was already highly economically developed by then, producing, for example, 77 per cent of the world's manufacturing output by 1900. As a result, Western capitalism did not feel intense redistributive democratic pressures until very late. In contrast, independent India was born with extensive poverty and universal franchise.

Second, as franchise expanded in the West, to include the lower classes, welfare states, with public expenditures reserved for low-income groups, also began to emerge virtually everywhere. The first welfare state was born in Bismarck's Germany in the 1880s, as all male adults got the right to vote; it emerged in 1910-11 in the UK and in 1932 in the US, as franchise became larger. Welfare States have been of different types but, basically, all democracies feel the political necessity to attend to the well-being of the masses, not leaving it to markets alone.

Third, unlike in the West, the poor in India have come to vote much more than the rich. Over the last two and a half decades, India's poor have defined democratic theory, which says that the rich and the educated tend to vote more.

What inferences does this comparative sketch allow? As at some historical point in the other market-based democracies, capitalism and democracy are at odds in India today. And because universal franchise was instituted at a low level of income and the less educated and the poor have started voting more than the rich, India's democracy has felt an acute pressure to develop a welfare state even *before reaching a high level of income.* Moreover, since most of India's low-income population comes from four social categories—the scheduled tribes, the scheduled castes, lower OBCs and Muslims—the policy has moved quite decisively towards their concerns. Given the continuing tale of mass deprivation, it may not look that way on the urban streets and rural pathways, but India's policy and voting space has an unmistakable plebeian thrust today, both economically and socially.

What mainstream economists derisively call the reckless populism of India's government is, in fact, the call of a poor democracy—very substantially, if not wholly. It is not only the UPA government that has supported rights to food, education and rural employment; all political parties have. Indeed, non-Congress State governments in Tamil Nadu and Chhattisgarh have run bigger welfare programmes. Narendra Modi's critique of the food security bill was that it was not sufficiently ambitious.

Only a third of India, at best, can be classified as middle class. Democratic politics is unlikely to prioritise their concerns over those of the remaining two-thirds, especially if the middle classes, for a whole variety of reasons, vote less than the rest. Mainstream economists would like India's governments to rely on long-term, growth-based plans for poverty alleviation, interfering little with the market. Politicians, however, have to wind the next elections. Something concrete must be done here and now. Long-run considerations often do not work well in electoral politics.

But mainstream economists are absolutely right in one sense. If, in the process of attending to the bottom half or two-thirds, India's democracy adopts policies that choke the growth process, it will not be able to provide mass welfare either. Revenues to fund welfare programmes depend heavily on economic growth, which in turn is substantially dependent on investment. Therefore, regardless of what the masses want, democracies must also please investors.

That is where UPA 2 has erred. It had to walk on two legs : one that increases the investment rate, makes it easier to do business and enhances growth, and the other that attends to mass welfare. It concentrated on the second leg, taking investment and growth for granted. It assumed that India had become a land of business opportunity, but it did demonstrably little to nurture that belief.

But it is not too late. India's economic malaise is not yet a full-blown economic crisis. The morale of the narrative sketched above is quite simple. If investment and growth have serious implications for mass welfare, restore investor confidence with greater incentives and simpler rules of doing business. It is not anti-poor to be pro-investment.

Side effects of parliamentary polls

India is going to vote for the 16th Parliament. Out of the population of one hundred twenty crore, only eighty crore may elect five hundred forty-three candidates to rule this wonderful nation of different castes, races, communities and languages.

Some say this is going to change the future of Indian people, yet, others believe nothing remarkable is going to take place. this would be the same election like all others we have seen and voted for. Opinions vary from person to person, party loyalists and the leaders and workers are duty bound to project that their party is for over all change in the society so if voted to power by the people the face of India will certainly change.

This is the sweet talk we are hearing from here and there but the moot question is whether the voters properly use their power to form a government? Why there is enmity among the political parties on the personal level? If everybody wants India to kiss the sky and be the world leader then why the lectures of our beloved leaders are becoming cheaper and the expression lower?

In the name of freedom anything and everything is being said by campaigners. Asking vote for the party is one thing and using a bad language is another. Under such circumstances voters are getting confused whether they should go to vote or not.

But the fact is really different. People notwithstanding all this, are from the core of their heart interested to go to vote for they still feel that something may come out of the mess created by the leaders of all political parties. Election took place in some places, showed the turnout of the voters was beyond expectations. In some states it has touched 80% and the average has come to sixty percent.

India they say is a poor country. We agree with those who believe that we are poor people. In the changed world politics there is glamour in remaining poor. Let us not go into the discussion of poor and rich. We know that poverty is there in our country from time immemorial and all know that the poor are generally emotional and they can do and undo anything under the fit of emotions. Indians on that count are famous the world over, so the process of election also makes them more than necessary emotional. The crowd in the rallies, the debates on the paan thelas and the tea stalls and also in the government offices where the babus miss no opportunity to stop working, one can very well see how we feel and how we connect ourselves with the leaders and the parties. It is a common sense that two or more persons while discussing the prospects of the parties start fighting with each other. Not only this husband and wife also enter into the hot debate over this or that party's win. The entire environment is fully surcharged and there remains no chance to talk of the main issues like unemployment, inflation, education, national security, price control fast economic growth and many more things. Election becomes expression of emotions giving no importance to the real issues. This happens because the love for a person makes all emotional.

Being emotional is good or bad is a matter of discussion but generally emotions give bad results. This election is no exception to that rule. There is news from Bareilly of U.P. that a young man of 35 years has immolated self in the polling station premises on not finding his name in the voter list in Bhamaura area of this district "Hariram (35) had gone to cast his vote at Ram Bharose Inter College polling station in the Aonla parliamentary constituency which falls in Bareilly district. Police said." When he was told that his name was not there in the list, he doused himself with kerosene and set himself afire." Someone may say that the person was insane or stupid for committing suicide for the silly cause but that is not the correct interpretation of this very said event. The hysteric propaganda launched by all parties and the way rallies are organized seems to be the real cause behind this tragedy. The behaviour of the person may appear to be abnormal but the abnormality has taken place due to the constantly entering the words into his ears which worked like bomb inside. It appears that the vote to him had become a prestige point and the refusal played the worst game causing his death. Our politicians talk more, speak more without thinking how it is going to affect those who take all that is said very seriously. This death must teach them a lesson that airy talks and big unrealistic promises must go out of election propaganda. Poor men and women are emotional; they love the leaders and even pay for their victory everyday so it is the job of the leaders also to be cautious and attentive in speaking out in public meetings. But politicians never learn and never try to read the writing on the wall for they think they are destined to rule and nobody has the authority to tell them the truth, they believe that they know the truth which can be altered and amended according to the need of the time.

Enlightened voter knows nothing is going to change and the situation will remain the same but among 80 crore voters some are really serious and again we must know that all such voters are poor people.

Political democracy

Political Democracy, on the other hand, was growing towards its adulthood. Ideology of nationalism was on the wave particular with the passing away of the charismatic leaders. Now there was a generational change of leadership all across the political spectrum. With the operation of political democracy as impacted by development strategy was throwing up the leadership from regions. People of strata at the lower end of the spectrum were searching for political spaces having realized the power of their vote. Some aspirants among them, having a perception of being by-passed from the stream of development, took to militancy also. Compulsion of political democracy were now before the second generation leadership. For winning an election, they had to address the constituency of vast majority of the poor. In case these constituents felt that a particular political party failed to come upto their expectations, its future was black. The elections of 1967 effectively demonstrated that the Congress party could not assume support of the poor for granted. With the dawn of such realities in the political democracy front, there was bound to be change in economic development strategies. Emphasis of economic development shifted towards agriculture with the twin objective of making the country self-reliant in food and also co-opting the farmers and peasants as more vigorous participant in the benefits of economic development.

A list of subsidies were introduced in the farm sector lowering the costs of inputs of fertilizers, seeds, water, power or credit and providing higher costs to their outputs by way of procurement prices for producers. Such programmes benefited undoubtedly the rich peasantry, which was a political compulsion of the time. A separate set-up programmes were initiated to target the landless and poor farmers to generate employment opportunities for them. Rather an attractive slogan was coined directed at the poor *i.e. Garibi Hatao*. With a view to demonstrate Governments credentials to bring about socialist pattern of society, banks were nationalized and privy purses of the Princes were abolished. These policies were dictated by the compulsions of political democracy. A hope was raised that with the nationalization of Banks, Government would assume social control on them to direct the credit to subserve greater goal of the people of different strata. Differential rate of interests were introduced for credits to the disadvantaged sections.

With such initiatives, there was rapid growth in agriculture making the country self-sufficient in food grains and ensured food security. With this growth, there was growth in savings, investment and also expenditure. This revived the industry. There were immediate political dividends. The Congress party returned to power in 1971 decisively. However, there is continuous dynamism in democratic processes. This phenomenon has been more pronounced in India because of its pluralities and structured relationships among the hierarchy of castes. Diversity of social structures varies widely from region to region yet different regions are emotionally integrated to one another because of several historical and cultural factors.

The mandate received by the Government in 1971 was massive; rather than this leading to stability sharpened the aspirations of hitherto excluded classes, to lend their voices to the mainstream development and be participants in the associated economic and social changes. Leadership to emerging movement among these classes, who were termed as backward classes yet not included as scheduled castes, was being provided by student leaders such as Lalu Prasad Yadav and Nitish Kumar under the veteran leader Karpoori Thakur articulating inclusion of backward classes in the developmental processes. There was simmering discontent in Gujarat seeking probity in public life.

The regional movements became pan India movement when Jaiprakash Narayan, a veteran Gandhian, agreed to take command of the movements. While these movements were on, Indira Gandhi was unseated from her seat in Parliament following a verdict of the Allahabad High Court on the petition which was filed challenging her election. Instead of taking the verdict as one within the Constitutional framework, the process of democracy was sought to be stifled and resort was taken to the emergency provisions of the Constitution and fundamental rights were suspended and leaders who had been participating in the movement were imprisoned. However, such a State of affairs could not continue as by this time democratic mindset of people at large was firmly rooted. Within two years of the invoking of emergency provisions, fresh elections had to be called to let the democracy have free play. In the ensuing elections, there was realignment of political forces and different factions of the political spectrum vied for sharing power. In fact the outcome of the election results was stunning for the observer at the marco-level. Indira Gandhi herself lost election and Congress party which has a resounding performance in the earlier election, lost out in numbers. Resultantly, the others put their parties together hurriedly to clobber up a coalition to form a Government styled as Janata Government. Thus coalition was of those groups who had come together for a common cause of fighting emergency and had no ideological bounding or well thought out common programme. Resultantly there were squabbles and development process had a setback. Political democracy once again responded by voting back Congress Party in 1980 with the message that economic development and that too inclusive one involving people of different strata must be taken up *a priori*. So the process of economic development was reordered to accommodate all groups and thus it had to be populistic and not necessarily most efficient.

Cynical Democracy

India's great churning will continue in the coming year. There is new momentum towards change. The momentum will be most manifest in glimpses of a new institutional order that is coming into being. India's progressive moment is now beginning to find its feet, with a clamour for a governance architecture that is more horizontal, transparent, decentralised, based on public reason and allows for new political formations to emerge. This process will continue. The flotsam of the old order will continue to be visible, and will often disguise the new undercurrents forming. More poison may come out of the system as partisan competition intensifies. But amid all the high-decibel exchanges, a quiet revolution will continue.

But the revolution will be most palpable in a subtle reorientation of attitudes. The most besetting sin of Indian democracy over the last couple of years has been its corrosive cynicism. It was cynical democracy with much to be cynical about. But the cynicism had become a self-fulfilling prophecy. Few believed anything could change, so little changed. There were no texts, there were only subtexts. Virtue was nothing but deception. We converted it into such an art form that there was cynicism about everything that pretended to be anything other than cynicism.

The cynicism was compounded by what Amartya Sen has made India's badge of self-identification : the argumentative Indian. We thought arguing was generally a good thing, since it denoted a kind of freedom and engagement with learning. But we forgot the other side. An argumentative person is someone who goes on arguing, well after the matter has been settled. Much of our public argument had this character. It was not argument in the interest of learning; it was argument in the interest of going on and on. Few who came to the argument were open to being persuaded, few were open to any possibilities other than what they had already committed to.

Cynicism contributed to a contagion of littleness. Cynicism is corrosive, precisely because it denies the possibility of there being a real distinction between virtue and vice, it denies the possibility that change for the good can take place. We become cynical not just about the fact that anyone can live up to high standards of morality; we become cynical about those standards themselves. The worst kind of levelling a democracy produces is one where all fine distinctions are levelled, where no utterance can be taken at face value.

The cynicism actually served the status quo rather well. If everyone's motives could be distrusted, there was no possibility of credible critique. Cynicism made collective action impossible : when we cannot trust each other how can we work with each other? Cynicism was hollowing out democracy.

The most remarkable change over the last few months has been the overcoming of cynicism. In a small way, idealism does not seem so outlandish after all. There is a new democratic experimentalism in the air. Not only were voters in that most cynical of cities, Delhi, willing to take a chance on a new party, the AAP, they did so in ways that defy any neat narratives. The AAP's single biggest achievement has been to change the mood of significant sections of the country. Arvind Kejriwal injected that real tonic that a democracy needs from time to time the possibility of the new. But most importantly, it began to speak a language that we thought had become almost impossible in our democracy; the language of trust. The AAP's ideas were not that important. What was important was the novel claim that if people just discussed thing as equal, thins would get better. Instead of the needlessly argumentative Indian who had, in the name of freedom, undermined democracy, the AAP injected the thought that a people involved in collective deliberation could reach sensible agreement. It identified the key deficit of our democracy, which has always been founded on distrust. Its simple promise was that if people can more visibly and easily participate in governance, things can improve. The idea is itself not original. But making the very classes that have stood in the way of that ideal accept it, even if fleetingly, is an achievement. It crafted a symbolic vocabulary around that idea. Even if government as a daily plebiscite is not always an attractive ideal, it certainly had the virtue of not being cynical abut the virtue of ordinary citizens.

The older parties are, of course, weighed down by their complicity with older and corrupt structures. But in their own ways, they have been dragged to a point where they have to acknowledge that business as usual is no longer possible. Underneath the surface drama of familiar faces, and occasional reminders of reactionary ideas, we should not miss the fact that the BJP has also been trying to script a new narrative. It is easy to spot Narendra Modi's baggage. But critics missed his novelty. By gatecrashing his way to national prominence, he showed that he could create a new basis of appeal. He has been consistent on the theme that India should enlarge its aspirations. It is a politics based on will, not ideas, but that is exactly the kind of politics you would expect a cynical environment to generate. In a curious twist, the politician we had a lot of reason to be cynical about became the embodiment of a kind of anti-cynicism.

This is where Congress lost out. It was too causal in grasping the winds of change. Rahul Gandhi talked abut them, but with an odour of defeatism. If Modi managed to brush off his vices through sheer energy, Congress managed to make even its virtues look suspicious through sheer lethargy. Rahul Gandhi seems to be acknowledging that old corruption is no longer acceptable. But the way he embarrassed his own governments by publicly ticking them off, whether it was one the Adarsh scam or the matter of criminal politicians, made the right stance more about him, not about change. The party of sincerity became the embodiment of cynicism. It is finding it hard to shake that off.

Professional cynics will warn us not to replace cynicism with delusion : aam aadmis do not stay aam in power for too long, a leopard cannot change its spots. Energy and sincerity are also not enough for one particular area that needs urgent attention : the economy. We should not be cynical about these cynics. There is something to these warnings. But there is little doubt that 2014 will belong to the party that can most successfully capitalise on the new yearning to overcome cynicism. A major political realignment is in the air.

Changes in Policies

This led to important changes in policies. The sector qualifying for subsidies were widened to include fuel, fertilizers and exports resulting increased Government expenditure. Services such as irrigation, electricity and transport were underpriced. Products of pubic sector including steel and coal were also at concessional rates. There was munificence of Government for rich peasantry and industrialists. Liberal bank credit was also made available to the Industry besides cheap inputs from the Public sector units who carried losses. Loan waivers were also granted to the industrialist classes. Non-performing assets were taken over by Government which brought additional costs on Government. To boost the growth, private consumption was encouraged by increasing the salaries of Government employees. Government also took up poverty alleviation programmes in a big way. All these efforts, in economic sense, maintained levels of consumption to support the associated growth process. The outlays on the programmes described above left very little for education, health care and social security.

Economic Policies

Such a set of economic policies at the behest of centre, would naturally set in process the phenomenon of doing better than the other when the political parties compete for soliciting votes. This is what exactly happened at the State level also. All the parties, irrespective of their stated ideology, performed the same pattern of governance as at the Centre-including something for everybody sacrificing efficiency. This had several effects on the political process. The parties lost on their ideologies; the limited resources could not be adequate to meet all the promises made by parties. As the gap between the promises made and promises kept increased the country of State to manage conflicts dwindled. This resulted in politics of patronage and a class of Political Managers emerged who would manage the voters, in a variety of bewildering ways, who were otherwise disillusioned. Though, by increasing spending Government was able to demonstrate growth in National Income and somewhat reduction in rural poverty, seeds of fiscal crisis and debt crisis were sown. In the field of Political democracy, disturbing phenomenon of political management caught up with all political parties. The combined effect of the two was financial instability of Government and democratic process getting beset with process of management. Consequently, the role of money acquired a decisive edge in the battle of ballot. The elected representatives became a commodity who could be traded by the political managers. Thus profit maximization became an important motive for political acts or deeds; the resolution of conflict between the economics of markets and politics of democracy was circumvented.

Populist Politics

The populist politics and economies of subsidies and increased expenditure resulted in Government living beyond its means *i.e.*, on borrowed money. The day of reckoning had to come. In 1991, India's external debt position became critical and balance of payment position unmanageable. The spectre of high rate of inflation loomed large. Government had to set its house in order and had to shift to policy of economic growth with economic efficiency. Political management was through the development of a belief that overall economic growth would automatically bring about reduction in poverty. The State would reduce its role in market/economy. Private sector would take a lead in economic development under the impression that investible resources would be used towards optimal economic gains. The domestic prices and international prices would get linked with the opening of Indian Markets. Foreign capital and foreign technology would play an effective role. So a stage for market capitalism was set in replacing the State led capitalism. The change of policy brought about was crisis driven and not strategy based. Thus the trajectories of the interface of economics and politics in India would get redefined. The year of 1991 is thus a watershed for the economy.

Is Indian politics populist?

Populism has increasingly become a staple of the Indian news media's diet. Most recently, the term has become a firm favourite within the commentary on the food security bill. The "populist" label is particularly favoured by critics of both the bill and the UPA government that promulgated it. But what exactly these observers mean when they call the policy populist is either unclear or widely varying and at odds with how the term has been historically conceptualised.

In the writings of corporate analysts, populism is most often defined in terms of a preference for redistribution over growth (setting aside the contentious claim that there is a necessary trade-off between these objectives). It is in this spirit that the UPA has been accused of being "more populist than [the late Venezuelan president] Hugo Chavez". For other observers, populism is used to indicate any policy driven by narrow political calculations rather than the broader well-being of the nation. Here it is the timing of the food security bill, during an election year, that makes it a "populist" move by the UPA government. For some analyses written from this perspective, even non-economic election-year agendas, such as the BJP's revival of Ayodhya, qualify as populist.

Yet, within the study of global politics, populism has meant something entirely different, and far more conceptually specific. First, it refers to mobilisations led by a political outsider, someone who was not previously a major player within the existing party system. Second, populist leaders would use their outsider status to craft appeals that attacked the existing political establishment for being self-serving and deaf to the needs of the ordinary citizen. Finally, populist figures would deploy these anti-elite appeals in the service of establishing direct links with voters, favouring the development of a personalistic cult over a party brand. This conceptualisation was developed most thoroughly within the context of Latin America, which produced iconic examples such as Chavez in Venezuela, Alberto Fujimori in Peru and, more recently, Evo Morales in Bolivia.

This threefold criteria suggests there are far fewer true populists in Indian politics than our media suggests. It is certainly difficult to portray the current Congress as populist, given that it is a party led by the ultimate insiders of Indian politics. The CPM's opposition to economic liberalisation, or support for redistributive policies, has often earned it the populist label, but this is also misplaced. While the CPM certainly promotes an anti-elite platform, it prioritises a strong party apparatus over a single charismatic individual—even Jyoti Basu never had the monopoly on power that Chavez had. Narendra Modi fits the bill to the extent that he has controversially sought to create a personal cult independent of the BJP and its Sangh affiliates. Yet even his most ardent supporters would be hard-pressed to call his platform anti-elite, and survey evidence continues to confirm support for him remains highest among urban upper castes. Of the major players in Indian politics, Mayawati probably comes closest to earning the populist label, as a relative outside who used vociferous anti-elite appeals to craft significant (and jealously guarded) cult of personality.

How does any of this matter for everyday political discussion? Isn't this just a semantic discussion for stuffy academics? I do not think so. Using terms whose meanings are neither well understood nor consistent leads us to talk past each other, or worse. By constantly invoking "populism" for a disparate set of polices disliked for different reasons (we very rarely hear something praised for being populist), we have emptied the term of any specific analytic value, and replaced it with a vague negative connotation that enables obfuscation and slippery argumentation. Analysts can disparage policies for being populist, without having to clarify the stakes of their position.

Instead, the use of specific, appropriate and clearly understood terms is essential for transparent and responsible policy debates which surely we all agree are needed. Thus, if we mean to say a policy is redistributive, we should simply say so. Doing so will force analysts to explain why they oppose redistribution specifically. It will also force them to clarify and defend broader implication of this position, which is often that there is an inevitable trade-off between democratic politics (which they see as creating incentives for privileging redistribution) and a robust economy (which they see as needing to be freed from such electoral shackles) : the so-called "democracy penalty" for growth. For the record, the numerous global studies on this subject continue to disagree on whether such a penalty exists.

Similarly, if we mean to say a policy is electorally driven, we should state this explicitly. Doing so would force us to explain why that is an undesirable quality for a policy to have. After all, the ideas of a ruling party crafting policies that voters will reward it for is a sign of democracy working exactly as intended. We might further have to specify whether this critique is intended to imply the need for less democracy—should we leave policymaking to technocratic experts insulated from the voting public? Or does it conversely mean the problem is that such policy responsiveness only happens every five years, and that we need more democratic channels for public pressure to flow up to elected officials in non-election years?

This discussion brings us back full circle to the food security bill. The policy is certainly redistributive, and also clearly driven by electoral interests. To my mind, neither trait is a signal of a deep dysfunction in Indian politics (of which there are plenty). If politicians believe that the key to their electoral appeals lies in proposing policies that are popular among India's poor majority, that is a heartening development, even if far from sufficient for ensuring the policy will be effectively implemented. Indeed, for most of its history, India has been viewed by outside observers as puzzling because it has enacted far fewer of these policies than one would expect from such a poor democracy. Why is this the case? That is a question for another column.

NEP 1991 and thereafter, Globalisation Liberalisation and Privatisation

In would be worthwhile to summarise the achievements on economic and political fronts until 1991 when India had completed four decades for planning and also of democratic process. On the economic front India was on growth curve overcoming the stagnation that existed before independence, there was sufficiency of food. There was upswings in savings and growth. Government might have become bankrupt needing restructuring of its finances, country at large had developed inherent strengths in economy. However, the forces of development did not significantly improve the conditions of the common people. Persistent poverty and absolute deprivation remained the reality for a large majority. Despite significant reduction in the incidence of poverty during the 1980s, the number of poor in 1990 was larger than the total population of India in 1947. Thus the balance sheet of achievements in the four decades of economic growth led by State Capitalism demonstrates that objective or eradicating poverty of the people and placing the country on the path of sustained industrialization was not quite realized.

India has been through the phase of market led growth for two decades. The report card in respect of the condition of the poor despite visible significant growth of 8-9 per cent, remains the same if not worse. Thus the differential among the upward mobile industry and knowledge based segments have widened *vis-a-vis* the traditional societies. The benefits of growth have been siphoned off by a small segment of the population; while bulk of the people have been deprived of the trickle down benefits. Naturally, this is challenging in a democratic Government and to democracy itself, and it would impact the growth rate finally. It has been demonstrated time and again that the under classes have the knack of striking at the buckles in a silent way at the poll hustings. Their silence becomes more vocal if they perceive the disparities widening when they soured the "Shinning India" of the NDA regime in 2002 elections.

Historically such classes are also not averse to take on the militancy riding on the availability of recruits from the classes left out of the development process. Low intensity war is raging on in at least in 158 districts—amounting to between one-fourth to one-third of all administrative districts in India— are partially or entirely convulsed in Maoists or Naxalite violence, of which 35 districts have spun out of control of Government of India, being virtual fiefs of the insurgents. Aiyar fears that Democracy is very demanding. If disillusionment with development is not checked, it could lead disillusionment with democracy and this would be the loss of single most achievement since independence. The alternatives would be draconian for people and development.

Liberalisation; effect

During the liberalisation phrase commencing in 1991, the industrial development once again was reiterated to be the only way to lead to the economic growth. Every State in the Union led by respective Chief Minister started vying with one another in attracting the entrepreneurs by promising giving aways without taking into consideration the consequences that such give aways would be finally detrimental to the people living off agriculture and those dependent on agriculture. The entrepreneurs were allowed to choose areas for their projects which had connectivity, water and were bearing multiple crops. Some of the targeted areas were fragile from environment angle. Some areas were predominantly in tribal areas. Industrialization would result in displacement of population and rehabilitation plan of the displaced population remained unimplemented. In a densely populated country like India, it would be difficult to locate areas where the displaced could be settled and alternative means of employment avenues created. The State Machinery was wantonly used in acquiring land and in the process Constitutional protection as provided to Scheduled Tribes was compromised.

The directions on the States as provided under Articles 38 and 39 of the Constitution were set at naught. Even the rights as guaranteed under Article 21 of the Constitution stood usurped. National Rehabilitation Policy, 1994, Government of India mentions that 15.5 million people stood displaced and 74.52 per cent displaced people were still awaiting rehabilitation. 40 per cent of these displaced persons were tribals and another 20 per cent were dalits. One in every seven tribals is a displaced person. The stated policy of rehabilitating the displaced person remains an unfulfilled promise. When the State itself is perceived by a section of its people as the trigger towards violation of their Constitutional Rights and Human Rights, it would be causing the rise of Politics of Resistance. Cumulative effect has been that during the liberalization period, with the massive drive for acquisition of land and the shrinking avenues of employment, the Maoist movement has fanned out. The State has to bear huge costs to contain such uprisings and low intensity resistance. The projects in such areas stand detailed. Acquisition of Land has come to a standstill.

Government has woken up to realities which it should have anticipated and is hoping to contain the situation through a combination of development package and legislative responses like Land Acquisition Bill, Food Security Bill, Rehabilitation Bill etc. though the political consensus on the proposed legislations is yet to emerge. Schemes such as National Rural Employment Guarantee, and food grains to the poor at subsidized rates are sought to provide succour to the rural areas. The delivery mechanism is admittedly flawed. As reported in Times of India, dated 7th December 2010, a fair percentage of food grains meant for the poor is diverted to open market and according to another report it is being exported to neighbouring countries. In the shifting blame game of centre and States, the poor are not getting the relief meant for them. Thus the gap between promise and fulfilment further gets widened.

The Cumulative effect is that India perceived to be among the top ten countries of the world in Economic Development fares poorly and is along with sub Saharan countries as far as Human Development Index is concerned. Suffice to say that resultantly India is labelled as an area where infant mortality is high, number of malnourished people abound and illiteracy levels are high. Thus after two decades of market led development, India remains qualitatively worse as far as the poor are concerned. Undoubtedly, therefore, benefits of rapid growth in this period has been skimmed off by the upper edge. As on date, the affluence levels are so high that the Rich and Powerful of India are seconded to none in their class in their achievement and are competing well with their counterparts in all walks of life.

Two India

Thus, India stand divided truly in two India's broadly speaking. In a democratic society, we would term that there is one India which is dominant in market and lags in vote bank and there is another India which lags in market but is strong in vote. In a country which swears by being Socialist Democratic Country where disadvantaged would be specially taken care of such a situation is vitriolic.

Four decade growth v. Two decade growth;

It is obvious that in India, four decades of State led growth and two decades of market led growth have not been able to bring down the number of poor but both the systems did add upward mobility. Both the systems of growth gave primacy to Industrial Development and marginal support to agriculture and employment generation schemes. Half hearted efforts have been taken towards redistribution of assets. There are obvious constraints to industrialization in the sectors which need land and water which would be true for Mining, Manufacturing, Power, Infrastructure, Real Estate etc. There would be relatively less constraints on knowledge based sectors. Majority of the poor population is rural based and dependent upon agriculture. Their number is in millions and the capacity of industry can never be enough to address the employment concern of such a huge number. Deliberately greater emphasis need to be brought on agriculture and agriculture related infrastructure and associated employment generation so that the hinterland booms with economic activity surrounding agriculture. The mindset that industrialisation is synonymous with development need to be reversed in favour of agriculture as synonymous with development. Political consensus should be steered towards the direction that stability in rural area with increased productivity in agriculture and increased in agriculture related infrastructure employment would provide space necessary for industrial growth.

Agriculture is so indigenous to the genius of India that quietly it has made strides to place itself second world agricultural output. It is the largest producer in the world for milk, cashew nuts, coconuts, tea, ginger, turmeric and black pepper. It is the second largest producer of wheat, rice, sugar, groundnut oil and fish, it is the third largest producer in tobacco is home to 10 per cent of world food output and first in production of fruits like banana and sapota. Cattle population of the country at 193 million is highest in the world. Therefore there is abundant scope in boosting Agriculture linked infrastructure and industries with the Government and Media reorienting the thought process. India has the potential to become the food bowl of the world. Such an approach is inclusive of the indigenous pattern of culture and harmony glossing over of which has led us to the present state.

Vote for Development or Caste Politics; Bihar or Gujarat or U.P. or Tamil Nadu

Political mandate has been renewed for the Government of Bihar by the people of Bihar in the recent elections. Generally, the massive mandate has been interpreted as vote for development over the Caste politics hither to practised vigorously. At least it is a simplistic interpretation under the euphoria of massive victory. On a micro analysis, one would come to a conclusion that caste equations still subsist and it is the arithmetic of delimitation which has favoured one side at the cost of other though the stress on development for positive political mandate is healthy. It needs to be recalled that Bihar registered a growth of 11 per cent in the year gone by without any addition of industry worth its name. Bihar is blessed with fertile land and has abundance of water. Its people are sturdy and hardworking who have contributed to the economic activities throughout India, Bihar, where industrial development has shied away would be an ideal laboratory to test the model of Agriculture led growth and related infrastructure development with an arrowed objective that this State alone would be producing sufficient food to sustain the entire country and also the neighbouring countries in its North. If it follows the beaten track of Industry led growth it would also have similar constraints as other states are having. Right emphasis on agriculture, if it adds to income in the hands of the professions dependent on agriculture, would also take care of the endemic problem of failed delivery systems as such programmes in the present form may become redundant. May be India can bring about balance between the vote bank equations leading to flowering of democracy and growth.

Dynasty versus democracy

At the All India Congress Committee (AICC) session in Delhi on January 17, Rahul Gandhi, the Congress's election campaign chief, demonstrated his capacity to speak cogently about his motivations and plans, while taking the party's competitors head-on. But precisely 10 days later, his 80 minute long interview with Times Now virtually undid what he had achieved : he fluffed answers to questions that he should have expected—on the comparisons between the anti-Sikh riots of 1984 and the anti-Muslim carnage of 2002, and on corruption that, together, incidentally, occupied roughly 40 per cent of the interview.

Mr. Gandhi's vain efforts to stay on message—to talk about his efforts to democratise the system, and allow more voices to be heard—rather than get drawn into a conversation on the Bhartiya Janata Party's prime ministerial candidate failed. Unlike the speech he gave at the AICC session, where he was able to control the narrative, faced with questions from a skilled interviewer, he floundered.

So even as the Congress's media managers sought to do damage control, elaborating on what Mr. Gandhi should have said, a young Congress activist—who had attended the AICC session—told *The Hindu* sadly. "If Rahulji had participated in more debates in Parliament, and interacted regularly with the media, he would have known how to answer questions." The only point on which Mr. Gandhi scored over his principal political rival is that he—as party general secretary Digvijaya Singh said—stood his ground, neither expressing annoyance or walking out as Mr. Narendra Modi, the BJP's prime ministerial candidate has done on more than one occasion.

But in making himself accessible, in demonstrating that he was open to questions, in stressing that power by itself held no attractions for him, and that the collective was more important than the individual—all democratic traits—he rendered himself vulnerable.

Winds of change

At the AICC session, he said the United Progressive Alliance government had "deepened" democracy through rights based laws, its landmark Right to Information arming citizens to question the functioning of government. The citizen had to be empowered, he said, but not by destroying democratic institutions like Parliament. "Democracy", he reminded his listeners, "is not rule by diktat. It is not rule by one man. It is rule through empowered elected representatives."

He had also acknowledged—without referring to the Aam Aadmi Party (AAP)—that the Congress had no option but to address the demands of an aspirational citizenry. "The imperative before us, is not whether to change", he said stressing, "but when and how to change."

On January 18, as Mr. Gandhi met party delegates, State-wise, many noticed a change : "What was new", delegate from Uttar Pradesh told *The Hindu*, was that he wanted to hear what we had to say : I have met him many times but I must say his attitude was far more positive than it has ever been in the past."

But this delegate, like many others I spoke to, said the hope was that Mr. Gandhi would be able to "sustain" the momentum generated by the AICC session, and actually implement, for instance, fairer selection methods when it came to choosing functionaries or giving party tickets, and push the generational change visible that day. "The problem is, most decisions are still taken behind closed doors, the selection committees for the elections still have, by and large, the same people. When will the doors open?" asked a delegate from Madhya Pradesh. No one can fault either the passion or the content of Mr. Gandhi's speech at the AICC session, but the party's faithful are still waiting for its future leader to translate his ideas into action.

In his first five years, *i.e.*, till 2009, the spotlight was on Ms Gandhi who had achieved sainthood after rejecting the prime ministership in 2004. But after 2009, the focus shifted to him. He demonstrated his interest in issues—in the tribals versus development question, in the problems of land acquisition. Now, more recently, he has set in motion the revival of the party's SC department with the objective of identifying Dalit leaders from the block to the State-level, and helping Dalits access social welfare schemes. While it would be premature to comment on this latest venture, in the case of the first two, he was unable to sustain either the momentum or leverage them for electoral gains.

If he has worked consistently on any issue, it is in trying to put systems into place, selecting poll candidates through a fairer process, and democratising the party through internal elections, starting with the Youth Congress. The going has been tough, as there is resistance to beings organised; as for elections, the results have been mixed—certainly some new faces have emerged, but money power has ensured that entrenched elements have also managed to win elections. Party workers continue to complain that very few can get past a tight circle of advisers, while debunking his "scientific" method of choosing potential youth leaders through examinations.

Clearly, democratising the Congress is an uphill task, harder in a party where dynasty is still paramount. Mr. Gandhi is acutely aware of this paradox.

In 2012, when I asked him whether he was aware of the contradiction between being a member of a political dynasty and his efforts to democratise the Congress, he responded : "I agree it's a paradox. But I have got this opportunity. I could say I don't' want it. I'm saying I want to work for this country, let me try to steer it in a positive direction."

But more recently, at an informal interaction, he was not quite as conciliatory when posed the same question : instead, he pointed out that there were many other political dynasties flourishing in the country : from the Badals in Punjab, to the Yadavs in Uttar Pradesh to the Thackerays in Maharashtra, something he repeated in the Times Now interview.

To democratise a Congress brought up on dynasty is difficult because Rahul Gandhi's mere presence is enough to encourage sycophancy, as is evident at every party event. But can the Congress, given its history and culture, choose anyone—for the moment at least—other than Rahul Gandhi to be the face of its future?

There may be murmurs of discontent at the top of the food chain, but at the level of the delegates who filled the Talkatora Stadium on January 17 there seemed to be unanimity that the Nehru-Gandhi family held the party together and, currently, there was no leader outside it who had the same kind of pan India appeal. "The really successful rajas in the past", a delegate from a Hindi heartland State said, "wielded absolute power, while creating a democratic system below. That is what Rahul Gandhi has to do."

Checking the drift

It is not that the Congress had not anticipated the negative impact of corruption or of the changing aspirations of an emergent middle class. In December, 2010, at the party's plenary session in Burari, Ms Gandhi had set in motion the battle against corruption, resulting in a flurry of laws and the removal of discretionary powers in Congress-ruled States. In January 2013, at the *chintan shivir* in Jaipur, she said the Congress could not allow the "growing educated and middle-classes to be disillusioned and alienated from the political process."

But the Congress has failed to address these changes partly because there is hardly any sustained discussion or putting together of heads in a formal forum on key issues relating to the economy, foreign policy, development and reasons for growing social unrest. The Congress Working Committee seldom meets and the little discussion that takes place is in the informal core group that deals with emergent problems. the Congress is now a party where general secretaries and ministers themselves scramble for information, where intrigue replaced any world view as ideology a long time ago, and ginger groups are a thing of the hoary past.

As senior Congress leaders, a majority wearing the party's traditional Gandhi *topi,* walked in to attend the AICC session on January 17, a collective gasp had gone up in the media stands at Talkatora stadium. It should not have been an unexpected spectacle as the starched white khadi cap is customarily worn at formal party occasions.

But with that familiar cap—embellished with the slogan "*Main hoon aam aadmi*"—now a common sight on the streets of Delhi with the AAP in power in the national capital, the vision of Congressmen donning the once evocative symbol of the freedom struggle sent out a new message : it was time for the country's oldest party to reclaim the ground it had lost to its competitors.

But can an organisation currently bearing the brunt of people's disenchantment with the traditional political class and the burden of a decade-old corruption-scarred government, achieve that? If the AAP has jogged the Congress out of its complacency, the question is : can Mr. Gandhi retrieve the Gandhi *topi* and win back the affections of the *aam aadmi*?

Democratic Constitution

As we begin our task we quickly discover, however, that various associations and organization calling themselves "democratic" have adopted many different Constitutions. Even among "democratic" countries. We find, Constitutions differ in important ways. As one example, the Constitution of the United States provides for a powerful chief executive in the presidency and at the same time for a powerful legislature in the Congress; and each of these is rather independent of the other. By contrast, most European countries have preferred a parliamentary system in which the chief executive, a prime minister, is chosen by the parliament. One could easily point to many other important differences. There is, it appears, no single "democratic" Constitution.

We now begin to wonder whether these different constitutions have something in common that justifies their claims to being "democratic". And are some perhaps *more* "democratic" than others? What does *democracy mean*? Alas!, we soon learn that the term is used in a staggering number of ways. Wisely, we decide to ignore this hopeless variety of definitions, for your task is more specific; to design a set of rules and principles, a Constitution, that will determine how the association's decisions are to be made. And our Constitution must be in conformity with one elementary principle : that all the members are to be treated (under the Constitution) as if they were equally qualified to participate in the process of making decisions about the policies the association will pursue. Whatever may be the case on other matters, then, in governing this association all members are to be considered as *politically equal*.

Criteria for a Democratic Process

Within the enormous and often impenetrable thicket of ideas about democracy, is it possible to identify some criteria that a process for governing an association would have to meet in order to satisfy the requirement that all the members are equally entitled to participate in the association's decisions about its policies? There are, at least five such standards.

(i) Effective participation.—Before a policy is adopted by the association, all the members must have equal and effective opportunities for making their views known to the other members as to what the policy should be.

(ii) Voting equality.—When the moment arrives at which the decision about policy will finally be made, every member must have an equal and effective opportunity to vote, and all votes must be counted as equal.

(iii) Enlightened understanding.—Within reasonable limits as to time, each member must have equal and effective opportunities for learning about the relevant alternative policies and their likely consequences.

(iv) Control of the agenda.—The members must have the exclusive opportunity to decide how and, if they choose, what matters are to be placed on the agenda. Thus the democratic process required by the three preceding criteria is never closed. The policies of the association are always open to change by the members, if they so choose.

(v) Inclusion of adults.—All or at any rate most, adult permanent residents should have the full rights of citizens that are implied by the first four criteria. Before the twentieth century this criterion was unacceptable to most advocates of democracy. To justify it will require us to examine why we should treat others as our political equals.

Until the twentieth century, most of the world proclaimed the superiority of non-democratic systems both in theory and in practice. Until very recently, a preponderant majority of human beings—at times, all—have been subject to non-democratic rulers.

Fundamentals of Democracy

1. Democracy helps to prevent Government by cruel and vicious autocrats

Perhaps the most fundamental and persistent problem in politics is to avoid autocratic rule. Throughout·all recorded history, including our own times, leaders driven by megalomania, paranoia, self-interest, ideology, nationalism, religious belief, convictions of innate superiority, or sheer emotion and impulse have exploited the State's exceptional violence to serve their own ends. The human costs of despotic rule rival those of disease, famine, and war.

Consider a few examples from the twentieth century. Under Joseph Stalin's rule in the Soviet Union (1929-1953), many millions of persons were jailed for political reasons, often because of Stalin's paranoid fear of conspiracies against him. An estimated twenty million people died in labour camps, were executed for political reasons, or died from the famine (1932-33) that resulted when Stalin compelled peasants to join Sate-run farms. Though another twenty million victims of Stalin's rule may have managed to survive, they suffered cruelly.

Or consider Adolph Hitler, the autocratic ruler of Nazi Germany (1933-1945). Not counting tens of millions of military and civilian causalities resulting from World War II, Hitler was directly responsible for the death of six million Jews in concentration camps as well as innumerable opponents, poles, gypsies, homosexuals and members of other groups he wished to exterminate.

Under the despotic leadership of Pol Pot in Cambodia (1975-1979), the Khmer Rouge killed a quarter of the Cambodian population : an instance, one might say, of self-inflicted genocide. So great was Pol Pot's fear of the educated classes that they were almost exterminated : wearing spectacles or having uncalloused hands was quite literally a death warrant.

To be sure, the history of popular rule is not without its own serious blemishes. Like all Governments, popular Governments have majority, an oligarchic minority, or a benign dictator, is bound to inflict some harm on some persons. Simply put, the issue is not whether a Government can design all its laws so that none ever injures the interests of any citizen. No Government, not even a democratic Government, could uphold such a claim. The issue is whether in the long run a democratic process is likely to do less harm to the fundamental rights and interests of its citizens than any non-democratic alternative. If only because democratic Governments prevent abusive autocracies from ruling, they meet this requirement better than non-democratic Governments.

Yet just because democracies are far less tyrannical than non-democratic regimes, democratic citizens can hardly afford to be complacent. We cannot reasonably justify the commission of a lesser crime because others commit larger crimes. Even when a democratic country, following democratic procedures, inflicts an injustice the result is still an injustice. Majority might does not make majority right.

However, there are other reasons for believing that democracies are likely to be more just and more respectful of basic human interests than non-democracies.

2. Democracy guarantees its citizens a number of fundamental rights that non-democratic systems do not, and cannot, grant

Democracy is not only a process of governing. Because rights are necessary elements in democratic political institutions, democracy is inherently also a system of rights. Rights are among the essential building blocks of a democratic process of Government.

Consider, for a moment, the democratic standards. Is it not self-evident that in order to satisfy these standards a political system would necessarily have to insure its citizens certain rights? Take effective participation : to meet that standard, would not its citizens necessarily process a right to participate and a right to express their views on political matters, to hear what other citizens have to say, to discuss political matters with other citizens? Or consider what the criterion of voting equality requires : citizens must have a right to vote and to have their votes coupel farily. So with the other democratic standards : clearly citizens must have a right to investigate alternatives, a right to participate in deciding how and what should go on the agenda, and so on.

By defintion, no non-democratic system allows its citizens (or subjects) this broad array of political rights. If any political system were to do so, it would, by definition, become a democracy!

Yet the difference is not just a trival matter of definitions. To satisfy the requirements of democracy, the rights inherent in it must actually be available to citizens. To promise democrtaic rights in writing, in law, or even in a constitutional document is not enough. The rights must be effectively enforced and effectively available to citizens in practice. If they are not, then to that extent the political system is not democratic, despite what its rulers claim, and the trappings of "democracy" are merely a facade for non-democratic rule.

Because of the appeal of democratic ideas, in the twentieth century despotic rulers have often cloaked their rule with a show of "democracy" and "elections". Imagine, however, that in such a country all the rights necessary to democracy somehow become, realistically speaking, available to citizens. Then the country has made a transaction to democracy—as happened with great frequency during the last half of the twentieth century.

At this point one might want to object that freedom of speech, let us say, won't exist just because it is a part of the very definition of democracy. Who cares about definitions? Surely, the connection must be something more than definitional. And of course, correct. Institutions that provide for and protect basic democratic rights and opportunities are necessary to democracy : not simply as a logically necessary condition but as an empirically necessary condition in order for democracy to exist.

Even so, isn't this just theory, abstractions, the game of theorists, philosophers, and other intellectuals? Surely, it would be foolish to think that the support of a few philosophers is enough to create and maintain democracy. And you would, of course, be right. The existence of fairly widespread democratic belief's among citizens and leaders, including beliefs in the rights and opportunities is necessary to democracy.

Fortunately, the need for these rights and opportunities is not so obscure that it lies beyond the comprehension of ordinary citizens and their political leaders. To quite ordinary citizen in the late eighteenth century, for example, it was fairly obvious that they could not have a democratic republic without freedom of expression.

One of the actions of Thomas Jefferson the U.S.A. after he was elected to the presidency in 1800 was to bring an end to the infamous Alien and Sedition Acts enacted under his predecessor, John Adams, which would have stifled political expression. In doing so Jefferson responded not only to his own convictions but, it appears, to views widely held among ordinary citizens in his time. If and when many citizens fail to understand that democracy requires certain fundamental rights,or fail to support the political, administrative, and judicial institutions that protect those rights, then their democracy is in danger.

Fortunately, this danger is somewhat reduced by a third benefit of democratic systems.

3. Democracy insures its citizens a broader range of personal freedom than any feasible alternative to it

In addition to all the rights, freedoms, and opportunities that are strictly necessary in order for a Government to be democratic, citizens in a democracy are certain to enjoy an even more extensive array of freedoms. A belief in the desirability of democracy does not abolition of the State would produce unbearable violence and disorder—"anarchy" in its popular meanings—then a good State would be superior to the bad State that is likely to follow upon the heels of anarchy.

If we reject anarchism and assume the need for a State, then a State with a democratic Government will provide a broader range of freedom than any other.

4. Democracy helps people to protect their own fundamental interests

Everyone, or nearly everyone, wants certain things : survival, food, shelter, health, love, respect, security, family, friends, satisfying work, leisure, and others. The specific pattern of your wants will probably differ from the specific pattern of another's. Like most people, one will surely want to exercise some control over the factors that determine whether and to what extent we can satisfy our wants—some freedom of choice, an opportunity to shape our life in accordance with our own goals, preferences, tastes, values, commitments, beliefs. Democracy protects this freedom and opportunity better than any alternative political system that has even been devised.

No one has put the argument more forcefully than John Stuart Mill.

A principle "of as universal truth and applicability as any general propositions which can be laid down respecting human affairs," he wrote, "...... is that the rights and interests of every or any person are secure from being disregarded when the person is himself able, and habitually disposed, to stand up for them.... Human beings are only secure from evil at the hands of others in proportion as they have the power of being, and are, self-protecting." We can protect our rights and interests from abuse by Government, and by those who influence or control Government, he went on to say, only if one can participate fully in determining the conduct of the Government. Therefore, he concluded, "nothing less can be ultimately desirable than the admission of all to a share in the sovereign power of the State," that is, a democratic Government.

Mill was surely right. Even if we are included in the electorate of a democratic State we cannot be certain that all our interests will be adequately protected; but if we are excluded we can be pretty sure that our interests will be seriously injured by neglect or outright damage. Better inclusion than exclusion.

Democracy is uniquely related to freedom in still another way.

5. Only a democratic Government can provide a maximum opportunity for persons to exercise the freedom of self-determination—that is to live under laws of their own choosing

No normal human being can enjoy a satisfactory life except by living in association with other persons. But living in association with others has a price; we cannot always do just what we like. As we left our childhood behind, we learned a basic fact of life : what we would like to do sometimes conflicts with what others would like to do, we have also learned that the group or groups to which we want to belong follow certain rules or practices that as a member we too, will have to obey. Consequently, if we cannot simply impose our wishes by force, then we must find a way to resolve our differences peacefully, perhaps by agreement.

Thus a question arises that has proved deeply perplexing in both theory and practice. How can we choose the rules that we are obliged by our group to obey? Because of the State's exceptional capacity to enforce its laws by coercion, the question is particularly relevant to our position as a citizen (or subject) of a State. How can we both be free to choose the laws that are to be enforced by the State and yet, having chosen them, not be free to disobey them?

If we and our fellow citizens always agreed, the solution would be easy : we would all simply agree unanimously on the laws. Indeed, in these circumstances we might have no need for laws, except perhaps to serve as a reminder; in obeying the rules we would be obeying ourself. In effect the problem would vanish, and the complete harmony between we and our fellows would make the dream of anarchism come true, but Experience shows that genuine, unforced, lasting unanimity is rare in human affairs; enduring and perfect consensus is an unattainable goal. So our difficult question remains.

If we can't reasonably expect to live in perfect harmony with all our fellow human beings, we might try instead to create a process for arriving at decisions about rules and laws that would satisfy certain reasonable criteria.

(1) The process would insure that before a law is enacted we and all other citizens will have an opportunity to make our views known.

(2) We will be guaranteed opportunities for discussion, deliberation, negotiation, and compromise that in the best circumstances might lead to a law that everyone will find satisfactory.

(3) In the more likely event that unanimity cannot be achieved, the proposed law that has the greatest number of supports will be enacted.

These criteria we notice, are parts of the ideal democratic process. Although the process cannot guarantee that all the members will literally live under laws of their own choosing, it expands self-determination to its maximum feasible limits. Even when we are among the outvoted members whose preferred option is rejected by the majority of our fellow citizens, we may nonetheless decide that the process is fairer than any other that we can reasonably hope to achieve. To that extent we are exercising our freedom of self-determination by freely choosing to live under a democratic Constitution rather than a non-democratic alternative.

6. Only a democratic Government can provide a maximum opportunity for exercising moral responsibility

What does it mean to say that we exercise moral responsibility? It means, that we adopt our moral principles and make decisions that depend on these principles only after we have engaged in a thoughtful process of reflection, deliberation, scrutiny, and consideration of the alternatives and their consequences. For we to be morally responsible is for us to be self-governing in the domain of morally relevant choices.

This is more demanding than most of us can hope to meet and of the time. Yet to the extent that our opportunity to live under the laws of our own choosing is limited, the scope for your moral responsibility is also limited. How can we be responsible for decisions that we cannot control? If we cannot influence the conduct of Government officials, how can we be responsible for their conduct? We are subject to collective decisions, as certainly we are, and if the democratic process maximizes our opportunity to live under laws of our own choosing, then—to an extent that no non-democratic alternative can achieve—it also enables us to act as a morally responsible person.

7. Democracy fosters human development more fully than any feasible alternative

This is a bold claim and considerably more controversial than any of the others. It is, an empirical assertion, a claim as to facts. In principle, we should be able to test the claim by devising an appropriate way of measuring "human development" and comparing human development among people who live in democratic and non-democratic regimes. But the task is of staggering difficulty. As a consequence, though such evidence as exists supports the proposition, we probably should regard it as an assertion that is highly plausible but unproved.

Just about everyone has views about the human qualities they think are desirable or undesirable, qualities that should be developed if they are desirable and deterred if they are undesirable. Among the desirable qualities that most of us would want to foster are honesty, fairness, courage, and love. Many of us also believe that fully developed adult persons should possess the capacity for looking after themselves, for acting to take care of their interests and not simply counting on others to do so. It is desirable, many of us think, that adults should act responsibly, should weigh alternative courses of action as best they can, should consider consequences, and should take into account the rights and obligations of others as well as themselves. And they should possess the ability to engage in free and open discussions with others about the problems they face together.

At birth, most human beings possess the potentiality for developing these qualities. Whether and how much they actually develop them depends on many circumstances, among which is the nature of the political system in which a person lives. Only democratic systems provide the conditions under which the qualities I have mentioned are likely to develop fully. All other regimes reduce, often drastically, the scope within which adults can act to protect their own interest, consider the interests of others, take responsibility for important decisions, and engage freely with others in a search for the best decision. A democratic Government is not enough to insure that people develop these qualities, but it is essential.

8. Only a democratic Government can foster a relatively high degree of political equality

One of the most important reasons for preferring a democratic Government is that it can achieve political equality among citizens to a much greater extent than any feasible alternative. But why should we place a value on political equality? Because the answer is far from self-evident.

The advantage of democracy would tend to apply to democracies past and present. Some of the political institutions of the democratic systems with which we are familiar today are a product of recent centuries; indeed, one of them, universal adult suffrage, is mainly a product of the twentieth century. These modern representative systems with full adult suffrage appear to have additional advantages that could not necessarily be claimed for all earlier democracies and republics.

9. Modern representative democracies do not fight wars with one another

This extraordinary advantage of democratic Governments was largely unpredicted and unexpected. Yet by the last decade of the twentieth century the evidence had become overwhelming. Of thirty-four international wars between 1945 and 1989 none occurred among democratic countries. What is more, "there has been little expectation of or preparation for war among them either." The observation even holds true before 1945. We back into the nineteenth century, countries with representative Governments and other democratic institutions, where a substantial part of the male population was enfranchised, did not fight wars with one another.

Of course modern democratic Governments have fought wars with non-democratic countries, as they did in World War I and II. They have also imposed colonial rule by military force on conquered peoples. They have sometimes interfered in the political life of other countries, even weakening or helping in the overthrow of a weak Government. Until the 1980s, for example, the United States had an abysmal record of giving support to military dictatorships in Latin America; in 1954 it was instrumental in the military coup that overthrew the newly elected Government of Guatemala.

Nonetheless, the remarkable fact is that modern representative democracies do not engage in war with one another. The reasons are not entirely clear. Probably the high levels of international trade among modern democracies predisposes them to friendliness rather than war. But it is also true that democratic citizens and leaders learn the acts of compromise. In addition, they are inclined to see people in other democratic citizens and leaders learn the arts of compromise. In addition they are inclined to see people in other democratic countries as less threatening, more like themselves, more trustworthy. Finally, the practice and history of peaceful negotiations, treaties, alliances, and common defense against non-democratic enemies reinforce the predisposition to seek peace rather than fight wars.

Thus a more democratic world promises also to be a more peaceful world.

10. Countries with democratic Governments tend to be more prosperous than countries with non-democratic Governments

Until about two centuries ago, a common assumption among political philosophers was that democracy was best suited to a frugal people : affluence, it was thought, was a hallmark of aristocracies, oligarchies, and monarchies, but not democracy. Yet the experience of the nineteenth and twentieth centuries demonstrated precisely the opposite. Democracies were affluent, and by comparison non-democracies were, on the whole, poor.

The relation between affluence and democracy was particularly striking in the last half of the twentieth century. The explanation is partly to be found in the affinity between representative democracy and a market economy, in which markets are for the most part not highly regulated, workers are free to move from one place or job to another, privately owned firms compete for sales and resources, and consumers can choose among goods and services offered by competing suppliers. By the end of the twentieth century, although not all countries with market economics were democratic, all countries with democratic political systems also had market economics.

In the past two centuries a market economy has generally produced more affluence than any alternative fo it. Thus the ancient wisdom has been turned on its head. Because all modern democratic countries have market economies, and a country with a market economy is likely to prosper, a modern democratic country is likely also to be a rich country.

Democratic typically possess other economic advantages over most non-democratic systems. For one thing, democratic countries foster the education of their people; and an educated work force is helpful to innovation and economic growth. In addition, the rule of law is usually sustained more strongly in democratic countries; courts are more independent; property rights are more secure; contractual agreements are more effectively enforced; and arbitrary intervention in economic life by Government and politicians is less likely. Finally, modern economics depend on communication, and in democratic countries the barriers to communication are much lower. Seeking and exchanging information is easier, and far less dangerous than it is in most non-democratic regimes.

In sum, despite some notable exceptions on both sides, modern democratic countries have generally tended to provide a more hospitable environment in which to achieve the advantages of market economies and economic growth than have the Governments of non-democratic regimes.

Yet if the affiliation between modern democracy and market economies has advantages for both, we cannot overlook an important cost that market economies impose on a democracy. Because a market economy generates economics inequality, it can also diminish the prospects for attaining full political equality among the citizens of a democratic country.

Kangaroo Courts and Democracy

Kangaroo courts are biggest threat to democracy. Self styled local leaders cannot be permitted to take over the legally constituted courts of law. Their threats to witnesses result into causality of justice. They can not hold parallel courts so as to reduce the judicial system to insignificance by holding parallel proceedings of their own.

One of the major reasons for high rate of acquittal and the guilty getting aware in cases involving rape and sexual abuse is the social attitude and frequent interventions and interferences on these self styled leaders and Kangaroo Courts.

People's Courts and democracy.—In Naxal areas writ of the naxals runs effectively and at large. These are denial of State's law and are enemies of democracy.

"Nothing rankles more in the human heart than a brooding sense of injustice. Illness we can put up with. But injustice makes us want to pull things down. When only the rich can enjoy the law, as a doubtful luxury, and the poor, who need is most, cannot have it because its expense puts its beyond their reach, the threat to the continued existence of free democracy is not imaginary but very real, because, democracy's very life depends upon making the machinery of justice so effective that every citizen shall believe in and benefit by its impartiality and fairness."

B.R. Ambedkar and his Philosophy on Indian Democracy : An Appraisal

Dr. Bhimrao Ramji Ambedkar (1891-1956), 'a symbol of revolt' (as mentioned by Pandit Jawaharlal Nehru, the first Prime Minister of independent India), was one of the front-ranking nation-builders of modern India. He is popularly known as the 'pioneer' who initiated the 'liberation movement' of roughly sixty-five million untouchables of India. Yet, Dr. Ambedkar, the chief architect of Indian Constitution, notwithstanding all handicaps of birth, has made, by pursuit of knowledge in the humanities, social sciences, politics and law, an indelible imprint on the body politic of the country. A glance of his copious writings would evidently show that despite his preoccupations with the problems of the *dalits* (Untouchables), Ambedkar has in his own way, made significant contributions to the contemporary political ideas.

B.R. Ambedkar stood apart from his well-known famous contemporaries of India in three respects.

First, being a great scholar, social revolutionary and statesman, he had in himself a combination of these attributes that one rarely possesses which made him distinguished from other intellectual personalities of that time. As an intellectual, gigantic personality and creative writer, he had imbibed knowledge that was truly encyclopedic. The range of topics, width of vision, depth and sophistication of analysis, rationality of outlook and essential humanity of the arguments that he came-up with made him different from his illustrious contemporaries.

Secondly, Ambedkar never wrote merely for literary purpose. In his scholarly pursuit as in his political activities, he was driven by a desire to comprehend the vital issues of his time and to find solutions to the problems of Indian society. With this motivation, he intervened, at times decisively in shaping the social, economic and political development of the nation during its formative stage. There was hardly any issue that arose between the early 1920s and the mid-1950s in India to which Ambedkar did not apply his razor-sharp analysis, whether it was the question of minorities, reorganization of States, partition, Constitution or the political and economic framework for an independent India.

The third unique aspect of Ambedkar lies with the nature and kind of questions he delved into. What is probably most important in a thinker and intellectual is not so much the answer they provide but the question they raised. Ambedkar raised the questions that were simultaneously relevant and uncomfortable. Relevant as they were critical for the nation-in the making and uncomfortable as very few were willing to acknowledge the existence of those issues. Ambedkar raised certain pressing issues in his characteristic style that no one was willing to take up or deal with.

In course of his public life over three decades, Ambedkar was fully convinced that politics should be the instrument to fight for justice in adorning all sections of the Indian people with freedom. As such, he tirelessly worked the goal of justice for the untouchables in an unjust society, mainly through political means. In the course of these activities, Ambedkar developed his own ideas about society and politics of the contemporary India. Viewed from the subject of political science, those ideas obviously merit attention. But, scholars who have worked on Ambedkar's different ideas fail to bestow due importance on these aspects of his thinking.

Insight into B.R. Ambedkar's idea on democracy

He was a true democrat and advocated a democratic society based on the principles of natural justice, equity and classification according to aptitude, ability and profession. The roots of democracy lie not in the form of Government but in the social relationships. He considered caste system in India as a serious obstacle in the path of democracy. He said, "The first condition precedent for the successful working of democracy is that there must be no glaring inequalities in the society. Secondly, there must be statutory provisions to mitigate the sufferings and to safeguard the interest of the suppressed and oppressed people. The society must be based on the principles of liberty, equality and fraternity in order to ensure social endosmosis "

According to him, economic inequalities are inherent in the capitalist economy which makes political equality assured by democracy worthless. Thus, according to Ambedkar, the failure to recognize that political democracy cannot succeed where there is no social and economic democracy has vitiated parliamentary democracy. Ambedkar maintained therefore that though "parliament democracy developed a passion for liberty, it never made a nodding acquaintance with equality. It failed to realize the significance of equality and did not even endeavor to strike a balance between liberty and equality, with the result that liberty swallowed equality and left a progeny of inequalities.

General connotation of Democracy

Democracy is the most valued and also the indistinct political term in the modern world. The ancient Greek word 'democracy' means rule by the *demos*, which can be translated as either 'the people; or 'the mole' depending on one's ideological preference. By itself, democracy means little more than that, in some undefined sense, political power is ultimately in the hands of the whole adult population and that no smaller group has the right to rule. Democracy can only take on a more useful when qualified by one of the other word with which it is associated, for example, liberal democracy, representative democracy, participatory democracy or direct democracy. Although all free societies are democratic, democracies can fail to protect individual freedom. Countries are generally considered democratic to the extent that they have fair and frequent elections in which nearly all adults have the right to vote, citizens have the right to vote, citizens have the right to form and join organizations and to express themselves in alternative sources of information existed. Architects of democracy must determine the constitutional structure that best suits the needs of a particular country, alternative forms of constitutional democracy include parliamentary versus presidential forms of Government, plurality versus proportional representation system and federal versus unitary systems.

In a Parliamentary system, the Prime Minister is elected by the parliamentary process and can be removed from office by a vote of no confidence from the Parliament. Executive and legislative powers are fused in a Parliamentary System. In a Presidential system, the President is elected directly by the people and there is a formal separation of powers.

Plurality voting tends to produce a two-party system and greater Governmental stability, but it offers voters fewer choices. Proportional representation, on the other hand, encourages the formation of small or splinter parties, which can make Governments unstable.

A third constitutional choice is whether to set up a federal or unitary form of Government. In a federal system, authority is divided between central and State Governments. In a federal system, each State has its own legislative and executive and state exercise broad powers. In the late 20th Century, a democratic revolution spread around the world as more countries sought to establish democratic Governments. There democratic transitions raised hopes for better and more peaceful world. Francis Fukuyama asserted that democracy had triumphed over communism and other competing ideologies. He suggested that democracy would in time become universal. Samuel Huntington examines the history of democracy since its emergence in America. He concluded that there have been three waves of democratization and two reverse waves since democracy first washed up on America's shore.

During the first democratic wave (1828-1926), more than thirty countries became democratic. A reverse wave began when Benito Mussolini came to power in Italy in 1922. Between 1922-1942 reversals occurred in many new democratic countries succumbed to communist, fascist and militaristic ideologies. By 1942, only twelve countries were democracies.

A second wave of democratization followed World War II (1943-1962) when the United States and Allied occupation promoted democracy in West Germany, Italy, Austria, Japan and South Korea. The second reverse wave occurred from 1958 to 1975, marked by military coups in Latin America and Asia and the birth of a number of African Countries. By 1975, a third of the world's democracies had reverted to authoritarian rule. Reversal occurred in Brazil, Argentina, Chile, Greece, Turkey, India, Pakistan, South Korea, the Philippines and elsewhere. Virtually all newly independent African countries were authoritarian. Many social scientists began to think that democracy was not applicable to developing countries.

In the mid 1970's the third wave of democratization began in southern Europe—Portugal, Greece and Spain. It spread throughout Latin America, as the military returned to the barracks. It moved into Asia, with India, Pakistan, Turkey, the Philippines and South Korea restoring democracy. Finally, the spread to the communist countries of Eastern Europe. Between 1974 and 1990, some thirty countries made transitions from authorization to democracy, approximately doubling the world's number of democracies. The third wave of democratization occurred, in most cases, through negotiations, elections and non-violence.

An important factor that influences the consolidation of democracy is the country's level of economic development. It produces a more highly educated society and attitudes, such as trust and tolerance that are conductive to a democratic political culture. Greater economic wealth facilitates compromise and accommodation among different groups Democracy follows, to use Samuel Houtington's phrase, "a two step-forward, one-step-backward pattern." The consolidation of democracy is influenced by prior experience with democracy, the political institutions that are established and the level of economic development among other factors. In a democracy, the Government and opposition leaders must work together, which often requires basing from the previous experience of others.

Democracy in Indian context

According to Ambedkar, democracy means fundamental changes in the social and economic life of the people and the acceptance of those changes by the people without resorting to disputes and bloodshed. He wanted to establish the principle of one man, one vote and one value not only in the political life of India but also in social and economic life. He wanted political democracy to be accompanied by social democracy. He gave central importance to social aspects of democracy over political aspects, unlike many others whose discourse on democracy is confined to the political and institutional aspects. Ambedkar paid greater attention to social linkage among people than separation of powers and constitutional safeguards for democracy. The concept of power contained in his thinking has a direct relationship between social power and political power. He was conscious of the social and economic inequalities which corrode the national consciousness of the Indian people. Ambedkar said, "We must make our political democracy a social democracy as well. Political democracy cannot last unless there lies at the lease of it social democracy."

Ambedkar paid serious attention to religious notions that promote democracy. Ambedkar viewed the religious foundation of caste as the fundamental obstacle to democracy in India on the one hand and the Buddhist doctrine of liberally, equality and fraternity as the foundations for democracy on the other hand. He writes, "It is common experience that certain names become associated with certain notions and sentiments, which determine a person's attitude toward men and things. The names, *Brahmin, Kshatriya, Vaisha and Shudra* are hierarchical divisions of high and low caste, based on birth and act accordingly."

Ambedkar thinks of democracy from the viewpoint of practical life. He belongs to the realistic school of political scientists. He is not bothered about the principles and theories of political science. During the national improvement, his aim has to have justice and freedom for the people in the real sense. He aspired for having a Government of the people, for the people and by the people. According to Ambedkar, democracy means no slavery, no caste, no coercion. He wants free thoughts that choice and capacity to live and let live, which his conscience, would be the right path to democracy. Ambedkar says "Democracy is a mode of associated living. The roots of democracy are to be searched in social relationship, in terms of the associated life between the people who form the society."

Ambedkar is the greatest political thinker. Outwardly this may see strange that in India, life was the monopoly of caste and was completely denied to other castes for thousands of years. However, here no contradiction is involved. It was the very privileged position assigned to the *Brahmin* that became the cause of the retardation. In Indian society, property, illiteracy, caste distinctions are the positive dangers to democracy. In these situations, educational facilities and economic help should be provided for those who are illiterate and backward on one hand and on the other, who want to wipe on the roots of caste system in order to safeguard the interest of democracy. Ambedkar says, "If you give education to the lower strata of the Indian society which is interested in blowing up the caste systems, the caste system will be blown up." At the moment, the indiscriminate help given to education by the Indian Government and American foundation is going to strengthen the caste system. Giving education to those who want to blow up caste system will improve prospect of democracy in India and put democracy in safer hands.

In Indian society, class structure is a positive danger to democracy. This class structure made a distinction of rich and poor, high and low, owners and workers, and permanent and sacrosanct parts of social organization. "Practically speaking in a class structure there is, on the other hand, tyranny, vanity, pride, arrogance, greed, selfishness and on the other, insecurity, poverty, degradation, loss of liberty, self reliance, independence, dignity and self respect."

According to Ambedkar, the aim of democracy is essentially need for the interest of society as a whole, and not for any class, group or community. Therefore, Dr. Ambedkar, while speaking on "conditions precedent for the successful working of Democracy", in Poona, emphasized that, "The first condition which I think is a condition precedent for the successful working of democracy is that there must be no glaring inequities in the society. There must not be an oppressed class. There must not be a suppressed class. There must not be a class which has got the entire privileges and a class which has got all the burdens to carry. Such a thing, such a division, such an organization of society has within itself the germs of a bloody revolution and perhaps it would be impossible for democracy to cure them." To him, real democracy is opposed to the suppression of minorities. The suppression and exploitation of minorities in any form is the negation of democracy and humanism. If suppression is not stopped, then democracy degenerates into tyranny.

Ambedkar holds that the individual in society is in him and he has certain inalienable right in social relationship, which must be guaranteed to him by the consumption on certain reasonable conditions and be protected by the State.

The democratic principles of life, liberty and pursuit of happiness are considered to be the essentials of human life in Ambedkar's concept of democracy. He attaches more importance to human well being and human rights.

The effective opposition is an important factor in the working for a successful democracy. Democracy means a veto power. There are two aspects of the veto power.

One is the long term veto of five years and the other—an immediate one. There must be people in the parliament immediately ready there and then to challenging Government.

Secondly, there must be equality in law and administration for efficient functioning of democracy and there is need of a permanent civil service for implementing the policy of the Government. The importance of free opposition and consent is a needful requirement of popular Government, Ambedkar says "Democracy is unrealizable without freedom of political discussion. A right to vote gives a man no real part in controlling Government unless he is free to form his own opinions about his vote, hear what others have to say about the issues and to persuade others to adopt his opinion."

A modern-day enlightenment

In recent months there has been a vociferous demand from some sections of Dalit Intellectual and Ambedkarite opinion that the ideas of Dr. B.R. Ambedkar and Mahatma Gandhi not be compared, contrasted, or put into any kind of conversation with one another. In this view, to mention Gandhi in the same breath as Ambedkar is to take attention and importance away from Ambedkar, and to blunt the radical edge of Ambedkar's contribution, to make him part of the same national mainstream of modern political thought in which Gandhi, Nehru, Tagore and many others belong. In other words, there is a type of exceptionalism that attaches itself to Ambedkar. Proponents of this exceptionalism bristle at any attempt to discuss Ambedkar together with his peers and contemporaries, starting with Gandhi and including all kinds of thinkers and leaders, especially those who happened to be caste Hindus.

The Gandhi-Ambedkar dialogue

There is no doubt that Ambedkar was indeed exceptional in many respects—as an intellectual, a politician and a human being. He fought unimaginable odds to become one of the greatest men of the historical era in which he lived. But this does not mean that he existed, thought or worked in isolation, apart from a climate of ideas, cut off from a rich inter-subjective context of teachers, mentors. benefactors, patrons, friends, comrades, followers, critics, adversaries, supporters, interlocutors, commentators and interpreters. Like any historically significant individual in the thick of public life, with a long and complex career in law, politics, scholarship and religion, Ambedkar too was surrounded by other people, some of whom helped him while others hindered him. Moreover, even today, long after his death, many different groups continued to vie for his legacy. Dalits and Neo-Buddhists are of course at the forefront of staking a claim to this inheritance, and so they should be, but they are not alone. Anyone who wants to understand the political foundations of India's modernity has to engage seriously with Ambedkar and all that he stood for.

To think of Gandhi and Ambedkar as paired figures is not a new discursive move. By the early 1990s, the late D.R. Nagaraj had developed a nuanced understanding of their tortured dialogue, reluctant complementarity and intimate enmity. In his classic essay, "Self-Purification v/s Self Respect : On the Roots of the Dalit movement" (1993), Professor Nagaraj made several important points : first, that it was Gandhi who initially grasped untouchability as a political problem (albeit his own concerns were spiritual and not material); second, that Gandhi and Ambedkar debated their divergent approaches to the problem of untouchability in a vigorous manner both before and after the Poona Pact of 1932; and third, that by the end of their long encounter with one another, Gandhi and Ambedkar had internalised one anothers' ideas. Thus, Gandhi could recognise the village, which he had romanticised as a kind of indigenous utopia, to be a socio-economic space of exploitation and oppression. Ambedkar meanwhile could acknowledge that the yearning for equality and recognition is not answered by a struggle for political rights and social justice alone, but ultimately must assume the dimensions of a deeper quest for transcendent religious truth.

Ambedkar exposed the swamp of caste prejudice that lay beneath the veneer of Gandhi's instinctive traditionalism, Gandhi alerted-Ambedkar to the dangers of fundamentalist modernism : violence against the self, estrangement from an organic community, loss of cultural memory, the return of repressed pasts in frightening, haunting forms, and the erosion of all bulwarks against the onslaught of capitalism. The arch-critic of modernity, Gandhi, and the arch-critic of tradition, Ambedkar, both transformed one another's views. The truth is that if caste is dehumanising, technology too, can be anti-human. If rural lie is steeped in darkness, urban lie too, can be hellish. ("Peepli Live? (2010). Anusha Rizvi and Mahmood Farooqui's brilliant film about farmer suicides and migrant labour, was a wryly ironic comment on this bitter reality). India today, as we know it, bears out the truth of both Gandhi and Ambedkar's views. On the one hand, electoral democracy has reinvented caste as an empowering vector of collective identity, and on the other hand, environmentally-aware social movements have shown up aggressive technological advancement and neo-liberal globalisation as impediments to human flourishing and political emancipation.

But Professor Nagaraj's abiding insight was to explain how the difference between "Harijan" and "Dalit" is the difference between the caste Hindu's struggle for self-purification and the outcaste's struggle for self-respect. The "self" in the two situations is not the same. Ambedkarites today are right to point out that because Gandhi's Harijan is a completely discredited and defunct category, which no longer has nor has had, in fact, for decades, any moral traction or political appeal. It is not necessary to invoke Gandhi together with Ambedkar in our ongoing discussions about caste. The caste system in Gandhi's polemics—a web of social relations typical of India, with an attendant set of basically benign religious beliefs and effective economic practices, minus any built-in or inevitable ideology of inequality—is non-existent as an empirically verifiable reality. No one experiences caste in this way; especially not those at the receiving end of its structural violence. Ambedkar raised this objection early on : today, nobody disputes that he was right.

Gandhi made an attempt to defend the Hindu social order on the basis of an innovative interpretation of its authoritative texts, but Ambedkar read those same texts—the Vedas, *shastras, puranas*, epics, the Gita, *etc.*—as justifying and reinforcing social inequality. For Ambedkar, beyond a point, reform, critique and reason, and even the most conscientious self-scrutiny, rigorous self-sacrifice and exemplary non-violence as advocated by the Mahatma, would fail against the unassailable wall of Hindu caste ideology, which for centuries had yielded the fruit of absolute social dominance, and often also political power for the upper castes. There was no choice, according to Ambedkar, but to "annihilate" caste, to migrate to another religion (namely, Buddhism), that had long ago successfully challenged and rejected the *varna vyavastha* taught and upheld in orthodox Brahminical texts. Accordingly he declared his intention to renounce Hinduism, in Yeola (near Nasik), in October 1935; some 20 years later, in October 1956, Babasaheb formally took Buddhist vows in Nagpur.

Returning to Ambedkar

Since we marked Dr. Ambedkar's 123rd birth anniversary on April 14, 2014, three questions have arisen. First, if Indians, by and large, accepted the new Constitutional regime of the independent nation-state and continue to abide both by the idea of equal citizenship and respect the rule of law, then why do caste prejudice, caste violence and social inequality based on caste hierarchy persist in such a rampant way? Second, if Babasaheb unequivocally won the argument against Gandhi, then why did not more people. Dalits as well as caste Hindus, follow him into Buddhism? Why are there numerically so few Ambedkarite Buddhists even today? Third, if the 2014 general election produces a national government led by the Hindu Right, then what kind of attitudes toward caste can we expect will re-enter the public imagination through the backdoor, if not explicitly and programmatically? Given that Hindutva is founded on a hatred of Gandhi, a dislike of all Gandhian values, and literally, the assassination of the person of Gandhi together with all that he stood for, will we see a glorification of *caturvarnya* greater caste pride, a renewed confidence in the religious legitimacy of caste differentiation, and newer forms of humiliation and exclusion inflicted upon Dalits?

It is high time we turned and returned to Dr. Ambedkar—not just within the confines of the Dalit community, whatever its undeniably special relationship with its greatest leader—but as Indians on the verge of entering into a reactionary phase in our political history. Whether through his conflict with Gandhi, or his rejection of Hinduism and adoption of Buddhism; whether through his work on the making of the Constitution and his creation of the basic outlines of a reservation policy, or as a believer in associational forms of collective life, fraternity, equal citizenship and fundamental rights—in all respects, Ambedkar suggested the way forward to a more egalitarian, democratic, and enlightened society than India has ever been. Only by retaining a commitment to his radically progressive vision not just for Dalits, but also for caste Hindus, and for India as a whole, will we be able to survive what promises to be dark chapter in the political life of the nation.

Criminalisation of politics is not the cause, but only a symptom, of dysfunctional democracy

In the current Lok Sabha 162 of the 543 members have criminal records against them. Seventy-six MPs are facing charges for serious criminal offences under the Indian Penal Code such as murder, rape, kidnaping, robbery, *etc.* This pattern is replicated in state assemblies and in local elected bodies, where supposedly one in five elected officials are charged with at least one case. Research has shown that during the 2009 Lok Sabha elections, a candidate with criminal charges, all else being equal, had a far greater probability of winning elections in comparison to a candidate with no criminal record.

This overwhelming presence of elected representatives facing criminal charges in legislative bodies of India is at the centre of the overarching public sentiment against politicians and electoral politics. During the agitations over the Lokpal Bill, Arvind Kejriwal's remark about criminals in the House compelled Parliament to issue a privilege notice against him. A defiant Kejriwal, in a four page reply to the House, asked, "[...] how can I respect Parliament of present times?" Recently, Jay Panda, an MP representing the Biju Janata Dal (BJD), has submitted three private members' bills in Lok Sabha to address the issue of criminal legislators. The current outrage against legislators with a criminal record is not new for Indian politics. Various government commissions in the past (especially the Vohra Commission in 1993) have recommended measures to deal with the criminal politician nexus. Civil society organisations have been calling attention to the criminalisation of legislative bodies in India. The Supreme Court intervened in 2002 and since then, all candidates contesting for elections have to compulsorily declare their criminal record, if any, and their assets.

In the face of this loud and persistent noise around the criminalisation of Indian politics, we ask whether, once elected, do MPs with a criminal record behave differently from their peers who do not have a criminal record? To answer this question, we collected five disparate measures of the performance of MPs. We looked at their attendance in Lok Sabha, their participation in Lok Sabha debates and questions raised by them in Lok Sabha. These data were complied by PRS Legislative Research. Second, we examined the utilisation of MPLADS funds that are allocated to MPs. this data came from the ministry of statistics website. Third, we collected data on the reported assets of MPs (the veracity of this information is questioned by many) and MPs' criminal records from the Association of Democratic Reforms (ADR). The data is drawn from affidavits filed by the MPs. ADR has meticulously collated, arranged the information to distinguish between two kinds of criminal records—serious (with charges like kidnapping, murder, *etc.*) and those who are charged with less serious crimes.

We find that MPs with criminal records are statistically *no different* from their peers with no criminal record on five indicators mentioned above. First, on average MPs are crorepatis, and MPs with serious IPC charges are likely to have more assets, but not much more. On average, an MP with no charges declared assets of Rs. 9.7 crore, whereas an MP with serious IPC charges declared assets of Rs. 5.8 crore.

Figure 1 demonstrates that MPs with criminal charges are less likely to attend Parliament. MPs with serious IPC charges have 70 per cent attendance record in Parliament, MPs with non-serious charges have 74 per cent attendance, and MPs with no charges have 79 per cent attendance record. However, when they do attend Parliament, MPs with criminal charges against them are more active than their peers. Figure 2 indicates that they are more likely to raise questions on the floor of the House. On average, MPs with serious IPC charges asked 272, MPs with non-serious charges asked 305, and MPs with no charges asked 232 questions, respectively. MPs with a criminal record are also equally likely to participate in debates on the floor of the House. the average participation rate among MPs is 31 debates.

Figure 3 suggests that there is no difference between MPs who have been charged with a crime in their utilisation of MPLADS funds. MPs with and without criminal charges against them have spent similar proportions of the funds allocated to them. These data shows quite clearly that as far as these indicators are concerned, there is no significant difference in the performance of an MP with criminal record and an MP with no criminal record.

There are, of course, some caveats to our analysis. Our analysis is limited to the 2009 Lok Sabha elections and is based on the information available with the three organisations mentioned above. Further, a deeper analysis may reveal that the nature of the questions posed by MPs with criminal charges against them are systematically different from the kind of questions asked by MPs with no charges against them. Similarly, it could be the case that the kind of MPLADS spending by MPs with criminal records is different from that of MPs without such a record. Only more sustained and systematic research can answer these questions.

Indeed, law-breakers should not be lawmakers. There is a clear moral position one can take against politicians with serious criminal charges against them. But our preliminary data analysis shows that once in office, politicians with criminal charges against them behave no differently from MPs with no criminal charges against them. The data we present suggests that to blame politicians with criminal records for everything that is wrong with our system would not be very prudent.

The criminalisation of politics is not the cause of the dysfunctional democracy in India, but a system of greater malaise in our democracy. Kejriwal's assertion and Panda's effort is commendable, but will only touch the symptom and not cure the cause. In the National Election Study (NES 2009), voters were asked whether they would prefer a candidate with a criminal record who gets work done or a clean politician who cannot get their work done. The rural poor said that they would not mind voting for a candidate with a criminal record if the candidate can get their work done. They also preferred an approachable politician to an honest politician. The poor's preference for a politician who can get things done "no matter what" is, in our opinion, because of the daily actions of a state that either treats the poor shabbily all year round, intimidates them, or is simply absent. That needs to be addressed.

Democracy—Form and method of Governance

Democracy to Ambedkar is "a form and a method of Government whereby revolutionary changes in the economic and social life of the people are brought about without bloodshed." In democracy, there should be no tyranny of the majority over the minority. The minority must always feel safe that although the majority carıying on the Government, the minority will not be hurt and that the minority will not be imposed upon. Ambedkar appreciated Harold Laski for his insistence on the moral order as a basic necessity of democracy. He says that if there is no moral order, democracy will get to pieces. It requires a "Public conscience". "A political democracy without an economic and social democracy is an invitation to trouble and danger."

Social democracy alone can assure to the masses the right to liberty, equality and fraternity. So, democracy is not only a form of Government but a way of life through which social justice can be established. Social justice ensures that society should promote the welfare of all. Democracy is a dynamic attitude towards human life. It attaches a great importance to virtues like tolerance and peaceful methods. Thus, parliamentary democracy involves non-violent methods of action, peaceful ways of discussion and acceptance of decision with faith and dignity. There are two other pillars on which parliament system rests. This system needs an opposition and free and fair elections. Ambedkar says, "In a Parliamentary democracy, there should be at least two sides. Both should know each other well. Hence a 'financial opposition', is needed opposition which is the key to a free political life. No democracy can be without it." In modern times, Dr. Ambedkar appears to educate and enlighten people to adopt the fair means for a change of Government."Election must be completely free and fair. People must be left themselves to choose whom they want to send to the legislatures."

The consequences of the caste system on politics and election are quite obvious. Caste are so distributed that in any area there are major castes carrying the seats of Assemblies and Parliament by sheer communal majority voting is always communal, because the minority communities are coerced and tyrannized for casting their vote in form of a particular candidate.

The democratic principles of life, liberty and pursuit of happiness are considered to be the essentials of human life in Ambedkar's concept of democracy. He attaches importance to human well being and human rights. The essence of democracy, to Ambedkar, is that as many members of a society as far as possible should share in the exercise of human rights. It means that there should be equal opportunities for all citizens and harmony among the claims of each person. Discrimination in human rights is the very negation of social and political democracy. Thus, Ambedkar puts emphasis on equality and liberty of human rights.

Centripetal & Centrifugal Democracy

Democracy the most desirable form of governance is not the oldest form like imperialism. However, the modern world has chosen to be electively democratic. Songs are sung in praise of democracy in abundance and also in extravagance in educational curriculum. A lot of variation exists in the formats of democratic governments. The leading patterns are of the USA and the Great Britain representing the presidential and the ministerial systems.

India having been ruled by the British borrowed and imbibed the so called Westminister model. Taking a cue, inspiration and even persuasion from the west in the context of the political happenings the Indians drafted the Constitution for creating an era of democracy after the independence.

The Constitution divides the Government in the legislature, the executive and the judiciary. Times have proved that the legislature has not come up to the expectations of the people. Most of the chosen representatives of both houses of Parliament and the states would not take legislative interest but eyeing on limited immediate political dividends. The judiciary is given the task of examining and interpreting the legislative mandate. Somehow the judiciary at times would not microscopically examine the intent and imperatives of law. Some other times would be enthused or obligated to enter into the field of judicial activism at times even disproportionate.

The basic burden of governance lies in the executive being the council of ministers. It being a Herculean task for the Constitution makers to create a balance among the executive officers incharge of day-to-day administration in addition to policy formulations and political vision. The Constitution framers perhaps did not intensively realize that they themselves were not only very highly educated and accomplished juridical brains but were chosen by the moderately educated electorate then constituting 27.05 per cent of the population. The right of adult franchise conferred on every Indian citizen although a laudable gesture yet election after election has been proved that not only the lack of education has adversely affected the choice of the correct representatives but even the educated class has been lent into the cobweb of political campaigning resulting in wrong selection of the rulers. It was expected that the people in general would have an adequate political and moral control over the chosen representatives to smoothen the function of democracy. Times have experienced that the system as also the psyche of the people would not let them keep an enlivened interest in the nuances of governance. Even otherwise the Indian people have been a subdued lot.

With the exception of Gandhi and disciples advocating or the grass root village administration, the prominent front rank Indian leaders Nehru, Patel, Ambedkar and many more were enamoured of the British model with supremacy of parliament and its nucleus being the council of ministers. The first Prime Minister, Jawaharlal Nehru became the centre of political governance but also of a dream of a future India that was to be shaped. His daughter Indira Gandhi after initial hurdles consolidated her position in the centre stage of politics partly because of the strategic designs but substantially due to the submissiveness and hero-worshipping traits of the Indians unmatched in the world.

The NDA Government led by an elastic and accommodative Atal Behari Vajpayee the people became fond of him based on his popular image. With a clear majority the current BJP Prime Minister Narendra Modi with support of NDA allies is in a commanding position. Modi has claimingly innovated and revolutionized the composition and functioning of the Prime Minister's office as the pivot of the entire government. The people always expect a leader at the altar of firmament as a saviour of their lives and aspirations. The citizen's intrinsically do not believe in quintessence of democracy in terms of their responsibilities, involvement and reciprocal interest to act as a watchdog of the doings and misdeeds of the government. Due to the evil fallout of the bureaucratic system the electorate is convinced about the name sake constitutional duty of casting the votes only. Hence the virus of corruption is created and multiplied in the incurable various diseases in governance.

the Prime Ministers like Nehru, Indira Gandhi and Modi due to their absolute majority in the Indian House of Commons have grown beyond their office. They would interfere in every ministry or department and their discretion would be ultimate. This is not so in Britain. The concept of collectivism among the council of ministers has fast evaded in India. It is only when a weak prime minister would take the reins of the country or does not enjoy a majority support that the concept of collectivism would become discernible to the people. Even a weak and timid P.V. Narasimharao with a suspected majority showed his strength and command at times to the surprise of many.

The wisdom of the experienced leaders in political parties would not become integral to the governing dimensions. Lal Krishna Advani, Yashwant Sinha, Murli Manohar Joshi, even foreign minister Sushma Swaraj and many such stalwarts would be of no use to the government of the day. The erstwhile Congress president Dev Kant Barooah once foolishly announced Indira is India, which was ridiculed across the world. The Congress presidency continuing in Nehru Gandhi family has evaporated the concept of collective leadership. Psychophancy may be the rule among the Congressmen. BSP led by Mayawati, SP of Mulayam Singh, RJD led by Laloo. TMC of Mamata Banerjee, BJD led by Naveen Patnayak, AIADM's J. Jayalalitha, PDP's Mehbooba Mufti and Badal father and son leading the Akali Dal are similar illustrations.

Due to the muddled political scenario the general feeling is that Modi is the centripetal force of the entire governance. The political aspirations, strategies, concept of development, good governance, foreign relations, technological advancement, agrarian reforms, multiple industrialization, weeding out corruption, innovations in administration are all designedly attributed to a single leader being the prime minister.

The moot question is in the largest democracy in the world whether the centripetal force or the centrifugal force in distribution of responsibilities should govern the fate of the people.

Parliamentary democracy

According to Ambedkar, parliamentary democracy has all the marks of a popular Government, a Government of the people, by the people and for the people. In parliamentary democracy, there is the executive who is subordinate to the limitative and bound to obey the legislative. The Judiciary can control both the executive and legislative and keep them both within prescribed bounds. Ambedkar says, parliamentary democracy has not been at a standstill. It was progressed in three directions. It began with equality of political rights by expanding in the form of equal suffrage. Secondly, it has recognized the principle of equality of social and economic opportunities. Thirdly, it has recognized that the State cannot be held at bay by corporation which is anti-social in their purpose. Parliamentary democracy produces the best result in the long run, because it assigns great significance to virtues like ability and cooperation, mutual respect and self help, discipline and devotion to work, for the happiness of the millions of people.

The system of parliamentary democracy, thus, embodies the principle of change and continuity to which Ambedkar attaches great importance. To him, only the spirit of the people can help parliamentary democracy to function well. People and democracy are closely related to each other. Ambedkar says, democracy is another name for equality. It is, therefore, a matter of some surprise that there has been a revolt against parliamentary democracy although not even a century has elapsed since its universal acceptance and inauguration. There is revolt against it in Italy, in Germany, in Russia and in Spain, and there are very few countries in which there has not been discontent against parliamentary democracy. Why should be this discontent and dissatisfaction against parliamentary democracy?

There is no country in which the urgency of considering this question is greater than it is in India. India is negotiating to have parliamentary democracy of the erroneous ideologies which have been responsible for the failure of parliamentary democracy. I have no doubt that the idea of freedom of contract is one of them. The idea became sanctioned and was uphold in the name of liberty. Parliamentary democracy took no notice of economic inequalities and did not care to examine the result of freedom of contract on the parties to the contract, in spite of the fact that they were unequal in their bargaining power. It did not mind if the freedom of contract gave the strong opportunity to defraud the weak. The result is the parliamentary democracy in standing out as a protagonist of liberty has continuously added to the economic wrongs of the poor, the downtrodden and the disinherited class.

The U.S. Supreme Court decision to overturn a 1960s law that helped enfranchise minorities is a stern reminder that law and politics in a democracy must together attend to its social divides

Has the United States Supreme Court killed the Voting Rights Act? No—but with *Shelby County, Alabama* v. *Holder*, handed down on June 27, the court has radically reframed the Act's constitutional meaning. Nearly a half century into the life of the Act, the court has resurrected a long-forgotten premise, one that initially informed the Act's enactment in 1965—that the Act is in principle temporary legislation because ordinarily the States, and not the federal government, regulate voting.

Back to centre stage

Consequently, voting rights have returned to centre stage in American politics. Some States are generating measures that make voting harder—for instance, requiring identification to vote. But other (if fewer) States are making it easier—by providing, for instance, for same day registration. On the whole, the reality on the ground is unsettling. Several States—Alabama, Mississippi, and Texas—which had been barred by the Act from proceeding with restrictive voter identification measures now plan to implement them.

One way forward is for Congress to accept the new decentralisation that the court has engineered, and led the State experiment. Alternatively, Congress could re-design a durable, national system for protection of voting rights. But that would be very hard work, especially given the Republican Party's commitment to tough voters eligibility standards, and thus to voter identification legislation. Also, any presidential pressure on Congress would be very polarising. Barack Obama is the first President since Lyndon Baines Johnson to truly support voting rights, unlike the Republican Presidents who previously presided over extensions of the Voting Rights Act. Yet in the current context of partisan rancour, he must keep quiet and let Congress lead. Maddeningly, though, a bipartisan coalition that would answer the court appears unlikely.

The seeds for the current crisis were sowed in 1965, when Congress framed the Voting Rights Act as emergency legislation. The end of the mid-1960s crisis in American democracy—so vividly dramatised by official violence against African—American protesters in March 1965, in Selma, Alabama—was not obvious. But the initial congressional guess was 1970—which proved to be the year that the Act was first renewed.

The renewal, in 1970, was harbinger of the Act's gradual institutionalisation. As time went on, both political parties deemed the Act a success that deserved semi-permanent status. To be sure, everyone knew that some day African-American voting rights would no longer require federal protection. Yet it was taken for granted that the when and the how of such a decision were up to Congress. And certainly no one anticipated, either then or during the Act's several renewals in 1970, 1975, 1982 and 2006, that the Supreme Court would step in for Congress.

The 14th and 15th Amendments to the Constitution give Congress the power to enforce them. The court can certainly construe the statutes that Congress writes. It has, in fact, been a close partner in such construction since 1966, when the court first reviewed the Voting Rights Act. Until June 27, Congress and the court worked together cooperatively in a process of updating and implementing the many powerful provisions of the Act. The court's conservative members thus shattered a long-standing alliance between Court and Congress when they suspended most of the Voting Rights Act's operation.

To be sure, in 2009, in a case from Texas, the Chief Justice warned that this might happen. But *Shelby* is a genuine shock to the system. The last time the Supreme Court invalidated a voting or civil rights statute was 130 years ago, in the still controversial *Civil Rights* cases of 1883, which struck at the 1875 Civil Right's Act.

The substantive basis for the rupture is equally startling. the court held in *Shelby* that the 2006 renewal of the Voting Rights Act offended the constitutional requirement that the States in the Union must be treated equally by the federal government once any unequal treatment of these States becomes outdated. The States and jurisdictions targeted by the Act's coverage formula, in Section 4 of the Act, no longer experience deep racial conflict, the court claimed. By inference, there is also no trouble in the States of Alaska, Arizona, California, and Texas and in counties or boroughs in Florida, New York City, North Carolina, or South Dakota, all of which historically experienced *Latino* v. *Anglo* or *Native-American* v. *White* conflict in electoral politics.

In fact, when Congress renewed the Act in 2006 it irresponsibly pretended—or so the 5-4 majority suggested in what amounts to a rebuke of how Congress works—that the South and the other covered jurisdictions were frozen in time. The court pictured Congress as blind to the obvious : discrimination in voting is a thing of the past.

Embracing the democratic progress since the 1960s, the court thus held that the 2006 coverage formula is unconstitutional (although interestingly nowhere can the Shelby majority find *constitutional text* to support this claim). The result is that administrative scrutiny by the Department of Justice of changes in State and local election law and districting (per Section 5 of the Act) are now on hold. There is nothing to administratively review, since the jurisdictionally targeted coverage of Section 4 is dead.

Imprudent experiment

Of course there is more to worry about here than disdainful judicial reprimands of America's national assembly. America's tortured development as a political democracy frame the court's weakening of the Voting Rights Act as overly optimistic. As the Southern writer William Faulkner once wrote. "The past is never dead. It is not even past." The *Shelby* decision imprudently experiments with America's deepest social and political cleavage.

We had a Reconstruction, the First Reconstruction after the Civil War, and for a time it was a considerable success. We had African-American members of Congress, Louisiana briefly had a black governor, and the South Carolina Supreme Court had an associate justice who was African-American. The University of South Carolina Law School was briefly fully integrated. Also, the public schools in New Orleans were integrated. The turnout rate among African-American adult male voters was about 80 per cent in presidential elections. There was plenty of conflict and terrible violence, to be sure. The First Reconstruction was nonetheless one of the world's greatest experiments in democracy.

But the First Reconstruction was killed off, and black voting and office-holding were reduced literally to zero by about 1900. It took until the 1960s to rebuild the strength of black politics and to force the country to enact the Voting Rights Act. American democracy has required a *Second* Reconstruction, to use the coinage of the great American historian, C. Vann Woodward.

Nothing like the stunning reversal of democracy that happened by 1900 is on the cards today. The Democratic Party is strongly committed to minority voting rights, and all Republicans pay lip service to the ideal—and some are very strongly committed to protecting them, such as the main author of the 2006 renewal, Rep. James Sensenbrenner of Wisconsin. Also the Supreme Court rather surgically invalidated the coverage formula of the Voting Rights Act, but left the rest intact—thus encouraging use of the federal courts. To be sure, litigation was the time-consuming, uncertain remedy that existed before 1965. But the difference between then and now is that there are many more election lawyers, and in general the lower federal courts are more liberal on voting rights than the Supreme Court. Also, there is a great deal of talent and capacity in the Civil Rights Division of the Justice Department, which has been active in one form or another since the late 1930s.

America is much different from 1965—or even 2006. The court was right about that. Not only did an African-American with a Kenyan name win the presidency in 2008, but that same controversial President also decisively won re-election last November. Still, the historical shadows over this decision are long and deep. We've seen in America how democratic revolutions can go backward. If the voting rights revolution of the past generation weakens seriously, then it will not be the first turn in such a cycle. Ironically, the first country in the world to have mass suffrage is still caught in contestation over protection of the right to vote. In that sense, Faulkner put his finger on a deep truth of American politics.

Economic democracy

Ambedkar says, the second wrong ideology which has initiated parliamentary democracy is the failure to realize that political democracy cannot succeed where there is no social and economic democracy. Some may question this proposition. To those who are disposed to question it, I will ask a counter question. Why parliamentary democracy collapsed so easily in Italy, Germany and Russia? Why did it not collapse so easily in England and the U.S.A.? To any mind, there is only one answer—namely, there was a greater degree of economic and social democracy in the latter countries than it existed in the former. Parliamentary democracy developed a passion for liberty. It never mode even a nodding acquaintance with equality. It failed to realize the significance of equality and did not even endeavor to strike a balance between liberty and equality.

A right to growth.—Don't people in a democracy have a right to good governance?

Economic growth represents opportunity. India's per capital GDP growth was 1.5 per cent during the notorious Licence Permit Quota (LPQ) Raj from 1950 to 1980 (Nehru, Indira Gandhi 1). The reversal of these failed policies in the 1980s (IG2, Rajiv Gandhi) almost doubled the per capita growth rate to 3 per cent. This was further raised to about 5 per cent (1992 to 2012) by the reforms of the 1990s (Narsimha Rao, Atal Bihari Vajpayee). The decline of per capita growth to 2 per cent in 2012-13 has come as a shock to the youth who have grown up in the decade of 6 per cent average growth.

The media exposure of high-level corruption at the Centre and pervasive governance failure across the country has heightened the outrage against the Government for depriving them of this new hope of a bright future. There is also a perception that the decline in growth is due partly to the indifference of the ruling party and its ministers to the role of economic growth in creating opportunities for all, including the generation of revenues so essential for enhancing opportunities for the poor through the supply of public goods (public health, basic education and employable skills). for instance, despite decades of talk about supply bottlenecks in infrastructure, lack of productivity in agriculture, leakages in PDS-FCI and abysmal sewage systems, there is little public evidence that state and Central ministers responsible for the areas critical to growth and opportunity are applying their minds and efforts to solving them. Don't people in a democracy have right to good governance?

Perhaps we need a "Right to Growth and Good Governance Act" to ensure that government at every level—from the ASHA worker or primary worker in the village to the humblest babu in the Block office, to the collector or magistrate at the district level, to the chief secretary of the state and all politicians holding office in State Governments or autonomous bodies—can be held accountable for economic growth.

The Chinese experience suggests that this could be an effective way of achieving sustained development and faster poverty reductions. Since 1980, when the Communist Party of China (CPC) instituted market reforms, China has had an average per capita growth of 8.8 per cent, double the 4.3 per cent average achieved by India. One of the major factors has been its primary focus on economic growth for enhancing national welfare. The objective of maximising economic growth has helped in achieving an effective governance system that is highly decentralised in operation while maintaining the unchallenged authority of the general secretary and the top organs of the party.

The basic objective of growth maximisation filters down not only to every level of government and party, but also to every state, provincial and party-related enterprise. Within this overall objective, party cadres, government officials and enterprise managers are relatively free to experiment on the means to achieve faster growth. More importantly, they are effectively rewarded for achieving growth targets. The intensity with which local officials compete to attract investment and the red carpet they lay out for FDI is apparent to anyone who has visited an enterprise zone in China.

At its higher levels, the party continues to provide overall guidance on the broad directions of growth. For instance, the growth objective was achieved by incentivising overseas Chinese entrepreneurs to shift their entire labour-intensive export manufacturing facilities to special zones in China. When the opportunity was exhausted, they turned their attention to more sophisticated FDI from developed countries. When export opportunities in developed countries appeared to flag and the Asian crisis struck, the higher-level direction changed to using infrastructure investment and import substitution of the export supply chain to sustain high growth. Thus, the use of growth achievement to measure the performance of party members and bureaucrats, and to reward them appropriately through promotion and economic opportunities for their family members, has allowed them to develop a unique blend of centralisation and decentralisation that has sustained growth for a historically unprecedented 30 years.

Though it is impossible to replicate the CPC-controlled Chinese system in a democratic country, we can and should give much greater importance to the growth objective, and also use it to reward bureaucratic functionaries to promote good governance. All public authorities responsible for licensing, permits, quotas and inspection would be judged by the growth of economic activity in their areas. The electricity department could be linked to the growth of metered electricity sale and consequent increase in production. Similarly, public health workers could be held accountable for the number of workers in their respective areas falling sick due to water-borne or communicable disease, and thus reducing production and growth.

If the right to food act can eliminate leakages, corruption and inefficiency in the PDS, FCI, as evidenced by the government's calculation of fiscal costs, a "Right to (8 per cent) Growth Act" can achieve wonders in eliminating corruption, improving governance and raising the rate of growth of the economy to its full potential of 8 per cent.

Two classes—ruler and ruled

Ambedkar says, 'I have referred to the wrong ideologies which in my judgment have been responsible for the failure of parliamentary democracy. All political societies get divided into two classes—the rulers and the ruled. If the evil stopped here, it would not matter much. But the unfortunate part of it is that the division becomes stereotyped and stratified so much so that the rulers are always drawn from the ruling classes and the classes of the ruled never becomes the ruling class. People do not govern themselves, they established a Government and leave it to govern them, forgotten that is not their Government. That being the situation parliamentary democracy has never been a Government of the people or by the people, and that is why has never been a Government for the people. Parliamentary democracy, not withstanding the paraphernalia of a popular Government, is in reality a Government of a hereditary subject class by a hereditary ruling class. It is those vicious organizations of political life which have made parliamentary democracy having not fulfilled the hope it held out to the common man of ensuring to him liberty, property and pursuit of happiness.'

Self-Government rule

Dr. Ambedkar was one of the admirers of freedom and self-Government of India. And he stood for a democratic system of administration. Dr. Ambedkar preferred the elected rulers or the Government to hereditary rulers for a good and democratic administration. He emphasizes that the administration must be free of corruption and dishonest ways of administering things. He says, everyone must share the responsibilities for the successful working of the democratic institutions in the land, otherwise; the feelings of public welfare and co-operation would not be strengthened.

Civil liberties

He says, "Democracy cannot function in the absence of basic civil liberties—which enables the community to vindicate itself against the State furthermore, the right to criticize, if it is to be effective, must include the right to organize opposition through political parties. Representative democracy is essentially procedural. It is characterized by free expression, free parties and free election." To Ambedkar, "Political parties are indispensable in parliamentary democracy, for democracy without a party system is unconceivable. There should be a regular party system." Ambedkar preferred that at east two parties are essential in democracy for its fructification. 'A party is necessary to run Government. But two parties are necessary to keep Government from being a despotic. A democratic Government can remain democratic only if it is worked by two parties—a party in power and a party in opposition."

Ambedkar fought against caste and injustice because he found that there were no human rights for a large majority of the people. He rebelled against such a social organization. He wanted to vitalize the masses in India, for equal human rights. For removing the social, economic, political and religious disabilities of the untouchables, it was necessary to establish Government of the people, for the people and by the people. Only under a democratic system of Government could social economic, political and religious freedom be ensured equally to every man and woman. His ultimate aim of life was to create a "real social democracy".

Social democracy

The concept of his social democracy included human treatment and human rights to all, without which it can not be sure and stable political life anywhere. The 19th century meaning of democracy is that each individual should have a vote, does not stand up to full test of social and political democracy. Without social democracy, neither political liberty, nor the unity of the nation can be maintained. According to him, political democracy rests on four premises :—these are—

(a) "The individual is an end in himself.

(b) The individual has certain inalienable rights which must be guaranteed to him by the Constitution.

(c) The individual shall not be required to relinquish any of his constitutional rights as a condition precedent to the receipt of a privilege.

(d) The State shall not delegate powers to private persons to govern others."

Human rights

The dignity of the individual, political liberty, social progress and human rights are necessary constitutional safeguards which form Ambedkar's basic decent democratic ideals in the political democracy. To him the ground plan means the social structure of a community to which the political plan is sought to be applied. Political democracy and liberty are nothing if not beaked and bucked up by equal social patterns, because the political structure rests on the social structure. "Indeed, the social structure," he says "has a profound effect on the political structure. It may modify it in its working. It may nullify it or it may even make a chery of it." It is therefore, essential that before passing any Judgment on any scheme of political relationship even making plans for economic reforms, the people must consider the ground plan that means social relations, Democracy should be regarded as both a social and a political method.

"The soul of Democracy", he says, "is the doctrine of one man, one value". This principle finds intrinsic worth in the individual personality of each man in political and social relation. This stands for the economic well being of the people, without which democracy, to him, has no value." The sum of democracy, according to him, essentially consists in the economic welfare of all men living in a particular society, besides its realization in political relation. Otherwise, democracy would kill its own soul and democracy without soul would be useless unrelated to human aspirations.

In India, to Ambedkar, the people have not realized that it is equally essential to prescribe the shape and form of the economic structure of society for the benefit of the majorities of men. They have not escaped hopes for economic democracy and emancipation, one vote after the long five years, has no meaning to the starving man. It has no significance to the man who is always exploited, rebuked and repressed. It has no value to him for whom there is no sympathy, no love and no give and take of life's hopes.

Artificial Barriers and Electoral Democracy

Civil society and the political establishment need each other to make democracy work

Many middle-class Indians, when questioned are quick to answer that they are 'non-political'. The same people would strongly advocate that every adult should vote—the most obviously political act in an electoral democracy. Politics act in an electoral democracy. Politics permeates almost every aspect of our lives, and to create artificial divisions between our politics, and ourselves, causes confusion in how both our society and our politics is shaped.

No social movement could therefore fail to recognise its relationship with political thought and action. The discourse in recent times has created arbitrary lines separating social and political movements. It has projected the 'political' as being tainted and this separation has alienated many of us from reasoned political thought and action.

"Civil Society" in the immediate context, is a buzword wrapped in ambiguity. The media has helped project. The media has helped project it as an utopian monolith expected to cleanse the rot in the political system. Even the way we define 'civil society' spells exclusiveness. It was expected to bring together an intrinsically hierarchical and divisive society which would confront politicians and their institutions. A popular protest can bring these divergent sectors together for some time.

However, it would be a mistake to romanticise or worse, equate 'civil society', with a movement. A campaign needs to work out details, and a movement needs to have its own internal logic. Sweeping away all complexities and reducing the debate to black and white, raises a threat to democracy itself. Social movements recognise this complexity, and see themselves as a part of a larger political process. There is an innate understanding of the politics of fighting oppression and exclusion and many have enriched and used democratic spaces that electoral politics does not offer.

The leaders of the independence movement were political but with symbiotic connections with a vast range of social movements with sated ideologies. Social movements had strong ideological and political differences, but they demonstrated a deep commitment to democratic debate, with a fundamental respect for difference and dissent. The Independence movement was therefore a collection of a variety of socio-political movements of depth and vision; some sustained the political parties they shaped. Gandhiji, Ambedkar, Netaji, M.N. Roy, the communists and many more, continued to influence our political future. They fought for independence from the British, despite sharp differences of a vision of India. Those visions were shaped by the social movements they helped establish. Some took public office, others like Gandhiji and Jayaprakash Narayan, did not. Embedded as they were in political discourse, these visionaries believed that sustained change would primarily emerge from participatory democratic processes. Leaders not to give birth to movements; on the contrary leaders emerge from them.

A legal frame-work by itself is insufficient, and is only a consequence of a movement that has already drawn large numbers of people into a sustained process. Social movements relied on their belief in the involvement of ordinary people, to pressurise the system for delivery and accountability. It developed the politics of conscience, to temper the simplistic reduction of democracy to numbers.

Post-Independence social movements, based on this tradition of grassroots work and struggle, have raised concerns of the weakest and most marginalised Groups have worked tirelessly and unacknowledged for years on a host of important issues in multiple ways. To quote both Gandhiji and Shankar Guha Niyogi—the murdered architect of the CMM, and organiser of the poorest tribals of Bastar—Sangharsh (struggle), Seva (service) and Nirman (development) are equally important to build political awareness and pressure.

India has a rich tradition of struggle without funding from agencies, foundations or the Government. Today, India's social movements are seen as powerful and independent. Most movements have kept away from public office,and therefore have been less prone to corruption.

The explosion of NGOs is in another framework, and they also need to be transparent and accountable. Each formation for struggle, whether NGO or movement is carefully watched by their own constituencies, and the standards of transparency, accountability and democratic functioning must cover everyone working in the public domain.

While it is undoubtedly true that political parties are facing a crisis of credibility, it is also unwise to berate the political class and their institutions for all failures. The "civil society" group that just joined the ranks of the political class has consistently attacked them. It is to be seen how they perform in their new *avatar*. They are grossly mistaken to believe that the Lokpal will only be enacted when and if they come to power.

We need to appreciate and nurture the very important role that will always be performed by socio-political movements. The movement for the Right to Information, and the Right to Work grew out of small but intense struggles of very ordinary people. Issues had to be understood, analysed and internalised to prepare the grounds to frame an appropriate law. The fact remains that it was Parliament that passed the laws. However, the implementation of radical enactments at the grassroots, where dreams turn to reality, is a continual challenge. The political class would do well to return to its socio-political base, and "civil society" to realise the intrinsic value in politics. Democracy demands a dialestical relationship between the two, to make promises real.

Vote by Defence Personnels and democracy

Vote bank politics is a commonly bandied about expression in the election season, which is no surprise. But a new vote bank of Armed Forces personnel is now looking a step closer to reality with the Supreme Court directing the Election Commission (EC) to allow defence personnel to vote as general voters in peace stations. This is somewhat unusual. The Supreme Court merely reiterated the law it laid down in an earlier judgment in 1971, though the circumstances of that case were somewhat different. The Representation of the People Act, 1950 defines the term 'ordinarily resident' in Section 20, a qualification required to get registered as a vote. Armed forces personnel are among the few categories of people defined as persons with 'service qualification' in Section 20(8) and are given a special dispensation in Section 20(3) and Section 20(5). This category can be declared while living at a place 'ordinarily resident status at another place where they would have normally lived, if it were not for the exigencies of service. Implicit faith was to be placed on their declaration and they would be registered at the place they indicated as their place of ordinary residence, most likely their native place, and as a corollary the place of their posting could not be their ordinary place of residence.

Place of posting v. residence

In a matter arising from the Nagaland Assembly Election in 1969, the court did not accept the argument that for service personnel, the place of posting cannot *ipso facto* be the place of residence. Instead, the declaration of the Assam Rifles personnel, who had spent 10 years in one location claiming it as a place of ordinary residence under Section 20(5), wherein but for their service qualification also they would have been ordinarily resident and not merely because of it, found favour with the Court. The Court declared that the statutory fiction in Section 20(3) gave the right to the personnel to claim registration at their home town or village but "the fiction cannot take away the right of persons possessing service qualification to get themselves registered at a constituency in which they are actually residing though such place happens to be their place of service."

The law gave a special dispensation to a service voter in that his declaration designating a place as his place of ordinary residence and certified by his organisation was not to be questioned by the Electoral Registration Officer (ERO) but simply accepted. It was intended to avoid the delay in registration if an enquiry were to be done independently by the ERO as in the case of ordinary voters.

Interpreting that judgment as mandating the registration of a service voter at the place of his posting and by cleverly using the provision under Section 20(5), a campaign was mounted in the run-up to the Punjab Assembly Election in 2007 by Brig. H.S. Ghuman (retd.) and his All India Veteran's Core Group (AIVCG) to have service personnel posted in several cantonment town in Punjab to register as ordinary voters there. A total of 7,274 service personnel were registered as voters, of whom 850 were from towns and villages of Punjab and 6,424 from other States. All applications were in Gurumukhi script, but most of the signatures were not in that language, therefore providing a clue to what really went on. The highest registration was in Kahnuwan constituency in Gurdaspur district with an Army cantonment, where 3,488 personnel registered. Of them, 70 were from Punjab and the rest from other States. It was alleged by the Akali opposition candidate that the Congress candidate P.S. Bajwa's relative, a retired Brigadier, was the prime mover for this large-scale registration. The formation commander was accused of collusion. Mr. Bajwa won that contest with a margin of 5,288 votes. Evidently, Mr. Bajwa used the tactics more effectively in the 2009 Parliament election. He seems to have won the Gurdaspur seat by a margin of 8,000 votes, with 11,000 votes from the cantonment cast in his favour against the 13,345 votes polled by servicemen.

Since then, retired service officers and others including a Member of Parliament have lent their support to this campaign culminating in the latest verdict of the Supreme Court. But as a note of caution that was sounded in many border States—that the local voters population may be small and can be outnumbered by the service personnel—the Court restricted the applicability of the order only to peace stations. In other words, only in peace stations can service persons claim they are ordinary residents and vote locally. If their units move out to non-peace stations, they cannot register themselves there. Imagine a serviceman who hails from Odisha and is posted in Jalandhar and gets himself registered there. He can vote in the Lok Sabha election but cannot vote for the Odisha Assembly election being held simultaneously. If his unit moves to a non-peace station, he can neither register himself there nor can he vote in the next Parliament or Assembly election unless he is registered again at some other place.

If peace stations are defined in a location-specific manner, this can lead to anomalies. If Itanagar or Leh are defined as peace stations but not Tawang or Nubra, it may be kosher for vote bank politics but will create disaffection among the local population in both places, given the small-sized constituencies and the thin margins of victory. Distinctions based on unit-specific roles in the same station will entitle men of the non-operational unit to register as voters and of the operational unit ineligible. So States have to be in either category to avoid anomalies.

More problems

As a large number of service personnel would be in the many cantonments in Haryana and Punjab, competitive canvassing by politicians there can bring in its wake other problems. A normal movement of a unit can be questioned by rival politicians as favouring one or the other candidate or party. The formation commanders can be accused of favouritism as happened in the Punjab Assembly election in 2007. Will the Election Commissioner be petitioned to effect the transfer of a formation commander because of his perceived partiality as is done in the case of Collectors, Superintendents of Police, Deputy Inspector Generals of Police, etc.? Only time can tell. But if a perfectly routine exercise by a detachment of the Army can be hyped to raise fears of a coup, pre-election movement of Army units and posting of formation commanders can become the subject of political mudslinging with obvious adverse consequences.

Since the new dispensation would not extend to all the defence personnel and since many service personnel may still remain registered in their native towns and villages by choice, the postal ballot system or its alternative—the proxy voting facility—would still be relevant. A study done at the behest of the EC by the Collector of Thanjavur district in 2007 showed that only 34.54 per cent of the postal ballot papers issued to service personnel returned in time to be included in counting. A significant 12.63 per cent of the ballot papers which were received late missed the counting. Worse, 25.39 per cent of ballot papers were returned undelivered, which meant that their addresses were not updated by the the Record Office.

Transmission time can be cut down if blank ballot papers are sent electronically, providing more time for their return. Better still would be to develop on-line voting and what better way than to provide it to the group that deserves it the most? We certainly owe it to our Armed forces personnel to do all that is possible to enable them to exercise their franchise.

Election and Democracy

Whether Election Commission or any other Constitutional Institution like President, Governor, Supreme Court, High Courts, Parliament, Public Service Commission and now Gram Panchayat, Municipalities etc. sacred cow? Can the argument survive that the institutions mentioned in text of Constitution cannot be touched? Those in, who argue those to be sacrosanct, those not in who argue to the opposite? How does a neutral lawyer look at this issue? A lawyer needs not to be committed to any. He argues for the brief. Herein both the sides are proposed to be examined and honest attempt would be made to adopt a neutral view.

Sanctity is *laissez faire* product. Indian Constitution was a compromise document wherein social, individual and a public interest stand equidistanced and persistently engrossed in tug-of-war like situation. Sometimes individual interests push back the other one or the second one and thus result privatization and other time social and political interest push back the individual interests and result in nationalization or socialization. Which does what depends on the system that prevails there and the policy that the Government stands for or follows; the capitalism, socialism, democracy, all owe to this scenario.

Indian Constitution provides for Part III (clamour to be sacrosanct). It provides for Part IV (DPSP). The Indian Supreme Court has balanced the two. Part III hitherto but no more. Part IV o.k. but know its limits. It has to respect people who constitute State, society, nation or country. All these are for the people, for their protection, for their welfare, security and safety. The protector cannot be allowed to devour the protected.

Constitution of India is Supreme. People of India are sovereign. The executive (President, Governors and Councils of Ministers) Parliament (Lok Sabha-Rajya Sabha) legislators (Legislative Assemblies and Legislative Councils of States) and Supreme Court and High Courts of states. Regional and District Councils are organs of Government. All work within areas (assigned to by the provisions of the Constitution. Election Commission, S.C./S.T./O.B.C. Commissions U.P.S.C. and P.S.C.'s of States are various constitutional bodies that discharge the functions given to them by the basic document of the sovereign, socialist, secular, democratic, republic which India that is Bharat is, and is so constituted by "we the people of India".

None of these institutions that are created by the Constitution can claim to be sacred cows. What is aimed at by the Constitution by creating these is that all these will work together to secure to all its citizens; justice, social, economic and political, liberty of thought expression, belief, faith and worship, equality of, of assuring dignity of Individual (Article 19-32) and unity and integrity of nation (Article 19(2) to (6).

The Constitution of India is supreme and sacred document of country (Article 12-13). Despite, that it is amendable under constituent power (Article 368). Many of its parts can be altered under legislative power beyond what is there is Article 368 (Article 2, 3 and 4). Now reply to query entitle is, that all parts of Constitution (barring basic features) are amendable, how can institutions created by it claim to be sacred cow? 'yes' it is true one organ cannot hit at the other. Live and let live, work and let others work, 'cooperate not kill' is crux of Ganga Jamuni cult of the country. Let not them fight *inter se*, rather fight against common enemies of humanity or of the country that is terrorism, poverty, naxalism, extremism, illiteracy and evils like sex discrimination, untouchability, corruption and black money. No organ is superior or inferior, no one should think of controlling the other, none is big brother, none step brother. All must swim or sink together with the system and the Constitution.

Electoral Reforms and Election Laws; Great Challenge to Constitutionalism

Article 54 and 55 (Election of President), 66 (vice president), 79, 80, 81 (Lok sabha, parliament), Article 168, 170, 171 (state legislatures), Part XV (Article 324-334) (Elections), Chapter IX-A of IPC (offences relating to Elections) Sections 171A to 171-1 (9 sections) and Section 505, Representation of People Act 1950 (32 sections and four Schedules), Representation of People Act, 1951 (Section 1-170) as amended in 1966, 1988; Delimitation Act 1972 (Sec. 1-11), The Presidential and vice-presidential Elections Act, 1952 (Sec. 1-23). Model Code of Conduct for the guidance of political parties and candidates (1 to VII) issued by CEC, the Conduct of Election Rules 1961 (1-99) as amended in 1999 and Removal of disqualification Acts passed by Andhra Pradesh, Arunachal, Assam, Bihar, Goa, Daman, Diu, Gujarat, Haryana, H.P., Jammu Kashmir, Karnataka, Kerala, M.P., Maharashtra, Manipur, Meghalaya, Nagaland, Odisha, Punjab, Rajasthan, Tripura, Sikkim, Tamilnadu and West Bengal and Delegated Legislation Provision Act as amended in 1985 are relevant election laws in India.

Nehruvian model of democracy

We have adopted Nehruvian model of democracy. This model follows. 'Top to bottom formulas' for the planning and development. The schemes are formulated by experts at the top and plans are executed by machinery for those at the grass root. Gandhi ji advocated grass root democracy. Planning at the grass root, at village level and then it be executed accordingly. The murder of Gandhi Ji left Nehruvian model as sole choice and country went for it. Nehru ji was great champion of western system of governance. The Parliamentary system of England needed not to be experimented. It was time tested in London. It was known to Indian administrative set up. As such alternative model of presidential form was not accepted. In parliamentary form, election of representatives of people is *sine quo non*. We have been following it since 1952.

Democracy, weak Parliament and strong court

Parliament consists of the representatives of the people whereas Supreme Court consists of top legal brains available and willing to serve in the country. The Supreme Court has always attempted to stick to the soul of the Constitution. Parliament has always tried to clarify that soul by amending the Constitution. There has been almost a tug of war resulting on account of ego of leaders like Nehru and Indira Gandhi who were always in conflict with Supreme court and perceived it as obstruction in way of egalitarian society. But our democracy survives. Is it not great achievement of our people?

The case that saved Indian democracy.—The judgment in *Kesavananda Bharati* v. *State of Kerala*, was crucial in upholding the supremacy of the Constitution and preventing authoritarian rule by a single party. Exactly forty years ago, on April 24, 1973, Chief Justice Sikri and 12 judges of the Supreme Court assemble to deliver the most important judgment in its history. The case of *Kesavananda Bharati* v. *State of Kerala* had been heard for 68 days, the arguments commencing on October 31, 1972, and ending on March 23, 1973. The hard work and scholarship that had gone into the preparation of this case was breathtaking. Literally hundreds of cases had been cited and the then Attorney-General had made a comparative chart analysing the provisions of the Constitution of 71 different countries!

Core question

All this effort was to answer just one main question : was the power of Parliament to amend the Constitution unlimited? In other words, could Parliament alter, amend, abrogate any part of the Constitution even to the extent of taking away all fundamental rights?

Article 368, on a plain reading, did not contain any limitation on the power of Parliament to amend any part of the Constitution. There was nothing that prevented Parliament from taking away a citizen's right to freedom of speech or his religious freedom. But the repeated amendments made to the Constitution raised a doubt : was there any inherent or implied limitation on the amending power of Parliament?

The 703 page judgment revealed a sharply divided court and, by a waferthin majority of 7 :6, it was held that Parliament could amend any part of the Constitution so long as it did not alter or amend "the basic structure or essential features of the Constitution." This was the inherent and implied limitation on the amending power of Parliament. This basic structure doctrine, as future events showed, saved Indian democracy and *Kesavananda Bharati* will always occupy a hallowed place in our constitutional history.

Supreme Court v. Indira Gandhi

It is supremely ironical that the basic structure theory was first introduced by Justice Mudholkar eight years earlier by referring to a 1963 decision of the Supreme Court of Pakistan. Chief Justice Cornelius—yes, Pakistan had a Christian Chief Justice had later, a Hindu justice as well—had held that the President of Pakistan could not alter the "fundamental features" of their Constitution.

The *Kesavananda Bharati* case was the culmination of a serious conflict between the judiciary and the government, then headed by Mrs. Indira Gandhi. In 1967, the Supreme Court took an extreme view, in the *Golak Nath* case, that Parliament could not amend or alter any fundamental right. Two years later, Indira Gandhi nationalised 14 major banks and the paltry compensation was made payable in bonds that matured *after 10 years*! This was struck down by the Supreme Court, although it upheld the right of Parliament to nationalise banks and other industries. A year later, in 1970, Mrs. Gandhi abolished the Privy Purses. This was a constitutional betrayal of the solemn assurance given by Sardar Patel to all the erstwhile rulers. This was also struck down by the Supreme Court. Ironically, the abolition of the Privy Purses was challenged by the late Madhavrao Scindia, who later joined the Congress Party.

Smarting under three successive adverse rulings, which had all been argued by N.A. Palkhivala, Indira Gandhi was determined to cut the Supreme Court and the High Courts to size and she introduced a series of constitutional amendments that nullified the *Golak Nath, Bank Nationalisation and Privy Purses* judgments. In a nutshell, these amendments gave Parliament uncontrolled power to alter or even abolish any fundamental right.

These drastic amendments were challenged by Kesavananda Bharati, the head of a *math* in Kerala, and several coal, sugar and running companies. On the other side, was not only the Union of India but almost all the States which had also intervened. This case had serious political overtones with several heated exchanges between N.A. Palkhivala for the petitioners and H.M. Seervai and Niren De, who appeared for the State of Kerala and the Union of India respectively.

The infamous Emergency was declared in 1975 and, by then, eight new judges had been appointed to the Supreme Court. A shocking attempt was made by Chief Justice Ray to review the *Kesavananda Bharati* decision by constituting another Bench of 13 judges. In what is regarded as the finest advocacy that was heard in the Supreme Court, Palkhivala made an impassioned plea for not disturbing the earlier view. In a major embarrassment to Ray, it was revealed that no one had filed a review petition. How was this Bench then constituted? The other judges strongly opposed this impropriety and the 13 judge Bench was dissolved after two days of arguments. The tragic review was over but it did irreversible damage to the reputation of Chief Justice A.N. Ray.

Constitutional rights saved

If the majority of the Supreme Court had held (as six judges indeed did) that Parliament could alter any part of the Constitution, India would most certainly have degenerated into a totalitarian State or had one-party rule. At any rate, the Constitution would have lost its supremacy. Even several later admitted that the basic structure theory preserved Indian democracy. One has to only examine the amendments that were made during the Emergency. The 39th Amendment prohibited any challenge to the election of the President, Vice-President, Speaker and Prime Minister, irrespective of the electoral malpractice. This was a clear attempt to nullify the adverse Allahabad High Court ruling against Indira Gandhi. The 41st Amendment prohibited any case, civil or criminal, being filed against the

President, Vice-President, Prime Minister or the Governors, not only during their term of office but forever. Thus, if a person was a governor for just one day, he acquired immunity from any legal proceedings for life. If Parliament were indeed supreme, these shocking amendments would have become part of the Constitution.

Old idea of India and New one

The closer the election, the clearer it becomes that this is the most important general election since 1977. In that distant year, Indian voters were offered a choice between a dictator and her son on one side and a raggedy, disparate caboodle of crusaders for democracy on the other. They chose the caboodle mostly because they had learned the hard way what losing democracy meant. This time the choice increasingly appears to be between the past and the future, between an old idea of India and a new one. Those selling the old idea, in their different ways, are the Congress, the Aam Aadmi Party and the 'secular socialists' who banded together last week as a third front.

What is the old idea of India? It is the one bequeathed us by Nehruvian socialism whereby we have created India as she is today. A land in which a vast infrastructure of politicians, officials, clerks and peons govern badly an angry and restless populace that no longer understands why basic needs are so hard to meet. A land in which young people demand to know why the sons of officials and politicians live like billionaires while they hunt desperately for jobs in a market that in the past 10 years has dried up. So crony capitalism is a favourite catchphrase with the AAP lot, without them noticing that this is always a creation of the state. In the eyes of AAP, it is corporate India that is to blame.

What is most depressing is that if you talk to leaders of the parties in the old India club, the solutions they offer are no different to the ones we have already tried. In their campaign speeches, they talk of secularism and socialism, poverty alleviation schemes and empowering women. On corruption, the Lokpal is a 'new' idea that has been around for 40 years. They know that they offer nothing new, so they throw in dark references to the man they most fear and loathe. Narendra Modi.

The reason why they fear and loathe him is because his popularity, according to recent polls, has increased dramatically despite repeated attempts by the old India club to remind voters that he is a *'maut ka saudagar'*. A merchant of death as Sonia Gandhi famously called him. What they seem not to have noticed is that his popularity has increased because he has succeeded in selling voters a new dream of India. In a sales pitch to businessmen in Delhi last Thursday, he offered a detailed account of what his priorities will be if he becomes prime minister.

After making it clear that he believed that India's strengths were "democracy, demography and demand" and its weaknesses were serious deficits of governance, trust, morality and hope, Modi made the case for what he thinks can be done. He said nothing could improve without "good governance". He did not say in so many words that by this he meant massive administrative reforms, but used anecdotes from Gujarat to make this point.

Then he talked of needing to improve "the quality of life" for the average Indian. It was vital to make India a country in which young people could live with hope and dignity, he said, and for this they needed jobs and the amenities that remain mostly unavailable to rural Indians. Electricity, clean water and a standard of living that could be described as a standard of living. He said, "We need in rural India to keep the soul of the villages but provide people with the utilities and services available in urban centres." He reiterated that he saw urbanisation not as a problem but as an opportunity.

What touched my own cynical soul to its core was his suggestions, when talking of healthcare, that we pledge to make India clean and sanitary by the 150th anniversary of Gandhiji's birthday. This was the best tribute that could be paid to Gandhiji, Modi said, because he had worked so hard to convince Indians of the importance of sanitation and hygiene. In modern terms, Modi emphasised, the benefit would be a huge reduction in India's healthcare bills, because it would shift the emphasis to prevention from cure.

He talked of many other things and in talking of them made it sound as if there was no reason at all why they could not be done. Listen to the whole speech on You Tube and you may discover the real reason why Modi leads the race to become India's next prime minister. He offers hope in a time of deep despair and he offers a dream of prosperity at the end of a decade when the Indian economy has sunk to its lowest ebb in recent memory. The old India club offers only 'poverty alleviation' to people sick to death of poverty.

The people and their representative institutions

To understand how and why the Supreme Court widened its reach in India, we must first turn to the country's representative institutions. It is the power of these bodies that the judiciary traditionally monitors with its review authority. Which people these institutions represent and how these bodies attempt to address their problems have a defining effect on how courts operate in a country.

India's social question.—In the opening paragraphs to *Democracy in America*, Tocqueville wrote that he was struck by Americans' "equally of conditions" and how this equality (amongst those who voted), more than anything else, shaped the governance of the then young United States. In contrast, since independence, India's situation has much more closely resembled that of eighteenth-century France than eighteenth-century America. India faced the same "social question" of millions of poor citizens needing economic upliftment that Hannah Arendt argued ultimately doomed the french Revolution. By almost continuously remaining a democracy since independence, India has defined the wisdom of thinkers, from Aristotle to Arendt, why argue that a stable democracy requires a large middle class electorate and little poverty. India's poor have not doomed the country's democracy, but they have dramatically shaped its representative institutions and judiciary.

Poverty in India is widespread and deep. The Indian government developed its current standard for measuring poverty in the early 1970s. At that time, nearly 55% of the population was considered below the national poverty line. In 1999-2000 this figure was down to nearly 26%. However, these current numbers do not provide an accurate picture, given the relatively low level at which the government has set the poverty line. According to the World Bank, in 1999-2000, nearly 35% of Indians lived on less than one dollar a day, and almost 80% of Indians lived on less than two dollars a day. The first government census in 1951 found that just 18% of the population was literate. Though the literacy rate has grown steadily since then, it still officially stood at only about 65% in 2001.

Despite its poverty, India generally has a high voter turnout, averaging around 60% in general elections. Indeed, turnout seems to be higher amongst poorer and less educated groups in India. This fact can be seen in the rural-urban divide in voting patterns, as urban areas on an average have more educated and wealthier population. In the 2004 general election, voter turnout was over 58% nationwide. For Delhi it was 47%. The other five largest metro areas averaged a voter turnout rate 11.84% lower than the average for their state.

Many of India's elite (and ordinary citizens) question the quality of the parliament elected by India's poor and uneducated "teeming millions", as one member of the constitutional assembly described the majority of Indians. This argument has two primary variants. First, there is a belief that a parliament elected by the masses will be corrupt and ineffective at furthering the interests of the poor people who elect it and the country as a whole. Because so many voters are destitute, they do not have the education or resources to determine what political platform would best represent their needs. They are, therefore, easily "misled" by caste, communal, or patronage politics, all of which are rife in India. Further, even if the public did know what policies are best, it simply does not have the resources to effectively monitor politicians or otherwise engage with the political system to keep abuses in check and its desires prioritized.

Second, there is a fear that Indians will elect a parliament that promises to quickly right the nation's social injustices through mass redistribution of property. Such a platform could lead to violence, and undermining of liberal democracy, and even the breakup of the country.

Overridden constitutional constraints.—Although the Constitution was designed to check the more radical tendencies of Parliament and help calm fears created by having an economically poor electorate, Parliament has traditionally treated amending the Constitution like legislating by other means. The Constitution has had ninety-four amendments between 1950 and 2007, averaging 1.65 amendments per year. There were only seventeen years during this fifty-seven year period when no amendments were added to the Constitution, and the pace and volume of amending has only increased independence.

Part of the reason why there have been so many amendments is that the Indian Constitution, more than most, details the administration of governance. This feature has its roots in the political elite's underlying distrust of a popularly elected Parliament, which goes all the way back to India's founding. Dr. B.R. Ambedkar, a leading Dalit politician and chairman of the Constitutional Drafting Committee, was famous for criticizing the Congress Party leadership for being Brahmin-dominated and contemptful of the common man. Yet, when introducing the draft Constitution to the Constituent Assembly, even he reasoned that "democracy in India is only a top-dressing on the Indian soil, which is essentially undemocratic. In these circumstances it is wiser not to trust the Legislature to prescribe forms of administration. This is the justification for incorporating them in the Constitution." If in Tocqueville's America the people were the word of God, in India there was far more skepticism of their wisdom.

Perhaps amending the Constitution would have been made more difficult (most amendments only require a two-thirds vote of Parliament) if the Constituent Assembly felt it had more representational legitimacy. The Assembly was elected indirectly by the state legislative assemblies, which themselves were elected under the Government of India Act, a 1935 British statute that did not provide for universal suffrage. Some Assembly members questioned their ability to bind what would be a parliament elected more directly by the people. Dr. Ambedkar accepted that the Assembly was not as representative of the people, but pointed out that the Indian Constitution was easier to amend than that of other countries. Tellingly, he also justified the Assembly's constituent power by arguing that any future parliament elected on the basis of adult suffrage would be likely to have less wisdom than the Constituent Assembly.

Poor parliamentary governance.—Not only are many Indians afraid of the spectre of an unchecked Parliament, but they also view the institution as often abandoning its governance functions. Even Members of Parliament ("MPs") agree with this view and state that as a result the public trusts the higher judiciary more than Parliament to govern.

It is difficult and dangerous to try empirically to show how well the Indian Parliament has governed, but the perception of incompetence and simple abdication of responsibility is widespread There are also some telling statistics. In 2006, for instance, almost sixty-five per cent of MPs said nothing in the Lok Sabha (Parliament's lower house) on a legislative issue, while forty per cent of bills received less than one hour of debate.

To be fair, anti-defection laws in India mean that MPs cannot deviate from their party in votes on legislation, giving them a disincentive to engage in legislative issues. Further, because there are 553 members of the Lok Sabha, it is difficult to find time for every representative to speak on each bill. Additionally, an MP's staff budget is currently barely enough for a single secretary to help with research on bills. However, that sixty-five per cent of Members of Parliament had nothing to say does seem to indicate a high level of apathy on legislative issues amongst many MPs.

Parliament sessions are also filled with frequent political posturing that disrupts the legislative process. From the fall of 2004 to the fall of 2006, only approximately twenty per cent of "in session" time was spent on actually debating legislation. At the end of the budget session in the spring of 2007, an exasperated Prime Minister Singh chastised Parliaments "to reflect and think whether the frequent disruptions enhance the standing of Parliament in the eyes of the people...

Adding to these difficulties, India has one of the highest population-to-representative ratios in the world. Each member of the up to 552 member strong Lok Sabha represents on average two million people (the upper house, or Rajya Sabha, is limited to 250 members, most of whom are elected by state and territorial legislatures, although twelve are appointed by the President). With such large constituencies, it is difficult and time-consuming for a Member of Parliament to attend to all the demands of the citizens he or she represents.

In one of the more frequently cited examples of perceived parliamentarian neglect, the Supreme Court laid down guidelines in 1997 to protect women against sexual harassment in the workplace because none had ever been enacted by Parliament. The Court found that having no law violated women's fundamental rights and wrote its own guidelines for the country with inspiration from the Convention on the Elimination of All Forms of Discrimination Against Women ("CEDAW"), which India had ratified. Although the Court said the guidelines it crafted could be overridden by legislation, Parliament has passed no legislation to do so in more than ten years since.

India's Parliament has a reputation for not only underperformance, but also corruption and even criminality. In December 2005, a television station ensnared eleven MPs in a sting operation in which it paid them money to ask questions in Parliament on behalf of a fictitious body. In 2008, before a major trust vote, opposition members waved money inside the Lok Sabha, claiming that they had been offered bribes to abstain during the vote. Criminals have even begun to become politicians themselves. In 2006, the National Social Watch Coalition reported that criminal cases were pending against almost twenty-five per cent of members of the Lok Sabha. Half of these were for charges that could carry a sentence of five or more years in prison.

All of these factors contribute to large sections of the public seeing Parliament as having largely abdicated its governing responsibilities. In this climate, the Supreme Court has been able to more easily assert that it has the power and duty to take on many of Parliament's responsibilities.

A fractured parliament.—Parliament's highly splintered composition has further aided the Court's rise. No political party—even Congress during its years of dominance—has ever received more than fifty per cent of the popular vote in India. Districts are won on the basis of who receives the most votes, and a majority is not required. In the current Lok Sabha, sixty per cent of members did not gather more than fifty per cent of the votes in their district. Such an electoral set-up helps fuel the numerous regional, case, and tribal-based parties that permeate and fracture Indian politics as they compete for only the forty, or even thirty, per cent of the vote they need to win. It also means that even parties that have won well over half of Parliament's seats have not necessarily been given a mandate from over half of India's population.

Despite never winning more than half of the national popular vote, the Congress Party was the dominant party in the decades after independence. Until 1967, it not only had a majority of seats in the Lok Sabha, but also had over the two-thirds seats required to amend the Constitution (a super majority it would later reclaim in the elections of 1971, 1980 and 1984). Yet since 1989 there have been only coalition governments, with no party winning a majority of seats on its own. The current Manmohan Singh led government is comprised of an uneasy alliance of fourteen coalition parties.

Executive and State level governance.—The executive, whose ministers are composed of different members of the ruling coalition, has also been susceptible to the problems that plague Parliament more generally. The executive often becomes preoccupied with keeping political alliances together in the center, or even with simply trying to keep the country together. In 2006, the Ministry of Home Affairs reported active, armed resistance against the government in nineteen of twenty-eight states. The executive's focus on attempting to control appears fractured and political alliances while combating violent threats to the state has left it with less time to focus on the nuts and bolts of governing. Moreover, several ministers have been involved in high-profile corruption and criminal scandals.

State-level representative institutions are also plagued by many of the same problems found at the center. These shortcomings have prodded the higher judiciary to expand its public interest litigation jurisprudence to take on a broader role in areas traditionally overseen by State Government. From independence until 1967, the Congress Party largely ruled the states without serious political challenge, and its internal power structure helped smooth center-state relations. Since 1967, however, and particularly after Congress's massive defeat at the center in 1977, there has been widespread fracturing of political power at the state level, leading to governing and legitimacy problems similar to those found in the center. Differences in ruling parties at the state and center have often led to strained relations. Further, corruption and capacity challenges are often worse at the state level. For example, in Uttar Pradesh about forty per cent of the legislative assembly faced criminal charges in 2008.

The corresponding rise of the court.—The Emergency in the 1970s, as we will see, undercut the political legitimacy of Parliament and the executive, as well as their claims to constitutional supremacy. It is their poor governance record, though, along with the fracturing of the electorate, that has continued to weaken and distract India's representative institutions. Since the Indian military, although highly respected, has traditionally been under strong civilian control, and the President is largely a figurehead, the

Supreme Court, as one of the few truly unified national institutions, has been able to increase its governance role relatively unchallenged. In this climate of both fear of Parliament's power and exhaustion at its perceived misgovernance, the Supreme Court has reshaped the American judicial model it inherited into one that, it has argued, is better suited for India's social and political situation. As Chief Justice Balakrishnan stated in 2008 :

It is often argued that the Supreme Court should maintain restraint and should not violate the legitimate limits in the exercise of its powers. However, this argument fails to recognize the constant failures of governance taking place at the hands of the other organs of State, and that it is the function of the Court to check, balance and correct any failure arising out of any other State organ.

The growth of unelected bodies.—The rise of the Supreme Court is part of a larger trend present in India and across the globe that takes decision-making power away from representative institutions and transfers it to independent or quasi-independent unelected bodies. Bruce Ackerman and Edward Rubin have pointed to the rise of these institutions more generally as a reason why we should discard our traditional conception of three branches of government. The rise of such bodies in India was likely aided by a Supreme Court that has not found a strict separation of powers in the Indian Constitution. The prominence of these unelected institutions may herald the rise of a post-democratic era in which the expanding power of unelected bodies and their legal and technocratic restrictions render democratic engagement largely impotent to effect fundamental political change. Democracy is left in name, but only as a shell that gives legitimacy to unelected institutions and unassailable laws and principles that guide the polity.

From the beginning, India's founders were concerned that the politics, conflicts of interest, and corruption of the country's representative institutions could seriously hamper the young nation. To alleviate some of these fears, the Constitution set up a series of independent unelected bodies. These constitutionally-mandated bodies includes a commission to supervise elections, a comptroller and auditor general to check the government's accounts for legal irregularities, a finance commission to apolitically allocate tax revenue between the center and the states, and pubic service commissions at the union and state levels to oversee recruitment and promotion to government posts. The relatively independent Reserve Bank of India, which was created by the British in 1934, continued to regulate the money supply after independence and, after 1994, took on expanded powers to regulate the country's financial sector.

More recently, after its decision to liberalize the economy in the early 1990s, Parliament created a new set of independent or quasi-independent regulatory bodies. These entities include the Security and Exchange Board of India, the Telecom Regulatory Authority, the Insurance Regulatory and Development Authority, the Competition Commission, and central and state electricity authorities. The development of these bodies signaled a shift away from not only direct Parliamentary control over the economy through nationalized industries, but also Parliament's control over its regulation. In creating these institutions, Parliament was deeply influenced by advice from international development agencies (which themselves are another set of unelected bodies with a significant ability to control and shape governance decisions). It was hoped that if these Indian regulatory authorities had independence from the political process they would be less likely to grant "market-distorting" subsidies or be captured for political purposes, while reducing corruption and providing better services. In reality, these agencies are often not as independent as they are made out to be. Their actions are generally reviewed by Parliament, many of them can be reconfigured or outright disbanded through further legislation, and they must respond to many of the same political pressures as Parliament in order to retain their legitimacy with the public.

❑ ❑

SELECT BIBLIOGRAPHY

1. **Julius Stone,** The Province and Function of Law, Part II, Chs., 1, 8-16 (2000). Universal, New Delhi.
2. **Cardozo,** The Nature of Judicial Process (1995), Universal, New Delhi.
3. **Henry J. Abraham,** The Judicial Process (1998), Oxford.
4. **J. Stone,** Precedent and the Law : Dynamics of Common Law Growth (1985), Butterworths.
5. **W. Friendmann,** Legal Theory (1960), Stevens, London.
6 **M.D.A. Freeman,** Lloyd's Introduction to Jurisprudence.
7. **Bodenheimer,** Jurisprudence—The philosophy and Method of the Law (1997) Universal, Delhi.
8. **Upendra Baxi,** The Indian Supreme Court and Politics (1980), Eastern, Lucknow.
9. **Rajeev Dhavan,** The Supreme Court of India—A Social-Legal Critique of its Juristic Techniques (1977), Tripathi, Bombay.
10. **John Rawls,** A Theory of Justice (2000), Universal, New Delhi.
11. **Edward H. Levi,** An Introduction to Legal Reasoning (1970), University of Chicago.
12. **J. Stone,** Legal System and Lawyers', Reasonings, 1999 Universal, New Delhi.
13. **Campbell,** T., Seven Theories of Human Society, OUP.
14. **Diamond. S.** 'The Rule of Law versus the order of custom' 38 Social Research, 1971, 42.
15. **Frank J.,** Law and the Modern Mind, 1958 Anchor Books edt.
16. **Fuller L.L.,** 'Human Interaction and the law', 1969.
17. **Gorden, R.W.,** 'New Developments in Legal Theory' 1982 Pantheon Books.
18. **Hart HL.A.,** 'Definition and Theory in Jurisprudence', 1854, 70 LQR 37.
19. **Holmes OW.,** 'The Path of Law' 1897 10 Harv. Law Rev. 457.
20. **Kelsen H.,** The Pure theory of Law, University of California.
21. **Llewellyn, K.N.,** 'Some Realism about Realism—Responding to Pound' 1931 HLR 1222.
22. **Pound R.,** Philosophy of Law.
23. **Pound R.,** Social Control through Law.

24. **Rawls. J.,** A Theory of Justice, OUP 1972.
25. **Raz J.,** 'The Problems about the Nature of Law', 1982 Martinus Nijhoff.
26. **Ross R.,** On Law and Justice Stevens & Sons.
27. **Twining W.,** Karl Llewellyn and the Realist Movement.
28. **Wicke J.,** Postmodern Identity and the Legal Subject, 1991 62 UCLR 455.
29. **Law Behind Law,** 29 Col. L. Rev. 113.
30. Stare decisis in Contemporary England, 82, L.Q.R. 203.
31. Precedents in Court of Appeal, 9 C.L.J. 339.
32. Precedents, 8 C.L.J. 118.
32. **Salmond** : Jurisprudence.
34. Precedents in England law—**Cross**.
35. **Montrose**, Ratio Decidèndi of a case, 20 Mod. L.R. 587 (1957).
36. **Goodhard**, Ratio Decidendi of a case, 22 Mod. L.R. 117 (1959).
37. **Simpson,** The Ratio Decıdendi of a case 22 Mod. L.R. 453.
38. **Stone,** As above at p. 597.
39. **Gray,** Judicial Precedents—A Short History in Comparative Jurisprudence 9 H.L.R. 242 (1896-97).
40. **Read,** Judicial Process in common law 37 Canadian Bar Review 265 (1969).
41. **Mc Guing**, Precedents and Policy in Supreme Court 45 Canadian B.R. 679 (1967).
42. Making the Punishment fit the crime 77 H.L.R. 1071 (1963-64).
43. Doctrine of Precedent in Continental Law (1946) 20 Journal of Comparative Legislation 34.
44. History of Judicial Precedents 46 L.Q.R. 207.
45. **Good Hart**—Precedents in English and Continental Law 50 L.Q.R. 40.
46. **Maxwell,** Interpretation of Statutes.
47. **Bindra**, Interpretation of Statutes.
48. **Craise**, Construction of Statutes.
49. Golden rule of Interpretation 22 Can B. Rev. 1033.
50. The problem of legal interpretation in France (1930) 12 Journal of C.L. 79 (3rd Series).
51. The so called Anglo American and Continental Schools of thought in International Law. 13 British Y.B. of Int. Law. 31.
52. Interpretation in English and Continental Law, 9 Journal of C.L. 153 (1927).
53. Interpretation of Statutes 5 Camb. L.J. 163.
54. Interpretation of Uniform Statutes; 62 L.Q.R. 278.
55. **Lalla Ram Tiwari,** Leading Cases in Hindu Law.

56. Mimansa Rules of Interpretation, **Dr. Kishori Lal Sarkar.**
57. Hindu Law in its Sources, **Dr. G.N. Jha.**
58. **Gutteridge**, Comparative Law (1946).
59. **R. Pound** : What may we expect from Comparative Law 122 A.B.A.J. 56.
60. *R. Pound,* Comparative Law 13, Am. J. of Comp. L. 507.
61. *M. Rheinstein*—Teaching Comparative Law 5 U. of CH. L.R. 616.
62. 32 Teaching of Comparative Law as an academic subject 82 L.Q.R. 40 (1966).
63. Comparative Law as a factor in English Legal Education; 23 J. Com. Leg. & International Law 132.
64. Comparative and Foreign Law in American Law Schools 50 Col. L. 616.
65. Aims of Comparative Law, 7 Temp. L.Q. 300.
66. International Committee of Comparative Law Enquiry on the organization and purposes of institutes dealing with Comparative Law. 4 am J. of Comparative Law 248-68.
67. **F.C. Auld**; Comparative Law 26 Can. B. Rev. 776.
68. Institute of Comparative Law, 47 Col. L. Rev. 231.
69. **Herome Hall**, Comparative Law and Social Theory (1963).
70. **Schmithoff**, The Science of Comparative Law 7 Camb. L. Journal 94 (1939-41).
71. **Amos and Walton**, Introduction to French Law.
72. Introduction to Roman Law by **Jolowicz.**
73. Codification in British India, **B.K. Acharya.**
74. Seven years of Indian legislation—**Hunter.**
75. Indian Codification, **Ilbert**, 5 L.Q.R. 354, 13 L.Q.R. 224.
76. **Whitely Stokes,** Anglo Indian Codes.
77. **Mcnaire,** Roman Law and Common Law.
78. **Schwartz,** French Administrative Law and the Common Law World.
79. Justice According to Law—Pond, 14 Col. L. Rev. 1 (1914).
80. The Business of the Supreme Court : 51 Har. L.R. 577 (1938).
81. Proposed Federal Administrative Law : 36 A.B.A.J. 13 (1950).
82. Safeguards in the exercise of functions by Administrative Bodies : 28 Can. B. Rev. 538 (1950).
83. Administrative Law in England since 1918 by **Robson.**
84. Scope of Review of Federal Administrative Action, 50 Col. L. Rev. 559.
85. Authority and Responsibility 51 Col. L.R. 838.
86. Development of Administrative Law in England 81 L.Q.R. 148.
87. Do we need a Philosophy of Law? 5 Col. L. Rev. 339?
88. Legality of Administrative Directions 8 J.I.L.I. (1966).

89. Right to fair hearing in Indian, English and American Administrative Law. J.I.L.I. 492 (1958-59).

90. House of Lords on Natural Justice 1963, Mod. L.R. 543.

91. The Reform of Indian Administrative Law : The tasks before Administrative Reforms Commission 2 Ben. L.J. 100-123.

92. **Prof. G.P. Tripathi**—Comparative Jurisprudence.

93. **Prof. G.P. Tripathi**—Indian Jurisprudence.

94. **Prof. G.P. Tripathi**—Constitutional law; new Challenges.

95. **Prof. G.P. Tripathi**—Law and Social Transformation.

96. **Acocella N**. (1999), In difesa del welfare state, in Acocella N. (ed.), *Globalizzazione e stato sociale*, Bologna, IIMulino

97. **Aghion P., Caroli E. Garcia-Penalosa C.** (1999), Inequality and Economic Growth: the Perspective of The New Growth Theories, "The Journal of Economic Literature", 37(4): 1615-1660.

98. **Anderson E.S.** (1999), What is the point of equality? "Ethics", 109: 287-337.

99. **Arneson R.** (1989), Equality of opportunity for welfare, "Philosophical Studies", 56, 77-93.

100. **Arneson R.** (2000), Luck egalitarianism and prioritarianism, "Ethis". 110: 339-49.

101. **Barcellona P.** (1998), I declino dello stato. Riflessioni di fine secolo sulla crisi del progetto moderno, Bari, Dedalo.

102. **Barr N.** (1998), The economics of the welfare state, 1st ed. 1987, Stanford, Stanford University Press.

103. **Barrotta P**. (1999), I demeriti del merito. Una critica liberale alla meritocrazia, Soveria Mannelli, Rubbettino.

104. **Ben-Ner A., Putterman L**. (1998), eds., Economics, values and organization, Cambridge, Cambridge University Press.

105. **Bobbio N** (1978), Eguaglianza ed egualitarismo, in N. Bobbioet al, Eguaglianza ed egualitarismo, Roma, Armando.

106. **Bobbio N.** (1999), Destra e sinistra. Ragioni e significati di una distinzione politica, Roma, Donzelli.

107. **Bowles S.** (1998), Endogenous preferences: The cultural consequences of markets and other economic institutions, "Journal of Economic Literature", 36: 75-111.

108. **Bowles S.**, Gintis H. (2000), Social capital and community governance, Dept. of Economics, University f Massachusetts, Dec. 22, mimeo.

109. **Carens J.H.** (1981), Equality, moral incentives and the market, Chicago, The University of Chicago Press.

110. **Carens J.H.** (1986), Rights and duties in an egalitarian society, "Political Theory", 14 (1): 31-49.

111. **Cohen G.A**. (1989), On the currency of egalitarianjustice, "Ethics", 99, 906-944.

112. **Dworkin R**. (1981a), What is equality? Part 1: Equality of welfare, "Philosophy & Public Affairs", 10, 185-246.
113. **Dworkin R**. (1981b), What is equality? Part 2: Equality of resources, "Philosophy & Public Affairs", 10, 283-345.
114. **Fehr E.,** Gachter S. (2000), Fairness and retaliation: the economics of reciprocity, "Journal of Economic Perspectives", 14 (3), 159-181.
115. **Fischer J.M.** (1999), Recent work on moral responsibility, "Ethics", 110: 93-139.
116. **Fleurbaey M** (1995a), Equal opportunity or equal social outcome? 'Economics and Philosphy", 11: 25-55.
117. **Fleurbaey M.** (1995b), Equality and responsibility, "European Economic Review", 39: 683-689.
118. **Fleurbaey M.** (2001), Review of Roemer (1998), "Journal of Economic Literature", 39: 131-2.
119. **Franzini M.** (1994), In cerca dell'eguaglianza Siusta, "Politica ed Economia", June.
120. **Franzini M.** (1997), La riforma dello stato sociale, mimeo.
121. **Frey B.S.** (1997), Not just for the money. An economic theory of personal motivation, Cheltenham,Elgar.
122. **Gerard-Varet L.-A., Kolm S.-C., Mercier Ythier J.** (2000), The economics of reciprocity, giving and altruism, Macmillan, London.
123. **Gilbert M.** (1989), On social facts, Princeton, Princeton University Press.
124. **Goodin R. E.** (1998), Social welfare as a collective social responsibility, in D. Schmidtz, R.E. Goodin, Social welfare and individual responsibility, Cambridge University Press, Cambridge.
125. **Goodin R.E., Headdey B., Muffels R. Dirven H.J.** (1999), The real worlds of welfare capitalism, Cambridge, Cambridge University Press.
126. **Granaglia E.** (2001), Modelli di politica sociale, II Mulino, Bologna.
127. **Hayek F.A.** (1960), The constitution of liberty, Chicago, The University of Chicago Press.
128. **Hayek F.A.** (1976), Law, legislation and liberty, vol. 2: The mirage of social justice, London, Routledge & Kegan Paul.
129. **Hild M., Voorhoeve A.** (2002), Roemer on equality of opportunity, mimeo, June.
130. **Kolm S.-K.** (2000), The logic of good social relations, "Annals of Public nd Cooperative Economics", 71: 171-89.
131. **Levine A.** (1998), Rethinking liberal equality: from a 'utopian' point of view', Cornell University Press, Ithaca.
132. **Mason A** (2001), Equality of opportunity, old and new, Ethics, 111: 760-81.
133. **Rawls J.** (1971), A theory of justice, Cambridge (Mass.), Harvard University Press.

134. **Ripstein A.** (1999), Equality, responsibility and the law, Cambridge University Press, Cambridge

135. **Roemer J.E.** (1985), Equality of talent, "Economics and Philosophy", 1: 151-87

136. **Roemer J.E.** (1995), Equality and responsibility, "Boston Review", 20: 3-16.

137. **Roemer J.E.** (1996), Theories of distributive justice, Cambridge (Mass.), Harvard University Press.

138. **Roemer J.E.** (1998), Equality of opportunity, Cambridge (Mass.), Harvard University Press.

139. **Scanlon T.M.** (1988), The significance of choice, The Tanner lectures on human values, vol. 8, Salt Lake City, University of Utah Press.

140. **Schmidtz D.** (1998), Taking responsibility, in D. Schmidtz, R.E. Goodin, Social welfare and individual responsibiity, Cambridge University Press.

141. **Sen A.K.** (1980), Equality of what? in S. McMurrin (ed.), The Tanner lectures on human values, vol. 1, Salt Lake City, University of Utah Press, reprinted in A.K. Sen, Choice, welfare and measurement, Oxford, Blackwell, 1982.

142. **Sen A.K.** (1992), Inequaity re-examined, Oxford, Oxford University Press.

143. **Steiner H.** (1997), Choice and circumstance, Ratio, 10 (3): 296-312.

144. **Steiner H**. (1999), Equalities and responsibility, Notizie di Politeia, 56: 25-9

145. **Sulloway F.J.** (1997) *Born to rebel: birth order, family dynamics, and creative lives*, Vancouver, Vintage Books.

146. **Veca S**. (1986), Una filosofia pubblica, Milano, Feltrinelli.

147. **Veca S.** (1998), La filosofia poitica, Bari, Laterza.

148. **Watson G**. (1996), Two faces of responsibility, "Philosophical Topics", 24: 227-48.

149. **Ackerman, Bruce**. (1991), We the people: Foundations (Cambridge: Harvard University Press).

150. **Allan, T.R.S.**. (2001), Constitutional Justice: A Liberal Theory of the Rule of Law (Oxford: Oxford University Press).

151. **Alexander, Larry, ed.** (1998), Constitutionalism (Cambridge: Cambridge University Press).

152. **Altman, Andrew**. (1990) Critical Legal Studies: A Liberal Critique (Princeton: Princeton University Press).

153. **Austin, J.L.** (1995) The Province of Jurisprudence Determined (Cambridge : Cambridge University Press).

154. **Bentham, Jeremy**. (1838-1843) "Constitutional Code", in Vol. 9, Works of Jeremy Bentham, pp. 119-124, Bowring ed.

❑ ❑

INDEX

❑ ❑

Standard Text Books on Law

(Subject-wise)

❖ **Administrative Law**	
U. P. D. Kesari	**Administrative Law**
Harloveleen Kaur	**Administrative Law**
K. C. Joshi	**Administrative Law**
❖ **Arbitration & Conciliation**	
S. C. Tripathi	**Arbitration & Conciliation**
Anupam Kurlwal	**An Introduction to Alternate Dispute Resolution System**
S. C. Tripathi	**Alternate Dispute Resolution System (ADR)**
❖ **Banking Law**	
Anjani Kant	**Lectures on Banking Law**
R. N. Chaudhary	**Banking Law**
❖ **Business Law**	
R.N. Chaudhary	**Business Laws**
❖ **Company Law**	
S. C. Tripathi	**New Company Law**
❖ **Competition Law**	
S. C. Tripathi	**Competition Law**
❖ **Civil Procedure Code**	
Avtar Singh	**Civil Procedure Code**
D. N. Mathur	**Civil Procedure Code**
❖ **Constitutional Law**	
Kailash Rai	**Constitutional Law of India**
K. C. Joshi	**Constitutional Law of India**
G. P. Tripathi	**Constitutional Law-New Challenges**
Shatakshi Johri	**Lectures on Constitutional Law (with Power Point Presentation)**
June L. D'Souza	**World Constitutions**
❖ **Consumer Protection Act**	
S. C. Tripathi	**Consumer Protection Act**

❖ **Law of Contract**	
S. S. Srivastava	**Law of Contract — I & II with Specific Relief Act, Sale of Goods Act, Partnership Act & Negotiable Instruments Act**
Kailash Rai	**Contract-I & Specific Relief Act**
Prabhat K. Gupta	**Contract-I with Specific Relief**
❖ **Copyright Law**	
Ishita Chatterjee	**Copyright Law**
❖ **Criminal Procedure Code**	
S. N. Misra	**The Code of Criminal Procedure**
❖ **Criminology & Penology**	
N. V. Paranjape	**Criminology & Penology with victimology**
❖ **Cyber Law**	
J. P. Mishra	**An Introduction to Cyber Law**
❖ **Easement Act**	
H. P. Gupta	**Indian Easement Act**
❖ **Law for Engineers**	
Vibha & Kunwar Arora	**Law for Engineers**
❖ **Environmental Law**	
S. C. Tripathi	**Environmental Law**
Sukanta K. Nanda	**Environmental Law**
Sanjeev K. Chadha	**Lectures on Environmental Law**
❖ **Equity & Trust**	
S. C. Tripathi	**Equity & Trust**
❖ **Evidence**	
Avtar Singh	**Principles of The Law of Evidence**
❖ **Forensic Science**	
Ishita Chatterjee	**Law of Forensic Science**
❖ **Hindu Law**	
U. P. D. Kesari	**Modern Hindu Law**
Basant K. Sharma	**Hindu Law**
❖ **Human Rights**	
H. O. Agarwal	**Human Rights**

Dr. Bhagyashree A. Deshpande	**Human Rights : Law & Practice**
❖ **Indian Penal Code**	
S. N. Misra	**Indian Penal Code**
R. N. Saxena	**Indian Penal Code**
N.V. Paranjape	**Indian Penal Code**
Kumar Askand Padey	**Principal of Criminal Law in India : Cases and Materials**
❖ **Information Technology**	
Ishita Chaterjee	**Law on Information Technology**
❖ **International Law & Human Rights**	
H. O. Agarwal	**International Organisation**
H. O. Agarwal	**International Law & Human Rights**
H. O. Agarwal	**A Concise Book On International Law & Human Rights (Nut shell)**
❖ **Private International Law**	
Sai Ramani Garimella	**Private International Law (Conflict of laws)**
❖ **International Trade Law**	
Ishita Chatterjee	**International Trade Law**
❖ **Intellectual Property Rights**	
J. P. Misra	An Introduction to **Intellectual Property Rights**
M. K. Bhandari	An Introduction to **Intellectual Property Rights**
Kush Kalra	**Landmark Judgments on Intellectual Property Rights**
❖ **Law of Insurance**	
Naresh Mahipal	**An Introduction to Insurance Laws**
R. N. Chaudhary	**General Principles of Insurance Law**
❖ **Interpretation of Statutes**	
R.D. Srivastava	**Text Book of Interpretation of Statutes & Legislation**
D. N. Mathur	**Interpretation of Statutes**

❖ **Judicial Process**	
G. P. Tripathi	**Judicial Process**
❖ **Jurisprudence**	
Nomita Agarwal	**Jurisprudence & Legal Theory**
N. Krishna Kr.	**Jurisprudence & Comparative Law**
S. P. Dwivedi	**Jurisprudence & Legal Theory**
M. K. Das	**An Introduction to Jurisprudence (Legal Theory)**
❖ **Labour Laws**	
S. N. Misra	**Labour & Industrial Laws**
Sunil Yadav	**Labour Laws**
❖ **Land Law**	
R. R. Maurya	**U. P. Land Laws**
D. N. Mathur	**Maharashtra Land Laws**
❖ **Law & Medicine**	
Nandita Adhikari	**Law & Medicine**
❖ **Legal Dictionary**	
Arora	**Supreme Law Dictionary** (English – Hindi)
❖ **Legal Ethics**	
Kailash Rai	**Legal Ethics, Accountability for Lawyers & Bench-Bar Relations**
❖ **Legal GK**	
Sushil Kumar Garg	**Legal General Knowledge**
S. C. Tripathi	**Legal Essays & Short Paragraphs**
❖ **Legal Method**	
G. P. Tripathi	**Legal Method**
❖ **Legal Language**	
S. C. Tripathi	**Legal Language, Legal Writing & General English**
Anirudh Prasad	**Outlines of Legal Language in India**
❖ **Legal & Constitutional History**	
S. C. Tripathi	**Indian Legal & Constitutional History**
G. P. Tripathi	**History of Courts & Legislation**

❖ **Indian Limitation Act**	
H. P. Gupta	**Limitation Act**
❖ **Law & Social Transformation**	
G. P. Tripathi	**Law & Social Transformation**
❖ **Media Law**	
Sukanta K. Nanda	**Media Law**
❖ **Muslim Law**	
M. A. Qureshi	**Muslim Law**
Mohd. Nazmi	**Mohammadan Law**
❖ **Moot Court**	
Kailash Rai	**Moot Court (Pre-Trial Preparation and Participation in Trial Proceedings)**
❖ **Practical Training**	
D. N. Mathur	**All India Bar Examination Guide**
D. N. Mathur	**Hand Book on Court Visits (An Essential Readings for Law Students & Budding Lawyers)**
N. Krishna Kumar	**LL.B. Entrance Examination Guide**
J. K. Upadhyay	**UGC-Net (JRF) Examinations Guide on Law**
Sharma, Diwakar & Saraf	**CLP's Ultimate Success CLAT & LLB Entrance Examination 2016-17**
❖ **Partnership Act**	
H. P. Gupta	**Indian Partnership Act**
S.C. Tripathi	**Indian Partnership Act**
❖ **Pleadings, Drafting & Conveyancing**	
R. N. Chaturvedi	**Pleadings, Drafting & Conveyancing**
❖ **Public Interest Litigation**	
Ajay Gulati	**Public Interest Lawyering, Legal Aid & Para Legal Services**
Kailash Rai	**Public Interest Lawyering, Legal Aid & Para Legal Services**
❖ **Research Methodology (Legal)**	
Mona Purohit	**Legal Education & Research Methodology**
G.P. Tripathi	**Legal Research & Research Methodology**
G.P. Tripathi	**Legal Education in India**

❖ **Right to Information Act**	
A. S. Yadav	**Right to Information Act, 2005 : An Analysis**
❖ **Sale of Goods Act**	
S. C. Tripathi	**Sale of Goods Act**
❖ **Taxation Laws**	
Atal Kumar	**Taxation Laws**
❖ **Transfer of Property Act**	
G. P. Tripathi	**Transfer of Property Act**
Prof. (Dr.) Ashok Kumar Srivastava	**The Transfer of Property Act with Easement Act**
Rajani Malhotra Dhingra	**Transfer of Property Act and Indian Easement Act**
❖ **Law of Torts**	
J. N. Pandey	**Law of Torts**
Siddharth Dubey	**Lectures on Law of Torts and Consumer Protection**
❖ **Women & Children**	
Anjani Kant	**Law Relating to Women & Children**
S. C. Tripathi	**Law Relating to Women & Children**
S. K. Chatterjee	**Offences against Children & Juvenile Offence**
❖ **Women & Criminal Law**	
S. C. Tripathi	**Women & Criminal Law**
❖ **Political Science for Pre-Law Students**	
Dr. Preetam V. Jain	**Political Science I (Political Theory)**
Dr. Alok G. Gupta	**Political Science II (Political Obligation)**
Neelam Kant	**An Introduction to Political Science**
❖ **Economics**	
Ratna Chatterjee	**An Introduction to Economics**
Surbhi Arora	**Economics for Law Student**
❖ **Sociology**	
Navendu Thakur	**An Introduction to Sociology**
❖ **General English for Law Students**	
S.C. Tripathi	**General English for Law Students**

Shweta Gupta	**General English and Legal Language**
❖ **Reference Books**	
Dr. Amita Verma	**Cyber Crimes in India**
Dr. A. Verma	**Cyber Crimes & Law**
Dr. S. Kaur	**Female Foeticide—A Frightful Reality**
Dr. Kavita Singh	**Human Rights and Anti-Terrorism Law's in India**
Dr. Bandopadhyay & Dubey	**An Introduction to Environmental Rights**
Dr. Sharma, Jaswal & Singh	**Protection & Promotion of Human Rights in India**
G. S. Randhawa	**Victimology & Compensatory Jurisprudence**
Dr. H.O. Agarwal	**Kashmir Problems – Its Legal Aspects**
Ishita Chatterjee	**Techno Legal Aspects of Scientific Evidence**
Dr. Anshuman Mishra	**Election Laws With Special Reference to Corrupt Practices**
Devinder Singh	**Child Labour & Right to Education**
Dr. Sharma & Jaswal	**Law as a Facilitator of Socio-Economic Reforms**
Dr. Chintamani Rout	**Personal Liberty and Human Rights**
Dr. Ajay Pratap Singh	**The Arms Act in India : A Study in Criminological Perspective**
Kush Kalra	**Matrimonial Disputes**
Kush Kalra	**Freedom of Speech and Expression**
June L. DSouza	**International Law of Billergency & Occupation : A Pedagogic Introduction**
Usha Tandon & Sidharth Luthra	**Human Right : Trafficking of Women and Children Legal and Policy Framework**
Dr. Sanjeev K. Chadha	**Environmental Jurisprudence**

Central Law Publications

107 Darbhanga Castle, Allahabad-211 002 (India)
Tel.: [0532] 2461178, Tel. Fax: [0532] 2461123.
Mobile : 9415340927
E-mail: clp.editorial@gmail.com
Website: www.clplawbooks.com

Dear Reader,

- Thanks for choosing this book published by our publication house.
- Register yourself and your colleagues on our website www.clplawbooks.com at student/teacher corner and get promotional offers and free legal updates.
- Connect with us by giving feedback/ mistakes/critical evaluation and suggestions for our books.

Thanks

CLP Editorial Team